Chinese Foreign Relations

ASIA IN WORLD POLITICS
Series Editor: Samuel S. Kim

Chinese Foreign Relations

Power and Policy since the Cold War

Fourth Edition

Robert G. Sutter

ROWMAN & LITTLEFIELD
Lanham • Boulder • New York • London

Published by Rowman & Littlefield
A wholly owned subsidiary of The Rowman & Littlefield Publishing Group, Inc.
4501 Forbes Boulevard, Suite 200, Lanham, Maryland 20706
www.rowman.com

Unit A, Whitacre Mews, 26-34 Stannary Street, London SE11 4AB, United Kingdom

British Library Cataloguing in Publication Information Available

Library of Congress Cataloging-in-Publication Data
Sutter, Robert G., author.
Chinese foreign relations : power and policy since the Cold War / Robert G. Sutter. — Fourth edition.
pages cm. — (Asia in world politics)
Includes bibliographical references and index.
ISBN 978-1-4422-5327-8 (cloth : alk. paper) — ISBN 978-1-4422-5328-5 (pbk. : alk. paper) —
ISBN 978-1-4422-5329-2 (electronic) 1. China—Foreign relations—1976– 2. China—Politics and
government—1976–2002. 3. China—Politics and government—2002– 4. World politics—1989– I.
Title.
DS779.27.S873 2016
327.51—dc23
2015036921

Printed in the United States of America

Contents

Acknowledgments

The fourth edition of this volume was undertaken with the strong support of Susan McEachern, vice president and executive editor, Rowman & Littlefield. Audra Figgins, assistant editor, and Jehanne Schweitzer, senior production editor, Rowman & Littlefield, expertly helped guide the manuscript through the production process.

In addition to information cited in source notes, the assessments in this volume benefited from close and frequent interchange with numerous colleagues in Washington, D.C., and throughout the United States and Asia who have a strong interest in Chinese foreign relations and share their perspectives during conferences, more informal meetings, and conversations in Internet groups. Special thanks go to the students who participate actively in the several classes I teach each year dealing with China and its role in world affairs.

Abbreviations

ABM	antiballistic missile
ACFTA	ASEAN-China Free Trade Agreement
ADB	Asian Development Bank
ADIZ	air defense identification zone
AG	Australia Group
AIIB	Asian Infrastructure Investment Bank
AIT	American Institute in Taiwan
APEC	Asian-Pacific Economic Cooperation
ARATS	Association for Relations across the Taiwan Strait
ARF	ASEAN Regional Forum
ASB	air-sea battle
ASEAN	Association of Southeast Asian Nations
ASEM	Asia-Europe Meetings
BJP	Bharatiya Janata Party
BMD	ballistic missile defense
BRICS	Brazil, Russia, India, China, South Africa group
C4ISR	command, control, communications, computers, intelligence, and strategic reconnaissance
CACF	China-Africa Cooperation Forum
CBMs	confidence-building measures
CCP	Chinese Communist Party

CDM	Clean Development Mechanism
CEPA	Closer Economic Partnership Arrangement
CIC	China Investment Corporation
CIS	Commonwealth of Independent States
DMZ	demilitarized zone
DOD	Department of Defense
DPJ	Democratic Party of Japan
DPP	Democratic Progressive Party
EAEC	East Asian Economic Caucus
EAS	East Asian Summit
ECFA	Economic Cooperation Framework Agreement
EDCA	Enhanced Defense Cooperation Agreement
EEZ	exclusive economic zone
EU	European Union
FDI	foreign direct investment
FMLF	Farabundo Martí National Liberation Front
FRF	Futenma Replacement Facility
FTA	free trade agreement
FTAAP	Free Trade Area of the Asia-Pacific
G7	Group of Seven
G20	Group of Twenty
GATT	General Agreement on Tariffs and Trade
GDP	gross domestic product
GEF	Global Environmental Facility
GNP	gross national product
GSP	Generalized System of Preferences
IAEA	International Atomic Energy Agency
IDF	Indigenous Defense Fighter
IISS	International Institute for Strategic Studies
IMF	International Monetary Fund
INF	intermediate nuclear forces
IPR	intellectual property rights

IT	information technology
JCC	Joint Cooperation Committee
KMT	Kuomintang
LDP	Liberal Democratic Party
LNG	liquefied natural gas
LOAC	line of actual control
MCAS	Marine Corps Air Station
MFN	most-favored-nation status
MOFA	Ministry of Foreign Affairs
MOFTEC	Ministry of Foreign Trade and Economic Cooperation
MTCR	Missile Technology Control Regime
NLD	National League for Democracy
NMD	national missile defense
NPC	National People's Congress
NPT	Nonproliferation Treaty
NSC	new security concept
NSG	Nuclear Suppliers Group
NTR	normal trade relations
NUC	National Unification Council
NUG	National Unification Guidelines
OAS	Organization of American States
OECD	Organization for Economic Cooperation and Development
PA	Palestinian Authority
PFP	Partnership for Peace
PFP	People First Party
PIF	Pacific Islands Forum
PKI	Indonesian Communist Party
PKO	peacekeeping operations
PLA	People's Liberation Army
PLO	Palestine Liberation Organization
PNTR	permanent normal trade relations
PPP	purchasing power parity

PRC	People's Republic of China
PSI	Proliferation Security Initiative
RCEP	Regional Comprehensive Economic Partnership
RMA	revolution in military affairs
ROC	Republic of China
ROK	Republic of Korea
SAARC	South Asian Association for Regional Cooperation
SALT	Strategic Arms Limitation Talks
SARS	severe acute respiratory syndrome
SBY	Susilo Bambang Yudhoyono
SCO	Shanghai Cooperation Organization
SDF	Self-Defense Forces
SEF	Taiwan's Straits Exchange Foundation
SEPA	State Environmental Protection Agency
SETC	State Economic and Trade Commission
SEZ	special economic zone
SOE	state-owned enterprise
SOFA	Status of Forces Agreement
SPC	State Planning Commission
TAC	Treaty of Amity and Cooperation
TMD	theater missile defense
TPA	trade promotion authority
TPP	Trans-Pacific Partnership
TRA	Taiwan Relations Act
TRIPS	trade-related aspects of intellectual property rights
TSU	Taiwan Solidarity Union
UAV	unmanned aerial vehicle
UNCLOS	United Nations Convention on the Law of the Sea
UNDP	United Nations Development Program
UNSC	United Nations Security Council
UNTAC	United Nations Transitional Authority in Cambodia
USAID	U.S. Agency for International Development

USTR	U.S. trade representative
WHA	World Health Assembly
WHO	World Health Organization
WMD	weapons of mass destruction
WTO	World Trade Organization

Chapter One

Continuity and Strategy in Contemporary Chinese Foreign Policy

This chapter addresses a question asked throughout this book: Are trends toward more accommodation and moderation seen in Chinese foreign relations since the Cold War likely to continue? The chapter also reviews the ongoing debate among Chinese and international specialists on whether Chinese leaders have developed a coherent strategy in international affairs.

Debates over continued moderation and strategy in Chinese foreign policy have intensified with the political transition in 2012–2013 bringing to power president and Communist Party leader Xi Jinping. Amid ambitious economic reforms, authoritarian initiatives to suppress dissent and strengthen domestic controls, and dramatic purges of government corruption, this seemingly powerful leader has underlined Chinese nationalistic ambitions with widely publicized and assertive foreign policy initiatives. Chinese international behavior has challenged China's neighbors, the United States, and a variety of established international institutions and norms.[1] The outlook for Chinese foreign policy is further clouded by a range of domestic and international uncertainties. Most notably, the future of Communist Party rule in China is in question. Several leading international specialists have departed from the prevailing view of resilient Communist Party rule in post–Cold War China to warn that the political foundation of Xi's prominent leadership is unsustainable and crumbling.[2]

Following the Cold War, Chinese foreign policy demonstrated much greater moderation, engagement, and integration with the existing world order than prevailed in the past. Some analysts in China and abroad foresaw a clear road ahead for China. They viewed Chinese leaders following a strategy that deals pragmatically with world conditions, conforms to international norms, and pursues international peace, development, and harmony seen in the interests of China, its neighbors, and other concerned powers, notably the United States. Others, including this writer, judged that China's approach to foreign affairs depends on many variables inside China and abroad that could change. Many of these variables are beyond the control of the Chinese leadership. The Chinese leadership also has sometimes contradictory approaches in dealing with them. As a result, this assessment judges that continuation of moderation in Chinese foreign relations will remain contingent on circumstances that could change. Amid major uncertainties at home and abroad, Chinese leaders are in no position to formulate and implement a coherent and lasting strategy in foreign affairs. China's neighbors and other concerned powers, including the United States, need to watch these variables carefully and influence those that they can in order to encourage China's continued moderation in foreign affairs.

Assessments of contemporary Chinese foreign policy show ever expanding Chinese interaction with the outside world through economic exchanges in an era of globalization and broadening Chinese involvement with international organizations dealing with security, economic, political, cultural, and other matters. They demonstrate greater transparency in Chinese foreign policy decision making and policy formation. As a result, there is considerable agreement backed by convincing evidence in these writings about the course and goals of contemporary Chinese foreign policy. Areas of continued strong debate among scholars and specialists focus particularly on the aspirations and longer-term goals of the Chinese government. Foreign critics sometimes portray Chinese leaders as authoritarians trying to hold on to power and following an approach of hiding intentions of dominance as China builds greater power through recent foreign interactions.[3]

In general, leaders of the Chinese Communist Party (CCP)–led government have focused on promoting China's economic development while maintaining political and social stability in China. Their efforts help support one-party rule in China. Foreign policy serves these objectives by sustaining an international environment that supports economic growth and stability in China. For many years, this was done through active and often moderate Chinese diplomacy designed to reassure neighboring countries and other concerned powers, notably the United States, the dominant world power in Chinese foreign policy calculations. Chinese leaders have tried to demonstrate that rising Chinese economic, military, and political power and influence should not be viewed as a threat but should be seen as an opportunity for greater world development. In the process, Chinese diplomacy gave greater emphasis to engagement with and conformity to the norms of regional and other multilateral organizations as a means to reassure those concerned with possible negative implications of China's increased power and influence.[4]

Chinese foreign policy places great emphasis on seeking international economic exchange beneficial to Chinese development. Foreign direct investment, foreign aid, foreign technology, and foreign expertise have been critically important in China's economic growth in the post-Mao period. China is the center of a variety of intra-Asian and other international manufacturing and trading networks; it is the world's largest trading nation and the largest consumer of a variety of key world commodities and raw materials. China today depends fundamentally on a healthy world economy in which Chinese entrepreneurs promote economic development as an essential foundation for continued rule of the CCP government. At the same time, the world economy depends increasingly on China. The Chinese government exerts ever greater influence in international economic matters as a key manufacturing center for world markets and an increasingly prominent trading nation with a positive balance of trade and large foreign exchange reserves used for increasing foreign investment.[5]

Chinese nationalism and Chinese security priorities also are important determinants in contemporary Chinese foreign policy. The CCP government has placed greater emphasis on promoting patriotism and nationalism among Chinese people as communism declines as a source of ideological unity and legitimacy. Nationalism supports the CCP's long-standing priority to prevent Taiwan's moves toward de jure independence and separation from China. The Xi Jinping government also has appealed to Chinese nationalism in advancing Chinese claims with coercive means short of direct application of military force in disputed territories in the East China Sea and the South China Sea. These territories are seen to have been taken from China by foreign powers when China was weak and vulnerable during the nineteenth and twentieth centuries; restoring them to Chinese rule is widely supported by Chinese elite and public opinion.[6]

Chinese leaders are in the third decade of double-digit increases in defense spending. They build advanced military power and voice determination to take coercive measures if necessary to achieve nationalistic goals, especially regarding Taiwan and other disputed territories, even in the face of opposition by the power of the United States and its allies and associates.[7] More broadly, Chinese leaders seek to build what they call "comprehensive national power"—particularly economic, military, and political power—as China seeks an as yet not clearly defined leading role as a great power in Asian and world affairs.

IS THERE A CHINESE STRATEGY IN FOREIGN AFFAIRS?

Despite considerable agreement among specialists about the course and many of the goals in recent Chinese foreign policy, there also is considerable uncertainty and debate over the durability of China's recent approach. The uncertainty and debate have grown as the Xi Jinping government has adopted more assertive foreign policies and behavior challenging China's neighbors, the United States, and existing international norms and institutions. On one side are some specialists who have judged that China's leaders are following a firm strategy widely endorsed by the Chinese government that is focused on peace and development and will last well into the twenty-first century.[8] American and some other foreign specialists much more critical of China's rise also have argued that China has a clear but largely hidden strategy that is denied by the Chinese government. This purported strategy seeks eventual regional and in some cases global dominance.[9] On the other side are specialists who have argued that China's approach is subject to change, particularly as major uncertainties and variables could push Chinese foreign policy in directions different from the recent course.[10] Some specialists see a clear strategy in the recent period, though they acknowledge that Chinese calculations and actions could change as China grows in power and influence and meets with international reactions that are hard to predict.[11]

Affirmative

Chinese government officials and some Chinese and foreign scholars and specialists emphasized in recent years that the mix of Chinese government priorities and prevailing conditions provide the basis of a Chinese strategy of peace and development that will last for decades. The Chinese leadership was seen as determined to avoid confrontation in Chinese foreign policy as it pursued economic development at home and abroad in the interest of enhancing the legitimacy and standing of the CCP government. China's cooperative diplomacy and international activism grew as China sought the role of a responsible world power endeavoring to preserve and enhance China's international rights and privileges while it pulled its weight with greater international contributions, commitments, and obligations.

Chinese leadership priorities regarding economic development and domestic stability also favored a foreign policy that is inclined to accept the world situation as it is and avoid the often disruptive and assertive Chinese initiatives in world affairs during the Maoist period (1949–1976). Thus, China's strategy was said to accept the prevailing international and regional balance of power and influence that is often dominated by the United States. It pursued China's advantage by working with existing regional and other international economic organizations and by cooperating more closely with international groupings dealing with security, politics, culture, the environment, and other matters.[12]

Beginning in 2005, the State Council of the People's Republic of China issued white papers and prominent Chinese foreign policy officials provided supportive commentaries that outlined this view of China's strategy in foreign affairs. What they called China's Peaceful Development Road stressed that achieving peaceful development has been the "unremitting pursuit" of the Chinese people and government for almost thirty years and that China's approach will remain along these lines and compatible with Chinese and international circumstances for decades to come. Key features of the Chinese approach were said to include striving to sustain a peaceful international environment helpful to Chinese development and the promotion of world development and peace, achieving Chinese development beneficial to China and its economic partners through growing economic interchange conforming to economic globalization, and doing China's part to build a harmonious world with sustained peace and common prosperity featuring more democratic international decision making than that prevailing in the past. While acknowledging problems and conflicts in contemporary world affairs, the overall optimistic assessment said that "there are more opportunities than challenges" in the world today and that the rise of China was one of the most salient international opportunities, as "China's development will never pose a threat to anyone."[13]

Among more detailed assessments of China's overall foreign policy strategy by prominent Chinese officials and specialists was an article at that time by two prominent specialists of the Chinese government organization the Academy of Social Sciences.[14] This study said that there were four core concepts underpinning China's strategy in world affairs: (1) a drive for great-power status in world affairs; (2) a need for a stable international environment supportive of China's economic development; (3) a restraint on the part of Chinese leaders in world politics in order to avoid onerous obligations and commitments that would hamper China's growth and development, a restraint that was strong during the leadership of Deng Xiaoping in the 1990s; and (4) a recognition by post–Deng Xiaoping (d. 1997) leaders that China's success at home and abroad depends on ever closer interaction with world affairs that requires China to take up more international responsibilities than in the past.

It went on to highlight four features of China's current strategy. They are related to the four concepts mentioned previously: (1) great-power diplomacy involving strong Chinese efforts to maintain good relations with the United States and other international powers and to underline China's image as a great power at home and abroad; (2) active and positive diplomacy and other interaction with China's neighbors to create a buffer[15] and hedge of protection in the event that the ups and downs of U.S.–China relations cause the United States to resume negative pressure against the Beijing government; (3) a growing but still incomplete Chinese interaction with regional and international organizations, many of which were viewed with suspicion by China in the past but have come to be seen as beneficial for Chinese economic, security, and other objectives; and (4) a selective but growing Chinese willingness to undertake international responsibilities and commitments that in the recent past were shunned as costly drains on Chinese development.

In practice, according to the two Chinese specialists, the Chinese strategy involves several important initiatives:

- Seeking comprehensive cooperation and partnerships with all states around China's periphery and important governments elsewhere in the world.
- Emphasizing and demonstrating Chinese self-restraint in order to add to a benign image of China as not a threat but an opportunity for the world.
- Willingness to put aside past repeated and vocal complaints against U.S. dominance and "hegemony" in world politics as long as the United States does not challenge core Chinese interests regarding Taiwan, Communist Party rule in China, and related issues.
- A Chinese approach to economic development that opens the Chinese economy ever more widely to international influence so that as China rises in economic importance, the benefits of its rise are spread widely throughout the world and China's new position is less likely to be seen as a threat to the international economy or to the economies of countries that interact with China.
- Ever greater Chinese involvement with regional and other multilateral bodies. This effort is designed to enhance China's international profile while it channels Chinese power into these institutions, thereby reducing the suspicions of neighbors and significant world powers, notably the United States.

Among foreign assessments, a cogent analysis by the prestigious Institute for International and Strategic Studies focused on the growing concerns in the United States and among some of China's neighbors in Asia over the rise of Chinese economic, military, and political power and influence as a key driver in contemporary Chinese strategy in world politics.[16] The strengthening of negative perceptions of China's rise by the United States and other powers would inevitably lead to the rise of new balancing coalitions against China, it averred, upsetting China's still incomplete efforts to develop and accumulate comprehensive national power sufficient to secure Chinese internal and international interests. Thus, a core objective in China's strategy in world affairs was to ensure the continued smooth growth of Chinese wealth and power while simultaneously preventing the emergence of balancing coalitions that might arise in response to such growth.

To do this, China settled on an approach affirming Beijing's permanently peaceful intentions; emphasizing good-neighbor relations designed to wean states, especially neighboring ones, away from potentially balancing behavior or coalitions; using China's economic strength as leverage to increase dependence on the part of potential rivals; and accommodating and appeasing the reigning hegemon, the United States—at least until the point where Beijing can cope with American power independently—while exploiting Asian and international dissatisfaction with the United States in order to enhance China's own efforts to create buffers and guard against U.S. pressure and dominance. China's broader international goals included giving notice of its arrival as a great power, forging friendly relations with more distant governments for the purposes of developing new allies and access to needed commodities, and preempting these countries from aiding the United States in any future effort to pressure China.

A lengthy authoritative assessment based on years of interviews among specialists and officials in China by prominent international relations scholar Avery Goldstein argued that the Chinese leadership, after a period of debate and uncertainty for several years in the wake of the Cold War, came to an agreed-on foreign policy line in the second half of the 1990s that provided a grand strategy for Chinese foreign policy that was likely to last well into the future.[17] The strategy promoted China's rise to great-power status within the constraints of a unipolar international system that the United States led. It endeavored to sustain conditions needed for China's continued economic and military modernization and reduce the risk that the United States and others will view China's increasing capabilities as a threat that must be constrained or destroyed.

Two key components of the Chinese approach involved on the one hand establishing various types of partnerships with other world powers, thereby creating linkages that make China an indispensable or at least very attractive actor whose interests the system's key actors are reluctant to undermine. The other component was an activist international agenda designed to establish China's reputation as a responsible member of the international community and mute widespread concerns about how Beijing was likely to employ its growing capabilities, thus reducing the incentives for others to unite in opposition to China.

Supporting many of the themes emphasized in the work of Goldstein and others, David Shambaugh inventoried an impressive array of Chinese advances in Asia as indicative of the emergence of a new order in Asia with China at the center.[18] Phillip Saunders in 2006 depicted an effective Chinese strategy of greater international activism that posed major concerns for the United States.[19] Bates Gill in 2007 focused on the notable advances in what he called China's "new security diplomacy." He highlighted a Chinese strategy that advanced China's international posture and influence in regional security mechanisms and through effective approaches to issues involving nonproliferation, arms control, sovereignty, and intervention.[20] David Michael Lampton in 2008 concluded that China was pursing an effective strate-

gy in foreign affairs that would last well into the twenty-first century, though
he was uncertain about the longer-term future. He acknowledged that the
recent China strategy could change as China grew to great-power status and/
or elicited negative reaction from the United States later in the century, and
he reaffirmed that view in an assessment coinciding with Xi Jinping's ascent
to leadership.[21]

Meanwhile, noted above are examples of a growing body of literature
from mainly U.S. specialists such as Aaron Friedberg, Michael Pillsbury,
Denny Roy, and Ashley Tellis focused on what they saw as a coherent
Chinese strategy that the Chinese government denied and allegedly tried to
keep hidden from view. These experts examined closely China's military
buildup along with other elements of state power. They assessed how Chinese leaders employed their forces in military exercises against notional
enemies—often the United States. They combed Chinese specialist and other
writings for insights into Chinese strategy. They assessed the longer-term
implications of expanding Chinese influence in Asian and world affairs,
often depicting a zero-sum situation where China's rise came at the expense
of others, again with a focus on the United States. Their bottom line was a
warning to America that China's rise was at American expense. They foresaw a dangerous power shift in Asia where rising China would fairly soon be
in a position to challenge American leadership in Asia and thereby precipi-
tate a major defeat for U.S. interests and influence in world affairs. As
tensions rose in Sino-American relations coincident with the Xi Jinping leadership's more assertive foreign posture against the interests of the United
States and many of China's neighbors in a stable environment in Asia, this
group of specialists received closer attention from American government and
nongovernment elites, contributing to a hardening of America's overall posture toward China in these recent years.

Negative

A range of specialists and scholars answer "no" to the question, "Is there a
Chinese strategy in foreign affairs?" In the area of Chinese national security,
Thomas Christensen argued in 2001 that while the priorities of the Chinese
leadership seemed clear, "many of the means to reach the regime's domestic
and international security goals are so fraught with complexity, and sometimes contradiction, that a single, integrated grand plan is almost certainly
lacking, even in the innermost circles of the Chinese leadership compound."
Christensen summed up China's strategic goals along lines widely accepted
by other specialists and commentators to include (1) regime security, (2)
preserving territorial integrity, and (3) gaining prestige, power, and respect
on the international stage. But he pointed out that this simple list contains "a
rich menu of sometimes contradictory goals in a complex world that does not

allow for a unified master plan." A graphic example of such contradictions and complexity involved Taiwan, China's commitment to territorial integrity, and related Chinese nationalism driving the Chinese government to give top priority to preventing Taiwan moves toward independence. In the event of such Taiwan moves, Chinese leaders repeatedly stated that China will use its burgeoning military buildup opposite Taiwan and attack the island and its U.S. military supporters despite the catastrophic effect this would have on China's peace and development, the otherwise central objective in China's contemporary foreign policy.[22]

Susan Shirk built on her experience as a key policymaker in the latter years of the Clinton administration to warn Americans in 2007 that China's moderate approach to the United States and other powers was fragile and easily broken. The mix of authoritarian Chinese leaders with uncertain legitimacy, strong Chinese nationalism, and salient issues posing direct threats to Chinese nationalism and Chinese leadership legitimacy provide the foundation for her argument that China's rise to international prominence is that of a fragile superpower. In particular, she illustrated how China does not control the actions of leaders in Taiwan, Japan, and the United States well, and this could lead to crises and major shifts in China's recent moderate approach to foreign affairs.[23]

American government assessments repeatedly underlined uncertainty about China's strategy and longer-term objectives and what they meant for China's neighbors and the United States. Throughout the often white-hot debates in the United States over policy toward China during the Clinton administration (1993–2001), U.S. leaders from the president on down emphasized that U.S. policy of engagement with China was premised on the belief that firm and constructive U.S. interaction with the Chinese leadership would steer the Chinese government away from possible assertive and disruptive policy leanings, which were major concerns for U.S. leaders, toward policies of accommodation and cooperation with the United States and the prevailing international order.[24] The George W. Bush administration adopted somewhat tougher policies than the Clinton administration in trying to deter possible Chinese aggression against Taiwan and on other issues, but on balance carried out a policy emphasizing firm and positive engagement with China that was designed to steer the Chinese government along paths compatible with U.S. interests.[25]

Speaking in Japan in March 2005 during her first trip to Asia as the secretary of state in the second term of the George W. Bush administration, Condoleezza Rice affirmed the basic judgment in U.S. government circles that while China's growth in economic, military, and political power and influence was a reality, it was unclear whether the Chinese government had determined to use this power in ways that benefited or undermined U.S. goals of regional and international stability and cooperation. She described

China's rising power as "a new factor" in world affairs that "has the potential for good or for bad," and she asserted that it was the role of the United States and its partners to "try and push and prod and persuade China toward the more positive course." She cited integrating China into the World Trade Organization and working closely with China in talks dealing with North Korea, antiterrorism, and the United Nations as examples of positive convergence of Chinese and U.S. policies. But she cautioned that "China's internal evolution is still underdetermined. And as we look at issues of religious freedom, issues of human rights, as we look to the relationship between Taiwan and China, we see that there are matters of concern that still might take a bad turn." She added that the United States needed to use its power and influence and work closely with Japan and other allies and partners to create in Asia and the world "an environment in which China is more likely to play a positive role than a negative role."[26]

A more moderate Bush administration view of China's rising international importance came to prevail later in the Bush government's second term. This viewpoint was publicly associated with former U.S. Special Trade Representative and Deputy Secretary of State Robert Zoellick, who in September 2005 publicly articulated a strong argument for greater U.S. cooperation with China over Asian and other issues as China rose in regional and international prominence.[27] This viewpoint held that the United States had much to gain from working directly and cooperatively with China in order to encourage the People's Republic of China to use its rising influence in "responsible" ways in accord with broad American interests in Asian and world affairs. This viewpoint seemed to take account of the fact that the Bush administration was already working closely with China in the six-party talks to deal with North Korea's nuclear weapons development and that U.S. and Chinese collaboration or consultations continued on such sensitive topics as the war on terror, Afghanistan, Pakistan, Iran, Sudan, Myanmar (Burma), and even Taiwan as well as bilateral economic, security, and other issues. Bush administration policy came to embrace this point of view of China's rise.

The Barack Obama administration adhered to the Bush administration's generally constructive and positive view as it sought closer collaboration with China over salient international issues involving the global economic recession beginning in 2008, nuclear nonproliferation, climate change, and antiterrorism. The results were mixed and complicated by perceived Chinese assertiveness over long-standing differences with the United States over Taiwan and Tibet and more recent differences over U.S. leadership in the world economy and the role of the United States and allied countries contesting Chinese claims in waters along China's eastern and southern flanks. The experiences reinforced continued U.S. uncertainty concerning the overall strategic direction of Chinese foreign relations. American Defense Department reports complained regularly about the lack of transparency regarding Chinese intentions.[28]

Meanwhile, prominent Chinese foreign specialist and adviser to the Hu Jintao administration Professor Wang Jisi of Beijing University advised throughout this period that international and external circumstances are so varied and volatile that China is compelled to continue to respond with "stopgap measures and piecemeal solutions." He told the media in late 2008, "I do not deny the importance of a 'grand strategy,' but at present there is no strategy that we could come up with by racking our brains that would be able to cover all the aspects of our national interests, so we can only determine priorities in a general manner."[29]

The debate within China over foreign policy strategy intensified during the Xi Jinping leadership. David Shambaugh warned in 2013 of the active debate in China over foreign affairs, with tough-minded realists and nationalists gaining the upper hand against others with a more internationalist perspective seeking to work constructively and in accommodating ways with the United States and the existing world system.[30] Prominent Chinese foreign affairs specialists like Tsinghua University Dean Yan Xuetong called for greater activism and Chinese leadership in pursuing Chinese ambitions in nearby Asia in ways that challenged the existing order and China's relations with the United States, Japan, and several Southeast Asian countries.[31] Responding to such domestic calls for less deference to the United States and less accommodation of U.S.-led international institutions and norms, Xi's government took strong measures to advance territorial claims and created new international banks and other organizations that competed with existing international and regional institutions. It still endeavored to avoid conflict with Washington, seeking to create a new type of great power relationship with America through summit meetings and other means. But its actions made clear that China's view of its role as a "responsible power" in world affairs differed markedly from that of the United States and its allies.[32]

UNCERTAINTIES INFLUENCING CHINA'S POLICY IN WORLD AFFAIRS

Those who argue for caution in defining and assessing Chinese strategy in contemporary world affairs are supported by a variety of recent scholarship and evidence highlighting major uncertainties governing Chinese foreign policy and behavior. For one thing, there is plenty of evidence that the evolving Chinese policy emphasis on peace and development has been contested and its progress has been far from smooth. China's record under Mao and even under Deng Xiaoping showed repeated episodes of ruthless pursuit of revolutionary or national goals at odds with regional and international peace.[33]

Even after the end of the Cold War, there have been many twists and turns, along with various international crises and policy debates in China, on the best course to take in prevailing circumstances. Chinese leaders decided to pursue a much more assertive stance against outside powers than that espoused by the current peace and development line when they launched China's tough stance and provocative military actions in the Taiwan Strait in 1995–1996. Chinese leaders openly debated whether to adopt a tougher stance against U.S. "hegemonism" following the U.S. bombing of the Chinese embassy in Belgrade in 1999. The Chinese government for several days allowed illegal violence against Japanese diplomatic and business installations during an upsurge of anti-Japanese sentiment in China in April 2005.[34]

Amid ongoing debates over the proper course in Chinese foreign relations at the turn of the last decade, Chinese officials and other commentators publicly supported a much tougher approach regarding disputes with the United States and some of China's neighbors regarding contested territorial claims, economic disputes, and other issues. The strident rhetoric and associated actions by Chinese security forces were widely seen as foreshadowing a more assertive phase in Chinese foreign relations in the years ahead, even though Chinese foreign policy leaders endeavored to reaffirm commitment to the moderate approach of recent years.[35]

Subsequent events underlined the change in China's international approach. The anti-Japanese demonstrations in 2005 paled in comparison to the massive state-directed demonstrations against Japan and accompanying violence against Japanese properties in China following the Japanese government decision in September 2012 to purchase some of the disputed Senkaku (Diaoyu) Islands in order to head off grave consequences posed by the proposed purchase of the islands by Japanese rightists intent on provoking China. China had not seen such large-scale demonstrations targeted at a foreign power since the height of the campaigns against U.S. imperialism during the Korean War. The upsurge in opposition to Japan resulted in continuing patterns of repeated Chinese military and coast guard shows of force against Japanese forces in control of the disputed islands. And they coincided with Chinese use of coast guard forces backed by military forces that intimidated Philippine fishermen and security forces and took control of disputed Scarborough Shoal in the South China Sea.[36]

Meanwhile, Chinese foreign policy pronouncements and actions showed that even basic goals in Chinese foreign policy have changed in the post–Cold War period. One salient example involved Chinese opposition to "hegemonism." This was one of the two guiding principles (the other was peace and development) in Chinese foreign relations for more than twenty years, mainly in the 1980s and the 1990s. It was a successor to the principle of anti-imperialism that framed Chinese foreign relations in the Maoist period. As China sometimes grudgingly accommodated to the continued strong superpower status of the United States during the George W. Bush administration, it dropped prominent treatment of antihegemonism as a goal in Chinese foreign relations. Chinese officials acknowledged in private that they continued to oppose hegemonism, and several indicated that George W. Bush was the most hegemonic U.S. president in world affairs that they had seen. However, the goal of antihegemonism was overshadowed by public and private Chinese efforts to persuade Americans that China's rise would not be a threat to the United States.[37]

A second example of changed goals in foreign affairs was the introduction of a major new goal of reassurance in Chinese foreign relations in this period. It began after the Taiwan Strait crisis of 1995–1996 and concurrent territorial disputes involving China and its neighbors in the South China Sea and elsewhere. From that time until very recently, Chinese officials and official pronouncements gave high priority to countering growing regional and international perceptions of an emerging threat coming from China. They did so by emphasizing efforts through diplomacy and other means to reassure China's neighbors and eventually the United States and other powers that rising China was not a danger but a source of opportunity. The new Chinese goal—to reassure neighbors and others—provided the foundation for Chinese formulations in the twenty-first century regarding China's "peaceful rise," China following "the road of peace and development," and China seeking a "harmonious" world order. As noted above, policy and practice under Xi Jinping are less interested in harmony and more active and assertive in advancing Chinese goals even at the expense of the regional order and smooth relations with neighbors and the United States.[38]

A third major change in Chinese foreign policy goals emerged in the past decade over China's need for energy, especially foreign oil. An upsurge in domestic demand caused a crisis in the Chinese leadership in 2003–2004 and prompted what has been authoritatively depicted as a poorly managed outreach for energy resources across the globe. The implications of China's growing dependence on foreign sources of energy and the fact that those sources and lines of communication from them to China often are controlled by the United States figure prominently in continuing debates in China on how to achieve energy security and what this means for Chinese foreign relations broadly and Chinese relations with the United States in particular. The goal of energy security—with all its uncertainty for China and resulting debate among Chinese decision makers—has been placed high on the list of contemporary Chinese foreign policy goals.[39]

Not only are key Chinese foreign policy goals subject to change, but also there is no clear view as to whether the prevailing Chinese approach to world affairs reflects Chinese confidence, strength, and determination to continue the current course or reflects vulnerability and uncertainty in the face of circumstances at home and abroad that could prompt change in China's international approach. The result is a mixed and often confusing situation pointing out Chinese leaders' confidence in some areas and uncertainty in others, with the level of confidence or uncertainty in some key policy areas prone to change over time with changing circumstances. This mixed situation provides a weak foundation for a coherent and lasting Chinese strategy in foreign affairs.

An example of the mix of confidence and diffidence is seen in the work of specialists who track Chinese officials' asserted confidence or uncertainty over the key issue of Taiwan. They have documented several cycles of optimism and pessimism by Chinese officials in recent years brought on by changing policies of the Taiwan administration. [40]

Examples of such mixed assessment are seen on the one hand in studies highlighting ever growing Chinese confidence in dealing with Asian affairs evidenced notably in the assessments in periodic white papers issued by the Chinese government that deal with international affairs. Bates Gill joined a number of international specialists who focused on Chinese policy approaches of constructive interaction with neighbors and other powers in bilateral and multilateral arrangements that "are both cause and effect of China's more confident perception of its international and global situation." This optimistic view of Chinese confidence in foreign affairs also was highlighted in works by Avery Goldstein, Aaron Friedberg, Evan Medeiros, and M. Taylor Fravel. [41]

By contrast, Susan Shirk focused on uncertainty and nervousness on the part of Chinese leaders as they surveyed Chinese foreign relations. Jonathan Pollack emphasized that "beneath the confident veneer about China's economic success and its enhanced international standing, a more contingent forecast predominates." He emphasized that Chinese wariness and uncertainties flow from many unsettled questions about the new regional order, "with the longer-term US strategy with regard to China being uppermost among these uncertainties." Fei-ling Wang asserted that despite recent accomplishments, "an increasingly strong sense of China's 'vulnerability' and even 'insecurity' is clearly present in Beijing." This vulnerability and insecurity came from the Chinese communist administration's strong sense of being under siege following the collapse of Soviet and international communism at the end of the Cold War and by a strong sense of nationalism that challenged the administration's ability to manage Chinese foreign policy in ways constructive for their interests. Wang advised that there would be a continuing "mixture of insecurity and secrecy" in Chinese domestic politics and decision making affecting Chinese foreign relations. Supporting Wang's prediction are the recent works of David Michael Lampton, Andrew Nathan and Andrew Scobell, and David Shambaugh, which highlight domestic and international vulnerabilities contributing to Chinese leaders' insecurities.[42]

Uncertainty over the course of U.S.–China relations also adds to uncertainty about the future direction of Chinese foreign policy. Relations with the United States are widely acknowledged as the most important bilateral relationship and a key determinant in Chinese foreign policy. Whether China's approach to international affairs continues along the self-proclaimed strategic direction of peace and development or whether it veers toward assertiveness and confrontation or in some other direction is widely seen in China and abroad to depend heavily of the state of play in China's relations with the United States.

Lack of clarity in predictions of the future course of U.S.–China relations underlines ambivalence about the future direction of Chinese foreign policy. Princeton University Professor Aaron Friedberg followed a stint as deputy director of the U.S. vice president's national security staff by writing an assessment in late 2005 dealing with underlying uncertainties in U.S.–China relations. He questioned whether U.S.–China relations over the next decades would be marked by convergence toward deepening cooperation and peace or whether there would be deterioration leading to growing competition and possibly war. Assessing the enormous consequences of either path for China, the United States, and the international order, Friedberg warned that despite these consequences and the many studies of U.S.–China ties, the bottom line was profound uncertainty, with few willing to predict the outlook without major caveats and conditions.[43]

Reinforcing Friedberg's judgment, U.S. and Chinese leaders have had considerable difficulty in sustaining positive engagement amid growing competition for influence in Asia and major controversy over other salient issues ranging from cyber security to human rights. China reacted negatively to President Obama's series of initiatives in Asia known as the rebalance policy that in many respects has been designed to compete for influence with China. The president used his State of the Union message and other pronouncements in 2015 to stress that his economic initiative in the rebalance policy, the advanced free trade agreement known as the Trans-Pacific Partnership (TPP), was designed to ensure that America and not China would determine international trade and investment rules and norms.[44] Against the background of the American initiatives, the Xi Jinping government has challenged U.S. influence and the influence of U.S.-backed international financial institutions like the International Monetary Fund (IMF), the World Bank, and the Asian Development Bank. It did so in a series of initiatives since 2013 backed by Chinese-pledged commitments of hundreds of billions of dollars. Among others, the commitments are to the so-called New Development Bank involving the five members of the BRICS group (Brazil, Russia, India, China, South Africa); to the China-led Asian Infrastructure Investment

Bank involving China and most East, South, and central Asian countries; and to countries along the interior Asian Silk Road Belt and along the twenty-first-century Maritime Silk Road in southeastern and southern Asia.[45]

WHERE THIS STUDY FITS AMONG ASSESSMENTS

On the basis of the considerations and evidence presented thus far, I judge that prudence requires U.S. policymakers and other international observers to hedge their bets regarding a hoped-for continuation of China's recent moderate approach in foreign affairs. At the same time, I do not agree with those who see recent Chinese moderation in foreign affairs as mainly a ruse in a hidden strategy to deceive America and thereby control the world. The evidence in recent Chinese behavior is ambiguous as to whether China has settled on a strategy in international relations that will focus on peace and development and establishing a harmonious world order for the next several decades. The record shows that the course of Chinese foreign policy in the post–Cold War period has been tortuous, full of twists and turns influenced by developments inside China and by events outside China affecting Chinese foreign policy. Most important inside China have been leadership changes and debates[46] and the success of China's economic and military modernization. Developments outside China that have an impact on China's foreign policy include notably the actions of the United States and of leaders of such key areas of importance to China as Taiwan, Japan, and North Korea.

In the view of this writer, it is hard to predict with certainty how these variables will behave in the future and what impact they will have on Chinese policy at that time. At bottom, the record seems to show Chinese leaders addressing foreign policy choices in a contingent way, assessing the costs and benefits for China's interests and their own, before coming to a decision. Were domestic or international circumstances to change in ways that would alter the current balance of costs and benefits affecting China's emphasis on peace and development, it is logical to conclude that the Chinese emphasis on peace and development would change as well.

Some scholars believe China has now reached such an important international position that the Chinese leadership is able to set the guidelines for international trends and carefully manipulate domestic Chinese developments, thereby ensuring that China will be able to pursue a coherent and firm strategy into the future without interruption. In contrast, the recent record of Chinese foreign relations demonstrates that the Chinese leadership is far from confident that it can manage without serious interruption the major challenges it faces at home and that it judges that China, while growing in influence, is far from dominant in Asia, not to mention other parts of the world that receive less Chinese attention in foreign policy. Chinese officials are careful not to confront America. They see the United States remaining the leading power in Asian and world affairs for the time being and perhaps for some time to come. American policy is viewed as a critically important determinant in China's discernment of costs or benefits of particular policies and the general direction of China's foreign policy. There is no certainty as to how the United States will behave, how it will endeavor to deal with China and its rising influence in Asian and world affairs, and what effect U.S. actions will have on China's overall strategy in international relations. A similar degree of uncertainty surrounds decision making in Taipei, Pyongyang, Tokyo, and other areas outside direct Chinese control that can have a critically important impact on Chinese foreign policy.

The recent record shows that U.S. leaders seem to understand the important American role in encouraging constructive and cooperative Chinese foreign behavior and deterring Chinese and other aggression and assertiveness disruptive of U.S. interests in regional and global peace and stability. The George W. Bush administration emphasized the positive in public interaction with Chinese leaders in frequent summit meetings, phone conversations, and other collaboration. This administration held the line against U.S. advocates of tougher policies toward China on trade and other issues. At the same time, it remained wary of possible negative implications of China's military buildup and greater prominence in Asian and world affairs, hedging against possible negative outcomes while encouraging Chinese international behavior deemed responsible by the United States.[47] This reinforced a cautious optimism that positive and constructive aspects in Chinese foreign relations would continue during the administration of President Barack Obama while Chinese assertive tendencies would remain held in check. As noted above, the record thus far during the Obama government is erratic, with a recent mix of competition versus cooperation, with competition rising in importance. In sum, considering the array of factors and influences that have an impact on Chinese foreign policy interests and decision making, it appears that Chinese leaders are not in a position to formulate and implement a coherent and lasting strategy in foreign affairs.

THE PURPOSE AND SCOPE OF THIS BOOK

In this book, I seek to explain thoroughly the determinants of and significant developments in Chinese foreign relations after the Cold War. In chapter 2, I assess the foreign policy priorities of Chinese leaders and the importance of these priorities relative to the Chinese leaders' domestic priorities. In chapter 3, I examine how the changing pattern of Chinese decision making and changing Chinese worldviews are in turn changing Chinese foreign policy and behavior.

In chapter 4, I assess the importance of Chinese economic development and economic globalization on Chinese foreign relations and how these lead to increasing Chinese involvement in regional and global organizations that deal with world governance. Chapter 5 is an examination of Chinese national security concerns and their effect on Chinese foreign relations, China's role in international nonproliferation and arms control regimes, and the role of the Chinese military in China's foreign relations. In the next six chapters, I assess China's relations with key powers or world areas, and in the last chapter, I examine the outlook for Chinese foreign relations.

Chapter Two

Chinese Leadership Priorities

Implications for Chinese Foreign Relations

An assessment of recent Chinese foreign relations needs to discern as well as possible the key determinants of Chinese foreign policy and behavior, especially the priorities of Chinese leaders. This task is complicated because the literature is divided between specialists who claim that the Chinese leadership gives top priority to China's search for great-power status and leadership in Asian and world affairs[1] and those specialists,[2] including this writer, who judge that prevailing evidence shows that Chinese leaders focus on domestic stability and economic growth. Seeing these as the key elements in determining its ability to stay in power, the Chinese Communist Party (CCP) leadership generally views them as the top priority. However, equal priority is given to managing issues of nationalism, like the Taiwan issue, that if challenged could threaten the viability of the one-party government. Though cross-strait relations eased after the election of Taiwan President Ma Ying-jeou in 2008, they were crisis prone for much of the past two decades; they have become more tense in the lead-up to January 2016 elections for Taiwan's new president. Chinese leaders are on record affirming that Taiwan moves toward independence mean China will use force. Against this background, I join other specialists who judge that the Chinese leaders view goals of regional leadership and international status as secondary in importance to these domestic issues.

This chapter reviews the development of Chinese foreign relations in the 1990s to provide a context for discerning Chinese foreign policy priorities after the Cold War and into the twenty-first century. It then explains and assesses China's foreign policy priorities. As in the case of Chinese goals of development and stability versus Chinese nationalistic goals involving Taiwan noted above, the goals often conflict with one another, precluding a clear and predictable strategy in foreign affairs.

THE EVOLUTION OF CHINESE PRIORITIES AFTER THE COLD WAR

The end of the Cold War saw the weakening and collapse of Soviet military power, which markedly improved China's overall security situation. For the first time, the People's Republic of China (PRC) was not facing an immediate foreign threat to its national security. However, the sharp international reaction to China's harsh crackdown on dissent after the June 1989 Tiananmen incident caught Chinese leaders by surprise. They reportedly had expected developed nations to restore stable relations after a few months. They had not counted on the rapid collapse of communism in Eastern Europe, the subsequent march toward self-determination throughout the Soviet republics, and ultimately the end of the Soviet Union in 1991. For several years, these unexpected events diverted the developed nations from returning to China with advantageous investment, assistance, and economic exchanges. They also called into question China's strategic importance as a counterweight to the Soviet Union and posed the most serious challenge to the legitimacy of the Chinese communist government since the Cultural Revolution (1966–1976). Taiwan's concurrent moves toward greater democracy and self-determination received growing positive attention in the United States and the West, adding to China's concerns about broad international trends and what to do about them.[3]

The United States was seen in Beijing as both China's greatest threat and its most important partner. In response to U.S.-led sanctions and criticisms in the late 1980s and early 1990s, the Chinese government used foreign affairs to demonstrate the legitimacy and prestige of China's communist leaders. High-level visits to Asian capitals and elsewhere in the non-Western world were used along with trade and security arrangements in order to strengthen China's image before skeptical audiences at home and abroad. To reestablish internal political stability, Chinese leaders also gave high priority to the resource needs of the military and public security forces. Thus began a long series of double-digit annual increases in China's defense budget that has persisted up to now and has made China Asia's leading military power and a much more formidable military competitor of the United States.[4]

Recognizing that communist ideology was not popular enough to support their continued monopoly of power, leaders in Beijing played up themes of patriotism and Chinese nationalism to support their rule. Criticism by the United States and other countries of the communist system in China were portrayed not as attacks against unjust arbitrary rule but as assaults on China's national integrity. These attacks were equated with "imperialist" pressures on China in the nineteenth and twentieth centuries.[5]

Meanwhile, Deng Xiaoping spurred economic reform and China's opening during a tour of southern China in 1992, making other senior Chinese leaders move away from their hesitant approach to economic modernization and reform after the Tiananmen crackdown. Deng called for faster growth and increased economic interchange with the outside world, especially the developed economies of Asia and the West. This call coincided with the start of an economic boom on the mainland that continued for several years of double-digit growth and then declined a bit to the still rapid pace of 7–8 percent annual growth. The growth caught the attention of foreign business and government leaders. American business interest in the China market grew markedly from 1992 and was credited with playing an important role in convincing the Clinton administration in 1994 to stop linking U.S. most-favored-nation trade treatment to improvements in China's still-poor human rights conditions.[6]

Deng Xiaoping and the new third generation of leaders headed by president and party leader Jiang Zemin continued the post-Mao policies, emphasizing fostering a better economic life for the people of China in order to justify their continued monopoly of political power. As the prestige of Mao and communism had faded rapidly, Chinese leaders found themselves depending heavily on foreign trade and related foreign investment and assistance for China's economic development. To ensure their political survival, China's leaders continued to emphasize the maintenance of a peaceful international environment, especially in nearby Asia, which would facilitate the continued trade, investment, and assistance flows so important to Chinese economic well-being.[7]

The leaders further put aside self-reliance. They broadened international contacts by increasing efforts to meet the requirements of the United States and others regarding market access, intellectual property rights, and other economic issues in order to become a member of the World Trade Organization (WTO). Chinese leaders accepted more commitments and responsibilities that stemmed from participation in such international economic organizations as the World Bank, the Asian Development Bank, and the Asia-Pacific Economic Cooperation forum.[8]

Chinese leaders remained sensitive on matters of national sovereignty and international security issues close to home. But they adjusted to world pressure when resistance appeared detrimental to broader Chinese concerns. Examples of this adjustment include Chinese cooperation with the international peace settlement in Cambodia in 1991, willingness to join the 1968 Treaty on the Nonproliferation of Nuclear Weapons and to halt nuclear tests by the end of 1996 under an international agreement, willingness to abide by the terms of the Missile Technology Control Regime, and efforts in 1994 to help the

United States reach an agreement with North Korea over the latter's nuclear weapons development program. Beijing also endeavored to meet international expectations on other transnational issues, such as policing drug traffic, curbing international terrorism, and working to avoid further degradation of the global environment.[9]

China's hard line against outside criticism of its political authoritarianism and poor human rights record continued to illustrate the limits of China's accommodation to international norms. China continued to transfer sensitive military technology or dual-use equipment to Pakistan, Iran, North Korea, and other potential flash points despite criticism from Western countries. Furthermore, Chinese political and military leaders were not reluctant to use rhetorical threats or demonstrations of military force to intimidate those they believed were challenging China's traditional territorial or nationalistic claims in sensitive areas such as Taiwan, the South China Sea, and Hong Kong.[10]

As a general rule, Chinese leaders tended to approach each foreign policy issue on a case-by-case basis, each time calculating the costs and benefits of adherence to international norms. This kind of approach applied especially to security and political issues, while Chinese leaders came to view economic norms differently, seeing China generally well served by embracing economic globalization and the norms associated with it. By 1991, Chinese officials saw that maintaining support for the Khmer Rouge in Cambodia would counter broader Chinese interests in achieving a favorable peace settlement in Cambodia and solidifying closer Chinese relations with members of the Association of Southeast Asian Nations (ASEAN), Japan, and the West—all of whom saw continued Chinese aid to the Khmer Rouge as a serious obstacle to peace. Similarly, in 1994, China announced its decision to stop nuclear testing by the end of 1996 and to join the comprehensive nuclear test ban, thereby ending the risk of major friction in its relations with the United States, Japan, Western Europe, and Russia.[11]

Influencing the case-by-case approach was a rising sense of nationalism among Chinese leaders and the Chinese people more broadly. Tending to view the world as a highly competitive, state-centered system, Chinese leaders were at first slow to embrace multilateralism and interdependence, though they came to accept these trends regarding economic issues. In security and political affairs, however, they were inclined to see the world in fairly traditional balance-of-power terms. They stressed that the world was becoming more multipolar (that is, a number of competing large nation-states), though in the face of undiminished U.S. dominance, they came to play down multipolarity for the time being.[12]

Chinese suspicions of the prevailing Asian and international order centered on the dominant role played by the United States and its allies and associates. These nations were seen as setting the agenda of many international regimes in order to serve their own particular national interests, in the process giving short shrift to the interests and concerns of newly emerging powers like China. In fact, as China's economic and military power grew, official Chinese commentary saw the United States and its allies as unwilling to share power with China and seeking to keep it weak for as long as possible. [13]

Chinese leaders recognized that the United States exerted predominant strategic influence in East Asia and the western Pacific, was a leading economic power in the region, and was one of only two powers (along with Russia) capable of exerting sufficient power around China's periphery to pose a tangible danger to Chinese security and development. As the world's remaining superpower, the United States was seen by Chinese officials in the 1990s as exerting strong influence in international financial and political institutions, such as the World Bank and the United Nations, that were particularly important to Beijing. The United States also played a key role in areas of great sensitivity to China's leaders, notably regarding Taiwan and international human rights. [14]

While Chinese leaders tried hard to work constructively with U.S. leaders in areas of mutual interest, more often than not they saw U.S. policy in Asian and world affairs as adverse to Chinese interests. Chinese leaders maneuvered carefully and sometimes forcefully to defend and protect key interests while accommodating American concerns in other areas. A military face-off with two U.S. aircraft carrier battle groups in the Taiwan area in 1996 and the trashing of U.S. diplomatic properties in China by Chinese demonstrators after the U.S. bombing of the Chinese Embassy in Belgrade in 1999 illustrated how far Chinese leaders were prepared to go in fending off perceived American pressure. Chinese media in these years were full of affirmations of Chinese determination to make necessary sacrifices to defend important interests against U.S. "hegemonism." [15]

As party leader and president, Jiang Zemin exerted increasing influence in Chinese policymaking during the 1990s. Jiang was successful in maneuvers against formidable leadership competition, notably from the likes of former president Yang Shangkun and his nephew Yang Baiping. He initiated a more flexible position that became a central tenet in the Chinese stance toward Taiwan, even though it was temporarily upset by Taiwan President Lee Teng-hui's visit to Cornell University in 1995 and the subsequent crisis and military standoff in cross-strait relations leading to the deployment of U.S. aircraft carriers to the Taiwan area in 1996. Jiang also worked with Vice Premier Zhu Rongji and other senior government leaders to bring inflation under control while sustaining strong economic growth. Jiang's policies generally were consistent with those set forth by Deng Xiaoping, whose health declined in the several years before his death in February 1997. [16]

Deng's passing allowed Jiang to assume the mantle and actual position of China's paramount leader. His overall standing, of course, was much weaker than that of Deng, whose prestige and leadership credentials traced back to the legendary Long March of the 1930s. But Jiang was especially active in foreign affairs, leading Chinese efforts to sustain an effective approach toward the United States, adjusting the mix of incentives and sanctions in Chinese policy toward Taiwan, and creating a more coherent and active Chinese policy toward its periphery in Asia.[17]

With Deng gone in February 1997, the three major tasks for the year were:

- The July 1, 1997, transition of Hong Kong to Chinese rule;
- The reconfiguration of Chinese leadership and policy at the Fifteenth CCP Congress in September 1997; and
- The Sino-U.S. summit of October 1997, which China hoped would show people in China and abroad that its leaders were now fully accepted as respectable world leaders following a period of protracted isolation after the 1989 Tiananmen crackdown.[18]

Generally pleased with the results of these three endeavors, President Jiang and his associates began implementing policy priorities for 1998. At the top of the list was an ambitious multiyear effort begun in earnest after the National People's Congress (NPC) meeting in March 1998, to transform tens of thousands of China's money-losing state-owned enterprises (SOEs) into more efficient businesses by reforming them (for example, selling them to private concerns, forming large conglomerates, or other actions). Beijing embarked on major programs to promote economic and administrative efficiency and to protect China's potentially vulnerable financial systems from negative fallout from the 1997–1998 Asian economic crisis. China's new premier, Zhu Rongji, initiated sweeping changes in China's banking and other financial systems designed to reduce or eliminate the vulnerabilities seen elsewhere in Asia.[19]

A new team was in place, managing policy without such powerful leaders of the past as Mao Zedong and Deng Xiaoping. On the whole, top-level leaders seemed to be working smoothly together to pursue Chinese policy interests.[20] There were few signs of disagreement among senior leaders over the broad recent policy emphasis on economic reform, though sectors affected by reform often resisted strenuously. China anticipated joining the WTO in 2001 or 2002, which strengthened the need for greater economic efficiency and reform. The reforms also exacerbated social and economic uncertainties, which reinforced the government's determination to maintain a firm grip on political power and levers of social control. By late 1998, instability caused by economic change and growing political dissent prompted the PRC leadership to initiate significant suppression of political dissidents and related activities. The repression continued through the next decade and has persisted off and on up to the present.[21]

Against this background, foreign affairs generally remained an area of less urgent policy priority. Broad international trends, notably improved relations with the United States and an upswing in China's relations throughout its periphery, supported the efforts by the Chinese authorities to pursue policies intended to minimize disruptions and to assist their domestic reform endeavors. The government remained wary of the real or potential challenges posed by a possible renewed Asian economic crisis, by Taiwan, by efforts by Japan and the United States to increase their international influence in ways seen as contrary to Beijing's interests, by India's great-power aspirations and nuclear capability, and by other concerns. The PRC at this time voiced special concern over the implications of U.S. plans to develop and deploy theater ballistic missile defense systems in eastern Asia and a national missile defense (NMD) for the United States. Chinese officials also voiced concern over the downturn in U.S.–China relations at the outset of the George W. Bush administration but appeared determined to cooperate with the U.S.-led antiterrorism campaign begun in September 2001.[22]

TWENTY-FIRST-CENTURY FOREIGN POLICY PRIORITIES

In the first decades of the twenty-first century, the policies and priorities of the Chinese leadership have depended on key internal and external variables that determine the future of the communist regime and its role in Asian and world affairs. For a time, a mainstream view among U.S. officials and non-government China specialists was that the Chinese communist-led government was resilient enough to deal with most anticipated problems internally. As noted in chapter 1, that view has recently been called into question by some leading international China experts. Meanwhile, China remains wary of the United States and is steadily building military power targeted against American and allied forces. But unless Beijing is challenged by circumstances, China is seen in this study as reluctant to confront the United States or to engage in military conquest and aggression. Alternative views include those who see Chinese leaders now ready and able to confront the United States and China's neighbors, using military attacks if necessary, over such key issues as Taiwan and territorial claims along China's periphery.[23]

Political Leaders and Institutions

China's "third-generation" leadership was under Jiang Zemin, with Mao's being the first generation and Deng's the second. This third generation was followed by the "fourth generation," led by president and party leader Hu

Jintao (2002–2012) and the "fifth generation," led by Xi Jinping (2012–present). A process of political regularity and institutionalization developed that made China's political behavior much more predictable than it was during the Maoist period (1949–1976). Political leaders generally were more technically competent and less ideologically rigid than past leaders. They were aware of the problems they faced and were prepared to deal with at least some of the most important ones.[24]

The level of political skills of the fourth generation showed as Hu Jintao and his colleagues handled more or less effectively a number of difficult domestic and foreign policy concerns ranging from sustaining economic growth during the global recession of 2008–2010 to repeated crises caused by North Korea's nuclear weapons development and other provocations.[25] The transfer of power to fifth-generation leaders beginning in 2012 was disrupted by the removal from power in March 2012 of politburo member Bo Xilai amid a major scandal involving Bo's wife and the murder of a British businessman long associated with Bo and his family, the arrest of Bo's lieutenant after he sought refuge in the U.S. consulate in Chengdu, and Bo's reported ambitions to seek a position on the Politburo Standing Committee at the Eighteenth CCP Congress in late 2012.[26]

Composed of technocrats, economists, managers, and other professionals, the fourth and the fifth generations have been seen as capable and pragmatic when confronted with economic and social problems. They had limited experience with and understanding of the West. In practice, the leadership attempted to adhere to existing policies promoting economic development, but the leaders also gave more attention to the disadvantaged and others left behind as a result of the sweeping economic changes. They remained strict in enforcing laws and regulations against those who would seek to challenge one-party rule in China, resulting in a wide range of human rights violations according to international observers.[27]

The institutionalization of China's politics was the result of a proliferation of institutions from the top down. Chinese Communist Party and NPC sessions and plenums were regularly scheduled and held, and planning and budgetary cycles were adhered to. The principles of class struggle were replaced by budgets geared to a socialist market economy and political constituencies. Socialist laws continued to be promulgated, although enforcement remained problematic.[28] The authorities endeavored to bring emerging economic and social elites into the Communist Party. Jiang Zemin successfully changed party practices to advance the recruitment of such wealthy and influential people into the party's ranks.[29]

President and party leader Xi Jinping has broken with some of the recent patterns of Chinese leadership. Xi has developed more personal charisma than his recent predecessors; the propaganda apparatus has fostered a personality cult centered on Xi. Xi's attack on corruption within the party, government, and military leaderships is unprecedented in scope and effect; top leaders have been brought down and more are likely to fall from power. Xi has positioned himself at the helm of such a wide range of leadership bodies dealing with salient issues ranging from widespread economic reforms to national security that observers wonder how one leader can sustain such a demanding work schedule. Xi's forceful leadership style in dealing with domestic corruption is married with an apparent willingness to risk opposition from the United States, Japan, and other neighboring countries to China's more assertive posture on differences with neighbors over territorial disputes and with the United States over competitive interests in the Asia-Pacific region, among other issues.

Whether Xi's posturing as a powerful leader reflects actual confidence and lasting authority and control remains subject to active debate among foreign specialists.[30] Key weaknesses include the uncertainty over the resilience of one-party communist rule in China noted earlier.

In foreign affairs, Xi's tough actions regarding disputed territorial issues have wide appeal in China, but thus far they have had mixed results. As discussed in later chapters, China faces seeming protracted problems along its eastern and southern periphery, by far the most important area of Chinese foreign policy concern. The Xi Jinping government has no solution for the dangerously volatile situation on its border posed by the erratic North Korean regime of Kim Jung Un, who is intent on developing nuclear weapons sure to destabilize Northeast Asia. Xi's tough policies have deeply alienated Japan, strengthening domestic support for closer Japanese military alignment with the United States, India, Australia, and others as Tokyo girds for a long struggle to protect itself from growing Chinese power. Most Southeast Asian nations remain reluctant to challenge China publicly over its recent advances in the South China Sea, but the Chinese expansion has put the United States on alert as it prepares with the assistance of Japan and Australia among others for contingencies; the Americans also garner overt and tacit support of key Southeast Asian governments. In southern Asia, the Xi government's mix of economic and political overtures along with military force demonstrations in disputed border areas and in the Indian Ocean have deepened suspicions in New Delhi as it actively advances diplomatic, economic, and security ties with the United States, Japan, and Australia as part of national strengthening to protect its interests as China grows in power. Meanwhile, comparatively tranquil situations in areas of acute Chinese concern in Taiwan and Hong Kong have experienced unanticipated mass demonstrations along with political developments and social trends sharply at odds with Chinese interests; in neither case is there a smooth path for spreading Chinese influence and control.

As a political force, the Chinese military has less influence than during the Mao and Deng periods. The military had less representation than in the past at the high-level CCP politburo. An urban, educated elite, the leadership is civilian based. In the past two decades, only two or three of the twenty-plus members of the Communist Party Congress Central Committee Politburo represent the military; none of the nine- or seven-member elite Standing Committee of the politburo has represented the military. Of course, China's remarkable military buildup has shown strong leadership support behind military modernization.[31]

Personal rivalries of senior leaders remain hidden. In maneuvering to succeed Hu Jintao two candidates, Xi Jinping and Li Keqiang, each backed by different leadership groups, emerged at the Seventeenth CCP Congress in 2007. Xi and Li were designated China's first- and second-ranking leaders at the Eighteenth Congress in 2012, but Xi has since created a large gap of power and prestige between himself and Li as well as other members of the top leadership. Xi's unprecedented anticorruption efforts are widely seen as focused on his opponents or others who might thwart his policies and ambitions. As noted earlier, whether Xi's ambitions go beyond his ability to control remains an open question.[32]

Economic and Social Trends

At the start of the twenty-first century, economic growth sustained the overall rise in the standard of living that characterized Chinese development over the previous two decades. A relatively young, well-trained labor force with modern technical skills increased in number. The rapidly improving infrastructure of rail, roads, and electronic communications greatly reduced perceived distance and helped link the poorly developed interior to the booming coastal regions.

Chinese development remained heavily dependent on foreign trade, investments, and scientific/technical exchange. The government faced daunting problems—notably ailing SOEs and a weak banking/financial system. The massive and often wasteful use of energy and other resources and a widespread shortage of uncontaminated water head the list of major environmental problems that appeared hard to resolve without large production cutbacks or expensive technology. China's foreign-invested manufacturing and infrastructure development seems at odds with the important goal since the Hu Jintao period to move China from dependence on foreign trade to an economy driven by domestic consumption. Chinese household consumption remains low. Government support for social services improved from a low base, but Chinese families continue to rely on personal savings to cover education, health care, and retirement expenses that in other countries were met with government funds. The interest payments on massive domestic savings are held artificially low, providing plenty of funding from banks to

SOEs but disadvantaging savers. Thus, people have less money to devote to consumer spending.[33]

The global economic crisis and recession of 2008–2010 saw sharp cutbacks in Western consumption of Chinese and other imports. In 2009 the overall Chinese economy turned sharply downward. Unemployment rose dramatically. The leadership took concrete steps to promote large-scale infrastructure and other domestic development and spending. In 2010 the Chinese economy resumed double-digit growth but faced new uncertainties with continued stagnation in major export markets in Europe and Japan and weak growth in the United States.[34]

Leadership differences reflecting diverging policy preferences and bureaucratic and institutional interests have influenced the Chinese policy process. One result of China's external outreach was the growing importance of ministries with responsibility in foreign affairs, such as the Ministry of Foreign Affairs (MOFA) and the Ministry of Foreign Trade and Economic Cooperation (MOFTEC). The latter, especially, became more important as Beijing joined the WTO. (In 2003, MOFTEC changed its name and became China's Commerce Ministry.) For many years, the National Development and Reform Commission of the PRC sustained broad and strong powers dealing with economic policies. Central regulatory bodies such as the State Economic and Trade Commission also became more important for a time.[35]

As leading officials in the central government agreed on a course of action, they often found their plans thwarted by poor implementation further down the bureaucratic chain of command or in the provinces. The decentralization of economic authority that had proven so effective in promoting growth in the post-Mao period meant that the central leaders often were unable to see their priorities implemented.[36] Thus, developed countries had long experience with the weaknesses of the implementation of central Chinese government guidelines on such sensitive economic issues as Chinese infringement of intellectual property rights (IPR). Lax Chinese administrative control hit home in 2008 when it was discovered that the Chinese supply of milk was widely tainted and had caused deaths and widespread illness among babies and small children.[37]

Manifestations of social discontent were widespread in recent years.[38] Available Chinese government figures showed the number and frequency of these demonstrations grew to 74,000 reported in 2004 and more than 80,000 in 2005. Official Chinese reporting for later years shows roughly 90,000 to 100,000 "mass protests" reported annually for several years. The importance of these demonstrations and protests grew with the strong advance of Internet communication in China.

Although certainly worrisome for Chinese leaders concerned with preserving stability and continued CCP rule, these developments seem to have a way to go before they pose a major or direct threat to the government.

Notably, the discontented need to establish communications across broad areas, groups need to establish alliances with other disaffected groups, and the alliances need to put forth leaders prepared to challenge the regime and gain popular support with credible moral claims. Success also requires a lax or maladroit regime response. The attentiveness of the government to dissidence and the ruthless crackdown on the Falun Gong beginning in 1999 strongly suggest that Beijing remains keenly alert to the implications of social discontent and prepared to use its substantial coercive and persuasive powers to keep it from growing to threatening levels.[39]

Security and Foreign Policies

At the dawn of the twenty-first century, China remained dependent on its economic connections with the developed countries of the West, Japan, and China's other Asian neighbors. Nonetheless, Chinese nationalism was one of the leading forces pushing Chinese policy in directions that resisted U.S. international leadership, the power of the United States, and U.S. allies in eastern Asia, notably Japan and the Philippines, and also Taiwan. Chinese leaders on the one hand attempted to stay on good terms with their neighbors and to keep economic and other channels with the United States open. On the other hand, they have endeavored over time to weaken overall U.S. power and influence in a long-term attempt to create a more "multipolar" world. Military modernization continues the rapid pace begun in the 1990s. The Chinese development of ballistic and cruise missiles and acquisition of advanced Russian weaponry pose notable dangers.[40] Recent concern in China has centered on perceived U.S. "containment" and military "encirclement" of China seen in the Obama government's rebalance policy emphasizing security and other American reengagement with Asia. The Chinese government has also worried about U.S. national and theater missile defense programs, and the potential for Japan and India to improve their regional force projection capabilities with the support of the United States. A drawback for China of the U.S.-led antiterrorism campaign was that it increased U.S. influence and presence along China's western periphery—adding to Beijing's overall sense of being surrounded by U.S. power and influence. American control of sea-lanes from oil-producing countries of the Middle East and Africa to China marks an added worry in China's growing concern over energy security. Taiwan, however, remains China's main security focus, and it is the biggest problem both politically and militarily in U.S.–China relations.[41]

THE OUTLOOK FOR REGIME SURVIVAL

Regime survival remains the central concern of China's leaders. The balance sheet of the challenges facing the administration and the strengths of the communist administration argued for its continuing in power, though there was considerable debate among specialists about the future. The communist regime's residual power, coercive capabilities, and other strengths probably still outweigh its weaknesses, at least for the time being. [42]

The sweeping structural changes necessitated by China's WTO entry and the broader demands of economic globalization and the information revolution have seriously tested the capacity of China's system and the competence and unity of a leadership facing repeated cycles of leadership change in the now-routine CCP and National People's congresses every five years. Developing succession arrangements and policies that sustain leadership unity, advantageous economic growth, and a modicum of popular support was essential to regime continuity. [43] The communist leadership maintains the command of strong military, police, and other security forces and uses them against a wide range of real or perceived opponents.

There is no clear alternative to communist rule, and there remains strong popular and elite aversion to fragmentation or chaos that could accompany regime change. Popular acquiescence to regime authority also comes from the positive performance of the economy. [44]

These strengths, however, are arrayed against the party's often growing weaknesses and challenges. Jiang Zemin's remaining in a senior leadership position while seeking the retirement of many of his Politburo Standing Committee colleagues headed the list of succession issues at the Sixteenth Party Congress in 2002. Succession issues were handled in a more business-like fashion as Hu Jintao retired after his ten-year tenure as party and state leader at the Eighteenth Party Congress in 2012. However, Xi Jinping's extraordinary hold on the reins of power while stoking fear at all official levels through the massive anticorruption campaign could prompt a major and potentially disruptive backlash. [45]

Decisions on economic opening and reform have benefited some Chinese groups while disadvantaging others, increasing the risk of leadership divisions. Other economic problems included massive debt, lagging reforms of SOEs, financial sector weaknesses, rising inequalities, large-scale unemployment, unsustainable levels of pollution, energy shortages, and the inadequacy of the national welfare, health, education, and pension systems. These problems remain interlocked, with reforms helping development in one area and having negative consequences in others, thus offering no easy solutions. [46]

The CCP has been able to recruit some talented newcomers, but ideological commitment remained weak despite recent efforts to reinvigorate ideological training and propaganda. Rampant corruption at all levels of party and state authority is being addressed by Xi's leadership.

Economic change has gone hand in hand with social changes, producing increasing pressure on the administration to adjust its policies. The flexibility of the leadership in adapting to new trends continues to be tested, with high potential for further dissonance between citizens and government and greater instability in both urban and rural areas. Aggrieved and disaffected groups present in all parts of society continue demonstrations and work stoppages.[47]

Seeking continued economic engagement with the rest of the world, PRC leaders try—with limited success—to control entry of perceived adverse outside information and other sources of pressure that come with greater economic openness and information exchange. Taiwan's separate status and democratic example challenge regime legitimacy and add to leadership debate, as to a lesser degree does the example of Hong Kong's greater freedoms. Pressure from the United States and other countries in support of principles championed by ethnic and democratic activists in China combined with the strong U.S. strategic posture to appear to Beijing as a challenge to the Chinese government's goals. China reacted defensively with internal security forces on alert in response to the Arab Spring popular protests that threatened and brought down long-standing autocratic rulers in northern Africa and the Middle East.[48]

The External Environment

Changes in the external environment continue to cause shifts in Chinese domestic policy and Chinese leaders' overall priorities and preoccupations. Particularly important was how China perceived the threat from abroad. Although they no longer saw a major military threat to China's national security, Chinese leaders continue to see influence from the outside world—notably the United States and Western-aligned countries—as constituting a major threat to China's stability; many of their comments about this threat appeared to be exaggerated rhetoric designed in part to justify a firm party grip. China also is concerned about the influence of Islamic countries on ethnic minorities in Xinjiang and other parts of northwest and southwest China, and this in part led China to support the U.S.-led antiterrorist campaign after September 11, 2001.[49]

Tensions across the Taiwan Strait, in the territorial disputes with Japan or India, in the South China Sea and the Yellow Sea, or in other areas near China increase China's perception of threat and result in more assertive security policies at home and abroad. Stronger disputes with the United States probably would have a similar effect. The recent record shows that Chinese leaders have been relatively unconstrained by foreign criticism in using force to crack down on internal dissidents or in suppressing public discussion of foreign policy issues. In circumstances of growing tensions with the United States or nearby powers, it seems likely that the use of nationalistic propaganda would become more evident.[50]

Other external developments also could have a significant effect on China's internal stability:

- Foreign economic developments often have helped or hindered China's economic growth. An increased ability to absorb China's exports fosters growth, but recessions among China's key trading partners or a significant drop-off in foreign direct investment hurts growth and contributes to social problems in China.
- Cultural change abroad spills over into China. China's opening to outside cultural influence, including foreign television, music, and other media, could amplify dissent—especially if the government does not permit greater openness and pluralism.[51]

CHINA'S GOALS IN FOREIGN AFFAIRS

Regime survival remains the leaders' top priority and continues to drive Chinese leadership preoccupations with the myriad domestic issues noted previously. Against this background, Chinese government policies and practices in international affairs on the whole are of somewhat less immediate importance and lower priority. They reflect goals and objectives in world affairs that have existed in China for decades. Further, these goals and objectives seem likely to continue well into the twenty-first century. Chinese leaders appear to have reached consensus on these objectives, although they frequently do not agree on the means by which to achieve them.[52]

To recap, Chinese leaders continue to share certain overarching objectives:

- They seek to perpetuate their power and avoid the fate of the Soviet Union and other Eastern European communist regimes.
- They pursue territorial unification and integrity, especially with Taiwan and, to a lesser degree, claims in the East China, South China, and Yellow seas and claims regarding India.
- They also seek to modernize China's economic, technological, and military capabilities and improve social conditions while maintaining stability.

In addition, China has strategic objectives that reflect its status as a rising power:

- Regional preeminence: Although U.S. and other foreign specialists offer differing opinions on China's long-term regional and world goals, a mid-range view sees China's leaders wanting to be in a position of sufficient strength (with both positive and negative incentives—carrots and sticks) so that other countries in the region and Asian regional organizations would routinely take China's interests and equities into account in determining their own policies. Beijing wishes to be seen as the leading power in Asia, higher in prestige or regional influence than its neighbors. It also wishes to be able to project power sufficient to counter hostile naval power and airpower.

• Global influence: A permanent member of the UN Security Council, Beijing desires status and prestige among the community of nations. It intends China to be a major player in the International Monetary Fund, the World Bank, the WTO, and other key international institutions. China's leaders have sought to assert influence on issues that are deemed important to China, not only to protect and defend Chinese interests but also to bolster China's standing as a major power. Chinese leaders believe that international power and prestige are an extension of national economic and technological prowess, which they intend to develop.

China's officials have approached the broad strategic objectives listed here in an international environment where Chinese leaders tend to view China's influence as growing at an impressive rate but far from dominant and where external and internal factors limit China's freedom of action and possible assertiveness in world affairs. At the start of the twenty-first century, Chinese perceptions of global trends appeared to be in flux and a matter of considerable internal debate. Chinese leaders, as reflected in official comments, had believed that the world was becoming multipolar, with the United States as the single superpower but increasingly less able to exert its will as other countries and regions opposed U.S. initiatives. This view changed sharply beginning in the mid to late 1990s because of the striking disparities between U.S. economic performance and that of other major powers and also because of U.S. leadership in the Balkan crisis, U.S. policy on missile defense, the U.S. war on terrorism, and other issues.[53]

The Chinese apparently concluded that the world would be unipolar in the near term, with the United States exerting greater influence than Chinese commentators had originally calculated. Chinese leaders often perceived that this influence might not be benign regarding China's key interests, notably Taiwan and around China's periphery.[54] Chinese commentary expressed concern about the expansion and strengthening of the U.S. alliance structure and the ability of U.S.-led alliances to intervene regionally and globally.[55]

Developments in the past decade appear to have altered Chinese perspectives of China's power and that of the United States. China's quick rebound and America's slow recovery from the global economic crisis and recession of 2008–2010 added to perceptions in China that a multipolar world—with China as a leading power and America in decline—was emerging. The perceptions fed into the ongoing Chinese foreign policy debate, with some officials and other commentators urging China to take more initiatives to enhance and secure its interests, even at the expense of smooth relations with the United States and its allies and associates. Partly in response to the recent

Chinese assertiveness, the United States launched the wide-ranging and widely publicized rebalance with the Asia-Pacific, thereby ushering in a new phase of Sino-American competition for influence in Asia.

Meanwhile, despite China's turn from traditional Marxist-Leninist-Maoist ideology, components of this tradition continue to influence the thinking of some leaders. Some Chinese officials see themselves locked in a struggle of values with the West and particularly the United States, which they see as bent on dividing or "Westernizing" China. Also common is the long-standing Chinese tendency to focus on a primary adversary in world affairs, to exaggerate its threat to China, and to seek domestic and foreign power to offset and counter this threat. Patterns of behavior reflecting this tendency can be seen repeatedly in later chapters examining Chinese leaders' policies and behavior toward the United States and its interests in Asia in the post–Cold War period.

Preoccupied with domestic issues of modernization and stability, Chinese leaders have tended at least until recently to be reactive to international developments. Deng Xiaoping stated that China should not get out in front on world issues but should take advantage of opportunities, bide its time, and gradually build Chinese power and influence; his successors generally held to this view. The Hu Jintao government reportedly saw the period until about 2020 as a "strategic opportunity" for China's leadership to modernize and develop national wealth and power in an international atmosphere that, if managed appropriately, would support Chinese domestic development goals.

However, Chinese leaders also have become more active in bilateral and multilateral diplomacy. In international forums (the United Nations, the WTO, arms control discussions, and other arenas), China increasingly has tried to ensure that it is one of the rule makers for the global environment of the twenty-first century.[56] Beijing has also perceived that it needs to continue to build its military capabilities to be able eventually to back up its diplomacy, especially over the status of Taiwan, other territorial claims, and a widening range of important interests regarding energy security and the security of sea lines of communication, space, and other global commons. In particular, China has shown that it is willing to use military-backed actions by an array of Chinese security forces, trade sanctions, violent and destructive demonstrations in China, and other means in pursuit of its goals regarding sensitive security, sovereignty, and other contested issues involving the United States and governments along China's rim in nearby Asia. The Xi Jinping government strongly shows these more active and assertive tendencies, foreshadowing difficulties for the United States and China's neighbors as they endeavor to deal with an increasingly powerful and newly assertive China.[57]

Chapter Three

Changing Patterns in Decision Making and International Outlook

The foreign policy and behavior of the People's Republic of China (PRC) is determined by leaders who make the decisions on the basis of what they think about the issues being decided. The patterns of decision making and the international outlook of Chinese leaders have changed in the post–Cold War period:

- China's greater opening to the outside world since the death of Mao and China's remarkable integration with international economic, security, political, and other multilateral organizations have accompanied much greater transparency and openness in Chinese foreign policy decision making.
- The number of people in and outside the Chinese government with an interest and influence in Chinese foreign policy decision making has grown enormously from the Maoist period. At that time, the Chinese Communist Party (CCP) chairman made most of the key decisions, often shifting policy in radical directions, with the assistance of a few advisers.
- The Chinese decision makers today also represent a much broader set of Chinese interests in international affairs, notably in international economics and overall global stability and welfare. This trend contrasts with the predominantly security-oriented interests that dominated Chinese leadership concerns over foreign affairs during much of the Cold War. These security-oriented interests were focused on narrower concerns about preserving national sovereignty and security against superpower opposition.
- The outlook of Chinese decision makers on international affairs at times appears more cosmopolitan and compatible with prevailing international trends and norms, with less emphasis than in the past on the need for China to be on guard and prepared to take assertive and forceful action

against dangerous and predatory powers seeking to exploit, oppress, and constrain China. At other times, guarded suspicion seems more salient.[1]

This chapter reviews highlights of what is known of the prevailing structure and processes in the Chinese government's decision making on foreign policy and salient features of the international outlook of Chinese decision makers. The assessment shows that in the Chinese government, the CCP, and the People's Liberation Army (PLA), the three key administrative groups governing China, the structure and processes in Chinese decision making on foreign policy are more regularized and institutionalized than in the past. Also in contrast to past practice, Chinese leaders often are more accommodating to international trends and more in conformity with prevailing international norms.

However, the assessment also shows significant areas of secrecy; long-standing suspicion of other world powers, especially in nearby Asia; nationalistic and military ambitions; and other trends that seem at odds with or contradict cosmopolitan and accommodating Chinese foreign policy and behavior. The net result reinforces a finding in this book that while much of the recent orientation of China's foreign policy should be encouraged and welcomed by the international community, world leaders should not assume that these Chinese policy trends will uniformly prevail. Leaders in China long have held conflicting views over how far to go in accommodating other countries and in conforming to international norms.

For instance, Chinese foreign policy in recent years repeatedly has shown abrupt shifts toward confrontation during international crises involving China. The accidental U.S. bombing of the Chinese embassy in Belgrade in May 1999 prompted a sharp turn toward the negative in China's approach toward the United States.[2] The danger of reversal in Chinese policy toward the United States surfaced again in 2001 as a result of the April 1 clash between a Chinese jet fighter and a U.S. reconnaissance aircraft in international airspace near China's southern coast.[3] In contrast with China's accommodating approach toward neighboring countries, labeled China's "good-neighbor" policy, mass demonstrations against Japanese diplomatic and business installations in China in 2005 resulted in damage and destruction that went on for several days until curbed by Chinese authorities.[4]

Most important in recent years, the scope and intensity of Chinese assertiveness regarding long-standing disputes with neighbors over maritime claims in the East China Sea and the South China Sea have come as unwelcome surprises to nearby countries and to the United States and other powers concerned with the regional order. They belie China's continued refrain stressing China's common interests in peace and development. They have deepened foreign suspicions that Beijing is playing a double game involving coercion intent on advancing control of disputed territory along with enough rhetorical reassurance and economic exchange to avoid military conflict, especially with the United States, or confrontation with a united front of aroused powers in the region.

An impressive buildup of Chinese naval, coast guard, fishing, oil exploration, and dredging forces and equipment has allowed repeated assertive actions to advance Chinese control. The PLA Navy, maritime surveillance forces, and Chinese foreign policy organizations have employed intimidation, coercion, and harassment along with stern verbal warnings against fishing, energy prospecting, maritime surveillance, and military and diplomatic actions by foreigners involving Chinese-claimed territorial and other rights in waters along China's rim. Efforts by Japan, South Korea, and several Southeast Asian nations to support their claimed rights and interests, along with complaints from the United States, Australia, India, and other concerned powers have been dismissed or have met with truculent Chinese attacks.

The year 2012 featured extraordinary demonstrations of Chinese use of this wide-ranging means of power and force short of direct military action, establishing the prevailing Chinese approach in following years. The means have involved repeated shows of force by Chinese civilian-controlled maritime security forces, diplomatic threats, economic sanctions at odds with established international norms, and in the case of Japanese claims in the East China Sea, mass demonstrations in over one hundred Chinese cities for a weeklong period in September 2012 that resulted in widespread violence including burning and looting of Japanese properties and beatings of Japanese citizens in China.[5] Chinese forces took control of Scarborough Shoal in the South China Sea from the Philippines; massive dredging created Chinese fortified islands in the South China Sea; coast guard and naval patrols chased neighboring fishermen, intimidated foreign oil exploration, and threatened small foreign occupation forces on disputed reefs. The forces pressed China's claims against Japan with repeated face-offs between the two sides' coast guard and air forces.[6]

Adding to the tentativeness and uncertainty among Chinese and foreign observers regarding how and why Chinese foreign policy decisions are made is the prevailing secrecy that continues to surround Chinese policy on key foreign policy questions. To this day, U.S. officials remain in the dark about how senior Chinese leaders deliberated in the weeks following the crises in May 1999 and April 2001.[7] Similar uncertainty pervades reviews of what is known of Chinese decision making during the April 2005 demonstrations against Japan, and in the repeated episodes of intimidation and assertiveness against neighbors in recent years. President Xi Jinping has demonstrated Chinese strength in promoting greater activism in foreign affairs, but assessors struggle to determine who actually is making decisions and what issues and priorities are driving those decisions.[8]

What the previously mentioned episodes show is that even though much more is known than in the past about Chinese foreign policy decision making, especially as it involves economic issues, major political and security issues remain shrouded in secrecy. This is the intent of the Chinese authorities. Those in China who reveal information that is defined by Chinese authorities as coming under a very broad purview of national security are arrested and prosecuted.

Even key Chinese decisions in international economics, such as the considerations that top leaders focused on in making the final decision for China to accept significant compromises in 1999 to reach agreement with the United States in order to join the World Trade Organization (WTO), are not clearly known. Discussions with U.S. officials about the days leading up to the final agreement in November 1999 show that Premier Zhu Rongji, backed by senior economic policy leader Wu Yi and other key officials, was instrumental in reaching the final agreement with the U.S. negotiating team. But the motives and arguments in senior Chinese leadership deliberations and those of President Jiang Zemin and other leaders with a role in or influence on the final decision remain unknown.[9]

One of the most important international security issues facing Chinese decision makers involves the international crisis brought about by North Korea's development of nuclear weapons and concurrent leadership transition. The range of Chinese interests in the crisis, including avoiding war, preserving stability in Korea and northeastern Asia, and preventing the spread of nuclear weapons, appears clear. Yet Chinese officials and specialists are frank in acknowledging that they remain in the dark and uncertain about what top Chinese decision makers actually say in conveying Chinese priorities during secret communications with the reclusive North Korean regime.

Thus, it was unknown in China and abroad whether Chinese leader Hu Jintao and his colleagues adopted a uniformly accommodating posture to North Korean leader Kim Jong Il during the latter's initially secret ten-day visit to China in January 2006 and his later visits in 2010 and 2011.[10] How much, if any, pressure the Chinese leader was prepared to exert on his North Korean counterpart in order to ensure that the North Korean crisis was managed along lines acceptable to China remained a mystery. In the event, China's leaders publicly supported the ailing Kim's arrangement transferring leadership to his inexperienced son, Kim Jong Un, after Kim's death in December 2011. The younger Kim's repeated provocations have seen President Xi Jinping pull back public demonstrations of support, but the scope and content of Chinese efforts to get Pyongyang to change course remain unknown.[11]

KEY DECISION MAKERS IN CHINESE FOREIGN POLICY

There is general agreement among Chinese and foreign specialists regarding the continued decisive role of the "paramount" leader at the top of the hierarchy of government, party, and military actors influencing Chinese foreign policy decision making. Mao Zedong, Deng Xiaoping, Jiang Zemin, and Hu Jintao played that role in the past, and today Xi Jinping holds power as Communist Party general secretary, government president, and chairman of the Central Military Commission; he is in this key final decision maker role. It is generally held that Mao and Deng were strong and decisive in guiding Chinese foreign policy, where Jiang and Hu were seen as much more consultative and cautious in their foreign policy roles. Xi Jinping moved quickly to establish control over foreign policy and national security. He established a new national security commission, which he heads, that provides leadership for Chinese national security policies both domestic and foreign.[12] His active personal involvement in defining initiatives stressing China's international priorities shows greater willingness than either Jiang Zemin or Hu Jintao to take risks short of applying direct military force in challenging existing norms, institutions, and other arrangements that are seen to work against China's ambitions.[13]

Supporting the paramount leader and influencing his decisions are his top-level colleagues in the CCP's Politburo Standing Committee. Under Hu Jintao's leadership (2002–2012) there were nine members of the Standing Committee, and many played important roles in foreign policy. In the lead was Prime Minister Wen Jiabao, who was more active than President Hu in dealing with foreign affairs. During the leadership of Jiang Zemin, who left his last official leadership post in early 2004, specialists assessed that the broader CCP Politburo and the CCP Secretariat under the politburo played supporting roles as the paramount leader made decisions. Like Xi Jinping and unlike Hu Jintao, Jiang sought and appeared to enjoy the limelight in international affairs.

Xi Jinping has six colleagues in the CCP Politburo Standing Committee. Though second-ranking party leader and Premier Li Keqiang is very active in foreign affairs, official Chinese media coverage and international attention clearly give top priority to Xi. The Chinese president makes use of politburo meetings, large foreign affairs conferences involving most senior Chinese leaders involved in foreign affairs, and the new national security commission to set China's foreign policy agenda.[14]

Xi Jinping also makes use of the so-called Leading Small Group for Foreign Affairs, which has been used by Chinese leaders over the years to set broad policy directions. Members of this group have changed at times but have usually included the president or the premier, the state counselor for foreign affairs, and top-level officials of the Foreign Affairs, Defense, and

State Security ministries. There are a variety of other small groups run by party, government, or military bodies. Several of these policy groups have strong implications for foreign affairs and Xi is leading many of them. Thus, he leads the Central Leading Group for Comprehensively Deepening Reforms, which is in charge of guiding China's current wide-ranging economic reform agenda. Xi leads the Leading Small Groups on Taiwan affairs and on financial and economic affairs; in the past the premier usually led the latter group. And Xi chairs the main military decision making body, the CCP's Central Military Commission and another new group to oversee military reform.[15]

One purpose of these leading groups is to allow key government, party, and military components to have input into important foreign policy decisions. A second purpose is to allow the paramount leader and his close advisers to benefit from these contributions as they seek to formulate effective policies that reflect the expertise and interests of relevant parts of the Chinese government, party, and military apparatus. Among administrative actors consulted in such decision making are the Ministry of Foreign Affairs, the Commerce Ministry, the Xinhua news agency, the International Liaison Department of the CCP, and components of the PLA dealing with intelligence, military exchanges, and arms transfers. The ability of the senior Chinese leader to control the actions of the myriad bodies involved in contemporary Chinese foreign affairs has repeatedly come into question as Chinese behavior has seemed to zig and zag between options of moderation and accommodation and options of truculence and assertiveness. The pattern underlines that China's seemingly authoritarian control in actuality is "fractured."[16]

THE FOREIGN POLICY CONCERNS AND WORLDVIEW OF CHINESE LEADERS

Few foreign specialists have had meaningful contacts with senior Chinese leaders to the point of understanding more than the general outlines of their thinking on world affairs and how this affects their leanings in foreign affairs. Thus, the judgments in their assessments remain tentative. Chinese specialists who have close contacts with senior Chinese officials generally say little about this subject. When they do address it, they tend to emphasize that those officials remain more wary of the United States and the U.S.-dominated international order than others in China who adopt a more moderate and relaxed view of the United States and the international situation. The Chinese specialists also emphasize that senior Chinese leaders show more sensitivity than others in China to perceived threats or affronts coming from foreign sources.[17]

Assessments of Chinese foreign policy thinking at the start of this century made the case that Chinese foreign policy and behavior were changing markedly in directions more in line with international norms, especially regarding economic and cultural matters and constructive participation in multilateral organizations. These changes in Chinese policy were seen as influenced by a more pluralistic range of Chinese decision makers whose diverse interests were reflected in foreign policy and behavior. These decision makers represented a variety of government, party, and military bureaucracies, government-affiliated and nongovernment think tanks, and provincial and local governments, as well as broad segments of Chinese people, reflecting aroused public opinion, especially on nationalistic issues. According to the assessments, the broad range of those influencing Chinese foreign policy meant that the Chinese foreign policy process needed to be more consultative and attentive to wide-ranging inputs. As a result, the decision-making process often was slower and more cumbersome than in the past, when the top leader could decide changes in policy on his own authority.[18]

As Chinese policy and practice became increasingly engaged in international relations, better-educated and younger officials and nongovernment specialists played a more important role in informing and guiding the decision-making process. They contributed on such complicated issues as economic regulations, intellectual property rights, environmental compliance, arms control regulations, human rights, and international law. Another feature of the recent foreign policymaking process in China was that foreign governments, businesses, and other nongovernment groups had more entry points that allowed them to influence some or all of the diverse range of Chinese actors that have influence in determining Chinese foreign policy and behavior. These outside influences tended to push China toward behavior more in line with international norms.

The assessments acknowledged the still secretive and hierarchic structure of Chinese foreign policy decision making, with the top-level party, government, and military leaders exerting dominant influence on final decisions, especially on national security questions.[19] They also highlighted a prevailing worldview among this elite that emphasized seeing international affairs in terms of competing states, with China required to maintain its guard against exploitation and oppression as it seeks to develop national wealth and power and greater influence in Asian and world affairs. Nonetheless, the assessments pointed out that these leaders needed the expertise and broad inputs that came from consulting the wide range of bureaucratic and nongovernment specialists and interests noted previously. To do otherwise risked ineffective or mistaken policies that could have a direct impact on top Chinese leaders, whose legitimacy rested heavily on demonstrating an ability to advance Chinese power and influence without major international complications or confrontation. In sum, there was some optimism that the recent trend of increasing Chinese foreign policy conformity with and adherence to international norms, along with continued emphasis on promoting general trends toward world peace and development, were likely to continue. [20]

On assuming the leading CCP position in 2002, Hu Jintao appeared to follow the pattern of generally cautious moves toward moderation in Chinese foreign affairs seen in the latter years of Jiang Zemin. Hu's leadership featured emphasis on "peaceful development" and supporting a "harmonious" world. [21] The recent Chinese assertiveness and truculence in foreign affairs highlighted earlier focused on the United States and China's neighbors and emerged during the later years of Hu rule; they have been reinforced under the activist foreign policy of Xi Jinping. They belie the earlier emphasis on peaceful development and harmony. China's current mixed message features "win-win" cooperative development on the one hand and a hard line advancing territorial control and other Chinese interests at the expense of neighbors and concerned powers on the other.

Roots of the recent Chinese assertiveness and toughness lie in the deep and rich soil of the world outlook of Chinese elites and public opinion. A review of the various worldviews propounded by leaders of the People's Republic of China since 1949 indicates how difficult it remains for China to fully accept existing international norms and an accommodating posture to the United States, Western countries, and China's neighbors with a large stake in the prevailing regional and international order. As specialists in China have repeatedly emphasized in recent years, China's rising international prominence has brought to the fore nationalistic and zero-sum realist foreign policy calculations on the part of a variety of influential foreign policy actors in China that have put those Chinese leaders arguing for progressive accommodation to existing international norms in a more defensive and increasingly less influential position. These nationalistic and realist calculations tap into strongly engrained Chinese views of world affairs that have been perpetuated by the communist government's massive propaganda apparatus for the sake of strengthening one-party communist rule.

There is little disagreement among Chinese and foreign specialists that Chinese officials and the rest of the Chinese people have long been conditioned through the education system and government-sponsored media coverage to think of China as having been victimized by international powers since the early nineteenth century. Emphasis on this historical conditioning was strengthened after the CCP crisis at the time of the Tiananmen demonstrations and bloody crackdown in 1989 and continues to the present. Sensing that communism no longer provided adequate ideological support for continued CCP rule, the authorities instituted a patriotic education campaign with related media coverage. The campaign was designed to encourage regime-supporting patriotism in China by recalling the more than one hundred years of foreign affronts to Chinese national dignity. With this focus, foreign complaints about human rights and other abuses in China after the Tiananmen crackdown were depicted as the latest in a long series of foreign efforts to abuse and victimize China. As such, they were likely to elicit negative responses from Chinese people directed at foreign governments rather than result in Chinese people agreeing with the foreign criticism of the abuses of Chinese communist rule. [22]

The historic record since the first Opium War (1839–1842), featured in Chinese indoctrination, education, and media efforts, provides a rich legacy for those seeking to view China as an aggrieved party in international affairs. [23] For example, foreign powers, mainly Great Britain but including the United States, used opium trade as a way to balance their purchases of tea and other commodities from China in the early nineteenth century. Backed by superior military power, British, and later joint British-French, military expeditions defeated Chinese forces and compelled the opening of several so-called treaty ports along Chinese rivers and coastal areas, where foreigners lived under their own jurisdiction, not Chinese law, and foreign missionaries were free to spread religious beliefs seen as heterodox by Chinese officials. Foreign military power coerced the Chinese government to give large swaths of territory to foreign rule. After Japan unexpectedly defeated China in a war over dominance in Korea and took Taiwan from China in 1895, the foreign powers seemed poised to divide up China into their respective colonies or spheres of influence. [24]

China probably would have been divided by the foreign imperialists had not the tensions leading to World War I caused the European powers to withdraw forces from China in order to prepare for war in Europe. The field was then open for Japan to dominate China, which it did. Other foreign powers did little other than object to Japan's expansion and eventual takeover of Manchuria.

In 1937, as full-scale war broke out between China and much stronger and technologically superior Japanese forces, China stood basically alone. Through brutal and rapacious attacks, 1 million Japanese soldiers occupied the most productive parts of China. With Japan's defeat in 1945, the United States sided with Chiang Kai-shek against the Chinese communists in three years of Chinese civil war, ending with the communist victory on the Chinese mainland in 1949 and Chiang Kai-shek's retreat to Taiwan.

The Chinese communists then confronted the United States following the June 1950 U.S. intervention into the Korean War as well as the U.S. intervention into the Taiwan Strait that prevented the communists from reunifying Taiwan with the mainland. In the Chinese view, twenty years of hostility, confrontation, and abuse of China at the hands of American leaders were followed by twenty years of similar treatment of China by the Soviet Union, which emerged as China's main security threat in the late 1960s. Finally, at the end of the Cold War, the PRC experienced an international situation where for the first time it did not face immediate danger of war with one or two nuclear-armed superpowers.

The lessons of this sordid experience, which continues to be strongly emphasized by Chinese education, media, and propaganda organs, heavily influence the world outlook of Chinese leaders and people:

- The world is viewed darkly. It is full of highly competitive, unscrupulous, and duplicitous governments that are seeking their selfish interests at the expense of China and others.
- To survive and develop, China needs power—military power backed by economic power and political unity. If there is disunity at home, foreign powers will use Chinese differences to exploit China, just as they did in the past.
- China is an aggrieved party. It has suffered greatly at foreign hands for almost two centuries. It needs to build its power and influence to protect what it has and to get back what is rightfully China's. This means restoration of Taiwan to Chinese sovereignty and securing other Chinese territorial claims.
- China does not dominate the world order; other powers do—during the Cold War, the United States and the Soviet Union; after the Cold War, the United States. China needs to work toward an international balance that helps Chinese interests and avoids outside dominance. In this vein, Chinese leaders in recent years have emphasized the benefits of a multipolar world order where China would have greater freedom of maneuver and security than in an international order dominated by the United States. [25]

Complementing this historical discourse showing China as the victim of predatory outsiders are other features influencing China's worldview to various degrees:

- The ideological and revolutionary drive of Mao Zedong and his colleagues to foster revolution in China and abroad has largely ended, though as noted in the previous chapter, China's leaders remain determined to preserve Communist Party rule in the face of perceived political challenges and values supported by the West.
- Chinese self-reliance, important in the latter Maoist period, has been put aside with China's ever-growing interdependence with the world, especially in economics and trade. Nevertheless, with the exception of North Korea, China scrupulously avoids alliances with or formal dependence on other states as it seeks ties with other countries based on the "win-win" formula that determines Chinese foreign relations recently. Chinese cooperation with others is contingent on a "win" for China that is within the

scope of a win-set defined narrowly in terms of tangible benefit for the Chinese state.

- Chinese officials recently have fostered an idealized depiction of benevolent Chinese imperial interaction with China's neighbors. The hierarchic order of international relations with China at the center seen during much of the Ming and Qing dynasties from the fourteenth to nineteenth centuries is depicted showing Chinese naval expeditions and other foreign interchange that reflects China's purported unwillingness to be expansionist. [26]

- Chinese official discourse and related scholarship tend to play down foreign depictions of Chinese leaders changing foreign policies and even overall alignments as Chinese interests shift with changing circumstances at home and abroad. Rather, they portray Chinese policies and practices as consistent, based on appropriate principles in line with broad moral goals, and aligning China's approach with the "progressive" forces in international affairs.

- Applying these principles to foreign practice involves China's "peculiar" operational code of conduct—"firmness in principle and flexibility in application," as Samuel Kim labels it. This process has troubling implications for China's international view and its relations with other states. For Kim and others there is a gap between principle and practice in Chinese foreign relations, with China repeatedly attempting to show through sometimes adroit and sometimes awkward use of a wide range of old and new sets of principles that interest-based changes in Chinese foreign relations remain consistent with righteous principles. [27]

- A major implication of such Chinese reasoning is an acute sense of Chinese exceptionalism. Many Chinese truly believe that the People's Republic of China has always followed morally correct foreign policies in the interest of progressive world forces. They believe China has done nothing wrong in world affairs; indeed the PRC is the only major international actor (possibly with the exception of my beloved Roman Catholic Church) never to have acknowledged making a wrong decision or taking wrong action in foreign affairs. Thus, if difficulties arise with neighbors, the United States, or other states over foreign policy concerns, the fault naturally lies with the other party or some other circumstance, but never with China. Such an international outlook is deeply rooted among Chinese elite and public opinion.

The overall result of China's acute sense of grievance against past international victimization of China on the one hand and the strong sense of righteousness in the foreign policy and practice of the PRC on the other hand support a Chinese popular and elite worldview of poor self-awareness of Chinese international shortcomings and sharp sensitivity to international pressure. This situation makes it very hard to deal with differences, especially with issues of wide interest in China like Taiwan, Japan, the United States, and the widely publicized maritime territorial claims.

Meanwhile, although some foreign and Chinese specialists look on the bright side and see China conforming more to international norms, more sober views see China adjusting to circumstances. They see that adjustments could shift in ways at odds with international stability if the circumstances were to change, say, for example, with a rise in Chinese power and decline of the power of the United States.

CHINESE ELITE AND POPULAR VIEWS OF THE UNITED STATES

This section focuses on Chinese views of the United States because in the post–Cold War period, the United States has been widely seen in China as the leading international power, a superpower determined to maintain dominance and hegemony in world affairs.[28] The conditioning of Chinese elite and popular opinion for many years by government-controlled education and media has reinforced a strong sense of patriotism and suspicion of the United States. The conditioning often stresses the need to speed China's drive for comprehensive national power in order to ensure China's rightful interests in the face of U.S. and other foreign pressures. At times of cooperative China–U.S. relations, Chinese government authorities play down the anti-U.S. stance, but it emerges often and with surprising vehemence at times of Sino-U.S. friction.[29]

Assessments by U.S., Chinese, and other specialists have continued to find that Chinese officials and the experts who advise them view U.S. policy and behavior with a great deal of suspicion. Wang Jisi, one of the most prominent Chinese specialists on U.S.–China relations and a frequent adviser to President Hu Jintao and key Chinese leaders, wrote in 2005 that despite some ups and downs in Chinese views of the United States since the end of the Cold War, "the official line continues to point to the United States as the mainstay of the 'hostile forces' that try to destabilize China and refers to the United States as the hegemonic power that threatens global security." He added, "to most Chinese observers, . . . the United States is an insatiable domineering country that believes only in its own absolute power, one that would never allow any other country to catch up with it." Given their perception of American intentions and hegemony, these Chinese elites tend not to trust U.S. motives. Although they see China benefiting from and heavily dependent on economic and other ties with the United States, they continue to fear American manipulation of China in international strategic terms, exploitation in economic terms, and subversion in political and ideological terms. As Wang advised Chinese readers in an interview in October 2008, "Pax Americana" is an unjust international order "under power politics," and

"China cannot accept being led by the United States" even as Beijing pursues cooperation with Washington for pragmatic reasons. Professor Wang teamed with a prominent American China specialist, Kenneth Lieberthal, to publish an important study in 2012 that reaffirmed the deep suspicions of Chinese and U.S. official elites toward one another.[30]

At the start of the twenty-first century, the list of Chinese charges and grievances against U.S. hegemonism was long and involved many issues of direct concern to China and nearby Asia. They included the large and growing U.S. defense budget; a strong tendency to use coercive measures in U.S. foreign policy; allegedly wanton disregard of international institutions and rules when deemed inconvenient; an aggressive agenda in promoting Western values; unilateral decisions to build missile defenses; endeavoring to restrict high-technology information to China and others; arrogant violations of other countries' sovereignty; unjustified expansion of U.S. alliances in Europe and Asia; and determination to contain emerging powers, notably China.[31]

To American policymakers and others interested in better U.S. relations with China, the clear tendency of Chinese leaders to exaggerate the negatives in the U.S. approach to China and to highlight the threat the United States posed to the key interests of the CCP leadership were major obstacles to improved relations. Remedying these tendencies was difficult. Part of the problem was how deeply rooted the inclination was for leaders in China (and the United States) to exaggerate the power and influence—usually seen as negative—posed by the other side.[32]

Chinese strategists throughout the Cold War tended to focus on how the United States and/or the Soviet Union could or did use "power politics" and outright coercion to force China to compromise over key interests. The exaggerated Chinese claims that the United States was seeking to split up, hold back, and contain China in the 1990s and later echoed this approach. Adding to the tendency was the long-standing Chinese leadership practice of analyzing world politics in terms of "contradictions" derived from Marxism-Leninism and developed by Mao Zedong. The Chinese international approach and worldview thus had a clear focus on the "main enemy" or danger to China and its interests. The United States played this role in the 1950s and 1960s; the Soviet Union was the main enemy in the 1970s and much of the 1980s. Beginning in the 1990s, despite China's strong need to promote advantageous economic and other relations with the United States, Chinese elite thinking and behavior showed that the United States again became the main target of Chinese international concern—that is, China's main "enemy."[33]

In order to mobilize domestic and international forces to deal with the main danger, Chinese leaders tended to portray the adversary in starkly negative terms. Often associated with this kind of international outlook was a "united front" policy. This involved Chinese efforts to win over other powers to assist in the focused attempts to counter the danger posed by the main adversary. Of course, China's dealings with the United States in the 1990s were not as clear-cut as its dealings with the Americans and the Soviets in the Cold War. The United States was not seen only as an adversary; it also was a competitor and a partner whose cooperation was essential to Chinese modernization. Thus, Chinese leaders endeavored to sustain a balanced approach to the United States that preserved a working relationship—especially economic relations—while continuing to view U.S. power as threatening many important Chinese interests. [34]

The episodes of greater Chinese assertiveness against the United States, its Asian partners, and others in nearby Asia began at the end of the previous decade and continue up to the present. They included a revival of exaggerated claims that the United States, now under the Obama administration, was using its avowed efforts to reengage with Asia-Pacific countries under the rubric of its rebalance policy as a thinly veiled effort to contain and hold back China's rising influence in the region and throughout the world. Slow U.S. recovery from the global economic crisis that started in 2008 and other perceived American weaknesses and contrasting economic, military, and other Chinese advances led many Chinese elite and popular observers to recalculate the international balance of power in China's favor. A weakened U.S. superpower and the rise of China and other nations meant that a multipolar world was not far off, allowing, in the calculations of these Chinese opinion leaders, for a more assertive Chinese policy regarding a range of differences with the United States. [35]

CHINESE OPPOSITION TO SUPERPOWER DOMINANCE IN ASIA

Another legacy of the past that influences Chinese officials' contemporary worldview and international behavior is the long record of Chinese policy and behavior in Asia that shows repeated maneuvering to keep China's periphery as free as possible from hostile or potentially hostile great-power pressure. Asia, especially the countries around China's periphery, has been the main arena of Chinese foreign relations for obvious reasons. Nearby Asia contains security and sovereignty issues (e.g., Taiwan) of highest importance. It is the main arena of interaction with the United States. Its economic importance far surpasses the rest of world (China is Africa's biggest trader but until very recently it did more trade with South Korea). Asian stability is essential for China's economic growth—the linchpin of communist rule.

Efforts to keep this periphery free of potentially hostile great-power presence and pressure are seen as central to Chinese security, and China has long used both offensive and defensive measures to thwart perceived great-power ambitions in the region. This trend has persisted, along with the growing

Chinese economic integration, increasing political and security cooperation, and active engagement with various states and multilateral organizations in the region. Thus, as Chinese officials declare greater confidence as China rises in influence in Asia, they work assiduously in trying to ensure that the United States and its allies and associates do not establish power and influence along China's periphery that is adverse to Chinese interests.[36]

Available scholarship[37] shows a growing acceptance by PRC leaders of interdependence in international economic relations but continued wariness regarding close interaction with and dependence on others regarding political, security, environmental, and other concerns. It indicates that it is still too early to know if Chinese leaders are genuinely internalizing and embracing global norms and values that would argue for greater stability and moderation in Asian and world affairs. Alternatively, they may be merely adapting to global norms to derive tactical benefits, biding their time to exert greater pressure and force to achieve Chinese goals when future circumstances are more advantageous. While Chinese leaders have moved over time to see their interests best served by full engagement with international economic norms, Chinese leaders generally seem to follow a case-by-case approach, doing cost-benefit analysis in making key foreign policy decisions. Interdependence with and moderation and accommodation toward powers involved in Asian and world affairs appear to prevail when the costs of a more assertive posture—one more consistent with Chinese nationalistic attitudes and evidenced in periodic recent assertive behavior toward Japan, India, Southeast Asian claimants to disputed territories in the South China Sea, and South Korea, as well as the United States, Taiwan, and others—outweigh the benefits. When the assessed cost-benefit calculus allows, China has appeared ready and willing to use coercion, intimidation, and violence to have its way in disputes in nearby areas.

Chinese foreign policy in the Maoist period strongly opposed U.S. and Soviet power and pressure, especially along China's periphery. Years of often violent resistance to American containment with the help of the Soviet Union evolved under Mao's revolutionary leadership to a break in the alliance with Moscow and China standing against both the United States and the Soviet Union by the early 1960s. Moscow's persisting military buildup and search for greater political and military influence around China's periphery eventually became the strategic focus of Chinese foreign policy in Asia and China's overall approach to world affairs by the late 1960s. After serious leadership disagreements were resolved by the deaths and imprisonment of much of the Chinese military high command and other involved leaders, China developed a fairly consistent approach, at first under the leadership of Premier Zhou Enlai and Chairman Mao Zedong and later under Deng Xiaoping. It attempted to use U.S.–Soviet differences pragmatically to China's advantage. The Chinese leaders recognized that only at tremendous cost and great risk could China confront the Soviet Union on its own. It relied heavily on international counterweights to Soviet power, provided mainly by the United States and its allies and associates in Asia and elsewhere. As the United States reevaluated its former containment policy directed against China and no longer posed a serious military threat to Chinese national security, Chinese leaders maintained a collaborative relationship with the United States and the West as a key link in its security policy against the Soviet Union. [38]

For post-Mao Chinese leaders, the highest priority was to accomplish modernization as well as to maintain national security and internal order. Chinese leaders recognized the fundamental prerequisite of establishing a relatively stable strategic environment, especially around China's periphery in Asia. The alternative would be a highly disruptive situation requiring much greater Chinese expenditures on national defense and posing greater danger to domestic order and tranquility. China did not control this environment. It influenced it, but the environment remained controlled more by others, especially the superpowers and their allies and associates. As a result, China's leaders were required repeatedly to assess their surroundings for changes that affected Chinese security and development interests. The result was repeated Chinese adjustments to take account of such changes. [39]

At the same time, Chinese leaders had nationalistic and ideological objectives regarding irredentist claims (such as Taiwan) and a desire to stand independently in foreign affairs as a leading power among "progressive" developing nations of what was called the Third World. These goals struck a responsive chord politically inside China. Occasional leadership discussion and debate over these and other questions regarding foreign affairs sometimes had an effect on the course of Chinese foreign policy. However, following Deng Xiaoping's rise to power in the late 1970s, the debates became less serious—at least until the leadership impasse in the late 1980s, which set the stage for the Tiananmen crisis and crackdown of 1989. Of course, that leadership crisis focused mainly on domestic issues, and China's foreign policy orientation toward strengthening national security and development was not altered fundamentally. [40]

Thus, in the two decades after the most violent phase of the Cultural Revolution ended in 1969, China's top foreign policy priority remained the pragmatic quest for a stable environment needed for effective modernization and development. Chinese leaders since the late 1960s saw the main danger of negative change in the surrounding environment posed by the Soviet Union. At first, Chinese leaders perceived Soviet power as an immediate threat to its national security. Over time, it came to see the Soviet Union as more of a long-term threat, determined to use its growing military power and other sources of influence to encircle and pressure China into accepting its dominance in the balance of influence in Asia. [41]

Chinese maneuvers to free China's periphery as much as possible from the potentially hostile and debilitating presence of great powers continue in the post–Cold War period and focus on Chinese concerns over the United States. For the first decade after the Cold War, Chinese officials adopted a rhetorically confrontational approach, featuring regular and strongly worded attacks on the U.S. alliance system in Asia and other reflections of what they saw as "Cold War thinking," "power politics," and "hegemonism" in U.S. policies and behavior. The Chinese approach failed in the face of Asian states unwilling to side with China against the United States and in the face of strong U.S. power and influence determined to confront if necessary Chinese assertiveness over Taiwan and other issues.[42]

Adjusting to the adverse balance of costs and benefits for Chinese interests, Chinese leaders changed policy. By 2003, they articulated a new policy that emphasized China's peaceful rise and peaceful development in Asian and world affairs. This policy continues up to the present, though the episodes of Chinese assertive actions and strident rhetoric against the United States, its Asian partners, and other nearby states since the end of the previous decade have raised serious questions about the policy's durability. Unlike previous Chinese policy and behavior, the policy approach since 2003 sought not to confront the United States publicly on most issues. Chinese leaders still register strong differences with U.S. dominance in Asian and world affairs and remain concerned about how that U.S. power hurts Chinese interests regarding Taiwan and other sensitive issues. They openly demonstrate this opposition when the costs and benefits of doing so are seen to favor Chinese interests. The mix of stated moderation and periodic forceful actions and strong rhetoric confuse the situation. Thus, Chinese officials' comments on the Obama administration's emphasis on closer engagement with Asia under the rubric of the so-called rebalance policy have been critical in carefully measured language, while Chinese media have been full of strident charges against alleged U.S. schemes to use the new policy in order to "contain" and "hold back China's rise."[43] In the main, top-level Chinese leaders still emphasize a policy that plays down differences, striving to keep U.S.–Chinese relations as well as Chinese relations with most Asian and world governments on the generally positive footing that is seen as needed for Chinese stability and economic development.[44]

UNCERTAIN OUTLOOK: CHINA, THE UNITED STATES, AND NEARBY ASIA

The Chinese assertiveness and truculence beginning at the end of the previous decade presumably was prompted by calculations of at least some Chinese leaders who perceived American decline and Chinese ascendance opening the way for China to adopt tougher public actions and positions on long-standing differences with the United States and a variety of Asian countries with important security and sovereignty disputes with China. Although top-level Chinese leaders toned down differences and reaffirmed interest in peace and development during summits and other meetings with U.S. counterparts, China also continued double-digit defense spending to build military forces focused on fighting Americans in Asia; it used coercive and intimidating measures to advance territorial claims at neighbors' expense that disrupted the regional order and challenged U.S. ability to serve as the area's security guarantor; and it initiated a variety of China-centered international bank and other investment programs, trade agreements, and political and economic multilateral organizations that were at odds with or excluded the United States.

These developments in nearby Asia—the most important arena of Chinese foreign relations—demonstrate that the future course of Chinese policy remains uncertain. Other reasons to remain uncertain about China's purported peaceful approach to regional and world affairs include long-standing viewpoints among the Chinese leadership registering deep suspicions of U.S. policy and behavior; the policies and behavior of Japan, India, Taiwan, and many other governments around China's rim; and other potential or actual world conditions adverse to Chinese interests.

Given the salience of the United States in Chinese foreign policy calculations over the years, it is important to assess the implications of Chinese wariness that appeared deepened by the American government's emphasis on its rebalance policy to Asia starting notably in 2011. China registered strong opposition to the elements of the policy calling for increased U.S. military deployments, activism, and growing security collaboration with Japan, Australia, the Philippines, and other allies and powers. Recent Chinese free trade and investment initiatives that exclude or challenge American interests countered the American-backed Trans-Pacific Partnership free trade arrangement, which seeks much more rigorous measures to restrict the kinds of state-directed economic interventions and abuse of intellectual property rights common in Chinese economic practices.

Meanwhile, the fact remains that optimistic projections about U.S.–China relations have been made at various times during the post–Cold War period when those relations seemed to be improving but then deteriorated into confrontation and acrimony as a result of a crisis or persisting differences.[45] Indeed, the record of U.S.–China relations since 1989 seems to favor a less rosy perspective, which available evidence and testimony by Chinese specialists indicate is the prevailing view among senior Chinese leaders. The less optimistic perspective takes account of the many deeply rooted differences that Chinese and U.S. leaders will continue to grapple with in the years ahead. As there is no guarantee that the conditions that came to hold those differences in check and gave rise to a more positive path at the beginning of this century will continue or that third parties (e.g., North Korea, Taiwan, Japan, Vietnam, the Philippines, India, and others) might not intervene in ways that disrupt U.S.–China relations, it is advisable to be cautious in predicting any long-term or fundamental change in Chinese policies involving the United States and related developments, especially in nearby Asia.[46]

The most important differences in U.S.–China relations that appear likely to remain relevant determinants of Chinese foreign policy include the following:[47]

- Taiwan: Taking office in May 2008, Taiwan President Ma Ying-jeou reversed the provocative pro-independence stance of the previous government of President Chen Shui-bian and reached out to China for progress in cross-strait relations. Economic and social contacts advanced, but progress was slower regarding China's ongoing isolation of Taiwan internationally and its buildup of military forces to intimidate Taiwan and its U.S. supporters. Strategists in the United States welcomed the increased dialogue and exchanges in cross-strait relations, but they saw the military buildup as a threat to the United States as well as Taiwan and responded by strengthening Taiwan and U.S. forces in the region, prompting China at times to threaten to or actually cut off U.S. military contacts and to publicly campaign against U.S. initiatives to reengage with Asia-Pacific countries. Domestic trends in Taiwan added to cross-strait tension as Ma's government approval ratings reached remarkable low points and his party did very poorly in islandwide elections in November 2014 against candidates of the opposition party that challenges key elements in Ma's rapprochement with Beijing. The lead-up to the Taiwan presidential election of January 2016 has seen Xi Jinping and other PRC leaders register strong concern with alleged moves toward Taiwan separatism.[48]

- Asia: China's leaders have long viewed China's rise in power and influence as eventually displacing U.S. military power around China's periphery, but at the start of the twenty-first century, U.S. superpower influence and military deployments grew around China's periphery to the point where the United States appeared more powerful in Asian affairs than at any time since before the Vietnam War. The wars in Iraq and Afghanistan and the global economic crisis beginning in 2008 weakened overall U.S. power; China became more assertive in dealing with long-standing differences with the United States over Asian and other matters. President Obama's response with American military, economic, and political reengagement with the Asia-Pacific region led to U.S.–Chinese tensions.[49]

- CCP legitimacy: Although the George W. Bush administration and the Barack Obama administration appeared to accept the legitimacy of CCP rule in China, strong forces in the U.S. government, Congress, media, and various nongovernment interest groups continued to work to change China's political system—anathema for China.[50]

- U.S. world leadership: Although generally reluctant to confront U.S. world leadership, particularly when other world powers often were unwilling to do so, China remained opposed to U.S. "hegemonism" and sought to use international organizations and multilateral groups to constrain U.S. power. Chinese officials hoped that this will lead over time to a diminution of U.S. power and a multipolar world.

Regarding important bilateral U.S.–Chinese differences, which are reviewed in the chapters below, they involve clusters of issues in security, political, and economic categories. Apart from Taiwan, bilateral security disputes have involved U.S. complaints over China's proliferation of weapons of mass destruction (WMD), China's large defense budget increases, Chinese use of cyber attacks and espionage against the United States; China's complaints and concerns over U.S. military actions and pressure, including the negative implications for China of U.S. missile defense programs; expanded U.S.-Japanese security cooperation; NATO expansion; and stepped-up U.S. military deployment throughout China's periphery.[51]

A key security flash point is North Korea. China has worked with the United States to seek to curb North Korea's nuclear weapons program. At the same time, Beijing is reluctant to follow the U.S. lead and apply significant pressure on North Korea. Many specialists argue that China would work against any U.S. effort to use force or serious economic pressure against North Korea because China has a much stronger interest than the United States in preserving North Korea as a viable state and avoiding the disruption that greater pressure on Pyongyang would cause.[52]

The interface of U.S. and Chinese military forces along China's periphery is not without significant incident, even as the two powers endeavored to resume more normal ties after the April 1, 2001, crash of a Chinese jet fighter and a U.S. surveillance plane, the EP-3. An unarmed U.S. Navy surveillance ship was harassed and rammed by Chinese boats in waters off the Chinese coast in 2002. A Chinese submarine was detected following a U.S. aircraft carrier in the western Pacific in 2006. U.S. surveillance ships encountered harassing Chinese boats in the South China Sea in 2008 and 2009. American surveillance aircraft along China's periphery routinely encounter Chinese fighters, sometimes at close quarters.[53]

Support by the United States for the Dalai Lama and continued criticism of Chinese policies in Tibet are seen by Beijing as challenging China's territorial integrity. When combined with U.S. support for Taiwan and criticism of Chinese repression of dissent in Xinjiang, U.S. actions regarding Tibet appear to some in China as part of a broader longer-term U.S. effort to break up China.[54]

Political concerns focus on powerful forces in the United States and China that incline toward harder-line policies that would exacerbate the differences. The wide range of U.S. interest groups that favor a tougher U.S. stance to China was well demonstrated during congressional and media debates over U.S. China policy in the 1990s. The U.S. preoccupation with the war on terrorism and major crises dealing with Iraq and North Korea curbed the attention these groups gained after 2001. The victory of the Democratic Party in the 2006 congressional elections foreshadowed stronger U.S. government criticism of China over trade and other differences, though it was muted by a U.S. need to cooperate with China on salient security issues like North Korean nuclear weapons and on the massive consequences of the global economic crisis beginning in 2008. The generally moderate and cooperative posture toward China of the Obama administration failed to hide continued differences between the two countries over a long list of issues highlighted by trade and economic disputes, conflicting strategies in the Asia-Pacific, and human rights.[55] In China, the prevailing nationalistic emphasis in leadership discourse and popular opinion reinforced suspicions of American intentions as debate continued on whether conditions justified a more demanding and "less submissive" posture toward the United States and its Asian and other international associates.

Economic issues center on the friction arising from asymmetrical growth in trade and commercial relations. American businesses are sometimes frustrated with conditions in China or lack of Chinese openness to their products. U.S. labor and other groups see the burgeoning trade deficit with China—the largest U.S. trade deficit with any country—as a threat to U.S. jobs and economic well-being. China resents strong U.S. pressures for greater market opening, curbing Chinese intellectual property theft, Chinese currency revaluation, and other measures. Chinese officials chafe at U.S. restrictions on high-technology transfers to China, while U.S. officials warn that such transfers increase China's ability to pose a national security threat to the United States. Meanwhile, debate continues in the United States and China over the wisdom of China's large purchases of U.S. government securities as part of China's massive holdings of foreign exchange reserves.[56]

Chapter Four

China's Role in the World Economy and International Governance

The greatest importance of today's China is as the world's second-largest economy. China's modernization and economic advance spread and deepen throughout the vast country and into all corners of the world. They support active diplomacy in multilateral and bilateral relations. They provide the basis for the fastest-growing military modernization of any country in the post–Cold War period and thereby change the security calculus of China's neighbors and other concerned powers, notably the United States.

China's role in today's world has depended fundamentally on the success of the almost forty years of economic reforms and international outreach begun in the post-Mao period by Deng Xiaoping and his successors. China's growing international economic footprint has increased its heretofore limited importance to a wide range of countries in the developed and developing world as a trading partner, a recipient and source of investment, and a creditor.[1]

Prior to that time, the People's Republic of China exerted important influence in world affairs in different ways and for different reasons. China's vast size, strategic location, revolutionary and nationalistic zeal, and broad popular mobilization made it a formidable opponent for both the United States and the Soviet Union and an important determinant in the foreign policy calculations of neighboring Asian countries. China's importance grew as it developed nuclear weapons and the ballistic missiles to deliver them to targets as far away as Washington, D.C. Ironically, China's prevailing backwardness in economic development for much of this period made China more difficult for the U.S. and Soviet superpowers to deter and to counter adverse Chinese moves, thereby increasing China's importance in their calculations.[2]

In part because of post-Mao China's dramatically growing economic interdependence, measuring Beijing's actual power and influence in the world economy and in international governing bodies remains difficult. As noted in chapter 1, some specialists in China and abroad consider Chinese leaders increasingly confident and powerful as they use China's large economic power to exert influence in line with China's long-standing ambitions of greater regional and global power. Others, myself included, view the Chinese leaders as continuing to follow contingent policies based on changing assessments of the costs and benefits for China that in turn depend on international and domestic circumstances. The amount of influence China exerts on the world economy is growing, but so is China's dependence on key variables in the world economy that the Chinese leadership does not control, including access to energy and other resources, protectionist tendencies among developed countries, and international disapproval of China's impact on climate change and the broader environment. Meanwhile, in 2013 China's domestic economy reached the most important turning point in its four-decade trajectory, prompting a vast array of difficult reforms with uncertain prospects. And despite a steady drumbeat of Chinese and international publicity to the new activism of the Xi Jinping government in organizations of global and regional governance, the fact remains that China's leaders use greater engagement in multilateral organizations defensively, notably to protect Chinese interests from unwanted U.S. interventions, as much as they use such involvement to enhance China's international prominence and importance. In the second decade of the twenty-first century, the reality seems to be that China remains an emerging power with a large and growing economy that is heavily dependent on important international and internal variables. Against this background, China's leaders generally continue to eschew major commitments in providing regional or international common goods or asserting international leadership that involve significant payments or costs for China that will not be paid back in some way. Exceptions, as in the case of China's secret aid to North Korea, generally involve cases with direct bearing on narrowly defined Chinese national interests.[3]

CHINA'S ECONOMIC IMPORTANCE

Since the beginning of economic reforms following the death of Mao Zedong in 1976 and the ascendance of Deng Xiaoping as China's top leader in the late 1970s, China has been the world's fastest-growing major economy. From 1979 to 2014, the average annual growth rate of China's gross domestic product (GDP) was about 10 percent. By 2010, China became the world's second-largest economy, after the United States. In 2011, it became the largest manufacturer, surpassing the United States. In 2012, it became the world's largest trader. The per capita GDP (a common measurement of a country's living standards) of China now surpasses $7,000. China also has become the second-largest destination of foreign investment, the largest holder of foreign exchange reserves, and the largest creditor nation.[4]

Measured in U.S. dollars using nominal exchange rates, China's GDP in 2013 was $9.5 trillion, about 56 percent the size of the U.S. economy, according to the IMF. Several predictions said that China was on track to surpass the United States, the world's largest economy, within a decade.[5]

Many economists contend that using nominal exchange rates to convert Chinese data (or that of other countries) into U.S. dollars fails to reflect the true size of China's economy and living standards relative to the United States. Nominal exchange rates simply reflect the prices of foreign currencies vis-à-vis the U.S. dollar; such measurements exclude differences in the prices for goods and services across countries. For example, one U.S. dollar exchanged for local currency in China would buy more goods and services there than it would in the United States. This is because prices for goods and services in China are generally lower than they are in the United States. Economists attempt to develop estimates of exchange rates based on their actual purchasing power relative to the dollar in order to make more accurate comparisons of economic data across countries, usually referred to as purchasing power parity (PPP). The PPP exchange rate increases the (estimated) measurement of China's economy and its per capita GDP. According to the IMF, which periodically does international price surveys, prices for goods and services in China are about 56 percent the level they are in the United States. Adjusting for this price differential raises the value of China's 2013 GDP from $9.5 trillion (nominal dollars) to $16.1 trillion. Thus, using PPP measurements, China's economy surpassed the U.S. economy to become the world leader in 2014.[6]

At the same time, Chinese growth rates have declined steadily from 12.8 percent in 2012 to around 7 percent in 2015. In 2013, Chinese leaders began a wide range of over sixty sets of mainly economic reforms to deal with existing or anticipated economic weaknesses involving the inefficient practices of state-owned enterprises (SOEs) and the state banking system, resource and energy scarcities, massive environmental problems, and China's strong dependence on the health of the global trading economy, which stalled following the financial crisis and recession begun in 2008.[7]

Economists generally attribute much of China's rapid economic growth since the late 1970s to two main factors: large-scale capital investment (financed by large domestic savings and foreign investment) and rapid productivity growth. The two factors appear to have worked together; economic reforms led to higher efficiency in the economy, which boosted output and increased resources for additional investment in the economy. Over the past decade, the rate of improvement in labor productivity has been declining steadily. This raises the danger seen elsewhere that as China's technological development begins to approach that of major developed countries (i.e., through its adsorption of foreign technology), its level of productivity gains, and thus, real GDP growth, could slow significantly from its historic levels unless China becomes a major center for new technology and innovation and/or implements new comprehensive economic reforms. Several developing economies (notably several in Asia and Latin America) experienced rapid economic development and growth during the 1960s and 1970s by implementing some of the same policies that China has utilized to date to develop its economy, such as measures to boost exports and to promote and protect certain industries. However, at some point in their development, some of these countries began to experience economic stagnation (or much slower growth compared to previous levels) over a sustained period, a phenomenon described by economists as the "middle-income trap." This means that several developing (low-income) economies were able to transition to a middle-income economy, but because they were unable to sustain high levels of productivity gains (in part because they could not address structural inefficiencies in the economy), they were unable to transition to a high-income economy. China may be at a similar crossroads now. The Economist Intelligence Unit (EIU) projects that China's real GDP growth will slow considerably in the years ahead, averaging 6.3 percent from 2014 to 2020 and 4.1 percent from 2021 to 2030.[8]

The Chinese concern over economic growth meshes with a long list of internal problems that the Xi Jinping government is endeavoring to address with economic and related reforms. Those problems involve the following:[9]

- Weak leadership legitimacy highly dependent on how the leaders' performance is seen at any given time.
- Pervasive corruption viewed as sapping public support and undermining administrative efficiency.
- Widening income gaps posing challenges to the communist regime ostensibly dedicated to advancing the disadvantaged.
- Widespread social turmoil reportedly involving 100,000–200,000 mass incidents annually that are usually directed at government officials and/or aspects of state policies; managing such incidents and related domestic control measures involves budget outlays greater than China's impressive national defense budget.[10]
- Highly resource-intensive economy (e.g., China uses four times the amount of oil to advance its economic growth to a certain level than does the United States, even though the United States is notoriously inefficient and arguably wasteful in how it uses oil).[11] Enormous and rapidly growing environmental damage is done in China as a result of such intensive resource use.

• Need for major reform of an economic model in use in China for over three decades that is widely seen to have reached a point of diminishing returns.

The Chinese leadership met and set forth in November 2013 an ambitious and wide-ranging agenda of economic and related domestic reforms. These proposed actions will deal with the problems noted above, among other things. How the sixty-plus sets of measures for reform will in fact be implemented and how they will be made to interact effectively with one another are widely seen to require a strong and sustained effort of top Chinese leaders, probably for many years.[12]

Foreign Trade and Investment in China

In foreign affairs, the growing importance of the Chinese economy was manifested most notably by the growth in economic interchange between China and foreign countries throughout the world. Most important in this regard was the growth of trade and foreign investment in China. More recently, Chinese investment abroad also has grown rapidly from a low base. Notable increases in Chinese commercial and concessional financing have assisted developing countries in Africa, Latin America, and Asia.

Trade continues to play a major role in China's rapid economic growth. In 2004, China surpassed Japan as the world's third-largest trading economy, after the European Union and the United States, and it was reported to have surpassed the United States as the world's largest exporter in 2007 and as the world's largest trader in 2012. Chinese exports grew dramatically in the years between China's joining the World Trade Organization in 2001 and the start of the global economic crisis and recession in 2008. They doubled in size from 2004 to 2007, with an average annual growth rate of 29 percent. One result was very large Chinese trade surpluses. In more recent years, trade growth has declined. In 2014, China's trade totaled $4.34 trillion, up 3.4 percent year on year. Exports were $2.34 trillion, up 6.1 percent year on year, and imports were $1.96 trillion, up 0.4 percent, with a resulting trade surplus of $382.46 billion, up 47.7 percent.[13] In the first quarter of 2015, trade contracted 13.8 percent, falling far short of the government's goal of 6 percent annual growth for the year.[14]

Official Chinese trade data on its major trading partners in 2013 (based on total trade) list in order the twenty-eight countries that make up the European Union (EU28), the United States, the ten nations that constitute the Association of Southeast Asian Nations (ASEAN), and Japan. China's top three export markets were Hong Kong, the United States, and the EU28, while its top sources for imports were the EU28, ASEAN, and South Korea. According to Chinese data, it maintained large trade surpluses with Hong Kong

($369 billion), the United States ($222 billion), and the EU28 ($119 billion) and reported large trade imbalances with Taiwan (-$116 billion) and South Korea (-$92 billion).[15]

In assessing China's major trading partners, it is important to keep in mind differences of Chinese trade data with those of some of its major trading partners. This is because a large share of China's trade (both exports and imports) passes through Hong Kong, which reverted to Chinese rule in July 1997 but is treated as a separate customs area by most countries, including China and the United States. China treats a large share of its exports through Hong Kong as Chinese exports to Hong Kong for statistical purposes, while many countries, including the United States, that import Chinese products through Hong Kong generally attribute their origin to China for statistical purposes. Trade data from the United States showed that the importance of the U.S. market to China's export sector was likely much higher than was reflected in Chinese trade data. Based on U.S. data on Chinese exports to the United States and Chinese data on total Chinese exports, it was estimated that Chinese exports to the United States as a share of total Chinese exports grew from 15 percent in 1986 to 33 percent in 2004.[16] Though China rapidly expanded and diversified in exports in later years, the U.S. market absorbed about 19 percent of Chinese exports in 2014.[17]

China's trade boom was heavily dependent on large inflows of foreign direct investment (FDI) into China. Annual utilized FDI in China (excluding the financial sector) grew from $636 million in 1983 to $119.6 billion in 2014. The cumulative level of FDI in China is well over $1 trillion. According to Chinese government data on nonfinancial FDI inflows, the largest sources of cumulative FDI in China for 1979–2013 were Hong Kong (47.0 percent), the British Virgin Islands (BVI), Japan, the United States, and Taiwan (both Hong Kong and the British Virgin Islands are viewed as tax havens that allow Chinese investors to gain advantage using off-shore locations to carry out investment in China and abroad).[18]

The largest sector for FDI flows in China in recent years was manufacturing, which often accounted for over half of total annual FDI in China. There were reportedly 445,244 foreign-invested enterprises (FIEs) registered in China in 2010, employing 55.2 million workers or 15.9 percent of the urban workforce. FIEs account for a significant share of China's industrial output ($25.9 in 2011); they are responsible for about half of China's foreign trade. FIEs in China dominate China's high-technology exports. From 2002 to 2010, the share of China's high-tech exports by FIEs rose from 79 percent to 82 percent.[19]

The large role of FIEs and their often extensive supply chain networks meant that a large portion of Chinese trade is so-called processing trade where firms in China obtain raw materials and intermediate inputs from abroad, process them locally, and export value-added goods. Estimates of the extent of such processing trade vary. Among higher estimates, two professors from Peking University reported in 2012 that thanks to China's encouragement of close interaction with foreign firms in special export zones and other means, processing trade constituted about half of China's total trade. Such processing trade saw China at times add only a small amount to the product; the finished product often depended on sales to the United States or the European Union. The trade of components and semi-finished products also resulted in extensive double counting in Chinese trade figures.[20]

Meanwhile, underlining the strong Chinese interdependence on the international economy, the Singapore ambassador in China told Chinese media in August 2013 that 60 percent of the goods that are exported from China and the ten Southeast Asian states of ASEAN are ultimately manufactures that go to the United States, Europe, and Japan. Only 22 percent of these goods stay in the China-ASEAN region.[21]

Growing Chinese Investment Abroad

In the early 2000s, the Chinese government urged Chinese companies to increase Chinese investment abroad. Overseas investment up to that point was quite limited; it remains difficult to measure with precision the extent and importance of these investments and their significance for data on foreign investment into China. For many years, well over half of Chinese overseas investment was shown in Chinese data to go to Hong Kong, the British Virgin Islands (BVI), and the Cayman Islands. The accounting rules in these locales were such that they were seen to provide tax havens and allow Chinese firms to seek advantage by investing there and from those locations to send investment back into China.[22] China's FDI outflows by destination for 2012 indicate that the largest destinations of total Chinese FDI through 2012 were Hong Kong (57.5 percent of total), the BVI, the Cayman Islands, the United States, and Australia. In terms of Chinese FDI flows in 2012, the largest recipients were Hong Kong (58.3 percent of total), the United States, Kazakhstan, the United Kingdom, and the BVI.[23]

By the end of 2006, Chinese government figures showed that over 5,000 domestic Chinese investment entities had established nearly 10,000 overseas direct-invested enterprises in 172 countries or territories around the world. The accumulated FDI stock reached $90 billion, of which nonfinancial FDI was $75 billion and finance-related FDI $15 billion. Of the total, $37 billion was in equity investments, $33 billion in reinvested earnings, and $19 billion in other kinds of investment. In 2006, FDI from China accounted for about 0.8 percent of global FDI stocks and 2.7 percent of global FDI outflows (thirteenth in the world).[24] By way of comparison, in 2006 the cumulative stock of FDI was over $2.8 trillion for the United States (as opposed to $90 billion for China).

The trend changed rapidly in following years, with strong growth in outbound Chinese investment. China was the world's fifth-largest foreign investor in 2010, with outbound Chinese investment valued at $59 billion.[25] According to UN data, China provided $101 billion in investment in 2013; it ranked as the third-largest source of global FDI that year. The stock of China's outward FDI through 2013 was estimated at $512 billion.[26]

Chinese companies invested outside China for many of the same reasons that other multinational firms do. They sought to do the following:

- Bypass trade barriers and use domestic capacity because the home market for their products was too small
- Service markets in order to secure access or to expand market presence
- Better compete with foreign-affiliated companies in the Chinese market and diversify manufacturing facilities
- Secure supplies of raw materials and resources
- Circumvent domestic government controls (by sending the investment funds to an offshore destination and then bringing them back as a foreign investment)[27]

The last motive, the need for "round-trip" investments, seemed to be specific to China and had an apparently important bearing on how to assess the scope and importance of Chinese investment data. This practice was seen to result in a significant overstatement of both outward and inward FDI in China. Studies estimated that 20 to 30 percent of capital leaving China was "round-tripped" back as foreign investment in the domestic Chinese economy. Much of this "round-tripped" investment was done through Hong Kong, but tax havens such as the Cayman Islands and the British Virgin Islands also were significant. As noted above, such havens remained the top three destinations for Chinese outward FDI.[28]

The more conventional Chinese motives for outward investment were driven by three main factors:

1. China's massive accumulation of foreign exchange reserves led government officials to seek more profitable ways of investing these holdings, which traditionally were put into relatively safe, low-yield assets, such as U.S. Treasury securities. In September 2007, the Chinese government officially launched the China Investment Corporation (CIC), under the direction of the State Council, in an effort to better manage its foreign exchange reserves. With an initial stake of $200 billion, the CIC was one of the largest sovereign wealth funds.

Initial investments proved to be less than successful, but the Chinese government seemed to continue support for this kind of investment.

2. To complement its reception of large amounts of foreign investment, the Chinese government attempted to promote the development of internationally recognized Chinese brands. One approach was to purchase existing companies and their well-known brand names (as well as their technology and management skills).

3. Acquisition of energy and raw materials was a major priority of China's recent overseas investment efforts. China sought to either purchase or invest in foreign energy and raw material companies, infrastructure projects such as oil and gas pipelines, oil refineries, mines, railroad, road, and port connections to oil and other raw materials, and related joint ventures.[29]

A major turning point in Chinese investment abroad came with the Xi Jinping government and its much greater emphasis on activism in foreign affairs than the previous Chinese governments. The investment and other economic initiatives abroad announced by President Xi, Prime Minister Li Keqiang, and other senior Chinese leaders received enormous publicity from China's massive state-directed propaganda apparatus. The leaders' proposals involved planned expenditures of hundreds of billions of dollars in investments, loans, and other mechanisms to promote development in less developed countries designed to advantage Chinese economic interests and international influence. Among the most important vehicles for the new loans and investment push were a $40 billion Chinese commitment to a Chinese Silk Road Fund; a $50 billion Chinese commitment to a China proposed Asian Infrastructure Investment Bank (AIIB); a $10 billion Chinese commitment to New Development Bank established by the five so-called BRICS countries (Brazil, Russia, India, China, and South Africa); and a Chinese proposed Shanghai Cooperation Organization (SCO) Development Bank involving China, Russia, and the four former Soviet Republics in central Asia that make up the core membership of the SCO.[30]

The new proposals were surprising to close observers of Chinese investment abroad; they came during a period of reassessment of the advantages and disadvantages of China's use of large-scale government lending and other means as part of a broad gauge "going-out" strategy over the previous decade. Similar to the Xi Jinping government's economic initiatives, Chinese leaders in the previous decade also offered and signed numerous agreements reportedly worth many billions of dollars that focused on building infrastructure in order to gain secure Chinese access to oil and other raw materials needed for China's resource-intensive economic growth. The costs of the Chinese loans and investment often were repaid in oil or other commodities. And in that period, Chinese leaders repeatedly called attention to multibillion-dollar funds created by China in support of Chinese investment plans in different parts of the developing world.

The official results of the reassessment of the decade of experience with the "going-out" strategy have not been announced. Available commentary in official Chinese media and international media shows a mixed record of accomplishment with many important shortcomings. For example, specialists that search beyond the headlines of multibillion-dollar investment plans and loan deals find that the deals more often than not are not executed as proposed or are not done at all. Large-scale infrastructure agreements worth many billions of dollars involving Nigeria, the Philippines, Myanmar, Sri Lanka, Mexico, and Greece have failed to go forward. Adding to this checkered record of accomplishment, major actual and proposed Chinese investments in Libya, Iraq, Sudan, Afghanistan, Syria, and other risky locations have collapsed in the face of war and domestic conflict in recent years.

Emblematic of these trends, the deputy dean of the National School of Development at Beijing University observed in *China Daily* in February 2015 that "over half of China's overseas investments are not profitable."[31] In part to offset the risk of investment in unstable parts of Africa, the Chinese government has seen the wisdom of avoiding bearing alone the risk of Chinese investments in unstable parts of Africa by launching in 2014 a $2 billion African Development Fund to be invested through the African Development Bank.[32] Meanwhile, China's hailed $3 billion investment in a large copper mine in Afghanistan and other purported and aborted investments in mining ventures are very common, with China Mining Association vice chairman Wang Jiahua telling the China Mining Congress and Exhibition in Tianjin in November 2013 that about 80 percent of China's overseas mining investments had failed.[33] Reflecting Beijing's current emphasis on promoting investment abroad, meetings between the Indonesian president and President Xi Jinping in 2015 featured agreements of $63 billion in planned investment. However, the Indonesian Investment Coordinating Board reported at this time that China had planned $24.27 billion of investment in Indonesia between 2005 and 2014, but only $1.8 billion, equal to 7 percent, was actually invested. The report showed that Indonesia was a difficult place for foreign investment but added that Japan, another major investor in Indonesia, was three and a half times more likely than China to follow through on its investment plans.[34]

Meanwhile, data and assessments provided by ASEAN, *The Economist*, and the *China-Latin America Economic Bulletin* show that the Chinese record of actual investment abroad has amounted to much less than one would expect after reading repeated news stories and commentary over the past decade of a variety of multibillion-dollar Chinese investment plans similar to those fostered by the Xi Jinping government. The data and assessments show that China's actual investment in Southeast Asia, Africa, and Latin

America has amounted to a significant but still modest amount for these areas, ranging from about 10 percent for ASEAN to around 5 percent each for Africa and Latin America. Even when one takes into account underreporting by the Chinese government of investment abroad, China's low percentage of investment after many years of pledges and plans to increase investment is a notable finding.[35]

The above background information provides a context for discerning realities in the Xi Jinping government's various investment proposals that are widely touted in international affairs. While it's probably too early to give a definitive assessment of the impact of Xi Jinping's varied economic initiatives on Chinese relations with developing Asian, African, and Latin American states, the brief assessment provided below, which is based heavily on the observations of Chinese specialists and officials, argues that it would be incorrect to assume that China is in a dominant economic position in any of these regions. The facts argue otherwise. For example, in nearby Southeast Asia, where China's investment level is twice that of its investment in Latin America and Africa, Chinese investment (including from Hong Kong) in ASEAN countries remains at modest levels—about 10 percent of foreign investment there according to ASEAN data. This comes despite repeated Chinese pledges over the past decade to enhance investment in Southeast Asia with a $10 billion fund, a $3 billion fund, and other initiatives. Investment by Japan and the European Union are much higher.[36]

The China-initiated Asian Infrastructure Investment Bank (AIIB) represents a work in progress. Chinese officials reportedly were surprised by the number of states seeking to join, despite reports of U.S. opposition. The Chinese Ministry of Finance announced on April 15, 2015, that fifty-seven nations were approved as founding members of the AIIB; they included all members of ASEAN. Official Chinese media reported China's commitment of $50 billion to the bank, but the commitments of other nations, the rules and regulations of the body, and a host of other issues were in the process of being resolved. Deliberations to decide on the distribution of each country's respective share of decision-making power in the bank and the selection of leading bank officials reportedly were expected in meetings of representatives of the founding members later in the year.

By contrast, the $40 billion China Silk Road Fund is under direct Chinese control and registered more concrete progress than the AIIB. The fund was established on December 29, 2014, and began operation on February 16, 2015. The scope of the fund's activities involved both the countries included in China's proposed Silk Road Economic Belt Initiative (mainly countries west of China going overland as far as Europe) and countries included in China's proposed 21st Century Maritime Silk Road Initiative (mainly countries along the sea routes from China through Southeast Asia and the Middle East to Europe). A map publicized by official Chinese television and print media on April 15, 2015, showed that the scope of the Silk Road Economic Belt and the 21st Century Maritime Silk Road involves all of the Southeast Asian countries as well as neighboring countries of the South Pacific.

Coincident with the March 2015 Boao Forum on Asia Annual Conference and Xi Jinping's keynote address there emphasizing China's "common destiny" with Southeast Asian and other neighbors, Chinese authorities released on March 28 a new action plan suggesting steps to be taken under the rubrics of the Silk Road Economic Belt and the 21st Century Maritime Silk Road initiatives. The plan was created by the National Development and Reform Commission, the Ministry of Foreign Affairs, and the Ministry of Commerce and was endorsed by the State Council. It was as much a vision statement as it was a plan of action. The main substance of the plan was in sections dealing with "framework" and "cooperation priorities" that detailed a very wide range of proposed or possible policies and practices. The details showed that while China has a focus on developing infrastructure projects connecting China more closely with its neighbors, Beijing is open to pursuing a broadly defined range of actions favored by China and neighboring states involving promoting enhanced policy coordination across the Asian continent, financial integration, trade liberalization, and people-to-people connections.[37]

Providing some clarity on what Southeast Asian and other neighbors can expect from the Silk Road Fund, official Chinese media announced the first project supported by the fund during President Xi Jinping's visit to Pakistan on April 20, 2015.[38] The project involves providing capital to build the Karot Hydropower project in northeastern Pakistan. That project is valued at $1.65 billion. It is part of a very ambitious Chinese plan to build a $46 billion, 3,000 kilometer China-Pakistan Economic Corridor from China's Xinjiang Uighur Autonomous Region through the Khunjerab Pass (elevation 15,397 feet) in the Karakorum Mountain range into Pakistan's Baluchistan region to the Chinese-built Gwadar Port on the far western Pakistan coast, thereby connecting China, Pakistan, and the Arabian Sea. It remains very difficult at this early stage to determine how and whether the $46 billion Chinese plan will be implemented and paid for, but the overall figure is staggering. By comparison, the United States was the main provider of assistance to Pakistan during the long U.S.-led war in Afghanistan since 2001. The total amount of U.S. assistance was about $31 billion, and the American assistance was forecast to decline sharply with the U.S. military pullback from Afghanistan.

According to *China Daily*, the hydropower project is emblematic of the kinds of medium- to long-term projects that will be supported by the fund in Asia and elsewhere within the broad scope of the fund. Specific information on the Pakistan project says that construction of the proposed power station will start at the end of 2015 and the station will be in operation by 2020. The station will be operated by a Chinese company for thirty years and then transferred to the Pakistan government.

Chinese media reporting showed a diffusion of Chinese funding mechanisms both supporting the Pakistan power project and supporting the broad Silk Road Fund. The media reporting did not provide a clear figure on how much of the $1.65 billion cost of the power project the fund will actually pay. What it said is that the fund will join "a consortium led by the Export-Import Bank of China" that is supplying the funding for the power station, according to a *China Daily* report of April 20, 2015. Meanwhile, the *China Daily* report also disclosed that the initial capital of the China Silk Road Fund amounts to $10 billion coming from a variety of sources including $6.5 billion from foreign exchange reserves; $1.5 billion from the sovereign wealth fund, China Investment Corporation; $1.5 billion from the Export-Import Bank of China; and $500 million from the China Development Bank.

Publicity surrounding the Boao Forum and President Xi's speech there and speeches on other recent occasions underlined Chinese motives seeking mutual benefit, peace, development, and ever greater cooperation and integration with Asian neighbors. Chinese leaders and commentary also repeatedly disavowed seeking advantage in competition for influence with the United States, Japan, and others.

Nevertheless, the surge of Chinese commentary also contained remarks by Chinese leaders and lower-level officials and commentators showing specific benefits China seeks from the Silk Road Fund, the AIIB, and related efforts in dealing with neighboring Asian countries. There are economic benefits and strategic benefits.[39]

The perceived economic benefits were as follows:

- China's massive foreign exchange reserves were said to be better employed in infrastructure development and investments abroad in Asia than being employed in U.S. government securities and such other low-paying investments abroad.
- Asia's massive need for infrastructure meshes well with China's massive overcapacity to build infrastructure after thirty years of rebuilding China. Meshing the two will allow competitive Chinese construction companies to continue productive growth in building Chinese-funded infrastructure in neighboring countries.
- Connecting remote western and southern regions of China with neighbors through modern infrastructure in Asia will serve to develop these backward Chinese regions more rapidly and thereby help to bridge the wide economic development gap between interior and coastal provinces in China.
- The Chinese-supported infrastructure will allow many Chinese industries with excess capacity or facing higher wage demands or more stringent

environmental restrictions in China to relocate to nearby Asian countries and continue to prosper and develop.

- The Chinese-funded connection with neighbors will facilitate trade and the increased use of Chinese currency in international transactions.
- Developing trade routes including road, rail, and pipeline connections to China from the Arabian Sea through Pakistan, from the Bay of Bengal through Myanmar, and overland through central Asian states and Russia is said to reduce China's vulnerability to possible foreign interdiction of sea-borne shipments of oil and other needed goods to China. In particular, Chinese strategists worry about such vulnerability of Chinese imports and exports passing through the Indian Ocean and the Strait of Malacca.

The perceived strategic benefits were as follows:

- South China Sea territorial disputes and Chinese intimidation and divisive tactics in dealing with ASEAN and its member states have led to what some Chinese commentators see as "negativity" in recent China–Southeast Asian relations. The Silk Road Fund and related initiatives act to change the subject in China–Southeast Asian relations in ways that improve Chinese influence and image.
- The Chinese initiatives were seen as an effective way to use China's geographic location and large foreign exchange reserves in crafting policies and practices that offset American efforts to advance U.S. regional influence and standing through the Obama government's rebalance policy in Asia.

While generally emphasizing the positive, the surge of Chinese commentary also contained statements by Chinese officials and commentators showing reservations about the Silk Road Fund and related initiatives, seeing notable risks. They involved economic risks and political risks.[40]
    The perceived economic risks were as follows:

- Since the more viable investment opportunities in Asia have already been taken, China will be focused on less secure investment opportunities. Given this reality, some commentators warned against repeating the shortcomings noted earlier seen in China's "going out" efforts using Export-Import Bank and China Development Bank funding to seek energy and resources over the past decade.
- Beijing continues to emphasize that it is a "developing" country with major internal needs. Thus, the win-win formula governing Chinese funding abroad usually requires assurance that the funding will be paid back in some way. The long-term commitment to infrastructure development in less than secure countries heightens the chance for changes and unrest that

as noted above have destroyed or undercut massive Chinese investments carried out or planned throughout the developing world and even in Europe. Chinese commentary also noted that longer-term investment is more prone to loss due to corruption in such less-than-stable countries. All of the above undercut the likelihood of Chinese outlays being paid back.

The perceived political risks were as follows:

- China's Asian neighbors were seen as wary of coming under China's sway as a result of the closer economic connections called for in the Silk Road Fund and related plans. Chinese commentators warned Beijing against appearing as Japan did in the late 1980s when Tokyo prompted regional fears as it bought resources and deepened investment using its highly valued currency and other economic advantages.
- China also has a mixed reputation in its support for labor standards, environmental protection, the quality of work, and sustaining large Chinese-built infrastructure projects. Backlash has come in African and Latin American countries and is seen in changing attitudes working against China among rulers in Asian countries including Myanmar, the Philippines, Sri Lanka, and others.

Against the background of the above realities, prominent Asia-Pacific economic and political expert Zhang Yunling of China's Academy of Social Sciences advised *China Daily* on March 9, 2015, that the new Chinese investment plans may take a long time—"20 years, 50 years, or even 100 years to accomplish." He warned that the potential risks include "political instability in some countries, terrorism, global competition and concerns about China's growing presence in some regions."[41]

Taken as a whole, the above assessment shows that despite China's disavowals of seeking advantage at others' expense, China does seek a number of advantages in using recent economic initiatives to advance its relations and influence in Asia at the expense of the United States, Japan, and their allies and associates. At the same time, knowledgeable Chinese officials and specialists appear realistic about the risks involved in these economic initiatives. And, specialists in China and abroad argue on the basis of Chinese experience over the past decade that the actual Chinese impact of the recent investment initiatives may remain limited and far from dominant for some time to come. An implication for interested observers is that basing judgments on Chinese visions in action plans and pervasive publicity regarding Chinese largess has been off target in the recent past and in view of prevailing realities probably will be off target today.

Foreign Aid

China's foreign aid remains difficult to assess, given a lack of official and reliable data. The Chinese government's first white paper on foreign aid was released in April 2011; it provided an overall figure of China's cumulative foreign assistance and data on other trends, but not enough information to determine the cost of Chinese assistance to specific countries or during specific times. The *China Statistical Yearbook 2003–2006* released an annual aid figure of $970 million, but specialists judged that this did not include loans, a main form of Chinese aid. A former U.S. government foreign aid official, Georgetown University Professor Carol Lancaster, judged in 2007 that China's annual aid ranged in value between $1.5 billion and $2 billion.[42] Studies that inventoried various reports of loans, state-sponsored investment, and other official Chinese financing came up with much larger figures, though aid specialists judged that much of these efforts would not qualify as aid and that it was difficult to determine when and whether reported aid and loan pledges were actually ever made and disbursed. Chinese financing at times involved interest-free or concessional loans, but it also involved trade and investment agreements, including arrangements whereby Chinese loans were to be repaid by commodities (e.g., oil) produced as a result of the development financed with China's help.[43] Chinese aid efforts received an especially high profile in Africa. Some reports emphasized the benefit China received from offering assistance without the conditions that Western donors imposed; China followed a policy of "noninterference" in the internal affairs of governments being pressed by Western donors because of gross abuses of power or corruption. China also was able to expedite assistance without lengthy processes dealing with environmental and social standards, and the public buildings, roads, and infrastructure built with Chinese assistance often were completed expeditiously by Chinese contractors who had a tendency to use Chinese labor and served as prominent reminders of Chinese assistance. Deborah Brautigam, a specialist on foreign aid and Chinese involvement in Africa, estimated that Chinese aid in Africa in the past decade (2001–2009) amounted to $2.1 billion.[44]

The second Chinese white paper on foreign assistance was issued in 2014; it offered better information focused on the three-year period 2010–2012. China provided $14.4 billion in grants, interest-free loans, and concessional loans. Over half of that went to Africa, where fifty-one countries received Chinese aid. Thirty Asian nations received around 30 percent of China's foreign aid, and nineteen countries in Latin America and the Caribbean accounted for 8 percent. China's aid to Oceania accounted for 4.2 percent of its aid over the period 2010–2012. A plurality of China's aid (44 percent) went to economic infrastructure projects, which the white paper defined as transport and communications, broadcasting and telecommunications, and power supply construction. The second-largest spending category was social and public infrastructure (27 percent of the total aid), which includes the construction of schools, hospitals, and other civil construction. [45]

From 2010 to 2012, there was a big increase in concessional loans, which accounted for over half of Chinese aid, and a big fall in interest-free loans, which accounted for less than 10 percent. Compared with grants or interest-free loans, the use of concessional loans expanded the scope of Chinese foreign aid as it raised funds from the market. It reduced the financial burden on the Chinese government as it only covered the interest difference between concessional and commercial loan rates. The recipient country was required to pay back the debt. [46] Periodic reports showed that some developing countries, such as the poorly administered Kingdom of Tonga in the Pacific Islands, imprudently took on too much Chinese debt and faced strong pressure to pay what they owed. [47]

The official Chinese figures made it difficult to discern with precision the actual annual costs of Chinese foreign assistance. The Chinese outlays for 2012 were seen as in the same range as Norway and Sweden and far behind the United States, Great Britain, Germany, France, and Japan. Meanwhile, because China continued to receive considerable foreign aid, it was difficult to determine whether it was a net contributor or recipient of foreign assistance. *The Economist* in January 2015 reported that "as recently as 2010 it [China] was still a net recipient of foreign assistance." [48]

China was a leading recipient of international assistance in the 1980s and the 1990s. In the past decade, the World Bank annually provided about $1.5 billion in loans for China. The Asian Development Bank provided loans annually worth $1.3 billion. Reports by the Organization for Economic Cooperation and Development (OECD) showed that at least until recently Japan, Germany, and France provided China with official development assistance. The EU also maintained annual programs of assistance in China. Many EU members other than Germany and France, as well as other developed countries (e.g., Canada, Australia), maintained a variety of assistance programs in China, as did such prominent Western foundations and nongovernmental organizations as the Ford Foundation. China also benefited greatly from international donors' efforts to combat avian flu and to support the Global Fund for AIDS, Tuberculosis, and Malaria. [49]

In April 2010, Chinese media reported that twenty-four UN agencies, such as the UN Development Program, that provide assistance to China had reached an agreement to extend their assistance for another five years. The value of this assistance was not specified. The OECD issued a report later in 2010 that showed that donor countries provided China with an annual amount of aid valued at $2.6 billion a year. [50]

At this time it also became clear how China gained assistance through various climate change and environmental programs. The Clean Development Mechanism (CDM) under the Kyoto Protocol was reported to be an important source of China's clean technology acquisition from foreign countries. The CDM allowed developed countries with a greenhouse gas reduction commitment to invest in emission reduction projects in developing countries as an alternative to more expensive emission reductions in developed countries. As Georgetown University Professor Joanna Lewis pointed out in 2008, "The CDM has become a vehicle for China to help stimulate investment in projects that mitigate greenhouse gas emissions and to help cover the incremental cost of higher-efficiency or low-carbon technology."[51] China's National Development and Reform Commission said that China had approved a total of 2,443 CDM projects as of March 2010.[52] An independent study showed that China was among the highest beneficiaries among developing countries regarding CDM projects.[53] An unexplored but presumably important consideration for China's economic modernization is the role these technology transfers from developed countries have played in China's rapid ascent up the technology ladder to a position of global leadership in the production of renewable and clean energy equipment.[54]

Regarding foreign assistance, China is the largest recipient of environmental aid from the World Bank. It received 17 percent of the total funding for climate change projects from the Global Environmental Facility (GEF) through the World Bank during 1991–2002. The overall value of the aid was over $300 million. From 2002 to 2009, the value of GEF funding to China was $122 million. In 2008, a World Bank loan of $200 million funded a large energy-efficiency project in China. In 2010, the Asian Development Bank reportedly approved a loan of $135 million to support building so-called green power plants in China. The UN Development Program has been involved in an energy-efficiency project in China. Many foreign governments, including the United States, Canada, Australia, Switzerland, and Norway, have supported bilateral cooperation projects in China dealing with climate change.[55]

ASSESSING CHINA'S GROWING ROLE IN INTERNATIONAL ECONOMICS

The strong Chinese and international publicity supporting salient economic initiatives of the Xi Jinping government reflected the Chinese government's broader determination to demonstrate greater prominence and leadership in world affairs. China's enormous and growing economic size, the global scope of its economic influence, and the willingness of recent Chinese leaders to undertake important international initiatives support projections of advancing overall Chinese international leadership and perceived growing dominance, especially in nearby Asia. However, realities of deteriorating economic conditions in China and multiple and serious constraints abroad have important implications for China's ever more internationally interdependent economic growth; they undercut projections of ever greater leadership and sway, painting a more uncertain future.

As a result, there are differing views among Chinese officials and international specialists about how important China actually is in international economic affairs. The views differ as well about what this means for overall Chinese foreign relations, especially China's expanding role in regional and global international organizations that deal with economic as well as political, security, environmental, and other matters of importance to the world community in the post–Cold War period.

According to many Chinese officials and international observers, China's growing economy and its burgeoning international trade and investment relationships provide a solid foundation for China to play an ever more important role in influencing and managing world affairs. Debate shows periodically in mainstream Chinese media and abroad over whether China's economic success had reached a point where it provided a model to be followed by other countries. Many in the West in recent years saw the emergence of a "Beijing consensus" encompassing the main features of China's development approach; they judged that the Chinese government was in the process of spreading this development model throughout the world—a trend they viewed as adverse to Western values and goals, summed up as what they called the "Washington consensus."[56]

On the other hand, senior Chinese officials tended to eschew association with a Beijing consensus or a China model that would oppose Western norms. The Chinese leaders duly criticized Western efforts to impose their values and development norms on other countries through conditions on foreign assistance, sanctions, and other means interfering in other states' internal affairs. They launched international banks and other initiations that seemed to compete with Western-backed international financial institutions. A basic Chinese position was that foreign countries should be free to choose their desired development path and not feel obliged to follow one model or another. Some Chinese economic specialists were frank in highlighting the many shortcomings of the Chinese development model, suggesting that China had a long way to go before its economic development experience could provide a model for others to emulate.[57]

Based on its status as the world's largest trading partner and second-largest economy, China was looked to increasingly as a leader in Asian and world affairs. As discussed in later chapters of this book, government leaders throughout the world often consulted closely with Chinese leaders in bilateral exchanges and in international organizations, endeavoring to influence and govern international affairs to their mutual benefit.

Conforming to norms of economic globalization, Chinese leaders notably put aside past Chinese government suspicion of Asian and international multilateral organizations.[58] They embraced burgeoning Asian and international economic groupings, and they showed sometimes more guarded cooperation with other international organizations dealing with political, security, and other issues. On balance, Chinese engagement met with the general satisfaction of other regional and international participants.

Against this background, a number of foreign specialists and commentators in recent years portrayed China as a leader in international economic affairs, surpassing Japan, India, and the European powers, as it rapidly closes the gap with the United States.

Thus, they commonly asserted the following key judgments:

- China already is an economic superpower.
- It is likely to continue rapid growth and gather greater economic and geopolitical strength.
- China's growth is the main engine changing the post–Cold War Asian and international order, where the United States was dominant, into a more multipolar order where U.S. dominance is diminished by China's rising stature and importance.
- China's emergence is unique among major powers in that China has emerged by being widely open to economic interaction with the rest of the world, building international dependence on China's economy.
- The speed, scope, and scale of China's economic expansion on the global stage create very strong adjustment pressures on the United States, other developed countries, and many developing nations as well.[59]

LIMITATIONS OF CHINA'S INTERNATIONAL ECONOMIC INFLUENCE

A contrasting view of China's international economic importance comes from some international observers and some Chinese officials who are diffident about Chinese economic power and influence in world affairs. They frequently emphasize important limitations and preoccupations at home and abroad that act as a brake on China's adopting costly leadership initiatives anytime soon in international economic and other world affairs. A fundamental premise of the Chinese government's stress for much of the twenty-first century on China's adherence to the goals of peace and development was the argument that Chinese authorities faced many obstacles and problems at home and a variety of actual or potential obstacles abroad. Chinese leaders needed to encourage and sustain a peaceful and harmonious world order as they dealt with these concerns and pursued a longer-term goal of developing

China's "comprehensive national power."[60] The Xi Jinping government modified the adherence to peace and development in pursuing greater international activism by China, but I, along with some other foreign specialists, argue that China does indeed continue to face serious challenges at home and abroad that undercut the impact of recent Chinese initiatives and impede the advancement of Chinese influence to a status of dominance in regional or global affairs. In particular, because of domestic and international circumstances discussed throughout this book and given China's repeatedly demonstrated commitment to a status as a developing country with a carefully circumscribed willingness to undertake expensive international obligations, China will move slowly to bear the costs of regional and international leadership.

The arguments of the Chinese and foreign observers who are diffident about China's emerging power and influence in international economics and global governance start with the judgment that both China's future international role and the stability of the government led by the Chinese Communist Party (CCP) depend heavily on healthy growth of the Chinese economy. This in turn depends on the overall health of the world economy and on the Chinese government's effective implementation of reforms conducive to economic growth. The targets of economic and related reform in China are many, posing ongoing challenges for China's future economic growth and stability.[61]

Weaknesses and Challenges to China's Domestic Growth

The weaknesses and challenges include the following:

- Uneven economic growth: The global economic crisis has demonstrated to the Chinese government the dangers of relying too heavily on foreign trade and investment for economic growth. The abrupt drop in Chinese foreign trade in 2015 had serious implications.
- A manipulated currency policy: China does not allow its currency to float and therefore must make large-scale purchases of dollars to keep the exchange rate within certain target levels. Although the renminbi (or yuan) has appreciated somewhat since reforms were introduced in July 2005, analysts at various times have contended that it was highly undervalued against the dollar. Economists warned that China's currency policy made the economy overly dependent on exports and fixed investment for growth and promoted easy credit policies by the banks. These policies may undermine long-term economic stability by causing overproduction in various sectors, increasing the level of nonperforming loans held by the banks and boosting inflationary pressures.

- State-owned enterprises: Accounting for about one-third of Chinese industrial production and employing a large part of China's urban workers,
SOEs put a heavy strain on China's economy. Over half are believed to
lose money and must be supported by subsidies, mainly through state
banks. Government support of unprofitable SOEs diverts resources away
from potentially more efficient and profitable enterprises. In addition, the
poor financial condition of many SOEs makes it difficult for the government to reduce trade barriers out of fear that doing so would lead to
widespread bankruptcies among SOEs. Such trade barriers are a source of
serious dispute between China and the United States and some other leading trading partners.
- The banking system: Banking in China faces several major difficulties
because of its financial support of SOEs and its failure to operate solely on
market-based principles. China's banking system is regulated and controlled by the central government, which sets interest rates and attempts to
allocate credit to certain Chinese firms. The central government has used
the banking system to keep afloat money-losing SOEs by pressuring state
banks to provide low-interest loans, without which a large number of
SOEs would likely go bankrupt. In recent years, about 50 percent of loans
from state-owned banks went to SOEs, even though a large share of the
loans was not likely to be repaid. The high volume of bad loans now held
by Chinese banks and the overall uncertain financial state of the banking
system have made Chinese reformers reluctant to open the sector to
foreign competition. Corruption poses another problem for the banking
system; loans often were made based on political connections. In general,
the system promotes widespread inefficiency in the economy because savings often are not allocated based on obtaining the highest possible returns.
- The agricultural system: This system has been highly inefficient because
of government policies that have sought to maintain a high degree of self-
sufficiency in grains. These policies have diverted resources from more
productive economic sectors and have kept domestic prices for some agricultural products above world prices.
- Rule of law: The lack of the rule of law in China has led to widespread
government corruption, financial speculation, and misallocation of investment funds. In many cases, government and party connections, not market
forces, are the main determinant of success for firms in China. Foreign
firms sometimes find it difficult to do business in China because rules and
regulations often are not consistent or transparent, contracts are not easily
enforced, and intellectual property rights are not protected. The lack of the
rule of law in China limits competition and undermines the efficient allocation of goods and services in the economy. In addition, the Chinese
government does not accept the concept of private ownership of land and

assets in China, which is another obstacle to the efficient allocation of economic resources.

- Poor government regulatory environment: China maintains a weak and relatively decentralized government structure to regulate economic activity in China. Local government officials often ignore laws and regulations. As a result, many firms cut corners in order to maximize profits. In recent years, such practices led to a proliferation of unsafe food, medicines, and other consumer products being sold in China or exported abroad.

- Social issues: A number of social problems have arisen from China's rapid economic growth and extensive reforms. These include a widening of income disparities between coastal and interior regions and between urban and rural parts of China, and a number of bankruptcies and worker layoffs. These pose several challenges to the Chinese government, such as focusing resources on economic development in interior and rural areas and developing fiscal and tax systems to address various social concerns, such as poverty alleviation, education, worker retraining, and pensions. China's poor and inequitable health care system also has shown serious vulnerability to epidemics, such as SARS, avian flu, and HIV/AIDS.

- Growing pollution: The level of pollution in China continues to worsen, posing serious health risks for the population. The Chinese government often disregards its own environmental laws in order to promote rapid economic growth. The World Bank saw twenty out of thirty of the world's most polluted cities in China, with significant costs to the economy, such as health problems, crop failures, and water shortages. According to one government estimate, environmental damage costs the country 10 percent of the country's GDP, each year. The Chinese government estimated that over 300 million people living in rural areas drink water made unsafe by chemicals and other contaminants. China is the world's largest producer and consumer of coal, which accounts for about 70 percent of China's energy use. Although growing environmental degradation has been recognized repeatedly as a serious problem by China's central government, it has found it difficult to induce local governments to comply with environmental laws, especially when such officials feel that doing so will come at the expense of economic growth.[62]

International Challenges and Shortcomings

Internationally, economic growth and increased trade and investment enhance China's prominence, but I side with those observers who remain diffident and cautious about China's importance in international economics and see recent developments also reflecting various shortcomings, limitations, and contradictions that challenge and impede China's world role.[63] For one thing, increased trade and investment with neighbors in Asia do not automatically place China in a leadership position in Asia, much less in other areas farther from China's borders. Looking at China's efforts to create a positive profile in neighboring Asian areas, the growth in trade and South Korean investment in China provided the lead elements in improving China–South Korean relations, arguably one of the areas of greatest success in China's recent foreign policy, at least until recent years.[64] A similar pattern of Chinese trade and Southeast Asian investment in China saw China advance markedly in relations with the countries of ASEAN. Burgeoning Asian trade networks of processing trade involving Southeast Asia and China pushed China ahead of the United States as ASEAN's top trading partner. The Chinese government also set the pace in economic and other relations with the group of ten Southeast Asian states with initiatives involving a China–ASEAN free trade agreement.[65]

Nevertheless, the strong economic links were not sufficient to prevent a serious downturn in China's relations with South Korea and with several Southeast Asia governments in recent years over disputed territorial claims and approaches to regional problems. That better economic ties sometimes do not automatically translate into good overall relations showed most notably in China's relations with Japan. Booming trade with Japan and strong investment by businesses of Japan in China helped moderate political and security tensions between China and the neighboring government. Yet the Chinese government more often than not had difficulty in improving strained relations with Japan. Indeed, as reviewed in chapter 8, relations deteriorated sharply in 2012 over territorial disputes and other issues to the lowest point since World War II. After two years of acute tension, relations began slowly to return to some semblance of normal diplomatic and economic interchange, but with each side viewing the other with great wariness and suspicion.

Trade and economic interchange are less important but growing fast in China's relations with other neighbors—Russia, southern Asia, and central Asia. Russian arms sales and oil sales have been a key foundation of Sino-Russian ties. At odds with the United States and the West over Russia's takeover of Crimea and military aggression against Ukraine, President Vladimir Putin recently sought closer political ties with China and China reciprocated. Nevertheless, the Russian president has at various times in the recent past given higher priority to relations with the United States and the West, and China's leaders have done the same. The result has been behavior contrary to a depiction of Sino-Russian solidarity in foreign affairs.[66]

India's rapprochement with China receives great fanfare during summit meetings and gives an impression of forward movement on border disputes and in trade relations. However, the realities are that border progress is slow while the fundamental strategic problem for India caused by Chinese-backed Pakistan remains unaltered. Meanwhile, India recently has appeared to see its interests better served by cooperating closely with the United States and its allies while giving lower priority to improving relations with China.[67]

In South Korea, Southeast Asia, southern Asia, and elsewhere, manufacturers and their employees tended to view rising China as a threat to their existing business. More efficient production in China frequently meant that these entrepreneurs had to abandon their domestic enterprises and terminate employees in favor of integrating their manufacturing with production in China. Despite the Chinese rhetoric of "win-win" in dealing with economic relations with neighboring countries, Chinese officials were well aware that laborers in Asian and other international manufacturing enterprises that produce products that were also produced in China were more often than not put out of work. U.S., European, Asian, and Latin American laborers and manufacturers also were in the lead pressing for government protection against the onslaught of Chinese manufactured goods entering their markets.[68]

Chinese Investment Abroad and Foreign Assistance

The limitations of growing Chinese investment abroad and Chinese foreign assistance are discussed earlier in this chapter as well as in later chapters dealing with different world areas. Despite having almost $4 trillion in foreign exchange reserves and an avowed interest to assert leadership in international affairs, Chinese officials also sustain an identity as a developing country with major internal requirements. The latter condition usually precludes large commitments that will not provide a win in the narrow Chinese win-set seen in Beijing's ubiquitous "win-win" formula in international affairs. At bottom, China continues efforts to avoid outlays or risks that will not be paid back or compensated for in some tangible way beneficial to China's economic advancement and growth. As a result, China is seen by President Obama and other international commentators as a "free rider," benefiting from the common goods provided at great cost and considerable risk by the United States, other powers, and various global and regional international economic and financial institutions, but unwilling to bear significant costs and risks in support of those goods.[69] Chinese leaders and commentators resent and dispute such charges; they provide lists of Chinese contributions of common goods, but many are done in ways that get others to pay or have other tangible material benefits for China's development. China's behavior over the years provides plenty of examples supporting the free rider label. Notably, why China continues to receive significant amounts of foreign assistance that could be directed to many more needy countries as it rises to world leadership flush with cash seems consistent with the free rider label. Looking out, China's long-standing general requirement for repayment of its concessional loans and other means of investment will face a major test given its $46 billion plan to develop Pakistan, a nation of notorious corruption with a poor record of meeting debt obligations. None of the over $30 billion of U.S. assistance to Pakistan provided since 2001 will be paid back. Nevertheless, it is important to recall that China has been adroit in the recent past in allowing regional and global multilateral banks like the World Bank, the Asian Development Bank, and other international financial institutions to underwrite loans that support Chinese construction of infrastructure in developing countries. If such development occurs in the current case of Pakistan, this will benefit China's economy and may advance Chinese influence in the area, but it will reinforce the negative free rider label.

Uncertain Energy Security

The need to be on guard in the face of economic vulnerability appeared very much in the Chinese leaders' approach to China's fast-growing need for imported raw materials, particularly oil. China became the world's largest importer of oil and it consumes an ever growing share of other international raw materials, including iron ore, copper, aluminum, nickel, and timber. Chinese leaders at times adopted an overtly mercantilist approach to gaining access to oil and gas resources overseas. They showed serious reservations about the international market in these critically important commodities. This led Chinese purchasers of international oil to strive hard to diversify sources. In recent years, China's top suppliers were Saudi Arabia and Iran, but China bought even more oil from a diverse range of suppliers that includes Sudan, Russia, and Angola. Meanwhile, government-backed Chinese enterprises sought control of foreign oil fields that were available for purchase and paid a premium for the rights to develop such fields. China's growing dependence on imported oil and gas, especially Middle East oil, also means that China depends even more on U.S. forces to secure the sea lines of communication between the Persian Gulf and the Chinese coast. Some Chinese strategists worry that the U.S. Navy might close these channels and try to "strangle" China in the event of conflict over Taiwan or other issues. Despite predictions by some Western commentators and in Chinese government pronouncements about the expanding reach of China's emerging "blue water" navy, Chinese strategists have few realistic options to counter U.S. power so far from Chinese shores, at least over the next five years and probably longer.[70]

Environmental and Climate Change Issues

Another area involving international economics where Chinese leaders remain on the defensive has to do with the environmental practices in China and the consequences on the Chinese and world environment of China's rapid growth. For over a decade, Chinese leaders have been working hard, on the one hand, to avoid being considered an international laggard on environmental practices while, on the other, to avoid environmental obstacles to the rapid development of China's economy. On the positive side, Chinese leaders since the early 1990s have taken serious steps to deal with worsening environmental conditions in China. Premier Li Peng was particularly instrumental in putting ecology on the political map. Laws were passed on air, water, solid waste, and noise pollution. Enforcement mechanisms were bolstered, and funds for cleanup, inspection, education, and enforcement increased repeatedly in the 1990s. [71]

In January 1999, a top environmental official announced that China would boost spending on "green" projects to 1.5 percent of GDP between 1997 and 2000. In 1996 to 2000, plans called for investing almost $60 billion in environmental programs. State-owned banks and the State Environmental Protection Agency (SEPA) in 1997 announced that no loans would be issued to seriously polluting firms; in 1996, some 60,000 enterprises—mostly rural factories with no environmental safeguards—were shut down. In January 1997, Beijing set up a national center to disseminate environmentally sound technology, and on March 1, 1997, the government announced the adoption of five new sets of international environmental protection standards.

Despite good intentions at the top, Beijing had serious problems, especially compliance and follow-through with funding and implementation of promised programs. In the late 1990s, China had only about 20,000 enforcement officials nationwide to inspect industrial firms throughout the country; enforcement authority remained weak and fragmented; and penalties were anemic. Local officials tended to judge proposed projects by the number of jobs they created and the revenue they generated rather than by the environmental damage or good they did. [72]

With close to 10 percent annual growth and extensive foreign investment focused on manufacturing, China faced enormous environmental problems at the start of the twenty-first century. Demand for electric power grew rapidly and was met predominantly by coal-fired plants. Autos clogged roads in major cities. Air pollution went from bad to worse. Efforts to develop hydropower using dams on China's rivers were controversial, as the projects displaced large numbers of people and had major environmental impacts on people in China and other countries downstream from the new dams. Serious depletion of water resources in northern China was exacerbated by water pollution, pervasive throughout China. [73]

The Chinese leadership at the time gave more emphasis than its predecessors to the need for sustainable development in China. However, the results more often than not were mixed. Official Chinese media and Chinese officials noted significant improvement in water pollution levels in some Chinese rivers but not in others during the Tenth Five-Year Plan (2001–2005). Efforts to curb air pollution included 182 projects to reduce sulfur dioxide emissions and closures of over 6,000 heavily polluting enterprises. Air pollution levels were said to have improved in some cities, but sulfur dioxide remained a major problem.[74]

As they had done in the past, Chinese officials responsible for environmental protection agreed in 2006 that an investment of 1.5 percent of GDP was required to effectively curb pollution and that an investment of 3 percent of GDP was needed to substantially improve the environment. The Chinese government appeared more serious than in the past about reducing the wasteful use of energy in Chinese production, and significant progress was made in this area during the Eleventh Five-Year Plan (2005–2010). It also continued stronger emphasis on increasing the importance of renewable energy, notably hydroelectric power.

The nation still lacks a powerful national body that is able to coordinate, monitor, and enforce environmental legislation: SEPA is understaffed, has limited resources, and must compete with other bureaucracies for attention. The devolution of decision-making authority to local levels placed environmental stewardship in the hands of officials who often were more concerned with economic growth than the environment. Meanwhile, the deficiency of capital and the lack of will to promote the massive spending necessary to reverse several decades of environmental damage indicated that environmental restoration faced a steep uphill climb.

The international consequences of China's environmental problems were varied and usually negative. Dust storms from eroding land in northern China polluted the atmosphere in Korea and Japan, leading to popular and sometimes official complaints and concerns. Air pollution from China affected locales to the east as far away as the Pacific coast of the United States. Chinese dams on the Mekong River and other Asia rivers originating in Tibet had negative impacts on the livelihood of people in neighboring countries, complicating official relations. Extensive international publicity regarding China's poor environmental record made international opinion less patient with Chinese government explanations that China, as a developing country, should not be held to strict environmental standards. As a result, China's image in world affairs declined.[75]

China avoided the negative international spotlight when the United States refused to agree to the Kyoto Protocol to reduce polluting and other emissions. The U.S. position became the focal point of international criticism, with little attention devoted to China's refusal to agree to binding commitments on greenhouse gas emissions. In January 2006, China joined the United States and others in the inaugural ministerial meeting of the Asia-Pacific Partnership on Clean Development and Climate. The meeting elicited broad statements and promises by representatives from China, the United States, Japan, and others that were viewed by some as a positive step forward.

Others saw these statements as a diversion from these states' unwillingness to be bound by the international standards set forth in the Kyoto Protocol.[76]

In response to growing domestic and international pressures for stronger Chinese actions to curb environmental damage, the Chinese government adopted a number of measures in 2007 and 2008. China established senior-level working groups to deal with international pressure that China conform more to growing world efforts to curb the negative effects of climate change. Chinese diplomats and senior officials were in the forefront in bilateral and multilateral meetings in calling attention to China's concerns over climate change. They emphasized that China and other developing countries should not see their growth thwarted by environmental restrictions and that developed countries should bear the initial responsibility for concrete actions to deal with the growing issue. At home, Chinese officials took new measures to curb investment in energy-intensive industries and to improve the poor standard of energy efficiency in Chinese manufacturing.[77]

China was seen in the West as partly responsible for the collapse of the international climate change meeting in Copenhagen in December 2009. Chinese leaders defended their position that Chinese economic development should not be encumbered by binding commitments to reduce greenhouse gases. The energy intensity of Chinese production declined, according to goals set by the Chinese government for the Eleventh Five-Year Plan, though China's position as the world's largest emitter of greenhouse gases solidified, with ever larger Chinese emissions. The massive global economic crisis beginning in 2008 distracted attention from broad-gauge international solutions to climate change, reducing the negative spotlight on China's role and responsibility.[78] China in recent years showed strong interest in working with the United States and other developed countries in coming up with international accords that would curb the growth of greenhouse gas emissions without major complications for Chinese economic development. China's stress on greater energy efficiency in recent years and future plans are unlikely to offset projections that China's carbon dioxide (CO_2) emissions in 2035 will be double the amount seen in 2011.[79]

Tourism

The Chinese economy gains greatly from the influx of foreign tourists. China is one of the top tourist attractions in the world. China received 26.3 million "foreign" tourists (excluding those from Hong Kong, Macao, and Taiwan) in 2014. In turn, China's growing economy and rising middle class have seen Chinese tourism grow markedly. In 2013, there were 97 million Chinese trips abroad, making Chinese the largest group of outbound travelers. *The Economist* reported in 2014 that "nearly one in ten international tourists worldwide is now Chinese." Most Chinese trips abroad—an estimated three-quarters of such trips—are to Hong Kong and Macao. [80]

Chinese officials frequently endeavored to channel Chinese tourist groups to neighboring areas and faraway countries in an effort to win goodwill. [81] Chinese leaders and foreign officials interested in attracting visitors routinely gave a great deal of media attention to the prospect of future Chinese tourism to places as far away as Africa. For example, tourism is important to the Australian economy, and Chinese and Australian media in recent years were full of accounts of surging Chinese tourism adding to the Australian economy. At the same time, Chinese officials curbed tourism to countries China disapproved of. Chinese tourism to the Philippines declined because of Sino-Philippine frictions over disputed territorial claims in the South China Sea.

Meanwhile, the local reception to incoming Chinese tourists was not always positive. Neighboring populations sometimes resented Chinese visitors. Indeed, media reports in recent years highlighted boorish behavior of Chinese tourists and efforts by Chinese officials to "promote polite tourist behavior in order to boost China's soft power." [82]

CHINA, MULTILATERALISM, AND INTERNATIONAL GOVERNANCE

China's growing involvement with and dependence on the world economy heads the list of reasons explaining China's ever broadening and deepening involvement with various multilateral organizations. Most notably, scholars and specialists saw remarkable changes and increased Chinese activism in Asian regional multilateral organizations, with China taking a leading role in creating such structures as the China–ASEAN Free Trade Agreement and a regional security body that includes Russia and four central Asian states, known as the Shanghai Cooperation Organization (SCO). The Chinese approach in these endeavors strove to meet the interests of the other participants while ensuring that Chinese interests including development and stability were well served. China also has participated actively in recent years in loosely structured global groups, notably the G20, involving the world's twenty leading powers, and the BRICS group, involving Brazil, Russia, India, China, and South Africa. A highlight of very recent Chinese multilateral engagement was the China-fostered Asian Infrastructure Investment Bank (AIIB) discussed earlier. [83]

China's approach to multilateralism has changed markedly since China became an active participant in such endeavors on entry into the United Nations in 1971. At one level of analysis, there has been a steady trend since then toward closer Chinese government cooperation with the United Nations and an ever wider range of multilateral organizations and the international norms they support. The record of Chinese adherence to multilateral guidelines and norms remains somewhat mixed, however.[84]

Chinese engagement with international economic organizations has been the most active and positive. The reasons seem obvious: these organizations provide numerous material benefits for China's development, and China's active participation ensures that it will play an important role in decisions affecting the world economy on which Chinese development depends. There are some limits on Chinese cooperation with international economic institutions. For example, China does not cooperate closely with international organizations that seek to regulate scarcities in the global oil market. As noted previously, rather than rely fully on the global energy market and international groups that seek to facilitate its smooth operation, China at times pursues an independent approach to ensure that it has the energy it needs for economic growth. China gave little attention to international complaints of rising energy prices and other negative results for the world oil market that flow, for example, when China purchased foreign oil rights at high prices.[85]

For many years, China's more active and positive approach in Asian regional economic, security, and political organizations seemed to reflect a priority of the Chinese government to demonstrate that China's rising power and influence should not be seen by China's neighbors and the region's dominant outside power, the United States, as a danger. China did not want to prompt these states to seek measures to cooperate against the interests of the rising Chinese power. China's attentive diplomacy and deference to the interests of its neighbors reassured most of them about Chinese intentions, giving rise to significant improvement in Chinese relations throughout its periphery in the first decade of the twenty-first century. The ten ASEAN states, for example, warmly welcomed Chinese engagement, which they saw as generally consistent with the organization's emphasis on managing disputes through protracted consultations and avoiding interference in each other's internal affairs. On the other hand, the governments of Taiwan and Japan at various times were in the lead among those in Asia who judged that the recent rise of Chinese military power along with China's economic power and positive multilateral diplomacy was inconsistent with China's avowed peaceful intentions toward its neighbors and posed a serious threat to their security and regional stability.

As noted earlier, beginning in 2009 and 2010, China began to show more assertiveness toward its neighbors and the United States regarding regional territorial disputes and other differences. During the transition to the Xi Jinping government in 2012, Chinese officials and commentary began an approach prevalent up to 2015 that gave much less emphasis to reassuring neighbors and the United States, with some Chinese officials arguing that China's past accommodating stance had sent "the wrong signal" to neighboring disputants and the United States.[86] China's truculence was accompanied by coercive and intimidating behavior designed to cow the neighbors and other concerned powers including America. China also manipulated multilateral groups like ASEAN in ways that divided the membership on issues sensitive to China, allowing Chinese interests to prevail at the expense of the unity and effectiveness of the regional group.

Competition between China and the United States for influence among regional countries and for support for the respective preferred regional groups of America and China added to tension that in the recent past China sought to avoid. The reasoning of Chinese leaders for this significant change of course remains unknown. Many argue that China's growing economic and military capabilities combined with perceived U.S. weakness and decline during a period of military withdrawal from Iraq and Afghanistan led Chinese decision makers to feel less constrained as Beijing repeatedly applied its newly prominent power to pressure and intimidate weaker neighbors over territorial and various other disputes. [87]

Meanwhile, it was noted earlier that in the case of international regulation of environmental practices, China was reluctant to commit to international norms if they infringed on Chinese efforts to expand economic growth. And the Chinese government's approach to international human rights regimes long focused on engaging in protracted dialogue and cooperation where possible or needed in order to avoid international sanction. China nonetheless consistently avoided significant commitments that impeded its ability to coerce those in China who were seen as challenging the communist administration. [88] China's cooperation with international arms control measures grew steadily in the past two decades, although the Chinese government continued to avoid commitments that impeded Chinese independence in certain areas sensitive to important Chinese interests. [89]

There have been discernable stages in Chinese cooperation with multilateral organizations and international norms. In the 1970s and early 1980s, as China moved slowly toward greater engagement with international and regional multilateral organizations, it kept its involvement with the United Nations at a low level. It joined only a small number of UN agencies. One reason was Maoist suspicion that such international groups were dominated by foreign powers pursuing selfish interests at odds with China's. Another reason was the lack of experience and expertise in the Chinese Foreign Ministry and the overall Chinese government apparatus after the chaos of the Cultural Revolution. Meanwhile, Beijing focused on bilateral relations with the United States and the Soviet Union, endeavoring to position China effectively in the changing and often dangerous Cold War in Asia. Bilateral ties that could be controlled by Chinese elites without outside interference were also the focus of China's dealings with neighboring countries. The multilateral groups that China did join it joined with little actual cost to its sovereignty and ability to avoid constraints or costly commitments, while the symbolic benefits of membership (prestige, recognition, standing out as a leader for developing world interests, and having a voice in world affairs) were enhanced.[90]

This approach of limited involvement gave way to much greater participation during the late 1980s and the 1990s. China's membership in international organizations nearly doubled between 1984 and 1996 (from twenty-nine to fifty-one), and its membership in international nongovernmental organizations tripled over the same period (from 355 to 1,079). During this period, China also joined all the major intergovernmental organizations within the UN system.[91] China's participation in multilateral arms control treaties was faster than the increase in the number of new treaties themselves: between 1982 and 1996, China's accession to such treaties went from two to twelve.[92]

Having put aside the Maoist practices of the past, Chinese officials gained more experience in international organizations and better perceived the benefits of greater involvement. As China's international stature rose, it appeared necessary to become involved in a wider range of international organizations and activities in order to protect and foster the ever wider range of Chinese foreign policy interests. Indeed, China depended on some of these groups, notably the World Bank, the IMF, and the Asia Development Bank, for important assistance in its economic modernization plans.

As the bipolar Cold War order crumbled, China endeavored to promote a multipolar world where various power centers, including a rising China, would work within the United Nations and other multilateral forums to influence the course of world developments. Greater Chinese involvement in multilateral organizations and groups was also useful in projecting an activist image in Chinese foreign policy following the Tiananmen massacre of 1989, when the United States and other countries were isolating China. At the same time, such involvement reassured neighbors and others concerned with China's rapidly rising economic and military strength that Beijing was prepared to follow the international norms supported by these multilateral groups.

Specialists differed in assessing what this record of greater involvement actually meant for the Chinese government's attitude to international norms supported by the multilateral groups. A prevailing view held that Beijing was particularly reluctant to allow such participation to curb its freedom of action regarding key issues of security and sovereignty or to require costly economic or other commitments by China. Its participation involved maneuvering to pursue narrow national interests without great concern with international norms. It meant primarily burnishing China's global image, deflecting international opprobrium, and securing Chinese interests more effectively.[93]

Since the latter 1990s, China has been more active in its support and initiation of multilateralism and has moved further in adopting cooperative norms, particularly in economic and some security areas. In this period,

China has actively defended the United Nations and its Security Council as the legitimate locus of international security consultations, intensified its contributions to the ASEAN Regional Forum, joined the WTO, taken an active part in the ASEAN Plus Three process, established a China–ASEAN Free Trade Area, promoted multilateral cooperation in the six-member SCO, and worked to ease tensions on the Korean peninsula through the Chinese-fostered six-party talks. In the current decade, the foreign policy activism of the Xi Jinping government has seen China take significant initiatives like the China Silk Road Fund, the BRICS New Development Bank, the Asian Infra-structure Bank, and the Free Trade Area of the Asia-Pacific. The initiatives are in direct competition with initiatives supported by the United States, and they appear as challenges to the international financial institutions supported by the United States. Apart from these implications for Chinese competition with the United States, reasons for these more activist stances include the following:

- Chinese leaders became more confident of their progress—economically and diplomatically—since the 1990s and also came to recognize more clearly the benefits—especially in terms of international assistance to deal with its internal problems—of certain multilateral organizations.
- Beijing recognized that its economic and diplomatic success placed it in a more prominent position to operate more actively within regional and world affairs.
- China at the turn of the century seemed compelled by international real-ities to put aside for a time previous efforts to promote a multipolar world; promoting international multilateralism became a useful fallback position that guarded against U.S. unilateralism contrary to Chinese interests and built international coalitions in favor of a more "democratic" world order that would not be dominated by U.S. leadership.[94]

By this time, the Chinese government appeared truly to have accepted coop-erative multilateralism as a means to take advantage of its strengths as an attractive economic and trading opportunity.[95] A more mixed picture has continued to prevail on human rights, environmental, energy, and interna-tional security questions, including arms control. While more cooperative in several instances, China remained concerned to defend narrow Chinese sove-reign national interests, and it was particularly on guard in the face of pos-sible U.S.-led efforts to constrain Chinese power or compromise Chinese interests.[96] Examples included the following:

- Strong Chinese resistance to U.S.-led efforts to promote greater human rights and democracy through the United Nations and other international bodies

- Chinese reluctance to join international bodies led by developed countries to manage disruptive twists and turns in the world energy markets
- Chinese refusal to commit to international environmental regimes that might curb China's economic independence and rapid growth
- China's refusal to join the U.S.-led Proliferation Security Initiative and its reluctance for many years to participate in the U.S.-led Asian regional security dialogue, the Shangri-La Forum
- China's continued weapons development cooperation with key associates, notably Pakistan, despite U.S. and other international criticism that these steps are contrary to arms control commitments made by the Chinese government
- China's use of Asian regional organizations to exclude the United States from the region and to press for the reduction and withdrawal of U.S. forces from around China's periphery in Asia

Greater Chinese activism in international organizations and governance in the post–Cold War period notably is illustrated by the development of China's role in the United Nations and related organizations and the development of China's role in Asian regional organizations. Those developments are reviewed here. To protect and foster its ever growing international economic and other interests in other parts of the world, the Chinese government also became more involved in a variety of organizations in other world regions. Those involvements are treated in later chapters dealing with Chinese relations with different world areas.

The United Nations and UN-Related Organizations

Since joining the United Nations in 1971, the Chinese government has sought to maximize benefits and minimize costs while playing an increasingly prominent role in international governance through the United Nations and related organizations. Chinese economic reforms and international economic outreach saw China in the early 1980s join the World Bank and the IMF. China soon became the largest borrower from the World Bank and worked closely with the IMF in learning techniques and gaining advice important for Chinese economic reforms and development. Combined with loans and assistance from the Asian Development Bank, which China joined in the mid-1980s, and assistance provided by developed countries, China became the largest international recipient of foreign assistance in the 1980s and much of the 1990s. In recent years, China has sought a more prominent position in the IMF, consistent with its status as the world's second-largest economy. Frustration with the slow IMF process to grant a more prominent position to China reportedly influenced Beijing to move ahead over the past two years with the AIIB as well as the New Development Bank and the SCO Development Bank. [97]

China relied heavily on its position as a permanent member of the UN Security Council to ensure that its interests were protected regarding the many international issues considered by the council in the post–Cold War period. This was especially important as the United Nations changed its approach to international affairs. During the Cold War, the council tended to emphasize the articles of the UN charter that supported a state-based system of order. This met with the preferences of the Chinese government, which was reluctant to allow interference in its own and other nations' internal affairs. This emphasis has given way to greater concern in the United Nations with individual justice, a developing norm of humanitarian intervention, and a focus on the promotion of democracy—tendencies that often are seen as potentially or actually problematic by Chinese authorities, who remain concerned that such intervention could at some point be directed at China or Chinese interests abroad. [98]

Specific changes seen in UN policies and practices in recent years that pose important and sometimes negative implications for Chinese interests include the following:

- Today the veto is rarely used, and resort to its use is likely to be regarded as a breach of a developing informal norm of nonuse.
- There has been an increase in the scope and number of peacekeeping operations, many of which cite humanitarian motives as a part of the reason for intervention; these should more accurately be described as peace-building operations, to be used predominantly in internal conflicts with mandates that can include the holding of elections, refugee assistance, human rights protection, and economic reconstruction.
- Recent secretaries-general, especially Kofi Annan (1997–2006), promoted the idea of humanitarian intervention and the priority of individual sovereignty over state sovereignty. The UN secretary-general gave increased attention to human rights. In 1993, the United Nations appointed a high commissioner for human rights. The UN Security Council also created International Criminal Tribunals to try those indicted for war crimes.
- UN-related institutions such as the IMF and World Bank became more intrusive and extended their reach into the policymaking realm of domestic societies. The performance criteria on which loans were conditioned increased several-fold since the 1980s, and ideas of good governance were promoted.
- The numbers of nongovernmental organizations vastly increased in the recent decades and received better access to and more information from bodies such as the IMF, the World Bank, the Human Rights Committee,

the Committee against Torture, and other UN-related bodies that tended to intervene in states' internal affairs.[99]

In the post–Cold War period, China's position as one of the five permanent members of the UN Security Council (the Perm-Five) helped ensure that the United States and other powers could not continue to shun China as a result of the Tiananmen crackdown or for other reasons if they expected Chinese cooperation, or at least acquiescence, with their initiatives before the Security Council. Thus, despite past close Chinese association with the notorious Khmer Rouge in Cambodia, Western powers sought Chinese involvement and assistance in coming up with a 1991 peace plan for Cambodia that was backed by the Perm-Five. The United States and other Western governments tended to mute their recent criticism of Chinese human rights and other policies at the time of the international confrontation with Iraq following Baghdad's invasion of Kuwait in August 1990. Seeking UN Security Council endorsement for the use of force against Iraq made Washington and other Western capitals more sensitive to China's possible use of its veto power in the Security Council.

Beijing's general practice was to go along with whatever broad international consensus prevailed on particular issues being considered by the United Nations. Chinese representatives especially wished to avoid choosing sides on sensitive issues dividing the developing countries of what was called the Third World, and they generally kept a low profile on those issues. Beijing also was less inclined than in the past to join the Third World bandwagon against such isolated states as Israel, especially following the normalization of Sino-Israeli diplomatic relations in 1992. Beijing in the 1990s and, to a somewhat lesser degree, in the first decade of the twenty-first century did line up with anti-U.S. forces on issues where the United States was isolated—such as the U.S. effort to use military force against Iraq in 1997–1998 because of its failure to comply with UN mandates. In these cases, Chinese diplomats usually positioned themselves behind other powers and rarely took the lead in attacking the United States. China followed a similar practice in the lead-up to the U.S.-led military attack on Saddam Hussein's regime in 2003, standing in the UN Security Council a step or two behind Russian and French diplomats who led the criticism of the U.S.-led military operation. In the recent decade, China came to regret not standing against Western powers seeking military intervention in Libya in 2011, and it subsequently joined with Russia in blocking UN endorsement of such intervention in Syria.[100]

China's general opposition to international sanctions and other such pressure to coerce governments to conform to UN-supported norms has remained a feature of Chinese diplomacy up to the present, even though China sometimes bent its resistance in cases where strident opposition would isolate it or hurt other significant Chinese interests. In the case of U.S.- and European-led efforts since 2005 to pressure Iran to halt nuclear programs seen as promoting a nuclear weapons program, China worked closely with Russia to seek compromises and procedures that would avoid imposition of significant sanctions on a country that was an important energy supplier for China and a key Chinese political partner in the Middle East. China also held out against strong U.S. and other pressure in the United Nations for stronger UN-backed sanctions against the egregious human rights violations fostered by the Sudan government's practices in a civil conflict that claimed many thousands of lives and displaced millions. China endeavored to muster support from authoritarian and other governments that would be sufficient to head off binding sanctions that would seriously complicate China's strong interest in oil from the African nation. China also used its influence with considerable success to muster sufficient international support to prevent or moderate proposals for strong UN actions involving international sanctions being imposed on North Korea, Myanmar (Burma), and Zimbabwe for their illegal and repressive policies.[101]

On the other hand, China actively participated in a variety of UN peacekeeping operations designed to support UN-backed administrations against often strong and violent opponents. China did not obstruct international tribunals investigating crimes of former leaders in Serbia and Rwanda. It seemed to oppose an international tribunal to investigate war crimes of the Chinese-backed Khmer Rouge regime in Cambodia but did so discreetly, supporting the current Cambodian government as it delayed for years the start of the tribunal. As illustrated in the cases of the UN-backed intervention against Iraq for its invasion of Kuwait in 1990 and in the case of the U.S.-led military intervention into Iraq in 2003, China opposed the actions with varying degrees of intensity but was reluctant to take a strong stand of opposition that would jeopardize important interests in China's relations with the United States and other powers.[102]

Exceptions to China's low-risk strategy in the United Nations often centered on Taiwan. Chinese foreign policy gave top priority to blocking Taiwan from gaining entry into the United Nations or UN-affiliated organizations. To battle against efforts by Taiwan's diplomatic allies seeking to raise the issue of Taiwan's representation in the United Nations, Beijing in January 1997 used its veto power for the first time in twenty-five years. It did so to block approval for UN peacekeepers in Guatemala until Guatemala agreed to reduce its support for Taiwan's efforts to gain UN entry. In 1999, China repeated the pattern by blocking the continuation of UN peacekeeping operations in Macedonia, which had recently established diplomatic relations with Taiwan.

The Chinese authorities were seen to have mishandled the initial months of the SARS epidemic in China during 2002–2003, leading to the spread of the disease to Taiwan and other neighboring areas. Senior Chinese leaders subsequently adopted more effective policies and endeavored to change policy in directions favored by Chinese neighbors. However, they remained uncompromising in the face of Taiwan's efforts to gain entry as an observer to the World Health Organization (WHO), a UN-affiliated body directing the international effort against the epidemic. Beijing continued its tough stance against Taiwanese representation or participation in the WHO efforts to deal with the avian flu epidemic that was seriously affecting China and neighboring countries in 2005–2006. The coming to power in 2008 of a moderate Taiwan government intent on improving relations with China eased to some degree Taiwan–China competition involving the United Nations and affiliated organizations.[103]

The importance of the United Nations and related organizations in Chinese foreign policy in the post–Cold War period failed to hide China's reluctance in these bodies to undertake costly commitments or substantial risks. China's behavior seemed to reinforce its image in the United States and among Western powers as a "free rider" or at least a "cheap rider" in undertaking costs and commitments for common regional and global goods. China remained strongly wedded to its "win-win" approach in international relations. If China was going to extend effort and resources for a common good, it generally had to be shown that such actions resulted in tangible benefits for China defined in a fairly narrow Chinese win-set. For example, China repeatedly publicized its role as the largest participant among the permanent members of the UN Security Council to UN peacekeeping efforts. It rarely pointed out that its contributions until very recently were noncombatants, thus generally its personnel were positioned out of harm's way. It avoided highlighting the fact that the Chinese participants, like those from Bangladesh and other large contributors of UN peacekeepers, were paid from the UN peacekeeping budget. And China rarely noted the size of its peacekeeping budget contribution, which has risen from a very low base and for many years was at the same low level as that of Italy. It rose further in the 2013–2015 period to a level (6.64 percent of the overall budget) approaching the level of Great Britain; this level was far behind Japan (10.83 percent) and very far behind the United States (28.38 percent).[104]

Meanwhile, though China strongly supports the United Nations as the ultimate arbiter of international issues, it remained reluctant to see its allotment to the UN budget rise from its recent remarkably low level, which for many years was about the same as that of Spain. In 2012, the Chinese Institute of International Studies (an institute associated with China's foreign ministry) reported that China agreed to a "hefty" increase of its UN dues, from the previous level providing 3.19 percent of the UN budget to a level providing 5.15 percent. The new level was said to "overtake Canada and Italy" and to make China the sixth-largest contributor to the UN budget. Reflecting the kind of rhetoric used by China to minimize costs in the UN

and other international bodies, the report emphasized China's status as a
"developing country" that should receive "the preferential policy rate intended for 'low per-capita countries.'" Thus, the report stressed that the
increase in Chinese payment to the UN represented "a heavy burden." For
comparison purposes, the U.S. dues amount to 22 percent of the UN budget
and Japan's dues amount to 10.8 percent.[105]

China and Asian Regional Organizations

The end of the Cold War and the impact of economic globalization led to a
much more fluid dynamic among Asian governments and governments like
that of the United States that had a strong interest in Asia.[106] One salient
development was the growth of a variety of regional multilateral organizations to deal with economic, political, and security matters. Some of these
bodies, like the ASEAN Plus Three (ten ASEAN members plus China, Japan, and South Korea) and the SCO (made up of Russia, China, Kazakhstan,
Kyrgyzstan, Tajikistan, and Uzbekistan), deliberately excluded non-Asian
powers like the United States. Others, like the Asia-Pacific Economic Cooperation, the ASEAN Regional Forum, and the East Asian Summit included a
wide range of countries strongly involved with Asian affairs. China played
an active role in all these bodies.

China often took initiatives in working with ASEAN and fostering such
regional groups as the SCO and the six-party talks. During the previous
decade, its approach seemed accommodating to neighboring powers with the
notable exception of Taiwan and Japan. As noted earlier, this pattern changed
with advancing Chinese economic, military, and political capabilities enabling Beijing's pursuit of a more assertive and coercive stance in advancing
Chinese territorial ambitions and other interests at the expense of neighbors
and the United States. Against this background, the Xi Jinping government
launched the China-backed Asian Infrastructure Investment Bank and a
range of other regional economic plans well crafted to benefit China's economic advancement and spread Chinese influence at odds with competitors
in the United States and Japan.

Although ASEAN members suffered as a result of the Asian economic
crisis of 1997–1998, its organization of ten governments provided the basis
for many of the Asian regional groupings. Members of ASEAN had been
working together since the late 1960s and had established some basic norms
that facilitated cooperation. The members were at least outwardly more
cooperative and accommodating than the more powerful governments of
northeastern Asia—China, Japan, South Korea, and North Korea. The latter
remained at odds over serious historical, territorial, and strategic disputes and
rivalries, resulting in ASEAN providing the lowest common denominator for
many Asian regional organizations.

At the turn of the century, China took the lead among Asian and other powers in establishing new frameworks of cooperation with ASEAN.[107] China's proposal for a China–ASEAN Free Trade Agreement set the pace for other powers to follow with their economic proposals for ASEAN. China became the first major power to sign the ASEAN Treaty of Amity and Cooperation, prompting many other powers to follow suit. China's trade relations with ASEAN grew faster than those of other powers, and it became ASEAN's leading trading partner and a major destination for ASEAN's foreign investment. China supported Malaysia's hosting an inaugural East Asian Summit in December 2005. Malaysia and China initially favored a grouping based on the ASEAN Plus Three membership but bowed to pressures from Japan, Indonesia, and Singapore that membership be broadened to include India, Australia, New Zealand, and probably Russia, with the door remaining open to possible U.S. participation, which began in 2010. In more recent years, China was less likely to defer to those in ASEAN disagreeing with China on sensitive territorial and other issues; it was more likely than not to pressure and manipulate ASEAN leaders on such matters.

In northern Asia, the SCO was founded in 2001, based on an organization known as the Shanghai Five, which was established in 1994 with a membership including all present SCO members except Uzbekistan. China was a major financial supporter of the group and provided its headquarters in China. The group developed slowly; it endeavored at first to build mutual trust among members and to ease any concerns about military deployments and border issues. Concern with transnational terrorism also was a prime concern of the SCO members, which rose with the September 11, 2001, attack on America and the subsequent U.S.-led war against the terrorist-harboring Taliban regime in Afghanistan. For a time, most SCO members cooperated closely with the U.S.-led military effort; China remained wary of U.S. military presence along its periphery. In 2005, a prodemocracy uprising in Kyrgyzstan was successful in changing the government, while demonstrations for political change in Uzbekistan were put down harshly by the authoritarian regime. China and Russia backed Uzbekistan's subsequent demands that U.S. forces leave the country, and the SCO in mid-2005 said that Western military forces should set a deadline for departing the region.

China and Russia remained determined that the SCO would not allow U.S. membership, though nearby states were given observer status. Under the auspices of the SCO, China and Russia in August 2005 conducted a major military exercise near the Chinese coast that seemed to have little to do with long-standing SCO concerns with border security and combating terrorism and transnational crime. The large show of force involving long-range Russian bombers and thousands of Chinese troops seemed designed to send a strong signal to the United States, Japan, and Taiwan about Chinese and Russian military preparedness and resolve.[108] China and Russia became less concerned with the United States as the American-led forces in Afghanistan withdrew and bases for these forces were closed in central Asia.

China continued to play a key role in the recently moribund six-party (North and South Korea, the United States, China, Japan, and Russia) talks that began in 2003 to deal with North Korea's nuclear weapons development. Although not a formal multilateral organization, the talks held out the potential for development of a regional organization in northeastern Asia, if and when the various issues raised by the North Korean nuclear issue moved toward an acceptable resolution.

Chapter Five

Chinese National Security Policies

CHINA'S NATIONAL SECURITY CONCERNS AND MILITARY ACTIONS

There is probably no more important reason for continuing international uncertainty about China's approach to world affairs in the twenty-first century than the apparent disconnect between China's national development policy and China's national security policy. Chinese officials for many years articulated a relatively clear national development policy. That Chinese approach was laid out authoritatively in the December 2005 Chinese government document "China's Peaceful Development Road," and was repeated in similar documents in later years. This approach was consistent with the thrust of Chinese leadership pronouncements since the turn of the century, emphasizing Chinese leaders' determination to avoid trouble abroad and to seek international cooperation and a harmonious world order as China develops and rises peacefully in importance in Asian and world affairs in the twenty-first century.[1] Unfortunately, the December 2005 document and the follow-on documents and statements make little or no reference to military conflict, the role of the rapidly modernizing People's Liberation Army (PLA), and other key national security questions. When asked about this, one senior Chinese Foreign Ministry official said in May 2006 that China's national security policy was less clearly developed than China's national development policy.[2]

In fact, however, the broad outlines of Chinese national security policy are fairly clearly laid out in official Chinese documents and briefings.[3] They—and the remarkable recent advances in China's military modernization in the post–Cold War period—are in the lead among Chinese statements and behavior that have called into question just how peaceful and cooperative

China's approach to Asia and the world actually will be. Indeed, noted earlier was the heightened determination of the Xi Jinping government to advance China's disputed territorial claims and to show greater regional and international activism in competition with the United States and other powers, including several Chinese neighbors. Also noted was the decline in the Chinese emphasis in the recent past on reassurance and deference to neighbors and others in the interest of sustaining regional and global harmony and peace. Taken together with the most recent authoritative Chinese white paper on military modernization and strategy issued on May 26, 2015, a prudent conclusion is that China's peaceful development strategy is far from uniformly implemented and it does not represent the sum and substance of China's international approach. Rather it is accompanied by a range of statements and actions showing a significantly more muscular Chinese foreign policy under Xi Jinping.

Foreign specialists on the Chinese military pointed out seeming contrasts and contradictions in Chinese official pronouncements and actions dealing with trends in international security during the administration of Communist Party General Secretary and state President Hu Jintao (2002–2012). Authoritative Chinese foreign policy pronouncements emphasized China's view of an emerging harmonious world order in which China was rising peacefully in national strength and international influence. China often was seen as occupying its most influential position in world affairs in the modern era. In contrast, white papers on national security,[4] public presentations by authoritative Chinese military representatives, and the continuation of an impressive buildup and modernization of the Chinese military forces in recent years revealed Chinese leadership's strong concern about China's security in the prevailing regional and international order. This concern continued despite twenty years of double-digit-percentage increases in China's defense budgets and despite the view of many foreign specialists that China was becoming Asia's undisputed leading military power and an increasingly serious concern to American security planners as they sought to preserve stability and U.S. leadership in Asia.[5]

Chinese military modernization programs have been under way for thirty years. They have reached the point where they strongly suggest that the objective of the Chinese leadership is to build Asia's most powerful defense force.[6] China's military growth complicated China's relations with the United States and some Asian neighbors, notably Taiwan, Japan, India, Vietnam, and South Korea. Leaders from the United States and some Asian countries were not persuaded by Chinese leadership pledges to pursue the road of peace and development. They saw Chinese national security policies and programs as real or potential threats to their security interests.[7]

Chinese national security pronouncements duly acknowledged that with the end of the Cold War, the danger of global war—a staple in Chinese warning statements in the 1970s and 1980s—ended. However, recent Chinese national security statements rarely highlighted the fact that Chinese defense policy was being formulated in an environment that was less threatening to China than at any time in the past 200 years. Typically, in the 2010 white paper on national defense, the international system was represented as stable, but "international strategic competition" was "intensifying," "security threats" were "increasingly" volatile, and world peace was "elusive."[8] The critical Chinese response to the Obama government's emphasis since 2011 on military as well as economic and political reengagement with Asia under the rubric of the U.S. policy of rebalance in the Asia-Pacific region reflected sometimes thinly disguised and sometimes forthright Chinese suspicion of a revival of American efforts to constrain and contain China's spreading influence.[9]

PLA pronouncements and Western scholarship made clear that the United States remained at the center of the national security concerns of Chinese leaders.[10] The 2004 white paper presented a widening military imbalance of grave concern to China caused by U.S. military technological advances and doctrinal changes referred to as the "World Wide Revolution in Military Affairs (RMA)." Authoritative PLA briefings in 2008 presented growing U.S. military power as the most serious complication for China's international interests, China's main security concern in the Asian region, and the key military force behind Chinese security concerns over Taiwan, Japan, and other neighbors. Explaining China's concerns in the Asia-Pacific region, the 2010 white paper warned that "the United States is reinforcing its regional military alliances, and increasing its involvement in regional security affairs."

Chinese statements and the PLA buildup opposite Taiwan underlined that Taiwan was the most likely area of U.S.–China military conflict. And the United States and its military allies were portrayed as the principal sources of potential regional instability in Asia. China responded harshly to indications of closer U.S.–Japanese strategic cooperation over Taiwan, notably a statement supporting a peaceful resolution of the Taiwan issue that was released following the U.S.-Japan Security Consultative Committee meeting in February 2005. The Chinese Foreign Ministry claimed that U.S. Secretary of State Hillary Clinton's intervention about disputes in the South China Sea at the ASEAN Regional Forum meeting in Hanoi in July 2010 represented an "attack on China."[11]

PLA and other Chinese officials registered strong determination to protect Chinese territory and territorial claims, including areas having strategic resources such as oil and gas. As Chinese–Japanese and other territorial conflicts involving energy resources in the East and South China Seas grew in scope and intensity, they intruded ever more directly on these PLA priorities. Chinese concerns increased over U.S. and allied forces controlling sea lines of communication, which were essential for increasing oil flows to China. The Chinese government appeared uncertain as to how serious was the strategic danger posed by the vulnerability of China's energy flows from the Middle East and Africa through the Malacca Strait and other choke points in Southeast Asia and what should be done about it. Chinese national security officials openly debated these issues. [12] The Chinese government pursued solutions including overland oil and gas pipelines that would bypass the Malacca Strait, and the steady buildup of Chinese naval capabilities, including the development of Chinese aircraft carriers, that would provide more military power to protect Chinese trade, energy flows, and other maritime communications. [13]

Given the recent record of U.S. policies and behavior regarding China and Chinese interests, the concern Chinese leaders had over the strategic intentions of the United States regarding China and Chinese interests concerning Taiwan, Japan, Asia, and world affairs was not unwarranted. The George W. Bush administration worked more closely with Taiwan's government in efforts to support Taiwan's defense against China than any U.S. administration since the break in official U.S. relations with Taiwan in 1979. It also worked more closely in defense collaboration with Japan, which focused on Taiwan and other possible contingencies regarding China, than at any time since the normalization of U.S. and Japanese relations with China in the 1970s. Policy statements such as the National Security Strategy of the United States of 2002 and the Quadrennial Defense Report of 2006 made clear that the U.S. military was able and willing to take steps to sustain Asian stability in the face of possible adverse consequences of China's rising military strength. Bush administration leaders emphasized U.S. uncertainty over China's longer-term strategic intentions; they affirmed that they were not fully persuaded by Chinese pronouncements on peace and development and remained unsure whether China will be a friend or a foe of the United States. They built up U.S. forces in Asia and collaborated with Japan and other allies and partners, including India, in part to ensure that U.S. interests and Asian stability will be sustained in the face of possible disruptive or negative actions by Chinese military forces.

The Barack Obama administration continued American resolve in the face of China's military buildup as it carried out the most significant U.S. reengagement with the Asia-Pacific region in many years. Speaking to reporters on the way to Beijing in January 2011, Secretary of Defense Robert Gates publicly affirmed U.S. determination to deal effectively with advancing Chinese military capabilities. [14]

In this context, it appeared reasonable for Chinese leaders to carry out the acquisition, development, and advancement of military capabilities specifically designed to defeat U.S. forces, especially if they were to intrude in a confrontation regarding China's avowed top priority: restoring Taiwan to

Chinese sovereignty. And as the Chinese leaders devoted ever greater effort to this military buildup, the U.S. advancement of its military deployments and defense cooperation with Taiwan, Japan, Australia, India, and others also seemed logical in order to deter Chinese attack and preserve stability. Of course, the result was an escalating arms race and defense preparations that seemed very much at odds with the harmonious international environment Chinese leaders sought to nurture and sustain. In effect, the respective Chinese and U.S. defense buildups and preparations regarding Taiwan demonstrated that Chinese leaders were not prepared to pursue uniformly "the road to peace and development" set forth in the document "China's Peaceful Development Road." Peace and development and a harmonious international environment clearly were goals of Chinese foreign policy, but Chinese leaders at the same time were hedging their bets, notably with an impressive array of military acquisitions that provided capabilities they judged necessary.[15]

Overall, Chinese defense acquisition and advancement showed broad ambitions for Chinese military power. While they appeared focused on dealing with U.S. forces in the event of a Taiwan contingency, these forces can be used by Chinese leaders as deemed appropriate in a variety of circumstances.[16]

Salient Chinese defense acquisitions and modernization efforts include the following:

- Research and development in space and other surveillance systems to provide wide area intelligence and reconnaissance and the development of antisatellite systems to counter the surveillance and related efforts of potential adversaries
- Cruise missile acquisitions and programs that improve the range, speed, and accuracy of Chinese land-, air-, and sea-launched weapons, including submarine launched missiles that travel much faster than the speed of sound and target sea and land surface forces
- Ballistic missile programs that involve missiles with multiple warheads and that improve the range, survivability (through mobile systems in particular), reliability, accuracy, and response times of tactical, regional, and intercontinental-range weapons to augment or replace current systems
- Development of ballistic missiles capable of targeting U.S. or other naval combatants
- Construction and acquisition of advanced conventional-powered submarines with subsurface-launched cruise missiles and guided torpedoes and nuclear-powered attack and ballistic missile submarines to augment or replace older vessels in service
- Development and acquisition of more capable naval surface ships armed with advanced antiship, antisubmarine, and air defense weapons

- Air force advances, including hundreds of modern multirole fighters, advanced air-to-air missiles, airborne early warning and control system aircraft, aerial refueling capabilities, and unmanned aerial vehicles
- Air defense systems involving modern surface-to-air missiles covering all of Taiwan and much of the maritime rim of coastal China and air defense fighters
- Improved power projection for ground forces, including more sea- and airlift capabilities, special operations forces, and amphibious warfare capabilities
- Research and development of defense information systems and improved command, control, communications, and computer systems
- Development of cyber warfare capabilities
- Increasing the tempo and complexity of exercises in order to make the PLA capable in joint interservice operations involving power projections, including amphibious operations[17]

The Chinese advances mean that no single Asian power can match China's military power on continental Asia. With the possible exception of Japan, no Asian country will be capable of challenging China's naval power and airpower in maritime eastern Asia. Should Beijing choose to deploy naval and air forces to patrol the sea lines of communication in the Indian Ocean, only India conceivably would be capable of countering China's power.[18]

Looking to the future, it is possible to bound the scope of China's military buildup. Available evidence shows that it focuses on nearby Asia. The major possible exceptions include the long-range nuclear weapons systems that target outside Asia and Chinese cyber warfare and space warfare capabilities. China has used its long-range nuclear weapons to deter the United States and other potential adversaries by demonstrating a retaliatory, second-strike capability against them.[19]

The objectives of the Chinese military buildup seem focused first on Taiwan, preventing its move toward independence and ensuring that China's sovereignty will be protected and restored. More generally, Chinese forces can be deployed to defeat possible threats or attacks on China, especially China's economically important eastern coastline. Apart from conflict over Taiwan, they are designed to deal with a range of so-called local war possibilities. These could involve territorial disputes with Japan, Southeast Asian countries, or India or instability requiring military intervention in Korea. Meanwhile, the Chinese military plays a direct role in Chinese foreign policy; it seeks to spread Chinese international influence, build military relationships with neighboring countries and others, and support a regional and international environment that will foster China's rise in power and influence. This role likely will involve continued active diplomacy by Chinese military officials, increasing numbers of military exercises with Asian and other countries, some Chinese arms sales to and training of foreign military forces, and more active participation by Chinese national security officials in regional and other multilateral security organizations and agreements. [20]

The Chinese military is on course to continue a transformation from its past strategic outlook, that of a large continental power requiring large land forces for defense against threats to borders. The end of the threat from the Soviet Union and the improvement of China's relations with India, Vietnam, and others eased this concern. China is moving away from a continental orientation requiring large land forces to a combined continental/maritime orientation requiring smaller, more mobile, and more sophisticated forces capable of protecting China's inland and coastal periphery. Unlike the doctrine of protracted land war against an invading enemy prevalent until the latter years of the Cold War, Chinese doctrine probably will continue its more recent emphasis on the need to demonstrate an ability to attack first in order to deter potential adversaries and to carry out first strikes in order to gain the initiative in the battlefield and secure Chinese objectives.

To fulfill these objectives, Chinese forces will need and will further develop the ability to respond rapidly, to take and maintain the initiative in the battlefield, to prevent escalation, and to resolve the conflict quickly and on favorable terms. Chinese military options will include preemptive attacks and the use of conventional and nuclear forces to deter and coerce adversaries. Chinese forces will expand power-projection capabilities, giving Chinese forces a solid ability to deny critical land and sea access (e.g., Taiwan Strait) to adversaries and providing options for force projection farther from Chinese borders. [21]

To achieve these objectives, Chinese conventional ground forces will evolve, consistent with recent emphasis, toward smaller, more flexible, highly trained, and well-equipped rapid reaction forces with more versatile and well-developed assault, airborne, and amphibious power-projection capabilities. Special operations forces will play an important role in these efforts. Navy forces will build on recent steps forward with more advanced surface combatants and submarines having better air defense, antisubmarine warfare, and antiship capabilities. Their improved weaponry of cruise missiles and torpedoes, an improved naval air force, and greater replenishment-at-sea capabilities will broaden the scope of their activities and pose greater challenges to potential adversaries. Air forces will grow with more versatile and modern fighters; longer-range interceptor/strike aircraft; improved early warning and air defense; and longer-range transport, lift, and midair refueling capabilities.

These military forces will be used increasingly in an integrated way consistent with an emphasis on joint operations that involve more sophisticated command, control, communications, computers, intelligence, and strategic reconnaissance (C4ISR), early warning, and battlefield management systems.

Improved airborne and satellite-based systems will improve detection, tracking, targeting, and strike capabilities and enhanced operational coordination of the various forces.

Chinese strategic planners are sure to build on the advantages that Chinese strategic missile systems provide. Estimates vary, but it appears likely that Chinese plans call for over 1,500 short-, medium-, and intermediate-range solid-fueled, mobile ballistic missiles (with a range under 4,000 miles) and short-range cruise missiles with increased accuracy and some with both nuclear and conventional capabilities. China is also modernizing a small number of longer-range nuclear missiles capable of hitting the continental United States, and it seems likely to develop a viable submarine-launched nuclear missile that would broaden Chinese nuclear weapons options. Chinese nuclear missiles have smaller and more powerful warheads with multiple reentry vehicle capabilities. The emphasis on modern surveillance, early warning, and battle management systems with advanced C4ISR assets seen in Chinese planning regarding conventional forces also applies to nuclear forces.

These advances will build on China's existing military abilities. They pose concerns for the United States, Taiwan, Japan, and many other Chinese neighbors; they present an overall strategic reality of increasing Chinese military power that influences the strategic outlook of most Chinese neighbors. Those abilities include the following:

- The ability to conduct intensive, short-duration air and naval attacks on Taiwan as well as prolonged air, naval, and possibly ground attacks. China's ability to prevail against Taiwan is seen as increasing steadily, especially given lax defense preparedness and political division in Taiwan. Massive U.S. military intervention is viewed as capable of defeating a Chinese invasion, but Chinese area denial capabilities could substantially impede and slow the U.S. intervention.
- Power-projection abilities to dislodge smaller regional powers from nearby disputed land and maritime territories and the ability to conduct air and sea denial operations for 200 miles along China's coasts.
- Strong abilities to protect Chinese territory from invasion, to conduct ground-based power projection along land borders against smaller regional powers, and to strike civilian and military targets with a large and growing inventory of ballistic missiles and medium-range bombers armed with cruise missiles.
- A limited ability to project force against the territory of militarily capable neighboring states, notably Russia, India, and Japan.
- Continued ability to deter nuclear and other attacks from the United States and Russia by means of modernized and survivable Chinese nuclear missile forces capable of striking at these powers.

As China's military capabilities continue to grow more rapidly than those of any of its neighbors and as China solidifies its position as Asia's leading military power, the situation clearly poses serious implications for and some complications in China's foreign policy. As I have discussed, Chinese officials in the recent past worked hard and with some success to persuade skeptical neighbors, the United States, and other concerned governments that China's rising power and influence will be peaceful and of benefit to all. However, many neighboring officials and those in the United States and elsewhere, sometimes publicly and more often privately, remain concerned.

Such wariness was reinforced by the Xi Jinping government's truculence on China's territorial claims, notably in the East China Sea and the South China Sea. Moreover, the latest Chinese white paper on defense of May 26, 2015, had a special focus on strategy. On the one hand, it reaffirmed China's general theme emphasizing Chinese promotion of "peace and development" in international affairs. On the other hand, it took pointed aim at the Obama government's rebalance policy and the role of Japan in Asia and in regional and international affairs. It gave special emphasis on securing China's "maritime rights and interests" in the face of so-called provocations by neighbors supported by the United States, Japan, and others. And it added that China needed to keep advancing capabilities in order to "safeguard the security of China's overseas interests." Against this backdrop, the paper further shifted Chinese strategy toward a focus on maritime defense. It said with indirect but obvious reference to past Chinese practice, "The traditional mentality that land outweighs sea must be abandoned, and great importance has to be attached to managing the seas and oceans and protecting maritime rights and interests." It went on to forecast a much greater role for the PLA Navy on world waterways, avowing that the PLA Navy "will gradually shift its focus from offshore waters defense" to the combination of "offshore waters defense" with "open seas protection."[22]

Adding to the concern with such rhetoric in tandem with big advances in Chinese military capabilities is the view held by many of the officials of neighboring governments on what their countries experienced in dealing with the People's Republic of China. Though the Chinese government works hard to distort the historical record in its favor and most Chinese seem to believe the historical "party line" that China has never been aggressive toward its neighbors, the history of the use of force in Chinese foreign policy is well known among regional officials. The record provides little assurance that China's avowed peaceful development in the twenty-first century will be sustained. The PRC government has resorted to the use of force in international affairs more than most governments in the modern period. The reasons are varied and include Chinese determination to deter perceived superpower aggression, defend Chinese territory and territorial claims, recover lost territory, and enhance China's regional and global stature. Studies of Chinese leaders' strategic thinking have led to the conclusion that modern Chinese leaders, like those in the past, have been more inclined than not to see the use of military force as an effective instrument of statecraft. [23]

Although facing superpower adversaries with much greater military might, Mao Zedong frequently initiated the use of military force to keep the more powerful adversary off balance and to keep the initiative in Chinese hands. Deng Xiaoping was much more focused than Mao on conventional Chinese nation building; he sought to foster a peaceful environment around China's periphery in order to pursue Chinese economic modernization. However, Deng also undertook in 1979 strong Chinese military action against Soviet-backed Vietnam, and he continued for several years to confront Soviet power throughout China's periphery despite China's military weakness relative to the Soviet superpower. In the post–Cold War period, Chinese officials judged that the Taiwan president's visit to the United States in 1995 so challenged Chinese interests that it warranted nine months of military tensions in the Taiwan Strait. These tensions included live-fire military exercises, ballistic missile tests near Taiwan ports, and a private warning from a senior Chinese military leader of China's determination to use nuclear weapons to deter U.S. intervention in a Taiwan confrontation. [24]

China's growing stake in the international status quo and its dependence on smooth international economic interchange are seen to argue against Chinese leaders' resorting to military force to achieve international objectives. At the same time, the rapid development of Chinese military capabilities to project power and the change in Chinese doctrine to emphasize striking first to achieve Chinese objectives and advancing maritime control are seen to increase the likelihood of Chinese use of force to achieve the ambitions and objectives of the Chinese government. Against this background, it is not surprising that an active debate continues about Chinese national security intentions and whether they override the Chinese government's concurrent public emphasis on promoting peace and development in Chinese foreign affairs.

As part of the debate, policymakers in the United States and allied countries are asked to balance their concern over Chinese military advances with assessment of the many shortcomings seen in China's military modernization. Eight specialists at the RAND Corporation in 2015 focused attention on such Chinese gaps, arguing that if deterrence fails in the Taiwan Strait, in the East and South China Seas, or elsewhere, U.S. policymakers and strategic planners will need to understand and exploit the limitations of China's military modernization to ensure that the United States and its allies are able to prevent China from using force to achieve its policy objectives. Those limitations involve the following two groups of factors:

1. Regarding leadership and quality of personnel, highlighted limitations include an outdated command structure, serious gaps in quality of personnel, lagging standards of professionalism, and widespread corruption.
2. Regarding weaknesses in combat capabilities, noted areas needing substantial improvement include logistical weaknesses, insufficient strategic airlift capabilities, limited numbers of special mission aircraft, and deficiencies in fleet air defense and antisubmarine warfare.[25]

Adding to the list of Chinese vulnerabilities is weak ballistic missile defense, which could become seriously problematic were the United States to follow the advice of conservative American strategists and build conventional ballistic missiles to target China in response to China's large buildup of conventional ballistic missiles targeting U.S. forces and U.S. allies in Asia.[26]

WEAPONS OF MASS DESTRUCTION: DEVELOPMENT, PROLIFERATION, AND NONPROLIFERATION

The development and deployment of nuclear weapons and ballistic missiles capable of carrying those weapons are critically important to China's national defense. They also continue to play an important role in Chinese foreign policy as a source of international power and influence.[27]

For many years, the Chinese authorities followed sometimes avowed and sometimes secret policies involving the transfer of nuclear weapons, ballistic missiles, and related equipment and technology to selected countries for economic, foreign policy, or defense reasons. In the post–Cold War period, the Chinese government changed policies in these areas in important ways. While the pace and scope of Chinese nuclear weapons and ballistic missile development continue steadily to improve and expand Chinese capabilities in these areas, the Chinese government has stopped egregious proliferation policies of the past, supported and joined many leading international arms control regimes, and endeavored to change China's past international image as an outlier to a responsible member of the international arms control community.[28]

The recent record shows that Beijing continues to develop its modest nuclear forces capable of targeting the United States, Russia, and regional powers, while its much stronger short-range missile and cruise missile development increases its ability to intimidate Taiwan and other neighbors and to warn their U.S. backers. Chinese activities related to the proliferation of weapons of mass destruction (WMD) have narrowed and slowed markedly in the post–Cold War period as the People's Republic of China (PRC) has joined and adhered to varying degrees to a number of international proliferation regimes. Some Chinese proliferation activities continue to pose challenges for U.S. and others' interests, and they sometimes meet with criticism and economic sanctions from the United States. [29]

China's Development of WMD Capabilities

Nuclear Forces

Beijing's multifaceted nuclear forces have developed since the 1950s and have served a variety of missions, including the following:

- Deterring U.S. or Russian nuclear attack
- Deterring any regional threat to China's national security from superpower conventional forces or other powers
- Backing China's efforts to regain lost territory, seek regional prominence, and gain greater global stature

The variety of Chinese nuclear weapons and delivery systems reflects the changing nature of the perceived serious threat China has faced over the past sixty years—first the United States, then both the United States and the Soviet Union, then the Soviet Union, and finally neither. It also reflects the changing preferences of senior Chinese leaders, especially following Mao's death in 1976. Particularly important are challenges and opportunities posed by Beijing's mixed ability to keep up with technological advances important in the development of nuclear weapons and delivery systems.

China continues to develop a modest nuclear capability able to target Taiwan and Asia-Pacific states, U.S. forces in the Asia-Pacific region, the United States itself, and Russia. China's development of short-range ballistic and cruise missiles has increased its ability to intimidate Taiwan. Both U.S. theater missile defense (TMD) efforts on behalf of Taiwan, Japan, South Korea, and other regional partners and plans for developing an enhanced U.S. national missile defense (NMD) concern Beijing's leaders. Chinese officials have warned against closer U.S. defense cooperation with Taiwan and particularly U.S. TMD support for the island, and they are concerned about the effect NMD would have on the global strategic balance.

China ostensibly seeks an air-, sea-, and land-based triad for its nuclear weapons, though up to now it relies on land-based missiles. Backward Chinese aviation and at least up-to-now limited submarine capabilities mean that the United States and possibly others could neutralize most foreseeable PRC advances in air or naval delivery systems. Thus, Beijing's triad actually has focused on three categories of land-based ballistic missiles—long, medium, and short range.

Developing long-range, mobile, solid-fueled ballistic missiles is a top priority for the Chinese government and will strengthen Beijing's recently weak minimum deterrent to U.S. or Russian nuclear attack. Beijing's much stronger, well-developed, and rapidly growing array of shorter-range ballistic missiles, along with current or developing cruise missiles, provides greater opportunity to use force, notably either conventionally armed or nuclear-armed missiles.

Through missile modernization, China is striving to increase the credibility of its limited deterrent by improving the readiness and survivability of the force. Because of technological shortcomings and economic limitations, China cannot afford the technology or inventory needed to counter the United States warhead for warhead. Indeed, foreign specialists judge that China lacks the will to develop a massive WMD force; its concept of limited deterrence both creates a sufficient sense of security for China's leaders and helps forge the morale its war fighters need to persevere in a WMD environment.[30]

Specialists strongly debate whether Beijing's growing short-range missile capabilities mean that it is preparing to depart from its past defensive posture, which stressed China's public commitment not to be the first to use nuclear weapons nor to engage in offensive military activities using nuclear-capable weapons. Specialists also warn of Chinese use of these missiles, probably armed with conventional warheads, as a means to force Taiwan to come to terms on reunification and to reduce the likelihood of U.S. military intervention in a Taiwan conflict. Others disagree, stressing among other things that Beijing does not and will not soon have the combination of sufficient technological, intelligence, and other support to carry out such an offensive posture.[31]

Chemical and Biological Weapons

Much less is known about Chinese capabilities regarding chemical and biological weapons. Beijing publicly asserts that it adheres to international norms and does not have biological or chemical weapons. Chinese interest in both areas has a long history, dating back to charges that Japan widely used such weapons against Chinese forces in World War II. Such charges have been a mainstay in Chinese publicity against most of the nations China has fought in the past sixty years. The modernization of Chinese chemical, biological, and related technologies and industries means that the PRC has ample ability to produce most known chemical and biological weapons.[32]

China's WMD Proliferation and Nonproliferation Activities

Beginning in the early 1980s, China's weapons proliferation activities emerged as an issue of growing concern for U.S. and other international policymakers. This trend has persisted for over thirty years. Chinese companies were seen by U.S. officials and other observers to have exported to several countries a variety of goods useful in building nuclear weapons, chemical weapons, and ballistic and cruise missiles.[33] In some cases, China provided critical materials, equipment, and technical assistance to nations that could not otherwise acquire these items for their weapons programs. Most notably, China provided Pakistan with a basic nuclear weapons design and substantial assistance in fabricating weapons-grade nuclear material. Moreover, China provided some countries with production technologies, allowing these nations to build certain missile systems with little external assistance.

China's proliferation behavior improved dramatically in the post–Cold War period and especially since the mid-1990s. The Chinese government gradually agreed to sign a number of key nonproliferation treaties, such as the Nuclear Nonproliferation Treaty (NPT) and the Chemical Weapons Convention (CWC), and developed internal bureaucratic and regulatory structures to carry out these commitments. China still engaged in exports of concern to the George W. Bush administration. This U.S. government repeatedly imposed sanctions on Chinese entities (though not the Chinese government) for transfers related to ballistic missiles, chemical weapons, and cruise missiles to Pakistan, Iran, and other countries. At that time, senior U.S. intelligence and national security officials highlighted Chinese weapons proliferation regarding Iran and missile proliferation regarding Pakistan and reported Chinese missile proliferation to Iran and North Korea.[34] Between 2009 and 2015, the Barack Obama government imposed sanctions on eighteen occasions on numerous entities in China for weapons proliferation.[35]

Nevertheless, since the end of the Cold War, the overall scope of Chinese proliferation activities declined significantly. The geographic distribution of Chinese proliferation-relevant exports narrowed from almost a dozen countries to three: Iran, Pakistan, and, to a lesser extent, North Korea. The character of China's exports similarly narrowed from a broad range of nuclear materials and equipment (much of it unsafeguarded) and complete missile systems to exports of dual-use nuclear, missile, and chemical technologies in recent years. In addition, during much of the 1980s and 1990s, China's nuclear and missile assistance directly contributed to the nuclear and missile programs in other countries; in recent years, such assistance was indirect at best. The frequency of such exports also declined. Chinese leaders were loath to restrict China's own national defense programs; they appeared to weigh carefully the pros and cons of restrictions on Chinese weapons and weapons technology transfers abroad, leading to some ambiguities and loopholes in their commitments that were criticized by the United States and others.[36]

Regarding negotiations and agreements on arms control and disarmament, Chinese officials were active during the Cold War in UN-related and other international bodies dealing with these matters. They repeatedly asserted that the United States and the Soviet Union needed to undertake substantial cuts in their arsenals and programs before powers like China with smaller numbers of nuclear weapons could be expected to agree to restrict their weapons development. China rebuffed international criticism of its transfers of WMD equipment and technology abroad, its large sales of conventional weapons in the 1980s to Iran and Iraq (notably, China sold $5 billion worth of weapons to Iraq in 1983–1988), and its multibillion-dollar sale of several dozen intermediate-range ballistic missiles to Saudi Arabia. China sometimes denied transferring or selling weapons and equipment despite overwhelming evidence to the contrary.[37]

An upsurge in U.S. and international concern with nuclear and other WMD proliferation followed the end of the Cold War and the U.S.-led military attack in response to Iraq's invasion of Kuwait in 1990–1991. This upsurge prompted Chinese leaders to begin to see the wisdom of curbing egregious proliferation activities and joining and conforming to international agreements and norms supported by nations seeking to regulate WMD development and proliferation. China in the 1990s moved to adhere to international agreements on arms control in several areas.

China promised tentatively to abide by the Missile Technology Control Regime (MTCR) in November 1991 and February 1992 and later reaffirmed that commitment in an October 4, 1994, joint statement with the United States. The MTCR, set up in 1987, is not an international agreement and has no legal authority. It is a set of voluntary guidelines that seeks to control the transfer of ballistic and cruise missiles that are capable of delivering at least 500 kilograms (1,100 pounds) of payload at least 300 kilometers (186 miles). Presumably with the MTCR guidelines in mind, on November 21, 2000, Beijing said that it had no intention of assisting any other country in developing ballistic missiles that can be used to deliver nuclear weapons (missiles with payloads of at least 500 kilograms and ranges of at least 300 kilometers), and it promised to issue missile-related export controls "as soon as possible." The PRC published those regulations and a control list (modeled on the MTCR) on August 25, 2002.[38]

China formally acceded to the NPT on March 9, 1992. The NPT does not ban peaceful nuclear projects, and on May 11, 1996, the PRC issued a statement promising to make only safeguarded nuclear transfers. On July 30, 1996, China began a moratorium on nuclear testing and signed the Comprehensive Test Ban Treaty in September 1996, though like the United States, China has not yet ratified the treaty. The Chinese premier, on September 10, 1997, issued nuclear export control regulations in support of China's pledges on nuclear transfers.

China joined the Zangger Committee, which regulates international nuclear trade, on October 16, 1997. Also in October 1997, China acceded to strong U.S. pressure and promised not to start new nuclear cooperation with

Iran. This angered the Tehran government and led to a serious temporary decline in China–Iran relations. On June 6, 1998, the UN Security Council (including China) adopted Resolution 1172, which asked states to prevent exports to India's or Pakistan's nuclear weapons or missile programs (China had been a major supplier to Pakistan in both areas). The PRC issued regulations on dual-use nuclear exports on June 17, 1998. In May 2004, China applied to join the Nuclear Suppliers Group (NSG), which accepted China as a member after the U.S. government decided to support China's entry. [39]

In November 1995, China issued its first public defense white paper, which focused on arms control and disarmament. China formally signed the CWC in January 1993. On April 25, 1997, China deposited its instrument of ratification of the CWC before the convention entered into force on April 29, 1997. From 1993 to 1998, the PRC issued export control regulations on chemicals. In October 2002, the PRC issued regulations for export controls concerning dual-use biological agents and related technology. On December 3, 2003, China issued a white paper on nonproliferation that stated that China's control lists regulating Chinese transfers of possible WMD components were almost the same as those of such arms control groups and regimes as the Zangger Committee, NSG, CWC, the Australia Group (AG) on chemical and biological weapons, and MTCR.

Among some perceived gaps in Chinese adherence to international arms control efforts, China is not yet a member of MTCR or the AG. In June 2004, China expressed willingness to join MTCR. China did not join the ninety-three countries signing the International Code of Conduct against Ballistic Missile Proliferation in The Hague on November 25, 2002. China has not joined the Proliferation Security Initiative announced by President George W. Bush on May 31, 2003. China cooperated with UN-backed efforts against North Korea's missile and nuclear tests in 2006, 2009, and 2013, though it remained reluctant to impose sanctions or other pressure on Pyongyang. China also cooperated in varying degrees with U.S.-backed efforts to sanction Iran for its reported development of nuclear weapons capabilities. [40]

CHINA'S APPROACH TO INTERNATIONAL TERRORISM

Other features of Chinese national security policy that have a significant impact on China's foreign policy and overall approach to world affairs include Chinese policies and practices related to international terrorism. Chinese leaders broadly supported the U.S.-led war on terrorism that began after September 11, 2001. There were some initial reservations over U.S. policy and actions voiced by Chinese leaders during the lead-up to the war in Afghanistan, which toppled the terrorist-harboring Taliban regime. Chinese leaders registered concern in particular over the U.S. military presence in central Asia, and they worked in generally subtle ways to support regional efforts opposing long-term U.S. military presence in this area. Chinese leaders opposed the U.S.-led military intervention against Iraq, but they were careful that China's opposition, as voiced in the UN Security Council and other venues, was less salient than that voiced by fellow UN Security Council permanent members. Letting France and Russia take the lead, China avoided serious problems in Chinese efforts to sustain positive ties with the George W. Bush administration.

China avoided close association with the Barack Obama administration's escalation of military force against resurgent Taliban insurgents in Afghanistan. It duly endorsed the May 2, 2011, killing of Osama bin Laden by American special forces as "a positive development in the international struggle against terrorism."[41] After the 2014 announcement of the withdrawal of American and NATO combat troops from Afghanistan, China met with outgoing and incoming Afghan leaders, who urged China to take a leadership role in dealing with the conflict in the country. Repeated high-profile Chinese–Afghan leadership meetings failed to hide China's uncertainty about potentially costly commitments in a very unstable country on the one hand, while on the other hand China increasingly worried about terrorists from Afghanistan entering China and exacerbating already serious Chinese problems in pacifying violent dissent among ethnic Uighurs in Xinjiang Autonomous Region and elsewhere in China.[42]

Maoist China had a long record of using terrorist techniques to intimidate and resist opponents at home and abroad. Chinese foreign policy was replete with examples of close collaboration with and support for movements and governments that employed terrorist methods in order to achieve ends that the Chinese government supported. The more pragmatic Deng Xiaoping government saw Chinese foreign policy interests better served by preserving regional and international stability conducive to Chinese economic development. As a result, Chinese foreign policy cut back sharply on military, training, and other support for radical groups that engaged in terrorist methods. By 1980, China's long record of support for the Palestine Liberation Organization and some more radical groups that engaged in terrorist activities against Israel had changed. In contrast to its stance in the past, China clearly indicated its opposition to terrorist practices against Israel and supported Israel's right to exist. Eventually, improved China–Israel relations led to formal diplomatic relations between the two states in 1992.[43]

It took Chinese officials a long time to pull back support for governments that harbored terrorists or that engaged in gross terrorist activities at home or abroad. If other important Chinese interests seemed to require good relations with such states, Chinese government policy was to preserve good relations, giving antiterrorism a lower priority. Thus, in the 1980s and into the 1990s, Chinese officials provided strong support for the Khmer Rouge resistance in

Cambodia and for governments in Pakistan, Iran, Syria, and Libya that were associated with terrorist activities. China also provided some aid to the Taliban regime in Afghanistan. Even after the September 11, 2001, attack, China continued strong and constructive involvement with terrorist-harboring regimes, such as Sudan, Iran, and Syria.[44]

The Chinese government was anxious to advance relations with the George W. Bush administration and viewed the attacks of September 11, 2001, as an opportunity to improve relations. It voiced sympathy with the United States after the attacks, allowed President Bush to use the Asia-Pacific Economic Cooperation (APEC) leaders meeting in China in October to rally support for antiterrorist action, and began closer cooperation with U.S. antiterrorism, intelligence, and other officials. In December 2001, the U.S.–China interagency counterterrorism working group was established; it met periodically in the following years. It had representatives from the two countries' law enforcement, intelligence, military, diplomatic, and financial agencies. China joined in efforts against international money laundering and the U.S. Container Security Initiative (designed to screen cargo entering the United States) and allowed an FBI liaison office to open in Beijing in 2002. Also in 2002, Chinese officials welcomed the U.S. government's identification of the East Turkistan Islamic Movement, which targets China's Xinjiang Autonomous Region, as a terrorist group.[45]

The Chinese government worked with Russia and some central Asian governments to preserve regional stability and curb terrorist activity under the auspices of the Shanghai Five organization begun in 1996 (with China, Russia, Kazakhstan, Kyrgyzstan, and Tajikistan as founding members) and its successor organization, the Shanghai Cooperation Organization (SCO; founded in June 2001 with the addition of Uzbekistan). It showed particular concern over international support for dissident groups in the western Chinese region of Xinjiang that sometimes engaged in terrorist activities. On the one hand, Chinese officials welcomed the U.S.-led war that toppled the Taliban regime in Afghanistan because the latter was seen to support transnational terrorism, including groups in China. On the other hand, the Chinese government worked to use the SCO and China's bilateral relations with Russia and central Asian states to register opposition to long-term U.S. military presence in central Asia.[46]

From the outset of the global war on terrorism, the Chinese government stressed that the United Nations should play the leading role. This was in part designed to counter some actions by the United States in the war against Afghanistan and particularly in the period leading to the U.S.-led military invasion of Iraq—both justified in part by the George W. Bush administration as counterterrorism measures. China supported most international conventions against terrorism.

In Asia, China continued multilateral and bilateral antiterrorist activities with SCO members. It also held antiterrorism exercises with Pakistan, India, and other countries. Antiterrorism was a prominent feature of China's burgeoning cooperation with the Association of Southeast Asian Nations (ASEAN). China was a member of APEC's Counterterrorism Task Force, and China featured antiterrorism cooperation in interaction with the European Union and some European powers. China cooperated with a wide range of governments and international agencies in securing the 2008 Olympic Games in Beijing from terrorist threats.[47]

MILITARY DIPLOMACY, ARMS ACQUISITIONS AND SALES, AND PEACEKEEPING

After the Cold War, Chinese military diplomacy, arms acquisitions and sales, and peacekeeping operations became important features in Chinese foreign policy. Chinese military leaders have been among the most active Chinese officials to engage in international relations in this period. The PLA high command has broadened and accelerated senior-level international exchanges in an effort to expand China's international influence, to increase opportunities for arms sales and purchases of equipment and technology, to ease concern over China's rising power, and to deepen PLA leaders' international experience. Some of the top PLA leaders have taken a place among the world's most widely traveled and internationally experienced military leaders.[48]

A centerpiece of PLA efforts is cooperation with Russia, which was for three decades the key supplier of modern military equipment to the Chinese armed forces. Russian arms sales to China averaged $1–$2 billion annually. Chinese military leaders endeavored to develop close contacts with the U.S. military, but extensive contacts were cut after the Tiananmen crackdown in 1989. They were resumed by the second term of the Clinton administration, but the defense officials of the George W. Bush administration, backed by strong sentiment in Congress, reversed this trend and allowed only slow and incremental improvement in U.S. military ties with China. Chinese objections to U.S. arms sales to Taiwan led to China-initiated halts in military exchanges. Military exchanges improved in recent years, despite rising U.S.–Chinese differences over China's truculence and assertiveness over territorial disputes in Asia and America's rebalance to Asia in ways seen negatively by China.[49]

Chinese officials for a time worked hard to end the embargo on military sales to China undertaken by the European powers and Asian and Pacific powers aligned with the United States. They appeared to be having some success in getting the Europeans to end their arms embargo in 2005 until the

U.S. government intervened strongly against such action. Although closely aligned with the United States, Israel followed opportunities for significant sales of advanced military equipment and technology to China. The George W. Bush administration, however, had some success as it strongly pressed Israel to curb such sales to China.[50]

Chinese arms sales abroad were an important source of funds for the PLA and the Chinese government in the 1980s and part of the 1990s. China supplied a wide array of arms to both sides during the Iran–Iraq war of the 1980s. Reforms conducted in the latter 1990s removed the PLA from business ventures at home and abroad. This, plus the fact that Chinese arms often are not competitive with the more sophisticated equipment available from other suppliers, meant that promoting arms sales abroad became a somewhat less salient feature of recent Chinese foreign policy. From 2005 to 2009, China sold approximately $8 billion worth of conventional weapons systems worldwide. China surpassed Germany, France, and the United Kingdom to become the third-largest arms exporter (after the United States and Russia) in the period 2010–2014. China accounted for about 5 percent of the world's exports of arms.[51]

The bulk of Chinese international military interchange more recently involved visits of PLA leaders abroad and visits of foreign counterparts to China. Other elements included usually small military exercises with various countries, ship visits, and some training of foreign military personnel in China and of PLA officers abroad. A growing feature of Chinese military diplomacy is China's increasing role in UN peacekeeping operations. In 2008, China joined UN-backed efforts to escort merchant ships in the Gulf of Aden and waters off Somalia because of the danger of piracy.

Reflecting a pace and scope of exchanges that has been sustained for many years, in 1996 China hosted more than 140 military delegations from more than sixty countries and sent military delegations to forty countries. The pace in 1997 was even more active, with a broad focus that included neighboring countries (the Kazakhstan defense minister visited China twice in the year), major powers, and a wide range of others (for example, Greece and Uruguay). In November 1997, a PLA deputy chief of staff visited France and Japan, paving the way for higher-level Chinese military visits to both countries. Germany sent its military chief of staff to China for the first time in 1998, and Australia received the Chinese defense minister in 1998. In November 1997, the PLA also welcomed its first high-level officer (a vice chief of staff) from South Korea. In 1997, China's army invited over 150 delegations from sixty-seven countries; twenty-three of the groups were headed by vice premiers or defense ministers, and fifty were headed by a commander in chief, chief of the general staff, vice minister of national defense, or armed services commander. The PLA sent over 100 delegations to seventy countries; the total number of foreign embassies accredited attachés in China reached sixty-three.[52]

By 2000, it was common for the PLA's top six officers to each conduct one foreign trip abroad, covering a total of twenty to twenty-five countries.[53] Official Chinese media and other sources revealed that the number of foreign delegations that the PLA was involved with at home and abroad in the 1990s nearly doubled since the previous decade. From 1978 to 2002, senior PLA officers led over 1,600 delegations to more than eighty countries. The PLA welcomed over 2,500 military delegations from five continents, involving tens of thousands of people; more than half of the delegations were led by defense ministers, joint service commanders, chiefs of the general staff, and service commanders. China formed military diplomatic ties with 146 foreign countries and sent military attachés to 103 countries, while 74 foreign countries stationed military attachés in China. During the 1990s, the Academy of Military Sciences interacted with counterparts in twenty-seven countries. Since the National Defense University was founded in 1985, up to 2002, it received 749 military delegations from seventy-nine countries, involving 6,407 foreign military personnel. Sixty-nine of the delegations were led by general officers. From 1999 to 2002, the PLA sent over 20,000 people in more than 800 specialized technical delegations overseas to investigate, cooperate in research, and participate in studies.[54]

Building on this momentum, an official Chinese media account of military diplomacy in 2004 highlighted important Chinese security initiatives with regional groups like the ASEAN Regional Forum and the SCO and joint military exercises with Britain, France, Australia, Pakistan, India, and Vietnam. At the end of the decade, China reported that the PLA had held forty-four joint military and training exercises, done twenty-eight humanitarian missions abroad, and established defense dialogues with twenty-two states. In the previous two years, it had sent ships to visit more than thirty countries and welcomed ships of more than twenty nations visiting China; defense ministers or chiefs of staff of sixty countries visited China in the two-year period. Underscoring this trend, reports in 2015 showed Chinese military leaders planning for future interchanges after an active 2014. That year saw China host thirty-one joint exercises and other training programs. China participated for the first time in the Rim of the Pacific naval exercise hosted by the United States each year. The media highlighted China's priority in developing closer military ties with "major countries and neighboring countries," as the military does its part in playing "a bigger role" in China's diplomacy.[55]

Developing in parallel with expanding Chinese military diplomacy was China's participation in UN-backed international peacekeeping operations.[56] China had negative experience with UN military operations against it during the Korean War, and Chinese leaders for a long time remained wary of international efforts to use the United Nations or other means to intrude in other countries' internal affairs. Thus, China strongly supported Serbia in 1999 in the face of NATO-led military intervention seeking to curb repression and restore peace in Kosovo. As the United Nations supported more intrusive measures to ensure peace in the post–Cold War period, China did not block these efforts and showed increasing signs of joining them.[57] In 1990, China began sending military observers to UN peacekeeping operations. In 1992, China agreed to participate in the most intrusive UN peacekeeping operation up to that time, the UN Transitional Authority in Cambodia. China supported the mission politically and financially, and it sent an engineering battalion to participate. In January 2000, China sent fifteen civilian policemen to the UN Transitional Authority in East Timor, the first time that China sent civilian policemen to UN peacekeeping operations.

By 2002, China had sent more than 650 military observers, 800 engineering troops, and 198 civilian policemen to take part in UN peacekeeping operations. In 2003, China agreed to deploy 550 troops to Liberia as part of the peacekeeping mission there. In 2004, Beijing sent 125 police officers to Haiti to support the UN-led international effort to stabilize the country. In 2006, China agreed to send 1,000 peacekeepers to Lebanon. In December 2010, 1,955 Chinese personnel were serving in nine UN missions. By that time, China had dispatched 17,390 military personnel to nineteen UN peacekeeping missions; nine persons had died while on duty. Up to that time, China had not sent combat troops to peacekeeping operations. That pattern ended when China in 2014 deployed 170 combat troops as UN peacekeepers in Mali and in 2015 700 Chinese combat troops arrived in South Sudan for UN peacekeeping duty.[58]

As Chinese security personnel spread in several locations, their numbers surpassed those of any of the other UN Security Council Permanent Members. The more narrow national interests of China were served in these deployments in some respects. The UN peacekeeping budget paid for the services of the Chinese troops. The personnel gained valuable experience when they deployed and pursued operations in various foreign locales and in the company of troops from other nations. As noted in the previous chapter, China has increased its modest commitment to the UN peacekeeping budget. In 2010, its contribution was somewhat less than 4 percent of the overall peacekeeping budget; it now is over 6 percent.[59]

During the 1980s and 1990s, China abstained from UN resolutions that authorized the use of force for peace enforcement. Even when Iraq invaded Kuwait, China refused to vote in support of the U.S.-led military effort to drive Iraq out of Kuwait. However, after the September 11, 2001, attack on the United States, China for the first time voted to endorse an American-led military action against a foreign country. As noted earlier, China opposed the U.S.-led war against Iraq in 2003 but did endorse an intrusive UN Security

Council resolution to disarm Iraq. It regretted its failure to block UN support for the NATO military intervention in Libya in 2011, and it joined Russia in blocking UN support for military intervention in Syria's civil war. [60]

Chapter Six

Relations with the United States

Chapters 2 and 3 show the central importance of the United States in Chinese foreign policy in the period after the Cold War. They also show an erratic pattern in Chinese–U.S. relations featuring periods of acute tension and acrimony and periods of close engagement and cooperation. During the first half of this period, the United States appeared to hold the stronger hand in the relationship, with American policy initiatives often offensive to China prompting Chinese reactions. In some instances, such as China's militant behavior during the Taiwan Straits crisis of 1995–1996 and its response to the U.S. bombing of China's embassy in Belgrade in 1999, the Chinese reactions were strong and violent, compelling substantial adjustments in U.S. policy. Later, the United States became embroiled in protracted wars in Iraq and Afghanistan and faced acute economic problems during the global economic crisis and recession beginning in 2008. By contrast, China avoided costly international obligations and sustained strong economic growth during the world recession.

Against this background, China began a new phase in its foreign policy, which is featured prominently in the international activism of current Chinese president Xi Jinping. China took a series of initiatives designed to advance control of disputed territory in the East and South China Seas in coercive ways short of using military force that came at the expense of several neighbors and at the expense of U.S. interests and influence in regional affairs. In 2010, China pressed the U.S. government harder than in the recent past in seeking concessions on Taiwan and Tibet policy. More recently, it launched prominent trade and investment mechanisms in Asia and, more broadly, designed to exclude the United States and compete with U.S.-backed regional and international economic and financial institutions. President Xi Jinping and other top Chinese leaders ignored the complaints of the

U.S. president about Chinese practices. The complaints included China bullying its neighbors, engaging in cyber theft of economic property and other egregious violations of international economic norms, avoiding international responsibilities, and establishing rules and economic arrangements in Asia and the world at odds with the interests of the United States and other nations dependent on free trade and economic interchange. Lower-level officers and official Chinese media addressed, rebuked, and dismissed the U.S. complaints, and the offensive Chinese behavior continued.

Officials and prominent experts in the United States and China at different times in the past argued in favor of some overall framework for the China–U.S. relationship that would allow the two powers to cooperate more closely and manage their differences more effectively. Shared opposition to the Soviet Union provided the foundation of a strategic framework for the Sino-American cooperation initiated by U.S. President Richard Nixon and Chinese Chairman Mao Zedong. That framework lasted for two decades but shattered completely amid strident American reaction to the Chinese crackdown at Tiananmen in 1989 and the concurrent demise of the Soviet empire. Subsequent frameworks failed to move forward. Examples included the Clinton administration's effort to establish a strategic partnership with China that was abandoned by the incoming Bush administration, the Bush administration's call on China to become a "responsible stakeholder" in international affairs that met with an unfavorable response in China, and American calls for the Obama administration to establish a closer "G2" relationship with China as the key element in world politics that met with unfavorable responses from China in particular. Most recently, a China-backed framework to establish a "new type of great power relationship" with the United States seemed to be failing amid American suspicions that China was playing a double game in encouraging high-level bilateral discourse while pursuing policies undermining American interests. [1]

The main reasons for these failures are the strong Sino-American differences reviewed in chapter 3. Adding to the negative mix is the state-fostered Chinese elite and public view of foreign affairs and particularly their negative view of the United States reviewed in chapter 3. As shown there, China has a unique sense of self-righteous exceptionalism in foreign affairs that will not change easily. The United States also is known for exceptionalism in international affairs. And both countries are big—the world's most powerful; their approaches to each other will not be easily changed by smaller powers or other outside forces.

DEVELOPMENTS DURING THE GEORGE H. W. BUSH AND CLINTON ADMINISTRATIONS

Against this background, post–Cold War U.S.–Chinese relations have followed a tortuous course with many vicissitudes. Though he anticipated shock and disapproval at the Tiananmen crackdown from the United States and the West, Deng Xiaoping failed to foresee the breadth and depth of American disapproval, which would profoundly influence U.S. policy into the twenty-first century. The influence was compounded by the surprising and dramatic collapse of communist regimes in the Soviet bloc and other areas, leading to the demise of the Soviet Union by the early 1990s. These developments undermined the perceived need for the United States to cooperate pragmatically with China despite its brutal dictatorship because of a U.S. strategic need for international support against the Soviet Union. Meanwhile, Taiwan's authoritarian government was moving steadily at that time to promote democratic policies and practices, marking a sharp contrast to the harsh political authoritarianism in mainland China and greatly enhancing Taiwan's popularity and support in the United States. [2]

The Chinese government presided over strong economic growth beginning in 1993, and Chinese leaders reflected more confidence as they dealt with American pressures for change. However, they eschewed direct confrontation unless provoked by U.S., Taiwan, or other actions. The contentious American domestic debate over China policy was not stilled until the September 11, 2001, terrorist attack on America muffled for a time continued American concerns over China.

President George H. W. Bush (1989–1993) took the lead in dealing with severe problems in China–U.S. relations caused by the Tiananmen crackdown and the decline in American strategic interest in China as a result of the collapse of the Soviet bloc. He resorted to secret diplomacy to maintain constructive communication with senior Chinese leaders, but the latter remained fairly rigid and made few gestures to help Bush justify a continued moderate U.S. stance toward China. Though the Bush administration said all high-level official contact with China would be cut off as a result of the Tiananmen crackdown, President Bush sent his national security adviser and the deputy secretary of state on secret missions to Beijing in July and December 1989. When the missions became known in December 1989, the congressional and media reaction was bitterly critical of the administration's perceived duplicity. [3]

Bush eventually became frustrated with the Chinese leadership's intransigence and took a tough stance on trade and other issues, though he made special efforts to ensure that the United States continued most-favored-nation (MFN) tariff status for China despite opposition by a majority of the U.S. Congress and much of the American media. Reflecting more positive

American views of the Republic of China (ROC) government on Taiwan, the Bush administration upgraded U.S. interchange with the ROC by sending a cabinet-level official to Taipei in 1992, the first such visit since official relations were ended in 1979. He also seemed to abandon the limits on U.S. arms sales set in accord with the August 1982 U.S. communiqué with China by agreeing in 1992 to a sale of 150 advanced F-16 jet fighters to Taiwan worth over $5 billion.[4]

Presidential candidate Bill Clinton used sharp attacks against President Bush's moderate approach to China to win support in the 1992 election. For candidate Clinton, using China issues to discredit the record of the Republican incumbent proved to be an effective election ploy. Once in office, President Clinton showed little interest in China policy, leaving the responsibility to subordinates.[5]

Assistant Secretary of State for East Asia Affairs Winston Lord negotiated with congressional leaders in 1993 to establish the human rights conditions the Clinton administration required before renewing most-favored-nation tariff status for China. However, Chinese government leaders stoked American business pressures to get Clinton to intervene in May 1994 to reverse existing policy and allow for unimpeded U.S. renewal of MFN status for China.

Pro-Taiwan interests in the United States, backed by American public relations firms in the pay of entities and organizations in Taiwan, took advantage of congressional elections in 1995 giving control of Congress to pro-Taiwan Republican leaders. They pushed for allowing a U.S. visit by ROC president Lee Teng-hui. Under heavy domestic political pressure, President Clinton intervened again and allowed Taiwan's president to visit the United States.

China's militant reactions and a resulting military confrontation between the United States and China in the Taiwan Strait (1995–1996) eventually involved two U.S. aircraft carrier battle groups sent to the Taiwan area to deter China. Concurrently, the Clinton administration moved to a much more coherent engagement policy toward China. In moves welcomed by China's leaders, the president held U.S.–China summit meetings in 1997 and 1998. Other progress beneficial to China included U.S.–China agreement on China's entry into the World Trade Organization and U.S. agreement to provide permanent normal trade status for China.

As Clinton had sought partisan advantage in attacking George H. W. Bush's moderation toward China, the Republicans in control of Congress returned the favor in strident attacks against Clinton's new moderation toward Beijing. The president's engagement with China also came under attack from organized labor interests within the Democratic Party.[6] The Chinese government was anxious to keep the economic relationship with the United States on an even keel and was disinclined to punish such congressional critics or take substantive action against them. More likely were Chinese invitations to such critical congressional members for all-expenses-paid trips to China in order to persuade them to change their views by seeing actual conditions in China.

President Clinton's more active and positive engagement with China saw such high points as the China–U.S. summits in 1997 and 1998, the Sino–U.S. agreement on China's entry into the WTO in 1999, and passage of U.S. legislation in 2000 granting China permanent normal trade relations status. Low points in the relationship during this time included strong congressional opposition to the president's stance against Taiwan independence in 1998, the May 1999 bombing of the Chinese embassy in Belgrade and Chinese demonstrators trashing U.S. diplomatic properties in China, strident congressional criticism in the so-called Cox Committee report of May 1999 charging administration officials with gross malfeasance in guarding U.S. secrets and weaponry from Chinese spies, and partisan congressional investigations of Clinton administration political fund-raising that highlighted illegal contributions from sources connected to the Chinese regime and the alleged impact they had on the administration's more moderate approach to the PRC.

TWENTY-FIRST-CENTURY DEVELOPMENTS

The initial toughness toward China of the George W. Bush administration began to subside with the September 11, 2001, terrorist attack on America and later developments. There followed several years of generally cooperative relations where the two sides dealt with differences in a burgeoning array of official dialogues and worked together to address such sensitive issues as North Korea's nuclear weapons program and efforts by Taiwan's president to promote greater separation and independence of Taiwan from China. The Taiwan issue declined in importance as Taiwan president Ma Ying-jeou took power in May 2008 and carried out a policy of accommodation and reassurance toward China that was welcomed by both the PRC and U.S. governments.

The Barack Obama government strove in vain to preserve the overall positive momentum in U.S.–Chinese relations seen in the latter Bush years. Relations deteriorated over trade and related economic policies and a range of other issues, notably reaching a low point during the prolonged U.S. presidential primaries and election campaign in 2012, which featured often harsh attacks on China. Toward the end of the rule of Hu Jintao (2002–2012), China became more assertive in support of its interests at odds with the United States, notably claims to disputed territory along its rim, especially in the East and South China Seas. For its part, the Obama government focused on a new approach known as the "pivot" to and later as the "rebalance" in the broad Asia-Pacific region that had military, economic, and diplomatic dimensions at odds with Chinese interests. Amid widely publicized assessments of deep mutual suspicion and mistrust among Sino-American leaders, U.S.–China relations became overtly competitive as both powers sought greater influence and power in Asia. Overall, the developments seriously challenged but did not reverse the continued strong pragmatic interest on both sides to seek cooperation where possible and to avoid conflict and confrontation.[7]

RELATIONS DURING THE GEORGE W. BUSH ADMINISTRATION

George W. Bush became president in 2001 with a policy more critical of China than the policy of his predecessor. The new president was wary of China's strategic intentions and took steps to deter China from using military force against Taiwan. Relations deteriorated when on April 1, 2001, a Chinese jet fighter crashed with a U.S. reconnaissance plane in international waters off the China coast. The jet was destroyed and the pilot killed. The reconnaissance plane was seriously damaged and made an emergency landing in China. Amid intense negotiations and delays, the U.S. crew and eventually the plane returned to the United States.

Subsequently, both governments established a businesslike rapport that emphasized cooperation and played down differences. The course of U.S.–China relations became smoother than at any time since the normalization of U.S.–China relations. The terrorist attack on America on September 11, 2001, soon led to U.S. preoccupation with the wars in Afghanistan and Iraq and the broader war on global terrorism; U.S. strategic attention to China as a threat was secondary. Chinese leaders gave priority to managing a difficult leadership transition and sustaining an authoritarian regime amid a vibrant economy and rapid social change. Though a wide range of differences spanning Taiwan and Tibet to trade and human rights remained, the two powers showed cooperation in dealing with North Korea's nuclear weapons program and the pro-independence maneuvers of Taiwan President Chen Shui-bian.[8]

Both governments prepared for contingencies in case their counterpart turned aggressive or otherwise disrupted the prevailing order in ways adverse to their respective interests. Both powers used growing interdependence, engagement, and dialogues to foster webs of relationships that would tie down or constrain possible policies and actions deemed negative to their interests.[9] On the whole, the Chinese government of President Hu Jintao welcomed and supported the new directions in U.S. China policy. The U.S. approach fit well with the Chinese leadership's broader priorities of strengthening national development and Communist Party legitimacy that were said to require China to use carefully the "strategic opportunity" of prevailing international circumstances seen as generally advantageous to Chinese interests.[10]

As China expanded its military power along with economic and diplomatic relations in Asian and world affairs at a time of U.S. preoccupation with war in Iraq and other foreign policy problems, the Bush administration debated the implications of China's rise in Asian and world affairs.[11] Some U.S. officials judged that China's rise was designed to dominate Asia and in the process to undermine American leadership. A more moderate view came from U.S. officials who judged that China's focus was to improve China's position in Asia in order to sustain regional stability, promote China's development, reassure neighbors, prevent balancing against China, and isolate Taiwan. This school of thought judged that China was not focused on isolating and weakening the United States in Asia, but it held that China's rise was having an indirect and substantial negative impact on U.S. leadership in Asia, largely because of U.S. policies and practices seen in the region as much more controversial and maladroit than Chinese policies and practices.

A third school of thought was identified with U.S. Deputy Secretary of State Robert Zoellick, who by 2005 publicly articulated a strong argument for greater American cooperation with China. This viewpoint held that the United States should work cooperatively with China in order to encourage the PRC to use its rising influence in "responsible" ways in accord with U.S. interests. It put less emphasis than the other two on competition with China and more emphasis on cooperation. Bush administration policy came to embrace the third point of view. The U.S. administration increasingly emphasized positive engagement and a growing number of dialogues with China, encouraging China to act responsibly and building ever-growing webs of relationships and interdependence. This pattern fit well with Chinese priorities regarding national development in a period of advantageous international conditions while building interdependencies and relationships that constrained possible negative U.S. policies and behaviors.

The Republicans lost control of the U.S. House of Representatives and the U.S. Senate in the 2006 election, and the Bush administration faced greater criticism of its foreign policies, including policies toward China, from congressional Democrats backed by the American media. Congressional critics focused special attention on economic problems including the large trade deficit with China and a resulting loss of American jobs. Against this backdrop, Treasury Secretary Henry Paulson was appointed to lead a new Strategic Economic Dialogue with Chinese counterparts. They met twice a year in an effort to manage differences and ease tensions, especially over salient trade and related economic problems.

The overall positive stasis in U.S.–China relations that emerged in the latter years of the George W. Bush administration generally met the near-term priorities of the U.S. and Chinese governments. Neither the Chinese leadership nor the U.S. administration sought trouble with the other. Both were preoccupied with other issues. Heading the list of preoccupations for both governments was dealing with the massive negative consequences of the international economic crisis and deep recession begun in 2008. Other preoccupations of the outgoing Bush administration included Iraq, Afghanistan, Pakistan, Iran, broader Middle East issues, North Korea, and other foreign policy problems, which came on top of serious adverse economic developments. China for its part faced a major leadership transition in 2012. Differences remained, notably growing trade and economic disputes paired with continued military buildups along China's rim that worsened an ongoing security dilemma between the two powers.

RELATIONS DURING THE BARACK OBAMA ADMINISTRATION

As a presidential candidate in 2008, Barack Obama was unusual in recent U.S. presidential politics in not making a significant issue of his predecessor's China policy. Like President Bush, the new president showed a measured and deliberative course with China involving pursuing constructive contacts, preserving and protecting American interests, and dealing effectively with challenges posed by rising Chinese influence and power. [12]

A major theme in President Obama's initial foreign policy was to seek the cooperation of other world powers, notably China, to deal with salient international concerns such as the global economic crisis and recession, climate change, nuclear weapons proliferation, and terrorism. He and his team made vigorous efforts to build common ground with China on these and related issues. China's leaders offered limited cooperation, disappointing the Obama government. [13]

More worrisome, Chinese actions and statements in 2009 and 2010 directly challenged the policies and practices of the United States:

- Chinese government patrol boats confronted U.S. surveillance ships in the South China Sea.
- China challenged U.S. and South Korean military exercises against North Korea in the Yellow Sea.
- Chinese treatment of U.S. arms sales to Taiwan and President Obama's meeting with the Dalai Lama in 2010 was harsher than in the recent past.
- Chinese officials threatened to stop investing in U.S. government securities and to move away from using the U.S. dollar in international transactions.
- The Chinese government responded very harshly to American government interventions in 2010 urging collective efforts to manage rising tensions in

the South China Sea and affirming the U.S.–Japan security treaty during Sino-Japanese disputes over East China Sea islands.[14]

The Obama government reacted calmly and firmly to what Secretary of State Hillary Clinton called these "tests" of a new assertiveness by China. Asian governments also became more active in working closely with the United States and in encouraging a greater U.S. presence in the Asia-Pacific. Their interest in closer ties with the United States meshed well with the Obama government's broad effort under the rubric of the U.S. rebalance to Asia in order to "reengage" with the countries of the Asia-Pacific, ranging from India to the Pacific Islands.[15] Against this background, the Obama government made clear that the United States was prepared to undertake military measures needed to deal with the buildup of Chinese forces targeting Americans and American interests in the Asia-Pacific.[16]

The lead-up to the January 18–20, 2011, visit of President Hu Jintao to Washington saw China ease recent tensions. The harsh Chinese rhetoric criticizing American policies and practices subsided; the Chinese put aside their objections to high-level military exchanges, and Secretary of Defense Robert Gates reestablished businesslike ties at the top levels of the Chinese military during a visit to Beijing in early January 2011; China used its influence to get North Korea to stop its provocations against South Korea and to seek negotiations over nuclear weapons issues; China avoided undercutting international sanctions to press Iran to give up its nuclear weapons program; China allowed the value of its currency to appreciate in line with U.S. interests; and Chinese officials were more cooperative over climate change issues at an international meeting in Cancun than they were a year earlier.[17]

For his part, President Obama made clear during 2011 and 2012 that he would pursue closer engagement with China as part of his administration's overall new emphasis on American rebalance with the Asia-Pacific. Obama administration leaders from the president on down articulated the outlines of a new emphasis on American reengagement with the Asia-Pacific that promised more competition with China for influence in the region while averring strong U.S. interest in greater engagement with China. The effort culminated with the president's visit to the Asia-Pacific region in November 2011, where he articulated his vision of enhanced American security, economic interchange, and diplomatic engagement. In January 2012, the president joined his civilian and military chiefs in announcing a new U.S. military strategy for the years ahead.[18]

The Year 2012—A Turning Point?

The year 2012 saw new tests and challenges in China–U.S. relations.[19] There were unprecedented demonstrations of Chinese power short of using military force in advancing Chinese claims to disputed territories in the South and East China Seas. The demonstrations continued into later years and were directed against U.S. allies Japan and the Philippines and against Vietnam. The measures were accompanied by official Chinese commentary accusing the United States of having fostered the territorial disputes and of using them to advance U.S. influence in the Asian region to the detriment of China. The Chinese demonstrations of power resulted in extralegal measures and in some cases widespread violence and property destruction. The implications for regional order clearly took a negative turn in 2012.

The year was also one of leadership transition in China and a presidential election in the United States. At the Eighteenth Congress of China's Communist Party in November, President Hu Jintao passed party and military leadership positions to Xi Jinping, who was named president during the National People's Congress meeting in March 2013. As discussed in earlier chapters, Xi was more effective than Hu in consolidating his leadership power, and he used his prominence to push an activist and assertive foreign policy well beyond the more measured foreign actions of the Hu leadership. In the United States, President Barack Obama ended a long and acrimonious presidential campaign, defeating Republican nominee Mitt Romney in the U.S. elections of November 2012. Growing divergence and competition in Asia headed the list of issues in 2012 that challenged and tested the abilities of American and Chinese leaders to manage their differences. [20]

The Republican presidential primaries saw sharp and often hyperbolic attacks on Chinese economic and security policies. In the third presidential debate on October 22, President Obama joined the fray with harsh rhetoric not seen in his presidential campaign in 2008. The president publicly referred to China for the first time as "an adversary." He added, "We believe China can be a partner, but we're also sending a very clear signal that America is a Pacific power, that we are going to have a presence there. . . . And we're organizing trade relations with countries other than China so that China starts feeling more pressure about meeting basic international standards."[21]

American diplomatic activism in support of its rebalance policy saw senior U.S. leaders headed by President Obama traveling frequently to the region and participating actively in bilateral relations and existing and newly emerging regional groupings involving the United States. The United States also was more active in competing in support of its economic interests, highlighting the proposed Trans-Pacific Partnership (TPP) free trade agreement involving the United States and countries on both sides of the Pacific. The proposed agreement was viewed as competing with groupings favored by China that required less trade liberalization and that excluded the United States.

Chinese media and officials condemned the so-called China bashing seen in the American presidential election campaigns. Chinese leaders remained firm in deflecting American pressure on the value of China's currency and broader trade practices and strongly rebuffed U.S. efforts to get China's cooperation in dealing with certain sensitive international issues, notably the conflict in Syria. China continued close ties with the new North Korean leadership despite the latter's repeated provocations and U.S. calls for greater pressure on Pyongyang. Chinese commentary accused the United States of fostering neighboring countries to be more assertive in challenging China's territorial claims in an effort to "contain" China. Top Chinese leaders highlighted regional trade arrangements that excluded the United States in order to undermine American-led efforts to advance U.S. interests through a trans-Pacific trade pact.[22]

Mixed Signals

Both sides endeavored to manage growing competition and rivalry with continued close engagement and pragmatism. The more than ninety official dialogues dealing with all aspects of the multifaceted relationship remained active.[23] The on-again, off-again pattern of exchanges between the military leaders of both countries—the weakest link in the array of dialogues between the two countries—was on again with improved exchanges in 2012–2015. President Obama and President Xi avowed commitment to manage differences effectively during summit meetings in 2013 and 2014 and looked positively to their meeting slated for September 2015.

The so-called Taiwan issue—historically the leading cause of friction between the United States and China—remained on a recent trajectory of easing tensions. Taiwan's election in 2012 and the victory of incumbent president Ma validated the continued moderate approach to cross-strait relations, foreshadowing closer engagement along lines welcomed by both Beijing and Washington.[24] Local Taiwan elections in November 2014 nonetheless saw a resurgence of the opposition Democratic Progressive Party (DPP) and a decline of the ruling Nationalist (Kuomintang) Party. The DPP was viewed very suspiciously by Beijing. If it were to win the January 2016 Taiwan presidential elections, cross-strait relations could become tenser.[25]

Despite pervasive Sino-U.S. distrust, there were also episodes demonstrating notable cooperation and seeming trust building between the two powers. One instance was the Sino-American handling of the case of Chen Guangcheng. The prominent Chinese civil rights activist in April 2012 escaped house arrest and fled from his home province to Beijing, where he eventually took refuge in the U.S. Embassy. After several days of talks between U.S. officials working with Chen on one side and Chinese officials on the other, a deal was reached to safeguard Chen and his family and to provide Chen with medical treatment. Chen subsequently changed his mind and appealed for American support to go to the United States with his family.

Intensive renewed U.S.–Chinese talks concurrent with the annual Security and Economic Dialogue between top American and Chinese department leaders then under way in Beijing resulted in a second deal where Chen and his family were allowed to leave for the United States on May 19, 2012.[26]

Meanwhile, the Obama government after mid-2012 played down the emphasis seen in 2011 and early 2012 on American security and military moves that added directly to the growing security dilemma with China. National Security Adviser Tom Donilon went to extraordinary measures to emphasize the nonmilitary aspects of the rebalance and to play down U.S. competition with China prior to President Obama's trip to the region in November 2012. Concurrently, the secretary of defense and the secretary of state similarly emphasized the broad and multifaceted reasons for strong and sustained American engagement with Asia and played down competition with China.[27]

THE STATUS AND OUTLOOK OF CHINESE–U.S. RELATIONS

A review of the record shows that there is little certainty in the course of Sino-American relations since the Cold War. The vicissitudes in the relationship caused by strong differences between the two major powers are forecast to continue. On the one hand, China and the United States differ strongly on many issues. The issues include their respective treatments of maritime territorial disputes in East Asia; competing trade and investment initiatives especially in the Asia-Pacific region; clashing approaches to seeking change of regimes grossly exploiting or brutally suppressing their people, flouting accepted norms regarding nonproliferation of weapons of mass destruction, or fostering terrorists; what should be done about the large and growing mutual security dilemma along China's rim posed by buildups in Chinese and U.S. military forces targeted at each other and by related cyber and space warfare options; and what should be done about the range of bilateral economic disputes headed by the massive U.S. trade deficit with China. On the other hand, the two powers converge and show strong interdependence on such key issues as mutual trade and investment; tourism, student, and other interactions of the citizens of both countries; and sustaining a stable regional and international order favorable to both countries. Pragmatism and prudence seem to argue for both governments to avoid conflict and confrontation.

At bottom, a case can be made that the fragile but enduring positive engagement seen in China–U.S. relations in recent years probably will continue, but serious uncertainties remain and seem to be getting stronger. Sino-American leaders have important pragmatic reasons to continue positive engagement and avoid confrontation and conflict. In particular:

- Both governments benefit from positive engagement in various areas. Such engagement supports their mutual interests in stability in the Asia-Pacific, a peaceful Korean peninsula, and a peaceful settlement of the Taiwan issue; U.S. and Chinese leaders recognize the need to cooperate to foster global peace and prosperity, to advance world environmental conditions, and to deal with climate change and nonproliferation.
- Both governments see that the two powers have become so interdependent that emphasizing the negatives in their relationship will hurt the other side but also will hurt them. Such interdependence is particularly strong in Sino-American economic relations.
- Both leaderships are preoccupied with a long list of urgent domestic and foreign priorities; in this situation, one of the last things they would seek is a serious confrontation in relations with one another.

Looking ahead, it's hard to envisage how the Obama government would see its interests well served with a more assertive U.S. stance leading to a major confrontation with China. Indeed, as noted above, the U.S. government at times has adjusted its rebalance and related initiatives in the Asia-Pacific in ways that reduce public emphasis on military strengthening sensitive to China and to those many Asia-Pacific governments seeking to avoid the disruption that would be associated with serious Sino-American differences. President Obama reached out to President Xi Jinping and the new Chinese leadership in holding the 2013 summit and sought greater engagement through senior-level interchange in cabinet-level visits and structured dialogues. Senior Obama administration officials' criticism of Chinese economic practices adverse to American interests remains measured. The administration has responded firmly when Chinese actions over disputed territory along its maritime rim escalate tensions and endanger stability, underlining America's commitments to regional stability and the status quo. Its posture on the preeminent issue of Taiwan has been supportive of Taiwan president Ma Ying-jeou's reassurance of and greater alignment with China.

China's Advances and Competition for Influence in Asia

Less certainty prevails regarding China's calculus, especially given the continued assertive and repeated advances China has made recently in pursuing its claims at the expense of its neighbors and the recent economic initiatives challenging U.S.-backed institutions and proposals. Repeated episodes of Chinese assertiveness and expansion over territorial and other disputes involving U.S. allies and interests in recent years are supported by seemingly growing public and elite opinion in China arguing for stronger foreign policy initiatives to change aspects of the regional order seen adversely in China.[28]

China's tough stand on maritime territorial disputes evident in the 2012 confrontations with the Philippines in the South China Sea and with Japan in the East China Sea has endured through China's leadership transition and now marks an important shift in China's foreign policy, with serious implications for China's neighbors and concerned powers including the United States. China expanded the scope of the confrontations by causing a crisis with the unannounced deployment of an oil rig for exploration in the Paracel Islands, disputed with Vietnam, in May 2014. The result was a protracted face-off of massed Chinese and Vietnamese coast guard and fishing boats and demonstrations in Vietnam that turned violent, destroyed Chinese properties, and killed four Chinese.[29] China's avowed success in advancing its claims against the Philippines and Vietnam and in challenging Japan's control of disputed islands head the list of reasons that the new Chinese policy is likely to continue and perhaps intensify in the future. Only a few governments seem prepared to resist, and the United States and other concerned powers have yet to demonstrate viable ways to get China to stop.

China has established a pattern of employing force, short of military means, and other pressure to assert more actively claims over disputed maritime territories. The Philippines and sometimes Vietnam continued to complain loudly, and Japan resisted firmly. But most concerned governments came to recognize that China's "win-win" formula emphasizing cooperation over common ground was premised on the foreign government eschewing actions acutely sensitive to China over Taiwan, Tibet, and Xinjiang, and that the scope of China's acute sensitivity had now been broadened to include the maritime disputes along China's rim.

China's neighbors and concerned powers like the United States have been required to calibrate more carefully their actions related to disputed maritime territories. Unfortunately, the parameters of China's acute concerns regarding maritime claims remain unclear as they are growing. Meanwhile, the drivers of China's new toughness on maritime disputes include rising patriotic and nationalist sentiment in Chinese elite and public opinion and the growing capabilities of Chinese military, coast guard, fishery, and oil exploration forces. The latter are sure to grow in the coming years, foreshadowing greater Chinese willingness to use coercion in seeking advances in nearby seas.

For now, a pattern of varied regional acquiescence, protests, and resistance to China's new toughness on maritime claims seems likely. It raises the question about future Chinese assertiveness, challenging neighboring governments with disputes over Chinese claims and challenging American leadership in promoting stability and opposing unilateral and coercive means to change the regional status quo.

There are forecasts of inevitable conflict between the United States and China as they compete for influence in the Asia-Pacific, or of a U.S. retreat in the Asia-Pacific in the face of China's assertiveness.[30] Such forecasts are offset in this writer's opinion by circumstances in China and abroad that will continue to constrict China's leaders. The circumstances are seen to hold back Chinese leaders even if they, like much of Chinese elite and public opinion, personally favor a tough approach in order to secure interests in the Asia-Pacific.

Constraints on Chinese Assertiveness

There are three sets of restraints on China's tough measures in foreign affairs related to the United States that are strong and are unlikely to diminish in the foreseeable future.[31]

Domestic Preoccupations

The first set of restraints relates to Chinese leaders' preoccupations with domestic priorities. There is a consensus among specialists in China and abroad about some of the key objectives of Chinese leaders. They want to sustain one-party rule, and to do so they require continued economic growth that advances the material benefits of the Chinese people and ensures general public support and legitimacy for the communist government. Such economic growth and continued one-party rule require stability at home and abroad, especially in nearby Asia where conflict and confrontation would have a serious negative impact on Chinese economic growth. At the same time, the need for vigilance in protecting Chinese security and sovereignty remains among the top leadership concerns as evidenced by the long and costly buildup of military forces to deal with a Taiwan contingency involving the United States and more recent use of various means of state power to advance territorial claims in nearby disputed seas. There is less clarity among specialists as to where Chinese international ambitions for regional and global leadership fit in the current priorities of Beijing's leaders, but there is little doubt that domestic concerns get overall priority.

On this basis, analysts see a wide range of domestic concerns preoccupying the Xi Jinping leadership and earlier Chinese leaders. As listed in chapter 4, they involve:

- weak leadership legitimacy;
- pervasive corruption;
- widening income gaps;
- widespread social turmoil;[32]
- a highly resource-intensive economy and enormous and rapidly growing environmental damage, and

• the need for major reform of an economic model in use in China for over three decades that is widely seen to have reached a point of diminishing returns.

As discussed in chapter 4, it remains to be seen whether the ambitious and wide-ranging agenda of economic and related domestic reforms set forth by the Chinese leadership in November 2013 will be effectively implemented in ways that ease the Chinese domestic problems. At bottom, these reforms seem to require a strong and sustained effort of top Chinese leaders, probably for many years.[33] Under these circumstances, those same leaders would seem unlikely to seek confrontation with the United States. Xi Jinping's accommodation of President Obama in meeting in California in 2013 and his leadership's continued public emphasis on seeking a new type of major power relationship may underline this trend. Of course, Xi has also led China's greater assertiveness on maritime territorial issues and on regional and international financial and economic institutions that undercut U.S. interests and influence. Thus far, however, the Chinese probes generally have been crafted to avoid direct confrontation with the superpower.

Whether the many domestic priorities preoccupying Chinese leaders noted above can be equated with President Obama's domestic preoccupations arguing for a continued pragmatic American approach to China remains to be seen. On balance, they incline Chinese leaders toward caution and pragmatism.

Strong Interdependence

The second set of constraints on Chinese measures against the United States involves strong and ever-growing interdependence in U.S.-Chinese relations. At the start of the twenty-first century, growing economic interdependence reinforced each government's tendency to emphasize the positive and pursue constructive relations with one another. A pattern of dualism in U.S.–China relations arose as part of the developing positive equilibrium. The pattern involved constructive and cooperative engagement on the one hand and contingency planning or hedging on the other. It reflected a mix of converging and competing interests and prevailing leadership suspicions and cooperation.

The dualism showed as each government used engagement to build positive and cooperative ties while at the same time seeking to use these ties to build interdependencies and webs of relationships that had the effect of constraining the other power from taking actions that opposed its interests. While the analogy is not precise, the policies of engagement pursued by the United States and China toward one another featured respective "Gulliver strategies" that were designed to tie down the aggressive, assertive, and other negative policy tendencies of the other power through webs of interdependence in bilateral and multilateral relationships.[34]

The power of interdependence and dualism to constrain assertive and disruptive actions has limits. As seen in China's periodic outbursts over the Taiwan issue and against Japan, changing international circumstances mix with strongly nationalistic sentiment among Chinese elite and public opinion and expanding Chinese military capabilities and coercive power to support stronger Chinese measures to protect and advance Chinese interests in the face of perceived outside intrusions and pressures.[35] In these instances, China's interdependence with Japan and the United States seems to be put aside at least temporarily in the interests of a strong demonstration of resolve against perceived provocations.

In sum, the American approach to China seeks engagement for its own sake, but it also seeks to intertwine China into what the Council on Foreign Relations called a "web" woven by the United States and its allies and associates to ensure that rising China conforms more to international norms backed by the United States as it rises in world prominence. For its part, China deliberately builds interdependence with the United States and with regional and international organizations involving the United States as a means to buffer against and constrain possibly harsh U.S. measures against China. As time passed, both sides became increasingly aware of how their respective interests were tied to the well-being and success of the other, thereby limiting the tendency of the past to apply pressure on one another. In effect, interdependence has worked to constrain both sides against taking forceful action against each other.

China's Insecure Position in the Asia-Pacific

The third set of constraints on tough Chinese measures against the United States involves China's insecure position in the Asia-Pacific region. This factor does not receive the attention it deserves and is treated here in some depth. Major American government and nongovernment studies of China's military challenge to the United States do not consider how China's insecure position in Asia reduces the likelihood that Beijing would seek a military challenge and confrontation with the United States.[36] Even after over two decades of repeated efforts, China's rise in the region remains encumbered and has a long way to go to challenge U.S. regional leadership. Nearby Asia is the world area where China has always exerted the greatest influence and where China devotes the lion's share of its foreign policy attention. The region contains security and sovereignty issues (e.g., Taiwan) of top importance for China. It is the main arena of interaction with the United States. This is the world area where the People's Liberation Army (PLA) is most active and exerts its greatest international influence. The region's economic importance far surpasses the rest of the world (China is Africa's biggest trader, but until very recently it has done more trade with South Korea). Stability along the rim of China is essential for China's continued economic growth—the linchpin of leadership legitimacy and continued communist rule. Against this background, without a secure foundation in nearby Asia, China will be inclined to avoid serious confrontation with the United States.[37]

Among Chinese strengths in the Asia-Pacific region are the following:

- China's position as the leading trading partner with most neighboring countries and the heavy investment many of those countries make in China (as discussed in chapter 4, China's investment in neighboring Asia remains far below projections; Beijing's recent multifaceted push for greater infrastructure and other financing promises to increase Chinese investment substantially);
- China's growing web of road, rail, river, electric power, pipeline, and other linkages promoting economic and other interchange with nearby countries;
- China's prominent leadership attention and active diplomacy in interaction with neighboring countries both bilaterally and multilaterally; and
- China's expanding military capabilities and related civilian security capabilities.

Nevertheless, these strengths are offset by various weaknesses and limitations. First, some Chinese practices alienate nearby governments, which broadly favor key aspects of U.S. regional leadership. Thus, leadership in the region involves often costly and risky efforts to support common goods involving regional security and development. In contrast, Chinese behavior shows a well-developed tendency to avoid risks, costs, or commitments to the common good unless there is adequate benefit for a narrow set of tangible Chinese interests. Although it has $3–$4 trillion in foreign exchange reserves, China continues to run a substantial trade surplus and to accumulate large foreign exchange reserves supported by currency policies widely seen to disadvantage trading competitors in the Asia-Pacific and elsewhere. As discussed in chapter 4, despite its economic progress and role as an international creditor comparable to international financial institutions, China annually receives an estimate of over $6 billion in foreign assistance loans and lesser grants that presumably would otherwise be available for other deserving clients in the Asia-Pacific and the world. It carefully adheres to UN budget formulas that keep Chinese dues and other payments remarkably low. It tends to ensure that its contributions to the broader good of the international order (e.g., extensive use of Chinese personnel in UN peacekeeping operations) are paid for by others. At bottom, the "win-win" principle that undergirds recent Chinese foreign policy means that Chinese officials make sure that Chinese policies and practices provide a "win" for generally narrowly defined national interests of China. They eschew the kinds of risky and costly commitments for the broader regional and global common good that Asian leaders have come to look to U.S. leadership to provide. A major reason for China's continued reluctance to undertake costs and commitments for the sake of the common good of the Asia-Pacific and broader international affairs is the long array of domestic challenges and preoccupations faced by Chinese leaders. The actual impact of these domestic issues on the calculations of Chinese leaders is hard to measure with any precision, though their overall impact appears substantial.

Second, recent episodes of Chinese assertiveness toward several neighbors and the United States have put nearby governments on guard and weakened Chinese regional influence. They have reminded China's neighbors that the sixty-year history of the People's Republic of China (PRC) has much more often than not featured China acting in disruptive and domineering ways in the region.[38] Notably, Mao Zedong and Deng Xiaoping repeatedly conflicted with and invaded neighboring countries either with Chinese forces or with insurgents organized, armed, and trained by China.

Third, the record of China's success in reassuring neighbors and advancing influence in the Asia-Pacific in the post–Cold War period—a period now extending twenty-five years—is mediocre. China faces major impediments, many homegrown. China's long-standing practice of building an image of consistent and righteous behavior in foreign affairs blocks realistic appraisal of the wary view of China held by officials in most neighboring countries and the United States. The latter countries fear another in the long series of historical shifts in Chinese policy away from reassurance and toward past practices of intimidation and aggression.

Chinese elite and public opinion is well conditioned by China's extensive education-propaganda apparatus; they know little about this negative Chinese legacy of past widespread intimidation and aggression. Absorbed in Chinese publicity regarding China's allegedly exceptional position of consistent, moral, and benign foreign behavior, Chinese elites and public opinion have a poor appreciation of regional and American concerns. Such elite and public opinion restricts more realistic Chinese policies when dealing with disputes and differences with neighbors and the United States.

Most notably, the Chinese government has the exceptional position among major powers of having never acknowledged making a mistake in foreign policy. Analysis shows that the Chinese sense of exceptionalism and righteousness is much stronger even than that prevailing in the United States, known for its exceptionalism in foreign affairs. However, free media, open politics, regularly scheduled elections, and changes in administrations lead repeatedly to U.S. recognition of foreign policy failures in pursuit of new directions. Roughly comparable to China's outlook is the Roman Catholic Church, when the pope issues directives on faith and dogma. Thus Beijing joins the Vatican with Chinese exceptional exceptionalism, which reinforces among Chinese people and elites the Chinese government–fostered worldview of China always following a correct stance.

As a result, when China encounters a dispute with neighbors, the fault never lies with China. If Beijing chooses not to blame the neighbor, its default position is to blame larger forces, usually involving the United States. Adding to this peculiar negative mix, as discussed in chapter 3, Chinese elites and public opinion remain heavily influenced by prevailing Chinese media and other emphases on China's historic victimization at the hands of outside powers such as the United States, Japan, and others. In sum, they are quick to find offense and impervious to the need for change and recognition of fault on their part.[39]

Measuring China's Relationships

As will be discussed in later chapters, measuring significant limitations and shortcomings seen in China's recent relations in the Asia-Pacific—even after twenty-five years of efforts in the post–Cold War period—can start with China's relationship with Japan, arguably Asia's richest country and the key ally of the United States in the region. The record shows that China usually has been unsuccessful in winning greater support, and relations seriously worsened to their lowest point since World War II because of disputes involving territorial and resource claims in the East China Sea.[40]

India's interest in accommodation with China has been offset by border frictions and competition for influence among the countries surrounding India and in Southeast Asia and Central Asia. The limited progress in Sino-Indian relations became overshadowed by a remarkable upswing in India's strategic cooperation with the United States during the past decade.[41] Meanwhile, Russian and Chinese interest in close alignment has grown with President Putin's isolation from the West, but over the years it has waxed and waned depending on the two powers changing respective relationships with the West.[42]

Until recently, China had a very negative record in relations with Taiwan. The election of a new Taiwan government in 2008 bent on reassuring Beijing changed relations for the better. China's economic, diplomatic, and military influence over Taiwan grew. The government was reelected in 2012, but the political opposition in Taiwan remained opposed to recent trends and improved its standing with Taiwan voters as the percentage approval of the ruling president sometimes dropped to single digits.[43]

Despite close Sino–South Korean economic ties, South Korean opinion of China declined sharply from a high point in 2004, initially because of historical disputes. South Koreans also opposed Chinese support for North Korea, which seemed designed to sustain a viable North Korean state friendly to China. This objective was at odds with South Korea's goal of reunifying North and South Korea, with South Korea being dominant. China's refusal in 2010 to condemn North Korea's killing of forty-six South Korean sailors in the sinking of a South Korean warship and its killing of South Korean soldiers and civilians in an artillery attack strongly reinforced anti-China sentiment. Chinese efforts to improve ties with a new South Korean president in 2013 were complicated by provocations from North Korea and Chinese advances in disputed territory claimed by South Korea.[44]

Chinese diplomacy at various times endeavored to play down Chinese territorial disputes with Southeast Asian countries, but differences have become more prominent in recent years, especially over disputed claims in the South China Sea, seriously encumbering Chinese relations with the region. China's remarkable military modernization and its sometimes secretive and authoritarian political system raised suspicions and wariness on the part of a number of China's neighbors, including such middle powers as Australia.[45] These countries have endeavored to build their own military power and to work cooperatively with one another and the United States in the face of China's military advances.

The People's Republic of China's record of repeated aggression and assertiveness during the forty-year rule of Mao Zedong and Deng Xiaoping toward many Asian countries means that China has had few positive connections on which to build friendly ties with its neighbors. Chinese interchange with Asian neighbors has depended heavily on the direction and leadership of the Chinese government. Nongovernment channels of communication and influence have been limited. The so-called overseas Chinese communities in Southeast Asian countries have provided important investment and technical assistance to China's development and have represented political forces supportive of their home country's good relations with China. At the same time, however, the dominant ethnic, cultural, and religious groups in Southeast Asia often have a long history of wariness of China and sometimes have promoted violent actions and other discrimination against ethnic Chinese.[46]

Limitations and complications also showed up in the areas of greatest Chinese strength in Asia—economic relations and diplomacy.[47] As discussed in chapter 4, double counting associated with processing trade exaggerated Chinese trade figures. As half of Chinese trade was conducted by foreign-invested enterprises in China, the resulting processing trade saw China often add only a small amount to the product, and the finished product often depended on sales to the United States or the European Union. Taken together, these facts seemed to underscore Chinese interdependence with the United States and allied countries and to represent a major caveat regarding China's stature in Asia as a powerful trading country.

The large amount of Asian and international investment that went to China did not go to other Asian countries, hurting their economic development. Until very recently, China invested little in Asia apart from Hong Kong, a reputed tax haven and source of "round-trip" monies leaving China and then returning to China as foreign investment. As discussed in chapter 4, China in 2013–2015 repeatedly pledged tens of billions of dollars worth of Chinese investment for infrastructure development in countries along China's periphery. The pledges seemed credible given China's large foreign exchange reserves, and interest among countries in the region in using the funds was strong. It remained to be seen how China and its various neighbors would work out mutually agreeable arrangements that would accord with China's ubiquitous "win-win" formula that required a clear advantage for a narrowly defined Chinese win-set before China would move forward with such foreign assistance.

What is known shows that China's aid (as opposed to financing arrangements that require repayment in cash or kind) to Asia is very small, especially in comparison to other donors, with the exception of Chinese secret but reportedly substantial aid to North Korea and, at least until recently, Myanmar. In keeping with China's "win-win" diplomacy, the sometimes dizzying array of meetings, agreements, and pronouncements in active Chinese diplomacy in Asia did not hide the fact that China remained reluctant to undertake significant costs, risks, or commitments in dealing with difficult regional issues.

North Korea reflects an unusual mix of Chinese strengths and weaknesses in Asia. On the one hand, China provides considerable food aid, oil, and other material support. China is North Korea's largest trading partner and foreign investor. China often shields Pyongyang from U.S.-led efforts at the United Nations to sanction or otherwise punish North Korea over its nuclear weapons development, ballistic missile development, proliferation activities, and military aggression against South Korea. At times, the United States and other participants in the six-party talks relied on China to use its standing as the foreign power with the most influence in North Korea to get Pyongyang to engage in negotiations over its weapons development and proliferation activities. On the other hand, North Korea repeatedly rejects Chinese advice and warnings. North Korean officials tell American and other officials of their disdain for China. Nonetheless, Chinese leaders are reluctant to cut off their aid. An increase in pressure on North Korea to conform to international norms could cause a backlash from the Pyongyang regime that would undermine Chinese interests in preserving stability on the Korean peninsula and in northeastern Asia. The net effect of these contradictions is that while China's influence in North Korea is greater than that of other major powers, it is encumbered and limited.[48]

China and U.S. Leadership in the Asia-Pacific

A comparison of Chinese policies and practices in the Asia-Pacific with those of the United States underlines how far China has to go despite over two decades of efforts to secure its position in Asia if it intends to be successful in seriously confronting and challenging the United States. Without a secure periphery, and facing formidable American presence and influence, China almost certainly calculates that challenging the United States poses grave dangers for the PRC regime.[49]

U.S. weaknesses in the Asia-Pacific included the foreign policies of the George W. Bush administration, which were very unpopular with regional elites and public opinion. As the Barack Obama government has refocused U.S. attention positively on the Asia-Pacific region, regional concerns shifted to worry that U.S. budget difficulties and political gridlock in Washington would undermine the ability of the United States to sustain support for regional responsibilities.

As seen in the Obama government's rebalance policy and in recent American practice, U.S. priorities, behavior, and power mesh well with the interests of the majority of Asia-Pacific governments that seek legitimacy through development and nation building in an uncertain security environment and an interdependent world economic order. The drivers of America undertaking leadership responsibilities in the Asia-Pacific region remain strong:

- The region is an area of ever greater strategic and economic importance for the United States.
- The United States remains strongly committed to long-standing U.S. goals of supporting stability and balance of power, sustaining smooth economic access, and promoting U.S. values and accepted international norms in this increasingly important world area.

The basic determinants of U.S. strength and influence in the Asia-Pacific region involve the factors discussed below.[50]

Security. In most of Asia, governments are strong and viable and are able to make the decisions that determine the direction of foreign affairs. In general, officials see their governments' legitimacy and success resting on nation building and economic development, which require a stable and secure international environment. Unfortunately, Asia is not particularly stable, and most regional governments are privately wary of and tend not to trust each other. As a result, they look to the United States to provide the security they need. They recognize that the U.S. security role is very expensive and involves great risk, including large-scale casualties if necessary. They also recognize that neither China nor any other Asian power or coalition of powers is able or willing to undertake even a fraction of these risks, costs, and responsibilities.

Economic. The nation-building priority of most Asian governments depends importantly on export-oriented growth. As noted above, much of Chinese and Asian trade heavily depends on exports to developed countries, notably the United States. The United States has run a massive trade deficit with China, and a total annual trade deficit with Asia valued at over $400 billion. Asian government officials recognize that China, which runs an overall trade surplus, and other trading partners of Asia are unwilling and unable to bear even a fraction of the cost of such large trade deficits, which nonetheless are very important for Asian governments.

Government Engagement. The Bush administration was generally effective in interaction with Asia's powers. The Obama government has built on these strengths. The Obama government's wide-ranging rebalancing with regional governments and multilateral organizations has a scope going from India to the Pacific Island states to Korea and Japan. Its emphasis on consultation and inclusion of international stakeholders before coming to policy decisions on issues of importance to Asia and the Pacific has also been broadly welcomed and stands in contrast with the previously perceived unilateralism of the Bush government.

Meanwhile, the U.S. Pacific Command and other U.S. military commands and security and intelligence organizations have been at the edge of remarkably wide-ranging U.S. efforts to build and strengthen webs of military and related intelligence and security relationships throughout the region that are unprecedented in their scope and importance and that continue to grow strongly.

Nongovernment Engagement and Immigration. The United States for decades reaching back to past centuries has engaged the Asia-Pacific through business, religious, educational, media, and other interchange. Such active nongovernment interaction puts the United States in a unique position and reinforces overall U.S. influence.[51] Meanwhile, fifty years of generally color-blind U.S. immigration policy since the ending of discriminatory U.S. restrictions on Asian immigration in 1965 has resulted in the influx of millions of Asia-Pacific migrants who call America home and who interact with their countries of origin in ways that undergird and reflect well on the American position in the region.

Asia-Pacific Contingency Planning. Part of the reason for the success of U.S. efforts to build webs of security-related and other relationships with Asia-Pacific countries has to do with active contingency planning by many Asia-Pacific governments. As power relations change in the region, notably on account of China's rise, regional governments generally seek to work positively and pragmatically with rising China on the one hand, but on the other hand they seek the reassurance of close security, intelligence, and other ties with the United States in case rising China shifts from its current avowed benign approach to one of greater assertiveness or dominance.

Against the background of recent Chinese demands, coercion, and intimidation, the Asia-Pacific governments' interest in closer ties with the United States meshed well with the Obama government's engagement with regional governments and multilateral organizations. The U.S. concern to maintain stability while fostering economic growth overlapped constructively with the priorities of the vast majority of regional governments as they pursued their respective nation-building agendas.

In sum, the circumstances discussed here underline the judgment that China remains constrained in the Asia-Pacific region and is not in a position to confront the United States. The Obama government's rebalance toward the Asia-Pacific region fits well with Asia-Pacific dynamics while China continues a conflicted approach between reassurance and assertiveness in ways that reinforce regional interest in sustaining and advancing closer ties with the United States. The situation is subject to change. China may miscalculate regional realities and pursue more forcefully its ambitions at the expense of neighbors and the United States. Then the United States and its allies and partners may face a choice of withdrawal or resistance. Meanwhile, the United States may tire of leadership responsibilities and withdraw from the region; or it may overreact and follow aggressive policies leading to Sino-American conflict. At bottom, the Chinese and U.S. leaders will continue competition and maneuvering for advantage in this critically important world area.

OTHER CONTEMPORARY ISSUES AND THEIR IMPLICATIONS

The Chinese and American governments have proven to be difficult partners. As discussed in chapter 3, the Chinese harbor objectives strongly at odds with important American interests and Americans continue to pursue those interests despite Chinese opposition. American public opinion of China's government tends to be unfavorable, while American media and congressional officials often go beyond the Obama administration in complaining about various Chinese economic, security, and political policies and practices at home and abroad. On its part, Beijing explicitly favors a multipolar international order at odds with U.S. leadership in world affairs. It opposes the strengthening U.S. alliance system and the behavior of American security and other forces as the leading power along the rim of China. It builds and deploys an impressive array of military forces designed to counter and if necessary confront the American military along China's rim. It sharply criticizes American support for Taiwan, especially arms sales, and it attacks U.S. support for China's neighbors that contest expansive Chinese claims to territory in the disputed seas along China's periphery. The Chinese government is highly sensitive to signals of U.S. support for the Dalai Lama, ethnic Uighur dissidents in China's Xinjiang region, and other domestic Chinese oppositionists. State-directed Chinese outlets routinely portray U.S. policy intentions in worst-case assessments, seeing Washington as seeking to bring down the one-party system in China as it fosters regional efforts to contain Chinese power. Prevalent negative depictions of U.S. intentions are married with media-propaganda campaigns establishing China's identity as resisting many aspects of American leadership while reinforcing Chinese self-righteousness.

Against this background, a long list of salient issues in Sino-American relations will not be resolved soon or easily. In addition to the recent disputes over maritime issues discussed above, these issues focus on important security and economic questions, Taiwan, and human rights, democracy, and other international norms favored by the United States. [52]

Security issues have grown in importance in tandem with China's strong military modernization focused on Asian issues of key concern to the United States. The security dilemma over Taiwan has developed since the 1990s. The scope of the Sino-American security dilemma has broadened in recent years to include contested maritime areas along China's periphery. The broad security dilemma involves forces directly committed to the Asia-Pacific region supported by expanding Chinese and substantial American nuclear weapons; growing cyber, space, and other unconventional attack capabilities; and espionage directed at one another.

Economic issues center on the overall impact of Chinese growth, closer U.S.–China economic relations, and international economic globalization. On the whole, the impact has been highly beneficial to China's interests. Complaints and initiatives to change existing economic relations have come in recent years largely from the U.S. side. They reflect a wide range of American interests and constituencies concerned with perceived unfair or disadvantageous aspects of the massive U.S.–China economic relationship. They focus on the unprecedented U.S. trade deficit with China seen as caused by currency manipulation, massive cyber and other theft of commercial know-how and intellectual property, state-sponsored subsidies, coercion and intimidation of U.S and other foreign companies to force the sharing of sensitive technology, and refusal to abide by pledges made in China's accession to the WTO to open restricted sectors of China's markets where American companies would be competitive. Suspicions of Chinese espionage color the American reaction to China's expanding investment in the United States, and some Americans argue against U.S. reliance on China to purchase American government securities. [53]

As noted earlier, tensions in contemporary U.S.–China relations over Taiwan have eased remarkably in recent years, but they could rise again if the candidate of the now opposition DPP were to win the Taiwan presidential election in January 2016. The stakes are high; the respective Chinese and U.S. military buildups focused on a Taiwan contingency mean that Taiwan is one of only a few areas where the world's number-one and number-two powers could come to blows, with devastating implications for them and international affairs.[54]

Issues of human rights and international norms in Chinese–U.S. relations reflect a wide range of differing values dealing with economic, social, political, cultural, and other interests and concerns. Differences over these issues have long characterized Sino-American relations. The differences have their roots in the respective backgrounds of the American and Chinese societies, governments, and peoples. Those backgrounds foster the values that are often at odds.

In general, the United States has sought to prompt the Chinese authorities to adopt policies and practices in line with the international values and norms prevalent in modern developed countries of the West, and Chinese leaders have seen their interests better served by conforming to many of these international norms. Economically, China's government has embraced many of the norms of the globalized international economy and has adapted to economic market demands. There remain many problem areas, with President Obama and others seeing China use state-directed means to manipulate and undermine the liberal economic order in pursuit of narrow Chinese interests.[55] China's conformity to world norms in the security area has been slower but substantial, especially in areas involving such sensitive issues as the proliferation of weapons of mass destruction. China's leadership at times has appeared more in line with international norms regarding issues affecting political power and processes in China, but it repeatedly resorts to authoritarian measures to sustain one-party rule.

Looking ahead, given the recent foreign policy activism and assertiveness of the Xi Jinping government, it appears that as Chinese capabilities grow, Beijing is likely to take actions that will further challenge the United States regarding the above-noted issues and the broad international order supported by the United States.[56] The challenges to the security and stability of the Asia-Pacific have been clear and seem primed to continue and perhaps grow. China's erosion of international economic norms is more hidden. China seems to support free trade by the United States and others in its ongoing efforts to exploit this open environment with state-directed means, widespread theft, and intimidation and coercion of companies and governments in a wholesale grab of technology, know-how, capital, and competitive advantage in a headlong drive for economic development at the expense of others.

Americans will face continuing impediments from China in dealing with nuclear proliferation by North Korea and Iran, and China was of little help in dealing with Syria's use of chemical weapons or with Russia's coercion of Ukraine and acquisition of Crimea. Chinese leaders remain determined to support the Leninist one-party system in China that treats human rights selectively and capriciously, with an eye always focused on sustaining the communist state. Taken together, these difficulties, frictions, and frustrations represent the focus of the overall China challenge for the United States in what promises to be a tense and difficult period in China's relations with America in the years ahead.

Chapter Seven

Relations with Taiwan

Along with relations with the United States, Chinese leaders in the post–Cold War period have consistently given high priority to dealing with what they call the "Taiwan issue" in China's foreign relations. As in the case of Chinese relations with the United States, China's relations with Taiwan followed a sometimes tortuous path. In a broad sense, China's approach has involved three main elements: positive incentives, mainly involving ever growing economic exchanges, complemented by coercion, seen in the impressive Chinese military buildup focused on Taiwan and continued Chinese efforts to isolate Taiwan internationally. Sometimes, Chinese leaders appeared confident that the mix of positive and negative incentives will meet Chinese interests regarding Taiwan. But at other times, they appeared frustrated and uncertain about how to prevent Taiwan's moves toward permanent separation from China.[1]

Taiwan's moves toward permanent separation grew from 1989 to 2008. This trend seriously challenged China's leaders, who give high priority to preserving Chinese sovereignty and nationalistic ambitions. Beijing's response featured the large-scale buildup of Chinese military forces directed at Taiwan and the United States and others, such as Japan, which might possibly get involved in a military conflict over Taiwan. And it involved periodic assertions by China of its determination to use forceful means to prevent Taiwan's independence. These Chinese actions alarmed leaders from Taiwan, the United States, Japan, and a number of other countries. They also underlined the fact that however accommodating China's declared foreign strategy might appear, Beijing could change quickly and sharply toward a more confrontational one, notably if leaders in Taiwan move toward permanent separation or independence from China. The volatility of the Taiwan "hot spot" and its unpredictable consequences for China's overall foreign policy were enhanced by the fact that China often seemed unable to control the actions of the leaders in Taiwan, notably President Lee Teng-hui (1988–2000) and President Chen Shui-bian (2000–2008), who repeatedly pursued opportunities to enhance Taiwan's independence from China.[2]

Chinese concerns over Taiwan subsided markedly when Taiwan voters in 2008 repudiated the pro-independence initiatives of Lee Teng-hui and Chen Shui-bian and elected President Ma Ying-jeou, who focused on a policy of reassurance and deepening engagement with China. The United States and other concerned powers supported the easing of tensions in the Taiwan Strait. Cross-strait economic, social, and political exchanges grew impressively. Taiwan became ever more dependent on the Chinese economy. Taiwan's military declined sharply relative to China's strong defense buildup. Its diplomatic options were tightly constrained by China. President Ma was re-elected in 2012, but public approval of his government declined substantially. Islandwide local elections in November 2014 were a major defeat of Ma and the ruling Nationalist (Kuomintang—KMT) Party. Mass demonstrations in Taipei in March and April 2014 occupied the legislature in protests called "the sunflower movement" triggered by a proposed cross-strait service trade agreement supported by the Ma government. The protesters and opinion polls demonstrated rising anxiety on the island over Taiwan's growing integration with China. The concern in Taiwan over China's intentions was reinforced by China's firm stance against a largely nonviolent popular uprising in Hong Kong beginning in September 2014 demanding direct popular election of Taiwan's chief executive. Hong Kong's so-called umbrella movement meshed with Taiwan's sunflower movement to play to the advantage of Taiwan's opposition Democratic Progressive Party (DPP), which was widely seen on both sides of the strait as much better positioned to win the January 2016 presidential election than it was in 2012. DPP leaders disagreed with the stand of the Ma government on One China and its implications for Taiwan, which provided the basis for the increased Taiwan-China cooperation since 2008. DPP leaders were often seen in China as pro–Taiwan independence, anathema for Beijing. It remained very uncertain in mid-2015 how cross-strait relations would evolve in the event of a DPP victory in January 2016.[3] Meanwhile, the hardening of U.S. policy toward China, especially over the Xi Jinping government's assertiveness and expansion in the East and South China Seas coincided with increased debate in Congress, the media, and among specialists regarding stronger American military and other support for Taiwan as a means to counter growing Chinese expansion. The Obama government policy avoided significant change in policy toward Taiwan as it continued support for President Ma and his accommodations with China.[4]

THE IMPACT OF CHINA–TAIWAN TENSIONS, 1995–2008

The relevant context of the cooperation and easing of tensions over cross-strait relations since 2008 is the tumultuous period dating from Taiwan President Lee Teng-hui's visit to the United States in 1995 to the end of the administration of Taiwan President Chen Shui-bian in 2008. Tensions in cross-strait relations and the perceived danger of conflict in the Taiwan area rose dramatically in the mid-1990s, lasting until the election of Ma Ying-jeou. In the end, Taiwan voters reacted strongly against the extremes of Taiwan leaders in this period, establishing momentum of improvement of cross-strait relations. China welcomed the turn of events and supported the momentum.

Developments during Lee Teng-hui's Presidency

China's post–Cold War search for a stable and peaceful international environment prompted Chinese efforts to smooth over differences and emphasize common ground, especially with China's neighbors and major trading partners. These efforts did not work with Taiwan.[5] The Taiwan government was not prepared to accept the terms of the People's Republic of China (PRC) for establishing improved relations, especially demands that Taipei adhere to a "one-China principle" as defined by Beijing. And Beijing was not nearly as accommodating with Taiwan as it was with other entities with which it has had disputes.[6]

The so-called Taiwan issue rose to unique status as a driving force in Chinese international and security policy priorities in the 1990s.[7] Following the end of martial law in Taiwan in 1987, greater democracy emerged on the island. With it came a rising sentiment in favor of greater separation from the mainland and a more prominent and distinctive role for Taiwan in world affairs. At first, Chinese leaders judged that the concurrent growth in cross-strait trade and other exchanges would hold these Taiwanese sentiments in check, but gradually they became seriously concerned about a perceived movement toward political independence. China's concern reached fever pitch after President Lee Teng-hui visited countries that maintained official relations with the PRC and then visited the United States in 1995.[8]

Beijing saw the Clinton administration's reversal of policy—first denying Lee a visa and then granting him one amid broad media and congressional pressure—as a major setback in Chinese foreign policy. PRC policy hardened. China resorted to provocative military exercises designed to intimidate the people of Taiwan and their international supporters prior to important legislative and presidential elections on the island in December 1995 and March 1996, respectively. The military actions cowed Taiwan for a few months until the United States eventually sent two aircraft carrier battle

groups to the Taiwan area, showing Beijing the potentially dangerous consequences of provocative military action against Taiwan.

Beijing also intensified efforts to isolate Taiwan internationally.[9] Beijing
used aid, diplomatic pressure, and other means to whittle away Taiwan's
shrinking band of diplomatic allies.[10] Taiwan's leaders reciprocated in international competition with China. During the Asian economic crisis of
1997–1998, Taiwan succeeded in welcoming senior Singaporean, Malaysian,
and other officials in Taipei, and senior Taiwanese delegations traveled to
Singapore, the Philippines, Thailand, and Japan.[11] Not wishing to upset relations with Asian countries seeking financial help, the PRC at first adopted a
low-key response to Taiwan's maneuvers. But tougher Chinese warnings
soon began.[12]

China took advantage of the high-profile U.S.–China summits of 1997
and 1998 to portray a common U.S.–China front. Beijing sought stronger
U.S. pledges on limiting American relations with Taiwan and curbing U.S.
arms sales to Taiwan. Beijing endeavored to turn to its advantage President
Clinton's affirmation in Shanghai on June 29, 1998, of the "three nos"—no
support for two Chinas, or one China/one Taiwan; no support for Taiwanese
independence; and no support for Taiwanese representation in international
organizations where statehood is required.[13]

The limits of PRC influence in Taiwan were once again evident when Lee
Teng-hui, chafing under Chinese pressure, announced in an interview in
1999 his view that the China–Taiwan relationship was one between two
separate states, what Lee called a "special state-to-state relationship." Seeing
this as a bold step toward independence, Beijing reacted strongly, suspending
formal exchanges through the cross-strait offices and escalating military
pressures along the Taiwan Strait. Taken by surprise, U.S. officials endeavored to calm the situation. Lee's move solidified his reputation in the Clinton
administration as a troublemaker. He retained important support in Congress,
which was then in the midst of a white-hot debate with the president over
various sensitive aspects of China policy, including policy toward Taiwan.[14]

Chinese officials and senior leaders warned strongly against the DPP
candidate, Chen Shui-bian, in the 2000 presidential election. The Chinese
rhetoric helped Chen improve his very narrow margin of victory against the
runner-up candidate, who was more acceptable to Beijing. Chinese leaders
thus learned of serious unintended consequences from poorly applied pressure tactics on the Taiwan electorate; they have avoided such tactics since.[15]

Developments during Chen Shui-bian's Presidency

President Chen Shui-bian entered office in May 2000, ending fifty years of
rule by the Kuomintang Party. On cross-strait relations, Chen appeared more
moderate than was widely anticipated; his carefully worded inauguration

speech (reportedly the work of fifty advisers) avoided serious provocations against Beijing while it gave no ground on Taiwan's separate status. Chen and his advisers also appeared to be working smoothly with the U.S. administration, which was anxious to avoid added friction with China.[16]

During his May 2000 inauguration speech, Chen used formulas designed to eschew independence for Taiwan while not accepting China's demand that he agree to adhere to a "one-China" principle. Specifically, Chen stated "five nos"—no declaration of independence, no change of national title, no inclusion of the "two-state" theory in the constitution, no holding of a referendum on reunification or independence, and no abolition of the National Unification Guidelines and the National Unification Council (the Guidelines and Council were created under President Lee Teng-hui and provided a way and means toward eventual Taiwan–China reunification). Chen hoped this approach would reduce Chinese pressure on Taiwan, but China held Chen to the five nos and continued to refuse to return to a dialogue with Taiwan's government (which had been suspended following Lee Teng-hui's "state-to-state" comments in 1999). It increased strong efforts to isolate Taipei internationally and reached out to opposition parties as a means to isolate Chen.[17] Underlying Beijing's response was a fundamental lack of trust in Chen.[18]

Beijing appeared reasonably satisfied as Taiwan became mired in a serious economic downturn and saw trade and investment with the mainland as the way out. By 2003, the burgeoning mainland economy drew investments from half of the 1,000 top Taiwan companies. Government officials from Taiwan said that the level of Taiwanese investment in the mainland was over $100 billion. The PRC accounted for about three-quarters of Taiwan's total foreign investment in the previous decade. Bilateral trade amounted to over $40 billion in 2003, growing at an annual rate of 30 percent. About 1 million Taiwanese citizens were in mainland China. Also by this time, markedly improved U.S.–China relations were accompanied by strong U.S. affirmations of a "one-China" policy and repeated private assurances by President George W. Bush that he opposed Taiwan's independence.[19]

Chen Shui-bian shifted to a much more assertive and pro-independence stance against China in 2003–2004. In the run-up to the 2004 presidential election, Chen and his senior colleagues rejected the principle of one China, condemned China's pressure tactics, and pushed hard for legal and institutional reforms that affirmed Taiwan's identity separate from China.[20] Chinese and U.S. officials viewed the reforms as steps toward independence.[21] Chinese officials warned against proposed changes in Taiwan's Republic of China (ROC) constitution in ways that would establish a formal and legally binding status for Taiwan as a country permanently separate from China. U.S. officials feared China would launch a military attack on Taiwan if Chen made the proposed changes.[22]

While the PRC's long-term objective was reunification, Chinese leaders for the time being seemed focused on preventing Taiwan from taking further steps toward permanent separation. Proposals by Deng Xiaoping and Jiang Zemin, supported by current Chinese leaders, stated that Taipei could have a high degree of autonomy under future arrangements but insisted that Taiwan must recognize itself as part of one China. Although Beijing's vision of a unified China remained vague, China was clearer on what it would not tolerate. Backed by an Anti-Secession Law in 2005, China warned that moves by Taiwan toward greater separation, notably a declaration of independence, would be met with force.[23]

The Chinese Communist Party leadership saw its own legitimacy entwined with its ability to show progress toward the goal of reunifying Taiwan with the mainland. It was reluctant to deviate from past positions widely accepted in China, sticking to the mix of hard and soft tactics that—unfortunately for China—seemed at that time to drive Taiwan further away from China. Beijing also perceived Taiwan as a security problem; its alignment with the United States and possibly Japan posed a barrier to China's regional and global influence. Taiwan could serve as a base for subversion in case of domestic turmoil on the mainland.[24]

In Taiwan, political forces were divided on cross-strait issues. President Chen Shui-bian, his ruling DPP, and their more radical allies in Lee Teng-hui's Taiwan Solidarity Union Party represented the so-called pan-green camp—one side of the political spectrum that continued to push for reforms that strengthened Taiwan's status as a country permanently separate from China. On the other side was the so-called pan-blue camp, made up of the formerly ruling KMT party and their ally the People's First Party, which generally was more cautious in taking political steps that might antagonize China.[25]

Seeing the rise of instability and an increased danger of conflict in the Taiwan area, President Bush publicly rebuked Taiwan's president on December 9, 2003. Chinese officials urged U.S. and international pressure to rein in the Taiwan leader. They judged that among the few options acceptable to Chinese officials, a strident public Chinese stance probably would increase support for Chen in the prevailing atmosphere in Taiwan and thus be counterproductive for China's purposes.[26]

Chen's narrow reelection victory in March 2004 showed Chinese and other observers how far the Taiwan electorate had moved from the 1990s, when pro-independence was a clear liability among the Taiwanese voters. Chinese officials were pleased that U.S. pressure sought to curb Chen's more ambitious reform efforts that flirted with de jure independence, but they pushed for more overt U.S. pressure, including curbs on U.S. arms sales.[27] Officials from the United States continued to press Chen to avoid provocative actions but remained firm in maintaining military support for Taiwan as a means to deter China from using force against Taiwan. They intervened repeatedly in the lead-up to the December 2004 legislative elections to highlight differences between U.S. policy and the assertive positions of President Chen and his supporters.[28]

The poor showing of the DPP candidates in the legislative election of December 2004 was seen by President Chen as a public rebuke of his assertive stance, and he and his party reverted for a time to the lower profile on cross-strait issues that he had used prior to 2003. After the dramatic visits of KMT Chairman Lien Chan and James Soong to China in the first half of 2005, Chinese President Hu Jintao and other Chinese officials muted China's past insistence on reunification under the one country–two systems formula, which also was used to govern Hong Kong's return to China and which was long rejected by large majorities in Taiwan. He and other Chinese officials and commentators also avoided a discussion of a possible timetable for reunification of Taiwan with the mainland. President Hu and other Chinese officials instead focused on the need to avoid further steps by Taiwan toward independence and promised various cross-strait economic, cultural, educational, and other benefits for the Taiwanese people.[29]

By 2006, President Chen began to renew the kinds of pro-independence, anti-China initiatives that had caused the flare-up of tensions seen in 2003–2004. The president announced in 2006 that the National Unification Council (NUC) would cease to function and that the National Unification Guidelines (NUG) that the NUC created would cease to apply. The continuation of the NUC and NUG, dating back to the early 1990s, was a key element of the status quo that Chen, under pressure from the United States, had pledged not to change as part of his "five nos" 2000 inaugural pledge. The U.S. government pressed Chen to reverse the 2006 initiative, but the results did not fully satisfy the U.S. government and deepened Bush administration suspicion of the Taiwan president.[30]

The Chen administration wound down with a reputation for poor governance, rising corruption scandals, and low approval ratings. President Chen nonetheless pursued changes in education policies, changes in the naming of government places, organizations, and institutions, constitutional changes, approaches to the United Nations and related organizations like the World Health Organization (WHO), and broader international recognition—all with an intent to support Taiwan's status as a country separate from China. These steps usually were seen as provocative by China and by the Bush administration, with the U.S. government weighing in publicly against measures it saw as upsetting the stability in the Taiwan Strait. The Chen administration's relations with the United States reached a point where U.S. hosting of stopovers for Chen's transits on trips abroad became restrictive and involved locales as far away from Washington as possible.[31]

China duly registered public opposition to Chen's initiatives but placed more emphasis than ever on working in consultation with the Bush administration to deal with Chen's maneuvers. It continued to reinforce the impressive military buildup focused on Taiwan and to deepen Taiwan's economic interdependence with the mainland. Looking beyond the Chen administration, Chinese officials built on increasingly positive connections they developed with the opposition pan-blue leaders and broader segments of Taiwan business elites and other Taiwan opinion leaders. [32]

In the end, Chen's maneuvers and their negative consequences for cross-strait and U.S.–Taiwan relations, along with the Taiwan president's deep personal involvement in corruption scandals, undermined DPP candidates in Taiwan legislative elections in January 2008 and the Taiwan presidential election in March 2008. The result was a landslide victory for KMT candidates. The party gained overwhelming control of the legislature; the new president, Ma Ying-jeou, had a strong political mandate to pursue policies of reassurance and moderation in cross-strait relations. [33]

THE MOMENTUM OF IMPROVING RELATIONS: 2008–2015

President Ma reassured China that his government would not move Taiwan toward independence and stressed closer economic, social, and other contacts across the strait. The cross-strait agenda now focused on building closer and mutually advantageous economic and social ties. The growing Chinese military buildup opposite Taiwan and reaching agreement on Taiwan's desired greater international participation were harder to deal with. [34]

On the whole, the improvements in cross-strait relations were rapid and impressive. The security situation in the Taiwan Strait relaxed. A major economic development was establishing a free-trade agreement in 2010 known as the Economic Cooperation Framework Agreement (ECFA), which provided privileged access to Chinese markets and other economic benefits for various important constituencies in Taiwan. [35]

There was no significant reduction of China's powerful military presence directly opposite Taiwan. President Ma also was reluctant to engage in talks with China on a possible peace agreement, and he argued that discussion on possible reunification between Taiwan and China would have to await developments after his term in office.

The numerous cross-strait agreements saw burgeoning face-to-face interaction between Taiwan and Chinese authorities after decades of no direct dealings. The agreements were between ostensibly unofficial organizations—Taiwan's Straits Exchange Foundation (SEF) and China's Association for Relations across the Taiwan Strait (ARATS). They required officials of the two governments to deal with each other on a host of transportation, food safety, financial regulation, and law enforcement issues. In effect, three channels of communication were now active between the Taiwan and Chinese authorities: the SEF–ARATS exchanges; exchanges between the leaders of the Chinese Communist Party (CCP) and Taiwan's KMT; and widening government-to-government coordination and cooperation on a variety of cross-strait issues. Many of the agreements, interactions, and understandings focused on managing the large-scale trade and investment between Taiwan and China.[36]

Meanwhile, the Ma Ying-jeou government achieved a breakthrough in getting China to allow Taiwan to participate in the annual World Health Assembly (WHA) meeting as an observer using the name "Chinese Taipei." Other evidence of progress in China–Taiwan relations over issues regarding Taiwan's participation in international affairs was the diminishment of what had been intense Taiwan–China competition for international recognition.[37]

The Bush administration welcomed the efforts of the Ma government and China's positive response as stabilizing and beneficial for all parties concerned. President Ma worked hard to keep his transit stops in the United States discreet in ways that would not complicate U.S. relations with China. High-level contacts occurred between the U.S. and Taiwan governments in quiet and private ways that avoided upsetting China, and U.S. military consultations with and advice to Taiwan's armed forces continued.[38]

The Bush administration delayed until close to the last minute approval of a large arms sales package for Taiwan. It was worth $6.5 billion. Initial generous U.S. arms sales' offers during Bush's first year in office were repeatedly delayed and whittled down because of partisan bickering and funding delays in Taiwan. Later, the U.S. government was reluctant to provide arms that would appear to support President Chen Shui-bian's perceived provocative stance toward China. The package in 2008 represented about half of what Taiwan wanted; it did not include sixty-six F-16 fighters that Taiwan had been requesting for years. China strongly criticized the sale and suspended for a year military contacts with the United States.[39]

The incoming Barack Obama government in the United States welcomed the new stability in cross-strait ties. Like the outgoing Bush government, the Obama administration relied on President Ma and his team to continue to manage cross-strait ties in positive ways that would not cause the Taiwan "hot spot" to reemerge.[40] The Obama government followed through with a $6 billion arms package for Taiwan in 2010. The package did not include F-16 fighters; it prompted sometimes strident public complaints along with limited substantive retaliation from China.[41] Later U.S. arms sales included another large arms package worth over $5 billion in 2011 that proposed significant upgrades in the capabilities of Taiwan's existing F-16 fighters.[42]

Status and Outlook

Leading into Ma Ying-jeou's second term (2012–2016), cross-strait moderation and growing engagement developed smoothly. The overall trend appeared advantageous for China as momentum in the direction of closer China–Taiwan ties continued along with the Ma government's repeated rejection of independence. China's military buildup seemed effective in dissuading Taiwan from disrupting existing trends. In effect, China intimidated Taiwan and thereby prevented moves toward greater separatism and independence. The military balance in the Taiwan Strait changed markedly in China's favor. In the face of China's buildup, the Ma government failed to follow through with earlier promises to sustain a comparatively low level of defense spending at 3 percent of GDP. China's buildup featured annual double-digit increases.[43]

Taiwan became ever more dependent on China economically. Hillary Clinton in June 2014 was the latest in a long list of non-U.S. government notables and specialists warning Taiwan that overdependence on China economically will make the island more vulnerable to unwanted Chinese pressures.[44] Taiwan's total trade with China grew from $31.3 billion in 2000 to $124.4 billion in 2013 (a 297 percent increase). The PRC is Taiwan's largest trading partner, its largest export market, and its second-largest source of imports. According to Taiwan's Mainland Affairs Council (MAC), the share of Taiwan's exports to China rose from 3.2 percent in 1985 to 28.5 percent in 2013 (this increases to 39.7 percent if exports to Hong Kong are included), while the share of its imports from China rose from 0.6 percent to 15.8 percent (16.4 percent if Hong Kong is included).Taiwan has enjoyed large annual merchandise trade surpluses with the mainland over the past several years; it was $39.2 billion in 2013, with Taiwan exports valued at $81.8 billion and imports at $42.6 billion.[45]

Taiwan is a major source of foreign direct investment (FDI) flows to the PRC, although the exact level remains unknown. According to the Taiwan Investment Commission, Taiwan's approved FDI flows to China grew from $2.6 billion in 2000 to $13.1 billion in 2011 but declined during the next two years (totaling $8.7 billion in 2013). The stock of Taiwan's approved FDI to China from 1991 to 2013 was $133.7 billion, 80 percent of which was in manufacturing. It is often claimed that the total level of Taiwan FDI in China could be as high as $300 billion. That's partly because Taiwan investors are believed to invest in China through Hong Kong entities in order to avoid scrutiny by Taiwan's government. More than 1 million Taiwanese people are estimated to be residing in the PRC, many involved with the more than 70,000 Taiwan companies operating there.[46]

Taiwan has endeavored to break out of the Chinese-imposed diplomatic isolation of Taiwan and has negotiated with Beijing in achieving some breakthroughs in international recognition and involvement. However, the scope of Taiwan's involvement appears carefully controlled by China, and Taipei seems unable to do much to change the situation on its own.[47]

As noted at the outset of this chapter, the popularity of President Ma and the ruling Nationalist Party has declined markedly. Anxiety is rising in Taiwan over the pace, scope, and direction of Taiwan's closer engagement with ever more dominating China. Against that background, DPP candidates scored a major victory in islandwide elections in November 2014 and seemed well positioned for the January 2016 presidential and legislative elections. In sum, political dynamics in Taiwan are changing determinants in the recent cross-strait progress and raise major questions about future trends.[48]

INCREASED AMERICAN SUPPORT FOR TAIWAN

Also noted at the start of the chapter is change in U.S. support for and approaches toward Taiwan. This section examines that topic in detail and discerns some implications.[49]

In response to the dramatic shift in Taiwan's approach to China under President Ma Ying-jeou, the U.S. government played down past emphasis on Taiwan's role in cooperation with the United States in sustaining a favorable military balance in the Taiwan Strait. Rather, it sought to support Ma's new approach of reassurance as an important means to sustain stability and peace. Despite the shifts toward greater criticism and competition in U.S. China policy since Ma's ascendance, recent Obama government policy toward Taiwan has proven to be more durable and consistent. The Obama government has sold a large amount of weapons to Taiwan but has avoided provoking Chinese ire with the sale of advanced fighter aircraft or submarines requested by Taiwan. China has viewed with suspicion the Obama government's rebalance in Asia policy highlighted since 2011, which involves enhanced engagement with allies, friends, and others, including the Chinese government, as a means to deepen American influence in the region in competition with China. The Obama government was careful to keep Taiwan outside of the scope of the rebalance in its initial explanations of the new policy, and later official U.S. references affirming Taiwan's role avoided specifics or actions that would raise China's ire over the very sensitive Taiwan issue in U.S.–China relations.[50]

American policymakers concerned with Taiwan repeatedly highlight the very good state of bilateral relations and the calm that prevails in cross-strait ties, a welcome comparison to the headaches for U.S. policy posed by active nearby hot spots in the East and South China Seas and North Korea. Signs of low U.S. tolerance for Taiwan actions that could disrupt cross-strait ties included U.S. officials warning against the Democratic Progressive Party candidate's China policy following U.S. official meetings with the candidate prior to the Taiwan election in 2012. This episode marked a rare American official intervention into a friendly democracy's electoral process.[51]

Specialists and media highlighted declines in U.S. support for Taiwan under the Obama government. The administration strongly disagreed, but it followed policies in the rebalance, in dealing with sales of sensitive weapons, and in reacting to the approach of the DPP presidential candidate, noted above, that underlined declining support for policy initiatives that would support Taiwan but risk upsetting China and come at a possibly significant cost for U.S. relations with China. By contrast, George W. Bush started his administration with a strong rebalancing against perceived Chinese assertiveness in Asia by placing Taiwan at the center of his approach, warning that he would do "whatever it takes" to help Taiwan defend itself against Chinese attack.[52]

Congress at times has been the source of strong support for Taiwan and pressure on the administration to do more for Taiwan. But the weak congressional signs of support of Taiwan in the first term of the Obama government were overshadowed by declining interest and opposition to Taiwan's wishes. Few members visited the island and those who did sometimes came away with views adverse to Taiwan's interests. After visiting Taiwan in August 2010, Senator Arlen Specter came out against irritating China by selling Taiwan the F-16 aircraft sought by President Ma.[53] Likewise, in a public hearing in June 2010, Senate Intelligence Committee Chairman Dianne Feinstein cast U.S. arms sales to Taiwan as a liability for U.S. foreign policy and pressed Secretary of Defense Robert Gates for options to resolve the impasse between the United States and China over the issue.[54]

The decline in congressional support also was influenced by the fracturing and decline of the Taiwan lobby in Washington. Reflecting the often intense competition in Taiwan politics between the Nationalist or Kuomintang (KMT) Party and the Democratic Progressive Party (DPP) in recent decades, DPP representatives in Washington and like-minded U.S. interest groups such as the Formosan Association for Public Affairs on one side, and KMT representatives in Washington and supporting interest groups on the other side, repeatedly clashed while lobbying congressional members. Ma Ying-jeou's appointment of the head of the KMT's Washington office, a veteran of these partisan squabbles with the DPP, as his choice to lead the Taiwan government's office in Washington saw the partisan divisions persist. An overall result was confusion on Capitol Hill and a decline in Taiwan's influence there.[55]

Against this background, several respected and prominent former officials and specialists called for an American pullback from continued support for Taiwan roughly consistent with the approach of Senator Feinstein and some others in Congress. Former vice chairman of the Joint Chiefs of Staff William Owens argued in November 2009 that because of the need for friendly ties with rising China, the United States should reassess the Taiwan Relations Act and curb American arms sales to Taiwan. Academic China specialist Bruce Gilley argued in January 2010 that Taiwan's détente with China should seek neutralization along the lines of Finland's position in the Cold War and that such neutralization should be supported by the United States; it would remove a major sore point in Sino-American relations. International relations scholar Charles Glaser said in March that the key to avoiding U.S. conflict with China was accommodating Beijing by withdrawing commitments to Taiwan. In January 2011, Joseph Prueher, former ambassador to China and former commander of the U.S. Pacific Command, hosted prominent business leaders and China specialists and produced a report that called for reevaluation of U.S. arms sales to Taiwan that were seen to create strongly negative implications for U.S. interests. In the largest and most thorough study of issues in U.S.–Chinese relations in many years, Carnegie Endowment for International Peace China specialist Michael Swaine warned in 2011 of the potentially disastrous consequences for the United States of its ongoing commitment to defend Taiwan against rising Chinese power.[56]

Since 2012 and 2013, rising American tensions with China over disputes in the East and South China Seas have been accompanied by an increase in congressional, nongovernment specialist, and media attention to Taiwan's role in proposed American plans for dealing with Chinese assertiveness. For its part, the Obama government is generally mum on Taiwan's role in this regard. U.S. government representatives now say that Taiwan is part of the rebalance but they avoid how this will assist in dealing with Chinese assertiveness. One reason for Obama government restraint presumably is that such discussion would heighten attention to the Taiwan issue in U.S.–China differences in Asia, causing more serious friction in U.S.–China relations than the Obama government judges as warranted under the circumstances. The Obama government, congressional representatives, and specialists are in agreement in complimenting the actions of the Ma Ying-jeou government—a major stakeholder in the contested claims—for generally adhering to peaceful means in dealing with differences and in reaching pragmatic understandings with Japan and the Philippines over fishing rights in disputed territories. They also appreciate Taiwan's criticism of China's abrupt declaration of an air defense identification zone over the disputed East China Sea islands in late 2013.[57]

Pushing against Obama government restraint has been an array of congressional representatives, specialists, and commentators arguing in favor of greater U.S. attention to Taiwan in this period of tension with China. Generally, the hardened views against China of these observers have crowded out the arguments of only a few years ago noted above for neutralizing Taiwan, accommodating Chinese demands over Taiwan, and withdrawing U.S. support for the island.

The push against Obama government restraint regarding Taiwan and China is intensified by the now common discourse in congressional deliberations and media commentary that the Obama government has been too timid in the face of challenges in such sensitive international areas as Ukraine, Syria, Iraq, Afghanistan, and elsewhere.[58] Few observers support U.S. combat operations to meet American objectives, and the critics probably recognize that the president's policies today are in line with public opinion polls showing war weariness in America. Nonetheless, the critics see the stakes in competition with China as long term and serious; they argue for stronger American actions that would show negative costs for China's interests if it pursues its so-called salami slicing in nearby disputed territories. They are prepared to risk some of the negative consequences for the United States that would flow for serious disruption of the existing relationship with China.

Against this background, Taiwan is involved in some proposed American actions to counter China as the United States moves from the positive engagement side of the policy spectrum to an approach that balances against and endeavors to deter Chinese expansionism. Strategists and specialists argue that to effectively deter expanding China requires credible American strategies to deal with confrontation with China. Taiwan often is at the center of such proposed strategies and is seen by some as "the cork in the bottle" if the United States needs to shore up radars, defenses, and other anti-China military preparations along the first island chain running from Japan through Taiwan to the Philippines.[59] National Defense University strategist T. X. Hammes has proposed a strategy that relies on close integration of land-based air and sea defenses involving Taiwan at the center that is designed to deal with a Chinese confrontation through conventional arms in ways that do not involve direct attack on the Chinese mainland.[60]

What exactly could be done in Taiwan to help to check Chinese power presumably would be in line with proposed and actual steps the Japanese government is taking in deploying forces to its south and west, especially along the Ryukyu Island chain, and using sensors, land-based and other antiship missiles, and sophisticated mines in plans to cut off or greatly impede Chinese passage beyond the so-called first island chain.[61] Seemingly along these lines, Congressman Randy Forbes, a leading advocate of strong U.S. defenses in Asia, has introduced legislative provisions that would consider the pros and cons of integrating Taiwan's sophisticated early warning radar with U.S. missile defense and sensor systems.[62]

A different path leading to greater U.S. attention to Taiwan came as a former leading Asian affairs official in the Obama government highlighted Taiwan's importance regarding the origins of the nine-dashed line that Chinese maps use to designate Chinese claims over most of the South China Sea.

Jeffrey Bader argued that as the creator of the dashed line in the 1940s, the Taiwan Republic of China (ROC) government should reevaluate its position in line with existing international law. The judgment was that if Taiwan did so, it would demonstrate the extremity and unreasonableness of China's current claim, pushing Beijing to do a similar reevaluation. Meanwhile, Taiwan's government controls the official archives that would show what exactly the ROC government intended when it proposed the dashed line claiming the South China Sea in the 1940s. A study and disclosure of perhaps more limited intent than Beijing's current claims also was seen to assist American efforts to get China to back away from its excessive claims and deal more reasonably and peacefully with other disputants.[63] Thus far, the Taiwan government has shown little interest in taking either of these steps, presumably because they risk friction in Taipei's relations with Beijing.

Taiwan also is involved in options raised in congressional deliberations and specialist commentaries on what the United States could do in order to raise the cost for China of its continued salami slicing in the nearby seas. According to this view, by raising the costs to China with these Taiwan-related options (as well as other options), the United States could show Beijing that its interests would be better served with a less aggressive approach in the East and South China Seas.[64] The Ma Ying-jeou government has reacted very warily to these suggestions, while the Obama government has ignored them.

They include using the sale of advanced jet fighters to Taiwan as a way to upset Chinese security calculus along its periphery in ways costly to China with the implicit understanding that more such disruptions of Chinese plans will come unless it ceases its assertiveness and expansion in the East and South China Seas. Another option is for American officials to speak out more forcefully in support of popular demonstrations such as those led by Taiwan's so-called sunflower movement. U.S. support for the freedom to speak out against feared Chinese dominance shown during the sunflower movement presumably would show the United States to be more open to a change in Taiwan's existing approach to China. Beijing is wrestling with how to deal with rising criticism in Taiwan of the Ma government's growing engagement with China. The above U.S. move would add to China's problems and presumably enhance the chances for the election of an opposition candidate in the presidential election in 2016—an outcome very costly and complicating for China's approach to Taiwan. Meanwhile, another U.S. option regarding Taiwan builds on the Obama government's strong recent criticism of China's use of coercion and intimidation of neighbors involved with disputes in the East China Sea and the South China Sea. The new U.S. government rhetoric raises the question of why the United States has not shown the same concern with long-standing Chinese military coercion and intimidation of Taiwan. Strong American statements against Chinese intimidation of Taiwan, if backed by substantive support, would seriously complicate China's plans for what Beijing sees as the resolution of the Taiwan issue—a major cost to the Chinese government.

The increased attention to Taiwan related to hardening U.S. policy toward China is reinforced by other factors increasing American focus on Taiwan. Thanks in part to stronger efforts by the Taiwan office in Washington and to the particular interest in Taiwan by committee chairs and ranking members in the House and Senate, the numbers of members of Congress visiting Taiwan and the stature of these members have increased.[65]

In 2012, a general election year when overseas congressional travel usually declines, there were fifteen representatives who visited Taiwan. The highlight was the visit of Representative Ileana Ros-Lehtinen (R-FL), then chairwoman of the House Committee on Foreign Affairs, who led a congressional delegation to Taiwan in May 2012, in celebration of President Ma's inauguration for his second term as president.

In 2013, there were four senators and eighteen representatives who visited Taiwan. Chairman Ed Royce (R-CA) of the House Committee on Foreign Affairs led a congressional delegation to Taiwan in January; Senator James Inhofe (R-OK), ranking member of the Committee on Armed Services, also came in January; and Chairman Robert Menendez (D-NJ) of the Senate Committee on Foreign Relations visited in August.

In January–August 2014, one senator and fourteen representatives visited Taiwan. Chairman Ron Wyden (D-OR) of the Senate Committee on Finance visited in August and Chairman Buck McKeon (R-CA) of the House Armed Services Committee led a congressional delegation in August.

Congress has continued to pass legislation and urge the U.S. administration in various ways to encourage Taiwan's democratization, to meet Taiwan's self-defense needs, and to assist with Taiwan's bid to participate in regional economic integration and international organizations, such as the World Health Assembly (WHA) and the International Civil Aviation Organization (ICAO). In 2013, both the Senate and the House of Representatives passed H.R. 1151, a bill supporting Taiwan's participation in the ICAO as an observer. The bill was signed into law with a supporting statement by President Obama in July 2013.[66]

In commemoration of the thirty-fifth anniversary of the enactment of the Taiwan Relations Act (TRA) the House of Representatives unanimously passed H.R. 3470 on April 7, 2014, reaffirming the American commitment to the TRA and Taiwan, and on April 9 over half of the U.S. Senate sent a joint letter to President Obama calling for expanded dialogue with Taiwan and continued support for Taiwan's democracy, freedom, and economic prosperity. The House Committee on Foreign Affairs held a hearing on March 14, entitled "The Promise of the Taiwan Relations Act," and subsequently the Subcommittee on East Asian and Pacific Affairs of the Senate Foreign Relations Committee held a hearing on April 3 entitled "Evaluating U.S. Policies on Taiwan on the 35th Anniversary of the Taiwan Relations Act (TRA)." Both hearings provided platforms for members of Congress and officials of the Obama administration to reiterate their support for strong Taiwan–U.S. relations.[67]

The convergence in congressional-administration support for Taiwan came with important differences, with congressional representatives pressing the government to strongly reaffirm the so-called six assurances of the Ronald Reagan administration that have long governed U.S. support for Taiwan and with congressional requirements for reports and closer administration monitoring of Taiwan's defense needs.[68] Meanwhile, the Senate Foreign Relations Committee captured the views of many supporters of Taiwan in Congress and elsewhere who see Taiwan's future closely tied to its economic connections and role in Asian and world affairs, arguing that Taiwan's joining the U.S.-backed Trans-Pacific Partnership (TPP) international economic agreement is an essential step securing Taiwan's overall strength and well-being. The committee's report, "Rebalancing the Rebalance," urged the Obama government to include Taiwan in the TPP.[69]

Interviews with close observers of Congress and Taiwan showed important personal and constituent reasons for the increased positive congressional attention to Taiwan.[70] Chairman Royce of the 113th Congress House Foreign Affairs Committee and Senate Foreign Relations Committee Chairman Menendez have important Taiwan-American constituencies in their respective district and state. Royce in particular has a long personal attachment to Taiwan. The chair of the House Foreign Affairs Committee Asia Subcommittee in the 114th Congress is Representative Matt Salmon, who served as a missionary in Taiwan in the late 1970s. The House committee also features such rising members as Representative Gerald Connelly, who is cochair of the congressional Taiwan caucus. Congressional observers note Connelly's familiarity with conditions in Taiwan based on past involvement in and visits to Taiwan prior to becoming a member of Congress.

Of course, congressional deliberations also reflect perceived shortcomings and criticism of Taiwan's policies and practices. Senator John Coryn, a strong supporter of U.S. arms sales to Taiwan, expressed public frustration in February 2013 with Taiwan's seemingly halfhearted efforts to persuade the United States to sell advanced fighter jets to Taiwan.[71] A staff member supporting House Armed Services subcommittee chair Representative Randy Forbes told an audience in Washington in April that year that Taiwan had "slipped off the congressional agenda."[72] A strong supporter of Taiwan, American Enterprise Institute specialist Dan Blumenthal in February 2014 wrote about the prevailing fatalism in American opinion about Taiwan and the perceived weak American commitment to protect the island from Chinese coercion.[73] At that time, international relations scholar John Mearsheimer caused some controversy when he assessed cross-strait trends and advised America to "say goodbye to Taiwan."[74]

Assessing Recent American Attention to Taiwan

Although pragmatism has seen American and Chinese leaders in the twenty-first century strive to manage their many and long-standing differences in ways that do not seriously disrupt bilateral relations, those differences persist, and with them continues an inability to create a lasting framework for cooperation. Against that background, expect more erratic shifts along a spectrum of close engagement on one side and serious balancing on the other.

For now, U.S. tensions with China along the periphery of China are growing; with them comes greater American attention to Taiwan. The attention may be motivated by sincere American interest in Taiwan; it also may be motivated by America's search for options that will prove costly to China and can be used or be proposed for use in order to pressure China to halt its behavior in the East and South China Seas that is against U.S. interests. I argue here that the attention to these options is enhanced by prevailing discourse in congressional, media, and other foreign policy deliberations that the Obama government has been weak in the face of a long list of recent foreign policy challenges.

Thus far, the role of Taiwan in the hardening of American policy toward China has not had a major effect on Obama government policy on the so-called Taiwan issue. The U.S. administration seems determined to treat Taiwan matters in ways that do not undermine the pattern that has been established since Ma Ying-jeou's presidency, which serves to reassure China and avoid bringing the Taiwan issue to the top of the American policy agenda with China once again. Disrupting or destroying this pattern would cause major problems for U.S. policymakers dealing with China on a day-to-day basis. It also could signal the kind of rupture in Sino-American relations that most U.S. friends in Asia seek to avoid. Those countries support the Obama rebalance, but their support is premised on continued U.S. efforts to engage constructively with China.[75] A Sino-American blow-up over Taiwan could preclude such interchange with China for a long time, and in the process it could undermine much of Asian support for the Obama rebalance policy.

Against that background, for options dealing with Taiwan discussed above to become operational may require domestic American pressure. As noted earlier, some in Congress and a number of specialists and commentators are active in advocating for various options regarding Taiwan. However, there are major countervailing pressures that offset support for substantial deviation from the Obama government's existing policy toward Taiwan.

1. American concern with China's expansion in nearby disputed territory is lower in public and congressional priority than the problems in Ukraine, Syria, Iraq, Afghanistan, Iran, and the Israeli-Palestine dispute. Those who pay attention to the Chinese actions often show serious concern, but relatively few pay attention, and thus the pressure for new U.S. options involving Taiwan is reduced.

2. The options proposed for American actions to deter China risk confrontation with China that is not supported by American public opinion. And Congress today is not the assertive Congress that advanced control of foreign policy in the post–Vietnam War period, notably producing the Taiwan Relations Act. Congress has reverted to a deferential posture in foreign affairs. Specialist James Lindsay argues that in recent circumstances, Congress will press for foreign policy change when two conditions are met: (1) the president's policy seems to be failing—a case can be made that the Obama policies have failed to stop Chinese expansion; and (2) there is no danger for important American interests in adopting the policy changes urged by Congress—China's power and determination show that the proposed policy changes could risk serious negative consequences for U.S. interests.[76]

3. Taiwan's willingness and ability to respond effectively to increased American attention remains questionable and seems to continue to erode. Taiwan remains ever weaker in the face of China's military buildup; it becomes ever more dependent economically on China, and its diplomatic room for maneuver is regulated by China with a firm hand. Thus, Taiwan remains on the track toward ever closer ties with China, making it increasingly difficult for the island government to reverse course in conjunction with initiatives proposed by Americans outside the administration designed to compete with and deter China.[77]

In sum, the forces and advocates prompting more American attention to Taiwan are growing, but the proposed options seem to face firm opposition by the Obama government and they enjoy limited support in Washington and Taipei. If concern over Chinese expansion continues to grow in the United States, the pressure for greater American involvement with Taiwan along the lines of options discussed above will increase. The controversy may attract the attention of U.S. presidential candidates and other candidates for office, foreshadowing a possible substantial change under a new U.S. government in 2017 with the kinds of interest in Taiwan discussed in this book. The importance of this change on the United States would be enhanced if the DPP wins the January 2016 presidential election in Taiwan.

Chapter Eight

Relations with Japan and Korea

Among China's neighbors in Asia, Chinese leaders gave highest priority to relations with the governments of northeastern Asia: Japan, North Korea, and South Korea. The reasons included the strategic location of these nations close to the economic centers of China's modernization; their economic, political, and military power and importance to China; and their close involvement with the United States. The record of Chinese foreign relations in this area in the post–Cold War period was very mixed. Recent Chinese relations with Japan and North Korea were the worst during the entire history of the PRC.

Coming to power amid enormous Chinese demonstrations and nationalistic outrage against Japan's purchase of disputed Senkaku (Diaoyu) Islands in 2012, the Xi Jinping government for two years pursued a confrontational posture over territorial disputes reflecting the higher priority Beijing gave to advancing its claims in the East China Sea and South China Sea. Strident official statements and commentary repeatedly attacked and sought to demonize Japanese Prime Minister Shinzo Abe (2012–) who had Japanese forces stand against Chinese intrusions in the Japanese-controlled islands. Trade and investment dropped sharply. Japan did not buckle under Chinese pressure. It became China's main international opponent as it built defenses at home, maneuvered for advantage in Asia, and sought and received strong backing from an Obama government increasingly concerned with Chinese assertiveness and expansion. The adverse circumstances and poorly considered aspects of the Xi Jinping government's activist Japan policy saw China bend despite its image of strength and resolve in pursuing nationalistic goals. The Chinese leader met with Prime Minister Abe in November 2014 and began a process of limited but growing mutual accommodation amid continuing strong differences. [1]

Chinese leaders showed more skill in managing very difficult and often contradictory imperatives coming from North and South Korea, at least until recently. They endeavored to sustain China's position in Pyongyang and markedly advance China's relations with Seoul. China's priority interest in stability on the peninsula was seriously challenged by North Korea's missile and nuclear weapons development, provocative military attacks against South Korea, and the uncertain leadership succession from North Korean dictator Kim Jong Il (d. 2011) to his inexperienced son Kim Jong Un. China at times joined the consensus of concerned powers in applying some sanctions on Pyongyang, but its response to North Korea's repeated provocations avoided pressure that would risk North Korean backlash endangering stability on the peninsula and in nearby China.[2]

RELATIONS WITH JAPAN

The future stability of eastern Asia will depend heavily on the relationship between the main regional powers, China and Japan. Unfortunately, China's relations with Japan were as erratic and crisis prone as China's relations with the United States in the post–Cold War period. At first, both Asian powers adjusted their bilateral relations amicably following the demise of the Soviet Union and its strategic influence in eastern Asia. The rise of China's power and influence in Asian affairs in the 1990s, combined with Chinese military assertiveness over Taiwan and the South China Sea in the mid-1990s, coincided with a protracted period of lackluster Japanese economic performance and weak political leadership. This called into question the past disparity of the economic relationship between the two powers; added to ongoing differences over territorial, strategic, historical, and economic issues; and strengthened the wariness and occasional antipathy between the two countries.[3]

Subsequently, Chinese relations with Japan worsened, especially over historical and territorial issues. Chinese concerns with Japan's defense posture, including its notably strengthened alliance relationship with the United States, added to this trend in declining relations. Tensions in China's relations with Japan undermined Chinese influence in Japan. China's broader strategy in Asia in the first decade of the twenty-first century was based on a good-neighbor policy—with China seeking to enhance its influence by dealing with Asian countries in an accommodating way, putting aside differences, and seeking greater areas of common ground. The disputes with Japan complicated that strategy.[4]

Chinese strong objections over Japan's treatment of historical issues sensitive to China and others in Asia and repeated visits by Japanese Prime Minister Junichiro Koizumi (2001–2006) to the controversial Yasukuni war memorial succeeded in putting the Japanese government on the defensive.

Nonetheless, the harshly critical treatment of China's most important neighbor also seemed to belie Chinese broader declarations of goodwill, accommodation, and "win-win" solutions. It prompted Japan, possessing great wealth and Asia's most modern military force, to prepare for protracted difficulties and rivalry with China in Asia while adding to broader regional wariness over Chinese intentions.[5]

The George W. Bush administration worked assiduously to strengthen the U.S alliance with Japan and found a willing and effective partner in the Japanese administration of Prime Minister Koizumi. Both sides played down persisting trade and other disputes as the bilateral relationship reached new heights of strategic and political cooperation.[6] The alliance remained strong after Koizumi's departure, though later Liberal Democratic Party (LDP) governments (2006–2009) were short lived, politically weak, and less effective in developing their avowed goals of close alignment with the United States.[7]

Chinese–Japanese political and security relations deteriorated markedly despite burgeoning trade and large Japanese investment in China. Disputes ranged widely and involved competing and highly nationalistic views of Japan's military expansion in Asia prior to 1945, territorial and resource conflicts in the East China Sea, rising Japanese concerns over China's military buildup focused on Taiwan and Chinese concerns about Japan's closer cooperation with the United States regarding Taiwan, Chinese concerns over Japan's closer military cooperation with the United States over ballistic missile defense and in regard to international deployments of Japanese forces, Sino-Japanese competition for Russian and other energy resources, and Chinese opposition to Japan's efforts to obtain a permanent seat on the UN Security Council.[8]

The Democratic Justice Party (DJP) of Japan won the general election in 2009 and deposed the long-ruling and more conservative Liberal Democratic Party. Its pro-China gestures came to naught amid repeated disputes, particularly over salient territorial and trade issues. Anti-Japanese demonstrations took place in China, and public opinion of China in Japan reached new lows.[9]

Underlying the deterioration of relations was a continuing change in regional power relationships. China's rising power and influence in Asian affairs since the 1990s, combined with Chinese military buildup and assertiveness focused on Taiwan and territorial issues around its periphery, coincided with Japan enduring a second decade of poor economic performance. As China loomed larger as Asia's leader in economic growth, Japan responded with deepening concern over its place in Asian and world affairs. This added to ongoing differences over territorial, strategic, historical, and economic issues and strengthened the suspicion between the two countries. Meanwhile, stronger nationalism in both countries put them at odds over a variety of sensitive issues related to history and territorial claims.[10] Notable in this regard was Chinese concern over deepening U.S.–Japanese alliance relations seen directed at rising China.[11]

Salient Trends and Key Determinants in Sino-Japanese Relations

This sharp downturn in Sino-Japanese relations prompted debate among specialists about the determinants and direction of Sino-Japanese relations. Some experts predicted an increasingly intense competition, including likely confrontation and possible conflict in future Sino-Japanese relations.[12] They highlighted changes in attitudes of Japanese and Chinese decision makers, opinion leaders, and popular opinion about the status and outlook of their mutual relations. They tended to see initiatives reflecting strong Sino-Japanese friction and rivalry.[13] Signs of Sino-Japanese competition and rivalry included the following:

- Separate and seemingly competing proposals by China and Japan to establish free trade arrangements with the ten Southeast Asian nations in the Association of Southeast Asian Nations (ASEAN) and other signs of competition for leadership in Asian regional organizations, notably the Sino-Japanese struggle for influence in the lead-up to the East Asian Summit of December 2005
- Intensifying competition for control of energy and other resources and disputed territory in the East China Sea
- Active Chinese international lobbying against high-priority Japanese efforts in 2005–2006 to gain a permanent seat on the UN Security Council[14]
- Strong Japanese competition with China to gain improved access to Russian oil in the Far East
- Greater Japanese support for Taiwan at a time of stronger U.S. backing of Taiwan during the Bush administration[15]
- The first significant cutbacks in Japanese aid to China since the normalization of relations in the 1970s
- Increased Japanese willingness to deploy military forces in Asia in support of U.S. and UN initiatives
- Stepped-up Japanese efforts to improve security, aid, and/or other relations with Australia, India, and other nations on China's southern and western flanks, including strong Japanese aid efforts for Pakistan, Afghanistan, and central Asian countries[16]
- Increased Japanese efforts to solidify relations with South Korea and the United States to form a closer Japan–South Korea–U.S. alignment in reaction to China's refusal to condemn repeated North Korean aggression against South Korea in 2010 and related Chinese truculence over its territorial claims in the Yellow Sea[17]

Underlying changes in Japan said to foreshadow greater Japanese–Chinese rivalry involved the following:

- A focus by strategic thinkers in the Japanese government and elsewhere in Japan on China's rising power as the major long-term security concern for Japan after the collapse of the Soviet Union and the end of the Cold War.
- An increasing view by the Japanese of China as a rival for regional influence, due to China's continued remarkable economic growth, rising political and military standing, and periodic assertiveness against Japan.
- A lessening of Japanese sensitivity and responsiveness to Chinese demands for special consideration on account of Japan's negative war record in China seventy years ago. These changes were due to the passage of time, the change in Japanese leadership generations, and Beijing's loss of moral standing in Japan due to its crackdown after the Tiananmen incident, its nuclear testing in the 1990s, and its intimidating military actions against Taiwan and in the East China Sea and the South China Sea. [18]
- A strong sense of national pride and determination among Japanese leaders and the public to preserve Japanese interests in the face of perceived efforts by officials in the People's Republic of China (PRC) to use charges from the past and recent economic, political, and strategic issues to prompt Tokyo to give way to Chinese interests.

Meanwhile, changes in China said to be leading to greater friction with Japan included the following:

- Chinese strategists' long-standing concerns about Japan's impressive military capabilities, which increased as a result of U.S.–Japanese agreements from 1996 on and which to Chinese observers appeared to broaden Japan's strategic role in eastern Asia and provide U.S. strategic support for Japanese politicians wishing to strike a military posture in the region less deferential to China than in the past. [19]
- Chinese concerns about stronger Japanese strategic support for the United States seen in Japanese deployments of military forces to the Indian Ocean and Iraq early in the past decade and in more recent Japanese emphasis on collective self-defense allowing for greater scope of Japanese military actions in support of their American ally discussed below.
- Chinese government specialists' acknowledgment of changes in Japanese attitudes toward China and the judgment that Beijing appeared likely to meet even more opposition and gain less support from Japan. The Japanese decisions to cut aid to China seemed consistent with this trend.
- Chinese nationalism became a focal point of government-sponsored media and other publicity in recent years, especially following the Tiananmen incident and the collapse of communism in Europe and the Soviet Union

at the end of the Cold War. Appealing to the sense of China as having been victimized by foreign aggressors in the past, the publicity focused heavily on Japan, by far the most important foreign aggressor in modern Chinese history. Government-sponsored publicity elicited widespread positive response in China and soured the overall atmosphere of China's relations with Japan.[20]

A contrasting perspective—which I favored in the past but have been forced to modify in the face of the acute recent tensions in Sino-Japanese relations—gave greater weight to the common interests and forces that continue to bind Sino-Japanese relations and to limit the chances of serious confrontation or conflict. Mutual interests centered on strong, growing economic and strategic interdependence between Japan and China and the influence of the United States and other third parties, including other national powers in Asia—all of whom favored and appeared ready to work to preserve Sino-Japanese stability. The argument against the development of serious Sino-Japanese confrontation involved the following elements:

• Both the Japanese and the Chinese governments remained domestically focused and continued to give high priority to the economic development of their countries, which seemed to require peaceful and cooperative relationships with Asian neighbors, notably with each other.
• China valued Japan for foreign investment and technology and as a market for Chinese goods; Japan was increasingly dependent on China as a market, source of imports, and offshore manufacturing base.
• Personnel exchanges between Japan and China grew markedly. Each year, tens of thousands of Japanese and Chinese students visited or studied in China and Japan. Government-sponsored exchange programs fostered interchange, and even if they did not always promote positive feelings, they probably promoted more realistic mutual perceptions. Tourist flows grew dramatically.
• Few if any governments active in Asian affairs benefited from or sought to promote greater Sino-Japanese friction. This included the United States. Even the Bush administration was careful to balance its initially strong pro-Japanese slant with reaffirmation of continued interest in closer mutually beneficial relations with China.

The recent deterioration in China's relations with Japan discussed below shows that despite the above mitigating factors, strong rivalry and repeated confrontation prevail. The above factors appear sufficient to prevent war, but the Xi Jinping government's active foreign policy assertiveness, strident nationalism, and revanchist territorial claims have focused strongly on an uncompromising Japan. This mix has driven Sino-Japanese relations to their worst state since 1945.

Post–Cold War Relations

A period of several years after the Tiananmen incident was widely acknowledged as the most positive and cooperative period in China–Japan relations since the Pacific War. Japan's initial response to the incident was muted. Tokyo went along with Group of Seven (G7) sanctions against China. In July 1990, however, Tokyo diverged from the rest of the G7 to announce a resumption of lending to China. The Chinese government strongly supported the Japanese move, which ushered in a three-year period of cooperation and cordiality.[21]

A visit to China by Prime Minister Toshiki Kaifu in 1991 confirmed that Tiananmen was no longer an obstacle to a cordial relationship. The change in Japanese policy coincided with a surge in Japanese investment in China. Many Japanese business leaders judged that Chinese authorities had shown themselves to be capable of maintaining stability, and this and later rapid Chinese economic growth encouraged Japanese investment. In a notable departure from past Japanese practice emphasizing the primacy of relations with the United States and the U.S.–Japan alliance, Japanese Prime Minister Morihiro Hosokawa declared in late 1991 that Japan's relationship with China was as important as its relationship with the United States. A successful visit to China by the Japanese emperor in 1992 indicated just how far the two sides were willing to go in order to put the past behind them, at least for the time being. More forthright expressions of regret by Japanese leaders, including Hosokawa in 1993 for past Japanese aggression against China, also were appreciated by the Chinese. Economic relations developed rapidly, with China becoming Japan's second-largest destination for direct foreign investment after the United States. Official dialogues and intergovernmental cooperation expanded, including cooperation in military and security matters.[22]

In 1995, several difficult political and security issues surfaced. China's nuclear testing program drew strong protests from Japan, which was followed by the freezing of a small part of Japan's large aid program in China. Beijing responded by reminding Japan again of its record of aggression in China. The fiftieth anniversary of the end of the Pacific War was used in China as an opportunity for extensive media examination of Japan's military past.[23]

In November 1995, the presidents of China and South Korea held a joint press conference in Seoul in which they criticized Japan's alleged failure to address adequately its history of aggression.[24] Meanwhile, the Chinese military exercises designed to intimidate Taiwan in 1995 and 1996 alarmed many officials and opinion leaders in Japan and increased Japan's wariness of PRC ambitions in the region.[25] The broad trends in relations since the mid-1990s featured serious differences over historical, territorial, diplomatic, and security issues, even though economic ties and interdependence continued to advance.

China–Japan Differences

Strategic Issues

During the later years of the Cold War, Japan and China were preoccupied with the military dangers posed by the Soviet Union. This common threat helped reduce the salience of security and other strategic differences between the two powers. Thus, though Chinese elite and popular opinion often showed angst over alleged Japanese militarism, Chinese leaders generally supported Japan's military efforts to offset Soviet power in eastern Asia. Beijing also generally supported a strong U.S.–Japan security relationship aimed at countering the Soviet Union; China sometimes characterized this as part of an international "antihegemony front" directed at Moscow. Japanese leaders for their part soft-pedaled reservations they had over China's missile developments, nuclear weapons programs, and other defense preparations that were targeted against the Soviet Union but had implications for Japan's security.[26]

The collapse of the Soviet Union lowered the tide of Sino-Japanese strategic cooperation, exposing the rocks of security and strategic differences. The end of the Cold War and collapse of the Soviet Union dismantled the Cold War strategic framework for eastern Asia, removed Japan's number one security threat, and took away the initial rationale for Japan's post–World War II geostrategic bargain with the United States.

Japanese leaders came to view the strategic situation in eastern Asia as more unsettled than during the Cold War, with a number of near-term flash points, notably North Korea and Taiwan, and longer-term uncertainties, many centered on China.[27] Japanese concerns regarding a possible North Korean attack on Japan and possible negative implications of unification of the Korean peninsula both involved China in indirect but important ways. More significant was Taiwan. An outbreak of hostilities in the Taiwan Strait involving U.S. forces would draw Japan in under the U.S.-Japan Defense Treaty and U.S.-Japan Defense Guidelines. The extent and role of Japanese involvement in a China–Taiwan–U.S. military conflict would require difficult decisions of Japan as it weighed the need to support its ally against the costs such actions would entail for its future relationship with China.[28] The direction that U.S. security policy would take remained a key question for Japan.[29] Until the 1990s, Japanese policymakers were confident that the United States needed Japan and that the alliance was just as critical for

Washington's security strategy as it was for Tokyo's.[30] This confidence waned during the Clinton administration, with Japan unsure of its value to the United States, while China's importance for the United States seemed to rise.[31]

In thinking about China as a concern for Japanese policy, Japanese strategists for several years gave primacy to worries about possible social instability and political paralysis in China in the immediate aftermath of the Tiananmen crackdown in China and the collapse of the Soviet empire. Beijing's subsequent rapid economic growth, continued political stability, and more assertive military and foreign policies shifted Japanese concerns more toward dealing with the multifaceted consequences of the rise of a power of China's size. In particular, Japanese officials and other strategists became more concerned with Beijing's nuclear weapons testing and development; increased airpower and naval power abilities; and periodic assertions, backed by military force, concerning sovereignty and territorial disputes with Taiwan and other neighbors, including Japan. Incidents included Japanese discovery of a Chinese submarine attempting to secretly penetrate Japanese territorial waters and repeated episodes of Chinese military survey ships endeavoring to map waters near Japan.[32]

In China, concern focused on Japan's cooperation with the United States in strengthening the U.S.–Japan alliance. Those Chinese commentators and officials who in the 1990s and later saw the United States as determined to hold back or contain China's rising influence in eastern Asia suggested that the United States was using the alliance with Japan toward this end. They charged that Japan was a willing accomplice because Tokyo feared that China's rising influence would come at its expense.[33]

The closer U.S.–Japan security cooperation during the George W. Bush–Koizumi administrations saw a number of developments of particular concern to Chinese officials. One was a more active U.S.–Japanese dialogue over the situation in the Taiwan Strait. Another was the emergence of a formal U.S.–Japan–Australian strategic dialogue—establishing a broader web of U.S.-led alliance relationships in Asia that excluded China. Third were the Japanese military deployments in the Indian Ocean and other military measures to support the U.S.-led wars in Afghanistan and Iraq, which raised concerns in some quarters in China about the implications of strengthened U.S.–Japanese military cooperation in areas around China's periphery. Subsequently, the strengthening of the Obama administration's support for Japan and other Asia-Pacific allies and associates, alarmed by assertive China's positions over maritime territorial disputes, was criticized in China as efforts to impede China's rise and "contain" China.[34]

History Issues

Japan's aggression against China in the seventy years prior to Japan's defeat in World War II remained a potent issue in mainland China.[35] The concerns of Chinese strategists and opinion leaders, as well as broader Chinese public opinion, about a possible revival of Japanese military expansion or more general Japanese untrustworthiness were strong. This was partly because Japanese aggression against China was far more severe than that of any other power and the fact that Chinese government–supported media and other outlets repeatedly used accusations of Japanese militarism as a way to build nationalistic feeling in China, to put the Japanese government on the defensive, and to elicit concessions from the Japanese government in the form of aid, trading terms, or other benefits. As China loomed larger and more influential in Asian and world affairs at the start of the twenty-first century, Chinese officials and opinion leaders tended to see the military threat from Japan posed less by Japan taking independent action and more by Japan's ever closer defense cooperation with the United States and possibly closer ties with Taiwan.

For their part, Japanese officials sometimes exacerbated bilateral difficulties by denying the facts of history or equivocating on Japan's aggression against China up to the end of World War II. While many in Japan felt genuine regret about the war, repeated reminders from China seemed particularly self-serving and undermined positive feelings toward the PRC regime, which had already lost considerable support in Japan because of its human rights record, weapons proliferation, and assertive nationalistic policies in the post–Cold War period. Meanwhile, some Japanese commentators reflected much broader suspicions of elite and public opinion when they speculated that Beijing strove to use its rising economic, political, and military influence to exert a dominant influence in eastern Asia, placing Japan in a subservient position similar to the one that it held in the historical order in eastern Asia throughout most of the 2,000-year history of the Chinese Empire.[36]

Territorial Issues

Sino-Japanese tensions over territorial disputes involved islets in the East China Sea and claims to East China Sea resources, notably natural gas. Eight islets known as the Diaoyu Islands (in Chinese) or the Senkaku Islands (in Japanese) were uninhabited, but they occupied an important strategic location, and the region around them was considered highly prospective for gas and oil resources. The roots of the dispute went back to the nineteenth century. Japan had defeated China in a war and taken control of Taiwan in 1895. Following Japan's defeat in World War II, Taiwan was returned to China, but the uninhabited Senkaku (Diaoyu) Islands located north of Taiwan remained under U.S. control. Japan's claim to the islets appeared strengthened when the United States returned them to Tokyo's control along with nearby Okinawa in 1971. Subsequently, the U.S. government endeavored to keep from taking sides in the dispute.

In the 1970s, Tokyo and Beijing agreed to put the disputed islets issue aside as they normalized diplomatic relations and signed a peace treaty addressing issues stemming from World War II. Japanese rightists built a makeshift lighthouse on one of the islets in 1978. The Japanese coast guard patrolled near the islets and fended off efforts by fishermen and others from Taiwan, Hong Kong, and elsewhere to assert claims to the islets. In February 1992, Beijing passed a law reaffirming China's territorial claims to the islets. The Japanese government promptly protested Beijing's sovereignty law, while it also subsequently reasserted its claim to the islets.[37] Renewed activities by Japanese rightists on the islets in mid-1996 precipitated a period of Sino-Japanese tension over competing territorial claims.

Subsequently, periodic tensions involving fishing and other intrusions, surveillance by government ships and aircraft, and diplomatic protests alternated with times of relaxation of tensions. A spike in Chinese–Japanese friction coincided with assertive Chinese territorial claims, sometimes backed by military patrols, around its periphery in 2009–2010. Japan's arrest in September 2010 of a Chinese fishing boat captain whose ship was videotaped ramming Japanese coast guard vessels near the Senkaku (Diaoyu) Islands precipitated a standoff between the two governments that went on for two weeks, until Japan gave in to Chinese pressure and released the captain. Meanwhile, amid intensifying competition among China, Japan, and other major consumers for international energy resources in recent years, Japan sharply disputed China's actions, beginning in 2004, involving taking natural gas from East China Sea areas that Japan also claimed. Japanese officials also disputed China's challenge of the scope of the Japanese exclusive economic zone east of the main islands of Japan.[38]

Economic Issues

Economic relations between the two countries were troubled on several occasions despite Japan's status as one of China's leading trading partners, source of economic assistance, and source of direct foreign investment. China's economic vibrancy after the Cold War also led Japanese manufacturers and other businesses to highly value China as a platform for production destined for Japanese and foreign markets and as an economic market of large potential for Japanese goods and services. China sometimes resisted perceived inequities in the bilateral economic relationship. Alleged efforts by Japanese government–backed companies to dominate key sectors of China's market were an important focal point for anti-Japanese demonstrations in Chinese cities in the mid-1980s.[39]

More recent developments reflected a shift in the bilateral economic relationship, as China became a more important partner for Japan than Japan was for China and as China continued rapid growth while Japan had little growth. In this context, Japan altered the level and scope of its aid program in China to focus on areas that offered less challenge to Japanese industry and were more compatible with other Japanese interests (for example, the environment). Japan moved gradually to phase out the aid program. In addition, Tokyo did not budge in the face of Chinese complaints in the 1990s that the combination of the requirement that they repay Japanese loans in yen and the large rise in the value of the yen in relation to the U.S. dollar and China's currency over the previous decade put a heavy additional burden on China's economic development. Meanwhile, Japanese companies remained reluctant to share their most advanced technology with China, fearing that the technology would be used to compete with Japanese producers. China's restrictions on so-called rare earth exports to Japan, which were very important to Japanese manufacturers, came during a period of tense relations over territorial issues in 2010. The Chinese action alarmed Japanese leaders that the Chinese government would use growing Japanese economic dependence on China to compel Japanese subservience to China.[40]

Goods produced in China (often by Japanese companies) for Japanese consumers posed serious competition for the producers of similar products in Japan. Japanese opinion leaders and the public often showed alarm over the "hollowing out" of Japanese industries, farms, and enterprises that were no longer able to compete with China-based producers. Some favored protectionist trade measures against China, though such measures were inconsistent with the international trade regimes supported by the Japanese government and business leaders, who continued to work more closely with China in order to achieve the advantages of economic scale needed to keep Japanese firms competitive in the international economy.[41]

Domestic Politics

The domestic politics of China and Japan manifested trends of growing national assertiveness and pride that spread throughout eastern Asia in the post–Cold War period.[42] Government-sponsored nationalism in China coincided with rising nationalistic sentiment in Japan, notably over territorial disputes, trade issues, and prominence in the United Nations and international organizations. As a result, compromise on sensitive issues in Japan–China relations became more difficult.[43]

Mutual Interests in Japan–China Relations

The Japanese and the Chinese economies were becoming increasingly interdependent. Japan was China's top trading partner from 1993 to 2002. China became even more important for Japan as it surpassed the United States in 2008 to become the largest market for Japan's exports. Japan–China trade was valued at $302 billion in 2010. Trade declined by 8 percent amid high tensions and mass anti-Japanese demonstrations over territorial disputes in 2012 and declined another 8 percent in 2013.[44] Regarding foreign investment in China, Japan was in the top ranks along with the United States. Japanese companies' investments were valued at $7.68 billion in China in 2010; China was the second-largest investment destination for Japanese firms after the United States. Sharp declines followed beginning in 2012; in 2014 the value of Japanese investment in China was $4.33 billion. Japan's aid had been the most important in China a decade ago, but it declined in importance in recent years.[45]

Personal exchanges between Japan and China grew. Following the inauguration of the post-Mao reforms, hundreds of thousands of Chinese students traveled and studied in Japan. Japanese students visiting or studying in China numbered 20,000 in the mid-1990s. The number of Japanese students in China in 2004 was over 19,000. The number declined after the mass demonstrations of 2012. There were 21,000 Japanese students studying in China in 2012 and the number dropped to 14,000 in 2014. Numerous exchange programs—many fostered by the governments—worked to build mutual understanding and improve relations.[46]

Other governments tended to disapprove of Sino-Japanese friction. The United States sought regional stability, strong relations with Japan, and improved relations with China. Russia favored regional stability as it improved its relations with China while its relations with Japan remained complicated by territorial disputes in particular. ASEAN sought to reduce tensions and build mutual trust through dialogue among ASEAN, Chinese, Japanese, and other leaders. It cooperated closely with various economic and other initiatives in the ASEAN Plus Three (ASEAN plus Japan, China, and South Korea) framework.[47] Whatever interest there was in Taiwan in trying to side with Japan against China declined markedly as President Ma Ying-jeou gave top priority to constructive engagement with China.[48]

South Korean leaders sometimes lined up with Beijing to criticize Japan. Privately, South Korean officials also showed some interest in using improved relations with China to balance South Korea's strong dependence on the United States and Japan for security and economic-technological support, respectively. However, a serious increase of PRC–Japan tensions was seen to complicate the regional military and economic stability important to South Korea's development. South Korea's president Kim Dae Jung (1998–2003) reached some rapport with Japanese leaders during summit meetings in the late 1990s and early 2000s. President Roh Moo-Hyun (2003–2008) was more outspoken against Japan, notably voicing strong opposition, along with China, to visits of the Japanese prime minister to the controversial Yasukuni war memorial. President Lee Myung-bak (2008–2013) endeavored for several years to improve relations with Japan and avoided moves toward China adverse to Japanese interests. However, Lee at the end of his term became sharply critical of Japan's claims to the South Korean–controlled islet Dokdo (known as Takeshima in Japan). His successor Park Geun-hye strongly opposed Prime Minister Abe's visit to the Yasukuni Shrine and his statements seen to soft-pedal Japan's historical oppression of Korea.[49] Meanwhile, it was hard to see what benefit North Korea would get from rising Japan–China tensions.[50]

Recent Developments

The Asian economic crisis of 1997–1998 added to the already strong preoccupation of leaders in Tokyo and Beijing with their respective domestic problems, especially economic problems. At least for the time being, neither government sought to exacerbate tensions over the array of issues that continued to divide them. Thus, they went ahead with senior leaders' meetings in Tokyo and Beijing, capped by President Jiang Zemin's November 1998 visit to Japan. That visit saw Japanese officials stand firm in the face of Chinese pressure on issues related to Taiwan and the history of China–Japan relations. Chinese leaders adjusted their approach, as leaders in both capitals endeavored to emphasize the positive and give less public attention to important and often deeply rooted differences that remained unresolved.[51]

While he emphasized Sino-Japanese economic and other compatible interests, Japanese Prime Minister Koizumi tested Chinese tolerance on the sensitive history issue with his repeated visits to the Yasukuni Shrine. After his third visit despite Chinese admonitions, Chinese officials made it known in 2003 that the Japanese prime minister would not be welcome in Beijing, but they were flexible in arranging a meeting between the Japanese prime minister and China's recently installed President Hu Jintao at the sidelines of an international summit in Europe in mid-2003. In 2004 and 2005, there were several subsequent meetings between Koizumi and top Chinese government leaders, but none in Beijing. By late 2005, however, senior Chinese leaders seemed unwilling to meet the Japanese prime minister under any circumstances because of his continued visits to the controversial war memorial.

A turn for the worse in China–Japan relations came during the violent anti-Japanese demonstrations in China during April 2005. Several events preceded the 2005 demonstrations, and later developments exacerbated tensions. Prime Minister Koizumi remained unapologetic about visiting the Yasukuni Shrine.[52] As happened several times in the past, a textbook seen to whitewash Japanese aggression prior to 1945 was approved for publication by Japanese government officials, actions seen negatively by China and Korea in particular. First China and then Japan engaged in exploitation of gas in disputed waters in the East China Sea. Russia vacillated between strong incentives from Japan and China in determining whether to favor one or the other in building a pipeline to eastern Asia for Siberian oil. Repeated intrusions into Japanese-claimed waters by Chinese "research" and other ships presaged the intrusion of a Chinese nuclear-powered submarine that Japanese forces found and tracked in Japanese territorial waters near Okinawa. Growing Japanese concern about the implications for Japanese interests posed by the rapid Chinese military buildup focused on Taiwan elicited more explicit Japanese government expressions of concern and a variety of countermeasures, many involving strengthening Japan's alliance relationship with the United States. In this context, Japan engaged in bilateral consultations with the United States over the Taiwan situation, worked in a trilateral forum with Australia and the United States that dealt with Taiwan and other Asian issues, was explicit in noting Japanese government concerns over the Taiwan situation, and backed the United States in seeking curbs on European and Israeli arms sales to China.[53] A large Chinese–Russian military exercise involving naval and air forces in the East China Sea in August 2005 was followed by Japan's detection in September of a flotilla of Chinese warships sailing near a Chinese gas rig that was exploiting resources in the East China Sea that were claimed by Japan.[54]

Japan's impressive aid and relief efforts after the tsunami disaster in southern Asia in December 2004 led to an increase in Japan's international profile. Japanese leaders used this enhanced profile to launch a series of high-level international visits and associated economic and other gestures in an effort to garner support for a permanent seat for Japan on the UN Security Council. Despite strenuous government efforts, China remained in the second echelon among tsunami relief donors. The Chinese government opposed Japan's UN bid. Public opinion in China was negative.

In these circumstances, whether by design or happenstance, tens of thousands of Chinese responded to an Internet campaign against Japan's UN bid by taking to the streets in April 2005, with many attacking Japanese businesses and diplomatic properties. For several days, the Chinese police attempted to regulate but did not attempt to stop the violent anti-Japanese acts, bringing bilateral relations to the lowest point since the normalization of relations in 1972.[55]

Subsequently, government officials on both sides endeavored to restore order and maintain mutually advantageous business ties. However, neither side gave ground on the various political and security disputes.[56] Fresh from his success in leading his party to a decisive victory in the diet election in September 2005, Prime Minister Koizumi again visited the Yasukuni Shrine in October, prompting shrill Chinese protests and a cancellation of talks to improve relations.[57]

The weak Liberal Democratic Party governments that followed Koizumi's departure from office in 2006 were welcomed by China. The Democratic Justice Party (DJP) administrations that followed in 2009 also received cordial receptions. Nonetheless, salient differences over fishing, territorial disputes, and trade in so-called rare earth important to Japanese manufacturing brought relations to another low point in late 2010.[58]

The election victory of the Democratic Party of Japan (DPJ) in 2009 also was of indirect but important relevance to Japan–China relations as it had an important impact on U.S. policy in dealing with China and Japan. Over the years, American policymakers disagreed on Japan's priority in U.S. foreign policy. In broad terms, U.S. policy toward the Asia-Pacific since the 1960s saw President Richard Nixon and some later presidents give top priority to developing cooperative U.S. relations with China, and in the process they neglected or downgraded U.S. relations with Japan. In the post–Cold War period, as Japan was economically stagnating and its political leadership sometimes appeared weak, some in the U.S. government believed that the United States was better off seeking to enhance its interests and influence in the Asia-Pacific by working more closely with rising regional powers, notably China. Others strongly disagreed. They stressed that without Japan as an ally and without access to military bases in Japan, U.S. influence in the Asia-Pacific would be severely constrained. According to this view, China's rapidly growing economic and military power represented major challenges as well as opportunities for the United States. To manage the challenges effectively in line with American interests appeared to require close U.S. cooperation with Japan. Common interests and values were said to bind the United States closely to Japan in an alliance relationship demonstrating mutual trust deemed essential in sustaining American security, economic, and political interests in the Asia-Pacific region.[59]

The George W. Bush administration in its early years clearly favored the latter view. Reflecting the judgments of a cohort of strongly pro-Japan leaders headed by Deputy Secretary of State Richard Armitage, the Bush administration's relations with Japan were given top priority in the Asia-Pacific and probably received more favorable U.S. administration attention than any other U.S. bilateral relationship during the early years of Bush's presidency.[60]

In its later years, however, Bush administration leaders came increasingly to rely on consultations and coordination with Chinese counterparts to manage salient Asia-Pacific hot spots, notably North Korea's nuclear weapons program and the pro-independence initiatives of Taiwan's president. On the other hand, U.S. leaders and Japanese leaders continued to reinforce political and economic cooperation and closer security ties, some of which served as a hedge against rising Chinese power and influence.[61]

As discussed in chapter 6, the Barack Obama government sought to advance the Bush government's positive engagement with and attention to China. By contrast, Japan became a more negative element in American policy calculations. Political uncertainty accompanied major leadership change in Japan. The election victory of the Democratic Party of Japan (DPJ) in 2009 challenged U.S. alliance relations in serious ways.

DPJ leader Yukio Hatoyama campaigned with pledges to reexamine the planned realignment of U.S. forces in Japan agreed to by previous Japanese governments and to pursue a more balanced foreign policy between the United States and Japan's neighbors, notably China. On entering office, Prime Minister Hatoyama moved quickly to reassess a 2006 Japan–U.S. agreement to realign U.S. troops in Japan, with a particular focus on the large and controversial U.S. bases in Okinawa, and to revise the U.S.–Japan Status of Forces Agreement (SOFA). Both topics were keenly sensitive issues in alliance relations. The 2006 agreement represented a delicate compromise reached after protracted negotiations that had a number of provisions calling for actions in future years that appeared difficult to implement. Hatoyama was pressured by his party's coalition partners, the Social Democratic Party and the People's New Party, which held swing votes in Japan's upper house, to switch that part of the 2006 agreement involving the U.S. Marine Corps Air Station (MCAS) Futenma Replacement Facility (FRF) in Okinawa. Thus, Hatoyama urged that the FRF site be switched from Henoko Bay, Okinawa—the location stipulated in the U.S.–Japan arrangements in the 2006 agreement—to some location off the island of Okinawa. He pressed his case publicly in initial official meetings with President Obama. The U.S. government remained firm in support of the provisions stipulated in the 2006 agreement. The FRF issue became the most important problem in U.S.–Japan relations and ultimately led to Prime Minister Hatoyama's resignation in 2010.[62]

Hatoyama's and other DPJ leaders' calls for a more balanced Japanese foreign policy seemingly aligned Japan less closely with the United States and gave more attention to China. Hatoyama notably favored an East Asian Community that initially seemed to leave out the United States. While trying to appeal to China, the DPJ found China to be wary of the Japanese initiatives. Beijing saw them as a means for Japan to assert leadership in regional affairs in competition with China.[63] Sino-Japanese relations subsequently foundered over the increasingly contentious territorial disputes, which became acute when Japan arrested the Chinese fishing boat captain for ramming Japanese coast guard ships in 2010. Two years later, DPJ Prime Minister Yoshihiko Noda sought to limit the damage to Japan–China relations caused by Japanese right-wing politicians seeking to purchase some of the Senkaku (Diaoyu) Islands and use them to antagonize China. Noda decided in September 2012 to have the Japanese government purchase the islands instead.

As discussed earlier, the Chinese reaction was extraordinary. An intense and massive propaganda barrage; authoritative government, party, and military pronouncements; and remarks by the full range of top leaders all urged Chinese people to register their "righteous indignation" over the Noda decision. The demonstrations in 120 Chinese cities, with associated burning and looting of Japanese properties, followed.[64]

Prime Minister Noda failed to appreciate that his seemingly pragmatic decisions came amid heightened public Chinese determination to defend territorial claims along China's maritime rim and followed China's successful use of coercion and intimidation to force Philippine fishing boats and security forces out of the disputed Scarborough Shoal in the South China Sea in mid-2012. Chinese assertiveness now had a much more important target than the Philippines. Chinese used coast guard forces, legal and administrative measures, trade pressures, diplomatic threats, and other means to force Japan to reverse its actions and negotiate with China over the disputed islands. The DPJ woes contributed to the landslide election victory of the Liberal Democratic Party (LDP) under Shinzo Abe in late 2012. Abe was firm in the face of Chinese pressure; protracted tensions ensued.[65]

The Obama government welcomed Abe's ascendance. The LDP administration promised better adherence to past agreements and a strong Japanese emphasis on the alliance. America shifted from a mediating role to a tougher stance critical of China's coercive behavior.[66] The U.S. position overlapped closely with Abe's defensive but firm stance toward China. China stridently attacked Abe as he sought support against Chinese pressures by strengthening defense at home and seeking support in visits to all members of ASEAN as well as India, Australia, and others. In contrast, President Obama, visiting Japan in April 2014, embraced close collaboration with Japan in Asia and underlined America's defense commitment to all areas under Japanese administrative control including the Senkaku (Diaoyu) Islands. Prime Minister Abe's visit to the United States in April 2015 advanced defense cooperation and international coordination between the two allies. President Obama took the opportunity to rebuke China for "flexing its muscles" to intimidate neighbors and gain control of disputed territory.[67]

Prime Minister Abe embraced the alliance with the United States and the Obama government rebalance policy initiatives. He increased Japan's defense budget for the first time in ten years, carried out defense reforms that enhanced Japanese military capabilities, and secured approval for the construction of the controversial new U.S. Marine Corps base on Okinawa. He entered Japan into the U.S.-led Trans-Pacific Partnership free trade agreement negotiations and sought economic reforms favored by many in the United States.

Abe's December 2013 visit to the Yasukuni Shrine surprised American officials, who had discouraged such action. The U.S. government took the unusual step of criticizing the prime minister's visit. U.S. leaders were working hard to bridge differences between South Korea and Japan over historical and territorial disputes. In particular, the United States sought to bring the three allies together in a united effort to deal with North Korea. The trilateral arrangement was also deemed useful in deterring China from destabilizing behavior.[68]

Beijing now regularly deployed maritime law enforcement ships near the disputed Senkaku (Diaoyu) Islands and stepped up what China called "routine" patrols to assert jurisdiction in "China's territorial waters." Chinese military surveillance planes at times reportedly entered airspace over territory that Japan considers its own. Such encounters saw both countries scramble fighter jets, and, according to the Japanese government, a Chinese navy ship locked its fire-control radar on a Japanese destroyer and a helicopter on two separate occasions.

China's patrols appeared to be an attempt to demonstrate that Beijing has a degree of administrative control over the islets and to underline that Japan must acknowledge that the territory is in dispute and begin negotiations with China on the dispute. Japan refused to acknowledge that the islands are in dispute. China and Japan did reach a four-point agreement announced at the time of the first Xi-Abe meeting in November 2014 that said the two sides "recognized that they had different views as to the emergence of tension situations in recent years in the waters of the East China Sea, including those around the Senkaku Islands." Such compromise wording was said to be sufficient to meet China's demand that Japan recognize the territorial dispute and begin negotiations with China on the dispute. In fact, there was no mention in the document of the territorial dispute and the Japanese government still did not recognize the dispute nor did it begin talks with China about the dispute.[69]

A highlight of Chinese assertiveness was Beijing's November 2013 announcement that it would establish an air defense identification zone (ADIZ) over the East China Sea including the disputed Senkaku (Diaoyu) Islands. Outside of China, the ADIZ was widely interpreted as a challenge to Japanese administration of the Senkaku (Diaoyu) Islands. Washington weighed in strongly against China's actions. China had not consulted with affected countries, and so they were unprepared; the announcement used vague and ominous language that seemed to promise military enforcement within the zone; the requirements for flight notification in the ADIZ went beyond international norms and impinged on freedom of navigation; and the overlap with other countries' ADIZs could lead to accidents or unintended clashes, thus raising the risk of conflict in the East China Sea.[70] The United States and Japan coordinated closely and at a high level in their individual and collective responses to the new situation. American officials expressed appreciation for Japan's measured response in what could have been a combustible situation.

Looking out, Japan faces serious domestic challenges as it attempts economic revival after decades of stagnation and the disastrous fallout from the March 2011 Fukushima tsunami/nuclear reactor disaster. Internationally, the confrontation in the East China Sea underlines China as the largest and growing factor in Japan's security calculations. Japan faces a protracted struggle where China has employed sometimes extraordinary coercive measures short of direct use of military force to pressure Japan to recognize China's claim, enter negotiations on terms agreeable to China, and follow conditions set by Beijing. Thus far, Japan seems prepared to resist, building its own strengths and working with the United States and others in the Asia-Pacific to offset the pressures from China. [71]

Chinese expansion also tops Japanese concerns over the stability of sea lines of communication and regional order in Southeast Asia and the South China Sea. Instability in Southeast Asia could jeopardize sea lines of communication, threaten Japanese nationals, and disrupt regional security dynamics. Japan's security interests are largely compatible with those of the United States, Australia, India, and the countries of Southeast Asia—they are: preventing regional hegemony, supporting a regional U.S. presence as a stabilizing force, and endeavoring to influence China's regional role as it grows in power. Japan likely will increase support where appropriate regarding the Philippines and Vietnam in their respective standoffs with China over disputed territory in the South China Sea. [72]

RELATIONS WITH THE KOREAN PENINSULA

With the collapse of the Soviet Union and the demise of East–West and Sino-Soviet competition for influence in the Korean peninsula after the Cold War, Beijing adjusted Chinese relations to take advantage of economic and other opportunities with South Korea while sustaining a leading international position in relations with North Korea. The international confrontation caused by North Korea's nuclear weapons program and related ballistic missile programs, and the sharp decline in economic conditions and the rise of political uncertainty there following the sudden death of Kim Il Sung in 1994, raised concerns in China about the future stability of the peninsula. In general, Chinese officials used economic aid and continued military and political exchanges to help stabilize and preserve Chinese relations with the North, while working closely with South Korea and at times the United States in seeking a peaceful resolution to tensions on the peninsula. In response to the crisis created by North Korea's provocative nuclear proliferation activities beginning in 2002, China was even more active, taking a leading role in international efforts to seek a diplomatic solution that would preserve China's influence and interests in stability on the peninsula.[73]

Foreign observers often judged that China had a longer-term interest in seeing a growth of Chinese influence and a reduction of U.S. and Japanese influence on the peninsula.[74] However, Beijing generally was careful not to emphasize China's challenge to U.S. leadership in Korean affairs. It apparently judged that Chinese interests were best met with a posture that allowed for concurrent improvements in China's relations with South Korea and effective management of China's often difficult relations with North Korea. The result up to the middle of the past decade was a marked increase in China's relations with South Korea and continued Chinese relations with North Korea closer than any other power, without negatively affecting Beijing's relations with the United States.

However, striking the right balance between sometimes conflicting Chinese objectives in relations with North and South Korea, without alienating the United States, has proven to be very difficult in recent years. This was especially evident during the unsteady North Korean leadership succession beginning with Kim Jong Il's stroke in August 2008 and subsequent rushed succession arrangements that featured egregious North Korean nuclear proliferation and military aggression. At first, China showed strong support for Kim Jong Il and the succession to his son, Kim Jong Un. This came despite North Korea's military attacks on South Korea and nuclear weapons and ballistic missile tests. China was seen as enabling North Korean aggression and provocations, and its relations with South Korea and the United States declined. As the Kim Jong Un government continued provocations and rebuffed Chinese influence and advice, notably by executing Kim's uncle Jang Sung Taek, who had close ties to China in 2013, China hardened its stance toward North Korea. It curbed oil shipments and other economic benefits of great importance for the regime. China's relations with North Korea declined to their lowest point.

Relations with South Korea

China steadily improved relations with South Korea, reaching a high point in the middle of the past decade. The Chinese advances coincided with the most serious friction in U.S.–South Korean relations since the Korean War. Adding to China's importance to South Korea was U.S. policy toward North Korea during much of the past decade. The Bush administration worked closely with China to facilitate international talks on North Korea's nuclear weapons program. North Korea preferred to deal directly with the United States on this issue. While such bilateral interchange with North Korea presumably would have boosted U.S. influence relative to that of China in peninsula affairs, the Bush government for some time saw such U.S.–North

Korean contacts as counterproductive for U.S. interests in securing a verifiable end to North Korea's nuclear weapons program. As a result, China saw its influence grow in the eyes of South Korea and other concerned powers as it joined with the United States in the multilateral efforts, notably the six-party talks involving Japan and Russia along with the two Koreas, the United States, and China, to deal with the North Korean nuclear weapons issue. At the same time, China sustained its position as the foreign power having the closest relationship with the reclusive North Korean regime. [75]

Against this background, widespread predictions that China would supersede the United States in relations with South Korea proved to be wrong. The latter part of the decade saw serious frictions in South Korean–Chinese relations and shifts in South Korean opinion against China. South Korean and U.S. leaders strengthened efforts to shore up their alliance relationship in order to safeguard their important respective interests in the face of North Korean threats, rising China, and other uncertainties in northeastern Asia. [76]

The upswing in Chinese–South Korean relations saw China become South Korea's leading trade partner. Trade was valued at $171 billion in 2010. Trade rose in subsequent years but fell back to $171 billion in 2014, a 25 percent decline from 2013. China still accounted for one-quarter of South Korea's foreign trade. China was the recipient of the largest amount of South Korean foreign investment (totaling $30 billion in 2010). The buildup of investment continued in 2014 with South Korean investments valued that year at $3.97 billion according to Chinese data. After South Korean efforts to stabilize South Korea's currency with the help of a $30 billion line of credit from the U.S. Federal Reserve in October 2008, China joined Japan in December in pledging its own $30 billion currency swap with South Korea. China was the most important foreign destination for South Korean tourists and students. In the face of the Bush administration's tough stance toward North Korea in 2001–2006, South Korea and China were close and like-minded partners in dealing more moderately than the United States with issues posed by North Korea's nuclear weapons program and related provocations. [77]

As relations developed, China's economic importance for South Korea was seen in both negative and positive ways. Periodic trade disputes came with growing concerns by South Korean manufacturers, political leaders, and public opinion about competition from fast-advancing Chinese enterprises. China's economic attractiveness to South Korean consumers declined markedly because of repeated episodes of Chinese exports of tainted consumer products to South Korean and other markets. South Korean leaders strove to break out of close dependence on economic ties with China through free trade agreements and other arrangements with the United States, Japan, and the European Union that would ensure inputs of foreign investment and technology needed for South Korea to stay ahead of Chinese competitors.

South Korea and China in November 2014 signed an agreement signaling movement toward conclusion of a proposed bilateral free trade agreement.[78]

Other differences between the two countries focused on competing Chinese and Korean claims regarding the scope and importance of the historical Goguryeo kingdom, China's rejection of international pressure in response to North Korean aggression against South Korea, longer-term Chinese ambitions in North Korea, and Chinese treatment of North Korean refugees in China and of South Koreans endeavoring to assist them there. The disputes had a strong impact on nationalistic South Korean political leaders and public opinion. During the government of President Lee Myung-bak (2008–2013), public opinion polls showed a significant decline in South Korean views of China and its policies and practices.[79] President Park Geun-hye (2013–) advanced relations with frequent friendly meetings with Chinese President Xi Jinping, prompting improvement in South Korean public opinion of China.[80]

Converging PRC–South Korean Foreign Policy Interests, 1992–2004

Converging South Korean–Chinese foreign policy interests supported economic and other trends to greatly enhance China's position in South Korea up to the middle of the last decade. By the early 2000s, China enjoyed a much more positive image than the United States in South Korean elite and public opinion. South Korean government officials also welcomed the improved ties with China as a means to diversify South Korean foreign policy options, reduce dependency on the U.S. alliance, secure South Korean interests on the Korean peninsula, and enhance South Korea's economic development.

South Korean motives for good relations with China often included foreign policy concerns. At times in the 1990s and later, South Korean officials viewed better relations with China as a useful way to preclude possible Chinese expansion or pressure against South Korea as China grew in wealth and power during the twenty-first century. They also saw good relations with China as providing protection against possible pressure from Japan in the future.[81] Officials in Seoul were careful to add that relations with China also broadened South Korean foreign policy options, allowing South Korea to appear to break out of the constraints imposed by what they saw as a U.S.-centered foreign policy since the 1950s. South Korean opinion leaders judged that with better relations with China, Seoul could afford to be more assertive and less accommodating in relations with the United States—although South Korean officials and scholars also often asserted that relations with China or other foreign policy options provided no substitute for the essential South Korean alliance relationship with the United States.[82]

Meanwhile, given continued difficulties in U.S.–China relations in the 1990s, South Korean officials sometimes expressed an interest in acting as a mediator between these two powers, both of which had friendly ties with Seoul. The position as mediator would have boosted South Korea's international stature. South Korean officials also asserted that South Korea wanted to avoid a situation where it might have to choose between Washington and Beijing if U.S.–Chinese tensions in Asia were to rise sharply.

According to South Korean experts, China also viewed good relations with Seoul as a possible hedge against Japanese power, although Chinese officials emphasized that their interests were focused on regional peace and stability and on setting a good example in relations with a smaller neighbor, South Korea, in order to reassure China's other neighbors about Beijing's foreign policy intentions. More broadly, Chinese intentions were said by some South Korean experts to reflect a desire to use better relations with South Korea against perceived U.S. efforts to contain or hold back China's growing power and influence in Asian and world affairs. In particular, Chinese specialists and officials voiced concern at times that the United States might use its alliance relationships with Japan and South Korea in order to check or build a barrier against the allegedly expanding "China threat" in northeastern Asia. Closer China–South Korean relations would complicate any such U.S. strategic scheme.[83]

In this context, South Korea and China markedly increased cooperation in Asian regional groups.[84] China's greater willingness in the 1990s and 2000s to cooperate more closely with and play a more active role in Asian multilateral organizations assisted this trend. Previously, Chinese officials had viewed Asian multilateral groups with more wariness and skepticism. Thus, China's greater willingness to cooperate with South Korea and others in the economic deliberations of Asia-Pacific Economic Cooperation (APEC) and in the security-related interchanges in the ASEAN Regional Forum enhanced Chinese–South Korean relations.

The two powers also participated actively in regional forums that excluded the United States. Both South Korea and China played significant roles in the biannual Asia-Europe Meetings initiated in 1996 to encourage greater cooperation between eastern Asia and the developed countries of Europe—in part as a counterweight to the U.S.-led APEC. The Asian economic crisis of 1997 prompted stronger regional cooperation efforts led by South Korea and China under the ASEAN Plus Three rubric. This group became a leading regional grouping in eastern Asia, with frequent meetings of senior ministers and state leaders that occasioned major economic and some political and security initiatives, notably proposals by China, South Korea, Japan, and others for free trade agreements in the region and security plans dealing with eastern Asia.

These actions reflected strong interest in China and South Korea in deepening intraregional cooperation, first in economic areas but then in political and security areas, in order to ease long-standing mutual suspicions among eastern Asian states and enhance prospects for peace and development in the region.[85] China's public stance at that time focused on its new security concept (NSC), announced in 1997. The NSC was a reworking of the Five Principles of Peaceful Coexistence, which were the mainstay of moderate and accommodating phases in Chinese foreign policy for fifty years. The NSC was well received in South Korea and along with other Chinese policies and behavior provided a vague but sufficient basis for many in South Korea and elsewhere in Asia to deal with China's rising power and influence in constructive ways.

When the NSC was initially proposed, Chinese foreign policy was strongly critical of and endeavored to reduce the influence of the United States and its foreign policies. Chinese officials repeatedly used the NSC to counter the U.S.-favored alliance structure in Asian and world affairs. Following the moderate turn in China's public posture toward the United States in 2001, Chinese officials and commentary generally avoided calling on South Koreans or other Asians to choose between China's NSC and the previously emphasized "Cold War thinking" and "power politics" exemplified by the U.S. insistence on maintaining and strengthening U.S.-led alliance structures in Asia and elsewhere. This more positive Chinese approach, which Chinese officials said would lead to a "win-win" situation in Asia for all concerned powers, including the United States, South Korea, and China, was well received in South Korea and helped strengthen Sino–South Korean relations.

Cooling in South Korea–China Relations

South Korean popular and elite opinion toward China showed a tendency to be volatile. A positive "China fever" reached a high point in South Korea in mid-2004 and subsided.[86] Significant differences emerged that increased South Korean public and elite wariness about China's rise and strengthened South Korean interest in preserving a close alliance relationship with the United States. These developments occurred for several reasons:

- South Koreans reacted negatively to continued disputes with China about Korean claims regarding the historical Goguryeo kingdom.
- Territorial disputes between Korea and China over the so-called Gando region emerged, while differences continued to fester over trade and refugee disputes.
- China's economic influence in North Korea increased (over half of North Korea's cross-border trade in 2009 was with China; Chinese investment in 2008 was valued at $41 million). The Chinese economic role surpassed

that of South Korea and appeared to many in South Korea to compromise and complicate South Korean efforts to use a gradual asymmetrical engagement policy to facilitate reunification of Korea under South Korea's leadership. Chinese economic engagement and support of North Korea was seen as designed to perpetuate the North Korean state and the prevailing division on the Korean peninsula.[87]

South Korean government officials generally remained focused on seeking an advantageous position for their government and country in the prevailing fluid international situation surrounding the Korean peninsula.[88] While Seoul moved closer to China on a variety of economic, political, and other issues, it had few illusions about Chinese objectives. South Korean officials saw China using improved relations with South Korea in part to compete with the United States and Japan, among others, for influence in the Korean peninsula and northeastern Asia and to preclude the United States and Japan from working closely with South Korea to pressure China.

As a result, South Korea continued to try to avoid a situation where it might have to choose between Washington and Tokyo on one side and Beijing on the other if U.S.–Japanese–Chinese tensions in Asia were to rise. Reflecting ongoing angst by South Korean government officials seeking to preserve a proper balance in maintaining the alliance with the United States while improving relations with China, these officials continued to emphasize that the U.S.–South Korea alliance should allow for positive U.S. and South Korean relations with China and should avoid friction with China. Against this background, South Korean officials remained unwilling to follow the United States in pursuing policies that China opposed. South Korea also continued to be reluctant to agree to allow U.S. forces in South Korea to be deployed to other areas in eastern Asia, in part because those forces might be deployed to the Taiwan area in the event of a U.S.–China military confrontation in the Taiwan Strait.[89]

From 2004, however, South Korean officials also endeavored to improve relations with the United States and thereby sought to preserve an advantageous balance in South Korea's relations with the United States, along with other powers, while pursuing closer ties with China. Thus, they played down past rhetoric that was opposed by many in the United States and supported by the Chinese government that emphasized South Korea's role as a "balancer" between the United States and China and Japan and China. They undertook important sacrifices, notably sending 3,000 combat troops to Iraq—a move opposed by most of the legislature and South Korean public opinion—in order to strengthen the alliance with the United States. They agreed to various high-level dialogues with U.S. officials in order to deal effectively with alliance issues, and they took the risk of pushing for a bilateral free trade agreement with the United States that if enacted would be sure to alienate many South Korean constituents. (The agreement was reached in April 2007 and entered into force in 2012.) And they modified their past reluctance to join the U.S.-supported Proliferation Security Initiative (PSI) and attended a PSI exercise as an observer.[90]

These steps accompanied South Korean efforts to sustain a working relationship with Japan despite differences over territorial and historical issues and South Korea's independent approaches to Russia, the European Union, and others. South Korean officials were privately explicit that these measures helped ensure, among other things, that South Korea would maintain its ambitions for a greater international role and would not come under the dominant sway of neighboring and growing China.

The equilibrium in South Korea's posture toward China, the United States, Japan, and others shifted further with the coming to power of the Lee Myung-bak government in 2008. The special envoys selected by the president to visit the three powers showed lower priority for China. The close personal relationship Lee established with President Bush and later with President Obama was not duplicated by the more businesslike relationship with Chinese President Hu Jintao. South Korea clearly wanted closer cooperation with Washington, Tokyo, and Beijing, but the priority seemed to have changed in favor of the United States. The adjustment reinforced signs of a broader wariness of Chinese policies and practices on the part of various elites and South Korean public opinion and a desire to solidify the South Korea–U.S. alliance for the uncertain period ahead.[91] As discussed below, President Park Geun-hye endeavored to improve relations with China while strengthening ties with the United States.

Relations with North Korea—Seeking Stability and Influence

American and South Korean officials and commentators were surprised and angered by China's refusal to condemn North Korea's military provocations: the sinking in March 2010 of the South Korean warship *Cheonan*, killing forty-six South Korean sailors; and the artillery attack on South Korea's Yeonpyeong Island in November 2010, killing some South Korean soldiers and civilians. China's deepening leadership ties and growing economic relations with and support for Pyongyang during a period of leadership transition in North Korea also appeared to enable North Korea's egregious nuclear proliferation, despite UN sanctions and international pressures in place since the North Korean nuclear tests of 2006 and 2009. Pyongyang's disclosure in November 2010 of what appeared to be a fully operational uranium enrichment facility, a major step forward in North Korea's nuclear proliferation, came following China's months-long block of the release of a report by UN experts charging North Korea with supplying nuclear technology to Syria, Iran, and Myanmar.[92]

At one level, the Chinese behavior and actions represented the latest episodes in China's often twisted relations with North Korea since the end of the Cold War. The record shows China repeatedly put in a reactive position as it was compelled to deal with crises caused by North Korea's nuclear weapons development, often abrupt and disruptive swings in North Korea's posture toward its neighbors and the United States, and economic crises and leadership transition in Pyongyang. U.S. policy toward North Korea and that of South Korea also have changed markedly over time, forcing adjustments in Chinese policies and practices.[93]

The stakes for China were high. With the possible exception of Taiwan, there was no more important area around China's periphery for Chinese domestic and foreign policy interests than the Korean peninsula. The stakes grew with rising Chinese equities in improving relations with South Korea, and often intense U.S. and other regional and international involvement to curb North Korea's advancing nuclear weapons development.

China's frustration with North Korea followed its nuclear weapons tests in 2006 and 2009 and other provocations.[94] The North Korean actions brought a halt to the six-party talks, which were promoted by China as the main diplomatic means to deal with North Korea's nuclear proliferation and its impact on the Korean peninsula. Contrary to past practice, the Chinese government allowed a public debate where relations with North Korea often were depicted as a liability for China, requiring serious readjustment in Chinese policy. Nevertheless, the overall record of Chinese policy and practice showed continuing caution; China endeavored to preserve important Chinese interests in stability on the Korean peninsula through judicious moves that struck an appropriate balance among varied Chinese relations with concerned parties at home and abroad. China remained wary that North Korea, the United States, and others could shift course, forcing further Chinese adjustments in response.

Chinese leaders recognized that their cautious policies failed to halt North Korea's nuclear weapons development. They probably judged that they would be living with a nuclear North Korea for some time to come, even as they emphasized continued diplomatic efforts to reverse North Korea's nuclear weapons development and create a nuclear-free peninsula. They appeared resigned to joining with U.S. and other leaders in what is characterized as "failure management," as far as North Korean nuclear weapons development is concerned.[95] They endeavored to preserve stability and Chinese equities with concerned powers. As in the recent past, they continued to avoid pressure or other risky initiatives on their own, waiting for the actions of others or changed circumstances that would increase the prospects of curbing North Korea's nuclear challenge and allow for stronger Chinese measures to deal with nuclear North Korea.

China's often-repeated, overarching goal in the Korean peninsula re-mained "stability." China's behavior in the face of various crises initiated mainly by North Korea seemed to underline this goal; by emphasizing stabil-ity, Chinese officials and commentators helped explain why China eschewed pressure on North Korea that could provoke a backlash or other develop-ments adverse to stability on the peninsula. At the same time, China also was seen to have a longer-term interest in strengthening Chinese influence and reducing U.S. and Japanese influence on the peninsula.[96] Recent Chinese policy and practice have not highlighted this goal, though China's strong objections for several months in 2010 to U.S. and South Korean military exercises in the Yellow Sea raised questions about China's continued will-ingness to coexist with the U.S.–South Korea alliance. Also, in the past year, China publicly pressured South Korea not to allow the planned U.S. deploy-ment of the advanced THAAD (Terminal High Altitude Area Defense) mis-sile in South Korea as a means to defend against North Korean ballistic missile attack. Beijing argued that the advanced American missile defense system had negative implications for Chinese security.[97]

As noted above, Beijing was careful not to emphasize challenging U.S. leadership in dealing with North Korea's nuclear proliferation and broader Korean affairs.[98] The Chinese government strove for concurrent improve-ments in China's relations with South Korea and effective management of China's difficult relations with North Korea. During the repeated crises over North Korea's nuclear program since 2002, China's cooperation with the United States, South Korea, and other concerned powers in seeking a nego-tiated solution to the problem enhanced overall positive development in Chi-na's relations with these countries, while managing tensions over the North Korean program in ways that avoided conflict or helped reduce the instability caused by Pyongyang's provocative actions.

China's cautious and incremental efforts to strengthen its influence in the Korean peninsula and thereby reduce U.S., Japanese, and other potentially adverse influence in this critically important bordering area were in line with China's overall approach in the period up to and during the Hu Jintao government (2002–2012) to advancing its interests in Asian and world affairs in the post–Cold War period. This pattern of Chinese post–Cold War interac-tion with neighboring states was to slowly but surely spread Chinese influ-ence though diplomatic, economic, and security interaction that emphasized the positives and played down the negatives in the Chinese–neighboring country relationships. China also relied heavily on the steady growth of what senior Chinese foreign policy officials call China's "weight" to cause neigh-bors to improve their relations with China over time, eschew foreign connec-tions and practices opposed by China, and thereby create a regional order more supportive of Chinese interests. The Chinese officials suggested that China's "weight" included its salient and rapidly growing economic importance to Asian neighbors, its leadership in Asian multilateral groups and international diplomacy, and the rapidly expanding reach of advanced Chinese military forces.[99]

The Chinese government generally was patient in pursuing regional influence. Domestic Chinese priorities required continued regional stability. While there remained active debate among commentators and officials in China over how assertive China should be in dealing with Asian and world affairs, the central leadership appeared to have stuck to a cautious approach that continued to avoid risks, costs, or commitments with potentially adverse consequences for the Chinese government's goals, which centered on sustaining their role in a supportive environment in China and abroad.[100]

In sum, when assessing reasons for China's refusal to cooperate closely with the United States and South Korea in response to North Korea's provocations, it was important to look beyond immediate concerns with stability on the Korean peninsula. China's approach to North Korea also was driven by a broad, albeit slow-moving and low-risk, drive to establish an order in the Korean peninsula more influenced by China and less influenced by foreign and other elements seen as adverse to Chinese interests. In this context, growing Chinese frustration with the twists and turns of North Korean behavior, especially Pyongyang's nuclear weapons development, did not result in a major change in China's reluctance to pressure North Korea to conform to international norms and eschew provocations and confrontation. China's focus was to preserve stability in an uncertain environment caused by internal pressures and international provocations of North Korea, and sometimes erratic policies by the United States and South Korea. China continued to follow practices that gave priority to renewed negotiations in the six-party talks. At least until recently, it tried to use positive incentives rather than pressure in order to elicit North Korean willingness to avoid further provocations and to return to negotiations on eventual denuclearization.

As noted above, the Xi Jinping government is committed to a more activist and higher-profile foreign posture that is more assertive and demanding on key issues, notably disputed territory. The Xi government's assertiveness has had profound impact on China's relations with the United States, Japan, and countries in Southeast Asia with an interest in the South China Sea. Regarding Korea, the new Chinese posture may explain Beijing's recent public complaints about the THAAD missile and also may explain the mysterious statement by the Chinese foreign minister at the National People's Congress in March 2014. He told a press conference in remarkably bold language that China had a "Red Line" regarding Korea that cannot be crossed and that was that China "will not allow war or instability on the Korean peninsula." Consistent with the image of Chinese foreign policy pronouncements during the Xi government, the remarks conveyed strength, initiative, and control by China. However, there was no clear reference to the causes of war or instability; it was unclear whether the target of the warning was North Korea, the United States, or some other actor; given the continued instability evident in the North Korea leadership purges since that time, it's hard to know exactly where China's new Red Line actually is. At bottom, Xi Jinping's international activism thus far has not changed fundamentally China's overall approach to the difficult choices Beijing faces dealing with North Korea and preserving stability on the Korean peninsula.

Developments in China–North Korean relations in the two decades following the Cold War can be divided into three periods:[101]

- 1989–2000 featured Chinese angst over North Korean leadership transition, instability, and economic collapse and crisis with the United States prompted by North Korea's nuclear weapons development.
- 2000–2001 featured a period of unprecedented détente, where China facilitated North Korean outreach and endeavored to keep pace with expanding North Korean contacts with South Korea, the United States, Russia, and others.
- 2002–2009 featured periodic and intense North Korean provocations and wide swings in U.S. policy, ranging from thinly disguised efforts to force regime change in North Korea to close collaboration with Pyongyang negotiators. South Korean policy also shifted markedly from a soft to a harder line in dealing with North Korea.

China's frustration grew with North Korea's continued development of nuclear weapons and other provocative actions. Chinese officials obviously miscalculated when they argued in the past that North Korea's nuclear weapons program was not a serious one but represented an effort to elicit aid and other support from the United States, South Korea, and others. China's more recent working assumption seemed to be a more realistic one—North Korea is intent on keeping nuclear weapons. In response, China was more willing, albeit with continued reservations, to join U.S.-backed efforts in the United Nations to criticize and impose limited sanctions on North Korea until it resumes negotiations leading to denuclearization. Meanwhile, the debate about the need to shift Chinese North Korean policy toward a harder line became part of a wider public debate about the future of Chinese foreign policy.[102]

Complementing the modest hardening in China's stance toward North Korea were a series of recent positive steps China took to offer unspecified but apparently substantial economic and other incentives to North Korea amid a major burst of high-level official engagement between the two sides.[103] The mix of Chinese actions, seemingly involving more carrots than sticks, underlined Chinese concern to preserve stability and China's position as the foreign power with the best relationship with both North and South Korea. China was prepared to acquiesce to a continued nuclear North Korea for the foreseeable future, rather than risk dangers associated with strong pressure on Pyongyang. The future of North Korea could be violent and disruptive. China sought to avoid such negative outcomes and to sustain a position of influence in determining the future of the peninsula.

Recent Developments—Steps Backward for China

China made gains in 2009–2011 in solidifying its position as the most important and avid supporter of the North Korean leadership, as Pyongyang witnessed the most significant leadership transition in a generation amid poor domestic conditions and generally unfriendly international circumstances. [104] China also deepened economic relations with both North and South Korea. Though China–North Korean discussions remain secret, it appeared that bilateral relations registered significant improvement despite differences over North Korea's proliferation and military provocations.

The same cannot be said about China's relations with South Korea. In 2010, those ties reached the lowest point since the establishment of China–South Korea diplomatic relations. China's refusal to criticize North Korean military attacks against South Korea left a lasting and widespread impression of where China's priorities lay when choosing between North and South Korea. Against this background and contrary to China's longer-term objective to diminish U.S. and Japanese influence on the Korean peninsula, China faced strengthened U.S.–South Korea and U.S.–Japan alliance relationships, and for a time closer strategic coordination between South Korea and Japan. Adding to South Korean and U.S. differences with China was Beijing's unexpectedly strong public opposition in 2010 to U.S.–South Korea military exercises in the Yellow Sea that were targeted at showing allied resolve and deepening deterrence against further North Korean military provocations. [105]

Chinese Advances

China's top leader Hu Jintao was in the vanguard of Chinese representatives seeking to underline Chinese support for the leadership transition in North Korea. Hu hosted visiting North Korean leader Kim Jong Il during three trips to China, in May and August 2010, and May 2011. The visits presumably were related to the beginnings of a formal transition from Kim Jong Il to leaders, including Kim's son Kim Jong Un, who were elevated to top positions at the first Workers Party of Korea party conference in forty-four years in September 2010. There followed a blizzard of speeches and publicity marking close China–North Korea relations, including important speeches by China's heir apparent, Vice President Xi Jinping, and a wide range of high-level party and security exchanges throughout the rest of the year and into 2011.[106]

The public displays of solidarity came along with some reports of differences between Beijing and Pyongyang over North Korea's proliferation activities and military attacks against South Korea. On balance, the Chinese leadership was clearly emphasizing the positive in its public posture toward Pyongyang. It backed up its support by thwarting South Korean–led efforts in the United Nations and elsewhere to press North Korea to bear consequences for sinking the *Cheonan* and attacking Yeonpyeong Island, and for its nuclear proliferation activities at home and abroad.

China also advanced various economic ties with North Korea. According to Chinese customs data, China–North Korea trade in the first half of 2010 amounted to $1.29 billion, a 16.8 percent annual increase. North Korea imported $940 million in goods from China and exported $350 million during the period. North Korea's imports from China rose markedly, with flour imports rising by 383 percent. North Korea's crude oil imports from China remained the same. Minerals and other natural resources continued to account for a large portion of North Korean exports to China. China also provided unspecified humanitarian assistance in 2010. China's trade and aid ties with North Korea raised concerns about the effects of those ties on UN and other international sanctions. Meanwhile, roads, railways, bridges, and other projects facilitating transportation between China and North Korea were under construction.[107]

As noted above, economic ties also grew between China and South Korea. The China–South Korea trade of $171 billion in 2010 was a 21 percent increase from $141 billion in 2009. South Korean investment in China in 2010 represented 21 percent of South Korea's total foreign direct investment (FDI). Meanwhile, the number of Chinese visitors to South Korea rose 48 percent in 2009, reaching 1.21 million. South Korean tourists were the largest group of foreign tourists visiting China in the first half of 2010, totaling 1.95 million; this marked an increase of 30 percent from the same period in 2008 and accounted for 15.5 percent of the total foreign tourists in China.[108]

Chinese Setbacks

China's response to the *Cheonan* incident and other military provocations and proliferation activities placed the greatest strain on China–South Korean relations in a generation. They brought relations to a new low. They sparked significant debate in South Korea, highlighting the relative weakness of China–South Korea political and security ties and strategic coordination despite close trade and investment ties. These weak links contrasted sharply with Beijing's concurrent strengthening political ties with the current leadership in

Pyongyang and increasing trade and economic exchanges at a time of stalled inter-Korean relations. [109]

Among other setbacks for China were the following:

- China's political and economic support of North Korea at a time of international condemnation of Pyongyang undermined perceptions of China's regional and international role as mediator of the six-party talks and as a responsible stakeholder in the international community. President Obama seemed to capture the sentiment of many world opinion leaders in criticizing China's "willful blindness" in the face of North Korean provocations. [110]
- North Korea's provocations introduced a high level of frustration into China's relations with not only South Korea but also the United States, Japan, Australia, and a number of Western powers.
- North Korea's provocations pushed the North Korean issue to the top of the U.S. policy agenda with China; China's failure to act to curb North Korea was accompanied by senior American leaders, including Secretary of Defense Robert Gates, warning bluntly in public that the North Korean nuclear program was now viewed as a direct threat to the United States. An implication was that if China didn't act to rein in North Korea, the United States would have to take action on its own. [111]
- China's weak response to North Korea's provocations and its unanticipated assertions in 2010 that U.S.–South Korea military exercises to counter North Korea were a threat to China helped solidify the already close U.S. relationship with South Korea. They also enhanced trilateral cooperation among the United States, South Korea, and Japan in order to deal effectively with North Korea in the absence of significant support from China. [112]

In sum, China faced a Korean peninsula marked by growing tension and deepening involvement by the United States and Japan at odds with Chinese interests. China's credibility and broader international reputation were battered. In return, China had solidified relations with North Korea.

Unfortunately for China, there remained large questions about North Korea's future trajectory. North Korea's uranium enrichment program and other proliferation activities showed nuclear ambitions opposed to Chinese efforts to lead North Korea to denuclearization. North Korea's emphasis on self-reliance as its national development strategy contradicted Chinese efforts to promote Chinese-style reform and opening of the North. The new leader Kim Jong Un posed great challenges for Chinese interests. He engaged in repeated provocations directed at South Korea, the United States, and the United Nations. Though talks and tentative agreements were reached with the new North Korean government and the United States on freezing nuclear weapons development and ballistic missile development in return for food aid and other matters in February 2012, Kim Jong Un insisted on conducting a long-range missile launch in defiance of UN restrictions in April, thereby ending the deal. There followed repeated North Korean threats of nuclear attacks against the United States. Numerous missile tests in defiance of UN restrictions came along with a third nuclear weapons test in February 2013. Against this background, the abrupt execution of Jang Sung Taek in December 2013 capped a series of gross affronts to Chinese interests.

The Xi Jinping government showed its displeasure by cutting back previous support and keeping the unpredictable North Korean government at arm's length. Beijing appeared to be marking time, awaiting changes in North Korea or elsewhere that would allow Chinese action in support of its interests without the major risk of North Korean backlash.

Apart from the March 2014 statement of China's so-called Red Line on Korean matters, there was little of the nationalistic rhetoric touting China's strength and determination to achieve its objectives in sensitive areas of foreign affairs. Along with the big drop of China's overall foreign trade, China–North Korea bilateral trade dropped by 13.4 percent in the first quarter of 2015. Trade in 2014 and 2013 were valued at $6.39 billion and $6.54 billion, respectively. Neighboring Chinese provinces reportedly continued investing in opportunities seen in North Korea's economy, making China the largest foreign investor in North Korea. Official data showed that China had not exported any crude oil to North Korea in 2014, a significant change from past practice that saw North Korea rely on oil exports from China. It was unclear how much food aid China was recently providing to the North Korean regime. China had been an important supplier in the past.[113]

Meanwhile, Xi Jinping improved relations with South Korea through friendly summit meetings and cordial diplomacy. China's Asian Infrastructure Investment Bank and various Silk Road investment plans elicited strong interest and support from South Korean officials and entrepreneurs. South Korea and China worked together in regional economic groups that excluded the United States, but South Korea also showed interest in the U.S.-backed Trans-Pacific Partnership that was a centerpiece of the Obama government's rebalance policy in Asia.

Chapter Nine

Relations with Southeast Asia, Australia, New Zealand, and the Pacific Islands

SOUTHEAST ASIA

For much of the post–Cold War period, China's attentive diplomacy and growing trade, investment, infrastructure, and other economic linkages supported cooperative relations with Southeast Asian neighbors. China joined and worked constructively with regional groups led by ASEAN in seeking to advance mutual interests focused on promoting development and sustaining stability. China for many years reassured Southeast Asian neighbors that China's remarkable military buildup, periodic violent displays of military force or threats to use military force against Taiwan and the United States, and sometimes forceful demonstrations of Chinese state power in advancing Chinese control in the disputed South China Sea should not be seen as a threat. The moderate and cooperative Chinese behavior recalled Beijing's positive approach to Southeast Asia during the period of "peaceful coexistence" in the 1950s when for a few years China and Southeast Asian nations advanced conventional diplomatic and economic ties. That period did not last long; China's interest in cooperative neighborly ties was superseded by higher priority interests in China's competition with the United States and the Soviet Union.[1]

The durability of China's moderate approach to Southeast Asia in the post–Cold War period also came into question when China gave higher priority to pursuing ambitions to control disputed territory at neighbors' expense. China's determination to pursue control of disputed territory grew with the rapid development of Chinese capabilities in military, coast guard, oil drilling, fisheries, and other aspects of state power with applications in the South China Sea. State-sponsored efforts to foster patriotism after the Tiananmen crisis of 1989 increased Chinese nationalism and led to demands of popular and elite opinion to defend strongly Chinese South China Sea claims and to reverse the steps other states had taken to use South China Sea resources and to advance their claims to areas claimed by China.[2]

Beijing's overall approach to the region was repeatedly complicated by conflicting goals. On the one hand, China had strong interests to break out of international isolation at the end of the Cold War and to expand Chinese influence throughout its periphery in ways that supported stability and development conducive to China's primary goal of economic modernization. Those interests seemed well served by advancing cooperative relations with moderate diplomacy and mutually beneficial economic exchanges with Southeast Asian countries. On the other hand, China's strong determination to defend sovereignty and achieve national unification showed repeatedly during the post–Cold War period. In Southeast Asia, this determination focused on defending and advancing control over disputed territory in the South China Sea. It saw Beijing resort periodically to coercion and threats that sought to intimidate neighbors and assert Chinese dominance over the contested areas.[3]

Reflecting these competing goals, China in practice shifted its approach toward Southeast Asia four times after the Cold War. Chinese behavior was not as erratic or crisis prone as its policies toward the United States, Taiwan, or Japan, but it was not consistent and often seemed hard to predict.

The shifts and the different stages in China's approach to the region in the post–Cold War period are discussed below. That discussion leads off with a brief review of the forty-year record of the behavior of the People's Republic of China toward Southeast Asia during the Cold War in order to understand the causes of past and recent shifts and to assess what they mean for the durability of a moderate Chinese approach to Southeast Asia of cooperative and accommodating interaction that is sought by the neighboring countries.

The overall record shows no coherent Chinese strategy in the course of PRC interaction with Southeast Asia. It shows repeated and often dramatic changes in the Chinese approach to Southeast Asia caused by sharp shifts in China's foreign policy priorities. As a rule, Southeast Asia has been an important arena where Beijing has pursued broader but often changing foreign policy goals. In that context, China over the years has given decidedly secondary priority to fostering close and cooperative Chinese–Southeast Asian relations for their own sake.

Cold War Developments

During the forty years of the Cold War, the changing Chinese approaches to Southeast Asia went through dramatic shifts that repeatedly featured ruthless, violent, and very disruptive Chinese behavior at the expense of its Southeast Asian neighbors.[4]

- The PRC's initial revolutionary emphasis on resisting U.S.-led imperialism saw close Chinese collaboration with and strong logistical and military support for Vietnamese communist armies in the defeat of U.S.-backed French forces in Indochina.
- China followed the post-Stalin (d. 1953) Soviet leadership in seeking an interlude of reduced tensions during a few years of so-called peaceful coexistence in the 1950s.
- That phase ended in 1958 with renewed Chinese militancy (e.g., confronting America in the Taiwan Strait, supporting Vietnamese communist armed struggle against U.S.-backed South Vietnam, and breaking with the USSR because of, among other things, the latter's perceived overly accommodating posture to America and its allies, notably in Asia). Supporting armed resistance against its enemies, China provided large amounts of military supplies, training, financial assistance, and political support to indigenous Communist Party–led insurgencies against Western-leaning governments in Thailand, Malaysia, and the Philippines. Chinese clandestine support for the Communist Party of Indonesia (PKI), then the largest nonruling communist party in the world, went hand in hand with China's active wooing of the radical militancy of the Indonesian regime of President Sukarno. A coup attempt in 1965 against the leadership of the Indonesian armed forces led to an enormous backlash that saw a half million deaths, including many thousands of ethnic Chinese, and that destroyed the PKI and Chinese influence in the country.
- China's Cultural Revolution begun in 1966 radicalized Chinese policies to opponents worldwide, including in Southeast Asia. Support for armed insurgencies now also targeted Indonesia. Neutral Burma reacted violently against Chinese Maoist demonstrations in 1969, causing China to create, fully support, and direct a fighting force of over 20,000 armed insurgents under the rubric of the Burmese Communist Party that represented the most serious security threat to Burma for the next twenty years. Strident anti-Soviet Red Guards disrupted the shipments of Soviet arms passing by rail through China to support the Vietnamese communists against America, seriously alienating Vietnam.[5]
- Mao Zedong's China came under heavy Soviet military pressure and saw the wisdom of a breakthrough with President Richard Nixon, who sought rapprochement with Beijing for strategic reasons, including seeking lever-

age against the increasingly powerful USSR. Chinese support for the Vietnamese communists and the various insurgencies in Southeast Asia continued, but Hanoi became very suspicious of China's new direction with
America and sought to rely more on the USSR. The latter move deepened
Chinese suspicions of Vietnam.

- Soviet-backed Hanoi's victory over U.S.-supported South Vietnam in
  1975 opened the path to fifteen years of armed struggle between China
  and Vietnam.[6] China solidified its long-standing clandestine support for
  the radical Khmer Rouge regime that defeated the U.S.-backed military
  regime in Cambodia in 1975. China sustained strong material and political
  support for the regime as it carried out its catastrophic consolidation of
  power (resulting in the deaths of 20 percent of the population of the
  country) and pursued armed challenges to Vietnam over territorial and
  other issues. As the Vietnamese prepared to invade Cambodia and topple
  the regime, it tried to purge Vietnam of ethnic Chinese, resulting in a
  massive exodus of hundreds of thousands of ethnic Chinese to China and
  neighboring countries.
- The Vietnamese invasion of December 1978 destroyed the Khmer Rouge
  government, but China ensured that strong-armed resistance by the guerrillas continued in Cambodia. Beijing worked with the United States and
  its allies and with ASEAN in opposition to the Vietnamese-installed regime and the Vietnamese military occupation. Hundreds of thousands of
  Chinese forces invaded northern areas of Vietnam for several weeks in
  1979, and Chinese forces fired artillery barrages and carried out other
  violent military operations along the Sino-Vietnamese border for the next
  ten years.[7]
- The violence focused on Cambodia didn't end until the end of the Cold
  War. The weakened Soviet Union curbed support to Vietnam, which in
  turn saw the need to end its military occupation and seek peace. The
  Chinese were eventually persuaded to pull back support for the Khmer
  Rouge, allowing a peace agreement to be reached in 1991.

China and ASEAN. The Cambodian struggle saw China's first substantial
interaction with ASEAN. Heretofore, Beijing had been suspicious of AS-
EAN's pro-Western leanings. China also was well aware that ASEAN leading members Indonesia and, to a lesser degree, Malaysia had grave reservations about how struggling against and weakening Vietnam would open the
way to what Jakarta and Kuala Lumpur feared would be Chinese expansion
in Southeast Asia at odds with their interests.

Post–Cold War Developments

The collapse of the Soviet threat with the demise of the USSR in 1991 at the end of the Cold War greatly relieved the PRC's security concerns around its periphery, including Southeast Asia. For this and other reasons, China was less prone than during the Cold War to resort to armed struggle and gross violence. However, in reaction to the Tiananmen crackdown of 1989, the United States led efforts to isolate and pressure China, looming as a serious threat to continued communist rule in the country.

As discussed in chapter 2, from this period up to the present, the PRC leadership has focused on important foreign policy priorities designed to sustain communist rule, support Chinese economic and military development, enhance Chinese security, and advance Chinese nationalistic sovereignty claims. As noted above and discussed at greater length below, these goals often led to conflicting Chinese policies and practices in Southeast Asia, and elsewhere.[8] Up to this point, Chinese foreign relations with Southeast Asian neighbors have gone through three distinct phases and have begun a fourth phase under President Xi Jinping. The shifts from one phase to the next have seen Chinese leaders reverse or revise policy actions and goals seen as having failed or otherwise become counterproductive for Chinese interests, and to add policy actions and goals better suited to advancing Chinese interests. Against this background, it seems prudent to expect continued shifting in China's policies and practices in Southeast Asia depending on circumstances in the region and on other influences in Chinese foreign policymaking.[9]

China–Southeast Asia Relations, 1989–1996

The first phase witnessed strong Chinese efforts to break out of the post Tiananmen isolation and pressure imposed by the United States and Western-aligned countries by means of more active Chinese diplomacy. Chinese diplomacy focused on neighboring countries and other developing states that were more inclined to deal with China pragmatically and without pressure regarding China's political system or other internal affairs.

In this period, China resumed normal diplomatic relations with Indonesia and established diplomatic relations with Singapore. It accommodated international pressure leading to a peace settlement in Cambodia in 1991 and in the process shifted Chinese support from the reviled and discredited Khmer Rouge to its former adversary, Cambodian strongman Hun Sen, whom China had sharply criticized in the past. Later developments advanced Chinese relations with Hun Sen. The withdrawal of the Vietnamese forces from Cambodia and the peace agreement of 1991 provided a foundation for normalization of China's relations with Vietnam. Beijing leaders also solidified China's position as the main international backer of the military regime that grabbed power in Myanmar after aborted elections in 1988. China provided military equipment, training, and economic and political assistance to the internationally isolated regime. [10]

China in this period viewed positive interaction with ASEAN as increasingly important. It engaged actively with ASEAN in order to improve political relations, build collaborative mechanisms, and curb the ability of the United States to pressure China over human rights and other sensitive issues. [11]

The rapid growth of trade and other economic interchanges was the most important indication of Chinese–Southeast Asian cooperation in the post–Cold War period. By 1992, Sino-ASEAN trade was fifteen times the volume it was in 1975. In 1993, Sino-ASEAN trade amounted to 5.4 percent of China's foreign trade, making ASEAN China's fifth-largest trading partner after Japan, Hong Kong, the United States, and the EU. Trade increased by about 30 percent in 1994 and by 40 percent in 1995, reaching a level of $20 billion annually. ASEAN in the mid-1990s accounted for about 7 percent of China's foreign trade, and China accounted for just under 5 percent of total ASEAN trade. In general, imports and exports in China–ASEAN trade were in balance. [12]

The composition of China–ASEAN trade changed. In the early 1990s, ASEAN exports to China tended to be natural resources and primary goods and materials. By 2001, Chinese imports and overall ASEAN–China trade items were predominantly manufactured goods, notably machinery and electric equipment. Chinese exports to ASEAN long had been diversified, including agricultural commodities, metals, and mineral products, along with manufactured goods. By 2001, manufactured goods, including machinery and electrical equipment and apparel and footwear, amounted to over 60 percent of Chinese exports to ASEAN. [13]

ASEAN–China investment also grew rapidly in the post–Cold War period, though it was mainly ASEAN investment in China and not the other way around. The pattern was supported by ASEAN entrepreneurs seeing their interests well served by integrating their enterprises with China's rapidly growing and internationally competitive economy rather than by endeavoring to compete directly with Chinese manufacturers in international markets. By the end of 1991, ASEAN states had committed $1.41 billion in 1,042 projects approved by Beijing. Singapore led the ASEAN states in trade and investment in China. By mid-1994, Singapore became China's fifth-largest overseas investor, after Hong Kong, Taiwan, the United States, and Japan. By that time, Singapore had invested in 3,834 projects in China with a promised investment of $6.8 billion. Most notable was the agreement to jointly develop a multibillion-dollar industrial park in China's Jiangsu Province. By early 1996, the Chinese government had approved 10,926 projects involving

ASEAN-country investments, with agreed investments of $26.4 billion (of which $6.2 billion was already paid). By the end of that year, there were 12,342 approved investment projects, valued at $34 billion (of which $9.4 billion was already paid).[14]

Chinese investment in ASEAN was much smaller in scale. It was less than $1 billion in the 1990s. ASEAN–China economic accords included the Joint Committee on Economic and Trade Cooperation, agreed to in 1994. Some of the ASEAN states signed agreements on joint scientific and technological cooperation with China, and ASEAN as a whole signed an agreement with China to set up the ASEAN-China Joint Committee on Scientific and Technological Cooperation in 1994.[15]

China and the ASEAN countries established various bilateral mechanisms for regular high-level political dialogue, and such dialogue between China and ASEAN developed markedly. Each year beginning in 1991, the Chinese foreign minister attended, by invitation, the annual ASEAN foreign ministers' conference. In 1995, China asked to become a "full dialogue partner" of ASEAN at this annual meeting, and this was accepted in December 1997. On security issues, ASEAN China invited in 1994 to become a consultative partner in the regional security dialogue carried on by the ASEAN Regional Forum (ARF).[16]

Continued opposition to U.S. international dominance prompted Chinese leaders to join with others in the region in fostering Asia-only economic, political, and security groups that excluded or marginalized U.S. leadership. The Chinese government was a strong supporter of the Malaysian prime minister's call in the 1990s for the establishment of the East Asian Economic Caucus (EAEC). The proposed EAEC was viewed warily by the United States, which was to be excluded from membership in the group. The United States strongly supported the more inclusive APEC forum, which had been actively dealing with regional economic issues for several years.[17]

China–Southeast Asia Relations, 1996–2001

China's imperative to protect and advance nationalistic sovereignty claims also rose in the 1990s. China passed a territorial law in 1992 asserting strongly claims to disputed territories, especially along China's eastern and southern maritime borders. The Chinese military and civilian security forces backed efforts by Chinese oil companies, fishing enterprises, and others to advance Chinese claims in the Spratly Islands of the South China Sea against the expansion of such activities by Vietnam, the Philippines, Malaysia, and other claimants. A major incident in 1995 saw Chinese forces occupy Mischief Reef, located near and claimed by the Philippines. Leading states of ASEAN were alarmed by Chinese territorial expansion and the United States also publicly weighed in, voicing support for peaceful resolution of regional disputes. Meanwhile, the nine months of off-and-on large-scale Chinese military exercises against Taiwan in 1995–1996 saw few of China's neighbors explicitly side with China or the United States. But many in Southeast Asia were seriously concerned with the implications for their interests of China's assertiveness and ambitions.[18]

Trying to reduce growing regional fear of the "China threat," Chinese leaders at this time began efforts to play down military actions and assertive commentary as they demonstrated more concern to reassure neighbors in Southeast Asia and other countries of Chinese peaceful intentions.[19] They propounded principles related to a "new security concept" that built on the moderate approach China had adopted at times in the past, notably in the mid-1950s cited above, regarding the so-called five principles of peaceful coexistence in international affairs. Chinese diplomacy was very active in bilateral relations, establishing various types of special partnerships and fostering good-neighbor policies. China also increased positive interaction with ASEAN, the ASEAN Regional Forum, and other Asian regional organizations. In the 1990s, top-level Chinese leaders like Jiang Zemin, Li Peng, and Zhu Rongji and the Chinese foreign and defense ministers traveled to ASEAN countries. When their Southeast Asian counterparts visited China, they received warm welcomes. In December 1997, President Jiang Zemin attended the informal ASEAN summit in Kuala Lumpur, and China and ASEAN issued their first joint statement. Earlier in 1997, ASEAN and China set up an umbrella panel, called the ASEAN-China Joint Cooperation Committee (JCC), to oversee ASEAN–China relations. The JCC was to identify projects to be undertaken by ASEAN and China and to coordinate four other parallel mechanisms:

- ASEAN–China senior officials' political consultations
- The ASEAN–China Joint Committee on Economic and Trade Cooperation
- The ASEAN–China Joint Committee on Scientific and Technological Cooperation
- The ASEAN Committee in Beijing[20]

China preferred to deal with territorial issues bilaterally, as was evidenced in the Sino-Philippines agreements reached in 1996 on a military code of conduct, military exchanges, and the establishment of some communications between military detachments in disputed areas in the South China Sea. China and the Philippines also reached agreement regarding joint maritime scientific research, fishing, control of piracy, and other endeavors. This convergence did not prevent continued friction, however. Indonesia succeeded in gaining China's participation in an annual multilateral workshop on "managing potential conflicts in the South China Sea." In the workshop, participants exchanged ideas on dealing with the disputed territories. Southeast Asian officials also discussed the territorial issues in ASEAN–China meetings of senior working-level officials.[21]

Chinese trade relations with Southeast Asian and other neighboring countries generally grew. The Chinese economy remained stable amid the Asian economic crisis of 1997–1998. China did not devalue its currency, it sustained economic growth, and it supported some international efforts to assist failing regional economies—developments that boosted China's stature in the region.

At odds with China's reassurance of its neighbors was the concurrent strong public opposition to perceived U.S. efforts to pressure and weaken China and strong public opposition to U.S. domination and "hegemonism" in various world areas, notably including Southeast Asia. Beijing told neighboring states that its "new security concept" opposed the archaic "cold war thinking" seen in U.S. efforts to sustain and strengthen alliance relations, including U.S. alliance relations or closer military relations in Asia, notably with Japan, South Korea, Australia, and some Southeast Asian nations. Beijing indicated that these states would be wise to follow China's approach and to eschew closer alliance and military ties with the United States.[22]

China–Southeast Asia Relations: 2001–2012

As discussed in chapter 6, the coming to power of the George W. Bush administration coincided with another shift in China's policy in Asia and elsewhere. The initially tough Bush administration approach to China involved supporting Taiwan, opposing China's military buildup and Chinese proliferation practices, strengthening U.S.–Japan alliance relations, and developing ballistic missile defenses in Asia. These steps did not elicit strident criticism by Chinese officials and in official Chinese media, whereas in the recent past, even less serious U.S. steps against Chinese interests were routinely denounced as perceived manifestations of U.S. hegemonism and cold war thinking.

Over time, it became clear that China was endeavoring to broaden the scope of its ongoing efforts to reassure its neighbors that China was not a threat. The broadened efforts now included and focused on the United States. The previous Chinese efforts attacking U.S. policies and alliance structures in order to get Asian governments to choose between closer relations with China under the rubric of China's new security concept and closer relations with the United States had failed and were put aside. In their place emerged a new and evolving Chinese emphasis focused on Washington as well as on Asian and other powers that China's "rise" would be a peaceful one that represented many opportunities and no threat to concerned powers. China's initial emphasis on "peaceful rise" eventually evolved into the even more moderate rubrics focused on "peaceful development" and seeking "harmony" in relations with all powers.[23]

The shift in China's approach reinforced the positive momentum in China's relations with Asian neighbors, notably in Southeast Asia and ASEAN. The webs of agreements China established with ASEAN and its member states grew rapidly. China initiated in 2002 an ASEAN-China Free Trade Agreement (ACFTA) that Japan, India, South Korea, and other powers endeavored to duplicate in later years. It agreed that year in negotiations with ASEAN to the Declaration on the Conduct of the Parties in the South China Sea, which set guidelines on how territorial disputes should be managed. China also prompted other powers to follow its lead in being the first to sign ASEAN's Treaty of Amity and Cooperation (TAC) in 2003. It played an active role in ASEAN-convened international groups, with China's preference at the time being ASEAN Plus Three (China, Japan, and South Korea), which notably excluded the United States. China worked closely with Malaysia in influencing the creation of the ASEAN-convened East Asian Summit during Malaysia's tenure as ASEAN's annual chair in 2005. The plan was for China to host the 2006 meeting and for membership to be restricted to ASEAN Plus Three. The plan was thwarted because of opposition by Japan, Indonesia, Singapore, and others, fearing Chinese dominance in the group. ASEAN's chair remained the host of the East Asia Summit and membership was opened to India, Australia, and New Zealand, with Russia and the United States joining later.[24]

Trade continued to grow rapidly. The global economic crisis of 2008–2009 briefly curbed China–ASEAN trade, but the value of trade grew markedly in 2010, reaching $292.7 billion according to Chinese statistics, making China ASEAN's leading foreign trading partner and ASEAN China's fourth-largest trading partner. Investment by Southeast Asian countries into China was substantial, while Chinese investment in those countries remained comparatively much smaller. Investment patterns also showed China and ASEAN directly competing for investment funds from Western and advanced Asian countries. In 2002, China became the world's largest recipient of foreign direct investment (FDI), gaining about half of the FDI going to Asia, excluding Japan. In the early 1990s, China had received less than 20 percent of FDI to developing Asia, while ASEAN countries received over 60 percent. This shifted sharply during the 1990s, and by the end of the decade, the figures were reversed, with China receiving over 60 percent and ASEAN under 20 percent. Predictably, the increase in FDI added to China's overall competitiveness in such manufactured products as electronics and consumer goods, which were a mainstay in ASEAN exports to advanced economies.[25]

China's salience in Southeast Asia also showed in other ways; in 2010, there were 6,000 Chinese-language volunteers teaching 50,000 Southeast Asian students in classes sponsored by, among others, thirty-five Confucius

Institutes. By that time, almost 800 flights took place every week between major cities in China and Southeast Asian countries. Between January and October 2009, 4 million people from ASEAN countries visited China and 3.7 million Chinese visited ASEAN countries. Chinese visitors ranked among the top three foreign countries visiting ASEAN countries, representing over 6 percent of foreign visitors to ASEAN countries.[26]

Perhaps the most concrete and lasting dimension of China's improved economic relations with Southeast Asia came in the form of a wide range of highway, railroad, river, power generation, power grid, and pipeline connections that integrated China ever more closely with those Southeast Asian countries that border China. Some of the projects had the support of such international financial institutions as the Asian Development Bank. Achievements by the start of this decade included modern highways linking southeastern China with neighboring countries; the development of smoother rail transportation between China and neighboring states; the start of pipelines linking China and coastal Myanmar, thereby bypassing the choke point of the Malacca Strait; the building of hydroelectric facilities in neighboring countries and in China and building related electric transmission infrastructure that would advance access to electric power in neighboring countries and southeastern China; and Chinese alteration of the Mekong River and other rivers connecting China and neighboring Southeast Asian countries so as to remove rapids and other obstacles to smooth river transportation.[27]

The new developments and infrastructure opened heretofore inaccessible areas to greater economic development; they were welcomed by the Chinese and Southeast Asian governments and placed the economies of nearby Southeast Asian areas into ever closer relationships involving China. The hydroelectric and river alteration projects prompted serious international criticism as well as some criticism in China on grounds of environmental damage, population dislocation, and negative effects on downstream fishing and other interests.[28]

After the setback in seeking Chinese leadership in the East Asia Summit, China's attention to Southeast Asia and ASEAN appeared to decline for a few years. Although Chinese officials continued to talk about ASEAN taking the lead in Asian multilateralism, they also privately and sometimes publicly showed impatience with the slow pace of progress under the leadership of ASEAN governments, many of which were beset with fundamental problems of political unrest and instability. China's ability to advance relations with ASEAN and the region were postponed when Thailand had to cancel and reschedule the annual ASEAN summit and related meetings in late 2008 because of political turmoil in Bangkok that closed the airports in the city. The Chinese efforts faced an added setback when the rescheduled meeting in Thailand in April 2009 was canceled and foreign delegates evacuated as hostile demonstrators invaded the meeting site. In this period, China found itself following the United States and others rather than leading the foreign powers in interaction with ASEAN. Notably, China delayed as the United States considered and finally made the appointment of an ambassador to ASEAN. As a result, China's later appointment of an ambassador to ASEAN seemed to be following the U.S. lead rather than setting the pace as China did earlier in the decade in dealing with the ACFTA and signing the Treaty of Amity and Cooperation. China also followed the U.S. lead in setting up a representational office with the ASEAN headquarters in Jakarta.[29]

Changes under Xi Jinping (2012–present)

As discussed earlier, beginning in 2009–2010 China adopted what many outside of China and some in China assessed as "assertive" practices, particularly regarding territorial claims with its Southeast Asian and other neighbors and the United States. For a time, the Chinese actions were mixed with strong reaffirmations of reassurance and peaceful intent, creating a muddled situation regarding China's overall intent toward Southeast Asia.

In the lead-up to and under the leadership of Xi Jinping since 2012, Chinese intentions in the South China Sea and other territorial disputes became clearer. In effect, Beijing was playing a double game.

On the one hand, domestic nationalism and demands for a less deferential and more activist Chinese foreign policy drove Chinese policy. The Xi government's widely publicized policies met with domestic approval as they advanced Chinese South China Sea claims. Rapidly expanding Chinese military and paramilitary capabilities along with impressive oil rigs, fishing fleets, dredging machines, and construction abilities allowed and probably prompted China's leaders to expand in areas that have long been claimed by China. China's advance also was in reaction to the Obama government's rebalance policy opposed by Beijing.

On the other hand, Xi's China married its tough policy on South China disputes with visionary publicity of China's proposed Silk Road Belt, Maritime Silk Road, and related proposals such as the still-forming Asian Infrastructure Investment Bank (AIIB) and related economic initiatives. In effect, China set forth a choice for the Philippines, Vietnam, other Southeast Asian disputants of China's South China Sea claims, ASEAN, and other governments and organizations with an interest in the South China Sea, notably the United States. Pursuit of policies and actions at odds with Chinese claims in the South China Sea would meet with more of the demonstrations of Chinese power seen in China's takeover of Scarborough Shoal from the Philippines in 2012, its deployment of an oil rig and a massive armada of defending ships near islands very sensitive to Vietnam in 2014, and its recent massive land reclamation for force projection in the far reaches of the South China Sea. At the same time, Southeast Asian and other neighbors' moderation and/or ac-

quiescence regarding Chinese South China Sea claims would result in mutually beneficial development flowing from Chinese economic largess.

In 2012, Chinese authorities took extraordinary measures and used impressive demonstrations of Chinese security, economic, administrative, and
diplomatic power to have their way in the South China Sea: [30]

- China employed its large and growing force of maritime and fishing security ships, targeted economic sanctions, and repeated diplomatic warnings
  to intimidate and coerce the Philippines to respect China's takeover of
  disputed Scarborough Shoal.
- China deployed one of the world's largest (32,000-ton) fish processing
  ships and a fleet of thirty fishing boats supported by a supply ship to fish
  in disputed South China Sea areas.
- China created a new, multifaceted administrative structure backed by a
  new military garrison that covered wide swaths of disputed areas in the
  South China Sea. A state-controlled Chinese oil company offered nine
  new blocks in the South China Sea for foreign oil companies' development that were far from China but very close to Vietnam, with some of the
  areas already being developed by Vietnam.
- China ensured that the 2012 ASEAN chair, Cambodia, prevented South
  China Sea disputes from consideration at the annual ASEAN Ministerial
  Meeting. The result was a remarkable display of ASEAN disunity in the
  first failure of the annual ASEAN Ministerial Meeting to conclude with an
  agreed-upon communiqué in the forty-five-year history of the group.

At the same time, Chinese officials and official Chinese media commentaries
emphasized the material benefits for regional countries in strengthening economic interaction with China. Thus, what emerged was a Chinese approach
having two general paths:

- One path showed South China Sea claimants in the Philippines, Vietnam,
  and others in Southeast Asia, as well as their supporters in the United
  States and elsewhere how powerful China had become in disputed South
  China Sea areas, how China's security, economic, administrative, and
  diplomatic power was likely to grow in the near future, and how Chinese
  authorities could use those powerful means in intimidating and coercive
  ways short of overt use of military force in order to counter foreign "intrusions" or public disagreements regarding Chinese claims.
- The other path forecast ever closer "win-win" cooperation between China
  and Southeast Asian countries, ASEAN, and others *provided* they avoided
  public controversy and eschewed actions challenging or otherwise complicating the extensive Chinese claims to the area. China emphasized the
  importance of all concerned countries to adhere to efforts to implement the

2002 Declaration of the Conduct of the Parties in the South China Sea (DOC). It duly acknowledged recent efforts supported by ASEAN to reach the "eventual" formulation of a code of conduct (COC) in the South China Sea, implying that the process of achieving the latter may take some time.

The most notable advance of Chinese intimidating and coercing other claimants in the South China Sea came in 2014 and involved Vietnam. China's abrupt deployment in the disputed Paracel Islands of the South China Sea on May 2 of a forty-story oil rig along with a protecting armada of over 100 fishing, coast guard, and reportedly military vessels shocked the region and particularly Vietnam, the other main claimant to these islands. Concurrent disclosures showed large-scale dredging creating Chinese-controlled islands on previously submerged reefs in the disputed Spratly Islands with China fortifying some of these sites for surveillance and power projection far from the Chinese mainland.[31]

The egregious Chinese advances demonstrated to audiences at home and abroad how far Beijing was prepared to go in confronting its neighbors, the United States, and other powers concerned with regional stability in order to advance its broad territorial claims in the South China Sea. The Chinese moves to defend and advance control in the South China Sea elicited uniformly positive treatment in Chinese media while Chinese leaders exuded confidence in facing predictable negative international reactions.

Nevertheless, probably unanticipated by Beijing's planners were mass demonstrations in Vietnam that turned violent, killing five Chinese and injuring many more while causing widespread damage to Chinese and other Asian invested enterprises. Sharply critical rhetoric and moves at odds with Chinese interests by the United States, Japan, Australia, and some Southeast Asian countries also underlined deepening wariness and growing diplomatic and security measures directed at China. Chinese delegates at the annual Shangri-La defense forum in late May were on the defensive in the face of direct attacks on China led by the United States and Japan.

Against this background, China's removal of the rig and its protective fleet in mid-July, much earlier than expected, was widely interpreted outside China as designed to reduce tensions, at least for a time. China denied this interpretation. It nonetheless toned down harsh rhetoric while continuing to defend the rig deployment. High-level Sino-Vietnamese talks in Beijing on August 27 reduced bilateral tensions.

There was no easing of the disputes over Chinese dredging to create outposts for power projection in the far reaches of the South China Sea. Those issues worsened and provided the focus on American and allied complaints at the 2015 Shangri-La defense forum.

The regional reaction to the Sino-Vietnamese confrontation appeared to show unwillingness by most Southeast Asian countries to take a stand against China. The Philippines was very critical of Chinese actions, and Manila collaborated with Hanoi in seeking options. The United States came into the lead of international critics of Chinese coercion; Japan and Australia usually weighed in supporting the American stand. However, most Southeast Asian countries remained on the sidelines. Although Malaysian officials continued to affirm claims to South China Sea territory also claimed by China, the Malaysian prime minister visited China for six days in late May 2014 and had meetings with President Xi Jinping without any apparent discord over the South China Sea or other issues. The Singaporean foreign minister ended a visit to China in mid-June pledging to avoid "finger pointing" and to serve as a "bridge" between China and ASEAN as Singapore undertakes the role of coordinating country for China–ASEAN relations in 2015. Adding to uncertainty in the face of China's challenge was that the Obama government's rhetoric had yet to be supported with concrete actions as part of a clear strategy to get China to stop its coercive advances of territorial control at the expense of its neighbors.

An overall implication of the Chinese double game in Southeast Asia and with ASEAN was that Beijing seemed to judge that regional circumstances would require acceptance of China's new assertiveness. The Southeast Asian countries and ASEAN on their own seemed too weak and divided to resist; whatever will to resist would be undermined by China's growing economic sway over neighboring countries.

In fact, China's apparent calculation may be incorrect. China's economic influence over ASEAN continued to grow but it remained far from dominant. According to ASEAN statistics, China, including Hong Kong, accounted for almost 18 percent of ASEAN's foreign trade in 2013; and growing Chinese investment in ASEAN saw Chinese plus Hong Kong investment account for 10.5 percent of foreign investment to ASEAN in the 2011–2013 period.[32] Of course, as shown in chapter 6, China's economic importance for ASEAN has a variety of limitations that make it less than likely that the regional governments will fall under China's sway for economic reasons. For example, ASEAN receives much more investment from Japan and several times more from the EU. And ASEAN does proportionately less trade with China than does either Australia or South Korea, middle powers that have repeatedly made clear to Beijing that their independence of action will not be compromised despite possible consequences for their economic relations with China. Meanwhile, as noted in chapter 3, it is probably incorrect to view the massive Chinese publicity in support of new Chinese lending to Southeast Asia and other countries along China's periphery as making China's neighbors bow to Chinese expansion in the East China Sea and the South China Sea. Most notably, the propaganda fails to hide China's mediocre record in Southeast

Asia and other developing countries in following through with repeated multibillon-dollar foreign investment pledges and other promises of economic support.

Further complicating purported Chinese dominance is the Obama government's multifaceted rebalance policy of broad engagement that is widely welcomed in Southeast Asia and strongly supported by U.S. allies Japan, Australia, and the Philippines. American leaders from President Obama on down have taken the lead internationally in warning China against coercive moves to change the regional status quo. They have begun to escalate military and other actions to deter China and support those subjected to Chinese intimidation. Against this background, the outlook for continued coercive Chinese advances seemed unclear and uncertain.[33]

AUSTRALIA, NEW ZEALAND, AND THE PACIFIC ISLANDS

Disputes over the South China Sea, stronger involvement of Australia and New Zealand in Asian regional bodies, and the expanded U.S. role in the area under President Obama's rebalance policy strengthened Chinese interests in relations with Australia, New Zealand, and the Pacific Island countries. China's economic and political prominence has grown. China's relations with Australia have improved markedly over the years, based notably on an upswing in Australian raw material exports to China and a marked increase in Chinese exports to Australia. Official Chinese attention to Australia, New Zealand, and the Pacific Islands has been extraordinary, with numerous high-level and other official visits. Nonetheless, officials and elites in regional governments often register wariness as they carefully calculate the pros and cons of closer China ties.[34]

The newly installed conservative government of Prime Minister John Howard endorsed the U.S. show of force during the 1996 Taiwan Strait crisis, a stance that reinforced a Chinese tendency to view Australian policy in the region as the same as that of the United States. As the United States moved to solidify alliance relations with Tokyo and Canberra, Chinese officials worried about U.S.-backed efforts to encircle and "contain" China. Chinese efforts to improve relations with Australia were widely seen in Canberra as designed to weaken Australian cooperation with the United States against Chinese interests.[35]

Howard's departure and the election of Kevin Rudd's center-left Labor Party in November 2007 suggested a possible shift away from Howard's pro-U.S. strategic orientation. Rudd used his fluency in Chinese to good effect in an exchange of visits with Hu Jintao, and Australia began a ministerial-level strategic dialogue with China. Rudd's government also opposed the expanding of the U.S.–Japan–Australia strategic dialogue to include India—a step of concern to China. At the same time, Australia reinforced its strategic relations with both Washington and Tokyo. The Rudd government also called for substantial defense increases to deal with changing power dynamics, notably the rise of China.

Shifts in Australian domestic politics saw Rudd replaced as prime minister by Julia Gillard in 2010, but he stayed on as foreign minister. The Gillard administration won a general election in August 2011. It pursued a deepening defense relationship with the United States in the face of China's military buildup and assertiveness over territorial and other issues, while sustaining positive economic ties with China. Rudd replaced Gillard as prime minister before elections in 2013 that brought the more conservative Liberal Party to power with Tony Abbott as prime minister. Abbott and his administration sustained the close economic relations with China along with the deepening alliance relationship with the United States and stronger economic and security interaction with Japan. The Australians were in the lead in the Asia-Pacific in support for the Obama government's rebalance initiatives in the region. They also were more forthright than any other regional powers with the possible exception of Japan in sharply criticizing China's coercive and intimidating advances of control at neighbors' expense in the disputed seas along its rim.[36]

Meanwhile, Taiwan's international activism under Lee Teng-hui (1988–2000) and Chen Shui-bian (2000–2008) saw Beijing intensify efforts to undermine Taiwan's position among the small Pacific Island countries. The Pacific Island regimes often switched recognition from Beijing to Taipei or vice versa in a bidding war. The China and Taiwan "money diplomacy" undermined efforts by Canberra and Wellington to condition aid in the hope of promoting better governance and viable conditions for sustainable economic development.[37] Australia and New Zealand welcomed the advent of the Ma Ying-jeou government in Taiwan in 2008, which promised to halt the use of money diplomacy and competition for diplomatic recognition in the Pacific Islands.

Australia

Australia established diplomatic relations with China in the early 1970s and became a major trading partner of China. China's rapid economic development required increasing imports of energy, iron ore, grain, and other resources, which Australia willingly provided; Chinese exports of manufactured goods to Australia also grew. A close ally of the United States, Australia generally adhered to a moderate policy and developed positive approaches in engagement with China, seeking to avoid the acrimonious disputes and controversies that sometimes marked the erratic course of U.S.–Chinese relations in the recent period. However, Australia publicly sided with Washington during the Taiwan Strait crisis of 1996. In the face of China's steady military buildup and assertive policies along its rim in recent years, Australia adopted a planned military buildup in 2009 and coordinated closely with the United States in countering perceived Chinese coercive practices in nearby seas and in support of the American strategic reengagement with the Asia-Pacific, including deployments of U.S. forces to Australia.[38]

Australian business representatives, politicians, and public opinion on the whole tended to be positive about China during the Cold War. There was widespread awareness of China's role as an increasingly important importer of Australian raw materials.[39] Of course, representatives of Australian manufacturers and unions tended to fear competition from China.[40] Australian government officials in the Howard, Rudd, Gillard, and Abbott administrations sustained a carefully balanced approach to China that avoided excessive enthusiasm as Australia sought to capitalize on new opportunities in the China market and other areas. The Australian government gave top priority to relations with the United States. They judged that U.S. power and influence in Asia were important in keeping China moving in constructive directions. Despite the decline in the U.S. image in Australia and elsewhere, U.S. power and influence were viewed as a foundation of Australian interests in the Asia-Pacific region.[41]

China became Australia's largest trading partner. In 2014, the annual trade was valued at $123 billion; over 23 percent of Australia's trade was with China. The foundation of the trade relations was China's purchase of Australian raw materials. China rapidly increased exports to Australia, so that Australia's overall trade balance with China was sometimes in deficit.[42] The two governments completed protracted negotiations over many years and signed a free trade agreement in June 2015. The agreement eased growing Chinese investment in Australia. China became the largest foreign investor in Australia the previous year. Cumulative Chinese investment in Australia was worth $1.5 billion in 2008. Cumulative Chinese investment in Australia was valued at close to $30 billion in 2014.[43]

In recent years Australia employed nonconfrontational dialogues rather than pressure tactics to encourage China to engage with the region and the world in more constructive ways. Australian officials were watchful for signs that China would use regional groupings and its growing stature in regional affairs to try to exclude the United States and Western interests and influence from Asia. They also kept a watchful eye on the rapid growth of the Chinese military's power projection capabilities.

On Taiwan, the Australian government tilted against Taiwan efforts to expand international influence and responded positively to China's call to criticize the moves by Taiwan President Chen Shui-bian to assert more independence in world affairs. Australia also came down harder on Taiwan than China in condemning the use of money and payoffs to top Pacific Island officials in order to garner diplomatic support among small Pacific Island states.[44] The shift in Taiwan's policy under President Ma Ying-jeou since May 2008 against "money diplomacy" and intense diplomatic competition with China and toward easing of tensions in the Taiwan Strait were welcomed by the Australian government.[45]

In 2009–2010, Australian relations with China were troubled over security concerns regarding China's military buildup, disputes over Chinese policies in Xinjiang and the visit of a Uighur activist to Australia, disputes over Chinese efforts to buy stakes in Australian firms, and the highly publicized criminal investigation and conviction of an Australian businessman. Vice President Xi Jinping and Vice Premier Li Keqiang—the top representatives of the new generation of Chinese leaders that gained control of the Chinese administration in 2012—visited Australia in efforts to mend fences.[46]

President Xi returned to Australia and the region in November 2014. In an unprecedented indication of top-level Chinese attention to Oceania, Xi spent ten days there, starting with his participation in the 15–16 November G20 summit in Brisbane. After the summit, Xi spent several days each in Australia, New Zealand, and Fiji.[47]

New Zealand

China and New Zealand established diplomatic relations in 1972. New Zealand sought economic opportunities in China because of post-Mao economic reforms and supported China's entry into the World Trade Organization. In 2004 it was the first developed country to recognize China's market economy status. In 2008 New Zealand was the first developed country to sign a free trade agreement with China.[48]

China surpassed Australia as New Zealand's most important trading partner in 2014 with bilateral trade valued at $18 billion. The two countries also maintained active political and defense interchanges. Among differences, New Zealand joined Australia to criticize sharply the competition between China and Taiwan in the Pacific Islands. And like Australia, New Zealand warmly welcomed the Obama government's rebalance initiatives in the Asia-Pacific, which China viewed negatively.[49] New Zealand officials relied strongly on the United States to maintain regional order in line with New Zealand's interests. Dealing effectively with China's rise added to reasons for New Zealand officials to seek to improve New Zealand's relations with the U.S. government, which saw a breakthrough during the Obama administration.[50]

The Pacific Islands

Chinese policy toward the Pacific Islands became clear in the 1990s. Chinese security interests seemed limited. China did build a satellite-tracking station in 1997 in the equator-straddling country Kiribati, but China had to dismantle that operation a few years later when the island government switched sides and established diplomatic relations with Taiwan. China sought support in the United Nations and other international bodies on issues of importance to China. This included Chinese efforts to block Japan's bid for a UN Security Council seat.[51]

On balance, however, the main driver of Chinese interest in the islands seemed to center at least until very recently on competition with Taiwan. In the 1990s, four regional states—the Solomon Islands, Nauru, Tuvalu, and Tonga—had long maintained diplomatic relations with Taiwan. Tonga switched to Beijing in 1998. Nauru switched to Beijing a couple of years later, but then after a few years switched back to Taiwan. The Marshall Islands switched from Beijing to Taipei in 1998. Palau also chose Taipei over Beijing, and Kiribati switched to Taiwan a few years after the opening of the Chinese embassy and tracking station in 1997. Others in the region—including such regional leaders as Papua New Guinea and Fiji—recognized China. In 2015, Taiwan was recognized officially by Kiribati, the Marshall Islands, Nauru, Palau, the Solomon Islands, and Tuvalu. Taiwan also was an unofficial "special dialogue" partner with the main regional organization, the South Pacific Forum.[52]

The most important development in China's efforts over the past decade to woo support from Pacific Island countries and undermine Taiwan came in Prime Minister Wen Jiabao's April 2006 visit to Fiji. Wen attended a meeting of the China–Pacific Island Countries Economic Development and Cooperation Forum. This group advances Chinese development and assistance to island countries. Excluded from the meeting (and the benefits provided by China) were those Pacific Island countries that maintained diplomatic relations with Taiwan.[53] China at the time maintained official relations with the Cook Islands, Fiji, Micronesia, Papua New Guinea, Tonga, Vanuatu, and western Samoa.[54]

China and Taiwan competed by providing aid to island governments. Unlike Western donors, the aid often came without principles of accountability, governance, transparency, or human rights as conditions for assistance.[55] Both governments also regularly hosted lavish and elaborate state visits for leaders of friendly island states.[56]

Taiwanese–Chinese maneuvering and aid giving bordering on bribery infuriated concerned officials and nongovernment elites in Australia and New Zealand. As discussed in chapter 7, the informal diplomatic truce between the moderate Ma Ying-jeou government in Taiwan and the Chinese government dampened the two governments' competition in the Pacific Islands.

Chinese economic interests in the region involved thousands of state and private Chinese companies that conducted business in the region ranging from hotels to logging. China established a Pacific Trade Office in Beijing. In 2004, China joined the South Pacific Tourism Organization and granted "approved destination status" to several island countries.[57]

At the November 2013 Second China–Pacific Islands Countries Economic and Cooperation Forum in Guangzhou, China, Vice Premier Wang Yang announced a $1 billion increase in low-interest Chinese loans to be provided over the next four years to eight Pacific Island nations having official relations with China. Chinese media said that 150 Chinese companies invested about $1 billion dollars in the countries and the value of Chinese projects built in the countries was $5.12 billion.[58]

An analysis by Australian specialists found that loans for projects came mainly from the Export-Import Bank of China and reflected the wishes of Pacific Island rulers. The result in some cases was an unsustainable debt burden. Given the constraints, they concluded that much of the $1 billion in promised Chinese financing may not be lent.[59]

Nevertheless, President Xi Jinping's unprecedented trip to the region in November 2014 saw discussion of economic cooperation in meetings in Fiji with Pacific Island leaders with official relations with China. China's media campaign supporting various "silk road" initiatives over the past year made clear that China's broadly defined 21st Century Maritime Silk Road included the Pacific Island countries.[60]

Antarctica

China began to play a more active role in Antarctica when Chinese scientists joined an Australian research expedition to the continent in 1979. In the 1980s, China set up its own scientific expedition bases and launched independent expeditions. China in the recent decade stepped up funding for upgrading existing Antarctic bases, establishing a new base, and increasing research involving Antarctica. During his visit to Australia in 2014, President Xi Jinping signed an agreement with Australia on further Antarctica cooperation, visited the Australian Antarctica research operations in Hobart, spoke by video-link with Chinese and Australian researchers working in the Antarctic, and visited the Chinese polar expedition research ship *Snow Dragon*, which was docked in Hobart. Overall, China's involvement on the continent remained modest.[61]

Chapter Ten

Relations with Southern Asia and Central Asia

The end of the Cold War, the collapse of the Soviet Union, and improvement in Russia–China relations posed opportunities and challenges for China in countries to China's south and west. Maintaining close ties with Pakistan, China found India, previously aligned with Moscow against China, more open to improved relations. The new central Asian republics also were open in a regional environment less controlled from Moscow.

Seeking to stabilize China's periphery, Chinese officials improved relations with India and in the process moderated somewhat China's past support for Pakistan on Kashmir and other issues between New Delhi and Islamabad. They secured boundaries and advanced relations with newly independent central Asian states. China's advances in central Asia came notably through the Shanghai Cooperation Organization (SCO), begun in 2001, which limited direct competition with Russia and strengthened cooperation among China, Russia, and four central Asian states. The group excluded the United States.

The U.S.-led war in Afghanistan begun in 2001 quickly toppled the terrorist-harboring Taliban regime and had a major effect on China's relative influence in southern and central Asia. The United States became the most influential foreign power in Afghanistan, Pakistan, and India, and had a few military bases in central Asia. Chinese leaders generally adjusted pragmatically and continued incremental improvements in regional relations.

The withdrawal of U.S. and NATO forces from Afghanistan came with the Obama government's strong focus on India as a western anchor in the U.S. government's rebalance policy of enhanced engagement in Asia. U.S. involvement in Afghanistan, Pakistan, and central Asia declined. The U.S. moves raised China's profile in the now more unstable Afghanistan situation and in Pakistan; the moves also complicated Chinese influence in India. The

231

foreign policy initiatives of President Xi Jinping highlighted multibillion-dollar infrastructure plans for the central Asian republics and Pakistan. Chinese toughness on border issues under Xi's rule caused friction in India.[1]

RELATIONS WITH SOUTHERN ASIA

After the Cold War, China improved relations with New Delhi, now devoid of a close strategic alignment with Moscow and more open to international economic and political exchange. The progress came to some degree at the expense of traditionally close Sino-Pakistani relations. Chinese leaders did their best to persuade Islamabad that Pakistan's interests were well served by a Sino-Indian rapprochement. China reportedly also continued support for Pakistan's nuclear weapons, ballistic missile, and other defense programs. Beijing continued some economic support for crisis-prone Pakistan, though the United States led international economic efforts to shore up the Pakistani government during the war in Afghanistan.[2]

Indian nuclear tests carried out in May 1998 by a newly installed nationalistic government in New Delhi posed the most serious challenge to China's policy in the region since the end of the Cold War. Subsequently, Chinese officials demonstrated a carefully calculated reaction that endeavored to avoid debilitating entanglements in southern Asia while checking Indian aspirations for greater regional and nationalistic prominence and preserving the close Chinese relationship with Pakistan. Beijing sought to work closely with the United States in the process, hoping to capitalize on their common interests and to avoid international publicity regarding China's role as a key supporter of nuclear weapons proliferation in Pakistan.[3]

Chinese leaders showed more balance in their approach to India and Pakistan during the Indian–Pakistani military confrontations over disputed territories in Kashmir. Seeking to avoid possible nuclear war in southern Asia, China refrained from past rhetoric strongly supporting Pakistani interests against India. Its evenhanded treatment of Indian–Pakistani differences during the so-called Kargil conflict of 1999 was followed by similarly balanced treatment during flare-ups of India–Pakistan tensions in 2001–2002.[4] China worked cooperatively with the United States, European powers, and others seeking to avoid war and limit instability in southern Asia.

Chinese officials adjusted to the sharp rise in U.S. power and influence in southern Asia as a result of the U.S.-led war in Afghanistan beginning in 2001. On the positive side as far as China was concerned, the more prominent U.S. commitment meant that Pakistan's government would once again enjoy strong support from the U.S. superpower. The U.S. material and military aid and strong political support would shore up shaky Pakistani government finances and enhance the Pakistani government's abilities to suppress militants and extremists promoting terrorism that affected China as well as others in the region. Growing U.S. involvement in India strengthened the U.S. ability to influence New Delhi to ease tensions with Pakistan and to avoid war in southern Asia.[5] At the same time, however, the new U.S. presence and influence had many negative implications for Chinese interests. Commentators in official Chinese media voiced concerns about an alleged U.S. ambition to encircle China militarily.[6] Chinese leaders played down these concerns as they continued to pursue constructive Chinese approaches designed to improve incrementally Chinese interests and influence in southern Asia. Using "dialogues," high-level visits, and other diplomatic measures, Beijing publicly emphasized the positive and minimized the negative with all its southern Asian neighbors, including India.[7]

China faced a difficult task in influencing India. India has long been at odds with China over territorial issues and over China's long-standing support for Pakistan. India and China also tended to be seen at home and abroad as rivals for influence and leadership in Asian and world affairs. In recent years, the two governments backed their industries, which competed actively for international energy, in order to fuel their respective burgeoning economies. Energy security added to factors influencing both powers to view warily their respective military improvements and alignments, especially those affecting transportation routes from the oil-rich Middle East.[8]

China and India fought a border war in 1962; India was humiliated. Incremental efforts to ease tensions and improve relations moved forward in the 1980s and appeared to receive an added boost from the collapse of the Soviet Union. For many years, the latter had fostered a close strategic relationship with India based in part on Soviet–Indian mutual suspicion of China. Prime Minister Rajiv Gandhi visited China in 1988, Premier Li Peng visited India in 1990, and President Jiang Zemin traveled there in 1996.[9] The regular exchange of visits by top-level Chinese and Indian leaders in following years were accompanied by many agreements, along with positive rhetoric asserting mutual determination to settle the border issue and other differences and to build on rapidly expanding economic cooperation and trade.[10]

As India and China improved relations, China continued to modify its long-standing support for Pakistan.[11] It was already evident in the 1970s that China was unwilling to take significant military action against India in the event of an Indo–Pakistani war. During the 1965 Indo–Pakistani war, Chinese forces did take assertive actions along the Indian border in order to divert Indian forces and weaken their assault against Pakistan. But when India defeated Pakistan in the 1972 war, which saw the dismemberment of Pakistan and the creation of an independent Bangladesh, China took no significant military action.

In the 1980s and 1990s, China further modified its public stance in support of Pakistani claims against India over territorial and other issues. Beijing notably adhered to an increasingly evenhanded approach over the sensitive Indo–Pakistani dispute over Kashmir. By 2008 it was reported that Chinese President Hu Jintao offered to mediate between India and Pakistan in order to help resolve the issues regarding Kashmir between the two countries. Terrorist attacks in Mumbai's financial district in November 2008 were linked to a Pakistani-based organization reportedly involved in resisting Indian control in Kashmir. China changed its past unwillingness to have the UN Security Council condemn the group and sided with a UN Security Council vote declaring the group to be a terrorist organization.[12]

China continued its close military and economic support for Pakistan. Numerous reports showed that China played a major role for many years in assisting Pakistan's development of nuclear weapons and related ballistic missile delivery systems, though Chinese officials denied this. In an interview published on June 3, 1998, President Jiang Zemin was asked, "Has China helped Pakistan to make its nuclear bomb?" He replied, "No, China has not helped Pakistan."[13] Continuing to benefit from Chinese military, economic, and political support, Pakistan chose to emphasize the positive in Sino-Pakistani relations and deemed counterproductive any significant show of irritation with Beijing's shift toward a more evenhanded public posture in the subcontinent. Recent high points of Chinese interaction with Pakistan included repeated visits by the Pakistani prime minister to China, reports of transfers of jet fighters and other advanced Chinese military equipment to Pakistan, and advances in China's nuclear power cooperation with Pakistan, reportedly in response to India's success in achieving a major nuclear cooperation agreement with the United States. Chinese Premier Wen Jiabao spent three days in Pakistan following a visit to India in December 2010. He announced an increase in what had been seen as a small (initially $10 million) Chinese donation for relief from a flood disaster in Pakistan in the summer and various commercial deals and assistance.[14]

As Sino-Indian relations improved, both sides saw their interests best served by giving less attention than in the past to continued significant areas of disagreement,[15] notably the following:

- Border issues: Large expanses of territory along India's northwestern and northeastern frontier remained in dispute. In many rounds of border talks since 1981, the two sides made slow progress in their putative effort to delineate the so-called line of actual control and other lingering problems. During Jiang Zemin's 1996 visit to India, the two sides codified many of the ad hoc confidence-building measures that had evolved over the years along the mostly quiet frontiers. Determination to settle the border issue was a focal point in senior-level dialogue between Chinese and Indian diplomats begun in 2003, though concrete results were slow to be an-

nounced, and occasional public assertions by Chinese and Indian government officials of claims to disputed border territories continued.

- Chinese ties with Pakistan, Myanmar, and other southern Asian states:
Long-standing close Chinese military ties with Pakistan and more recently
with Myanmar were viewed by some Indian officials as a Chinese "pincer
movement" to contain India. Long-standing Chinese ties with Bangladesh,
Sri Lanka, and Nepal added to the Indian suspicion that China sought to
use such ties to hobble India's ambitions by causing New Delhi strategic
concerns in southern Asia. China's military and political support assisted
the Sri Lankan government in its final victory in the long-running war
with the separatist Tamil Tigers in 2009, opening the way to closer strategic as well as economic and political cooperation. At times in the past,
some in India also saw the United States playing a supporting role through
its engagement policy toward China. Over the past decade, however, India
transformed this concern by nurturing a closer relationship, notably closer
military relations, with the United States. Officials in the United States
said that they were interested in developing these ties with India, along
with nuclear, economic, and other ties, for a variety of important reasons,
including as a strategic hedge in case of Chinese moves contrary to
American interests.

- Tibet: Beijing gave high priority to countering the efforts by the Dalai
Lama and his supporters to seek a greater international profile for Tibet.
Despite some greater Indian recognition of China's control of Tibet, China
remained at odds with New Delhi over India's continued hosting of the
spiritual leader and his government in exile.

- Trade, energy, and energy security: Continued Indian efforts to open the
economy and increase exports led to greater cooperation between the
economies of China and India but also Indian economic competition with
China for investment and markets and more direct competition for international energy resources. Concern over securing sea lines of communication from the oil-rich Persian Gulf saw India increase its already powerful
naval force in the Indian Ocean and prompted China to develop closer ties
with Pakistan, Myanmar, Sri Lanka, and others in developing port and
communications assets that would help secure Chinese access to Persian
Gulf oil and could involve Chinese naval forces in the region at some
point in the future.

- Asian and world leadership: India wanted a permanent seat on the UN
Security Council. China on the one hand said that it supported India's bid
and on the other made sure that UN reform was so slow that China would
remain Asia's only permanent member on the council. India reportedly
resented Chinese efforts to gain admission to the Indian-dominated South
Asian Association for Regional Cooperation, while New Delhi was
pleased that Japan and some Southeast Asian powers resisted Chinese

efforts to exclude India and other interested outside powers from the new East Asian Summit of December 2005. This allowed New Delhi to play a prominent role at the new organization. China appeared unenthusiastic in the face of India's efforts with support of Russia to gain observer status in the SCO. China, India, and others competed for influence in Southeast Asia through their respective free trade initiatives and involvement with efforts to secure sea lines of communication through the region. China also maneuvered unsuccessfully within the Nuclear Suppliers Group to thwart approval in 2008 of India's landmark nuclear cooperation agreement with the United States.

Recent Relations

In general, Sino-Indian relations settled on a path of limited cooperation that appeared likely to continue with no major diversion for at least several more years.[16] The prospects for another military conflict between China and India appeared to be low, and the chances that the two rivals would put aside their differences and become close partners also appeared to be low.

China and India were at odds over many issues that continued to make further rapprochement difficult. The relationship remained asymmetrical. The economic and strategic military disparities were wide. When viewing negative aspects of Chinese–Indian relations, Beijing regarded a more confident and prosperous India as a bothersome neighbor, a growing rival for influence in Asia, and a potential anti-China partner of the United States. Beijing, however, did not regard India as a major military threat or trade competitor. China, on the other hand, loomed larger in Indian calculations. Many Indians saw China as an undemocratic power that represented a long-term challenge to India's security.[17]

Key elements of the rivalry that did not seem likely to be resolved quickly or easily included the following:

- The role of Pakistan: Pakistan remained India's traditional and most immediate rival and also one of China's closest strategic partners—both relationships having a long history. Despite Pakistan's steep economic and political decline in recent years, Beijing still valued a stable and peaceful Pakistan that could assist in constraining India, protecting China's western flank from Islamic extremists, and facilitating Chinese entrée to the Persian Gulf and the Islamic world. By contrast, Indian hostility toward Pakistan was visceral. New Delhi regarded China's conventional military, missile, and nuclear weapons support to Pakistan as a hostile act.
- The border issue: Predictions of progress in the protracted border negotiations waxed and waned amid clear signs of serious differences. A border settlement that essentially formalized the status quo proved elusive amid

deep-seated mutual suspicions, both sides' firmness on territorial claims, and India's reluctance to set a precedent for settling the Kashmir dispute with Pakistan.

- Competition for influence elsewhere in Asia: China and India viewed one another as potential adversaries, and each was taking steps to counter the other's influence as both expanded power and influence in Asian affairs. China had a clear lead in spreading influence in Southeast Asia, but India competed with its own free trade agreements, diplomatic overtures to the Association of Southeast Asian Nations (ASEAN), military deployments, and, particularly, efforts to improve ties with Myanmar and Vietnam; it also sought strategically to foster closer cooperation in Asia with Japan and the United States.[18]

Limited but growing cooperation between China and India was occurring on a number of issues and seemed likely to continue.[19] For a time during the post–Cold War period, both looked for ways to promote a multipolar world order against the dominance of the U.S. superpower; this effort flagged first in India and then in China in 2000–2001. Both opposed U.S. missile defense proposals, but India moderated its opposition in 2001. Both cooperated in the U.S.-led antiterrorism campaign after September 11, 2001. Indian, Chinese, and Russian foreign ministers met periodically in sessions that were portrayed at times as opposed to U.S. international leadership. They added Brazil to form the so-called BRIC international grouping in 2009, and in 2011 they added South Africa to form the BRICS international grouping. The various groups' influence came more from the actions and importance of the member countries than from the trilateral, BRIC, or BRICS forums.[20] China and India seemed to stand together against Western demands that they take concrete measures to curb carbon emissions that cause climate change, and at times they joined coalitions opposed to plans in the World Trade Organization (WTO) for greater international trade liberalization.[21] They also sought to counter perceived Western infringements on state sovereignty that posed dangerous precedents for Tibet, Taiwan, and Kashmir.

The two powers also endeavored to expand bilateral trade. Trade grew from $350 million in 1993 to nearly $7 billion in 2003 and reached $70 billion in 2014. Unfortunately for India, its trade deficit with China that year rose to $37.8 billion. China was India's largest trade partner since 2008. India remained relatively less important as a Chinese trading partner, though it was China's largest trading partner in southern Asia. Trade grew despite the world economic crisis but as noted in chapter 4, Chinese foreign trade forecasts dropped substantially in 2015 as a result of international circumstances and changes in Chinese economic policies.[22]

Domestic politics were more important in determining possible shifts in India's policies than in China's. In China, the leadership seemed in basic agreement about the outlines of China's policy toward India, while the voices of those in India who benefited from or advocated improved ties with China were offset by defense planners, economic strategists, and politicians who were very wary of Chinese power and intentions. These strategists were resolved to maneuver effectively in order to protect Indian interests in anticipation of a possible shift toward a more assertive, less accommodating stance by Beijing.[23]

Certain catalytic events that appeared less than likely could steer the relationship on to more cooperative or competitive paths than the path cited previously, which was seen as most probable. More rapid movement toward a border settlement or a sharp deterioration of China–Pakistan relations could lead to closer relations between India and China. However, the coming to power of more hawkish leaders in India or an India–Pakistan conflict in which Pakistan's survival was in jeopardy would run the risk of another Sino-Indian military confrontation.[24]

President Clinton visited India in 2000. The Bush administration followed with high-level consultations that markedly improved U.S.–Indian relations even before the upswing in U.S.–Indian cooperation after September 11, 2001. Military ties between the United States and India developed rapidly, and a major nuclear agreement was the centerpiece of President Bush's 2006 visit to New Delhi—which reciprocated the visit of the Indian prime minister to the United States in 2005. The Barack Obama administration also carried out summit diplomacy to solidify India's prominent position in the U.S. government's overall rebalance policy in the Asia-Pacific. An important determinant in a more competitive Sino-Indian relationship is U.S. policy, where each Asian power—especially China—tends to see movement by Washington to court the other as a U.S. attempt at containment. A deepening Sino-Indian rivalry also could evolve as a by-product of close Indo–U.S. strategic cooperation or renewal of strong U.S. cooperation with China-backed Pakistan.

Conversely, possible U.S. military operations to implement international sanctions—which China and India viewed as potentially threatening to their own freedom of action in handling sensitive issues of sovereignty, such as Taiwan, Tibet, and Kashmir—could prompt closer Sino-Indian cooperation. A more cooperative Sino-Indian relationship probably would not preclude each side from pursuing advantageous economic and other bilateral relations with the United States.

Consultations in Beijing, New Delhi, other Indian and Chinese cities, and Washington in recent years[25] showed that high-level contacts and improvement in the atmosphere in Sino-Indian relations, along with advancing trading relations, pushed the relationship in a positive direction. Indian officials and opinion leaders in the past were quite wary of advancing relations with a rising China, but on the whole they recently seemed more confident and ready to pursue cooperative relations along common ground while remaining cognizant of remaining serious differences.

Among the latter, the perceived breach of trust by China in the 1962 war was not forgotten. Strong fears persisted concerning alleged Chinese ambitions to hobble India's rising power by using close Chinese support for Pakistan and developing Chinese relations with such regional nations as Myanmar. China's vibrant economy and active diplomacy often were viewed as in competition with Indian interests. Existing in a strategic area adjoining both powers, ASEAN was depicted as a key arena of Sino-Indian competition for economic benefit and political influence. China was more advanced than India in interacting with Asia-wide groups, and New Delhi was lagging behind Beijing in seeking a leading position in these bodies. In central Asia, China was seen supporting the now-ended refusal of the SCO to allow Indian participation, and despite its public posture, China was said to oppose India's gaining a permanent seat in the UN Security Council.

The previously mentioned issues, the broader historical experience of Sino-Indian relations, and especially the absence of substantial change in Chinese support for Pakistan tended to cause Indian specialists to reserve judgment about China's avowed benign intentions. Many Indian specialists judged that the recent positive Chinese approach toward India could change as a result of changes in China or abroad. They were not reassured by what they viewed as the less than transparent Chinese decision-making process. They looked to improved or continued strong Indian relations with the United States, Japan, and Russia as assisting India in case China changed to a harder line toward New Delhi. They also favored a continuation of the status quo in the Taiwan Strait, which they viewed as keeping China occupied with strategic concerns on China's eastern frontier and reducing the likelihood of assertive Chinese behavior toward India on the west. In recent years, New Delhi advanced its low-keyed unofficial relationship with Taiwan, much to the satisfaction of the Taiwanese government.[26]

Among key barometers of Chinese intentions monitored by Indian skeptics were Chinese missile and nuclear support to Pakistan and elsewhere in the region (China's intermediate-range ballistic missile sales to Saudi Arabia in the 1980s continued to be viewed negatively). A Chinese resort to force against Taiwan and disputants in the East China Sea and the South China Sea would reinforce Indian wariness toward the People's Republic of China (PRC), while Chinese military modernization, including missile developments threatening India or expanded naval forces in the southern Asian region, would be viewed with concern.

Weighted against elements of distrust and suspicion were growing positive conditions and perceptions in India regarding the status and outlook of relations with China and China's approach to Asian and world affairs. Heading the list was a perceived change in the asymmetry of power and influence between China and India. Until recently, it was argued, China tended to discount Indian power and influence, and India tended to fear Chinese power and influence. Several changes since the late 1990s altered this equation, giving Indian specialists a view that India was now dealing with China in a more equal way and from a position of improved strength. Key changes included India's demonstration of a nuclear weapons capability and missile delivery systems combined with a strong overall modernization of Indian conventional weapons; India's growing economy, which attracted investment and other interchange from the West, Japan, and other developed economies; and India's improved military and other ties with the United States, along with continued close ties with Russia and improving relations with the European Union and Japan.

These perceived changes in power relations compelled China to "come to terms" with India, resulting in greater positive Chinese attention to developing relations with India, according to some Indian specialists. Indian businesses were seen at least somewhat better able to deal with China's highly competitive manufacturers, who were feared in the past and were still viewed by many in India as a major threat to Indian industries.

According to Indian specialists, the heightened threat of international terrorism to China prompted Chinese officials to deepen antiterrorism cooperation with India, while Chinese leaders also came to view Pakistan as a liability as far as the terrorist threat to China was concerned. Chinese officials were said to express privately to Indian officials their concerns over anti-Chinese terrorists remaining active inside Pakistan; Chinese officials also expressed concern about Pakistani nuclear weapons and weapons technology exports and the possibility of such material getting into the hands of terrorists who were targeting China. Pakistan's weak economic conditions added to Chinese incentives to sustain close ties with India as a stable anchor of Chinese policy interests in southern Asia, according to Indian specialists.

The status and outlook of China's relations with India in 2015 showed momentum on the side of the positive aspects of India–China relations, while the negative aspects served as brakes slowing forward movement and precluding the kind of enthusiastic "China fever" seen from time to time in some other Asian states.[27] Indian government representatives and nongovernment specialists showed greater confidence in India's ability to deal with Chinese policies and behavior in pragmatic ways that would preserve and enhance Indian interests. Compared to a few years earlier, there was less alarm and seemingly more realistic views of the dangers posed by Chinese manufacturers to their Indian counterparts. In security areas, Indian officials and specialists seemed similarly less alarmed and more realistic about Chinese activities in Pakistan, Myanmar, Bangladesh, Nepal, and elsewhere in southern Asia. In the past, these activities had been viewed with deep concern as part of perceived Chinese efforts to encircle and contain Indian power and influence.

The China–Pakistan tie remained a counterweight to Indian leadership in southern Asia and Asian affairs, but Indian officials and nongovernment specialists seemed less concerned about Chinese activities in other nearby states. China also was seen as compelled by India's power and influence to deal pragmatically with the southern Asian power in order to foster and develop Chinese interests in the region.

Against this background, the publicity surrounding the exchanges of top-level visits was generally positive. It reflected advances in trade and other exchanges but indicated no breakthroughs on key differences, including the border issue. Reported "stand-offs" between Chinese and Indian border forces marred Xi Jinping's first visit to India as China's president in September 2014 and the first visit of Premier Li Keqiang to India in 2013.[28] Reports of respective military buildups along the frontier and occasional public spats between Chinese and Indian officials over the boundary remained a leading negative factor in bilateral relations. Xi's visit saw China promise efforts to invest $20 billion in India in the next five years. Prime Minister Modi's visit to China in May 2015 focused on strengthening mutually beneficial economic relations.[29]

Looking out, two major uncertainties in Chinese relations with southern Asia were posed by the U.S.-NATO withdrawal from Afghanistan and China's highly ambitious investment plans for Pakistan. The Afghanistan government of President Ashraf Ghani (2014–) sought China's assistance in dealing with the armed Taliban opposition and in investment in Afghanistan. China in February 2015 offered to mediate stalled peace talks involving the Afghan government and the Taliban. Afghanistan presumably would benefit from China's strong stress on investment as part of its Silk Road economic initiatives, but advancing investment in Afghanistan faced serious challenges on account of pervasive insecurity.[30]

President Xi Jinping's visit to Pakistan in April 2015 featured strong publicity in support of a very ambitious Chinese plan to build a $46 billion, 3,000 kilometer China-Pakistan Economic Corridor from China's Xinjiang Uighur Autonomous Region through the Karakorum Mountains to the Arabian Sea. As noted in chapter 4, it remained very difficult at this early stage to determine how and whether the $46 billion Chinese plan will be implemented and paid for. The implications of such deep Chinese investment in Pakistan for India and for China's relations with India seemed profound and largely negative. Meanwhile, some foreign experts on Chinese assistance efforts pointed to studies that said China's past promises of Chinese assistance valued at $66 billion to Pakistan in 2001–2011 had seen only 6 percent of the promises actually kept.[31]

RELATIONS WITH CENTRAL ASIA

After the end of the Soviet Union, China expanded ties across central Asia in order to stabilize its western frontier, gain access to the region's energy resources, and balance Western influence.[32] Improved ties with central Asian states shielded China's Xinjiang region and its ethnically Turkic Uighur population from outside Muslim and pan-Turkic influence. Central Asian leaders said they would not tolerate separatist groups targeting China, though China worried they might lack sufficient resolve to eradicate the threat. In this context, U.S., Russian, and Chinese efforts to support antiterrorist initiatives in central Asia beginning in 2001 seemed to reflect some important common ground among the three powers.[33]

China's regional energy projects sought secure supplies and diverse sources. Beijing concluded agreements to develop Kazakhstan oil and gas fields and constructed oil and gas pipelines with Kazakhstan, Uzbekistan, Turkmenistan, and other countries. The projects were expensive, logistically difficult, and complicated by inadequate energy-processing and transport systems. There were many signed agreements but slower progress toward completing the pipelines and filling them.[34]

Among the most notable energy-related developments, on September 24, 1997, China and Kazakhstan signed agreements worth $9.5 billion that involved development of two major oil and gas fields and the construction of pipelines in Kazakhstan, according to press reports. One pipeline was to cover 3,000 kilometers from Kazakhstan into western China and take an estimated five years to build. The pipeline was eventually built and began operation in 2006. By some estimates in recent years, exports of oil to China through central Asia amounted to about 10 percent of total annual Chinese oil imports.

Meanwhile, China signed an agreement with Turkmenistan in 2006 to export natural gas through a new pipeline reaching China through Uzbekistan and Kazakhstan. This pipeline was completed expeditiously and was supported by a separate natural gas pipeline linking Uzbekistan and Kazakhstan with China. The new efforts undercut what had been a situation of close control of the exporting of central Asian natural gas by Russian pipeline administrators.[35]

The continuing civil war in Afghanistan had important implications for central Asia as well as southern Asia. China generally urged all warring parties to stop fighting and to discuss their problems among themselves without any outside interference. China was willing to support international proposals for peace but typically supported a major role for the United Nations, where China had a permanent seat on the Security Council. The Chinese also were reported to suspect the Taliban faction in Afghanistan of being supportive of radicals in Xinjiang.[36]

In the years prior to U.S. withdrawal of most of its forces in 2014, when the Obama government increased combat operations against a resurgent Taliban threat, China straddled the fence and avoided commitments. China seemed close to the Pakistan security forces impeding U.S.-led attacks along the Afghan-Pakistan border. Chinese enterprises were said to do mining and some other economic efforts beneficial to the U.S.-backed Afghan government. As noted in chapter 5, China endorsed the May 2, 2011, killing of Osama bin Laden by American forces.[37]

Chinese commentary often viewed expanding NATO activities as U.S. efforts to extend influence in the region, squeeze out Russia, and contain China. Beijing sharply criticized a September 1997 exercise in Kazakhstan and Uzbekistan sponsored by NATO's Partnership for Peace, which featured a record-setting long-distance air transport of 500 U.S. troops to Kazakhstan.[38]

China's expanding influence in central Asia generally prompted little overt opposition from Moscow, which heretofore had jealously guarded the region's resources. For its part, Beijing regarded a central Asian power balance favoring Russia as advantageous to its own interests. China pursued its interests in central Asia cautiously, presumably in part to avoid risking a strong nationalist backlash from Russia's leadership.[39]

The Chinese interests included the following:

- Strategic position: China sought a stable and productive international environment around China's periphery while fostering a more widely accepted Chinese leadership role. Beijing also aimed to legitimate Chinese positions on major international issues, strengthen relations with Russia, and serve as a counter to U.S. power and influence. And China's diplomacy in central Asia aimed to prevent the region from becoming a distraction from China's internal development and more important foreign policy goals.
- Security: China tried to curb outside support to separatist Uighurs in Xinjiang Province. It saw common ground with regional governments in working against terrorist and criminal elements.
- Borders: China sought to demarcate, demilitarize, and stabilize borders with Russia, Kazakhstan, Kyrgyzstan, and Tajikistan. Border stability was central to Chinese development plans and foreign policy priorities.
- Economics: China's main economic interest in the region was energy. China sought growing amounts of oil and gas abroad, and central Asian countries—especially Kazakhstan and Turkmenistan—were promising partners.[40]

Chinese-developed economic and transportation links strengthened China's regional approach.[41] This pattern also was seen in Chinese efforts to deepen channels of trade and communication involving rail, road, river, pipeline, electric transmission, and other links with various southern and Southeast Asian countries bordering China. Following agreement with the Soviet Union in 1984 to build the first direct rail link between Xinjiang and Soviet central Asia (what is now Kazakhstan), the two sides agreed to broaden the cooperation on this "Eurasian land bridge." China double tracked some of its rail links leading to the cross-border line. It also built a line in the late 1990s into southwestern Xinjiang and used this line as the basis for plans to build a new rail link between Xinjiang and Kyrgyzstan. China also proposed building another rail link in northern Xinjiang, with a different crossing point into Kazakhstan. Highway links between Xinjiang and central Asia improved markedly beginning in the 1990s, with five hard-surface roads linking China and Kazakhstan and a new road to Kyrgyzstan. The China–Kazakhstan pipelines, as well as the natural gas pipeline linking China with Turkmenistan, added to China's connections to the region.[42]

China became the largest recipient of exports from Turkmenistan (68 percent of the country's exports), Uzbekistan (28 percent of exports), and Kazakhstan (22.7 percent of exports). It received 8 percent of Tajikistan's exports and 5 percent of Kyrgyzstan's exports. Chinese exports of manufactured goods spread throughout central Asia. China became the leading importer to Kyrgyzstan (51 percent of the country's imports), Tajikistan (40 percent of imports), Kazakhstan (30 percent of imports), and Uzbekistan (20 percent of imports). Chinese goods accounted for 13 percent of Turkmenistan's imports.[43]

Mongolia

Mongolia considers itself separate from central Asia; it nonetheless often is treated together with central Asia in broad assessments of Chinese foreign relations. A long and often hostile history with China made Mongolia more wary of China than were the states in central Asia. Without its Soviet ally, the Mongolian government moved toward free market and democratic reforms; it watched carefully for signs of Chinese dominance while seeking reassurances from other powers, especially Russia and the United States. Beijing demonstrated little overt concern over Mongolia as the government carefully avoided standing against Chinese interests.[44]

Recently, China dominates Mongolia's foreign trade. China receives more than 90 percent of Mongolia's exports and is Mongolia's largest supplier. China also is the country's largest foreign investor. Mongolia has relied on Russia for energy supplies, leaving it vulnerable to price increases; in the first eleven months of 2013, Mongolia purchased 76 percent of its gasoline and diesel fuel and a substantial amount of electric power from Russia.[45]

Balancing Russia and China and attempting to ensure independence and sovereignty, Mongolia has sought strong relations with "highly developed countries of the West and East" such as the United States, Japan, and Germany, as well as with India, South Korea, Thailand, Singapore, Turkey, Denmark, the Netherlands, Finland, Austria, Sweden, and Switzerland. The priority countries are Mongolia's so-called third neighbors, the United States, Japan, South Korea, Germany, and India.[46]

Mongolia supported the U.S. role in Asian security, in particular in northeastern Asia. It also backed the United States in the war on terrorism and sent some troops in support of the U.S.-led military action in Iraq. It has welcomed Obama administration officials visiting the country as part of the rebalance policy. The cornerstone of the Mongolian–Chinese relationship was the 1994 Treaty of Friendship and Cooperation, which codified mutual respect for the independence and territorial integrity of both sides. Mongolian leaders in private said that they continued to fear political forces in China that questioned Mongolian independence.[47]

The issue of Tibet was one of some sensitivity in Mongolian–Chinese relations. Mongolia shared with Tibet its brand of Buddhism and in the 1990s and 2000s received visits from the Dalai Lama despite Chinese protests. Mongolians sympathized with the plight of Tibet, recognizing that but for the backing of the Soviet Union, they might have suffered a similar fate. Realistically, however, they knew that they could do little for Tibet.

President Xi Jinping has taken the lead in his government in visiting Mongolia and all of China's central Asian neighbors.[48] The focus of Xi's often repeated high-profile visits to these countries has been to emphasize Chinese economic largess seen in Beijing's various Silk Road and related economic initiatives. The governments of these states reportedly remain wary of Chinese intentions, but the Chinese blandishments are attractive and there is little competition from other powers. Most notably, Russia's President Vladimir Putin seeks closer ties with China in a period of Russian tension with the West and sanctions registering Western opposition to Russia's forceful annexation of Crimea and continued aggression against Ukraine.[49]

Regional Multilateral Cooperation

China's interest in using multilateral organizations to pursue Chinese interests around its periphery in the post–Cold War period showed first in central Asia. Building on a growing "strategic partnership" with Russia, China hosted in Shanghai in April 1996 the first meeting of representative leaders of what became known as the Shanghai Five. The Shanghai Five consisted of China, Russia, and the three other former Soviet republics that border on China: Kazakhstan, Kyrgyzstan, and Tajikistan. The group focused at first on finalizing border settlements between China and the four former Soviet republics, demilitarizing their frontiers, and establishing confidence-building measures. These issues were dealt with in the 1996 Shanghai Five Agreement on Confidence Building in the Military Field along the Border Areas and the 1997 Agreement on Reducing Each Other's Military Forces along the Border Regions.[50] At their summit in July 2000, the Shanghai Five declared success in building a border belt of trust and transparency.[51] They also had begun collaborating against terrorism, arms smuggling, and a range of illegal transnational activities affecting their common interests. They agreed in 1999 to set up a joint antiterrorist center in Kyrgyzstan.

In the late 1990s, the Shanghai Five came to many agreements to institutionalize their procedures in dealing with border and security matters, and regularized meetings of the group's defense ministers and foreign ministers were established. Uzbekistan joined the group in July 2001, establishing the SCO, with six members: Russia, China, Kazakhstan, Kyrgyzstan, Tajikistan, and Uzbekistan. The declaration of the creation of the SCO showed strong attention to regional security issues involving terrorism, drug trade, and other transnational crimes affecting the countries. Work in subsequent annual summit meetings of the group included efforts to establish a charter and small budget for the organization, to start the small antiterrorism center in Kyrgyzstan, and to set up an SCO secretariat headquartered in Beijing and paid for by China to foster cooperation on terrorism and other transnational issues. Chinese leaders showed strong interest in broadening the scope of the SCO to include strong economic development efforts, notably in building transportation infrastructure that would benefit western China.[52] At the SCO prime ministers' meeting in Tajikistan in September 2006, Prime Minister Wen Jiabao announced that China had set a goal of doubling the current level ($40 billion) of Chinese trade with SCO members in the next few years.[53]

Chinese and other officials were careful to reassure the United States and others that the SCO was not adverse to U.S. interests or the concerns of other interested powers. However, they remained firm against proposals that would admit the United States or its allies to the group. They allowed Mongolia, Pakistan, Iran, and India to join as observers.[54]

Russia and China predictably used the Shanghai Five summit meetings and other occasions to issue statements and make speeches against U.S. domination and to call for a multipolar world, though such rhetoric dropped off once Russia and then China moderated toward the Bush administration by mid-2001. Until mid-2001, Chinese officials and media were uniform in calling attention to the Shanghai Five as a model of the type of mutually respectful, consultative, and equal state relationships favored by China's new security concept (NSC) in contrast to the "power politics" and "hegemonism" practiced by the United States.[55]

Reflecting some revival of an anti-U.S. emphasis, the SCO summit of July 2005 called on the United States and Western powers to set a deadline for the withdrawal of Western military forces from central Asia. The SCO military exercise of August 2005 involving about 10,000 Chinese and Russian troops had little to do with traditional SCO concerns about border security and antiterrorism; they were focused instead on a show of force in waters east of China that appeared directed at Taiwan, Japan, and the United States. The expulsion of U.S. forces in 2005 by SCO member Uzbekistan was welcomed by the group's leaders, Russia and China.[56]

Developing the SCO

The April 26, 1996, Shanghai summit meeting was the first meeting of the Shanghai Five and was initiated by China. China proposed the meeting in part to address issues regarding and to stabilize the sometimes tense 7,000-kilometer border China shares with the former states of the Soviet Union. The Treaty of Deepening Military Trust in Border Regions signed at the summit called on the signatories to invite the others to observe military drills and inform about any military activities within 100 kilometers of the border. It also forbade attacks on each other and restricted the scope and frequency of military maneuvers in border areas.[57] The next year, the Treaty on Reducing Military Forces in Border Regions was signed in Moscow. This agreement proposed to reduce the total number of military forces along the border to fewer than 130,400.[58] At a 1999 Shanghai Five summit in Bishkek, Kyrgyzstan, both the 1996 and the 1997 treaties were seen as successful, and the borders were said to be secure and stable.[59]

The Shanghai Five summit in Dushanbe, Tajikistan, moved beyond the previous emphasis on border security to stress a variety of regional issues of mutual concern. The gathered leaders discussed treaties to fight separatism, extremism, and terrorism—three "evils" stressed repeatedly by Chinese leaders. They also talked about dealing with drug trafficking and illegal immigration. In this context, the leaders agreed to hold regular meetings of officers from their justice, border control, customs, and public security departments.[60] They judged that developments and problems in the region had become more complicated and that the existing mechanisms under the Shanghai Five needed upgrading.[61]

At the summit in Shanghai in 2001, Uzbekistan was added to the group, prompting the declaration of the establishment of the Shanghai Cooperation Organization. The summit created a council of state coordinators to write a charter for the SCO and to establish regular meeting schedules.[62] The representatives of the six countries also signed the Shanghai Convention on Combating Terrorism, Separatism, and Extremism. The convention established a legal foundation for combating these problems.[63]

From that point on, SCO activities developed along several paths. In addition to the annual head of state meetings, regular meetings occurred at the levels of head of government, foreign minister, defense minister, and heads of law enforcement, energy, and trade departments. At the SCO summit in St. Petersburg in 2002, the group endorsed the SCO charter. It provided a legal basis of the principles, purpose, and tasks of the organization; the procedures for adopting new members; the legal effects of SCO decisions; and the means of cooperation with other multilateral organizations. [64] Reflecting China's strong role as a driving force behind the SCO's creation and development, Chinese Foreign Minister Tang Jiaxuan said at the summit that the SCO was no longer a "club for empty discussion but a viable institution capable to make an important contribution to the international war on terror." [65]

In January 2004, the SCO opened two permanent bodies: a secretariat in Beijing and a regional antiterrorism structure based in Tashkent. Chinese media highlighted UN Secretary-General Kofi Annan announcing at the opening of the secretariat that "an institutionally strengthened SCO has been evolving into an increasingly important regional security organization. The secretariat represents the logical extension of that process and the UN looks forward to multifaceted cooperation with our new regional partner." [66] Mongolia's foreign minister was present at the secretariat opening, and Iran, India, Pakistan, and Turkey expressed interest in joining. [67]

Chinese media were particularly insistent that the success of the SCO had to do with its "new security view." At the 2000 summit, it was declared that "a new security view that is built on mutual trust, equality, and cooperation are conducive to enhancing mutual understanding and good neighbor relations." [68] Chinese President Jiang Zemin called the "new view" the "Shanghai spirit." At the 2001 summit, Jiang declared that "the new model of regional cooperation represented by the 'Shanghai spirit' is a partnership not an alliance. It is an open mechanism not targeting any third party. In dealing with state-to-state relations it advocated the principle of equality and mutual benefit for the sake of win-win results and mutual development." [69] Of course, the ideas seen in this SCO development had their roots in China's Five Principles of Peaceful Coexistence of the 1950s, which emphasized respect for sovereignty, nonaggression, and noninterference as well the reworking of those principles seen in China's NSC of the 1990s, which advocated greater dialogue and mutual development and security. [70]

The smooth development of the SCO and China's interests in fostering regional cooperation and greater Chinese influence met serious challenge in 2008 because of Russia's invasion of Georgia and military support for and recognition of South Ossetia and Abkhazia, two small entities that broke away from Georgia with Russian support. On the one hand, China sought to sustain good relations with the newly assertive Russia and had little sympathy with Western-aligned Georgia and the proposed expansion of NATO to include Georgia. On the other hand, China was sensitive to its own secessionist problems in Tibet, Xinjiang, and Taiwan and wary of close alignment with Russia's resort to military action that placed it in direct opposition to the United States and the West. A summit meeting of the SCO in Tajikistan a few weeks after the Russian invasion placed the spotlight on China and its central Asian neighbors regarding their position on the Russian action. In the end, the SCO avoided strong support for the Russian action. Official Chinese commentary and expert opinion made clear that China remained focused on domestic concerns, sought to promote harmony in regional and world affairs, viewed the sharp decline in Russian relations with the United States and the rest of the West as a source of concern, and saw little benefit for China in taking sides in the disputes.[71]

Chinese Security Interests

China's stronger support for multilateral security mechanisms in the SCO showed that Chinese officials recognized that internal security issues could not be met only with confidence building and other such measures among sovereign states. Chinese rulers historically viewed central Asia as a source of threats to Chinese national security. The dissolution of the Soviet Union; the civil wars in Tajikistan, Afghanistan, and Chechnya; and the rise of Islamic unrest in western China created a tense and unstable regional situation of great concern to Chinese leaders. Militant attacks in Xinjiang were related to the rise of Islamic extremism in central Asia and the Taliban regime in Afghanistan. The Center for Strategic and International Studies reported in 2003 on over 200 militant attacks resulting in 162 deaths in Xinjiang over a decade after the end of the Cold War.[72]

Home to a large ethnic Turkish Muslim population of Uighurs who periodically resisted Chinese rule, Xinjiang remained central to Chinese concerns. Unrest and insurrection there would be especially troubling for Beijing given Xinjiang's large size, vast resources, and vital strategic location. There were considerable Uighur populations in many central Asian states, including 120,000 in Kazakhstan and 50,000 in Kyrgyzstan. Suppressing dissidents in Xinjiang affected China's relations with these neighboring governments. Nonetheless, rising militant activism directed against China and other SCO governments caused them to band together against the threat posed by militant Islam and the associated "three evils"—terrorism, separatism, and religious extremism.[73]

At the 2001 SCO summit in Shanghai, all the members pledged a collective response in defense of a government attacked by militants. In one sense, this agreement created a basis for China to project power abroad through a multilateral mechanism.[74] This was followed by an agreement at the 2002

SCO foreign ministers' meeting that endorsed Chinese actions fighting the "East Turkistan terrorists," along with Russian suppression of terrorists in Chechnya.[75] At a subsequent SCO defense ministers' meeting in Moscow, the SCO representatives issued a communiqué on military cooperation and established a senior defense official commission and a joint expert group responsible for coordinating military exercises among SCO participants.[76]

In addition to cooperating against terrorists, the SCO participants agreed to cooperate more regarding general emergency situations. In October 2002, Chinese and Kyrgyzstan militaries cooperated in a joint exercise in southern Kyrgyzstan, and in August 2003, five SCO members (not Uzbekistan) collaborated in a military exercise known as Coalition 2003.[77] That exercise had two parts, consisting of a mock hijacking of an airliner and a bus. Later notable exercises included the large exercise in 2005 noted earlier that seemed focused on the United States and its East Asian partners, the "Peace Mission 2007" joint antiterrorism exercise held in August that year, and the "Peace Mission 2010" involving 5,000 troops for two weeks of exercises in southern Kazakhstan.[78]

The rise in Russian assertiveness in areas bordering Russia in 2008–2009 posed a new development affecting the Chinese calculus in central Asia and more broadly in international affairs. The cautious Chinese reaction to the Russian military action in Georgia and its broader implications for relations with the West seemed to follow a path of least resistance between conflicting Chinese goals, notably regarding the maintenance of good Chinese relations with the United States and the West on the one hand and good relations with Russia on the other. The international economic crisis and sharp decline in energy prices seemed likely for a time to sap Russian economic strength and thereby possibly explained the more cooperative and less assertive Russian posture toward the West seen at the start of the Obama administration in 2009 and 2010. In turn, such developments helped China's sometimes awkward balance between Washington and Moscow by allowing Beijing to avoid having to choose between the two powers on important issues. Russia's shift in 2010 to a more cooperative stance with the United States and NATO on arms control, security, and economic issues nonetheless seemed awkward for China as it stood in contrast with Chinese truculence toward the United States at that time over Taiwan arms sales, Tibet, U.S. military surveillance near China, and economic issues. Of course, this phase passed with the sharp downturn in U.S.–Russian relations over Ukraine and Crimea and Xi Jinping's prominent solidarity with Vladimir Putin in the face of Western sanctions over the past two years. Meanwhile, how the Russian leadership would use energy resources and a somewhat revitalized military to its advantage among the relatively weak central Asia states and how it would act in the face of Chinese efforts to expand influence in central Asia remained open questions for Chinese policy.[79]

Chinese Economic Interests

China also saw the SCO and broader regional cooperation as helpful in expanding Chinese economic growth and influence in the region. Chinese and central Asian economies were complementary; central Asian states had raw materials that China needed (notably oil and gas), while China had consumer goods sought by the people in these states. Chinese leaders focused on Xinjiang were well aware that the bulk of the province's foreign trade was with central Asian states. As Xinjiang's economic development was part of Beijing's strategy to calm unrest in the area, Chinese leaders paid special attention to central Asian trade. As noted earlier, China became the largest foreign trader of the central Asian states with forecasts of growing Chinese economic importance for these countries.

Russia endorsed closer trade relations with China. President Putin said at an SCO summit in Shanghai in 2001 that "cooperation in economics, trade and culture is far more important than military cooperation."[80] A statement from a meeting of SCO trade ministers in 2002 said that "the SCO is different from the 'Shanghai Five' because regional economic cooperation is its main task."[81] A 2003 meeting of SCO prime ministers issued the Outline for Multilateral Economic and Trade Cooperation of the SCO, furthering economic progress among the members.[82]

A key driver in China's economic interest in central Asia is energy. With the rapid growth of China's economy, China became a net importer of oil. This greatly increased Chinese government interest in securing reliable supplies of foreign oil and natural gas. In this context, China's involvement in energy projects in Russia, Kazakhstan, Turkmenistan, Uzbekistan, and elsewhere was part of a broader Chinese effort to plan for the future.[83]

China's Recent Strength in Central Asia

As noted above, the Xi Jinping government gave high priority to improving relations with China's neighbors to the north and west, revitalizing and expanding broadly defined Silk Roads marking Chinese economic and strategic interests. The Xi government pushed for greater economic interchange in the SCO. At the fourteenth SCO summit in Tajikistan in September 2014, Xi focused on a long list of Chinese priorities for the SCO to increase economic involvement. Among the sometimes bewildering array of Chinese billion-dollar initiatives involving the Silk Road plans, Xi promised a Chinese loan of $5 billion to support economic cooperation among SCO states and promised to increase by $1 billion China's contribution to the China-Eurasia Economic Cooperation Fund, which was launched in 2013, to $5 billion.[84]

As discussed in chapter 11 dealing with Chinese-Russian relations, China's professed neutrality regarding Russia's takeover of Crimea and continued aggression against Ukraine was accompanied by repeated summits with President Putin concerning consolidation of close economic relations and security ties. China stood against Western sanctions and other such interference. Progress with the Shanghai Cooperation Organization was not impeded as Beijing-Moscow ties strengthened across the board.[85]

Overall, Chinese foreign policy in central Asia was effective in promoting border security, curbing transnational crime and terrorism, and supporting greater economic interaction. Chinese active participation in the Shanghai Five and SCO marked clear advances in Chinese government willingness to engage vigorously with multilateral organizations and to put aside past Chinese suspicions that such international groups would invariably be influenced by forces hostile to Chinese interests. As President Jiang Zemin said in reference to the SCO at the St. Petersburg summit in 2002, "Facts have proven that the establishment of this organization was correct and I am fully confident of its future."[86]

Nevertheless, the shortcomings and relative weakness of the SCO and of China's overall influence in central Asia also were evident at various times. China and its central Asian allies did little of consequence in dealing with the Taliban and the problems in Afghanistan. After September 11, 2001, the U.S.-led Operation Enduring Freedom accomplished more in the area in five months than the Shanghai grouping had accomplished in five years. The SCO members remained wary of one another, and there were numerous obstacles to greater economic, political, and military cooperation. By contrast, at various times many of these governments, including Russia and China, were willing—and several were eager—to cooperate to varying degrees with the sharp increase in U.S. military activity and presence in central Asia after 2001.[87]

Economically, China's trade with the post-Soviet central Asian republics expanded, while Russia's trade with them generally declined. Yet Russia was still an important trading partner. The central Asian countries also turned their trade attention to Turkey and the European countries, which became important trading partners for these states.[88] As central Asia was rapidly transformed after September 11, 2001, from a peripheral area of U.S. concern to a front line in the war on terrorism, China saw its increased influential position in central Asia, built incrementally over the previous decade, diminished in comparative terms. The military, economic, technological, and political capabilities of the United States seemed to offer more to the central Asian states than they could hope to obtain from China. China was put into a secondary role in central Asia. However, its persistent drive to incrementally improve its stature and work with the SCO in the process was part of an apparent longer-term effort to sustain Chinese interests and relevance in regional political, economic, and security trends. The Chinese also took advantage of adverse developments affecting the U.S. position in central Asia, such as Uzbekistan's decision in 2005 to expel U.S. forces from the country.[89]

Looking out in 2015, China's approach to the central Asian region seemed coherent, generally successful, and likely to continue along existing lines. While Chinese leaders have had several important interests and goals in pursuing relations with central Asia, they have managed them without significant conflict, reinforcing the likelihood of continuity and durability in China's approach to the region. Notably in contrast to Chinese approaches in eastern and southern Asia, there has been less tension between China's national development emphasis on promoting peace and development abroad and Chinese national security, territorial, and national unification objectives that emphasize China's use of force against foreign threats in ways that alienated and alarmed some of China's neighbors and other concerned powers.

Chinese interests and goals in central Asia continued to focus on the following:

- Borders and security, curbing outside support to separatists in Xinjiang province, and seeking common ground with regional governments in working against terrorist and criminal elements
- Access to central Asian oil and gas supplies and development of strong trade relations
- Fostering a stable and productive environment along this segment of China's periphery while enhancing China's regional and international prominence through effective bilateral and multilateral diplomacy

One of the reasons that China's government has been able to develop and sustain a coherent approach in post–Cold War central Asia despite potentially conflicting goals is that external forces that the Chinese leaders do not control and that strongly influence Chinese foreign policy in other areas do not play much of a role in China–central Asian relations. For example, Taiwan is insignificant in central Asia. Chinese threats to use force against Taiwan separatism have much less disruptive impact on China's central Asian neighbors than they do elsewhere around China's periphery. Japan's role in central Asia also is relatively small. China's sometimes strident reactions to disputes with Japan have a less disruptive impact on China's relations with central Asia neighbors than on Chinese relations with neighbors in other parts of China's periphery.

The upswing in U.S. military presence and influence in central Asia after the terrorist attack on the United States was an important change and had an impact on China's strategic calculus in central Asia. However, its overall importance has been offset by the fact that the foundation of U.S. power in central Asia is much weaker than in other parts of China's periphery. In addition, the record of relatively low levels of follow-on U.S. aid and official involvement in the region and Russia's continued leading importance among the central Asian republics also have diminished Chinese concerns about the U.S. military presence and influence in central Asia. Finally, the withdrawal of U.S. and NATO forces from Afghanistan has reinforced a decline in American interest in central Asia. The countries of the region are not included within the broad scope of the Obama government's rebalance policy to the Asia-Pacific region.[90]

Meanwhile, changes in Chinese foreign policy and behavior influenced by Chinese leaders' lack of confidence and uncertainty in their legitimacy at home and abroad are less in the case of central Asia than in other parts of China's periphery.[91] Notably, the need for Chinese leaders to adopt tough policies on territorial or other nationalistic issues with central Asian neighbors is less than in the case of Chinese relations with some neighbors to China's east and south. Part of the reason is that the Chinese government has been successful in keeping Chinese media and other public attention focused away from territorial and nationalistic issues with central Asian neighbors. In addition, Chinese territorial and nationalistic issues with central Asian neighbors seem less salient to core Chinese interests in development and national power than such Chinese issues with some other neighbors. And the generally authoritarian central Asian governments have endeavored to deal constructively and pragmatically with China over territorial and other disputes, a contrast with the nationalistic posturing of some of China's eastern and southern neighbors.

Although the course of China's strategy toward central Asia seems more stable than in other areas of Chinese foreign relations, there remain significant uncertainties clouding the longer-term outlook. For one thing, specialists are divided on China's long-term goals in the region and how these goals could lead to a major change in China's approach to the region. Some emphasize strongly that the prevailing Chinese interest in regional stability and energy trade will remain the important determinants of Chinese policy and will reinforce continuity in the Chinese policy and behavior we see today.[92] However, others argue that recent accommodating and moderate Chinese policies and behavior presage the creation of an emerging central Asian order dominated by China that will be reminiscent of the Sino–central Asian relationship during the strong dynasties in Chinese history.[93]

Meanwhile, China's influence in central Asia and developments in the region depend heavily on the power and policies of Russia. Russian weakness in the 1990s provided the opportunity for expanding Chinese influence in central Asia and the foundation of Russian inclination to cooperate closely with rising China on trade, including arms trade, and a variety of international issues. Under the leadership of Vladimir Putin, Russia has endeavored to rebuild elements of national strength and to use them to reassert Russian interests against those perceived as encroaching on Russian interests. Thus far, the Russian relationship with China generally has remained cordial and cooperative, though Russia–China competition for influence in central Asia and over other issues continues.[94] If China were to be seen to seek regional dominance in central Asia, Russia might adopt more competitive and perhaps confrontational policies that would have a major impact on China's existing approach to the region. At the same time, if Russia successfully pursues a more assertive leadership role in the region, China's leaders presumably would be forced to choose between accommodating rising Russian power and possibly losing Chinese equities and influence or resisting the Russian advances.

Chapter Eleven

Relations with Russia and Europe

With the demise of the Soviet Union following the end of the Cold War, Beijing's relationship with Moscow improved amid massive changes in the relative power between the two former adversaries. China advanced dramatically in economic modernization and international prominence, becoming the world's second power. Russia floundered for a decade, losing the military, economic, and other elements that had made the Soviet Union a major power in Asian as well as European and global affairs. The sparsely populated Russian far east saw steep declines in population, living standards, and military readiness as neighboring China boomed and its military modernized rapidly, partly with the help of Russian weapons and technical specialists.

Since the start of the leadership of Vladimir Putin fifteen years ago, international energy demand and the more disciplined Russian administration have raised Russia's economic importance as an exporter of oil, gas, and other commodities to Asian as well as other consumers. Russia was positioned as a key player in international disputes such as the controversies over the U.S.-led invasion of Iraq, Iran's nuclear development program, and the civil war in Syria. Russia also was critically important for Chinese interests in central Asia and for supplies of modern weaponry. However, Chinese efforts in the 1990s to forge a united front with Russia against U.S. "hegemonism" failed, in part because Putin in early 2001 steered Russian policy in a direction that gave primacy to businesslike relations with the United States. China soon followed suit.

Chinese and Russian leaders subsequently issued occasional joint statements and engaged in military exercises and diplomatic activities in opposition to U.S. interests and international leadership. Under Putin's rule, Russia often shifted to varying degrees to a tougher stance against the United States and the West on a variety of issues, including perceived intrusions on Russia's power and influence along its periphery, notably NATO expansion and deployment of U.S.-backed antiballistic missile systems in the Czech Republic and Poland. China gave some political support to Russian complaints against the perceived Western encroachment on Russian security interests. But when Russian military forces in August 2008 attacked Western-backed Georgia over territorial issues, Chinese leaders avoided taking sides. The weakness of any Russian–Chinese commitment against the United States and the West showed again when Russia shifted for a time in 2010 to a more cooperative stance with the United States and NATO on arms control, security, and economic issues that stood in contrast with Chinese truculence toward the United States at that time over Taiwan arms sales, Tibet, U.S. military surveillance near China, and economic issues.

Xi Jinping came to power with determination to pursue high-profile foreign policy where China was prepared to be assertive in advancing Chinese interests in a wider range of what China called core interests. Consolidating relations with Russia was high on his list of priorities; his first trip abroad as president in March 2013 was to Russia, where he met with Putin for the first of what became a pattern of frequent summits each year between the two presidents. The substance of the meetings saw agreements on building pipelines providing large amounts of Russian gas and sales of some of Russia's most advanced weapons. Xi's assertiveness toward U.S. Asian allies and the United States coincided and meshed well with Russia's shift toward a harder stance toward the West after a brief thaw in 2010. China's professed neutrality regarding Russia's takeover of Crimea and continued aggression against Ukraine failed to mask Chinese strong support for the Russian president and his provocative actions against Western interests.

Overall, the post–Cold War period shows that Chinese relations with Russia remained among the top priorities in Chinese foreign policy. Russia's geographic location, energy resources, nuclear arsenal, great-power position, and relatively modern weaponry warranted continued close attention by Chinese leaders.

In contrast, the developed countries leading the European Union (EU) were far away from China. They engaged in few military activities in areas of key importance to China. As a result, they tended to receive lower priority in Chinese foreign relations. However, China's trade depended increasingly on access to European markets, and European investment in China was an important boost to China's modernization. Educational and technical contacts between China and Europe grew along with economic relations. Chinese leaders also sought to encourage European opposition to U.S. policies, notably making thus far unsuccessful efforts to get the European countries to override U.S. opposition and end their embargo on transfers of military equipment to China. Burgeoning Sino-European economic and cultural ties along with strong common antipathy among leading European states and

China regarding controversial Bush administration policies, notably the U.S.-led invasion of Iraq, led to predictions of ever closer Sino-European alignment against Washington. However, such predictions soon foundered on the realities of widely diverging interests and values between China and European countries.[1]

RELATIONS WITH RUSSIA

Following the Cold War, China's relations with Russia developed in positive and constructive ways that endeavored to minimize differences and at times allowed Beijing and Moscow to use the image of closer cooperation to boost their respective international leverage, especially against the United States. For Beijing, the "strategic partnership" with Moscow provided a model for Chinese efforts to ensure stable relations with neighbors and major world powers. Facing an embargo on Western military sales to China following the Tiananmen crackdown of 1989, China turned to Russia for large-scale purchases of advanced equipment. The equipment was necessary as China built up military forces directed notably against Taiwan and possible U.S. involvement in a Taiwan contingency.

Wary of China's rising power along Russia's sparsely populated and weakly controlled Asian periphery, Russian leaders nonetheless found the advantages of arms sales and defense cooperation with China irresistible. The value of annual sales averaged $2 billion a year by the late 1990s. Bilateral economic relations also grew, but from a low base. Russia's importance to China in this regard was as a supplier of oil and other resources. Bilateral trade with Russia represented a very small percentage of China's overall foreign trade, though it was a higher percentage of Russia's more limited foreign trade.[2]

Chinese leaders showed keen awareness of the limits of Russian economic strength and political stability. The Russian leadership under Vladimir Putin established a clearer priority, where relations with China generally ran second to Russia's relations with the United States and the West. For many years, it was rare that Chinese and Russian leaders allowed rhetorical, political, and military gestures in support of Russian–Chinese assertiveness and independence against the West to get in the way of their respective strong interests in maintaining working relations with the United States and its allies and close associates; they also had difficulty forging a common front against the West even when one or the other, particularly Russia in recent years, seemed inclined to do so.[3]

Background to Improved Relations

China and Russia have had a long and often troubled history. Czarist Russia's expansion into the Far East came largely at the expense of the declining Chinese Empire. Nineteenth-century treaties saw vast stretches of territory formerly under China's rule become part of the Russian Empire. China's internal weakness and political dislocation during the first half of the twentieth century provided opportunities for Vladimir Lenin and Joseph Stalin to seek allies and foster revolutionary movements favorable to the Soviet Union. Soviet involvement was often ham-handed and, on occasion, worked against the immediate interests of the communist guerrilla movement in China led by Mao Zedong.[4]

Seeking economic support and strategic backing in the face of an indifferent or hostile West, Mao Zedong's newly formed People's Republic of China (PRC) sought an alliance with Stalin's Soviet Union in 1949. After many weeks of hard bargaining, the alliance was signed on February 14, 1950. The alliance relationship was essential to China's security and its military, economic, and social development in the 1950s. Soviet aid, advisers, and guidelines were key features fostering the changes under way in China. But steadily escalating differences arose over strategy toward the United States and international affairs, the proper ideological path to development, and the appropriate leadership roles of Mao Zedong and Nikita Khrushchev in the world communist movement. Soviet aid was cut off in 1960. Polemics over strategy and ideology led to more substantive disputes over competing claims to border territories. Armed border clashes reached a point in 1969 at which the Soviet Union threatened to attack Chinese nuclear installations, and Chinese leaders countered with a nationwide war preparations campaign against the "war maniacs" in the Kremlin. Party relations were broken, trade fell to minimal levels, and each side depicted the other in official media as a dangerous international predator.

The start of Sino-Soviet talks on border issues in October 1969 eased the war crisis, but each side continued preparations for the long-term struggle against its neighboring adversary. As the weaker party in the dispute, China attempted to break out of its international isolation and gain diplomatic leverage against perceived Soviet efforts at intimidation and threat. Beijing's opening to the Nixon administration was an important element in this policy. The Soviet Union continued its previous efforts to build up military forces along the Sino-Soviet and Sino-Mongolian borders in order to offset any perceived threat from China. It also pursued this course to provide a counterweight against any Chinese effort to exert pressure on countries around China's periphery that were interested in developing closer relations with the Soviet Union (for example, India and Vietnam).

The death of Mao Zedong in 1976 and the gradual emergence of a more pragmatic leadership in China reduced the importance of ideological and leadership issues in the Sino-Soviet dispute, but the competition in Asia again reached a crisis in 1979. China countered Soviet-backed Vietnam's invasion of Cambodia by launching a limited military incursion into Vietnam. The Soviet Union responded with warnings and large-scale military exercises along China's northern border. China also denounced the Soviet invasion of Afghanistan in 1979 and sided with the U.S.-backed anticommunist guerrillas in Afghanistan.

Chinese leaders spent much of the two decades from the late 1960s building military defenses and conducting diplomatic and other international maneuvers to deal with the perceived dangers of the prime strategic threat to China posed by the Soviet Union. Particularly important were the buildup of Soviet military forces along the Sino-Soviet and Sino-Mongolian borders and Soviet military and political presence and influence in key areas along China's periphery, notably Vietnam, Laos, Cambodia, India, Afghanistan, North Korea, and the western Pacific and Indian Oceans.[5]

Over time, both countries attempted to moderate the tensions. Soviet leader Leonid Brezhnev made several public gestures calling for improved economic, government, and party relations with China before he died in 1982. This prompted the start of a series of political, economic, technical, and cultural contacts and exchanges.

By 1982, the Soviet leadership concluded that its post-1969 strategy toward China (including the massing of forces along the eastern sector of the border and media campaigns against China's domestic and international policies) had backfired. The post-1972 normalization of China's relations with the United States and Japan and the signing of the 1978 China–Japan friendship treaty showed a strategic convergence among the United States, China, and Japan, which added to the Soviet defense burden and worsened the security environment on its long, remote, and thinly populated eastern flank. To undo this problem, Brezhnev and later leaders held out an olive branch to the Chinese leadership. Political contacts and trade increased and polemics subsided, but real progress came only after Mikhail Gorbachev consolidated his power in the mid-1980s and made rapprochement with China a priority.

Gorbachev was prepared to make major changes in what China referred to as the "three obstacles" to improved Sino-Soviet relations: Soviet troops in Afghanistan, the buildup of Soviet forces along the border (including the deployment in Mongolia), and the Soviet-backed Vietnamese military occupation of Cambodia.[6] Motivated by a desire to repair relations with China, to ease the defense burden on the Soviet economy, and to reciprocate China's reduction of its 4 million troops to 2.95 million from 1982 to 1986, the Soviet government announced in 1987 that a phased reduction of its troops (roughly 65,000 in total number) from Mongolia would be initiated with the aim of eliminating the deployment by 1992.[7] The Soviet formations in Mongolia had been kept at a higher level of readiness than others along the border, and the Chinese had long viewed them as a first-echelon strike force aimed at Beijing. In December 1988, Gorbachev announced at the United Nations that Soviet conventional forces would unilaterally be reduced by 500,000. Soviet spokesmen later clarified that, of the total, 120,000 would come from the troops arrayed against China and that remaining far eastern units would progressively be configured in a defensive mode. In late 1989, following Gorbachev's visit to Beijing in May, Chinese and Soviet officials began negotiations on reducing forces along the border, and during Prime Minister Li Peng's visit to Moscow in April 1990, an agreement was reached on governing principles regarding force reductions. By the time the Soviet Union collapsed in 1991, five rounds of talks on force reductions had been conducted.

The reduction of the conventional threat to China was complemented by the 1987 U.S.–Soviet intermediate nuclear forces treaty, under which Moscow dismantled all its medium- and intermediate-range nuclear missiles, including 180 mobile SS-20 missiles that were based in the Asian regions of the Soviet Union. Meanwhile, the Soviet Union agreed under the April 1988 Geneva Accords to withdraw its combat forces from Afghanistan by May 1989 and encouraged Vietnam to evacuate its troops from Cambodia by the end of 1989.

High-level political contacts helped alter the adversarial character of Sino-Soviet relations, the most important being the visits of Foreign Minister Eduard Shevardnadze and Gorbachev to Beijing in 1989 and of Li Peng and Chinese Communist Party General Secretary Jiang Zemin to Moscow in 1990 and 1991, respectively. Talks on resolving the border dispute, derailed by the Soviet invasion of Afghanistan, resumed in 1987. A treaty delimiting the eastern sector of the border was signed in May 1991. These military and political transformations in Sino-Soviet relations were supplemented by a significant growth in trade—especially along the border—and agreements providing for thousands of Chinese workers to be employed in construction projects in Siberia and the Soviet far east.[8]

Relations with the Yeltsin Administration

The collapse of the Soviet Union in 1991 removed the Soviet military threat that had been the central focus of Beijing's strategic planning since the 1960s. The changes came at a time when Chinese leaders were beleaguered in the face of national and international resentment over their handling of the Tiananmen Square demonstrations of 1989. Representing one of the few surviving communist regimes in the post–Cold War world, Chinese officials were especially suspicious of Boris Yeltsin and his proposed democratic reforms, which were anathema to Chinese leaders determined to maintain the Communist Party's monopoly of political power. Nevertheless, more pragmatic consideration of the national interests of China and Russia saw Yeltsin and Chinese leaders continue the process of gradually improving relations begun in the 1980s.

Regarding political issues, the ideological grounds for polemics between Moscow and Beijing were basically removed in the Gorbachev years—party-to-party ties were reestablished during the 1989 Deng Xiaoping–Gorbachev summit. The end of Communist Party rule in Russia coming against the background of the reforms that China had embarked on since 1978 rendered the old schismatic disputes about "revisionism," "social imperialism," and "hegemonism" irrelevant. Russia criticized Beijing's poor human rights record and its use of force to suppress the Tiananmen demonstrations, but they did not become major problems in government-to-government relations. In addition, Russia did not allow its expanded economic ties with Taiwan to offend Beijing. Meanwhile, progress on resolving Russo–Chinese border disputes continued. The May 1991 eastern sector border agreement was followed by the signing of an agreement in September 1994 on the western sector of the border. As a result, except for some small areas, the entire Russo–Chinese border was delimited.[9]

Both countries maintained the momentum of political contacts at the highest levels. In the 1990s, the presidents and premiers of China and Russia visited each other an average of once every two years. In addition, there were numerous meetings between foreign ministers, defense ministers, and economic officials of both countries.

Concerning military issues, in 1992 Yeltsin's government completed the withdrawal of troops from Mongolia initiated by Gorbachev in 1987. By May 1996, Russia reportedly had cut 150,000 troops from its far eastern deployment, and the Pacific Fleet had been reduced from its 1985 level by 50 percent. At the eighth round of negotiations on force reductions along the border in December 1992, both sides agreed to pull their formations back 100 kilometers from the border. Offensive weapons (tanks, strike aircraft, artillery, and tactical nuclear weapons) were to be reduced in the 200-kilometer zone that resulted.[10]

Efforts to reduce forces and institute confidence-building measures (CBMs) along the border became multilateral with the addition of the Soviet successor states Kazakhstan, Kyrgyzstan, and Tajikistan—all of which share borders with China—to a joint Commonwealth of Independent States (CIS) delegation. Guidelines, including force reductions, warnings preceding military exercises, and the attendance at exercises of observers from the signatories, were incorporated into an agreement signed by the leaders of the four CIS states and China in Shanghai during Yeltsin's April 1996 visit. As discussed in chapter 10, this initiated the Shanghai Five, a precursor to the

Shanghai Cooperation Organization (SCO), which was formed in June 2001 as the first multilateral organization involving Sino-Russian cooperation in central Asia in the modern period. [11]

A joint declaration signed at the end of Yeltsin's visit to China in December 1992 called for reducing troops along the border to "a minimal level" and for increased contact between Chinese and Russian military personnel. Each party also pledged to eschew the use of force against the other, including the use of force in the domain of third countries, and to refuse to enter any "military and political alliances" directed against the other party or sign with third countries any treaties or agreements detrimental to the state sovereignty and security interests of the other party. [12]

In July 1994, the Russian and Chinese defense ministers agreed on measures (such as preventing accidental missile launches, ending the electronic jamming of communications, and establishing signals to warn aircraft and ships in danger of violating the other side's border) to reduce the danger of inadvertent military escalation. In September 1994, the two sides agreed to the principle of no first use for nuclear weapons and to retarget nuclear missiles away from each other's territory. In May 1994, Chinese warships from the North China Fleet visited Vladivostok. Units of the Russian Pacific Fleet called at Qingtao that August. Local Chinese commanders also visited Russian military districts. [13]

China became the largest customer for Russian arms. Major purchases in the Yeltsin era included 200 Su-27 fighter–ground attack aircraft, fifty T-72 tanks, 100 S-300 surface-to-air missiles, ten Il-76 transport aircraft, several Kilo-class (diesel electric) submarines, and two Sovremenny-class destroyers. Moscow was also providing China with technology to improve the accuracy of surface-to-surface and air-to-air missiles and training in Russia for personnel who would operate the weapons purchased. Several of the sales agreements were difficult to reach. The Su-27 transaction was in the works for years. The first twenty-four aircraft were delivered in 1992, but additional deliveries were held up by various disputes. Eventually, the way was cleared for the delivery of forty-eight Su-27s, and an agreement was reached (reportedly worth $2 billion) allowing China to manufacture this high-capability aircraft under license. [14]

These sales reflected a pragmatic marriage of important bilateral needs. For Russia, arms sales to China supplied much-needed hard currency and allowed for the purchase of consumer goods from China; provided orders for severely distressed Russian defense industries; and reduced the tendency of the United States, Japan, and others to take Russia for granted in the post–Cold War Far East. Russia's political disarray also facilitated these arms sales, as reduced central control from Moscow gave defense industries more independence to make such deals. For China, the Russian equipment was relatively cheap, compatible with the existing Chinese inventory, and came without political or other preconditions. Both Russian and Chinese leaders were sensitive to concerns in the United States and Japan and among Asian governments along China's periphery that the Russian transfers substantially added to China's power projection and altered the prevailing military balance in East Asia. In general, Russian and Chinese officials said that China had a long way to go before it could use the recently acquired Russian weapons effectively or project the augmented power in ways that would have seriously upset the military balance in the region. There was debate in the West over when and if such weapons would alter the regional balance.[15]

Regarding economic and social interchange, trade between the two countries grew substantially from a low base. In 1985, Sino-Soviet trade was $300 million. Russian–Chinese trade reached $7 billion in 1995, and cross-border trade, which resumed in 1982 and was conducted largely in barter, accounted for a third of the volume, although its proportion began to decline in the mid-1990s in accordance with the desire of both governments to exert better control over cross-border interchange. China became Russia's second-largest trade partner after Germany.[16]

Along the economically more important eastern section of the Russo–Chinese border, roads and rail connections linked nineteen working border checkpoints between the two sides; two more checkpoints were planned for the latter 1990s. In addition, direct postal and telephonic links were created between northeastern China and the Russian far east. Russia also signed contracts to build nuclear and hydroelectric power plants in China. Both countries planned extensive pipeline and other projects to carry Russian oil and natural gas to Chinese consumers. These agreements on expensive infrastructure projects were very slow to be implemented; they required financing and other inputs that were difficult to arrange.[17]

Problems caused by an influx of Chinese into the Russian far east, particularly an influx of those who remained in violation of visa regulations, led Russia and China to work out a more stringent visa regime in 1994, but the problem of Chinese migration into the Russian far east persisted. Both countries faced the unprecedented challenge of managing the movement of what could be millions of people across a long border. Russia, in particular, could not afford to pump large sums of money into securing that border more effectively. There was a structural supply-and-demand dynamic at work: The high population density and unemployment that prevailed on the Chinese side stimulated people to cross into the Russian far east, which traditionally suffered from severe labor shortages. The entire eastern third of Russia (east of Lake Baikal, a territory almost the size of the United States) had fewer than 20 million inhabitants—and its population was shrinking as people migrated toward Russia's European heartland. This was exacerbated by economic distress in the Russian far east that was worse than in most other regions, including severe food and energy shortages and wage arrears.[18]

Convergence and Divergence in the Late 1990s

The improvement of Russian–Chinese relations in the late 1990s was marked by frequent high-level visits laced with anti-U.S. rhetoric. These prompted some Western experts and commentators to warn of an ever closer Russo–Chinese strategic alignment. They saw the beginnings of this structure in joint Russo–Chinese statements supporting a multipolar world, in increasing military cooperation, and in efforts by Russia and China to work together politically and diplomatically to thwart U.S. efforts at the UN Security Council and elsewhere to pressure countries like Serbia, Iraq, Iran, Libya, and others to conform to international norms supported by the United States. [19]

Others argued that there were serious limitations to Russian–Chinese cooperation and major obstacles to a strategic alliance between them. [20] The condition that would be most conducive to the emergence of a Sino-Russian strategic alliance was seen to be a crisis or rupture in Russia's or China's relations with one of the other major powers, such as the United States or Japan. The hypothesis here was that if Russia or China—and particularly both of them—were to become locked in a protracted geostrategic confrontation and hostility with the United States and/or a resurgent Japan, this could push Moscow and Beijing to forge a strategic alliance to counter their powerful enemy. Absent such developments, the limits to Russian–Chinese cooperation seemed substantial and the obstacles to a strategic alliance formidable. [21]

During this period, both China and Russia found that their relations with the advanced industrial democracies, particularly the United States, remained difficult. China faced problems over human rights abuses, trade and weapons proliferation questions, the status of Tibet, and especially the Taiwan question. For Russia there were problems concerning its relations with other Soviet successor states, Russian military operations in Chechnya, tension over NATO enlargement, and nuclear proliferation. Internationally, Russia supported China's position on Taiwan, and China backed Russia's opposition to NATO enlargement. Each opposed international interference in what the other viewed as its internal affairs. Some Chinese and Russians viewed themselves as outsiders in relation to the Group of Seven (G7), which they saw as the "rich countries' club." As still-developing economies, they tended to resist certain G7-supported economic and trade policies in areas such as protectionism, dumping, intellectual property rights, transparency, and government regulations.

Russia badly needed the China market to export arms and industrial products for which, for various reasons, it had relatively few other buyers who could afford to pay. Food and inexpensive consumer goods from China played a vital role in helping sustain the Russian far east. Although China was economically far less dependent on Russia, Russia provided needed advanced weapons, nuclear reactor technology, and other industrial products that might have otherwise been much more costly for Beijing or unavailable for political reasons.

Both Russia and China used their improving bilateral relations for leverage in relation to the West, particularly the United States. Many Russian officials, for example, warned that U.S.-backed NATO enlargement could drive Russia into a much closer cooperation, even a strategic alliance, with China.[22]

China and Russia shared some other common interests that strengthened the basis of their cooperation. For example, both saw the possible spread of radical Islam in central Asia as a threat to their own domestic stability and national security. Both countries desired regional stability in Asia, wanted to avoid crisis on the Korean peninsula, and wished to forestall the reemergence of Japan as a major military power.[23]

Despite the broad basis for Russian–Chinese cooperation, there were serious limits to that cooperation—and even more to the creation of a meaningful strategic alliance between them. In the aftermath of the collapse of the Soviet Union and the loss of its peripheral territory and population, Russia's relative economic weakness and political instability in relation to China made many Russians nervous. Russia's population (roughly 150 million) was about half that of the former Soviet Union—and the already sparsely populated Russian far east was losing people. Russia's economy had contracted significantly during the still far from complete transition to a market economy. Industrial production appeared in the late 1990s to be as low as 50 percent of the 1991 level.[24]

With President Yeltsin's ailments and other problems, the political situation remained unstable. One aspect of that instability was the difficulty Moscow had in controlling distant regions, such as eastern Siberia and the far east. Leaders in those resource-rich regions sought greater autonomy from Moscow, and some flirted with the idea of separatism. Finally, many Russians were keenly aware of the deterioration of their country's military strength. The Russian army's remarkably poor performance in cracking down against armed insurgents in Chechnya was one indication of this.

In contrast, from Moscow's perspective, China—with its dynamic economy; huge and growing population; apparent national self-confidence and assertiveness; stable, authoritarian political system; and large and modernizing army—seemed strong. Some among the Russian policy elite found Beijing's example admirable and saw in China both a model to emulate and a natural ally. Others—mindful of Russia's declining power in relation to China and of the history of Russia's seizure of vast territories in eastern Siberia and the Russian far east from China in "unequal treaties" in the latter part of the nineteenth century—saw China's renaissance and burgeoning power as a challenge and potential threat. A Russian nightmare scenario from this perspective was that a resurgent China might try to retake vast, thinly populated territories from a weakened Russia.[25]

Although Russia's sale of advanced weaponry to China was widely believed to be motivated in large part by economic necessity on Russia's part and was strongly supported by the Russian defense industrial sector, the Russian security community had serious reservations about the sales. Some Russian commentators questioned the wisdom of helping modernize the military of a country that might become a threat to Russian security in the future. These reservations reportedly extended to the Russian military's general staff.[26]

On the Chinese side, too, there were significant limitations and constraints on cooperation with Russia.[27] Radical swings in Soviet and Russian domestic politics and foreign policy since the mid-1980s inevitably made Russia appear somewhat unreliable in Chinese eyes. Russia's economic, political, and military weakness was duly noted by Chinese strategic planners, who nonetheless remained vigilant for any signs of a revival of Russian strength that could affect Chinese interests in Asia.

In addition, Russia was much less important economically to China than the United States and other developed countries. Russia accounted for less than 2 percent of China's $300 billion in annual foreign trade in the late 1990s. China's trade with and credits and investments from the G7 countries weighed far more heavily in Beijing than did Russo–Chinese trade. China presumably would have been loath to jeopardize its vital economic relations with the advanced industrial democracies on Russia's behalf. The markets, financing, and technology of the West and the developed countries of eastern Asia represented a key link in China's ongoing program of economic modernization—and economic modernization and the concrete benefits it gave to the broad masses of Chinese people were the key sources of political legitimacy for the post-Mao leaders. It was difficult to imagine circumstances in which Chinese leaders would have allowed closer military, political, or other ties with an economically anemic Russia to jeopardize China's vital links with the world's most important economies—unless China faced a major crisis or geostrategic confrontation with the United States or Japan.

Thus, the pattern of China's relationship with Yeltsin's Russia showed Beijing giving priority to keeping relations with the often unstable Russia as calm as possible. China also sought military equipment and some advanced technology. When Chinese relations with the United States, Japan, and NATO were strained, Chinese officials fell back on relations with Moscow as a possible source of political leverage against the Western-aligned states. But when Beijing's higher-priority relations with the United States and the developed powers were in reasonably good shape, Beijing tended to keep at some distance from the Russians and their desire to gain Chinese support for a strong, public, anti-U.S., anti-Western stance on sensitive issues. In general terms, Russian leaders tended to use their relationship with China in a similar way, with the state of Russian relations with the United States as the more important determinant. Even though Beijing—like Moscow—said it wanted to see a multipolar world order develop, with the U.S. superpower as only one power among many, it saw only limited benefits from tilting strongly toward Russia as it opposed U.S. and Western policies. In this period, it saw more to be gained from a positive and constructive engagement with the United States and Western-aligned states—a higher priority in Chinese foreign policy.

Relations under Vladimir Putin and Hu Jintao

The course of Russian–Chinese relations in the early twenty-first century under new leaders—Vladimir Putin (2000) and Hu Jintao (2002)—followed the same mixed pattern seen in the 1990s. Both sides placed priority on promoting an evolving "strategic partnership." Economic cooperation improved from a low base, and Russian oil exports to China increased bilateral trade levels. A strong arms sales and defense technology–sharing relationship provided critically important support for China's military buildup, though there was a widely publicized drop-off in such cooperation for a few years beginning in 2005 that foreshadowed fewer but still important sales in following years. Political cooperation against U.S. interests varied, with Russia's Putin and then Chinese leaders moving to moderate anti-U.S. invective in the face of U.S. resolve and power, especially at the start of the George W. Bush administration. When Putin later adopted a tougher stance against the United States and its allies at the end of the Bush administration, China offered only limited political support. China seemed similarly uninvolved when now Prime Minister Putin and Russian President Dmitry Medvedev responded positively to overtures from the Barack Obama government for advances regarding arms control, NATO, and economic issues.

Putin showed a notably positive response to the United States during his first meeting with George W. Bush in the spring of 2001. He played down heretofore strong differences over missile defense and NATO expansion in the interest of fostering closer cooperation with the United States and the West. Cooperation between the United States and Russia was intensified following the September 11, 2001, terrorist attack on the United States. Russian support was essential in facilitating U.S.-led military operations in central Asia directed against the Taliban regime in Afghanistan. Russia saw its interests served by fostering closer economic and strategic cooperation with the United States and the West and by playing down past major differences.[28]

Maneuvering in the United Nations in the months prior to the war in Iraq in 2003 saw Russia join with France and others (including China to some degree) in standing against U.S. military actions to topple Saddam Hussein without renewed UN approval. It was unclear whether this reversal in Russian–U.S. cooperation was an episode prompted by key Russian concerns involving economic and other interests in Iraq and broader concerns regarding anticipated hostile Islamic reaction in the region and among the sizable Russian Muslim population or if it was part of a broader Russian decision to reverse course and seek to join with other world powers to resist and weaken the U.S. superpower. After the U.S.-led coalition succeeded militarily in toppling Saddam Hussein and senior Bush administration officials made significant gestures to ease tensions with Moscow, Russia appeared prepared to resume a more cooperative stance toward the United States. [29]

Seeing Russia trim its opposition to the United States in 2001 caused China to lose some steam in its then strong anti-U.S. rhetoric. China was critical of the American posture on missile defense and NATO expansion. Russia's actions added to Chinese imperatives to moderate China's stance toward the United States by mid-2001, setting the stage for the most important improvement in U.S.–China relations since the end of the Cold War. [30]

In this context, the improved Russian–Chinese relationship continued to grow, but it appeared to have less negative implications for U.S. interests in sustaining a leadership position and promoting U.S. objectives in Asia and elsewhere. Russian arms sales to and military cooperation with China continued the pattern of the past decade and increased somewhat as China stepped up the pace of military modernization focused on Taiwan. Economic relations also picked up, with higher trade figures caused especially by sales of Russian oil to China. Political cooperation against U.S. interests subsided from the intensified level of the late 1990s and early 2000s, which had at least partly resulted from various U.S. actions (such as the intervention in Kosovo, posturing over Chechnya and Taiwan, U.S. missile defense plans, and NATO expansion) that Moscow and Beijing perceived as contrary to their mutual interests. [31]

The relationship proved to be mixed and somewhat volatile regarding political cooperation despite the signing of a Russian–Chinese friendship treaty in 2001 and numerous bilateral agreements:

- Arms sales and technology transfers kept growing, primarily because Russian economic difficulties and Putin's emphasis on defense industries complemented China's need for advanced military equipment and technology to prepare for regional contingencies. China had difficulty integrating some of the new arms and technology, but on balance many foresaw improvements in Chinese capabilities to engage hostile forces at increasing distances from its shores.
- Economic relations moved forward. For a time, Putin tried to link arms sales to an expansion of commercial trade, but this did not succeed, espe-

cially given Moscow's need for the arms sales and Beijing's limited interest in other Russian exports. As China showed greater interest in Russian oil and other resources, Putin tried, again with little success, to link provision of these Russian supplies with demands that China purchase more Russian industrial goods. Negotiations, declarations, and agreements on large-scale energy and infrastructure projects—some dating back to the early Yeltsin period—continued. The flow of Russian oil to China increased via rail shipment. More efficient and expensive pipelines were slow to develop.

- Russia and China continued to pursue good-neighborly relations and bilateral CBMs. Although both moderated their respective public criticism of U.S. leadership in Asian and world affairs, in principle they remained opposed to the regional and global domination of a single power and occasionally jointly criticized evidence of U.S. "unilateralism" or "interventionism."[32]

There was an upsurge in public Russian–Chinese assertiveness against the United States in 2005. The Russian and Chinese leaders met in July and issued a formal statement widely seen as an attack on U.S. international leadership. Both governments joined with the SCO that month in calling for U.S. and allied forces to set a deadline for withdrawal from central Asia. They subsequently backed the authoritarian government of Uzbekistan, which disputed U.S. support for political opposition in the country, and called for U.S. forces to withdraw from Uzbekistan. In August, about 10,000 Chinese and Russian forces held sophisticated military exercises, ostensibly under the auspices of the SCO, that were focused in waters east of China and appeared directed at warning Taiwan and its supporters in Japan and the United States.[33] Both Russia and China resisted U.S.-backed efforts in 2005–2006 to pressure Iran to end suspected nuclear weapons development. These developments added to differences in Russian relations with the United States over Putin's authoritarian internal policies and other issues. Taken together, they complicated U.S. efforts to manage relations with Russia and China but did not appear to change the overall orientation of Russian and Chinese policies, which continued to give primacy to relations with the United States over relations with one another.[34]

Putin visited China in March 2006, initiating the "year of Russia" celebrations in China that Russia would reciprocate with "year of China" celebrations in 2007. Highlights of various agreements signed during the visit included three deals on developing Russian energy supplies and selling them to China via rail and future pipelines. Putin noted that trade had increased by 37 percent in 2005 to a value of $29.1 billion. He complained that China was purchasing Russian oil and other resources and not Russian manufactured goods, while some Chinese complained about Russian inability to provide sufficient oil to meet Chinese needs. The Chinese side reportedly was particularly irritated by Russian vacillation in determining the routing of an oil pipeline in Siberia. One route favored exports to Japan and another favored China, and Russia seemingly was using vacillation to extract concessions from Japan and China. The joint statement marking Putin's visit reiterated standard positions on Russian–Chinese cooperation over border issues, with the SCO, and over such controversial international issues as Iran's nuclear program.[35]

Russian–Chinese political cooperation against the United States remained limited, as both Moscow and Beijing seemed to maintain a grudging respect for U.S. power and influence and a calculation that constructive bilateral relations with the United States and its allies were essential to their respective development and reform programs. Russian–Chinese political cooperation also was limited by historical mutual suspicions, their respective concerns about each other's long-term threat potential, their occasional maneuvers at the other's expense for international advantages, and the preoccupation of both leaderships with domestic priorities.[36] As noted above, Russia's assertive stance against the United States and military intervention into Georgia in 2008 saw China straddle the fence; Russia's moderation with the Obama administration in 2010 was at odds with China's harder line toward the United States at that time.[37]

Economic cooperation focused on trade in energy. Bilateral trade dropped from $56.8 billion in 2008 to $38.8 billion in 2009 and returned to the 2008 level in 2010.[38] Trade relations also reflected repeated signs of China–Russia differences. Moscow's maneuvering between Japan and China over the Russian oil pipeline in Asia reached a new stage in 2009 when China agreed to a large, $25 billion loan to Russia in return for oil shipments and the Russian decision to construct and open earlier than expected an oil pipeline spur to China on the proposed Russian oil pipeline to the Russian Pacific coast.[39] Friction also was reported between Russia and China over the Russian leadership's efforts to control the export of oil and gas from central Asian republics, on the one hand, and Chinese efforts to build pipelines outside of Russian control and encourage exports of these commodities from central Asian countries to China on the other.[40]

The resiliency of the strong mutual interests behind China–Russia cooperation in arms sales and military technological cooperation was tested as the two sides endeavored to overcome differences resulting in a marked decline in the arms sales beginning around the middle of the past decade. The decline contrasted with the record of the previous ten years, when $25 billion worth of Russian air, naval, and ground military equipment was delivered to China. A major part of the problem was Russian complaints about Chinese reverse-engineering Russian arms; also involved was Russian inability to fulfill some contracts.[41] There were conflicting reports in late 2010 about when and if strong Russian arms sales to China would be resumed.[42]

Relations under Vladimir Putin and Xi Jinping

Sino-Russian developments of the previous decades highlight the incentives and constraints likely to influence the remarkable convergence of Chinese-Russian relations seen under President Xi Jinping and President Vladimir Putin. Past practice underlines the tendency of both sides to use their relationship for other reasons, to show solidarity when interests overlap, and to change course with one another when other foreign policy options seem more advantageous.

Putin's Russia found little international support for its coerced annexation of Crimea and continued thinly veiled military aggression against Ukraine. Resulting Western sanctions punished the Russian economy and shunned its leaders. The political upheaval in Ukraine and the Russian takeover in Crimea and aggression in Ukraine came as a surprise to China. Xi and his government professed neutrality, but the Chinese leader and the Chinese government made clear their continued strong support for the Russian president in the face of economic sanctions and diplomatic isolation from the West. Russia found that Xi Jinping's China was one of the few world powers willing to closely associate publicly with the controversial Russian president.

To compensate in part for lost opportunities in the West, Russian leaders sought economic advantage in closer relations with China. The two powers became more closely bound, especially regarding Russian energy sales to China. In the process, Moscow's leverage in making large energy deals with China was widely seen as reduced. A $400 billion gas deal signed in May 2014 said that Russia would supply China with 38 billion cubic meters (bcm) of gas annually from 2018 for thirty years. At China's insistence, the gas is to come from new fields in eastern Siberia; it will flow through a pipeline to be built. Among others, *The Economist* judged that this arrangement helped to reassure China that the Russians would not divert the gas to other consumers. In addition, a preliminary deal was signed in November 2014 calling for Russia to supply an added 30 bcm of gas to China through a proposed pipeline in western Siberia. Those experienced with Russian-Chinese energy negotiations were aware of hard bargaining on price; they judged that Russia's need for sales to China worked to Beijing's advantage in seeking a low price for the Russian gas.[43]

Meanwhile, the active Russian-Chinese arms sales relationship also showed Chinese leverage over Russia. Russia's agreement to sell China its most advanced surface-to-air missile system in a $3 billion deal was said to show Russia's need to cater to Chinese requests in the current adverse situation faced by Moscow. Along the same line of reasoning, Russia in November 2014 agreed to sell its most advanced Sukhoi-35S combat aircraft. Moscow initially insisted on a sale of forty-eight aircraft in order to compensate for losses it would incur from China's anticipated copying and reverse engineering of the advanced technology of the plane. However, Chinese leverage reportedly compelled the Russians to accept a sale of twenty-four aircraft. [44] Regarding military exercises, stronger overlapping interests against the West showed in recent years in expanding the scope of bilateral military exercises beyond the regularly scheduled Sino-Russian military exercises targeted at the United States or U.S. allies in the Asia-Pacific to include joint Chinese-Russian naval exercises in the eastern Mediterranean Sea and the Black Sea. [45]

Looking out, one set of variables yet to be determined is the scope and depth of China's various Silk Road initiatives and what they might mean—pro or con—for Russian interests in what Moscow calls the "near abroad." There are possible circumstances where Chinese–Russian cooperation could markedly improve, notably in the event of a harder U.S. policy approach toward the two powers. [46] There are also prospects for a decline in relations. The two sides could diverge seriously over key U.S. policies (as they did to some degree in 2001 over U.S. missile defense plans), or they could find themselves in competition in seeking eased relations with the United States. In any scenario, the chances of Moscow and Beijing reestablishing a formal alliance—especially one with a mutual defense component—appeared low. Bitter memories of their failed alliance in the 1950s, deep-seated mutual suspicions, and the specter of potentially serious political and economic repercussions remain powerful deterrents to the formation of an anti-Western military pact. [47]

RELATIONS WITH EUROPE

There was debate among specialists in the middle of the past decade regarding the priority of relations with Europe in Chinese foreign policy and their overall importance in international relations in the twenty-first century. American Chinese affairs expert David Shambaugh highlighted in 2004 the development in recent years of extensive economic and political contacts between China and Europe to argue that the relationship represented a centerpiece of Chinese foreign policy, creating an "emerging axis" independent of the United States that would be of major consequence in world affairs in the new century. [48] In contrast, French Chinese affairs expert Jean-Pierre Cabestan in 2006 tended to emphasize the limitations on China–European cooperation, highlighting in particular weaknesses and lack of coherence and unity in European approaches to China; major differences between the two sides; and much stronger U.S. than Chinese influence in Europe, which served as a brake to significant European actions with China that would challenge prevailing dynamics in European behavior or U.S. interests in regional and world affairs.[49]

The record of European–Chinese relations since the end of the Cold War provided evidence for both perspectives. On balance, however, it demonstrated that growing Sino-European trade and other connections had to overcome substantial obstacles and diverging interests before consideration of a China–Europe partnership with major international consequences would appear warranted. By the latter part of the decade, initial optimists of Chinese–European convergence changed their assessments, with David Shambaugh warning that relations had become more "complicated" and that for Europe the "China honeymoon was over."[50]

Indeed, China–Europe relations deteriorated to new lows in 2008 over such salient issues as Tibet, human rights, and the massive European trade imbalance with China. China canceled at the last minute the eleventh China–EU summit because of planned visits by the Dalai Lama with the French president and other European leaders. The sharp decline and rising friction in Chinese relations with Europe stood in marked contrast with general improvement in China's relations elsewhere, including often-troubled Chinese relations with Japan, Taiwan, and the United States.

Chinese Premier Wen Jiabao endeavored to halt the decline in a European visit in early 2009 that saw proposals to reschedule the China–EU summit and friendly visits to several European countries—but notably not France, because of the French president's meeting with the Dalai Lama in 2008. China and France subsequently patched up relations. In 2010, China engaged in top-level meetings with Western Europe's leading powers: France, Great Britain, Germany, and Italy, along with lesser powers, including Greece and Portugal, which were in financial distress on account of the protracted international economic crisis. Official Chinese media characterized China's activism as a "full scale push into Europe as it tries to be a major partner with European nations reeling from the global financial crisis." The European leaders welcomed Chinese trade deals and investments, but their impact was offset to some degree by domestic protectionist pressures against deepening economic ties with China. Sino-European differences also were evident in negative reactions in the continent to China's position during the international climate change conference in Copenhagen in December 2009; Chinese threats against Norway, European powers, and others as part of strident Chinese condemnation of the awarding of the Nobel Peace Prize in 2010 to a prominent Chinese dissident; and Chinese criticism of NATO's military actions in 2011 against the regime of Libya's Muammar Gaddafi.

Against this background, it seemed fair to conclude that the priority Chinese leaders gave to relations with Europe appeared to be growing. New momentum came in March 2014 when Chinese President Xi Jinping participated in the two-day international nuclear summit in the Netherlands and spent a total of eleven days in Belgium, France, Germany, and the Netherlands. Xi became the first Chinese president to visit the European Union. At that time, China issued its second policy paper on relations with the EU; the first was issued at a high point in Chinese enthusiasm about Europe in 2003. Xi's visit and the policy paper in 2014 duly registered China's appreciation of Europe's continued economic importance for China, but overall Europe still seemed to be a complicated area of generally secondary concern in Chinese foreign policy.[51]

Post–Cold War Relations

In general, relations with Europe were not of primary importance in Chinese foreign policy priorities in the aftermath of the Cold War. Relations with the United States, Japan, and powers along China's periphery continued to receive top foreign policy attention. Burgeoning economic contacts, along with political and security concerns related to Chinese and some European governments' interest in creating a multipolar world and using cooperation in multilateral organizations to curb the U.S. superpower, supported rapidly developing relations by the latter 1990s that continued into the new century.[52]

European leaders gradually eased diplomatic isolation of China after the 1989 Tiananmen crackdown, and the rapidly growing Chinese economy became a focal point of interest for a wide array of senior European visitors. Senior Chinese officials reciprocated, visiting various European countries in order to establish closer ties under the rubric of "strategic partnerships." This rubric at first focused on China's relations with larger European and other world powers, but it saw increasingly wider use in Chinese relations with smaller European governments and wider use among large and small countries in other world areas.[53]

Reflecting in large measure the European desire to become more closely linked with China's rising market among the dynamic Asian economies in the post–Cold War period, the EU (an entity of twenty-eight nations in 2014 as opposed to sixteen before 2004) became unusually active in the 1990s in building ties with China. The highlights included major policy pronouncements, high-level exchanges, and multifaceted assistance programs, backed by EU–China trade flows that expanded much more rapidly than the impressive pace of growth of the Chinese economy.[54]

In contrast, broader political and security cooperation remained hampered and constrained. The Chinese administration reflected mixed views of the importance and likelihood of substantial cooperation with Europe in these areas. The European powers were in the lead in supporting the expansion of NATO and the NATO-led intervention in Kosovo in the late 1990s. These were strongly opposed by China, which saw them as manifestations of U.S.-led hegemonism in world affairs. China moderated its anti-U.S. stance and opposition to NATO expansion by 2001 and hoped that improved China–Europe ties would prompt the European countries to end the embargo on military sales to China that had been in place since the Tiananmen crackdown of 1989. However, strenuous U.S.-led opposition to ending the arms embargo caused the Europeans to delay and vacillate and to respond positively to U.S. requests for closer U.S.–European consultations on China policy.

Against this background, the European powers and the EU were seen by some in China as too weak, divided, and dependent on the United States to allow Europe to become an active great power in international relations. Moreover, the European powers, despite many differences with the United States, also seemed to share the same political values and strategic objectives as the United States in areas sensitive for the Chinese administration. In particular, they supported China's movement toward democracy despite the strong determination of the Chinese government to maintain one-party rule, and they opposed Chinese threats to resort to force in dealing with the Taiwan issue. Even the positive development of European–Chinese economic relations was marred, from China's perspective, by numerous European efforts to curb rapidly growing Chinese exports to European markets, to join with the United States in complaining about alleged unfair Chinese trade practices, and to refuse strong Chinese efforts to gain recognition for China as a "market economy" under World Trade Organization (WTO) guidelines.[55]

In the 1990s, the EU represented sixteen nations, including the large majority of the countries of Western Europe. In the 1990s, the EU was unusually active in building ties with Asia, particularly China. The efforts saw several exchanges of high-level visits, cultural exchanges, and the use of development assistance and training aid. Highlights included the EU's 1994 statement, "Towards a New Asia Strategy"; the summit meeting between EU leaders and those of the East Asian countries at the so-called Asia-Europe Meeting (ASEM) in Bangkok on March 1–2, 1996; the EU's July 1995 statement titled "Long-Term Policy for Europe-China Relations"; the ASEM summit of April 1998; the EU–China summit of April 1998; and the March 1998 EU document titled "The Establishment of Full Partnership with China." The Asian economic crisis of 1997–1998 dampened European enthusiasm for investment in the region, but China weathered the crisis relatively well, and its continued growth proved to be a magnet for European trade and investment and accompanying interest from visiting European leaders.[56]

Chinese leaders appeared anxious to reciprocate the heightened European interest. Senior leaders, including President Jiang Zemin and Premiers Li Peng and Zhu Rongji, made highly publicized visits to European countries during the latter 1990s. Those visits were accompanied by reports of major sales by European countries of sophisticated transportation and other equipment to China.[57]

Impressive statistics, especially in the area of trade, rested behind the European nations' growing interaction with China. Members of the EU saw their overall trade with China triple in ten years, from $14.3 billion in 1985 to $45.6 billion in 1994. The pace of growth was accelerating as time went on, with trade in 1993 seeing a 65 percent increase over the previous year. China became at this time the fourth-largest trading partner of the EU countries. This trend came within a broader wave of European–Asian trade, which saw the two sides' trade with each other become roughly equal to their trade with the United States. The Asian economic crisis saw trade growth stabilize for a while, with China's trade with EU states amounting to $43 billion in 1997, but levels of EU–China trade increased by about 15 percent in 1998.[58]

The French government was in the lead among European powers at that time in seeking closer ties with China. The government saw this as a means to foster a multipolar world order that would implicitly curb the power of the remaining superpower after the end of the Cold War, the United States. France, along with Russia, was among the first international powers to establish a strategic partnership with the Chinese government of President Jiang Zemin, which emphasized this new form of Chinese relations with key world powers in the latter 1990s.[59]

U.S. officials duly marked Sino-European cooperation in various areas and saw mixed implications in the emerging European–Chinese relationships. On the one hand, improved European–Chinese relations provided a number of benefits for U.S. policy and interests. They exposed China to more Western ideas and institutions, which over time might encourage the type of change in China favored by the United States. They provided greater European experience in dealing with China, which helped achieve improved U.S.–EU communications on China-related questions. On the other hand, U.S. officials and American opinion leaders sometimes complained that greater European involvement with China complicated U.S. efforts to prompt the Chinese government to conform more closely to internationally accepted norms that were important to the United States. Thus, European country representatives and EU representatives were depicted as less stringent than their U.S. counterparts in dealing with China on sensitive issues like human rights, market access, intellectual property rights, and other questions.[60]

The incentives for increased contacts in European–Chinese relations in the 1990s came mainly from the Europeans. The moves by the EU toward China came in the context of a general sense among European leaders that the EU and its members needed to take more decisive action in order to continue to be seen as important actors among the growth economies of Asia, especially in eastern Asia and notably China. This was deemed particularly important as it became evident in Europe in the early 1990s that eastern

Asia's economic growth would surpass that of other major markets and that Europe's future economic health would be determined by how well EU members adjusted to and profited from the opportunities in the region. The Europeans were said to be concerned that they had missed an opportunity to be included in the Asia-Pacific Economic Cooperation (APEC) forum uniting economic powers of the Pacific Rim. The Europeans also judged that China's rising power and influence were central in determining eastern Asia's prosperity and that the EU and the individual member states needed to focus special efforts on building closer relationships with China.

The European statements on China at that time also made it clear that EU members placed emphasis on China's importance to broader European interests regarding such issues as the world trading system, the proliferation of weapons of mass destruction and related technology, environmental concerns, and others. China was seen as especially important in determining the future importance of the WTO, which was a top priority of the Europeans, and in influencing the future stability of the Korean peninsula—EU members were concerned about nuclear proliferation and stability there. Britain and Portugal had special concerns with China because of the reversion of their respective colonial possessions, Hong Kong and Macao, to Chinese control in 1997 and 1999.[61]

Nonetheless, amid economic attraction, the rhetoric of strategic partnerships, and European determination to build closer ties with China were several realities limiting European–Chinese relations, according to European and Chinese experts.[62]

China's View of Europe

Beijing was anxious to gain economically from improved relations with Europe. Beijing also was interested in fostering greater European political and strategic independence from the United States. This was part of broader PRC efforts at the time to develop a multipolar world more advantageous to China than the prevailing international order with the United States in the leading position. Throughout the 1990s and until 2001, Beijing publicly chafed under an international order where the Chinese saw the United States as the dominant power; this international order often pressed the PRC hard on a variety of sensitive international and domestic questions. Thus, for China, relations with Europe were viewed with an eye to other Chinese interests; Europe was said to represent a kind of "card" that could be played by China in the more important contest of U.S.–Chinese relations.

This line of thinking underscored limits of Chinese interests in Europe. It reflected the fact that in the order of PRC foreign policy priorities, primacy was given to the United States, followed by Japan and important countries in the Asian area; Europe and other areas more distant from China came in behind them.

China notably opposed NATO expansion and tried from time to time to play up intra-alliance rivalries and differences, especially between the U.S. and French governments. But this effort was largely in vain, given the strong alliance support for U.S.-led NATO and its expansion. Chinese officials also had a long history of thinking of the EU and its members as oriented to protectionist tendencies that would try to impede the flow of Chinese exports to European markets.

European Limitations

Because of organizational and institutional weaknesses, the EU and its members had a hard time developing a comprehensive and coherent policy toward China. As Europe's interest in China was mainly economic, the EU and its members were seen as most effective when dealing with a country like China based on economic issues, with other channels of interaction remaining weak.

As a diplomatic actor or as a force on security issues, the EU and its members were said to be less well suited to take action in relation to China, especially as EU members were reluctant to allow the EU very much leeway to deal with important defense and security issues. The EU was very slow to come out in support of the American show of force off the Taiwan Strait in the face of provocative PRC military exercises in 1996, though some member governments were prompt in supporting the move.

Twenty-First-Century Trends

As noted earlier, developments in Sino-European relations led some observers for a time to point to the development of "a comprehensive and multidimensional relationship," "a strategic partnership," and "a new axis in world affairs."[63] Other specialists took a less positive view of the significance and outlook of China–Europe relations, emphasizing substantial limitations and differences. On balance, the recent record along with past practice suggests that the growing China–Europe ties will remain hampered by substantial and sometimes growing problems and competing interests.

Trade and economic ties are the foundation of the relationship. According to Chinese trade data in early 2005, the EU in 2004 surpassed Japan and the United States to become China's largest trade partner, and China became the second-largest trade partner of the EU following the United States (those one and two positions continued for the next ten years).[64] The expansion of the EU to twenty-five members in 2004 obviously increased the size of the Chinese trade figures with the EU, though the main EU countries involved in

China trade were listed among the Western European states that were long-standing EU members—Germany, Holland, the United Kingdom, France, and Italy, which were said to account for 72 percent of EU trade with China at that time.[65] According to European sources, the main items that EU countries sold to China were manufactured goods, such as automobiles and aircraft. China, for its part, shipped mostly computer equipment, mobile phones, digital cameras, and textiles to European markets. Trade grew impressively until the economic crisis of 2009. It rebounded and reached a value close to $500 billion in 2010. Trade grew steadily after that, amounting to $559 billion in 2013 and $615 billion in 2014.[66]

Chinese sources reported in late 2010 that the EU countries were the third-largest source of foreign investment in China. The total stock of European foreign direct investment in China amounted to more than $70 billion. In 2013, the EU remained one of the top five foreign investors in China, but annual investment declined from 10 billion Euros in 2012 to 8.2 billion Euros in 2013. Chinese investment in the EU grew from a low base. It was valued at 4.2 billion Euros in 2013. In a victory for China discussed in chapter 4, many European countries joined as founding members of the China-initiated Asian Infrastructure Investment Bank, even though the United States viewed Chinese motives with suspicion. According to Chinese and European sources, the European countries also were the largest exporter of technologies to China, which allowed for upgrades to Chinese manufacturing and related capabilities. China and the EU also participated in a number of joint technology projects, including the world's largest cooperative science and technology research project, the EU-China Framework Agreement. Meanwhile, Chinese investment in Europe became more significant. By 2009, it amounted to $6.28 billion, involving 1,400 Chinese-funded enterprises. Of this total, Chinese investment in Europe in 2009 alone amounted to $2.97 billion.[67]

That not all was positive in China–Europe economic relations was seen in the fast-growing trade deficit Europe ran with China. It tripled in size in five years, amounting to around $127 billion in 2005. The deficit grew at a rate four times the growth of Europe–China trade and made trade with China the source of Europe's largest trade deficit. The trend was exacerbated by the fact that China remained the main beneficiary of the EU's Generalized System of Preferences program, which granted trade preferences to China. In 2010, the trade deficit was $142.8 billion. It remained over $100 billion in following years.[68]

The large trade deficit and Chinese commercial competitiveness fed sentiment in Europe against Chinese imports. Significant curbs were introduced beginning in 2005 against incoming Chinese textiles, shoes, televisions, and other products. Later curbs included restrictions on Chinese solar panels. European complaints against Chinese trade practices, intellectual property rights protection, and currency valuation policies grew.[69] Concurrent world-wide Chinese efforts to gain market economy status from WTO partners had some success in some quarters (Association of Southeast Asian Nations, Australia, New Zealand, and some Latin American countries), but the EU and many of its members, along with the United States, stood firm against strong Chinese pressure. China's status as a nonmarket economy meant among other things that the EU did not have to rely on cost figures given by Chinese exporters when determining if goods were being sold below cost in the EU. The EU instead could consider cost and price data from other countries when it decided whether to apply duties to Chinese exports in defense of European producers or to launch antidumping procedures.[70]

Official EU reports and widespread European media coverage highlighted growing frictions over economic issues. Scandals in 2007–2008 over the safety of consumer products from China added to the negative reporting. Economic data from the European Commission[71] showed a mixed and somewhat negative picture for European interests in trade with China. The European stake in the foreign-invested enterprises in China amounted to 8 percent of such foreign investment in the country. China was the fastest-growing export market for Europe, growing 75 percent between 2003 and 2007 to a level valued at well over $100 billion a year. Nonetheless, the EU still exported more to Switzerland than it did to China. Barriers to trade in China were estimated to cost EU businesses close to $30 billion in lost trade opportunities annually, and major losses came from counterfeiting and intellectual property rights violations in China. China was the largest target of trade defense investigations by the EU. European service companies repeatedly complained about Chinese restrictions on granting telecom licenses and on investment in banking, construction, and other sectors.

In the political realm, Chinese and European leaders held regular meetings. President Hu Jintao and Premier Wen Jiabao visited Europe on official business annually. President Xi Jinping and Premier Li Keqiang followed this pattern.[72] During the same period, China hosted a wide range of senior European and EU leaders. Since 1997, the annual China–EU summit has rotated between Brussels and Beijing. Both the EU and China learned how to deal with one another in the sometimes difficult EU–China negotiations notably concerning China's entrance into the WTO.

As noted above, China cancelled the China–EU summit in 2008 over the French president's planned meeting with the Dalai Lama. Smooth relations took over a year to revive. Chinese leaders were particularly active in visiting European capitals and hosting European leaders in 2010. Chinese and foreign media portrayed China as able and willing to make investments and promote mutually beneficial economic relations even with European countries with questionable credit ratings following the 2009 economic crisis. Xi Jinping and Li Keqiang highlighted China as a growing investor in Europe.[73]

The EU continued to issue major policy pronouncements about China. The EU's partnership with China included a multifaceted program of economic, scientific and technological, and educational and legal cooperation. The program aimed in particular at strengthening bilateral political contacts and trade relations, as well as better controlling pollution, alleviating poverty, and favoring the establishment of a modern government system under the rule of law in China. The programs had the financial support of the EU, the largest source of official development assistance in the world. In 2003, the EU Commission calculated that programs it was running in China amounted to annual expenditures of over $300 million. These programs did not take into account the sometimes large (e.g., in the case of Germany) assistance programs in China offered by individual European countries.[74]

The Chinese statement, China's EU Policy, in October 2003 contained a series of statements about convergence in EU and Chinese views, notably about the need for a more democratic and multipolar world, that seemed directed against U.S. international leadership. It paired that with demands that EU members avoid contacts with Taiwan and the Dalai Lama and that "the EU must lift as soon as possible its arms embargo against China in order to eliminate the obstacles preventing EU–China cooperation in the military industry and technologies sectors."[75]

The Chinese EU statement coincided with a Chinese offensive against the EU arms embargo. China secured the support of the French government on this issue, and the French promised to persuade other EU members to lift the ban that had been in place since 1989. France managed to get the German government to change its view and to erode British opposition. However, U.S. opposition was strong and firm, leading to a major crisis with the EU over whether to end the embargo. The United States was backed by many within Europe, including the new government in Germany in 2005, and had the strong support of Japan, which agreed with the United States that lifting the embargo would enhance the ability of Chinese forces to confront America and its allies in the event of a conflict over Taiwan. China's passage of a tough Anti-Secession Law directed at Taiwan in March 2005 halted the European movement to lift the embargo, at least for the time being. European leaders also showed greater interest to coordinate policies with the United States on sensitive issues involving China, including the buildup of Chinese military forces and its implications for Taiwan and broader Asian security and stability.[76]

According to Jean-Pierre Cabestan, this string of setbacks for Chinese interests combined with rising trade frictions in EU–Chinese relations caused Chinese leaders to reassess European policy. While clearly determined to develop advantageous economic and other ties with European counterparts, Chinese officials were more realistic about developing any sort of a meaningful strategic partnership with Europe for the foreseeable future.

The EU and its members were seen as collectively too weak, divided, and dependent on the United States to become an independent great power in international relations. Thus, China tended not to see the EU as an advantageous partner for China in its rise to power and influence in world affairs. Further, the EU was much more prone to side with the United States than with China on issues sensitive to China involving democracy and the rule of law in China, stability in eastern Asia, the implications of China's growing trade surpluses with both the United States and the EU members, and antiterrorist efforts and curbs on nuclear weapons proliferation in Iran.[77]

This backdrop put the continuing array of agreements and of well-publicized contacts between China and Europe in a more realistic setting. Led by the United States, NATO remained far more important to European powers than being designated as a "strategic partner" by China or carrying out exchanges of senior military delegations and small military exercises with the Chinese military. Both the French and the British governments engaged in annual "strategic dialogue" with Chinese civilian and military security experts, and Chinese military officers were being trained in German, French, and British military staff colleges, among others.[78]

At the nongovernment level, Europe welcomed the over three million Chinese tourists visiting European sites each year,[79] but this seemed insufficient to offset European concerns about the economic disruption and perceived threat posed by massive Chinese imports. Moreover, there were broadening concerns about Chinese illegal immigration into Europe at a time of continued high levels of economic unemployment in many European countries. The number of Chinese students in Europe grew to nearly 100,000 in 2004 and rose to over 200,000 in later years, with about half in the English-speaking United Kingdom.[80]

The latter years of the Hu Jintao presidency saw some dramatic events in China–Europe relations caused notably by Tibet, climate change, human rights, and other issues.[81] German Chancellor Angela Merkel met the Dalai Lama in 2007 despite strenuous Chinese protests. The result was a notable cooling in Chinese relations with Germany. The Chinese government's suppression of violent Tibetan demonstrations in March 2008 coincided with the Olympic torch relay through European capitals. Pro-Tibetan demonstrators disrupted the relay in London and Paris, and European leaders equivocated on whether they would attend the 2008 Beijing Olympic Games. The result further strained EU–China relations over the Tibet issue. When French President Nicolas Sarkozy indicated that he would meet the Dalai Lama and then did so in late 2008, China's reaction was strong. Beijing abruptly postponed the planned EU–China annual summit scheduled to be held in France.

Premier Wen Jiabao traveled to Europe in early 2009 in an effort to shore up China–European relations, but he also continued Chinese efforts to isolate the French president until the French administration worked to fix the damage caused by the meeting with the Dalai Lama. China's efforts to improve ties with European countries were complicated by widespread disapproval in Europe over what was seen as China's role as a major impediment to progress at the international conference on climate change in Copenhagen in December 2009. Also, China alienated many in Europe with its strident reaction and pressure on Norway and other European governments participating at the Nobel awards ceremonies in honor of a Chinese dissident receiving the 2010 Nobel Peace Prize.[82]

A gradual Chinese–French reconciliation culminated in Hu Jintao's visit to Paris in November 2010—part of a trip to European capitals seeking advantageous economic ties with China during a period of protracted economic recession in the West. French President Sarkozy traveled to China in 2011 to further cement ties, but that visit was overshadowed by differences in China–Europe relations, in this case Hu Jintao's and other Chinese complaints about NATO's employing military force against the regime of Libya's Muammar Gaddafi.[83]

The Xi Jinping presidency has seen nothing like these dramatic events in relations with Europe. China–European relations reflected the mix of positive developments and sustained differences evident since the outset of the twenty-first century. In 2015, neither side seemed prepared to give high priority to changing the status quo. Europe had enormous economic preoccupations and a very difficult relationship with Russia. Xi Jinping's China had a wide array of domestic challenges while its activism in foreign affairs focused closer to home, along China's periphery.

Canada and the Arctic

A NATO member with strong ties to Europe and the United States, Canada was among the first of leading Western nations in establishing diplomatic relations with China, in 1970, as China reached out for greater international contact and support in the face of the growing power and pressure of the Soviet Union at that time. It became a major trading partner of China. China's rapid economic development required more imports of energy, foods, and other resources, which Canada willingly provided, while Chinese exports of manufactured goods to Canada grew enormously, leading to a large trade deficit for Canada.

Generally following a moderate course in dealing with China, Canada usually sought to avoid the acrimonious disputes and controversies that sometimes marked the erratic course of U.S.–China relations in the recent period. An exception was the leadership of Prime Minister Stephen Harper whose government for several years in the first decade of the twenty-first century highlighted political disputes with China, notably over human rights and Tibet, before calming disputes in a more pragmatic pursuit of closer economic contacts.[84]

China since 2008 sought to become a permanent observer on the Arctic Council, an exclusive regional forum of eight member states (Canada, Denmark, Finland, Iceland, Norway, Russia, Sweden, and the United States) created in 1996 to promote collaboration and cooperation on Arctic issues. It became an observer in 2013. The five coastal states bordering the Arctic Ocean, Canada, Denmark, Norway, Russia, and the United States, signed a declaration in 2008 signaling that by virtue of their sovereignty, sovereignty rights, and jurisdiction in large areas of the Arctic Ocean, they are uniquely positioned to address the evolving contemporary issues of the Arctic. The declaration represented an explicit statement that there was no need for a comprehensive Arctic Treaty on the lines of what exists in Antarctica. Chinese commentary has taken the position that the Arctic region possesses a "shared heritage of humankind," suggesting China could oppose some of the Arctic states' sovereignty claims and assert claims of its own as the melting ice creates easier access to resources in the area and eases barriers to more efficient sea transportation between China and European and North America ports.[85]

Chapter Twelve

Relations with the Middle East, Africa, and Latin America

The remarkable resource-intensive growth of China's export-oriented economy in recent years was accompanied by an upsurge in development of Chinese infrastructure and expanded urbanization and industrialization in China. As a result, there was a major increase in Chinese imports of oil, metals, timber, and other raw materials and agricultural products needed for Chinese economic development and industrial production. An authoritative Chinese commentator in 2010 said that China consumed over four times the amount of oil to advance its GDP than the United States did, and over eight times the amount of oil to advance its GDP than did Japan. The voracious need for energy and other resources China did not have in adequate supply in turn increased the importance of Chinese foreign relations with resource-rich countries throughout the world, notably in the Middle East, Africa, and Latin America.[1]

Those areas of the developing world received steady but generally low levels of Chinese government attention in the 1990s. The importance of the three regions to China grew in tandem with the growth of Chinese trade and other economic involvement focused on Chinese purchases of oil and other raw materials. Striving to balance Chinese imports and pursue economic opportunity, the Chinese government fostered programs that facilitated widespread use of Chinese companies in construction projects and rapid development of Chinese exports of manufactured goods to these regions. The impressive influx of Chinese merchants, construction laborers, and others saw close to 1 million Chinese working for 1,600 Chinese firms in Africa in 2010. As China grew to become the world's second-largest economy, largest trader, and largest holder of foreign exchange reserves, increased Chinese trade, investment, and foreign assistance activities in these areas received prominent attention in international media. The growth in China's economic profile included a large and growing share of foreign economic interactions in these regions. In contrast to sometimes sensational media reports, however, China did not dominate the economic interaction, as the Western-oriented developed countries led by the United States, countries of the European Union, Japan, and international financial institutions played a far more important role than China as investors, aid providers, and markets for regional exports.[2]

The increased Chinese economic involvement was accompanied by political activism and some military support that backed improved Chinese relations with governments throughout the three regions. The imperatives of economic development underlined pragmatism in Chinese diplomacy. China sought to maintain good relations with all countries that eschewed formal contacts with Taiwan. It tried to avoid taking sides or alienating important actors in salient disputes such as the Middle East peace process and international efforts to curb Iran's suspected development of nuclear weapons. It adjusted in practical ways to changes affecting its energy and other interests, notably the breakaway of oil-rich southern Sudan as an independent country after a long armed struggle against the Chinese-backed regime in Khartoum. Though some Chinese initiatives sought to reduce the power and influence of the United States, Chinese officials generally gave secondary priority to undermining American authority.

The foreign policies of the Xi Jinping government saw China remain active in the Middle East, Africa, and Latin America, even though the priority of the government's high international profile focused more on the periphery of China. As discussed in chapter 4, Chinese economic reforms now stressed less resource-intensive production and curbed investment in domestic infrastructure, which was seen to have reached the point of diminishing returns. As a result, greater emphasis was placed in foreign economic policy on initiatives seen in Chinese Silk Road plans that pledged tens of billions of dollars of Chinese investment in and financing of large transportation, electric power and other infrastructure projects to be built by the massive excess capacity of Chinese construction firms no longer able to find work in China as a result of recent economic policy changes. In line with these changes, Chinese policy in the Middle East, Africa, and Latin America continued to seek to build infrastructure that provided access to needed resources. Even with the ongoing economic reforms, China's need for imported oil and other commodities continued to grow, albeit at a more modest pace than in the recent past. At the same time, Chinese policy in these regions gave much more attention to deals involving Chinese infrastructure projects like high-speed rail lines, roads, power plants, and airports that President Xi Jinping, Premier Li Keqiang, and other senior leaders promised would be supported with promises of multibillion-dollar Chinese financing arrangements.

As discussed in chapter 4, coincident with China's intense publicity on its Silk Road initiatives, there was a growing awareness in China and abroad about the serious shortcomings of China's emphasis since the start of the previous decade on investment and financing in seeking oil and other resources abroad. On the positive side, trade to the Middle East, Africa, and Latin America grew rapidly and benefited a wide range of Chinese firms. Millions of Chinese went to the three regions to seek economic advantage. Multibillion-dollar Chinese and sometimes World Bank and other foreign financing supported numerous Chinese-built projects that provided good access to raw materials needed by China. Chinese debts for these efforts were often repaid in oil or other commodities. On the negative side, the decline in oil and raw material prices in recent years caused countries where China had a heavy debt exposure such as Venezuela, Ecuador, and Angola to seek debt relief that China was reluctant to grant without some compensation or other assurance of repayment. Meanwhile, as noted in earlier discussion of Indonesia and Pakistan, the vast majority of widely publicized Chinese investment deals there failed to materialize. China's worldwide foreign investment efforts resulted more often than not in unprofitable ventures. Mining ventures were particularly volatile, with over 80 percent failing to be realized. Such shortcomings also were common in the Chinese interaction with the Middle East, Africa, and Latin America. Also, the Chinese practice to build infrastructure with Chinese firms and minimizing local involvement, and a variety of Chinese practices involving labor standards, environmental standards, and corrupt dealings with partner governments ran up against sometimes violent opposition by affected interest groups and people.

Against this background, the Xi government basically stuck with the playbook of the previous government, with less emphasis on seeking resources and more emphasis on infrastructure to be built by Chinese firms. The heavy publicity Xi's public actions received from Chinese propaganda organs meant that foreign policy in these regions often seemed to have a higher public profile than in the past. In fact, however, China's emphasis in foreign affairs was more on China's periphery. In the Middle East, Africa, and Latin America, China's trade position was strong but not growing as fast as in the recent past, and was not dominant; its position as an investor remained surprisingly small against the backdrop of Chinese leaders' repeated multibillion-dollar pledges. China probed for political advantage in competition with the United States, but it generally took care to avoid high-profile political or military actions that would seriously complicate relations with Washington.

RELATIONS WITH THE MIDDLE EAST

Chinese policy and behavior toward the Middle East in recent years followed a pattern seen in Chinese policy and behavior toward other regions of developing countries far from China—Africa and Latin America. On the one hand, there was an upswing of Chinese attention to the region, notably because of growing Chinese need for oil and other energy sources and resources that are required to support China's remarkable economic growth. On the other hand, China's close relations with Iran and some other energy and resource exporters complicated China's efforts to stay on good terms with the United States and developed countries important in Chinese foreign policy.[3] In recent years, Iran continued to be seen as a major deviant from world norms regarding nuclear weapons proliferation, terrorism, human rights, and other sensitive issues that were supported by the United States, the EU, and other powers of importance to China. The Chinese government was more reluctant than in the 1990s to take strong public positions against the United States and its allies in dealing with Iran, as well as Iraq and other issues of controversy, as it gave higher priority to managing differences and advancing common ground with Washington.[4]

Because of its geographic distance from Chinese territory, the Middle East was never a top security concern for China, although the region's importance to the Chinese government grew with China's growing oil and other resource needs.[5] Following the Tiananmen crackdown and the end of the Cold War, Chinese leaders were concerned with a wide range of more pressing domestic and international priorities. In the 1990s, they gave generally secondary attention to relations with the region, though China did make some significant gains in pursuing multifaceted political, economic, and strategic interests. It endeavored to boost Beijing's role as an interested party in the Middle East peace process and in international disputes with Iraq. Consistent with China's often tough public line at the time against U.S. "hegemonism" and "power politics," Chinese officials and commentary made clear China's opposition to U.S. strategic dominance in the Persian Gulf and elsewhere in the region. However, the Chinese government generally did not allow its pervasive anti-U.S. rhetoric to spoil its more important effort to stabilize U.S.–China relations. Meanwhile, Chinese policy aimed at keeping on good terms with all sides, including notably Israel, in the often contentious politics of the region. In this way, China could serve its economic interests of ensuring diverse supplies of oil and access to regional markets for economic benefit and arms transfers.[6]

During the Cold War, Chinese officials viewed the Middle East as a key arena of East–West competition for world domination and of resistance by so-called Third World states and liberation movements against outside powers and their local allies. Beijing lined up on the side of the reputed progressive forces resisting U.S. and/or Soviet dominance and provided some military aid, training, and other support to some resistance movements. In general, however, Chinese leaders saw the Middle East as distant from primary Chinese foreign policy concerns.

The end of the Cold War and the collapse of the Soviet Union did not change this basic calculus. Yet because of China's isolation from Western and other governments as a result of the Tiananmen incident of 1989, Chinese officials endeavored to build closer ties with many authoritarian governments in the Middle East region. President Yang Shangkun, Premier Li Peng, and Foreign Minister Qian Qichen traveled widely in the area, as well as in other Third World locales, in an apparent effort to persuade audiences at home and abroad that the Chinese government could not be effectively isolated. Beijing continued to gain both economically and politically from active arms sales to the region, notably during the Iran–Iraq war of the 1980s. And it solidified the establishment of diplomatic relations with Saudi Arabia in 1990 with the multibillion-dollar sale of older Chinese intermediate-range ballistic missiles. China also improved relations with Israel and established formal diplomatic relations with the country in 1992.[7]

China's economic and global interests seemed to lead China toward policies that would avoid offending any major Middle Eastern country and open opportunities for trade and for imports of oil. In addition to arms sales and Chinese–Middle Eastern trade valued at $3 billion a year by the early 1990s, Beijing had earned on average over half a billion dollars annually from labor contracts involving construction projects in the region since the late 1970s.[8]

The Persian Gulf War in 1990–1991 added to regional economic difficulties, which included Western sanctions, crimped regional economic development, and curbed opportunities for Chinese economic interchange and arms sales. Meanwhile, the U.S.-led victory in the Persian Gulf War came at China's political expense, in the sense that Beijing's efforts to keep on good terms with all sides in the conflict counted for little as U.S.-backed power moved to dominate the region. Coming on top of U.S.-backed efforts to isolate China and pressure it to change in accordance with international standards supported by the United States, this development prompted Beijing to seek opportunities to undercut U.S. world influence while building Chinese ties with countries in the region. It was at this juncture that Chinese officials moved forward in relations with many Arab governments and with Iran, partly as a move to counter U.S. dominance and pressure.[9]

In general terms, the Middle East in the mid-1990s also was seen as important to China because of its relationship to China's unstable western areas, especially Xinjiang. Beijing worried about support from the region to Islamic separatists or other radicals in China. Chinese crackdowns in Xinjiang met with public and private disapproval from some Middle Eastern governments.

As China became a net importer of oil in 1993, Beijing worked harder to diversify its international supplies, and the Middle East loomed large with its abundant oil and gas reserves. China's oil consumption grew at 7 percent a year in the mid-1990s; its import bill was about $5 billion in 1997, with half coming from the Middle East. The Chinese also sought to develop trade in military items and technologies with countries that were on poor terms with the United States (for example, Iran), in part to use those ties as leverage in dealing with suspected U.S. plots to contain and pressure China. China also purchased military equipment from Israel in order to modernize its military despite the Western arms embargo against China. Meanwhile, Chinese officials, though victorious over Taiwan in establishing diplomatic relations with the conservative Saudi Arabian government, devoted strong efforts to curb any Taiwan inroads in the Middle East as well as elsewhere. [10]

Continuing past Chinese efforts to build productive ties with all Middle Eastern countries, Beijing's relations with Israel flourished in trade, political exchanges, and defense ties. Chinese officials continued to lean toward the Arab and Palestinian positions on Middle East peace issues but duly acknowledged the legitimacy of Israeli concerns. Chinese officials disapproved of U.S.- or Western-backed pressure against so-called rogue states like Iraq, Iran, Libya, and Syria, though Chinese policy usually followed the international consensus in the United Nations when it dealt with Iraqi recalcitrance or other issues. [11]

The improvement in U.S.–Chinese relations after 1996 and especially the summit meetings of 1997 and 1998 had an indirect impact on Chinese policy in the Middle East. On the one hand, it reinforced the judgment by some in China that Beijing had more to gain by working more or less cooperatively with the United States than by lining up with states in the Middle East or elsewhere that were strongly hostile to the United States. It also encouraged China to be more active on regional issues that heretofore had been the prime domain of other powers and to do so in ways that at least outwardly seemed supportive of U.S. goals involving stability and peace. Thus, for example, Chinese leaders during 1997 and 1998 summit meetings with the United States promised to stop cooperation with Iran on nuclear development, to halt sales of antiship cruise missiles to Iran, and to halt support for Iran's ballistic missile development. Beijing also strove to work in support of U.S.-led efforts to revitalize the stalled Middle East peace process, notably through the visit of Vice Premier and Foreign Minister Qian Qichen to frontline states in December 1997 and his subsequent interchanges with U.S. officials on Middle East peace issues. [12]

The transition toward a Middle East posture more in line with U.S. interests remained muddled, however. At times Beijing still saw its interests as well served by staking out tough public anti-U.S. stances on sensitive regional questions. [13]

Partly to avoid serious difficulties with the United States and other concerned powers, Chinese officials were prudent in their exchanges and generally cooperative with UN-backed restrictions on Iraq.[14] Nonetheless, Beijing signaled through commentaries and official interchange that its long-term interests in developing a more multipolar power configuration in the region were well served by outcomes of diminishing U.S. power.[15] With regard to Iraq, China repeatedly joined Russia and others in trying to moderate U.S.-backed pressure on Baghdad over weapons inspection issues, urging diplomatic negotiations over the use of force and reiterating calls for the eventual easing of sanctions.[16] Regarding the stalled Middle East peace talks Beijing announced in early December 1997 that Foreign Minister Qian Qichen would visit Lebanon, Syria, Israel, Egypt, and the Palestinian Authority (PA) from December 18 to 26. This marked the highest-level Chinese visit to either Israel or the PA and the first visit to nearly all the so-called frontline states.[17] During his visit to the frontline states, Qian Qichen boosted China's pro-Arab profile on the peace process and took the opportunity to register Beijing's growing impatience with U.S.-backed international sanctions against Libya and Iraq. Reflecting improved Chinese ties with Israel since the establishment of diplomatic relations in 1992, Qian was moderate in his talks with Israeli leaders. He said China understood their security concerns and strongly opposed terrorism. At other stops, however, Qian blamed Israeli Prime Minister Benjamin Netanyahu's government for the impasse in the peace process.[18]

Returning to Beijing on January 2, 1998, Qian was typically circumspect in addressing China's role in the Middle East peace process, an issue evidently still of secondary importance in Chinese foreign policy. He said China would introduce no major policy initiatives and would not serve as a formal mediator, but it would use its permanent seat on the UN Security Council (UNSC) and other means to facilitate the peace process.[19]

Mirroring what Chinese officials perceived as the "two-handed" U.S. policy of engagement and containment toward China, the Chinese government came up with a two-pronged policy of its own with regard to U.S. interests in the Middle East: China employed strategic partnerships, such as those forged with France and Russia, and historical affinity with the region's developing countries to endeavor to weaken U.S. dominance. At the same time, it promoted cooperation and avoided direct confrontation in ongoing dialogue with the United States on key regional issues. Taken together, these elements presented a somewhat muddled and conflicted Chinese approach.

Meanwhile, Chinese leaders also tried to show balance in dealing with Prime Minister Benjamin Netanyahu, who visited China in May 1998. The Chinese officials told the Israeli leader of their great concern about the stalemate in the peace process, they blamed Israel's failure to commit to signed agreements with Arab parties concerned, and they voiced Chinese support for Palestinian people in particular and the Arab people in general. China supported the land-for-peace principle as the basis for a just, comprehensive settlement. At the same time, Chinese officials acknowledged Israel's security concerns. They insisted that China was not playing the role of a "middleman" in the peace process but was trying to work together with the United States and others in the international community to bring about a peaceful solution. Press reports also indicated that the two sides discussed ways to boost the $300 million annual bilateral trade relationship, as well as to increase a reported several hundred million dollars in annual secret military trade. According to Israeli Radio, Premier Zhu Rongji told Netanyahu that China would not sell nuclear and missile technology to Iran.[20]

TWENTY-FIRST-CENTURY POLICY CONTRADICTIONS AND DILEMMAS

Chinese policy and behavior in the Middle East in the twenty-first century featured a series of decision points involving often contradictory imperatives. These imperatives posed sometimes serious dilemmas for Chinese leaders and seemed to require pragmatic and careful cost-benefit assessments by Chinese officials. One-sided decisions ran the risk of serious negative consequences for Chinese interests. In general, the Chinese leaders adopted positions that were well balanced, had the broadest international appeal, and did the least damage to China's often conflicting interests in the Middle East. At the same time, the kind of muddled overall message seen in China's actions in the Middle East in the 1990s continued into the new century. One result was that while China's State Council issued statements on many foreign policy issues and regions, it offered no such guidance on relations with the Middle East. Presumably this gap came because offering such a clear statement of policy would very likely alienate more than one of the important regional powers and undermine some significant Chinese interests in the sensitive matrix of the Middle East.[21]

Heading the list of complications and conflicting imperatives in Chinese policy toward the Middle East was Chinese leaders' need to strengthen their relations with oil and gas exporters, including targets of U.S.-backed international pressure (like Iran) and countries that periodically wished to show greater independence from the United States (like oil-rich Saudi Arabia). Building better Chinese relations with these two energy giants was further complicated by their deep mutual suspicion and conflicting interests.

Also in the past decade, Chinese leaders were seeking to tone down their anti-U.S. posturing seen in the 1990s in order to strengthen Chinese moderation toward the United States; this was in the interest of avoiding conflict and convincing the United States and its partners of China's determination to conform to international norms as it sought greater economic development, international influence, and power. China also did not wish to appear to challenge the long-standing U.S. relationship with Saudi Arabia for fear of seriously antagonizing the United States. Chinese strategists saw their access to the energy resources of the Persian Gulf heavily influenced by the strong U.S. military presence in the Gulf and the broader Middle East. Taken together, the previously mentioned imperatives and trends were often at odds. They appeared contradictory, and they complicated China's approach toward the region.

Deepening the trend of the previous decade, Chinese policy aimed as much as possible at keeping on good terms with all sides in the often contentious politics of the region.[22] The logic behind the Chinese approach to the Middle East seemed clear, even though the Chinese goals seemed in conflict and the resulting Chinese actions appeared to be somewhat ambivalent and confusing. Chinese domestic economic growth and political stability depended on stable energy supplies. The main sources of Chinese energy demand involved industrial activities, infrastructure development, and transportation growth. The large increase in the number of cars in China strengthened the need for imported oil. Despite China's efforts to diversify the sources of oil imports, the Middle East accounted for over half of China's overall imports, with Saudi Arabia and Iran being the biggest or among the biggest suppliers in the region.[23]

Graphic examples of China's stronger drive for international energy resources included a variety of high-level Chinese visits and energy-related agreements with Iran, as well as even more interactions and agreements with the major energy power in the region, Saudi Arabia. Saudi Arabia was the largest supplier of oil to China for most recent years, accounting for about 15 percent of Chinese imports. In 1999, President Jiang Zemin visited Saudi Arabia and signed accords, including a Strategic Oil Cooperation Agreement, that opened the Saudi oil and gas market to China. Later, Saudi Arabian enterprises reached agreements to expand and modernize oil refineries in China.[24] In 2006, the head of state of Saudi Arabia visited China in his inaugural trip abroad. President Hu Jintao reciprocated a few months later. The Chinese president followed up with a widely publicized visit in 2009. While more oil sales and closer bilateral relations seemed in the offing, it was unclear how far the two governments would go in solidifying their bilateral relationship and what meaning this would have for the United States, which historically was the major power backing the Saudi ruler. Although Saudi Arabia reportedly had an interest in showing greater independence from the United States, Chinese interest in posturing against the United States in such a sensitive area as relations with Saudi Arabia seemed low. China notably continued to rely on the U.S. military to ensure secure transit for its growing energy imports from Saudi Arabia and other Middle Eastern suppliers. Further, Chinese leaders continued to emphasize to U.S. counterparts China's interest in seeking partnership with the United States.[25]

By the time of Chinese President Hu Jintao's visit to Saudi Arabia in February 2009, Sino–Saudi Arabian trade amounted to over $42 billion a year. Bilateral trade declined along with international energy demand during the global economic downturn in 2009, but it rebounded to a value of $43 billion in 2010. It grew to $73 billion in 2013. China became the largest importer of Saudi oil. Chinese trade with the Middle East at this time was well over $200 billion a year.[26]

Meanwhile, even though China was well aware that Saudi Arabia and Iran had a number of serious differences and were often on opposite sides regarding Middle Eastern problems, China pursued its long-standing ties with Tehran given China's ever growing energy needs. In October 2004, the Chinese government agreed with Iran to buy large quantities of Iranian natural gas over a twenty-five-year period. China later agreed to develop an oil field in western Iran, and in 2009 a deal worth over $3 billion was reportedly reached involving Chinese development of a natural gas field in Iran. Chinese firms also were deeply involved in developing the Tehran subway, electricity, dams, and other industries and infrastructure. These steps reinforced Chinese reluctance to see sanctions or other pressure imposed on Tehran by the United States and Western powers concerned with Iran's nuclear development program, though China also continued to avoid standing alone against such international opposition.[27] Top-level Chinese leaders visited Iran less frequently than Saudi Arabia, but they met cordially with the controversial Iranian president in China and at international meetings elsewhere. Iranian officials said in 2011 that direct Chinese trade with Iran was valued at $29 billion, and indirect trade through countries neighboring Iran brought the total to $38 billion in 2010. They added that Iran is currently China's third-largest supplier of crude, providing China with roughly 12 percent of its total annual oil consumption. Trade was slated to reach a value of $50 billion in 2015.[28] Active collaboration between Iranian and Chinese energy firms indicated that China would continue to rely on imports from the country, though projections that China will rely on the Middle East for 70 percent of its oil imports in 2015 (up from 44 percent in 2006) were premised on big increases in Chinese oil imports from the five Arab states in the Gulf Cooperation Council. In 2014 China imported 9 percent of its foreign oil from Iran.[29]

At the same time, strong examples of China's moderation toward the United States and its interest in the Middle East included China's reluctance to stand against the U.S.-led military assault against Saddam Hussein in 2003. Beginning in 2002, Chinese officials repeatedly assured U.S. officials that China would not block the U.S.-led attack. They also were careful that the level of their public opposition to the U.S. action stayed below that of

Russia, France, and Germany; the latter two governments—and not China—bore the brunt of U.S. resentment and anger over the international opposition to the U.S. move. The relatively mild Chinese government position in opposition to the U.S.-led military attack on Iraq compared notably with China's more strenuous opposition to much less offensive U.S. actions against Iraq during the 1990s. As one Chinese diplomat said in an interview in 2007, "China will not challenge the presence of the United States in the Middle East." Instead, China will focus on strengthening relations with Middle Eastern countries beneficial for the supply of oil and other energy to China.[30]

Regarding the more recent controversy over Iran's nuclear program, the Chinese government acted as though it did not want to choose between its important energy and other ties with Iran and its concern to nurture the continued cooperation of the United States, the EU, and others who have strongly pressed Iran over a variety of issues, notably its suspected efforts to develop nuclear weapons. Chinese officials at times endeavored to slow and delay actions in the United Nations that would result in condemnation of or sanctions against Iran, and at times they worked closely with Russia in fending off pressure from the United States and the EU powers for more decisive UN action. However, China tried to avoid standing alone against Western pressure, and it bent to such pressure in allowing the issue to be brought before the UN Security Council despite earlier pledges to resist such a step. In June 2010 China voted for a UN Security Council resolution approving new sanctions against Iran on account of its suspected nuclear weapons development.[31]

Chinese relations with Israel posed another set of contradictions and complications for Chinese foreign policy in the Middle East. China benefited greatly from economic and military transfers from Israel; the latter were especially valuable to China because of the continued Western arms embargo against China. China resented U.S. pressure to curb Israeli military transfers to China.[32] Beijing accepted Israel's right to exist and eschewed past support for radical elements aiming at Israel's destruction—steps that significantly improved China's relations with the United States and other concerned Western powers. At the same time, China supported the PA in its opposition to various Israeli pressures and maneuvers seen as designed to weaken the PA and to reduce its legitimate territorial claims. It was sharply critical of Israel's December 2008 invasion of Gaza and the resulting humanitarian crisis. The victory of the radical Hamas movement in PA legislative elections in the middle of the decade and growing control of the radical movement over the PA posed a serious complication. China was low keyed in accepting Hamas in the face of strong U.S. and Israeli opposition to international support for what they deemed a terrorist organization. The Chinese foreign ministry spokesperson welcomed the April 2011 agreement between Hamas and its

Fatah rival, paving the way to the formation of an interim government to prepare for elections determining the future administration of the PA. [33]

A more serious set of complications was raised by the war in July–August 2006 between Israel and Hezbollah forces based in southern Lebanon. Chinese commentary moved from a more or less evenhanded position to one that sided against Israel and to a degree the United States. China did not want to seriously alienate any major party or make major commitments or take risks in the volatile situation; this was illustrated by the bland and noncommittal remarks of its Foreign Ministry "special envoy" sent to tour the region and by much of Chinese media commentary. The United States, European powers, Israel, Iran, and Syria loomed much more important in the conflict and the efforts to resolve the conflict. As one veteran scholar of China–Middle East relations concluded, China's behavior during the crisis showed that Beijing continued to talk much and do little regarding serious regional issues. [34] China did respond to UN and European requests for peacekeeping forces and agreed to provide 1,000 personnel for the UN peacekeeping operation in Lebanon. The Chinese personnel were used in support functions, according to Chinese diplomats. [35]

An additional set of contradictions was posed by China's ongoing efforts to suppress dissent and splitist activities by Muslim adherents in Xinjiang. It was deemed essential that these elements be suppressed in order to preserve order and stability in China. At the same time, the tough Chinese measures negatively affected China's image among the Islamic governments in the Middle East. Finally, Chinese antiterrorist efforts at home and abroad, notably in the Shanghai Cooperation Organization (SCO), were seen as vital to Chinese national security and regional stability and an important foundation for greater Chinese cooperation with the United States and other Western powers. At the same time, China's interests with Iran required Chinese leaders to allow the president of Iran to participate in the elaborate fifth-anniversary summit of the SCO in Shanghai and later meetings of the group, despite strong accusations from Israel, the United States, and Western powers that Tehran supported terrorist activities against Israel, in Iraq, and elsewhere. More recent Chinese fence straddling showed in avoiding a veto of UNSC Resolution 1973 against the Gaddafi regime while complaining at the highest levels about the violence in Libya resulting from NATO forces employing military coercion in the country under the auspices of the UNSC resolution. [36]

Middle East Gap in Xi Jinping's Foreign Policy

President Xi Jinping wrestled with these contradictory imperatives. Though advancing a higher profile for China in other parts of the world, Xi and his colleagues were unable to get beyond China's traditional low profile in the Middle East. Though Chinese economic interests in the region continued to grow along with the rapid rise of oil imports and Chinese exports of manu-factured goods, the Chinese president and prime minister did not visit the region up to mid-2015. The main reasons had to do with the pervasive vio-lence throughout the region and resulting danger to the safety of Chinese leaders.

Caution and practicality determined China's reaction to the upsurge of mass demonstrations against authoritarian regimes throughout North Africa and nearby Asia in 2011. The Chinese government focused internally, tight-ening already extensive Chinese internal controls to guard against possible spillover effects that might challenge continued one-party rule in China. In the region, Chinese officials adjusted pragmatically to the new administra-tions taking form in Tunisia and Egypt. The armed conflict in Libya cost Chinese enterprises invested there dearly; the Chinese government was effec-tive in facilitating the evacuation of over 30,000 Chinese nationals from the country. China seemed to depart from its past practice in abstaining rather than blocking UN Security Council Resolution 1973 in March 2011 authoriz-ing all measures, including military action, against the Libyan government of Muammar Gaddafi, then engaging in armed resistance to populist forces struggling for his ouster. An examination of the costs of blocking the meas-ure showed that they outweighed benefits China would have derived from vetoing the measure.[37]

Beijing came to regret this decision and began to oppose NATO military action against Gaddafi. It joined Russia in blocking UN action in opposition to the Bashar al-Assad government in the Syrian civil war. Still supporting the Assad government in Syria, China avoided full endorsement of U.S. calls for strong action against the radical Islamic State in Iraq and Syria. Regional turmoil spread with the fall of the government of Yemen to militants in early 2015. Saudi Arabia intervened with bombing raids against the militants. Xi Jinping had been planning a visit to Saudi Arabia and Egypt along with Pakistan and Indonesia in March 2015. He changed plans in the wake of the Saudi bombings, scrapped plans for both the Saudi Arabia and Egypt visits, and confined the trip to Pakistan and Indonesia. The Xi trip predictably underlined Chinese Silk Road economic initiatives that included the states in the Middle East, but security dangers combined with the various contradic-tions facing Chinese policy inclined Chinese leaders at least for now to avoid a potentially dangerous and counterproductive higher profile in the volatile Middle East.[38]

RELATIONS WITH AFRICA

In the 1990s, China devoted considerable political attention to African coun-tries in order to compete with Taiwan for international recognition, to build solidarity with members of the Third World bloc in the United Nations and other world organizations, to facilitate some advantageous trade in oil and other commodities, and to portray itself internationally as a power with growing international stature and influence. The Chinese government generally eschewed commitments that would involve substantial Chinese aid or other resources or that would antagonize disputants in the continent's many conflicts. Although Chinese media at the time often focused on themes of opposition to U.S. dominance and hegemony in world affairs, the generally low level of U.S. or allied powers' involvement in African affairs meant that Beijing devoted a low level of media and political attention to criticizing U.S. and other powers' policies that were incompatible with Chinese goals on the continent.[39]

The history of Chinese relations with Africa is full of often visionary and sometimes quixotic efforts to throw off outside influence and foster rapid development and social progress. Chinese officials to this day continue a long-standing practice of comparing Africa's suffering under the European colonialists with China's so-called hundred years of humiliation. Chinese aid efforts have waxed and waned according to the urgency of changing Chinese priorities. At times during the Cold War, Beijing was an important supplier of basic military equipment and training to a number of liberation groups and newly emerged governments. Chinese leaders proclaimed that Africa was ripe for revolution in the 1960s and provided a variety of assistance to groups. The assistance ranged from providing help to dissident factions opposed to the UN-backed regime in Congo-Leopoldville to providing backing for the regime of President Mobutu Sese Seko in Zaire to help check Soviet-backed incursions from Angola in the 1970s. The Chinese were key backers of liberation fighters against the Portuguese in Angola and Mozambique, they supported Robert Mugabe in his struggle against white-ruled Rhodesia, and they backed other radical groups in South Africa and elsewhere.[40]

China relied heavily on backing from African countries in its efforts to rally Third World support in order to gain entry for China and to remove Taiwan from the United Nations in 1971. Competition between China and Taiwan for diplomatic recognition continued. It intensified when Beijing gave higher priority to checking Taiwan's flexible diplomacy, especially following the visit by Taiwan's president, Lee Teng-hui, to the United States in 1995.

Large-scale demonstration projects also characterized Chinese policy in Africa. The Tan-Zam Railway, which links Zambia's copper fields and the Tanzanian coast, was undertaken by Chinese engineers even though it was previously judged ill advised by Western and other international experts. Despite great obstacles, Chinese government workers completed the project after many years of effort, the loss of many lives, and great expense.

Post-Mao Chinese leaders were much less interested in spending money overseas, especially when their political standing at home rested heavily on their ability to improve economic conditions for the Chinese people. Thus, by the late 1970s, the overriding focus of domestic modernization led to a reduction in Chinese enthusiasm for funding expensive African assistance programs. Chinese officials also recognized that past efforts to roll back superpower influence in the region had not worked well. Aid levels dropped markedly in the late 1970s and remained around $100 million annually for the whole world. Chinese assistance increasingly took the form of training, export credits for Chinese goods, or joint financing plans. As the Chinese export-oriented economy grew, so did Chinese trade, from about $300 million with Africa in 1976 to $2.2 billion in 1988. Of course, this still was only a small fraction of overall Chinese trade.[41]

As post-Mao China was willing and anxious to receive foreign aid from the World Bank, the International Monetary Fund (IMF), and other international bodies and donor countries, this put China in direct competition with African states seeking aid from the same sources. The newly open Chinese economy also was seen by some to be taking foreign investment that might have gone to African ventures. African grumbling over these trends grew. Even some longtime African friends felt increasing ambiguity in their ties with China. With mixed results, Chinese officials used diplomacy, propaganda, and exchanges to preserve Beijing's self-described position as an intimate supporter of struggling African states. While acknowledging Chinese political support, African governments often recognized that they had to follow China's example in cultivating ties with developed economies, including the United States, Europe, and Japan, if they expected markedly to boost their modernization efforts. Meanwhile, long-standing Chinese efforts to offer university and other training for African students were clouded by several publicized incidents showing apparent Chinese social bias against Africans in the late 1980s.[42]

Chinese incentives to improve relations with African countries increased after the Tiananmen incident of 1989.[43] Officials anxiously sought African and other Third World support to offset Beijing's isolation and to reduce international pressure against China. The period also saw Taiwan launch its pragmatic or flexible diplomacy policy. Taipei used offers of aid or other means to woo aid-dependent African countries and to have them establish official diplomatic relations with Taiwan even though they had diplomatic relations with Beijing. Whenever this occurred, Beijing broke ties with the African state concerned, providing a net diplomatic gain for Taipei.

Chinese leaders shortly after Tiananmen directed PRC diplomats to focus on resuming and developing relations with old friends, including African states that remained supportive of Beijing. Foreign Minister Qian Qichen visited eleven African countries one month after Tiananmen. African states, which seemed to be marginalized as major Western and Asian investors turned their attention elsewhere in the post–Cold War period, generally welcomed China's renewed emphasis on strengthening ties.[44]

High-level Sino-African exchanges in the post–Cold War, post-Tiananmen period resumed in full force in July 1992 when President Yang Shangkun, Foreign Minister Qian Qichen, and a PRC trade delegation visited Morocco, Tunisia, and the Ivory Coast. Chinese media played up the visit as a major event in Sino-African relations, noted China's sensitivity to the widening political and economic gap between the developed countries and Africa, and hailed Yang's reaffirmation of cooperation with the Third World as a basic tenet of China's foreign policy. An active travel schedule continued through the decade:

- During a seven-country trip in July–August 1995, Vice Premier Zhu Rongji laid out a four-point formula for joint ventures and limited direct assistance of possible projects.
- During a six-country swing in May 1996, President Jiang Zemin declared China and Africa to be "all-weather friends," signed twenty-three economic and technical agreements, and promised that China would always stand firmly alongside Africa.
- In January 1997, Foreign Minister Qian Qichen visited six countries, noted overall improvements in PRC–African relations, and hammered Taiwan for allegedly attempting to buy diplomatic relations with African states.
- During a seven-country visit in the spring of 1997, Premier Li Peng praised African states for supporting China on human rights and Taiwan issues and stressed that, unlike Western countries, China provided assistance to Africa without political conditions.
- In December 1997, Foreign Minister Qian Qichen visited South Africa to sign a joint communiqué normalizing relations and officially switching South African diplomatic recognition from Taipei to Beijing.
- In January–February 1999, Vice President Hu Jintao visited four African countries.[45]

The Chinese military also was active in Africa in exchanges, training, and a variety of small arms sales. The deputy chief of the People's Liberation Army's General Staff, Xiong Guangkai, offered a perceptive view of Chinese assessments of African conditions during a speech at the Zimbabwe Defense Staff College in 1997.[46] He assessed Africa's many problems stemming from "internal wars" and "sustained economic difficulties," "the old irrational institutional economic order" that provided low profits for producers of most primary products and raw materials, and interference in African affairs by "hegemonism and power politics."

Xiong strongly reaffirmed ties between China, "the largest developing country in the world," and Africa, "the largest developing continent in the world." China supported African efforts to determine their own political and economic systems without outside interference. It pledged to continue "model" Sino-African ties for "sincere, equal, friendly and cooperative relations." Citing Chinese support for the reelection of the African Boutros Boutros-Ghali as UN secretary-general—a stance that enjoyed wide support in Africa but was opposed by the United States—Xiong strove to portray broad common ground in Sino-African political relations. He capped his talk with reference to Jiang Zemin's May 1996 visit to Africa, during which Jiang set forth five points that were to continue to govern Sino-African relations into the twenty-first century. These were to be sincere and friendly and to be each other's reliable all-weather friends; to stand on an equal footing, respect each other's sovereignty, and not interfere in each other's internal affairs; to be equal and mutually beneficial and seek for common development; to strengthen consultation and cooperate closely in international affairs; and to create a better world with an eye toward the future.

By the late 1990s, against the backdrop of the long-standing Chinese emphasis on strengthening ties with developing countries in Africa and elsewhere, PRC leaders typically characterized PRC–Third World solidarity as essential for promoting China's multipolar worldview, defending PRC positions in international forums such as the United Nations, and standing firm against U.S. global dominance. Aspiring to more equal status with the world's great powers, China also viewed positive relations with African states and other developing countries as important for pressing forward on national priorities of securing vital energy and mineral resources, expanding exports (including conventional arms), and pressing for eventual Taiwan–mainland reunification.

A heightened PRC focus on these priorities was on display across Africa in the late 1990s[47] as China pursued oil deals, notably with Nigeria, Sudan, and Angola; mineral extraction rights with Democratic Republic of Congo and Zambia; exports of textiles, consumer goods, machinery, and other manufactured goods to multiple countries, and notably a multimillion-dollar trade-investment package deal with South Africa; Chinese involvement in construction of infrastructure projects throughout Africa financed by international and Chinese sources; arms sales to several African states; and a one-China policy throughout the continent. Taiwan's diplomatic ties in Africa fell to eight mostly small countries, following Beijing's success in winning over South Africa and establishing formal diplomatic relations on January 1, 1998. In early 1999, Taiwan had official diplomatic relations with the following countries in Africa: Burkina Faso, Chad, Gambia, Liberia, Malawi, São Tomé and Príncipe, Senegal, and Swaziland.

Continued Chinese success in Africa hinged on several factors, not the least of which was Beijing's drive to compete with other large powers, especially the United States. There were some signs in the late 1990s that Beijing was losing interest in this effort. For one thing, Beijing found it difficult to compete with U.S. power. Unlike the proxy battles in the 1960s and 1970s, China increasingly considered that its competition in Africa with the big powers during the 1990s and beyond would be primarily economic in nature. China's trade with Africa at that time was comparatively small and represented only about 2 percent of Africa's total trade volume; Sino-African trade continued to rise, nearing $5.7 billion in 1997, and was about the same level in 1998.[48] To differentiate China from Western and Japanese suitors competing for African market shares, Beijing continued to play up themes of PRC–African solidarity while criticizing its competitors for their alleged colonial or hegemonic track records of plundering less developed countries; for their offers of assistance with requirements regarding improved democracy, human rights, and government integrity; and for their decisions to divert investments away from Africa after the Cold War.

Reflecting a temporary shift away from an anti-U.S. stance in Africa, Chinese media complaints about U.S. policies and behavior during President William Clinton's landmark African trip in 1998 were lower keyed than those dealing with Secretary of State Madeleine Albright's visit to seven African countries in late 1997.[49] As time went on and U.S.–China relations improved, Beijing seemed to see Chinese interests as better served by cooperating with U.S. power in ways that would advance Chinese influence as well, rather than viewing U.S. and Chinese influence in zero-sum terms.

China also faced a major challenge in trying to continue its relationship as Africa's "all-weather friend." As most African countries developed slowly or not at all and post-Mao China averaged 9 percent annual growth, the gap between China and African countries widened and seemed hard to bridge. China found it more difficult to appeal for African sympathy and support on the basis of common status as developing countries. And yet, despite a variety of trade deals, loans, and high-profile stadium, road, and other construction projects (often built with Chinese labor), China avoided large outlays of foreign assistance to African countries and continued to reap the benefits of large-scale assistance from international financial institutions, leaving less for African states.[50]

Twenty-First-Century Chinese Advances in Africa

The new century showed a deepening and broadening of Chinese interaction with African countries along the lines set down in the 1990s. The upsurge in Chinese trade, investment financing, and high-level official interaction with African countries stood in contrast with the often stagnant and contentious relations African countries had with developed countries and international financial institutions. A marked increase in Chinese purchases of oil and other raw materials from Africa, a concurrent effort to foster Chinese exports to African markets, and an increase in Chinese construction projects throughout Africa were new and important drivers of Chinese interest in the continent. Otherwise, the patterns of the post–Cold War period continued without major change. China continued to devote strong political attention to African countries in order to compete with Taiwan, enhance solidarity with members of the Third World bloc in the United Nations and other world organizations, facilitate growing trade, and portray China internationally as a power of growing stature and importance. The Chinese government had an active aid program in several African countries, but the cost of the program to China (that is, the amount of funds leaving China to aid African countries that were not guaranteed to be paid back in commodities or other forms) remained small. With a few exceptions, Chinese arms transfers to Africa were small. China avoided taking positions that would be seen to be interfering in the sometimes controversial internal affairs of African countries or that would antagonize disputants in the continent's many conflicts. Consistent with its recent emphasis on avoiding antagonism with the United States and other powers as it endeavored to pursue a path of "peaceful development," the Chinese government tended to avoid media and other political attention seen as criticizing U.S. and other powers' policies that were incompatible with Chinese goals on the continent.[51]

In general, the advance of Chinese relations in Africa faced fewer complications than concurrent Chinese advances among developing countries in the Middle East or Latin America. In the latter two areas, the security, political, and economic roles of the United States, European countries, and other foreign powers generally were significantly more important than China's newly rising prominence. Taken together, the roles of these other foreign powers added to factors constraining the influence China exerted in those regions. In the case of Africa and especially sub-Saharan Africa, however, China's involvement reached high prominence in a setting where other powers appeared less vigorously involved. Assessments of China's status in Africa varied,[52] but available data up to 2015 did not show Chinese dominance, nor did China seem to reach a status of Africa's leading foreign power. China's trade had grown impressively but slowed recently; Chinese investment remained low; China's non-commercial interests in Africa seemed limited. *The Economist* in January 2015 assessed the situation and saw China as "one among many" large outside powers that have had and continue to have a major impact on African development over the years.[53] That said, China in recent years clearly played a leading role in regional affairs along with the United States and European countries and the international organizations they support. The latter powers sometimes criticized aspects of Chinese involvement in Africa, but they also moved to consult with and work more closely with China in dealing with regional issues. Meanwhile, though the Chinese government usually sustained good relations with African government leaders, it found that China's increasing impact on Africa resulted in mixed reactions below the national government level, with some strong negative responses on the part of constituencies adversely affected by Chinese interaction with their countries.[54]

A landmark in China's efforts to formulate a comprehensive outreach to Africa came in October 2000 when China's leaders and the leaders of forty-five African countries met in Beijing to form the China-Africa Cooperation Forum (CACF). They agreed that CACF would meet every three years to further mutual economic development and cooperation. The Chinese government endeavored to enhance cooperation by using the first CACF meeting to pledge forgiveness of $1.2 billion in African debt covering thirty-two nations and to expand Chinese foreign aid to Africa. At the second ministerial CACF conference held in Addis Ababa, Ethiopia, in December 2003, China promised to cooperate with Africa in priority sectors identified in the African governments' New Partnership for African Development. These African priorities included infrastructure development, prevention and treatment of diseases such as HIV/AIDS, human resources development, and agricultural development. China also agreed to begin negotiations on reducing tariffs to zero for some exports to China of the least-developed African countries.[55]

Continued high-level attention to Africa included the release in January 2006 of the Chinese government's first official white paper on African policy, prior to Foreign Minister Li Zhaoxing's visit to several African countries. The document was broad ranging and basically restated official Chinese positions on Africa, which were also highlighted in President Hu Jintao's visit to Morocco, Kenya, and Nigeria in April 2006. This was followed by Prime Minister Wen Jiabao's visit to seven African countries in mid-2006. At the time, Chinese media reported that Chinese trade with Africa reached $40 billion in 2005, up rapidly from $10 billion in 2000.[56]

China hosted the CACF summit in November 2006. Representatives of forty-eight African countries and Chinese leaders capped the meeting with a joint declaration that provided an action plan for the next three years. The emphasis in the declaration was on expanding exchanges, trade, investment, and mutually beneficial ties as well as calling on the United Nations and the international community to strengthen support for African interests. At the summit, China pledged $5 billion in preferential loans and credits and to double aid to Africa by 2009. It announced support for health and education efforts in Africa and said that trade would expand from the 2005 level of $40 billion to reach $100 billion by 2010. Meanwhile, Chinese companies signed fourteen commercial contracts and agreements valued at $1.9 billion.[57]

Chinese government figures estimated that the number of Chinese companies operating in Africa in June 2004 was 674, with a total investment of $1.5 billion. *China Daily*, an official Chinese newspaper, said in a report on Africa on April 26, 2006, that "by the end of 2005, the accumulated investment from China to Africa had reached $1.25 billion."[58] A *China Daily* report in August 2006 said, "China's direct investment in African countries amounts to US$1.18 billion with more than 800 Chinese enterprises operating on the continent."[59] At the time of the November 2006 African summit, *China Daily* said, "So far China has invested US$6.27 billion in Africa."[60] Whatever the reasons for these varying figures, it seemed clear that the figures would grow, particularly in light of recent Chinese oil deals in Africa (which are discussed later in this chapter). However, these significant but still comparatively modest investment figures provided by the Chinese government regarding Chinese investment in African countries contrasted with the sometimes hyperbolic media reports in recent years of massive Chinese investments of several billions of dollars each in various African nations.

The latter reports sometimes confused a memorandum of understanding or an agreement on a feasibility study with a formal contract, and they also at times confused China's agreement to purchase commodities from an African country with a Chinese commitment to invest in the country. Even the respected U.S.-based Council on Foreign Relations said in its January 2006 study on Africa that Chinese investment in Sudan alone was $4 billion.[61] It is not clear how the council arrived at this figure, when official Chinese media at the time said that the level for all of Africa was just over $1 billion. These differences are important for those seeking to understand the scope and effect of Chinese foreign relations. The much larger figures cited by the Council on Foreign Relations and other respected media and analytical groups may reflect exaggerations in media reports about Chinese agreements, other sources of investment in projects involving China, or other factors.[62] In any event, a Chinese government official put a recent rise in Chinese investment in Africa in some perspective during an interview with *China Daily* in April 2011. The official said that Chinese investment in Africa, then "about $1 billion" a year, was "dwarfed by the West" in contributions to overall annual foreign investment in Africa amounting to $80–$90 billion.[63]

Chinese foreign assistance to African states also received prominent treatment in Chinese and international media and among concerned international relations specialists, even though the actual amounts of Chinese assistance to Africa seemed modest and much less than that provided by developed countries and international financial institutions.[64] As discussed in chapter 4, for a variety of reasons, the actual amounts of Chinese foreign assistance were not released in a comprehensive way by the Chinese government. China did issue an official document on Chinese foreign assistance in April 2011, but the information was very broad ranging. The second Chinese white paper on foreign assistance was issued in 2014; it offered better information focused on the three-year period 2010–2012. China provided $14.4 billion in grants, interest-free loans, and concessional loans. Over half of that went to Africa, where fifty-one countries received Chinese aid.

Against that background, foreign analysts continued to rely on piecing together information supplied by Chinese media and other official sources and on data from foreign sources in order to discern contributions and costs regarding specific countries and programs. Prime Minister Wen Jiabao was reported by Chinese and international media to have pledged at the CACF meeting in Ethiopia in 2003 that China would gradually increase aid to Africa, provide training for 10,000 Africans over three years, and increase Chinese tourism to Africa. At the November 2006 CACF summit in Beijing, Chinese leaders promised to double Chinese aid to Africa over the next three years. The Council on Foreign Relations reported in 2006 that there were 900 Chinese doctors serving in Africa at that time.[65]

Many of these noteworthy developments continued long-standing Chinese assistance practices—for example, many thousands of African students (along with many thousands of African liberation fighters) were educated and trained in China in past decades. They also followed the recent practice of the Chinese government in avoiding large outlays of Chinese money in support of African aid projects. A U.S. congressional report listed salient Chinese assistance projects in African countries in the period 2003–2005. Most involved loans for relatively small amounts (under $100 million), with a few grants of lesser amounts to build government buildings, roads, and sports stadiums and provide disaster relief. The projects often were highly visible in the African countries concerned, providing positive publicity for China at relatively low cost.[66]

The main exceptions to this prevailing pattern of modest Chinese investment and even more modest Chinese aid outlays in Africa involved deeper Chinese involvement with some of the main oil- and resource-producing African states such as Sudan, Angola, and Congo. Reflecting its ever growing need to secure international sources of oil and other resources, China came by 2005 to account for 31 percent of the global growth in oil demand and imported 28 percent of its oil from Africa.[67]

Even in this regard, however, there are important points needing clarification. In particular, in assessing the importance and impact of Chinese aid and investment abroad, further research and analysis are needed involving the role of Chinese companies and Chinese workers in doing these aid and investment projects. As seen in the case of Sudan and elsewhere, Chinese projects often involve large numbers of Chinese workers in the employ of Chinese entities. What needs further research and analysis concerns how these workers (and the many other Chinese workers involved in various aid and infrastructure projects in Africa and elsewhere) were (and are) paid. If they were paid by Chinese entities in China and the money stayed in China (for example, placed in workers' bank accounts or given to their families in China)—and when abroad if the Chinese workers lived in areas supplied by China and used equipment and materials supplied by China and these costs were paid for in China—the result would involve much less Chinese government spending abroad. In effect, the bulk of such projects would be paid for by the Chinese government to Chinese entities in China. Such an approach would maximize the economic benefit for China from the project. And the Chinese government could argue to Chinese domestic critics of foreign aid that it was not spending large amounts of money abroad when there were pressing domestic needs at home. Its monies were being spent mainly in China. The foreign country would benefit from the completed project but would get little extra economic benefit in the form of technology transfer, work experience, employment, and spending by foreigners for goods and services in their country.[68]

Salient data underlining the importance of Africa in Chinese foreign relations in 2011 included the following:

- Leadership attention and contacts: President Hu Jintao visited four African countries in February 2009, marking his fourth visit to Africa since becoming president in 2003. Premier Wen Jiabao led China's delegation to the fourth China-Africa Cooperation Forum (CACF), held in Egypt in November 2009. He pledged to double the $5 billion low-cost loan for African development promised at the 2006 CACF, and he detailed a wide range of debt relief, environmental, education, training, and other Chinese offers and opportunities for African countries. China had diplomatic relations and embassies in all but a small handful of African states (four still recognized Taiwan), maintained extensive party ties with African political parties, and developed growing relations with regional and subregional organizations like the African Development Bank.
- Economic relations: China's trade with Africa grew by 30 percent a year in the previous decade, reaching $106.8 billion in 2008. The trade was spread among various countries, with Angola and South Africa being the most important trading partners. Chinese success in selling manufactured and other goods to Africa generally balanced China's large-scale imports of African commodities. Trade dipped in value in 2009 but revived to a level of $114.8 billion in 2010. In 2009 China became Africa's largest trading partner, surpassing the United States and the European Union. The Chinese government also set up a series of commercial and investment centers called special economic zones that provided special privileges and incentives to Chinese firms in Africa. China's cumulative investment at the end of 2010 was said to be worth $9.3 billion by official Chinese

media. Chinese aid included forgiveness of debts to China by poorer African countries valued at almost $3 billion; several billions of dollars of financing provided by a special Sino-African development fund; and financing, including loans from official Chinese banks backed by commodities and other collateral, in support of large-scale infrastructure projects in Angola, Sudan, Congo, and other resource-rich countries. China's provision of such financing engendered serious controversy among Western countries and some African constituencies concerned with China's provisions to support corrupt or otherwise unsavory regimes.

- Social, cultural, and other interchange: The over 1 million Chinese working in Africa included professionals in Chinese commercial and government institutions, Chinese laborers working on projects throughout the continent, and Chinese traders and small-business people focused on selling Chinese commodities to African consumers. The Chinese government followed past practice in pursuing active cultural exchange programs with African countries and sending Chinese medical personnel to Africa. Chinese-funded Confucius Institutes, whose mission is to spread Chinese language and culture abroad, were established in a dozen locations in Africa.
- Military relations: China sustained an active program of military exchanges throughout Africa. Chinese arms sales generally remained at a low level, though Chinese arms sales to controversial governments like Sudan and Zimbabwe received critical attention in international media. Chinese military and other security forces were active participants in UN-backed peacekeeping efforts in several African countries. Since 2009, China maintained warships along the Horn of Africa to work with international security efforts to counter pirate attacks against international shipping off the coast of Somalia.[69]

Continuity and Change in Xi Jinping's Africa Policy

The highlights of Chinese interaction with Africa during the Xi Jinping government included President Xi Jinping's visit to South Africa, Tanzania, and the Democratic Republic of the Congo on his first official trip abroad in March 2013. Premier Li Keqiang visited Ethiopia, Nigeria, Angola, and Kenya in his first trip to Africa in May 2014. China's trade with Africa reached $210 billion in 2013 and grew to around $230 billion in 2014. Chinese investment was growing rapidly from a low base. It amounted to $2.52 billion in 2012. There were 2,500 Chinese firms operating in Africa.[70]

The majority of recent Chinese foreign policy initiatives in Africa were, as in the past, commercial. The Xi Jinping government did take a few steps that increased China's foreign policy profile in non-commercial areas. China agreed for the first time to send combat troops to support UN peacekeeping missions; they were in Africa and involved deployments of 170 troops to

Mali and 700 troops to South Sudan. China's special envoy for Africa took an active role in endeavoring to mediate the conflict in South Sudan. China's naval ships that participated in international antipiracy efforts off the Horn of Africa also were used to evacuate Chinese and other civilians from nearby crisis areas, most recently Yemen in 2015; they also were part of Chinese contingents participating in naval exercises with Russia in the eastern Mediterranean Sea and the Black Sea. Presumably to support the increased Chinese navy activities, China in 2015 engaged in discussions with Djibouti for what the Djibouti president said was "a military base." China in the past has strongly opposed foreign bases.[71]

As in the Xi government's various Silk Road initiatives and proposed investment, loans, and financing plans supporting Chinese interacting with other developing countries, Chinese officials and commentary emphasized Chinese investment and support for large infrastructure projects where Chinese construction firms would play a leading role. As noted in chapter 4, China's stress in the past decade on Chinese-provided infrastructure to gain access to oil and other raw materials declined somewhat given the change in Chinese domestic priorities and economic reforms.

Reflecting the new priority, the leader of the Chinese Export-Import Bank told African representatives in November 2013 that China would invest the heretofore unimagined sum of $1 trillion in Africa over the next decade. He advised that the funds would be focused on the construction of transnational highways, railways, and airports. He noted in particular that China was preparing to spend as much as $500 billion on a rail network that would span the continent, recalling to veteran African observers the dream of Cecil Rhodes of a Cape to Cairo rail link.[72] While eschewing such grandiosity, Li Keqiang made the focus of his African trip plans connecting African capitals with Chinese high-speed rail technology. He pledged an extra $12 billion of Chinese financial assistance to Africa and focused on the provision of rail lines linking African capitals with high-speed railways. He also said that China would boost its credit lines to Africa by $10 billion over the existing $20 billion credit line. Li presided over the signing of a railway deal in Kenya. Following Li's visit to Nigeria, in November 2014 China Railway Construction Corporation signed China's largest-ever overseas investment deal, agreeing to build a 1,400-kilometer railway along the coast of Nigeria. Another proposal involves a five-nation train line in East Africa.[73]

Subsequently, Foreign Minister Wang Yi reaffirmed China's commitment to assist Africa to develop "Three Major Networks"—railway, road, and regional aviation. China signed a deal with the African Union (AU) during the AU heads of state meeting in Ethiopia in 2015. It was publicized as "the most substantive project the AU has ever signed with a partner." It promised to connect Africa by road, rail, and air transportation. Meanwhile, consistent with recent Chinese efforts to move offshore to more advantageous situations excess Chinese industrial capacity, China's largest steel maker in late 2014 announced plans to shift 5 million tons of annual production (11 percent of its annual output) to South Africa.[74]

Unfortunately for observers in China, Africa, and elsewhere seeking a realistic view of what actually China will accomplish and over what period of time, the uniformly positive and supportive official Chinese commentary on the very ambitious projects provided no hint of the now well-known constraints China has faced with such plans in the recent past and will likely face in the future. Several points discussed earlier in this book highlight the kinds of constraints and limitations encountered by recent multibillion-dollar Chinese proposals throughout the developing world. It is argued here that these constraints must be considered before forecasting the kind of economic leadership in Africa or elsewhere highlighted by official Chinese publicity; the latter seems to give very high priority to showing the high profile and new activism in China's foreign policy under President Xi Jinping rather than a balanced picture of China's achievements.

For example, as seen in chapter 4 and elsewhere, evidence that China implements only a fraction of its seemingly very expensive pledges is strong and growing as government officials and specialists study the projects that are promised but are not implemented (a subject that official Chinese media usually avoids). Thus, China's recent record of implementing its proposed multibillion-dollar projects in Indonesia and Pakistan has shown that less than 10 percent of the projects actually get done. It also shows that 80 percent of proposed Chinese mining deals (an important feature of Chinese economic interaction in Africa) fail to be implemented. And it shows that Chinese satisfaction with the push for greater Chinese foreign investment abroad is tempered by the fact that the Chinese enterprises more often than not are losing money in foreign invested deals.

Though a comprehensive study of failed Chinese implementation in Africa has not been done, there are plenty of examples of very large promises followed by little implementation for a variety of reasons on the Chinese side and the side of the foreign partners. In Nigeria, for example, where official Chinese commentary focuses on the massive 2014 deal to build Nigerian railways noted above, little is said of the fact that Chinese companies and Chinese multibillion-dollar loans have been involved in failed deals to rebuild Nigeria's rail system since the 1990s.[75] Meanwhile, in July 2005, China and Nigeria signed an $800 million crude oil sale agreement involving the projected purchase by China of 30,000 barrels of oil a day for five years. In April 2006, the Chinese state-owned company China National Offshore Oil Corporation (CNOOC) said that it had completed a deal to buy a share of a Nigerian oil license. The deal marked CNOOC's "biggest-ever overseas acquisition," costing over $2 billion. To win the bid, China agreed to build a hydropower station and to take over a privatized Nigerian oil refinery that was losing money. Foreign experts warned that the oil blocs won by China were in contested areas of the Niger Delta region that were plagued by insurgency, banditry, and oil thefts. As it happened, several large Chinese deals with Nigeria fell through because of various reasons later in the decade. In 2010, the Chinese Consul General in Lagos told the media that steadily growing China–Nigeria trade had reached an annual value in 2009 of over $6 billion. The composition and balance of the trade showed Chinese exports, mainly manufactured goods, were valued at $5.47 billion, while Nigerian exports to China were less than $1 billion. The Chinese official said this reflected the fact that "very limited crude oil is currently exported to China," an indication that earlier plans for Chinese purchase of Nigerian oil had failed to materialize.[76]

Corrupt practices, nontransparent agreements with unaccountable African governments, unstable conditions in many African countries, and China's changing need for imported raw materials all complicated the implementation of promised Chinese support. African labor unions and other politically active constituencies often resented China's tendency on the one hand to import Chinese labor crews in carrying out Chinese-supported projects and on the other hand to be less attentive to international labor standards when employing Africans. The environmental impact of Chinese development projects prompted the often active civil society groups in African countries to mobilize protests against Chinese practices.[77] Those African countries well endowed with oil or other raw materials sought by China, notably Angola, recently faced repayment of large Chinese loans with commodities that were markedly less in value. They sought debt postponement and other relief from Chinese creditors assiduous in ensuring that China would be paid back.[78]

The goodwill China wins with African governments with their loans and financing is balanced by a clearer awareness of Chinese self-interest. Africa also is on the receiving end of increased interest by the United States, India, and others. A concrete indicator that China—as noted by *The Economist*—does not dominate Africa but is "one among many" foreign powers influencing Africa is the fact that while China is Africa's largest trader there are many other important trading partners; China's share of 15 percent is hardly dominant. Foreign investment in Africa shows that China, even after all the pledges of multibillion-dollar "investment" deals, actually accounts for less than 5 percent of foreign investment in Africa.[79] Meanwhile, the net impact of the various widely touted Chinese-financed projects in Africa is less than first appearances if only for the fact that many and perhaps a majority of the proposed projects are not implemented in the end.

RELATIONS WITH LATIN AMERICA

Throughout much of the post–Cold War period, China followed a low-keyed and pragmatic effort to build better relations with Latin American countries. Beijing was well aware of China's limited standing in the region. The region has long been dominated by U.S. power and influence and has also been developing improved economic and political relations with European powers, Japan, South Korea, and others. Radical movements in the region in the past looked to Moscow rather than Beijing for support and guidance. Throughout the 1990s and into the next decade, China seemed content to maintain an active diplomatic presence; to engage in a wide variety of government-sponsored political, economic, and military contacts; and to see China's economic relations with the region grow to a point where China–Latin America trade, while only a small fraction of Chinese overall trade, surpassed Chinese trade with Africa by the late 1990s. [80]

A rapid increase in Chinese purchases of Latin American commodities along with widely publicized Chinese leaders' visits to the region in 2004, 2005, and 2008 appeared to mark a significant change in China's approach to Latin America. President Hu Jintao's regional tour and participation at the November 2004 Asia-Pacific Economic Cooperation (APEC) summit in Chile saw an outpouring of media and specialist commentary that provided often grossly exaggerated assessments of China's rising investments and other economic interests in Latin America. They also exaggerated Chinese support for such regional leaders as Venezuela's president, Hugo Chavez, who were determined to stand against U.S. interests and influence in the region. Subsequent assessments provided a more sober view of China's increased interest in the region. China's interest appeared to focus heavily on obtaining access to resources needed for Chinese economic development; it showed little sign of a Chinese desire to undertake the costs and commitments involved in challenging the United States or adopting a significant leadership role in Latin America. The increased Chinese interest in acquiring Latin American resources generally was welcomed by regional leaders but also was accompanied by strong opposition and complaints over the impact of Chinese economic relations on regional economies. [81]

Throughout the post–Cold War period, Chinese motives in Latin America were similar to Chinese motives in the Middle East, Africa, and other developing countries without major strategic significance for China. Beijing sought to nurture common bonds with Latin American countries and strove to win their support for China's positions in the United Nations and other international organizations. Latin America, especially Central America and the Caribbean, represented the main battleground in Beijing's international competition with Taiwan. Chinese officials went to extraordinary lengths, even using China's veto power in the UN Security Council, in order to curb the still strong support for Taiwan on the part of many regional states.[82] Chinese commentaries until 2001 also routinely criticized U.S. policy in Latin America and highlighted European and Japanese resistance to U.S. efforts to have its way in the region. The rhetoric fit into the broader Chinese tendency at that time to see and encourage signs of emerging multipolarity in the world when the U.S. superpower met resistance from other powers determined to protect their interests in an economically and politically competitive world environment. As a result of the improvement in U.S.–Chinese relations in 1997–1998, Chinese officials and commentary devoted less attention to these themes. This trend became more pronounced because in mid-2001 China muted most routine rhetoric against U.S. hegemonism and later adopted an emphasis on peaceful development that sought closer partnership and cooperation with the United States.

China historically has paid less attention to Latin America than to any other Third World region. Geographic distance and China's preoccupation with issues closer to home put Latin American issues low on China's list of priorities. In the East–West and Sino-Soviet competition for global influence during the Cold War, Beijing at times tried to make headway among radical Latin American groups. In general, however, there was little to show for this effort. The power and influence of the United States remained very strong among most established governments in Latin America, while leftists in Cuba, Chile, Nicaragua, and elsewhere tended to look to the Soviet bloc for tangible assistance rather than to seek the political advice and rhetorical support offered by Maoist China.[83]

Post-Mao leaders pursued pragmatic approaches in order to build conventional political, economic, and military relations with the established Latin American governments. As in other parts of the developing world, Chinese leaders eschewed the tendency of Maoist leaders to take sides on Latin American issues, especially those having symbolic value in the East–West and Sino-Soviet competition for global influence. Instead, they sought to align China with whatever consensus was emerging among Latin American states over sensitive issues. Chinese officials also repeatedly emphasized Chinese–Latin American common ground in seeking greater "South–South" economic cooperation. (Beijing refers to "South–South" cooperation as cooperation between and among states that are economically developing as opposed to developed countries.)[84]

Although Beijing had some contact with leftist anti-Soviet parties in Latin America during the radical phases of China's Cultural Revolution, post-Mao leaders minimized or cut those ties. Beijing ignored the Maoist-oriented Sendero Luminoso in Peru, and its contacts with the Farabundo Martí National Liberation Front guerrilla front in El Salvador were minimal. By contrast, China markedly increased its exchanges with ruling parties and governments in Latin America, endeavoring to improve state-to-state relations wherever possible.[85]

The economic imperative behind China's policy in the 1990s was illustrated in official Chinese commentary. A year-end assessment in December 1997 emphasized the recent economic dynamism of Latin American economies. It said the region's overall growth had reached a seventeen-year high of 5 percent, and it highlighted Latin America's new openness to trade, investments, and other economic interchange with various world economic centers. The commentary emphasized substantial growth of Latin American trade with Asia. China's trade with the region had more than doubled since 1990, growing from $3 billion in that year to $8 billion in 1998.[86]

Chinese commentary at the time showed that Chinese economic aid to the region was minimal.[87] Political relations for over a decade into the post–Cold War period saw a steady stream of generally second-level Chinese leaders travel to Latin America and warm Chinese welcomes for visiting Latin American dignitaries.[88] Official Chinese commentary during those exchanges underscored China's determination to be seen as a close friend of Latin American countries, as sharing common feelings and experiences in the struggle for economic development and nation building. As was typical during that time, in May 1998 the number two leader of China's National People's Congress paid an extensive visit to Brazil, Chile, and Peru.[89] Visiting many places in each country, he promoted greater mutual understanding and cooperation, especially between China's parliament and the parliaments of these Latin American states. Also at this time, a senior leader of China's united-front political organ, the Chinese People's Political Consultative Conference, paid a visit to Brazil to foster greater Sino-Brazilian understanding and cooperation.

Post–Cold War Sino–Latin American relations featured a wide range of military leadership exchanges. The Chinese defense minister and other senior military leaders hosted Latin American visitors. Defense Minister Chi Haotian led a delegation to Mexico and Cuba in early 1999.[90] There were few major Latin American recipients of Chinese military sales or aid, though Chinese defense officials used small-scale training opportunities and military equipment transfers to establish and build up good relations with their Latin American counterparts.[91]

From the early 1990s, Beijing sought to avoid controversy in Latin America, with two major exceptions: Taiwan and U.S. policy. China was unrelenting in its diplomatic efforts and commentary against Taiwan's influence in the region. Reports of secret aid offers, advantageous trade deals, and other means to gain Chinese influence at Taiwan's expense were common. Both Beijing and Taipei remained locked in a kind of nonviolent guerrilla war for recognition. In the process, Beijing was not reluctant to use coercive means to get what it wanted. In 1997, for example, China used its UN Security

Council veto for the first time in over twenty-five years in order to block the sending of cease-fire monitors to Guatemala, whose government maintained official relations with Taiwan. Among the several countries in Latin America that supported Taiwan, Guatemala strongly backed the government's efforts at that time to gain entry into the United Nations. A compromise was soon reached, allowing the cease-fire monitors to go to Guatemala, which was reported to have moderated its support for Taiwan's UN entry. After China used the veto in this way, Beijing used the threat of a veto for authorization of peacekeepers to Haiti in order to encourage Haiti, one of several countries in Latin America that maintained official relations with Taiwan, to reduce its support for Taiwan and its efforts to gain entry into the United Nations. It later relented, once Haiti took steps to adjust its policy toward Taiwan and the mainland.[92]

Criticism of U.S. dominance in Latin America was a staple of Chinese propaganda for decades. Commentary in the 1990s highlighted the U.S. struggle to preserve its economic advantage in the face of a vigorous challenge by the EU. And it focused on European, Canadian, and other opposition to the sanctions imposed by the United States as a result of the Helms-Burton Act, which regulated foreign companies dealing with Cuban companies involving properties appropriated from the United States forty years earlier.[93] The moderation in the late 1990s of Chinese criticism of U.S. policy in Latin America probably was related to Chinese desire to sustain positive momentum in U.S.–China relations at the time of summit meetings in 1997 and 1998. Chinese invective against U.S. policies resumed soon after.[94] However, Chinese leaders made a more lasting change in muffling anti-U.S. commentary in mid-2001. As a result, China's public posture in Latin America since that time generally has eschewed controversy regarding U.S. policy. This left Taiwan as the sole exception to the Chinese government's general practice of avoiding issues of controversy in relations with Latin America.

At the start of the twenty-first century, the broad outlines of China's approach to Latin America appeared reasonably clear. The priority Chinese leaders gave to the region was relatively low, similar to Chinese attention to the Middle East and Africa. Chinese activities reflected multifaceted political and economic interests focused on competition with Taiwan and a search for advantageous trade opportunities. Beijing also nurtured relations with Latin American countries to ensure their support in the United Nations and other world bodies.[95]

As China became increasingly interested in obtaining oil and other needed resources in the twenty-first century, Chinese interest in Latin America rose markedly, as did Chinese interest in the Middle East and Africa, for similar reasons. This increased China's public profile in Latin American affairs, and some in the region sought to cultivate ties with China in opposition to the United States. Chinese leaders for their part welcomed positive attention from the region but remained reluctant to take any leadership role that would involve major commitments or compromise their efforts to sustain businesslike relations with the United States. They also found that rising economic relations with Latin American countries came with significant complaints and resentments that complicated Chinese relations with several countries in the region.

Economic Relations

By all accounts, economic relations between China and Latin American countries took off in the previous decade. Growth in trade and investment was large. Two-way trade flows increased over 500 percent, from $8 billion in 1999 to $40 billion in 2004, and kept growing. Much of the activity centered on Chinese efforts to secure access to natural resources. As a result, the large increases in trade focused on a few Latin American countries that provided the raw materials that China was seeking, notably copper, nickel, iron ore, petroleum, grains, wood, frozen fish, fish meal, sugar, leather, and chemical substances. Increased trade also saw a large upsurge in Chinese manufactured goods exported throughout Latin American markets. From 1990 to 2003, Latin American exports to China grew 21.1 percent annually, while imports from China increased by 30 percent annually. The pattern continued in later years. [96]

These developments meant that the relative importance of China as a trading partner for Latin America increased markedly. However, it was easy to exaggerate the extent of the China–Latin America relationship. In 2011, total China–Latin America trade flows remained one-fourth of the trade that occurred between Latin American countries and the United States. Canada and the European Union remained major Latin American trading partners. The relative importance of Latin America to China was likewise not overwhelming, especially given that the expansion of Chinese trade on a global level was remarkable in recent years. [97]

Although China's economic role in Latin America was not that prominent on a regional level, the story was different for certain countries. In the case of Peru, China jumped from its eighth-largest trading partner in 2001 to number two in 2004. [98] China that year also was Chile's second-largest trade partner and number three for both Brazil and Cuba. [99]

As the decade wore on, China's rapid economic development saw a large rise in Chinese trade with Latin America. Bilateral trade reached $120 billion in 2008. This was more than Chinese trade with Africa, but it still represented only about 20 percent of the value of U.S.–Latin American trade and less than half the value of Latin American trade with the EU. China's top trading partners were Brazil, Mexico, Chile, Argentina, Peru, and Venezuela. There was a rough overall balance between exports and imports in Chinese trade with the region. Chinese exports were mainly computers, telecommunication equipment, clothing, shoes, and electronics, while Chinese imports were mainly raw materials. The downturn in the U.S. and other Western economies during the economic recession beginning in 2008 and numerous large Chinese investments and multibillion-dollar lines of credit to secure energy and other resources in Latin America saw China emerge as the top trading partner of Brazil and a leading trader in several other Latin American countries. China–Latin America trade was valued at $130 billion in 2009. It grew rapidly in 2010, reaching $178.6 billion. The trade was balanced, with Chinese exports to Latin America valued at $88.3 billion and imports valued at $90.3 billion. Brazil was the standout in the growing economic ties with China. Bilateral trade in 2010 was valued at $56.2 billion. Commodities such as iron ore made up the vast bulk (90 percent) of Brazilian exports, and manufactured goods were the products imported from China.[100]

Reports of large amounts of Chinese investment in Latin America, including a reported $100 billion in investment projected up to 2015, were featured during President Hu Jintao's widely publicized visit to Latin America in late 2004.[101] At first, actual investments were slow in coming, and Chinese officials sometimes dampened enthusiasm about such reports of massive Chinese investment. In reference to the purported $100 billion investment, a senior Chinese official told the *Miami Herald* in 2005, "I have no idea where that figure came from."[102]

For several years, Chinese outflows of foreign direct investment (FDI) were very small. The cumulative stock of Chinese FDI totaled only $33.2 billion in 2003, 14 percent of which was in Latin America.[103] Up to 2006, Chinese investments abroad remained limited, around $10 billion a year for the entire world. Latin America received 36.5 percent and 46 percent of Chinese FDI in 2003 and 2004, respectively. Compared to FDI arriving in Latin America from other sources, China's portion was very small. In 2004, 0.71 percent of Latin America's cumulative stock of FDI was from China; Chinese FDI represented 2.46 percent of inflows to Latin American countries that year (compared to 29 percent from the United States).

Later multibillion-dollar projects represented a significant shift in Chinese investment trends, which emerged as China's economy and its foreign exchange holdings grew. The turn of the decade registered a big increase in Chinese investment. Official Chinese media reported in April 2011 that cumulative Chinese investment in Latin America had reached $41.2 billion at the end of 2009. The upswing continued in 2010, with Brazil being a major target of investment. Various Chinese investment deals in Brazil in 2010 were valued at $17 billion. If China does ultimately invest $100 billion in Latin America by 2015, China's portion of Latin America's cumulative stock likely would still be a distinct minority share. In 2010, over 90 percent of foreign direct investment flowing into Mexico and Brazil, the region's two biggest economies, came from developed countries. [104]

While it is impossible to know China's investment intentions, it did appear clear in recent years that China's investments are directed toward projects that facilitated the procurement of natural resources (for example, roads and port facilities) and that they were concentrated in a few countries where the resources base is significant (Brazil, Argentina, Chile, Peru, Venezuela, and Ecuador). As Chinese investment abroad grew, it became more widely known that figures showing cumulative Chinese investment in Latin America could be exaggerated, as a large proportion [105] of this "investment" went to such tax havens as the British Virgin Islands and the Cayman Islands, and these tax havens also were the source of most of the Latin American investment going to China. [106]

As in the case of Chinese financing of infrastructure efforts in African and other developing countries, China has engaged in similar financing efforts to build roads, railroads, refineries, ports, and other facilities in Latin America. Little of this would be considered foreign assistance by Western standards, and Chinese foreign assistance to Latin America is thought to be very low. In 2009 and 2010, the China Development Bank extended multibillion-dollar lines of credit to energy companies and government entities, notably in Brazil, Ecuador, and Venezuela. The loans were secured by revenue earned from the sale of oil at market prices to Chinese national oil companies. The loans were distinguished by their large size and long terms. They were attractive at that time because many companies were postponing major investments in oil development because of cash flow problems, and other financial institutions were unwilling to lend such large amounts of capital for such long terms. [107]

The positive effects of growing economic ties on Chinese relations with Latin America were reduced by a variety of complications and negative features of the economic ties. If past practice in other developing countries was any guide, Chinese investments in Latin America were likely to come in the form of "tied loans," which carried low interest rates and led to the project being carried out by Chinese state-owned enterprises. In other words, while Chinese FDI might be an important source of foreign capital for Latin America—a region that experienced a decline in FDI since 2000—it was often less likely to be a driving force for major increases in local employment or marked poverty reduction. The conditionality associated with such investment reduced the goodwill and favorable image China garnered from the economic effort. [108]

Countries in Latin America that were not major exporters of resources tended to focus on the fact that they could not compete with incoming Chinese manufactured goods and that those goods also took their important markets in the United States and elsewhere. Countries that exported products similar to those of China (notably Mexico but also many Central American and Caribbean countries) experienced intense competition with China. The Inter-American Development Bank underlined the grim reality for these countries in noting,

> China has significant comparative advantages in the product categories that are crucial to Mexico and the countries of Central America (textiles, apparel, and electronics), in particular because these countries specialize in labor-intensive parts of the production chain in which China has an important edge. . . . Countries benefiting from FDI sources similar to those of China, or which receive FDI in similar sectors, are likely to see sharper declines in FDI flows.
>
> In 2008 Mexico exported just $2 billion worth of goods to China while importing goods valued at $34 billion, including clothing and electronics. An intense export rivalry emerged over the U.S. market, with the Mexican government accusing the Chinese of impinging on its export territory by flooding the United States with cheap goods manufactured in low-wage factories. Some reports pointed more optimistically to growing Mexican exports to a vibrant Chinese market and profitable Mexican investment in China-based factories to make products for the Chinese market and for export.[109]

Important constituents in the resource-exporting countries also have reacted negatively to incoming Chinese manufactured imports and overall Chinese competition for world markets. The complaints rose when the prospect of expanded resource exports to China prompted many Latin American governments to agree to China's request that they declare China a market economy. This status was sought by China for the positive international recognition that it provided and also for the practical matter that it made it more difficult under World Trade Organization rules for countries to impose antidumping duties on Chinese goods. Actions declaring China a market economy by Latin American governments that were anxious to export resources to China were criticized by constituents in Latin American countries representing important manufacturers and businesses. Brazil's Industrial Federation of São Paulo condemned the move by the Brazilian government to declare China a market economy as a "political decision" that left "Brazil industry in a vulnerable position" and would bring "prejudicial consequences to various industrial sectors." Similarly, reports that Brasilia and Beijing were soon to begin negotiations for a free trade agreement (FTA) were quelled when Brazilian business leaders feared that local businesses would not be able to compete with Chinese companies. Despite the rapid increase in Brazil–China trade and Chinese investment in the country, the new Brazilian president in 2011, Dilma Rousseff, steered policy in directions to defend Brazilian manufacturers suffering in the face of imported Chinese goods benefiting from the low value of China's currency; she also pressed China to open its market more to Brazilian aircraft and other manufactured goods.[110]

Chile actively sought an FTA with China. The deal was signed in August 2006. Peru and Costa Rica completed FTAs with China in 2010.[111]

Economic competition was not the only downside to China's commercial penetration in the region. Latin American countries had long been suppliers of raw materials to extraregional powers, and they often resented this role as well as the unfavorable terms of trade and environmental degradation that inevitably followed. As the pattern of Chinese trade and investment became more important and clear, past practice indicated that Latin American countries would see that the kind of relationship China was attempting to forge with the region was not all that different from the past imperialist and neoimperialist models that Latin America had come to resent. Extraction of natural resources, exposure to more competitive economies, and political arm-twisting in return for concessions was hardly an attractive evolution for Latin America. Some Chinese commentators expert in regional issues showed an awareness of negative features in China's developing relationship with Latin America; they urged steps to foster a more balanced and complementary relationship in the broad interests of both sides.[112]

Political Relations

The Taiwan factor continued to drive China's political relations in Latin America. Almost half of the governments that officially recognized Taiwan were in Latin America. Other than Paraguay, all were in Central America and the Caribbean. These countries were a major focus of Taiwan's foreign policy, and Taiwan maintained their loyalty with generous economic aid packages. In 2003, for example, Taiwan was the single largest aid donor to Haiti, Grenada, St. Kitts and Nevis, St. Vincent and the Grenadines, and Dominica.[113] In return, this bloc annually cosponsored resolutions in the UN General Assembly calling on the body to consider membership for Taiwan. Given the "dollar diplomacy" of Beijing and Taipei as they competed for international recognition, small countries often switched recognition when given a good offer from one side or the other.[114]

As noted in chapter 7, the coming to power in 2008 of the moderate Ma Ying-jeou administration in Taiwan changed the competition between China and Taiwan for international recognition. Seeking to reassure China and ease cross-strait relations, Ma reached an informal understanding with China whereby neither will pursue new advances in diplomatic relations at the expense of the other. Paraguay and perhaps other countries in Latin America were prepared to switch recognition from Taipei to Beijing, but such moves did not take place, presumably because of the informal Taiwan–China understanding.[115]

Latin America, including Central America and the Caribbean, also remained significant to China because of the number of votes the region represents in international bodies, especially the United Nations. A manifestation of the importance of having allies in international organizations was seen in the past two decades when the members of the UN Human Rights Commission voted on a U.S.-sponsored resolution considering criticism of China for its human rights record. China worked very hard and was consistently successful in shielding itself from criticism, but in each vote a handful of Latin American countries voted against China. Almost always, these countries were Central American nations that maintained diplomatic relations with Taiwan. The tendency of most Latin American countries to abstain in such votes was a reflection of an unwillingness to choose between the United States and China.[116]

While the diplomatic drama at the UN Commission for Human Rights was perhaps the most public international forum where China sought allies among Latin American countries, China also was quietly seeking admittance to a number of regional organizations. It has ties with the Organization of American States, the Association for Latin American Integration, the Caribbean Development Bank, and the Inter-American Development Bank.

China's relations with Latin American countries also had a South–South dimension that supported Chinese efforts to work over the long term against U.S. dominance and to create a multipolar world. China's support for Brazil's bid to become a permanent member of the UN Security Council, cooperation agreements in the areas of science and technology, and solidarity in pushing for a favorable international trade regime were part of Beijing's South–South agenda that has long existed in Chinese foreign policy. Chinese leaders also participated actively and often cooperatively with Brazilian leaders in various international groups dealing with global development and governance. Notably, China collaborated closely with Brazil, India, and Russia in a new international grouping known as the BRIC, an acronym containing each member country's first letter. Another new grouping included South Africa along with China, India, and Brazil. As noted earlier, South Africa was asked and agreed to join the BRIC countries in 2011, with that organization becoming BRICS.[117]

China's political relationship with Latin America's leftist leaders was more complicated. Available evidence suggested that China was being cautious in its relations with Venezuela, a country of strong interest in the PRC's increasingly active quest for oil and other energy resources. The reasons had to do with avoiding friction with the United States and close association with Venezuela's support of indigenous populism and antiglobalization causes. China did have special need for oil and did undermine U.S. interests to some degree by seeking to capitalize on the Chavez government's quest to reduce Venezuela's dependence on the U.S. market and divert supplies to China.[118]

Regarding Cuba, China developed a long-term relationship. From the end of the Cold War and the termination of Soviet aid to Cuba, Sino-Cuban relations increased. Since 1991, China's top leaders have visited the island, including Hu Jintao in 1997, 2004, and 2008.[119] Following Hu's stop during his 2004 Latin American tour, China announced that it would extend Cuba interest-free loans, donate $12 million for hospitals and school uniforms, and strengthen ties in the areas of biotechnology, oil exploration, mining, tourism, and telecommunications. There also were repeated reports of deepening China–Cuba military and intelligence cooperation. They centered on reported Chinese arms sales and Chinese acquisition of former Soviet-operated signals intelligence outposts in Cuba.[120] Whatever was taking place was not seen as posing a threat to the United States, according to U.S. officials.[121]

Another cluster of allegations against China focused on supposed Chinese maneuvers to control the Panama Canal. The concern stemmed from the fact that Hong Kong–based Hutchinson Whampoa Limited, a company that had links to China, owned the port facilities in Cristobel and Balboa, on both ends of the canal, and had received an offer to develop a former U.S. facility at Rodman's Point. Some judged that the company was a cover for the Chinese administration and that it engaged in surveillance and might resort to sabotage in the event of a Sino-U.S. war over Taiwan.[122] On reflection, most U.S. policymakers presumably found this scenario far-fetched; no action was taken.

Xi Jinping's Latin America Policy

The Xi Jinping government's policy toward Latin America advanced the same commercial features seen in Chinese policy toward other developing countries. There was heavy emphasis on Chinese investment in and loans for Chinese-supplied infrastructure, with the highlight being ambitious plans of Chinese support for transcontinental railways. Though the value of Chinese trade with Latin America ($260 billion in 2013) seemed to stall in recent years, President Xi said that trade would grow to $500 billion in ten years and he pledged $250 billion in Chinese investment in that period. Chinese media advised that China was the region's second-largest trading partner and third-largest source of foreign investment. It said that cumulative Chinese investment reached $68 billion at the end of 2012 and that investment in 2013 was $15 billion.[123]

President Xi Jinping visited Trinidad and Tobago, Costa Rica, and Mexico on a trip that took him to his first informal summit with President Obama in California in 2013. He traveled to Brazil, Argentina, Venezuela, and Cuba in 2014. Xi also established closer relations with and hosted a ministerial-level forum with the Community of Latin American and Caribbean States (CELAC) in Beijing in January 2015. Closer Chinese association with CELAC was notable for political reasons as the body, formed in 2010, excluded the United States and Canada and often was sharply critical of U.S. policy, especially regarding Cuba.[124] Prime Minister Li Keqiang made his first visit to South America in May 2015, traveling to Brazil, Chile, Columbia, and Peru.[125]

As in the case of Xi's and Li's visits to other developing countries, strong Chinese publicity stressing China's international importance and prominence featured multiple pledges of loans and investment in support of Chinese-supplied infrastructure development. As *Xinhua* said in a feature article on Xi's visits in 2014, "infrastructure construction has emerged as a highlight in the all-around cooperative China-Latin America partnership with the potential to drive bilateral cooperation to higher levels."[126] The kinds of problems constraining advances in Chinese investment and implementation of ambitious infrastructure projects backed by Chinese loans seen in other developing countries were common in Latin America. Venezuela had accumulated enormous debt from Chinese lending backed by oil. Its ability to pay back the debt was in serious question given the decline in the price of oil and other raw materials. Similar problems to lesser degrees faced leaders with loan repayments to China and declining values in exported raw materials in Ecuador, Brazil, and Argentina, among others.[127]

As many of the Latin American economies reliant on raw material exports saw their economic growth stagnate, it remained unclear how China would be able to advance trade levels and increase investments in line with Xi Jinping's predictions for the next decade. Meanwhile, the healing U.S. economy and the strong American dollar made Latin American exports to the United States of higher-value-added manufactured goods grow rapidly. China's share of Latin American exports remained around 10 percent at $92 billion in 2013; the U.S. share of Latin American exports was several times larger at $393 billion.[128] In investment, the gap between China and developed countries was larger. Despite the Chinese publicity, Chinese investment in Latin America accounted for only a bit more than 5 percent of foreign direct investment in Latin America in 2012.[129]

Chapter Thirteen

Prospects

The debate over China's rise and what it means for the world will continue into the twenty-first century. The debate intensified with the coming to power of President Xi Jinping. He and his government tightened political control domestically and actively advanced Chinese interests in ways that were increasingly at odds with neighbors, the United States, and others supportive of key elements of the existing international order fostered by America. The Chinese advances were supported by ever expanding Chinese capabilities backed by the impressive and growing economic and military power of China. Official Chinese media highlighted Xi's consolidation of control of party and state leadership as he was depicted in glowing accounts directing multifaceted Chinese initiatives abroad with confidence and authority in pursuit of his broad vision of a unified, powerful, and internationally respected China—what Xi and the Chinese publicists called "the China Dream."

In many respects, recent developments in Chinese foreign relations validated the view of many Chinese and international commentators that China had grown in power and confidence to the point that it could and would pursue a strategy of ever expanding influence and leadership in Asian and world affairs. The tipping point in the Asian order that many forecast with the United States in decline and China in ascendance was seen to have arrived. The choices for America were often depicted in stark terms. Some called on the United States to gird itself to prepare to resist in a "contest for supremacy." Others saw the need for America to give way to China's advance, making a choice that accepted China's leading power and influence in Asia as America pulled away.[1]

These choices are unattractive. They seem to involve risk of great power war on the one hand or American appeasement on the other. Fortunately, a close look at Chinese foreign policy and behavior in this volume underlines many uncertainties in China's recent rise in world affairs. It finds powerful constraints on Chinese influence in world affairs and large gaps and serious shortcomings in the foreign initiatives of the Xi government. Consideration of these realities at odds with the official discourse in China seems to undermine the argument that China is ready for Asian and world leadership. Readers are urged to consider these factors and be aware of further perhaps unexpected developments having an impact on China's rise as they assess the wide range of opinions under discussion on the trajectory and impact of China's rise.

Domestic Preoccupations

As discussed in chapters 2 and 4, the constraints on Chinese influence in regional and world affairs start at home. The Chinese leaders face an ongoing and major challenge in trying to sustain one-party rule in the massive, dynamic, and economically vibrant Chinese society. They want to sustain one-party rule; to do so they require continued economic growth that advances the material benefits of Chinese people and ensures general public support and legitimacy for the communist government. Such economic growth and continued one-party rule require stability at home and abroad, especially in nearby Asia where conflict and confrontation would have a serious negative impact on Chinese economic growth. At the same time, they seek to protect Chinese security and advance Chinese control of sovereign claims. This top concern is evident in the long and costly buildup of military forces to deal with a Taiwan contingency involving the United States and more recent use of various means of state power to advance territorial claims in nearby disputed seas. Of course, this priority seems to contradict the priority of stability in Asia for the sake of needed economic development. There is less clarity among specialists as to where Chinese international ambitions for regional and global leadership fit in the current priorities of the Beijing leaders, but there is little doubt that the domestic concerns get overall priority.

The wide range of domestic concerns preoccupying the Xi Jinping leadership explained earlier in this volume involve:

- weak leadership legitimacy highly dependent on how the leaders' performance is seen at any given time;
- pervasive corruption that saps public support and undermines government efficiency;
- widening income gaps that are contrary to comminist ideals and sources of social division;
- widespread social turmoil (reportedly involving 100,000–200,000 mass incidents annually) that requires domestic security budgets bigger than China's large national defense budget;

- highly resource-intensive economy and related enormous environmental damage; and
- over sixty major reforms proposed for an economic model at the point of diminishing returns with no clear plan of how they can be implemented.

Against this background, it is not surprising that there remains a strong debate among foreign specialists regarding the stability of one-party rule in China. A crisis and change in the Chinese political order would be unexpected largely because we know so little of the inner workings of the Chinese leadership; it probably would have a major impact on China's international role.

More immediately, what the above domestic preoccupations mean for Chinese foreign policy focus on China's continued unwillingness to undertake the costs and risks of international leadership because it has so many important requirements at home. China may not like American leadership in Asian and world affairs, but it has strong and enduring domestic reasons to avoid taking on the leadership mantle on its own.

Strong Interdependence

The second set of constraints on China confronting the United States and the existing international order supported by the United States involves China's strong and ever growing interdependence with the United States and with other aspects of the international order supported by the United States. As seen in chapter 6, both the U.S. and Chinese governments have built strong interdependence in U.S.–Chinese relations, especially economic relations. And China depends on the United States for secure passage of its growing imports of oil and gas from the Persian Gulf. Neither side can deal effectively with North Korea without the other. Additional areas of interdependence involve climate change, antiterrorism, nuclear nonproliferation, and cyber security. The Xi Jinping foreign policy initiatives maneuver in establishing international financial organizations led by China and outside the U.S.-backed existing international financial institutions. But China still relies on the latter for important support and avows no interest in taking on the burden of replacing these organizations. Meanwhile, Chinese confrontations with Japan and other neighbors have a major negative impact on Chinese foreign trade and investment into China; the surprising recent thaw in Xi Jinping's two-year-long harshly cold treatment of Prime Minister Abe may have come in part because Chinese strategists took better account of the economic implications for China of a cold war with Japan.

China's Insecure Position in Asia

As discussed in chapter 6 and later chapters, China's interests in Asia around the periphery of China have always been the main focus of the foreign policy of the PRC, and they have received heightened attention by the Xi Jinping government. By contrast, in the post–Cold War period, Chinese interests apart from nearby Asia generally have been much more limited, focused heavily on commercial interests. Despite their importance, however, China's relationships with its neighbors have been mediocre; China has had a hard time balancing contradictory imperatives to sustain stability, peace, and development on the one hand and on the other hand to pursue with coercive and intimidating means advances in Chinese control of territory also claimed by its neighbors.

Chinese media commentary applauding Xi Jinping's assertiveness and firmness in advancing Chinese interests at the expense of neighbors and in opposition to the United States played well with audiences in China imbued with a strong sense of self-righteous nationalism. It was depicted as consistent with China's aspiring for regional and international influence under the broad rubric of the president's avowed "China Dream." Unfortunately, the reality was an overall worsening in Chinese relations with key neighbors and concurrent instability in the most important arena in Chinese foreign relations.

As seen in earlier chapters, the Xi government's policies for two years drove relations with Japan to their lowest point since World War II. Japan's effective firmness backed by an increasingly concerned America saw Xi change course—predictably without acknowledging any failure of past policy—in seeking better relations with Japan in 2015. Xi's policies dealing with the conundrum in North Korea effectively drove relations with Pyongyang to their lowest point ever, underlining China's inability to secure its interests in this critically important area for China.

Most Southeast Asian nations remained reluctant to challenge China publicly over its recent advances in the South China Sea, but the Chinese expansion put the United States increasingly on alert as it prepared with the assistance of Japan and Australia among others for contingencies; the Americans also garnered overt and tacit support of key Southeast Asian governments. In southern Asia, the Xi government's mix of economic and political overtures along with military force demonstrations in disputed border areas and in the Indian Ocean deepened suspicions in New Delhi as it actively advanced diplomatic, economic, and security ties with the United States, Japan, and Australia as part of national strengthening to protect its interests as China grows in power. Meanwhile, comparatively tranquil situations in areas of acute Chinese concern in Taiwan and Hong Kong experienced unanticipated mass demonstrations along with political developments and social trends sharply at odds with Chinese interests; in neither case was there a smooth path for spreading Chinese influence and control.

The Xi government had an easier time advancing relations with various Silk Road and other initiatives in central Asia and in improving relations with Vladimir Putin and Russia now isolated from the West. But the bottom line remained a series of serious challenges in the most important arena of Chinese foreign relations that seemed almost certain to complicate any notion of China attaining regional dominance and leadership.

Gaps and Shortcomings in China's International Economic Policies

As seen in chapter 4 and later chapters, the focus of the Xi Jinping government's foreign policies in areas apart from nearby Asia involved a massive push for Chinese investment and financing abroad, advancing and modifying the strong "going out" policies of Chinese investment and financing in these areas seen in the previous decade. The previous effort focused on attaining access to oil and other raw materials needed for China's resource-hungry economy. Recent Chinese economic reforms sought to reduce such intense resource use. The new push for foreign investment and financing was to enable construction abroad of Chinese-supplied infrastructure provided by the enormous excess capacity of Chinese companies for such construction and supply now that major infrastructure development inside China was curtailed under recent economic reforms.

The image purveyed by Chinese officials and lauding Chinese commentary was one of enormous Chinese largess, seemingly unprecedented in the annals of world affairs. China was depicted using its over $3.5 trillion in foreign exchange reserves in seeking mutually beneficial development throughout the world. The results saw multibillion-dollar commitments to various Chinese Silk Road funds, new development banks led by China and regional initiatives in Africa and Latin America. China pledged infrastructure in unstable Pakistan valued at $46 billion, a responsible Chinese official said Beijing's overall plan for investment in Africa over the next decade amounted to $1 trillion, and Xi personally pledged investment in Latin America of $250 billion over the next decade. Foreign commentary often came to echo the Chinese commentaries in seeing Beijing as the leader of international economic relations in Asia and much of the developing world.

In contrast, the discussion in this book takes pains to show limitations in China's international economic involvement and to show weaknesses in the Chinese pledges and forecasts of investment and financing of infrastructure, based in particular on the weaknesses and shortcomings seen in the previous decade of China's push for investment and financing of infrastructure. China's trade is over 20 percent of the trade of some Asia-Pacific countries like South Korea and Australia, but the trade situation does not provide a basis for

Chinese dominance in those countries. China's important but lower percentage of trade in developing countries in Southeast Asia, Africa, and Latin America makes China, in the words of *The Economist*, "one among many" of the foreign powers influencing these regions.[2] China's role as an investor in all these regions is surprisingly small especially in view of all the attention Chinese leaders have given for over a decade to stronger Chinese investments abroad.

A major weakness of Chinese pledges of multibillion-dollar investment and loans is that China often implements only a fraction of its seemingly very expensive pledges. Other limitations are seen; for example, a responsible Chinese official averred that 80 percent of proposed Chinese mining deals (an important feature of Chinese economic interaction in developing countries) fail to be implemented, and others showed that Chinese satisfaction with the push for greater Chinese foreign investment abroad was tempered by the fact that the Chinese enterprises more often than not were losing money in foreign-invested deals. There was no accounting in official Chinese media of the losses incurred by Chinese enterprises that heavily invested in risky locales that became violent with domestic and international armed combat. Salient examples include Chinese investments in Iraq before the U.S-led invasion of 2003 and before the crisis caused by the attacks of the militant Islamic State, Chinese investments in Libya prior to the violent overthrow of the Gaddafi regime, and investments in Syria prior to the recent Syrian civil war. Corrupt practices, nontransparent agreements with unaccountable foreign governments, unstable conditions in many developing countries, and China's changing need for imported raw materials all have complicated the implementation of Chinese promised support. Foreign labor unions and other politically active constituencies often resent China's tendency on the one hand to import Chinese labor crews in carrying out Chinese-supported projects and on the other hand to be less attentive to international labor standards when employing local workers. The environmental impact of Chinese-development projects prompted local civil society groups to mobilize protests against Chinese practices. Those countries well endowed with oil or other raw materials sought by China recently faced repayment of large Chinese loans with commodities that were markedly less in value. They sought debt postponement and other relief from Chinese creditors assiduous in ensuring that China would be paid back.

The U.S. Position in Asia

A final point limiting China involves the United States. As discussed in chapter 6, the United States has large advantages over China in Asia. The Barack Obama administration is preoccupied with numerous problems at home and abroad, but its rebalance policy fits well with Asian regional dynamics and is being implemented with bipartisan support from Congress. The president has complained publicly about Chinese coercive and self-serving practices advancing their interests in Asia, international economics, and other arenas at the expense of the United States as well as many other countries. He averred that the Asian and international order is at stake in these Chinese challenges. Xi Jinping publicly ignores the president's complaints, and the Obama government has had little success in persuading the Chinese to stop.

The situation has prompted growing debate in the United States about how to deal with China. Most of the discussion calls on the United States to go further than existing Obama government policy in showing China that its behavior will not be without negative consequences for China.[3] There are varying paths proposed.[4] The strong American position in Asia and how it might be enhanced provide an important foundation to encourage China to curb assertiveness and return to a more cooperative policy with the United States seen in the first decade of this century.

The origins of that period of moderation over ten years ago came in the early part of the George W. Bush administration after a period of Chinese assertiveness and challenge of the United States in the latter 1990s regarding Taiwan, missile defense, the Middle East, and other issues. It was known as China's "peaceful rise" policy and later was modified as China's "peaceful development" policy. According to senior Chinese officials' conversations with a wide range of American and other foreign observers at the time, China was prompted by assessments of U.S. power and other circumstances to review the negative consequences of China's past confrontations with neighbors and the United States and to review the negative experiences of past rising powers in the twentieth century to come to a judgment that China was better off in pursuing a more pragmatic policy to reassure America, China's neighbors, and other concerned powers that China's rise would be peaceful.[5] The Xi Jinping government has publicly put aside such reassurance to the United States as it pursues national, regional, and global ambitions in line with the "China Dream." To get China to return to such a pragmatic approach of reassurance will require carefully crafted demonstrations of American influence and power. To repeat the point above, the existing American situation in Asia today provides a good foundation for such efforts to influence and shape China's rise in directions compatible with U.S. interests.[6]

Notes

1. CONTINUITY AND STRATEGY IN CONTEMPORARY CHINESE FOREIGN POLICY

1. Christopher Johnson, "Xi Jinping Unveils His Foreign Policy Vision," *Thoughts from the Chairman* (Washington, DC: Center for Strategic and International Studies, December 2014); Yun Sun, "China's Peaceful Rise: Peace through Strength?" *PacNet* 25, March 31, 2014; Yong Deng, "China: The Post-Responsible Power," *Washington Quarterly* 37, no. 4 (Winter 2015): 117–32; Center for a New American Security, *More Willing and Able: Charting China's International Security Activism* (Washington, DC: Center for a New American Security, 2015); Christopher Johnson, *Decoding China's Emerging "Great Power" Strategy in Asia* (Washington, DC: Center for Strategic and International Studies, June 2014).

2. David Shambaugh, "The Coming Chinese Crack-Up," *Wall Street Journal*, March 6, 2015, http://www.wsj.com; Michael Forsythe, "Q and A: Roderick MacFarquhar on Xi Jinping's High-Risk Campaign to Save the Communist Party," *New York Times*, January 30, 2015, http://sinosphere.bolgs.nytimes.com; Cheng Li, "The End of the CCP's Resilient Authoritarianism?" *China Quarterly* 211 (September 2012): 595–623.

3. Fei-Ling Wang, "Beijing's Incentive Structure: The Pursuit of Preservation, Prosperity, and Power," in *China Rising: Power and Motivation in Chinese Foreign Policy*, ed. Yong Deng and Wang Fei-Ling (Lanham, MD: Rowman & Littlefield, 2005), 19–50; Yong Deng and Thomas Moore, "China Views Globalization: Toward a New Great Power Politics?" *Washington Quarterly* 27, no. 3 (Summer 2004): 117–36; Aaron Friedberg, "'Going Out': China's Pursuit of Natural Resources and Implications for the People's Republic of China's Grand Strategy," *NBR Analysis* 17, no. 3 (September 2006): 5–35; David Michael Lampton, *The Three Faces of Chinese Power: Might, Money, and Minds* (Berkeley: University of California Press, 2008); Evan Medeiros, "Is Beijing Ready for Global Leadership?" *Current History* 108, no. 719 (September 2009): 250–56; David Shambaugh, *China Goes Global* (New York: Oxford University Press, 2013); Andrew Nathan and Andrew Scobell, *China's Search for Security* (New York: Columbia University Press, 2012); Denny Roy, *Return of the Dragon* (New York: Columbia University Press, 2013); Men Honghua, *China's Grand Strategy: A Framework Analysis* (Beijing: Beijing Daxue Chubanshe, 2005); Yuan Peng, "A Harmonious World and China's New Diplomacy," *Xiandai guoji guanxi* (Beijing) 17 (May 2007): 1–26.

4. Rosemary Foot and Andrew Walder, *China, the United States, and the Global Order* (New York: Cambridge University Press, 2011).

5. Wayne Morrison, *China's Economic Conditions*, Congressional Research Service Report RL33534 (Washington, DC: Library of Congress, 2014).

6. Elizabeth Economy, "China's Imperial President," *Foreign Affairs* 93, no. 6 (November–December 2014): 80–91; Peter Gries, *China's New Nationalism* (Berkeley: University of California Press, 2004); Suisheng Zhao, *A Nation-State by Construction: Dynamics of Modern Chinese Nationalism* (Stanford, CA: Stanford University Press, 2004).

7. Michael Swaine et al., *China's Military and the U.S-Japan Alliance in 2030* (Washington, DC: Carnegie Endowment for International Peace, 2013).

8. See, for example, Avery Goldstein, *Rising to the Challenge: China's Grand Strategy and International Security* (Stanford, CA: Stanford University Press, 2005); Bates Gill, *Rising Star: China's New Security Diplomacy* (Washington, DC: Brookings Institution Press, 2007).

9. See among others, Aaron Friedberg, *The Contest for Supremacy* (New York: Norton, 2011); Roy, *Return of the Dragon*; Ashley Tellis, *Balancing without Containment* (Washington, DC: Carnegie Endowment for International Peace Report, January 22, 2014); Michael Pillsbury, *The Hundred Year Marathon* (New York: Holt, 2015).

10. See, for example, Susan Shirk, *China: Fragile Superpower* (New York: Oxford University Press, 2007); Robert Sutter, *Foreign Relations of the PRC* (Lanham, MD: Rowman & Littlefield, 2013).

11. Lampton, *Three Faces of Chinese Power*; "Friend or Foe? A Special Report on China's Place in the World," *The Economist*, December 4, 2010, 3–16.

12. Zheng Bijian, "China's 'Peaceful Rise' to Great Power Status," *Foreign Affairs* 84, no. 5 (September–October 2005): 18–24; Wang Jisi, "China's Search for Stability with America," *Foreign Affairs* 84, no. 5 (September–October 2005): 39–48.

13. People's Republic of China State Council Information Office, "China's Peaceful Development Road," *People's Daily Online*, December 22, 2005; Dai Bingguo, "Stick to the Path of Peaceful Development," *Beijing Review* 51, December 23, 2010, http://www.beijinreview.com.cn.

14. Yunling Zhang and Tang Shiping, "China's Regional Strategy," in *Power Shift: China and Asia's New Dynamics*, ed. David Shambaugh (Berkeley: University of California Press, 2006), 48–70.

15. Such a buffer can be created in the event that China develops such a positive relationship with its neighbors that they would refuse to endanger their good relations with China by joining in a possible U.S. effort to contain or constrain China. See also Phillip Saunders, *China's Global Activism: Strategy, Drivers, and Tools* (Washington, DC: Institute for National Strategic Studies, 2006).

16. Institute for International and Strategic Studies, *China's Grand Strategy: A Kinder, Gentler Turn* (London: Institute for International and Strategic Studies, 2004).

17. Goldstein, *Rising to the Challenge*.

18. David Shambaugh, "China Engages Asia: Reshaping the Regional Order," *International Security* 29, no. 3 (Winter 2004–2005): 64–99.

19. Saunders, *China's Global Activism*.

20. Gill, *Rising Star*.

21. Lampton, *Three Faces of Chinese Power*; David Michael Lampton, *Following the Leader* (Berkeley: University of California Press, 2012).

22. Thomas Christensen, "China," in *Strategic Asia, 2001–2002*, ed. Richard Ellings and Aaron Friedberg (Seattle: National Bureau of Asian Research, 2001), 27–70.

23. Shirk, *China*.

24. Robert Suettinger, *Beyond Tiananmen: The Politics of U.S.-China Relations, 1989–2000* (Washington, DC: Brookings Institution Press, 2003).

25. Evan Medeiros, "Strategic Hedging and the Future of Asia-Pacific Stability," *Washington Quarterly* 29, no. 1 (2005–2006): 145–67.

26. Condoleezza Rice, remarks at Sophia University, Tokyo, Japan, March 19, 2005, accessed March 21, 2008, http://www.state.gov/secretary/rm/2005/43655.htm.

27. Remarks of Deputy Secretary of State Robert Zoellick, *Wither China? From Membership to Responsibility* (New York: National Committee for U.S.–China Relations, September 21, 2005), http://usinfo.state.gov/eap/Archive/2005/Sep/.

28. David Michael Lampton, "Power Constrained: Sources of Mutual Strategic Suspicion in US-China Relations," *NBR Analysis* (June 2010): 5–25; U.S. Department of Defense, *Annual Report on the Military Power of the People's Republic of China, 2010,* http://www.defenselink.mil.

29. Zhao Lingmin, "Optimistic View of Sino-US Relations—Exclusive Interview with Professor Wang Jisi," (Guangzhou) *Nanfeng Chuang,* October 8, 2008, 50–53.

30. Shambaugh, *China Goes Global,* 15–42.

31. "Yan Xuetong Interview: China Needs to 'Purchase' Friendship, Scholar Says," *Nikkei Asian Review* March 2, 2015, http://www.asia.nikkei.com.

32. Deng, "China: The Post-Responsible Power."

33. Sutter, *Foreign Relations of the PRC,* 29–90.

34. David Finkelstein, *China Reconsiders Its National Security: The Great Peace and Development Debate of 1999* (Alexandria, VA: CNA Corporation, 2001); James Przystup, "Japan-China Relations: No End to History," *Comparative Connections* 7, no. 2 (2005): 119–32.

35. Linda Jakobson and Dean Knox, "New Foreign Policy Actors in China," SIPRI Policy Paper 26 (September 2010); David Shambaugh, "Coping with a Conflicted China," *Washington Quarterly* 34, no. 1 (Winter 2011): 7–27.

36. Stephanie Kleine-Ahlbrandt, "Navigating Tensions in the East China Sea," *Huffington Post,* April 17, 2013, http://www.huffingtonpost.com.

37. See references to hegemonism in Robert Sutter, *China's Rise in Asia: Promises and Perils* (Lanham, MD: Rowman & Littlefield, 2005).

38. Bonnie Glaser and Evan Medeiros, "The Changing Ecology of Foreign Policy Making in China: The Ascension and Demise of the Theory of 'Peaceful Rise,'" *China Quarterly* 190 (2007): 291–310; Dai, "Stick to the Path of Peaceful Development."

39. Mikkal Herberg and Kenneth Lieberthal, "China's Search for Energy Security: Implications for US Policy," *NBR Analysis* 17, no. 1 (April 2006).

40. Richard Bush, *Untying the Knot: Making Peace in the Taiwan Strait* (Washington, DC: Brookings Institution Press, 2005); Alan Romberg, "Ma at Mid-Term: Challenges for Cross-Strait Relations," *China Leadership Monitor* 2010, no. 3 (June 28, 2010), http://www.hoover.org; Richard Bush, *Unchartered Strait* (Washington, DC: Brookings Institution Press, 2012).

41. Bates Gill, "China's Evolving Regional Security Strategy," in Shambaugh, *Power Shift,* 247–65. Gill elaborated this positive view in *Rising Star.* Similarly positive assessments of Chinese leaders' confidence are seen in Evan Medeiros and M. Taylor Fravel, "China's New Diplomacy," *Foreign Affairs* 82, no. 6 (November–December 2003): 22–35; Goldstein, *Rising to the Challenge.*

42. Shirk, *China*; Jonathan Pollack, "The Transformation of the Asian Security Order: Assessing China's Impact," in Shambaugh, *Power Shift,* 329–46; Wang, "Beijing's Incentive Structure"; Lampton, *Following the Leader*; Nathan and Scobell, *China's Search for Security*; Shambaugh, "The Coming Chinese Crack-Up."

43. Aaron Friedberg, "The Future of US-China Relations: Is Conflict Inevitable?" *International Security* 30, no. 2 (2005): 7–45.

44. The White House Office of the Press Secretary, "Remarks by the President in State of the Union Address," Washington, DC, January 20, 2015, http://www.whitehouse.gov/the-press-office/2015/01/20/remarks-president-state-union-address-january-20-2015.

45. Ralph Cossa and Brad Glosserman, "A Tale of Two Tales: Competing Narratives in the Asia-Pacific, *PacNet* 84, December 1, 2014.

46. Jakobson and Knox, *New Foreign Policy Actors in China*; Linda Jakobson, "China's Unpredictable Maritime Security Actors," Lowy Institute Report, December 11, 2014, http://www.lowyinstitute.org/publications/chinas-unpredictable-maritime-security-actors.

47. Medeiros, "Strategic Hedging."

2. CHINESE LEADERSHIP PRIORITIES

1. See among others, Aaron Friedberg, *The Contest for Supremacy* (New York: Norton, 2011); Denny Roy, *Return of the Dragon* (New York: Columbia University Press, 2013); Ashley Tellis, *Balancing without Containment* (Washington, DC: Carnegie Endowment for International Peace Report, January 22, 2014); Michael Pillsbury, *The Hundred Year Marathon* (New York: Holt, 2015).

2. Thomas Christensen, "China," in *Strategic Asia, 2002–2003*, ed. Richard Ellings and Aaron Friedberg (Seattle: National Bureau of Asian Research, 2002), 51–94; David Michael Lampton, *Following the Leader* (Berkeley: University of California Press, 2012).

3. Robert Sutter, *Shaping China's Future in World Affairs* (Boulder, CO: Westview Press, 1996), 32–33.

4. Harry Harding, *A Fragile Relationship* (Washington, DC: Brookings Institution Press, 1992), 235–39; Ashley J. Tellis and Travis Tanner, eds., *Strategic Asia, 2012–13: China's Military Challenge* (Seattle: National Bureau of Asian Research, 2012).

5. Joseph Fewsmith, *China since Tiananmen* (New York: Cambridge University Press, 2001), 21–43, 75–158.

6. Robert Suettinger, *Beyond Tiananmen: The Politics of U.S.-China Relations, 1989–2000* (Washington, DC: Brookings Institution Press, 2003), 194–99.

7. Sutter, *Shaping China's Future in World Affairs*, 33–34.

8. Andrew Nathan and Robert Ross, *The Great Wall and Empty Fortress* (New York: Norton, 1997), 158–77.

9. Sutter, *Shaping China's Future in World Affairs*, 33–34.

10. Shirley Kan, *China as a Security Concern in Asia*, Congressional Research Service Report 95-465 (Washington, DC: Library of Congress, December 22, 1994).

11. David Michael Lampton, ed., *The Making of Chinese Foreign and Security Policy in the Era of Reform, 1978–2000* (Stanford, CA: Stanford University Press, 2001), 34–36.

12. Evan Medeiros and M. Taylor Fravel, "China's New Diplomacy," *Foreign Affairs* 82, no. 6 (November–December 2003): 22–35; Zhang Yunling and Tang Shiping, "More Self-Confident China Will Be a Responsible Power," *Straits Times*, October 2, 2002, accessed October 4, 2002, http://www.Taiwansecurity.org; Denny Roy, "Rising China and U.S. Interests: Inevitable vs. Contingent Hazards," *Orbis* 47, no. 1 (2003): 125–37.

13. Sutter, *Shaping China's Future in World Affairs*, 35.

14. Chinese Academy of Social Sciences, *Trends of Future Sino-U.S. Relations and Policy Proposals* (Beijing: Institute for International Studies of the Academy of Social Sciences, September 1994).

15. David Michael Lampton, *Same Bed, Different Dreams* (Berkeley: University of California Press, 2001), 59–60.

16. Fewsmith, *China since Tiananmen*, 159–89.

17. H. Lyman Miller and Liu Xiaohong, "The Foreign Policy Outlook of China's 'Third Generation' Elite," in *The Making of Chinese Foreign and Security Policy in the Era of Reform, 1978–2000*, ed. David Michael Lampton (Stanford, CA: Stanford University Press, 2001), 123–50; Ye Zicheng, *Xin Zhongguo Waijiao Sixiang: Cong Maozedong dao Dengxiaoping* (Beijing: Beijing Daxue Chubanshe, 2001).

18. Robert Sutter, *Chinese Policy Priorities and Their Implications for the United States* (Lanham, MD: Rowman & Littlefield, 2000), 18.

19. Barry Naughton, "China's Economy: Buffeted from Within and Without," *Current History* (September 1998): 273–78.

20. Joseph Fewsmith, "China in 1998," *Asian Survey* 39, no. 1 (January–February 1999): 99–113.

21. Jean-Pierre Cabestan, "The Tenth National People's Congress and After," *China Perspectives* 47 (May–June 2003): 4–20.

22. Thomas Christensen, "China," in *Strategic Asia, 2001–2002*, ed. Richard Ellings and Aaron Friedberg (Seattle: National Bureau of Asian Research, 2001), 27–70, and "China," in Ellings and Friedberg, *Strategic Asia, 2002–2003*, 51–94.

23. C. Fred Bergsten et al., *China's Rise: Challenges and Opportunities* (Washington, DC: Peterson Institute for International Economics and Center for Strategic and International Studies, 2008); U.S.–China Economic and Security Review Commission, *2010 Annual Report to Congress*, accessed February 19, 2011, http://www.uscc.gov.

24. Cheng Li, ed., *China's Changing Political Landscape: Prospects for Democracy* (Washington, DC: Brookings Institution Press, 2008); Cheng Li, ed., *China's Emerging Middle Class* (Washington, DC: Brookings Institution, 2010).

25. Li, *China's Emerging Middle Class*.

26. Susan Shirk, "Power Shift in China—Part III," *Yaleglobal Online*, April 20, 2012, http://yaleglobal.yale.edu.

27. Cheng Li, *China's Leaders: The New Generation* (Lanham, MD: Rowman & Littlefield, 2001); Cheng Li, "Power Shift in China—Part I," *Yaleglobal Online*, April 16, 2012, http://yaleglobal.yale.edu; Lampton, *Following the Leader*, 47–77.

28. Alice L. Miller, "Institutionalization and the Changing Dynamics of Chinese Leadership Politics," in Li, *China's Changing Political Landscape*, 61–79.

29. Jing Huang, "Institutionalization of Political Succession in China," in Li, *China's Changing Political Landscape*, 80–98; Lampton, *Following the Leader*, 68–77.

30. Damien Ma, "The Year the Training Wheels Came Off China," *Foreign Policy*, December 31, 2014 http://foreignpolicy.com; Paul Dibb and John Lee, "Why China Will Not Become the Dominant Power in Asia," *Security Challenges* 10, no. 3 (2014): 1–21.

31. Dennis Blasko, *The Chinese Army Today* (London: Routledge, 2012).

32. Li, "Power Shift in China—Part I"; David Shambaugh, "The Coming Chinese Crack-Up," *Wall Street Journal*, March 6, 201, http://www.wsj.com.

33. Bergsten et al., *China's Rise*, 105–30; Wayne Morrison, *China's Economic Conditions*, Congressional Research Service Report RL33534 (Washington, DC: Library of Congress, 2014).

34. Wayne Morrison, *China's Economic Conditions*, Congressional Research Service Report RL33534 (Washington, DC: Library of Congress, June 24, 2011).

35. Tony Saich, *Governance and Politics of China* (New York: Palgrave, 2004), 135, 233–67; Bruce Dickson, "Updating the China Model," *Washington Quarterly* 34, no. 4 (Fall 2011): 39–58.

36. Bergsten et al., *China's Rise*, 75–90.

37. Wayne Morrison, *China's Economic Conditions*, Congressional Research Service Report RL33534 (Washington, DC: Library of Congress, November 20, 2008), 17–18.

38. Minxin Pei, *China's Trapped Transition: The Limits of Development Autocracy* (Cambridge, MA: Harvard University Press, 2006), 83–84, 189, 200–204; Thomas Lum, *Human Rights in China and U.S. Policy*, Congressional Research Service Report RL34729 (Washington, DC: Library of Congress, July 18, 2011), 28–29.

39. Lum, *Human Rights in China and U.S. Policy*, 6; Martin King Whyte, "Chinese Social Trends: Stability or Chaos," in *China's Future: Implications for U.S. Interests*, 67–84; Bergsten et al., *China's Rise*, 96–97, 103.

40. U.S. Department of Defense, *Annual Report to Congress: Military and Security Developments Involving the People's Republic of China 2012* (Washington, DC: U.S. Department of Defense, May 2012).

41. David Michael Lampton, *Three Faces of Chinese Power* (Berkeley: University of California Press, 2008), 40–42; Mark Manyin, coord., *Pivot to the Pacific? The Obama Administration's "Rebalancing" Toward Asia*, Congressional Research Service Report R42448 (Washington, DC: Library of Congress, March 28, 2012).

42. Dickson, "Updating the China Model."

43. Lampton, *The Three Faces of Chinese Power*, 208; J. Stapleton Roy, "Power Shift in China—Part II," *Yaleglobal Online*, April 18, 2012, http://yaleglobal.yale.edu.

44. Bergsten et al., *China's Rise*, 236; Morrison, *China's Economic Conditions* (2014); Susan Lawrence, *U.S.-China Relations: An Overview of Policy Issues*, Congressional Research Service Report R41108 (Washington, DC: Library of Congress, August 1, 2013).

45. Michael Forsythe, "Q and A: Roderick MacFarquhar on Xi Jinping's High-Risk Campaign to Save the Communist Party," *New York Times*, January 30, 2015, http://sinosphere.bolgs.nytimes.com.

46. Nicholas Lardy, *Sustaining China's Economic Growth* (Washington, DC: Peterson Institute for International Economics, 2012).

47. Elizabeth Perry and Mark Selden, *Chinese Society: Change, Conflict, and Resistance* (London: Routledge, 2010); Yongnian Zheng, "China in 2011," *Asian Survey* 52, no. 1 (January–February 2012): 28–41.

48. Richard Baum, "Political Implications of China's Information Revolution: The Media, the Minders, and Their Message," in Li, *China's Changing Political Landscape*, 161–84; Peter Mattis, "Executive Summary for 'China in 2012,'" *China Brief* 12, no. 2 (January 20, 2012): 1–3; Gideon Rachman, "China's Strange Fear of a Color Revolution," *Financial Times*, February 9, 2015,http://www.ft.com.

49. Michael Swaine, "China's Regional Military Posture," in *Power Shift: China and Asia's New Dynamics*, ed. David Shambaugh (Berkeley: University of California Press, 2005), 266–88; Manyin, "Pivot to the Pacific?" 8–9, 15–16, 18–19, 23–24.

50. Suisheng Zhao, "China's Pragmatic Nationalism: Is It Manageable?" *Washington Quarterly* 29, no. 1 (2005): 131–44.

51. Peter Gries refers to this kind of sensibility as "face nationalism." Peter Hayes Gries, "A China Threat? Power and Passion in Chinese 'Face Nationalism,'" *World Affairs* 162, no. 2 (Fall 1999): 67.

52. On Chinese leaders' goals, especially as they relate to world affairs, see the discussion in subsequent chapters and in the selected bibliography in this book.

53. Avery Goldstein, *Rising to the Challenge: China's Grand Strategy and International Security* (Stanford, CA: Stanford University Press, 2005); Yong Deng, "Hegemon on the Offensive: Chinese Perspectives on U.S. Global Strategy," *Political Science Quarterly* 116, no. 3 (Fall 2001): 343–65; Qian Qichen, "The International Situation and Sino-U.S. Relations since the 11 September Incident," *Waijiao Xueyuan Xuebao* (Beijing) 3 (September 25, 2002): 1–6.

54. Linda Jakobson and Dean Knox, "New Foreign Policy Actors in China," SIPRI Policy Paper 26 (September 2010); David Shambaugh, "Coping with a Conflicted China," *Washington Quarterly* 34, no. 1 (Winter 2011).

55. David Shambaugh, "China's Military Views the World," *International Security* 24, no. 3 (Winter 1999–2000): 52–79; Alan Tonelson, *A Necessary Evil? Current Chinese Views of America's Military Role in East Asia* (Washington, DC: Henry Stimson Center, May 2003).

56. Evan Medeiros, *China's International Behavior* (Santa Monica, CA: RAND Corporation, 2009).

57. Stephanie Kleine-Ahlbrandt, "Dangerous Waters," *Foreign Policy*, September 17, 2012, accessed October 7, 2012, http://www.foreignpolicy.com/articles/2012/09/17/dangerous_waters.

3. CHANGING PATTERNS IN DECISION MAKING AND INTERNATIONAL OUTLOOK

1. David Michael Lampton, ed., *The Making of Chinese Foreign and Security Policy in the Era of Reform, 1978–2000* (Stanford, CA: Stanford University Press, 2001); Evan Medeiros and M. Taylor Fravel, "China's New Diplomacy," *Foreign Affairs* 82, no. 6 (November–December 2003): 22–35; People's Republic of China State Council Information Office, "China's Peaceful Development Road," *People's Daily Online*, December 22, 2005, http://www.peoplesdaily.com.cn; Linda Jakobson and Dean Knox, "New Foreign Policy Actors in China," SIPRI Policy Paper 26 (September 2010); Yun Sun, *Chinese National Security Decision-making: Process and Challenges* (Washington, DC: Brookings Institution, May 2013).

2. David Michael Lampton, *Same Bed, Different Dreams* (Berkeley: University of California Press, 2001), 59–61; Robert Sutter, *China's Rise in Asia: Promises and Perils* (Lanham, MD: Rowman & Littlefield, 2005), 29.

3. John Keefe, *Anatomy of the EP-3 Incident* (Alexandria, VA: Center for Naval Analysis, 2002); Michael Swaine and Zhang Tuosheng, eds., *Managing Sino-American Crises: Case Studies and Analysis* (Washington, DC: Carnegie Endowment, 2006).

4. James Przystup, "Japan-China Relations: No End to History," *Comparative Connections* 7, no. 2 (July 2005): 119–32.

5. James Przystup, "Japan-China Relations," *Comparative Connections* 13, no. 3 (January 2013), http://www.csis.org/pacfor.

6. Ronald O'Rourke, *Maritime Territorial and Exclusive Economic Zone (EEZ) Disputes Involving China*, Congressional Research Service Report 42784 (Washington, DC: Library of Congress, December 24, 2014).

7. Consultations with U.S. government officials, Washington, DC, 1999–2001; Swaine and Zhang, *Managing Sino-American Crises.*

8. "Friend or Foe? A Special Report on China's Place in the World," *The Economist*, December 4, 2010, 3–16; Christopher Johnson, "Xi Jinping Unveils His Foreign Policy Vision," *Thoughts from the Chairman* (Washington, DC: Center for Strategic and International Studies, December 2014); Yun Sun, "China's Peaceful Rise: Peace through Strength?" *PacNet* 25 (March 31, 2014).

9. Consultations with U.S. government officials, Washington, DC, November 1999.

10. Interviews and consultations with Chinese officials and foreign policy specialists, Beijing and Shanghai, May–June 2006, Beijing, June 2010.

11. Scott Snyder, "China-Korea Relations: China's Post–Kim Jong Il Debate," *Council on Foreign Relations*, May 14, 2012, http://www.cfr.org/north-korea/china-korea-relations-chinas-post-kim-jong-il-debate/p28282.

12. Yi Qinfu, "What Will China's National Security Commission Actually Do?" *Foreign Policy*, May 8, 2014, http://foreignpolicy.com/2014/05/08/what-will-chinas-national-security-commission-actually-do.

13. Brad Glosserman and Denny Roy, "Asia's Next China Worry: Xi Jinping's Growing Power," *National Interest*, July 23, 2014, http://nationalinterest.org/blog/the-buzz/asias-next-china-worry-xi-jinpings-growing-power-10939?page=2.

14. Johnson, "Xi Jinping Unveils"; Glosserman and Roy, "Asia's Next China Worry."

15. Cary Huang, "How Leading Small Groups Help Xi Jinping and Other Party Leaders Exert Power," *South China Morning Post*, January 20, 2014, http://www.scmp.com/news/china/article/1409118/how-leading-small-groups-help-xi-jinping-and-other-party-leaders-exert.

16. Linda Jakobson, "China's Unpredictable Maritime Security Actors," Lowy Institute Report, December 11, 2014, http://www.lowyinstitute.org/publications/chinas-unpredictable-maritime-security-actors; David Michael Lampton, *The Three Faces of Chinese Power: Might, Money, and Minds* (Berkeley: University of California Press, 2008); Alice Miller, "The CCP's Central Committee's Leading Small Groups," *China Leadership Monitor* 26 (Fall 2008), http://www.chinaleadershipmonitor.org; Lu Ning, "The Central Leadership, Supraministry Coordinating Bodies, State Council Ministries, and Party Departments," in *The Making of Chinese Foreign and Security Policy in the Era of Reform*, ed. David Michael Lampton (Stanford, CA: Stanford University Press, 2001), 39–60.

17. Carola McGiffert, ed., *Chinese Images of the United States* (Washington, DC: CSIS Press, 2006), 9–22.

18. Lampton, *Making of Chinese Foreign and Security Policy in the Era of Reform*, 1–38.

19. Lu, "Central Leadership," 39–60; Fei-Ling Wang, "Beijing's Incentive Structure: The Pursuit of Preservation, Prosperity, and Power," in *China Rising: Power and Motivation in Chinese Foreign Policy*, ed. Yong Deng and Fei-Ling Wang (Lanham, MD: Rowman & Littlefield, 2005), 19–50.

20. Lampton, *Making of Chinese Foreign and Security Policy in the Era of Reform*; Evan Medeiros and M. Taylor Fravel, "China's New Diplomacy," *Foreign Affairs* 82, no. 6 (November–December 2003): 22–35.

21. "Priorities Set for Handling Foreign Affairs," *China Daily*, August 24, 2006, 1.

22. Suisheng Zhao, *A Nation-State by Construction: Dynamics of Modern Chinese Nationalism* (Stanford, CA: Stanford University Press, 2004); Peter Gries, *China's New Nationalism* (Berkeley: University of California Press, 2004); Anne-Marie Brady, *Marketing Dictatorship: Propaganda and Thought Work in Contemporary China* (Lanham, MD: Rowman & Littlefield, 2008), 151–74.

23. John Garver, *Foreign Relations of the People's Republic of China* (Englewood Cliffs, NJ: Prentice Hall, 1993), 1–28.

24. Sources for this historical review include Warren I. Cohen, *America's Response to China: A History of Sino-American Relations* (New York: Columbia University Press, 2010).

25. Yan Xuetong, "The Instability of China-US Relations," *Chinese Journal of International Politics* 3, no. 3 (2010): 1–30; Suisheng Zhao, "China's Pragmatic Nationalism: Is It Manageable?" *Washington Quarterly* 29, no. 1 (Winter 2005–2006): 131–44.

26. Among foreign studies on this subject, see David Kang, *China's Rising: Peace, Power and Order in East Asia* (New York: Columbia University Press, 2007).

27. Denny Roy, *China's Foreign Relations* (Lanham, MD: Rowman & Littlefield, 1998), 36–39; Samuel Kim, "China's International Organizational Behaviour," in *Chinese Foreign Policy: Theory and Practice*, ed. Thomas Robinson and David Shambaugh (New York: Oxford University Press, 1994), 401–5; Harry Harding, "China's Changing Role in the Contemporary World," in *China's Foreign Relations in the 1980s*, ed. Harry Harding (New Haven, CT: Yale University Press, 1985), 177–79.

28. Hu Guocheng, "Chinese Images of the United States: A Historical Review," in *Chinese Images of the United States*, ed. Carola McGiffert (Washington, DC: CSIS, 2006), 3–8.

29. Lampton, *Same Bed, Different Dreams*, 60.

30. Wang Jisi, "From Paper Tiger to Real Leviathan: China's Images of the United States since 1949," in McGiffert, *Chinese Images of the United States*, 12–18; Zhao Lingmin, "Optimistic View of Sino-US Relations—Exclusive Interview with Professor Wang Jisi," *Nanfeng Chuang* (Guangzhou), October 8, 2008, 50–53; Kenneth Lieberthal and Wang Jisi, *Assessing U.S.-China Strategic Mistrust* (Washington, DC: Brookings Institution, John Thornton China Center, 2012).

31. Rosalie Chen, "China Perceives America," *Journal of Contemporary China* 12, no. 35 (2003): 288–92.

32. Robert Ross and Jiang Changbin, *Re-Examining the Cold War: U.S.-China Diplomacy 1954–1973* (Cambridge, MA: Harvard University Press, 2001), 19–21; Lieberthal and Wang, *Assessing U.S.-China Strategic Mistrust*.

33. Wang, "From Paper Tiger to Real Leviathan"; Gong Li, "The Official Perspective: What Chinese Government Officials Think of America," in McGiffert, *Chinese Images of the United States*, 9–32.

34. The mix of challenge and opportunity posed by the United States for Chinese interests and policies in Asian and world affairs prompted differing assessments by Chinese and foreign specialists. Some emphasize positive and cooperative aspects of U.S.-China relations. See Medeiros and Fravel, "China's New Diplomacy"; Jia Qingguo, "Learning to Live with the Hegemon: Evolution of China's Policy toward the United States," *Journal of Contemporary China* 14, no. 44 (August 2005): 395–407; and Stephanie Kleine-Ahlbrandt and Andrew Small, "China's New Dictatorship Diplomacy," *Foreign Affairs* 87, no. 1 (January–February 2008): 38–56; others emphasize more negative and competitive aspects. See Joshua Kurlantzick, *Charm Offensive: How China's Soft Power Is Transforming the World* (New Haven, CT: Yale University Press, 2007); U.S.-China Economic and Security Review Commission, *Report to Congress*, 2008, http://www.uscc.gov; U.S. Department of State, *China's Strategic Modernization: Report from the Secretary's International Security Advisory Board (ISAB) Task Force*, 2008, accessed December 27, 2008, http://video1.washingtontimes.com/video/ChinaStrategic Plan.pdf; People's Republic of China State Council Information Office, "China's National Defense in 2006," Beijing, December 29, 2006.

35. Thomas Christensen, "The Advantages of an Assertive China," *Foreign Affairs* 90, no. 2 (March–April 2011): 54–67.

36. Andrew Nathan and Andrew Scobell, *China's Search for Security* (New York: Columbia University Press, 2012); "Yan Xuetong Interview: China Needs to 'Purchase' Friendships, Scholar Says," *Nikkei Asian Review*, March 2, 2015, http://asia.nikkei; Zhang Liping, "A Rising China and a Lonely Superpower America," in *Making New Partnership: A Rising China and Its Neighbors*, ed. Zhang Yunlin (Beijing: Social Sciences Academic Press 2008), 324–55.

37. Reviewed in Robert Sutter, *China's Rise in Asia (Lanham, MD: Rowman & Littlefield, 2005),* 35. For differing perspectives, see David Shambaugh, ed., *Power Shift* (Berkeley: University of California Press, 2005); Lampton, *The Three Faces of Chinese Power*; Bates Gill, *Rising Star: China's New Security Diplomacy* (Washington, DC: Brookings Institution, 2007); Shirk, *China*; Alastair Iain Johnston, "Is China a Status Quo Power?" *International Security* 24, no. 4 (Spring 2003): 5–56; Yong Deng and Thomas Moore, "China Views Globalization: Toward a New Great-Power Politics?" *Washington Quarterly* 27, no. 3 (Summer 2004): 117–36; Aaron Friedberg, *A Contest for Supremacy* (New York: Norton, 2011); Denny Roy, *Return of the Dragon* (New York: Columbia University Press, 2013); Nathan and Scobell, *China's Search for Security.*

38. Robert Sutter, *Foreign Relations of the PRC* (Lanham, MD: Rowman & Littlefield, 2013), 53–90; Garver, *Foreign Relations.*

39. Robert Sutter, *Chinese Foreign Policy: Developments After Mao* (New York: Praeger, 1986), 9.

40. Garver, *Foreign Relations*, 70–109.

41. Sutter, *Chinese Foreign Policy*, 10–12.

42. Sutter, *China's Rise in Asia*, 10–17.

43. Robert Sutter, Michael Brown, and Timothy Adamson, *Balancing Acts* (Washington, DC: Elliott School of International Affairs, 2013), 17–18.

44. Martin Indyk, Kenneth Lieberthal, and Michael O'Hanlon, *Bending History* (Washington, DC: Brookings Institution, 2012), 24–69.

45. Robert Suettinger, *Beyond Tiananmen* (Washington, DC: Brookings Institution, 2003); Lampton, *Same Bed, Different Dreams*; Mark Manyin, coord., *Pivot to the Pacific? The Obama Administration's "Rebalancing" Toward Asia*, Congressional Research Service Report R42448 (Washington, DC: Library of Congress, March 28, 2012); Robert Sutter, *U.S.-Chinese Relations* (Lanham, MD: Rowman & Littlefield, 2013).

46. Lieberthal and Wang, *Assessing U.S.-China Strategic Mistrust.*

47. Robert Sutter, *U.S.-Chinese Relations: Perilous Past, Pragmatic Present* (Lanham, MD: Rowman & Littlefield, 2010).

48. Lawrence Chung, "Xi Jinping Sounds Alert on Taiwan Independence," *South China Morning Post*, March 5, 2015, http://www.scmp.com/news/china/article/1729689/xi-jinping-sounds-alert-taiwan-independence.

49. David Finkelstein, *China Reconsiders Its National Security: The Great Peace and Development Debate of 1999* (Alexandria, VA: CNA, December 2000); Qian Qichen, "The International Situation and Sino-U.S. Relations since the 11 September Incident," *Waijiao Xueyuan Xuebao* (Beijing) 3 (September 25, 2002); Wang, "China's Search for a Grand Strategy"; Sutter et al., *Balancing Acts.*

50. Susan Lawrence, *China-U.S. Relations: An Overview of Policy Issues*, Congressional Research Service Report RL41108 (Washington, DC: Library of Congress, August 1, 2013).

51. Lawrence, *China-U.S. Relations*, 14–32.

52. Snyder, "China-Korea Relations."

53. Andrew Erickson and Emily de La Bruyere, "Going Maverick: Lessons from China's Buzzing of a U.S. Navy Aircraft," *Wall Street Journal China Realtime*, August 25, 2014, http://blogs.wsj.com/chinarealtime/2014/08/25/going-maverick-lessons-from-chinas-buzzing-of-a-us-navy-aircraft.

54. Lawrence, *China-U.S. Relations*, 47.

55. Sutter, *U.S.-Chinese Relations*, 161–81.

56. Wayne Morrison, *China-U.S. Trade Issues*, Congressional Research Service Report RL33536 (Washington, DC: Library of Congress, December 5, 2014).

4. CHINA'S ROLE IN THE WORLD ECONOMY AND INTERNATIONAL GOVERNANCE

1. See varying perspectives on these points in Arvind Subramanian, "The Inevitable Superpower: Why China's Rise Is a Sure Thing," *Foreign Affairs* 90, no. 5 (September–October 2011): 66–78; Carl Dahlman, *The World Under Pressure: How China and India Are Influencing the Global Economy and Environment* (Stanford, CA: Stanford University Press 2011); David Shambaugh, *China Goes Global* (New York: Oxford University Press, 2013); Wayne Morrison, *China's Economic Rise*, Congressional Research Service Report RL33534 (Washington, DC: Library of Congress, October 9, 2014).

2. Robert Sutter, *Foreign Relations of the PRC* (Lanham, MD: Rowman & Littlefield, 2013), 150–51.

3. David Michael Lampton, *Following the Leader: Ruling China from Deng Xiaoping to Xi Jinping* (Berkeley: University of California Press, 2014); Nicholas Lardy, *Sustaining China's Economic Growth* (Washington, DC: Peterson Institute for International Affairs, 2012); Michael Beckley, "China's Century? Why America's Edge Will Endure," *International Security* 36, no. 3 (Winter 2011–2012): 41–78.

4. Morrison, *China's Economic Rise*, summary page; Yu Yongding, "An Opportunity for China," *Japan Times*, April 12, 2015, http://www.japantimes.co.jp/opinion/2015/04/12/commentary/world-commentary/opportunity-china/#.VXLETdJViko.

5. "Catching the Eagle," *The Economist*, August 22, 2014, http://www.economist.com/blogs/graphicdetail/2014/08/chinese-and-american-gdp-forecasts.

6. Explained in Morrison, *China's Economic Rise*, 6–7.

7. U.S. China Business Council, *China Economic Reform Scorecard*, February 2015, https://www.uschina.org/reports/china-economic-reform-scorecard-february-2015 (the reviews are published four times a year).

8. Explained in Morrison, *China's Economic Rise*, 5.

9. See the treatment of these preoccupations in, among others, Lampton, *Following the Leader*, and Andrew J. Nathan and Andrew Scobell, *China's Search for Security* (New York: Columbia University Press, 2012).

10. Ben Blanchard and John Ruwich, "China Hikes Defense Budget, to Spend More on Internal Security," *Reuters*, March 5, 2013, http://www.reuters.com/article/2013/03/05/us-china-parliament-defence-idUSBRE92403620130305.

11. A Chinese government specialist wrote in an editorial in 2010 that China "consumed 0.82 ton of standard oil for every $1,000 increase in GDP value," while "in the U.S. and Japan, the figure was 0.20 ton and 0.10 ton respectively." Feng Zhaokui, "China Still a Developing Nation," *China Daily*, May 6, 2010, 12.

12. Stephen Roach, "China's Policy Disharmony," *Project Syndicate*, December 31, 2013, http://www.project-syndicate.org; Morrison, *China's Economic Rise*, 32–35.

13. People's Republic of China, Ministry of Commerce, "Brief Statistics on China's Import and Export December 2014," January 19, 2015, http://english.mofcom.gov.cn/article/statistic/BriefStatistics/201501/20150100871755.shtml.

14. *China Data Online*, April 13, 2015, http://chinadataonline.org/freesource/zixunshow.asp?id=846.

15. Morrison, *China's Economic Rise*, 20.

16. Wayne Morrison, *China's Economic Conditions*, Congressional Research Service Issue Brief 98014 (Washington, DC: Library of Congress, July 1, 2005), 6–8; Wayne Morrison, *China-U.S. Trade Issues*, Congressional Research Service Report RL33536 (Washington, DC: Library of Congress, January 7, 2011), 1.

17. U.S. Census Bureau, "Trade in Goods with China," accessed June 5, 2015, https://www.census.gov/foreign-trade/balance/c5700.html.

18. Morrison, *China's Economic Rise*, 12.

19. "Foreign Investment in China Hits Record in 2010," Agence France-Press, January 18, 2011, http://www.afp.com; Ding Qingfen, "ODI Set to Overtake FDI 'within Three Years,'"

China Daily, May 6, 2011; Morrison, *China's Economic Conditions* (2009), 4–9; Morrison, *China's Economic Rise*, 11.

20. Miaojie Yu and Wei Tian, "China's Processing Trade," *East Asia Forum*, October 27, 2012, http://www.eastasiaforum.org/2012/10/27/chinas-processing-trade.

21. Pu Zhendong, "Singapore Supports Strengthened Free-Trade Agreement with Beijing," *China Daily*, August 30, 2013, http://usa.chinadaily.com.cn/epaper/2013-08/30/content_16932418.htm.

22. Randall Morck, Bernard Yeung, and Minyuan Zhao, *Perspectives on China's Outward Foreign Direct Investment*, Working Paper (Washington, DC: International Monetary Fund, August 2007).

23. Morrison, *China's Economic Rise*, 16.

24. People's Republic of China, Ministry of Commerce, *2006 Statistical Bulletin of China's Outward Foreign Investment* (Beijing: Ministry of Commerce, 2007), 51.

25. Thomas Lum, coord., *Comparing Global Influence: China's and U.S. Diplomacy, Foreign Aid, Trade, and Investment in the Developing World*, Congressional Research Service Report RL34620 (Washington, DC: Library of Congress, August 15, 2008), 59.

26. Morrison, *China's Economic Rise*, 16.

27. Lum, *Comparing Global Influence*, 59–60.

28. Xiao Geng, *China's Round-Tripping FDI: Scale, Causes and Implications*, Working Paper (Hong Kong: University of Hong Kong, July 2004); Morck et al., *Perspectives on China's Outward Foreign Direct Investment*.

29. Morrison, *China's Economic Rise*, 15–16.

30. Reviewed in "Ambitious Economic Initiatives amid Boundary Disputes," *Comparative Connections* 17, no. 1 (May 2015): 57–61.

31. Huang Yiping, "Pragmatism Can Lead to Silk Roads Success," *China Daily*, February 25, 2015, http://repubhub.icopyright.net/freePost.act?tag=3.15484?icx_id=48971175.

32. Matina Stevis, "China Launches $2 Billion African Development Fund," *Wall Street Journal*, May 22, 2014, http://www.wsj.com/articles/SB10001424052702303749904579577881407374244.

33. Toh Han Shih, "Chinese Investors Warned about African Mining Risks," *South China Morning Post*, December 16, 2013, http://www.scmp.com/business/commodities/article/1381796/chinese-investors-warned-about-african-mining-risks.

34. Linda Yulisman, "Indonesia: Indonesia to Push China to Realize Investment," *Jakarta Post*, April 4, 2015, http://www.thejakartapost.com/news/2015/04/04/indonesia-push-china-realize-investment.html; Dinna Wisnu, "Indonesia: Jokowi's Visits to Japan and China: What's in It for Us?" *Jakarta Post*, April 7, 2015, http://www.thejakartapost.com/news/2015/04/07/jokowi-s-visits-japan-and-china-what-s-it-us.html.

35. Top ten sources of foreign direct inflows in ASEAN (table 27), accessed June 6, 2015, http://www.asean.org/images/2015/January/foreign_direct_investment_statistic/Table%2027.pdf; "China in Africa: One Among Many," *The Economist*, January 17, 2015, http://www.economist.com/news/middle-east-and-africa/21639554-china-has-become-big-africa-now-backlash-one-among-many; *2013 China-Latin America Bulletin*, 12, accessed June 5, 2015, http://www.bu.edu/pardee/files/2014/01/Economic-Bulletin-2013.pdf.

36. The assessment for the rest of this section is taken from "Ambitious Economic Initiatives amid Boundary Disputes," 57–61.

37. The plan is available at "Initiative Offers Road Map for Peace, Prosperity," *China Daily*, March 30, 2015, http://europe.chinadaily.com.cn/china/2015-03/30/content_19950708.htm.

38. Chen Jia, "Silk Road Fund Makes First Investment," *China Daily*, April 22, 2015, http://usa.chinadaily.com.cn/epaper/2015-04/22/content_20508778.htm.

39. "Ambitious Economic Initiatives amid Boundary Disputes," 59–60.

40. "Ambitious Economic Initiatives amid Boundary Disputes," 60–61.

41. "On the Silk Road to Shared Success," *China Daily*, March 9, 2015, http://usa.chinadaily.com.cn/epaper/2015-03/09/content_19757219.htm.

42. Carol Lancaster, *The Chinese Aid System* (Washington, DC: Center for Global Development, June 2007); Bao Chang and Ding Qingfen, "No Hidden Strings Tied to Aid," *China Daily*, April 27, 2011, 3.

43. Lum, *Comparing Global Influence*, 33–34.

44. Deborah Brautigam, *The Dragon's Gift: The Real Story of China in Africa* (New York: Oxford University Press, 2009), 168–69; *Africa and China: Issues and Insights—A Summary of a Conference* (Washington, DC: Georgetown University, November 7, 2008), http://www.asianstudies.georgetown.edu.

45. "Full Text: China's Foreign Aid," *Xinhua*, July 10, 2014, http://news.xinhuanet.com/english/china/2014-07/10/c_133474011.htm; Shannon Tiezzi, "China's Foreign Aid: Raw Numbers," *The Diplomat*, July 11, 2014, http://thediplomat.com/2014/07/chinas-foreign-aid-the-raw-numbers.

46. Denghua Zhang, *China's Second White Paper on Foreign Aid*, Australian National University INBRIEF 2014/26, accessed June 5, 2015, http://ips.cap.anu.edu.au/sites/default/files/IB-2014-26-Zhang-ONLINE.pdf.

47. Michael Field, "Uproar in Tonga: China's 'Gift' Troubles New Prime Minister," *NIKKEI Asian Review*, March 28, 2015, http://asia.nikkei.com/Politics-Economy/International-Relations/tonga.

48. "China's Financial Diplomacy: Rich but Rash," *The Economist*, January 31, 2015, http://www.economist.com/news/finance-and-economics/21641259-challenge-world-bank-and-imf-china-will-have-imitate-them-rich.

49. Thomas Lum, *U.S.-Funded Assistance Programs in China*, Congressional Research Service Report RS22663 (Washington, DC: Library of Congress, January 28, 2008), 3; Xin Zhiming, "Government Clears $5.4B World Bank Loan," *China Daily*, July 25, 2008, 13; Asian Development Bank and the People's Republic of China, *Fact Sheet*, 2015, http://www.adb.org/publications/peoples-republic-china-fact-sheet.

50. Fu Jing and Hu Haiyan, "China, UN Jointly Unveil Five-Year Aid Framework," *China Daily*, April 2, 2010; Gillian Wong, "China Rises and Rises, Yet Still Gets Foreign Aid," AP, September 27, 2010, http://www.ap.com.

51. Joanna Lewis, "China's Strategic Priorities in International Climate Change Negotiations," *Washington Quarterly* 31, no. 1 (Winter 2007–2008): 165.

52. National Development and Reform Commission, *China's Policies and Actions for Addressing Climate Change—The Progress Report 2009*, November 2009, 47.

53. Antoine Dechezlepretre et al., "Technology Transfer by CDM Projects," *Energy Policy* 37, no. 2 (2009): 1.

54. Keith Bradsher, "China Leading Global Race to Make Clean Energy," *New York Times*, January 31, 2010, http://www.nytimes.com.

55. World Bank, "Global Environmental Facility (GEF) Projects in China," July 2009; World Bank, "World Bank, GEF-Backed Energy Efficiency Program Expands in China," January 2008; Asian Development Bank, *Asian Development Bank and People's Republic of China: Fact Sheet*, December 2008, 3. The information in this and the previous four notes is taken from a seminar paper by Xinran Qi, Georgetown University, April 18, 2010.

56. "'China Model' Thirty Years On: From Home and Abroad," *People's Daily Online*, April 21, 2011, http://www.english.peoplesdaily.com.cn; Stefan Halper, *The Beijing Consensus* (New York: Basic, 2010).

57. Yu Yongding, "A Different Road Forward," *China Daily*, December 23, 2010, 9.

58. Zhang Yunling, "China and Its Neighbors: Relations in a New Context," in *Making New Partnership: A Rising China and Its Neighbors*, ed. Zhang Yunling (Beijing: Social Sciences Academic Press, 2008), 1–18.

59. Dahlman, *The World under Pressure;* Subramanian, "The Inevitable Superpower."

60. Zheng Bijian, "China's 'Peaceful Rise' to Great-Power Status," *Foreign Affairs* 84, no. 5 (2005): 18–24; People's Republic of China State Council Information Office, "China's Peaceful Development Road," *People's Daily Online*, December 22, 2005, accessed July 7, 2006, http://www.peoplesdaily.com.cn; Rosemary Foot, "Chinese Strategies in a U.S.-Hegemonic Global Order: Accommodating and Hedging," *International Affairs* 82, no. 1 (2006): 77–94; Susan Shirk, *China: Fragile Superpower* (New York: Oxford University Press, 2007).

61. Morrison, *China's Economic Rise*, 25–34.

62. Wayne Morrison, *China's Economic Conditions*, Congressional Research Service Report RL33534 (Washington, DC: Library of Congress, June 26, 2012), 26–32; Morrison, *China's Economic Rise*, 25–32.

63. The strengths and weaknesses of Chinese economic relations with various parts of the world are reviewed in greater detail in the following chapters.

64. Samuel Kim, *The Two Koreas and the Great Powers* (New York: Cambridge University Press, 2006).

65. Michael Glosny, "Heading toward a Win-Win Future? Recent Developments in China's Policy toward Southeast Asia," *Asian Security* 2, no. 1 (2006): 24–57.

66. Bobo Lo, *Axis of Convenience: Moscow, Beijing, and the New Geopolitics* (Washington, DC: Brookings Institution Press, 2008).

67. Alan Kronstadt, *U.S.-India Security Relations,* Congressional Research Service Report R42948 (Washington, DC: Library of Congress, January 24, 2013).

68. The reactions of Chinese trading partners are discussed in the following chapters.

69. Bree Feng, "Obama's 'Free Rider' Comment Draws Chinese Criticism," *New York Times*, August 14, 2014, http://sinosphere.blogs.nytimes.com/2014/08/13/obamas-free-rider-comment-draws-chinese-criticism/?_r=0.

70. International Crisis Group, *China's Thirst for Oil*, Asia Report 153 (Brussels: International Crisis Group, June 9, 2008); Erica Downs, *Brookings Foreign Policy Studies Energy Security Series: China* (Washington, DC: Brookings Institution Press, 2006); Aaron Friedberg, "'Going Out': China's Pursuit of Natural Resources and Implications for the PRC's Grand Strategy," *NBR Analysis* 17, no. 3 (September 2006): 1–35.

71. Robert Sutter, *Chinese Policy Priorities and Their Implications for the United States* (Lanham, MD: Rowman & Littlefield, 2000), 188.

72. Elizabeth Economy, "China's Environmental Challenge," *Current History* 105, no. 692 (September 2005): 278–79; Sutter, *Chinese Policy Priorities and Their Implications for the United States*, 189.

73. Elizabeth Economy, "China: A Rise That's Not So 'Win-Win,'" *International Herald Tribune*, November 15, 2005, accessed November 17, 2005, http://www.taiwansecurity.org.

74. Te Kan, "Past Successes and New Goal," *China Daily*, December 26, 2005–January 1, 2006, supplement, 9.

75. Zhou Shijun, "Green Future," *China Daily*, January 9–15, 2006, supplement, 1; Joanna Lewis, "The State of U.S.-China Relations on Climate Change," *China Environmental Series* 11 (2010–2011): 7–39.

76. Hua Jianmin, "Strengthen Cooperation for Clean Development," Chinese Foreign Ministry statement, January 12, 2006, accessed January 30, 2006, http://www.fmprc.gov.cn/eng.

77. Economy, "China"; Lewis, "The State of U.S.-China Relations on Climate Change"; Kenneth Lieberthal and David Sandalow, *Overcoming Obstacles to U.S.-China Cooperation on Climate Change*, John L. Thornton China Center Monograph Series 1 (Washington, DC: Brookings Institution Press, January 2009); Lewis, "China's Strategic Priorities."

78. Lewis, "The State of U.S.-China Relations on Climate Change."

79. Joel Kirkland, "Global Emissions Predicted to Grow Through 2035," *Scientific American*, May 26, 2010, http://www.scientificamerican.com/article/global-emissions-predicted-to-grow.

80. *2014 Chinese Tourism Facts and Figures*, accessed June 7, 2015, http://www.travelchinaguide.com/tourism/2014statistics/; Yang Wanli, "At 97M and Growing, China Has Most Outbound Tourists," *China Daily,* January 9, 2014, 4; "How the Growing Chinese Middle Class Is Changing the Global Tourism Industry," *The Economist*, April 19, 2014, http://www.economist.com/news/international/21601028-how-growing-chinese-middle-class-changing-global-tourism-industry-coming.

81. Guan Xiaofeng, "Record Number of Overseas Tourists Visit Capital," *China Daily*, January 26, 2006, 4; Xin Dingding, "More Chinese Traveling Overseas," *China Daily*, July 10, 2007, 2; Xin Dingding, "Mainland Tourists Big Spenders Overseas," *China Daily*, April 13, 2011, 3; Aurora Almendria, "Philippines Feels Force of Chinese Travel Warning," *BBC News*, October 22, 2014, http://www.bbc.com/news/world-asia-29684938.

82. Sasha Han, "China Tries to Teach Its Tourists Manners," *ABC News*, August 11, 2013, http://abcnews.go.com/International/china-teach-tourists-manners/story?id=19903241.

83. Jing-Dong Yuan, "China's Role in Establishing and Building the Shanghai Cooperation Organization (SCO)," *Journal of Contemporary China* 19, no. 67 (November 2010): 855–70; Wu Xinbo, "Chinese Perspectives on Building an East Asian Community in the Twenty-first Century," in *Asia's New Multilateralism*, ed. Michael Green and Bates Gill (New York: Columbia University Press, 2009), 55–77; Robert Sutter, *Historical Dictionary of Chinese Foreign Policy* (Lanham, MD: Scarecrow Press, 2011), citations for "G20" and "BRIC."

84. Jianwei Wang, "China's Multilateral Diplomacy in the New Millennium," in *China Rising: Power and Motivation in Chinese Foreign Policy*, ed. Yong Deng and Fei-Ling Wang (Lanham, MD: Rowman & Littlefield, 2005), 159–66.

85. David Zweig and Bi Jianhai, "China's Global Hunt for Energy," *Foreign Affairs* 84, no. 5 (September–October 2005): 25–38.

86. Remarks by a Chinese official during a workshop the author attended in Beijing, March 29, 2015.

87. Jianwei Wang, "China's Multilateral Diplomacy in the New Millennium," 166–77; Ellen Frost, *Rival Regionalisms and the Regional Order*, National Bureau of Asian Research Special Report #48, December 2014, http://www.nbr.org/publications/specialreport/pdf/free/021115/SR48.pdf.

88. Ming Wan, "Democracy and Human Rights in Chinese Foreign Policy," in Deng and Wang, *China Rising*, 279–304.

89. Evan Medeiros, *Reluctant Restraint: The Evolution of China's Nonproliferation Policies and Practices, 1980–2004* (Stanford, CA: Stanford University Press, 2007).

90. This framework of analysis benefited from conference presentations by Bates Gill; see Bates Gill, *Rising Star: China's New Security Diplomacy* (Washington, DC: Brookings Institution, 2007).

91. Samuel Kim, "China and the United Nations," in *China Joins the World: Progress and Prospects*, ed. Elizabeth Economy and Michael Oksenberg (New York: Council on Foreign Relations, 1999), 46–47.

92. Alastair Iain Johnston and Paul Evans, "China's Engagement," in *Engaging China: The Management of an Emerging Power*, ed. Alastair Iain Johnston and Robert Ross (London: Routledge, 1999), 235–72.

93. Bates Gill, "Two Steps Forward, One Step Back: The Dynamics of Chinese Nonproliferation and Arms Control Policy-Making in an Era of Reform," in *The Making of Chinese Foreign and Security Policy in the Era of Reform, 1978–2000*, ed. David Michael Lampton (Stanford, CA: Stanford University Press, 2001), 257–88; Johnston and Evans, "China's Engagement," 253.

94. Yong Deng and Thomas Moore, "China Views Globalization: Toward a New Great-Power Politics?" *Washington Quarterly* 27, no. 3 (Summer 2004): 117–36; Allen Carlson, "More Than Just Saying No: China's Evolving Approach to Sovereignty and Intervention," in *New Directions in the Study of China's Foreign Policy*, ed. Alastair Iain Johnston and Robert S. Ross (Stanford, CA: Stanford University Press, 2006), 217–41.

95. Margaret Pearson, "China in Geneva: Lessons from China's Early Years in the World Trade Organization," in Johnston and Ross, *New Directions in the Study of China's Foreign Policy*, 242–75.

96. Samuel Kim, "Chinese Foreign Policy Faces Globalization Challenges," in Johnston and Ross, *New Directions in the Study of China's Foreign Policy*, 276–308.

97. "China's Zhou Says IMF Members Frustrated with Quota Reform Delay," *Xinhuanet*, April 18, 2015, http://news.xinhuanet.com/english/2015-04/18/c_134160977.htm.

98. Kim, "China and the United Nations."

99. These insights from such specialists as Rosemary Foot, Bates Gill, and David Shambaugh came at an international meeting cosponsored by George Washington University and Centre Asie Ifri (Paris), January 2002; see, notably, Rosemary Foot, *Rights beyond Borders: The Global Community and the Struggle over Human Rights in China* (New York: Oxford University Press, 2000); and Rosemary Foot and Andrew Walter, *China, The United States and the Global Order* (New York: Oxford University Press, 2010).

100. Joseph Logan and Patrick Worsnip, "Anger after Russia, China Block UN Action on Syria," *Reuters*, February 5, 2012, http://www.reuters.com/article/2012/02/05/us-syria-idUSTRE80S08620120205.

101. Kim, "China and the United Nations," 42–89, and "Chinese Foreign Policy Faces Globalization Challenges," 276–308.

102. Carlson, "More Than Just Saying No," 217–41.

103. Jianwei Wang, "China's Multilateral Diplomacy in the New Millennium," 164–66; Jianwei Wang, "Managing Conflict: Chinese Perspectives on Multilateral Diplomacy and Collective Security," in *In the Eyes of the Dragon: China Views the World*, ed. Yong Deng and Fei-Ling Wang (Lanham, MD: Rowman & Littlefield, 1999), 75–81; "Beijing May Open Door to WHO for Taiwan," *South China Morning Post*, December 19, 2008, http://www.scmp.com.

104. "Financing Peacekeeping," *United Nations Peacekeeping*, accessed June 8, 2015, http://www.un.org/en/peacekeeping/operations/financing.shtml.

105. "Bearing More Responsibilities: China Increases Its Share of International Responsibilities," *China Institute of International Studies*, January 16, 2013, http://www.ciis.org.cn/english/2013-01/16/content_5674643.htm.

106. Robert Sutter, *China's Rise in Asia: Promises and Perils* (Lanham, MD: Rowman & Littlefield, 2005), 177–208, 249–64; Jianwei Wang, "China's Multilateral Diplomacy in the New Millennium," 166–86.

107. Zhou Gang, "Status Quo and Prospects of China-ASEAN Relations," *Foreign Affairs Journal* (Beijing) 80 (June 2006): 14–21.

108. Wang Haiyun, "Prospect for Sino-Russian Relations in 2006," *Foreign Affairs Journal* (Beijing) 79 (March 2006): 50–54.

5. CHINESE NATIONAL SECURITY POLICIES

1. People's Republic of China State Council Information Office, "China's Peaceful Development Road," *People's Daily Online*, December 22, 2005, accessed July 7, 2006, http://english.peoplesdaily.com.cn; "Full Text of Chinese President Hu Jintao's Speech at Opening Session of Boao Forum," *China Daily*, April 15, 2011, http://www.chinadaily.com.cn.

2. Interview, Chinese Foreign Ministry, Beijing, May 30, 2006.

3. I benefited notably from comprehensive briefings on China's national security policy given by leaders of the PLA's Academy of Military Science in Beijing in June 2008 and June 2011 and briefings by senior representatives of the academy at a public meeting at Georgetown University, Washington, DC, in October 2008.

4. People's Republic of China State Council Information Office, *China's National Defense in 2004* (Beijing: People's Republic of China State Council Information Office, December 27, 2004); *China's National Defense in 2006* (Beijing: People's Republic of China State Council Information Office, December 29, 2006); *China's National Defense in 2008* (Beijing: People's Republic of China State Council Information Office, January 2009); *China's National Defense in 2010* (Beijing: People's Republic of China State Council Information Office, March 2011); "Document: China's Military Strategy," *USNI News*, May 26, 2015, http://news.usni.org/2015/05/26/document-chinas-military-strategy.

5. Paul Godwin, "China as a Major Asian Power: The Implications of Its Military Modernization (A View from the United States)," in *China, the United States, and Southeast Asia: Contending Perspectives on Politics, Security, and Economics*, ed. Evelyn Goh and Sheldon Simon (London: Routledge, 2008), 145–66.

6. Chu Shulong and Lin Xinzhu, "It Is Not the Objective of Chinese Military Power to Catch Up and Overtake the United States," *Huanqiu Shibao* (Beijing), June 26, 2008, 11.

7. U.S. Department of Defense, *Annual Report on the Military Power of the People's Republic of China, 2008* (Washington, DC: U.S. Department of Defense, March 2008); *Annual Report on the Military Power of the People's Republic of China, 2009* (Washington, DC: U.S. Department of Defense, March 2009); and *Military and Security Developments Involving the*

People's Republic of China, 2010 (Washington, DC: U.S. Department of Defense, August 2010).

8. People's Republic of China State Council Information Office, *China's National Defense in 2010*, 4.

9. People's Republic of China State Council Information Office, *China's National Defense in 2010*, 4; Martin Indyk, Kenneth Lieberthal, and Michael O'Hanlon, *Bending History: Barack Obama's Foreign Policy* (Washington, DC: Brookings Institution, 2012), 61–62.

10. David Shambaugh, "Coping with a Conflicted China," *Washington Quarterly* 34, no. 1 (Winter 2011): 7–27; M. Taylor Fravel, "China's Search for Military Power," *Washington Quarterly* 33, no. 3 (Summer 2008): 125–41; briefings by Major General Luo Yuan and Senior Colonel Fan Gaoyue of the Academy of Military Science, Georgetown University, Washington, DC, October 2, 2008; People's Republic of China State Council Information Office, *China's National Defense in 2010*, 4.

11. Hu Xiao, "Japan and U.S. Told, Hands Off Taiwan," *China Daily*, March 7, 2005, 1; Academy of Military Science briefings, June 2008, October 2008; People's Republic of China State Council Information Office, *China's National Defense in 2004*; "Chinese FM Refutes Fallacies on the South China Sea Issue," *China Daily*, July 25, 2010, 1.

12. "China-Southeast Asia Relations," *Comparative Connections* 9, no. 3 (October 2007): 75, http://www.csis.org/pacfor.

13. "China-Southeast Asia Relations," *Comparative Connections* 10, no. 4 (January 2009), http://www.csis.org/pacfor.

14. Evan Medeiros, "Strategic Hedging and the Future of Asia-Pacific Stability," *Washington Quarterly* 29, no. 1 (Winter 2005–2006): 145–67; Elisabeth Bumiller, "U.S. Will Counter Chinese Arms Buildup," *New York Times*, January 8, 2011, http://www.nytimes.com.

15. Richard Bush and Michael O'Hanlon, *A War like No Other: The Truth about China's Challenge to America* (Hoboken, NJ: Wiley, 2007).

16. Dan Blumenthal, "Fear and Loathing in Asia," *Journal of International Security Affairs* (Spring 2006): 81–88; U.S. Department of Defense, *Military and Security Developments Involving the People's Republic of China, 2010*.

17. Godwin, "China as a Major Asian Power"; U.S. Department of Defense, *Military and Security Developments Involving the People's Republic of China, 2010*; Andrew Erickson and David Yang, "On the Verge of a Game-Changer," *Proceedings* 135, no. 5 (May 2009): 26–32.

18. Ashley J. Tellis and Travis Tanner, eds., *Strategic Asia 2012–13: China's Military Challenge* (Seattle: National Bureau of Asian Research, 2012).

19. Michael Swaine, "China's Regional Military Posture," in *Power Shift: China and Asia's New Dynamics*, ed. David Shambaugh (Berkeley: University of California Press, 2005), 266; David Michael Lampton, *The Three Faces of Chinese Power: Might, Money, and Minds* (Berkeley: University of California Press, 2008), 40–42.

20. David Shambaugh, "China's Military Modernization: Making Steady and Surprising Progress," in *Strategic Asia 2005–2006*, ed. Ashley Tellis and Michael Wills (Seattle: National Bureau of Asian Research, 2005), 67–104; Bates Gill, *Rising Star: China's New Security Diplomacy* (Washington, DC: Brookings Institution Press, 2007); Ashley Tellis, "China's Military Modernization and Asian Security," in *Strategic Asia 2012–13*, ed. Ashley J. Tellis and Travis Tanner (Seattle: National Bureau of Asian Research, 2012), 3–26.

21. The discussion here and in the following several paragraphs is adapted from Swaine, "China's Regional Military Posture," 268–72; see also U.S. Department of Defense, *Military and Security Developments Involving the People's Republic of China, 2010*.

22. "Document: China's Military Strategy."

23. John Garver, *Foreign Relations of the People's Republic of China* (Englewood Cliffs, NJ: Prentice Hall, 1993), 249–64; Thomas Christensen, "Windows and War: Trend Analysis and Beijing's Use of Force," in *New Directions in the Study of China's Foreign Policy*, ed. Alastair Iain Johnston and Robert S. Ross (Stanford, CA: Stanford University Press, 2006), 50–85; Robert Sutter, *Foreign Relations of the PRC* (Lanham, MD: Rowman & Littlefield, 2013), 10–14.

24. Robert Suettinger, *Beyond Tiananmen: The Politics of U.S.-China Relations, 1989–2000* (Washington, DC: Brookings Institution Press, 2003), 200–263.

25. Michael Chase, Jeffrey Engstrom, Tai Ming Cheung, Kristen Gunness, Scott Harold, Susan Puska, and Samuel Berkowitz, *China's Incomplete Military Transformation* (Santa Monica, CA: RAND Corporation, 2015).

26. Aaron Friedberg, *Beyond Air-Sea Battle: The Debate over U.S. Military Strategy in Asia* (New York: Routledge, 2014), 91–93.

27. Michael Swaine, "Chinese Views of Weapons of Mass Destruction," in U.S. National Intelligence Council, *China and Weapons of Mass Destruction: Implications for the United States*, Conference Report (Washington, DC: U.S. National Intelligence Council, November 5, 1999), 165–82; Bates Gill, "China and Nuclear Arms Control," *SIPRI Insights* 2010/4 (April 2010); M. Taylor Fravel and Evan Medeiros, "China's Search for Assured Retaliation," *International Security* 35, no. 2 (Fall 2010): 48–87.

28. Evan Medeiros, *Reluctant Restraint: The Evolution of China's Nonproliferation Policies and Practices, 1980–2004* (Stanford, CA: Stanford University Press, 2007).

29. The following section on China's development of WMD capabilities draws from Shirley Kan, *China and Proliferation of Weapons of Mass Destruction and Missiles: Policy Issues*, Congressional Research Service Report RL31555 (Washington, DC: Library of Congress, January 5, 2015). For Chinese views, see the periodic defense white papers referenced previously.

30. Bates Gill and James Mulvenon, "The Chinese Strategic Rocket Forces: Transition to Credible Deterrence," in U.S. National Intelligence Council, *China and Weapons of Mass Destruction*, 11–58; Shambaugh, "China's Military Modernization," 89–94.

31. William S. Murray, "Revisiting Taiwan's Defense Strategy," *Naval War College Review* 61, no. 3 (Summer 2008): 13–38; Ronald O'Rourke, *China's Naval Modernization*, Congressional Research Service Report RL33153 (Washington, DC: Library of Congress, December 23, 2014).

32. Eric Croddy, "Chinese Chemical and Biological Warfare (CBW) Capabilities," in U.S. National Intelligence Council, *China and Weapons of Mass Destruction*, 59–110; Kan, *China and Proliferation*, 16–18.

33. Medeiros, *Reluctant Restraint*; Kan, *China and Proliferation*.

34. See, among others, Bill Gertz, "U.S. Hits China with Sanctions over Arms Sales," *Washington Times*, January 25, 2002, and "CIA Sees Rise in Terrorist Weapons," *Washington Times*, January 31, 2002.

35. Kan, *China and Proliferation*, summary page.

36. Evan Medeiros, "The Changing Character of China's WMD Proliferation Activities," in U.S. National Intelligence Council, *China and Weapons of Mass Destruction*, 135–38; Kan, *China and Proliferation*.

37. Bates Gill, "Two Steps Forward, One Step Back: The Dynamics of Chinese Nonproliferation and Arms Control Policy-Making in an Era of Reform," in *The Making of Chinese Foreign and Security Policy in the Era of Reform*, ed. David Michael Lampton (Stanford, CA: Stanford University Press, 2001), 257–88; Garver, *Foreign Relations of the People's Republic of China*, 249–64.

38. Kan, *China and Proliferation*, 2–3.

39. Medeiros, "The Changing Character of China's WMD Proliferation Activities"; Kan, *China and Proliferation*.

40. Kan, *China and Proliferation*, 2–3, 7–18, 18–49.

41. Robert Sutter, *China's Rise in Asia: Promises and Perils* (Lanham, MD: Rowman & Littlefield, 2005), 77–94; Andrew Small, "China's Caution on Afghanistan-Pakistan," *Washington Quarterly* 33, no. 3 (July 2010): 81–97; "China Says Bin Laden's Death a Milestone for Anti-terrorism," *China Daily*, May 3, 2011, http://www.chinadaily.com.cn.

42. Zhao Huasheng, "Chinese View of Post 2014 Afghanistan," *Asia Policy* 17 (January 2014), http://www.nbr.org/publications/element.aspx?id=725.

43. Garver, *Foreign Relations of the People's Republic of China*, 168–73.

44. Bates Gill and Melissa Murphy, "China's Evolving Approach to Counterterrorism," *Harvard Asia Quarterly* (Winter–Spring 2005): 21–22.

45. Andrew Scobell, "Terrorism and Chinese Foreign Policy," in *China Rising: Power and Motivation in Chinese Foreign Policy*, ed. Yong Deng and Fei-Ling Wang (Lanham, MD: Rowman & Littlefield, 2005), 315.

46. Sutter, *China's Rise in Asia*, 256–59; Gill, *Rising Star*, 37–47.

47. Gill and Murphy, "China's Evolving Approach to Counterterrorism," 25–28; Scobell, "Terrorism and Chinese Foreign Policy," 311–18; "China Thanks Nations for Support for Olympic Security," *China Daily*, September 11, 2008, http://www.chinadaily.com.cn.

48. Kenneth Allen and Eric McVadon, *China's Foreign Military Relations*, Report 32 (Washington, DC: Henry Stimson Center, October 1999); Kristen Gunness, *China's Military Diplomacy in an Era of Change* (Alexandria, VA: CNA Corporation, 2006); Gill, *Rising Star*; People's Republic of China State Council Information Office, *China's National Defense in 2010*.

49. "Russia-China Relations," *Russian Analytical Digest* 73 (February 23, 2010), http://www.isn.ethz.ch; Shirley Kan, *U.S.-China Military Contacts: Issues for Congress*, Congressional Research Service Report RL32496 (Washington, DC: Library of Congress, June 10, 2014).

50. David Shambaugh, "China-Europe Relations Get Complicated," *Brookings Northeast Asia Commentary* 9 (May 2007), http://www.brookings.edu; U.S. Department of Defense–Israeli Ministry of Defense Joint Press Statement, News Release No. 846-05 (Washington, DC: U.S. Department of Defense, August 16, 2005).

51. Richard Grimmett, *Conventional Arms Transfers to Developing Nations*, Congressional Research Service Report RL34187 (Washington, DC: Library of Congress, September 26, 2007); U.S. Department of Defense, *Military and Security Developments Involving the People's Republic of China*, 9; "China Becomes the World's Third Largest Arms Exporter," *BBC News*, March 15, 2015, http://sinosphere.blogs.nytimes.com/2015/03/16/china-becomes-worlds-third-largest-arms-exporter/?_r=0.

52. Robert Sutter, *Chinese Policy Priorities and Their Implications for the United States* (Lanham, MD: Rowman & Littlefield, 2000), 192–93.

53. Kenneth Allen, *Showing the Red Flag: The PLA Navy as an Instrument of China's Foreign Policy* (Alexandria, VA: Center for Naval Analysis, 2003); Kenneth Allen, "PLA Air Force Foreign Relations," *Chinese Military Update* 3, no. 1 (2005).

54. "China's Military Diplomacy Forging New Ties," *Xinhua*, October 28, 2002, replayed by FBIS Document ID: CPP20021028000111.

55. "China's Military Diplomacy in 2004," *People's Daily Online*, January 5, 2005, accessed January 6, 2005, http://english.people.com.cn; People's Republic of China State Council Information Office, *China's National Defense in 2010*; Zhao Shengnan, "Military Outreach Gets New Emphasis," *China Daily*, February 2, 2015, http://www.chinadaily.com.cn/cndy/2015-02/02/content_19462377.htm.

56. International Crisis Group, *China's Growing Role in UN Peacekeeping*, Asia Report 166 (Brussels: International Crisis Group, April 17, 2009); Gill, *Rising Star*, 200–202; People's Republic of China State Council Information Office, *China's National Defense in 2010*.

57. Allen Carlson, "More Than Just Saying No: China's Evolving Approach to Sovereignty and Intervention," in *New Directions in the Study of China's Foreign Policy*, ed. Alastair Iain Johnston and Robert S. Ross (Stanford, CA: Stanford University Press, 2006), 217–41.

58. Huang Jingjing, "Keeping Peace in the Sahara," *Global Times*, November 12, 2014, http://backup.globaltimes.cn/DesktopModules/DnnForge%20-%20NewsArticles/Print.aspx?tabid=99&tabmoduleid=94&articleId=891479&moduleId=405&PortalID=0; "China Peacekeepers in South Sudan to Focus on Protecting Civilians," *Voice of America*, January 15, 2015, http://www.voanews.com/content/south-sudan-china-peacekeepers-unmiss/2599640.html.

59. "China Supports in UN Peacekeeping Operations," *China Daily*, March 31, 2011, http://www.chinadaily.com.cn; International Crisis Group, *China's Growing Role in UN Peacekeeping*; "Nation to Chip in More for UN Kitty," *China Daily*, December 31, 2009, 2.

60. Joseph Logan and Patrick Worsnip, "Anger after Russia, China Block UN Action on Syria," *Reuters*, February 5, 2012, http://www.reuters.com/article/2012/02/05/us-syria-idUSTRE80S08620120205.

6. RELATIONS WITH THE UNITED STATES

1. Robert Zoellick, "Whither China: From Membership to Responsibility," speech, September 21, 2005, http://2001-2009.state.gov/s/d/former/zoellick/rem/53682.htm; Elizabeth Economy and Adam Segal, "The G-2 Mirage," *Foreign Affairs* (May–June 2009), http://www.foreignaffairs.com/articles/64996/elizabeth-c-economy-and-adam-segal/the-g-2-mirage.

2. The findings of this chapter are treated in greater depth in Robert Sutter, *U.S.-Chinese Relations* (Lanham, MD: Rowman & Littlefield, 2013). For other perspectives see among others, David Shambaugh, ed., *Tangled Titans* (Lanham, MD: Rowman & Littlefield, 2012).

3. Michael Schaller, *The United States and China: Into the Twenty-First Century* (New York: Oxford University Press, 2002), 204–5.

4. Robert Sutter, *U.S. Policy toward China* (Lanham, MD: Rowman & Littlefield, 1998), 26–44.

5. James Mann, *About Face* (New York: Knopf, 1999), 274–78. Authoritative assessments of U.S.–China relations in the 1990s include David Michael Lampton, *Same Bed, Different Dreams* (Berkeley: University of California Press, 2001) and Robert Suettinger, *Beyond Tiananmen* (Washington, DC: Brookings Institution, 2003).

6. For this and the next two paragraphs, see Robert Sutter, *Historical Dictionary of United States–China Relations* (Lanham, MD: Scarecrow Press, 2006), lxix–lxx.

7. Assessments of US–China relations in this period include Jeffrey Bader, *Obama and China's Rise* (Washington, DC: Brookings Institution, 2012); Martin Indyk, Kenneth Lieberthal, and Michael O'Hanlon, *Bending History: Barack Obama's Foreign Policy* (Washington, DC: Brookings Institution, 2012), 24–69; Aaron Friedberg, *A Contest for Supremacy* (New York: Norton, 2011); Kenneth Lieberthal and Wang Jisi, *Addressing U.S.-China Strategic Distrust* (Washington, DC: Brookings Institution, March 2012); Andrew Nathan and Andrew Scobell, *China's Search for Security* (New York: Columbia University Press, 2012); Denny Roy, *Return of the Dragon* (New York: Columbia University Press, 2013); Nina Hachigian, ed., *Debating China* (New York: Oxford University Press, 2014); and Thomas Christensen, *The China Challenge* (New York: Norton, 2015). See also Sutter, *U.S.-Chinese Relations* and Shambaugh, *Tangled Titans*.

8. On Bush's reliance on China to deal with North Korea, see "Bush, Kerry Square Off in 1st Debate," *Japan Today*, October 1, 2004, accessed March 21, 2008,http://www.japantoday.com/jp/news/313422/all.

9. Condoleezza Rice, remarks at Sophia University, Tokyo, Japan, March 19, 2005, accessed March 21, 2008,http://www.state.gov/secretary/rm/2005/43655.htm; Evan Medeiros, "Strategic Hedging and the Future of Asia-Pacific Stability," *Washington Quarterly* 29, no. 1 (2005–2006): 15–28.

10. Rosemary Foot, "Chinese Strategies in a U.S.-Hegemonic Global Order: Accommodating and Hedging," *International Affairs* 82, no. 1 (2006): 77–94; Wang Jisi, "China's Search for Stability with America," *Foreign Affairs* 84, no. 5 (September–October 2005): 39–48; Yong Deng and Thomas Moore, "China Views Globalization: Toward a New Great-Power Politics," *Washington Quarterly* 27, no. 3 (Summer 2004): 117–36.

11. Sutter, *U.S.-Chinese Relations*, 129–30.

12. For an overview of the Obama government's approach to China, see notably Bader, *Obama and China's Rise*.

13. Indyk, Lieberthal, and O'Hanlon, *Bending History*, 24–69.

14. Bonnie Glaser and Brittany Billingsley, "Friction and Cooperation Co-exist Uneasily," *Comparative Connections* 13, no. 2 (September 2011): 27–40; Minxin Pei, "China's Bumpy Ride Ahead," *The Diplomat*, February 16, 2011, http://www.the-diplomat.com; Robert Sutter, *Positive Equilibrium in U.S.-China Relations: Durable or Not?* (Baltimore: University of Maryland School of Law, 2010).

15. Bader, *Obama and China's Rise*, 69–129; "Interview of Hillary Clinton with Greg Sheridan of the *Australian*," November 8, 2010, http://www.state.gov.

16. Elisabeth Bumiller, "U.S. Will Counter Chinese Arms Buildup," *New York Times*, January 8, 2011, http://www.nytimes.com; David Sanger, "Superpower and Upstart: Sometimes It Ends Well," *New York Times*, January 22, 2011, http://www.nytimes.com.

17. Sanger, "Superpower and Upstart"; "Beyond the US-China Summit," *Foreign Policy Research Institute*, February 4, 2011, http://www.fpri.org.

18. Bonnie Glaser and Brittany Billingsley, "Strains Increase and Leadership Transitions," *Comparative Connections* 14, no. 3 (January 2012): 29–40; Mark Manyin, coord., *Pivot to the Pacific? The Obama Administration's "Rebalancing" Toward Asia*, Report R42448 (Washington, DC: Library of Congress, Congressional Research Service, March 28, 2012).

19. Reviewed in Sutter, *U.S.-Chinese Relations*, 166–69.

20. Kenneth Lieberthal and Wang Jisi, *Addressing U.S.-China Strategic Distrust* (Washington, DC: Brookings Institution, March 2012).

21. Don Keyser, "President Obama's Re-election: Outlook for U.S. China Relations in the Second Term," China Policy Institute, Nottingham University, UK, November 7, 2012, http://blogs.nottingham.ac.uk/chinapolicyinstitute/2012/11/07/present-obamas-re-election-outlook-for-u-s-china-relations-in-the-second-term.

22. Ralph Cossa and Brad Glosserman, "Regional Overview," *Comparative Connections* 14, no. 3 (January 2013): 1–12; Bonnie Glaser and Brittany Billingsley, "US-China Relations: Strains Increase amid Leadership Transitions," *Comparative Connections* 14, no. 3 (January 2013): 29–40.

23. Daljit Singh, "US-China Dialogue Process: Prospects and Implications," *East Asia Forum*, November 2, 2012, http://www.eastasisforum.org.

24. Richard Bush, *Unchartered Strait* (Washington, DC: Brookings Institution, 2013), 213–50.

25. Aries Poon, Jenny Hsu, and Fanny Liu, "Taiwan Election Results Likely to Complicate Relations with China," *Wall Street Journal*, December 1, 2014, http://www.wsj.com/articles/taiwan-election-results-set-to-complicate-relations-with-china-1417366150.

26. Bonnie Glaser and Brittany Billingsley, "Xi Visit Steadies Ties; Dissident Creates Tension," *Comparative Connections* 14, no. 1 (May 2012): 29–30; Bonnie Glaser and Brittany Billingsley, "Creating a New Type of Great Power Relations," *Comparative Connections* 14, no. 2 (September 2012): 29.

27. Donilon's speech and U.S. officials' media briefing on the president's Asia trip were released on November 15, 2012, at http://www.whitehouse.gov/the-press-office.

28. Among treatments of this subject, see Timothy Adamson, "China's Response to the U.S. Rebalance," in *Balancing Acts: The U.S. Rebalance and Asia-Pacific Stability*, ed. Robert Sutter, Michael Brown, and Timothy Adamson (Washington, DC: George Washington University, Elliott School of International Affairs, 2013), 39–43.

29. "China-Southeast Asia Relations," *Comparative Connections* 16, no. 2 (September 2014): 59–61.

30. Aaron L. Friedberg, *Contest for Supremacy: China, America and the Struggle for Mastery in Asia* (New York: Norton, 2011); Andrew Nathan, review of *The China Choice*, by Hugh White, *Foreign Affairs*, January–February 2013, http://www.foreignaffairs.com/articles/138661/hugh-white/the-china-choice-why-america-should-share-power.

31. See the treatment of these preoccupations in, among others, David M. Lampton, *Following the Leader: Ruling China from Deng Xiaoping to Xi Jinping* (Berkeley: University of California Press, 2014), and Andrew J. Nathan and Andrew Scobell, *China's Search for Security* (New York: Columbia University Press, 2012).

32. Ben Blanchard and John Ruwitch, "China Hikes Defense Budget, to Spend More on Internal Security," *Reuters*, March 5, 2013, http://www.reuters.com/article/2013/03/05/us-china-parliament-defence-idUSBRE92403620130305.

33. Stephen Roach, "China's Policy Disharmony," *Project Syndicate*, December 31, 2013, http://www.project-syndicate.org.

34. This dualism and respective Gulliver strategies are discussed in Robert Sutter, "China and U.S. Security and Economic Interests: Opportunities and Challenges," in *U.S.-China-EU Relations: Managing the New World Order*, ed. Robert Ross and Oystein Tunsjo (London:

Routledge, 2010); see also James Shinn, *Weaving the Net* (New York: Council on Foreign Relations, 1996).

35. Robert Sutter, *Chinese Foreign Relations: Power and Policy since the Cold War*, 3rd ed. (Lanham, MD: Rowman & Littlefield, 2012), 3–13.

36. Such assessments of Chinese military capabilities include those by the Department of Defense, the Congressional Research Service (CRS), the Center for Strategic and International Studies (CSIS), and the Carnegie Endowment, which portray growing challenges and sometimes dire implications for the United States. The Defense Department assessments are annual; see http://www.defense.gov/pubs/2013_china_report_final.pdf. The CRS report is updated regularly; see http://fpc.state.gov/documents/organization/207068.pdf. The CSIS report is available at http://csis.org/publication/chinese-military-modernization-and-force-development-1; the Carnegie report is available at http://carnegieendowment.org/files/net_assessment_full.pdf.

37. Manyin, *Pivot to the Pacific?*; Phillip Saunders, *The Rebalance to Asia: U.S.-China Relations and Regional Security* (Washington, DC: National Defense University, Institute for National Security Studies, 2012). This section summarizes findings in Robert Sutter, *Foreign Relations of the PRC* (Lanham, MD: Rowman & Littlefield, 2013), 1–26, 311–27.

38. For a more detailed explanation of these findings, see Sutter, *Foreign Relations of the PRC*, 13–14.

39. Gilbert Rozman, *East Asian National Identities: Common Roots and Chinese Exceptionalism* (Stanford, CA: Stanford University Press, 2013).

40. Peter Ford, "Japan Abandons Bid to Make China a Key Pillar of Its Foreign Policy," *Christian Science Monitor*, November 17, 2010, http://www.csmonitor.com; James Przystup, "Japan-China Relations," *Comparative Connections* 14, no. 3 (January 2013): 109–17.

41. Lawrence Saez and Crystal Chang, "China and South Asia: Strategic Implications and Economic Imperatives," in *China, the Developing World, and the New Global Dynamic*, ed. Lowell Dittmer and George Yu (Boulder, CO: Rienner, 2010), 83–108; John Garver and Feiling Wang, "China's Anti-encirclement Struggle," *Asian Security* 6, no. 3 (2010): 238–63; Ashley Tellis, *India as a Global Power: An Action Agenda for the United States* (Washington, DC: Carnegie Endowment for International Peace, 2005).

42. Yu Bin, "China-Russia Relations: Guns and Games of August; Tales of Two Strategic Partners," *Comparative Connections* 10, no. 3 (October 2008): 131–38; Yu Bin, "China-Russia Relations: Putin's Glory and Xi's Dream," *Comparative Connections* 14, no. 1 (May 2014): 121–33.

43. Richard Bush, *Unchartered Strait* (Washington, DC: Brookings Institution, 2013).

44. Scott Snyder, "China-Korea Relations," *Comparative Connections* 12, no. 4 (January 2011), http://www.csis.org/pacfor; Scott Snyder, "China-Korea Relations," *Comparative Connections* 14, no. 1 (May 2014): 87–94.

45. Linda Jakobson, "Australia-China Ties: In Search of Political Trust," *Policy Brief* (Sydney: Lowy Institute, June 2012).

46. Sutter, *Foreign Relations of the PRC*, 319.

47. Yu Yongding, "A Different Road Forward," *China Daily*, December 23, 2010, 9.

48. Scott Snyder, "China's Post-Kim Jong Il Debate," *Comparative Connections* 12, no. 1 (May 2012): 107–14; Snyder, "China-Korea Relations," 87–94.

49. Robert Sutter, "Assessing China's Rise and U.S. Influence in Asia: Growing Maturity and Balance," *Journal of Contemporary China* 19, no. 65 (June 2010): 591–604; Sutter, *Foreign Relations of the PRC*, 321–26; Michael Beckley, "China's Century? Why America's Edge Will Endure," *International Security* 36, no. 3 (Winter 2011–2012): 41–78.

50. Author's findings based on interviews with over two hundred officials from ten Asia-Pacific countries discussed most recently in Robert Sutter, *Foreign Relations of the PRC*, 321–26.

51. During a speech in Manila in December 2013, Secretary of State John Kerry highlighted the millions of dollars of assistance to Philippine storm victims coming from such U.S. business partners as Coca-Cola, Proctor & Gamble, Dow Chemical, FedEx, Cargill, and Citibank. "Kerry Speaks in the Philippines," *Asian American Press*, December 17, 2013, http://aapress.com/ethnicity/filipino/kerry-speaks-in-the-philippines.

52. On Sino-American differences over these issues, see Susan Lawrence, *U.S.-China Relations: An Overview of Policy Issues*, Congressional Research Service Report R41108 (Washington, DC: Library of Congress, August 1, 2013); Sutter, *U.S.-Chinese Relations*, 183–272.

53. Andrew Dugan, "Americans View China Mostly Unfavorably," *Gallup Politics*, February 20, 2014, http://www.gallup.com/poll/167498/americans-view-china-mostly-unfavorably.aspx.

54. Vance Serchuk, "Obama's Silence on Taiwan Masks Its Significance in U.S. Relations with China," *Washington Post*, May 23, 2013, http://www.washingtonpost.com/opinions/obamas-silence-on-taiwan-masks-its-significance-in-us-relations-with-china/2013/05/23/a1b40470-c243-11e2-914f-a7aba60512a7_story.html; Daniel Russel, "U.S. Policy towards East Asia and the Pacific: Remarks at Baltimore Council on Foreign Affairs," Department of State Diplomacy in Action, May 29, 2014, http://www.state.gov/p/eap/rls/rm/2014/05/226887.htm; U.S. China Economic and Security Review Commission Hearing, "China and the Evolving Security Dynamics in East Asia," March 13, 2014, http://origin.www.uscc.gov/sites/default/files/transcripts/Hearing%20Transcript_March%2013%2C2014_0.pdf.

55. "China Very Aggressively Gaming World Trading System," *Economic Times*, October 7, 2011, accessed June 12, 2015, http://articles.economictimes.indiatimes.com/2011-10-07/news/30254012_1_currency-manipulation-trading-system-trade-deal.

56. For a review of the issues and disputes, see Lawrence, *U.S.-China Relations: An Overview of Policy Issues*.

7. RELATIONS WITH TAIWAN

1. Authoritative Chinese statements regarding Taiwan include People's Republic of China State Council Taiwan Affairs Office and Information Office, *The Taiwan Question and the Reunification of China*, September 1, 1993, http://www.gwytb.gov.cn, and *The One-China Principle and the Taiwan Issue*, February 21, 2000, http://www.gwytb.gov.cn; People's Republic of China State Council Information Office, *China's National Defense in 2002* (Beijing: People's Republic of China State Council Information Office, December 9, 2002); *China's National Defense in 2004* (Beijing: People's Republic of China State Council Information Office, December 27, 2004); *China's National Defense in 2006* (Beijing: People's Republic of China State Council Information Office, December 29, 2006); *China's National Defense in 2008* (Beijing: People's Republic of China State Council Information Office, January 2009); *China's National Defense in 2010* (Beijing: People's Republic of China State Council Information Office, March 2011); the 2005 Chinese Anti-Secession Law, text carried by *BBC News*, March 14, 2005, http://news.bbc.co.uk/2/hi/asia-pacific/4347555.stm; "Join Hands to Promote Peaceful Development of Cross-Strait Relations," speech by Hu Jintao, *Xinhua*, December 31, 2008.

2. Susan Shirk, *China: Fragile Superpower* (New York: Oxford University Press, 2007), 181–211.

3. Richard Bush, *Unchartered Strait* (Washington, DC: Brookings Institution, 2013); Richard Bush, "Hong Kong: Examining the Impact of the 'Umbrella Movement,'" testimony before the Subcommittee on East Asian and Pacific Affairs, U.S. Senate Foreign Relations Committee, December 3, 2014, http://www.brookings.edu/research/testimony/2014/12/03-hong-kong-umbrella-movement-bush; Shirley Kan and Wayne Morrison, *U.S.-Taiwan Relationship: Overview of Policy Issues*, Congressional Research Service Report R41952 (Washington, DC: Library of Congress, December 11, 2014); Shelley Rigger, "Coming Attractions: Election Season Hits Taiwan," Foreign Policy Research Institute *E-Notes*, June 2015, http://www.fpri.org/articles/2015/06/coming-attractions-election-season-hits-taiwan.

4. Robert Sutter, "More American Attention to Taiwan amid Heightened Competition with China," *American Journal of Chinese Studies* 22, no. 1 (April 2015): 1–16; Rigger, "Coming Attractions."

5. For Chinese perspectives, see, among others, Deng Xiaoping, "An Idea for the Peaceful Reunification of the Chinese Mainland and Taiwan," remarks delivered June 26, 1983, in

Selected Works of Deng Xiaoping (vol. 3, 1982–1992) (Beijing: Foreign Languages Press, 1994), 40–41; "One Country—Two Systems," remarks delivered June 22–23, 1984, in *Selected Works of Deng Xiaoping* (vol. 3, 1982–1992) , 70–71; and "Shemma Wenti Dou Keyi Taolun: Qian Qichen Fuzongli Jieshou 'Huashengdun Youbao' Jizhe Pan Wen Caifang," *Shijie Zhishi* 3 (February 2001): 14. For Taiwanese perspectives, see, among others, Lee Teng-hui, *Creating the Future: Towards a New Era for the Chinese People* (Taipei: Government Information Office, 1992); Zou Jingwen, *Li Denghui Zhizheng Gaobai Shilu* (Taipei: INK, 2001); and Su Chi, *Taiwan's Relations with Mainland China: A Tail Wagging Two Dogs* (London: Routledge, 2008).

6. For Chinese perspectives, see, among others, Deng Xiaoping, "An Idea for the Peaceful Reunification of the Chinese Mainland and Taiwan"; "One Country—Two Systems"; and "Shemma Wenti Dou Keyi Taolun." For Taiwanese perspectives, see, among others, Lee Teng-hui, *Creating the Future*; Zou Jingwen, *Li Denghui Zhizheng Gaobai Shilu*; and Su Chi, *Taiwan's Relations with Mainland China*.

7. Charles Freeman, "Preventing War in the Taiwan Strait," *Foreign Affairs* 77, no. 4 (July–August 1998): 6–11; Steven Goldstein, *Taiwan Faces the Twenty-first Century* (New York: Foreign Policy Association, 1997).

8. Nancy Bernkopf Tucker, "China-Taiwan: U.S. Debates and Policy Choices," *Survival* 40, no. 4 (Winter 1998–1999): 150–67.

9. John Garver, *Face-Off* (Seattle: University of Washington Press, 1997); Harvey Feldman, "Cross-Strait Relations with Taiwan: Implications for U.S. Policy," in *Between Diplomacy and Deterrence: Strategies for U.S. Relations with China*, ed. Kim Holmes and James Przystup (Washington, DC: Heritage Foundation, 1997), 141–62.

10. Robert Sutter, *Taiwan: Recent Developments and U.S. Policy Choices*, Congressional Research Service Issue Brief 98034 (Washington, DC: Library of Congress, December 29, 1999).

11. Ralph Clough, *Cooperation or Conflict in the Taiwan Strait?* (Lanham, MD: Rowman & Littlefield, 1999).

12. Robert Sutter, *Chinese Policy Priorities and Their Implications for the United States* (Lanham, MD: Rowman & Littlefield, 2000), 106.

13. *Taiwan–Mainland China Talks: Competing Approaches and Implications for U.S. Policy*, Congressional Research Service Report 98-887 (Washington, DC: Library of Congress, November 22, 1998).

14. Sutter, *Taiwan*.

15. Denny Roy, *Taiwan: A Political History* (Ithaca, NY: Cornell University Press, 2003), 235.

16. President Chen's many pronouncements and media interviews dealing with cross-strait issues and concurrent Chinese statements and pronouncements regarding Taiwan are assessed in Richard Bush, *Untying the Knot: Making Peace in the Taiwan Strait* (Washington, DC: Brookings Institution Press, 2005), 57–71, and in Steven Goldstein and Julian Chang, eds., *Presidential Politics in Taiwan: The Administration of Chen Shui-bian* (Norwalk, CT: East-Bridge, 2008).

17. David G. Brown, "Of Economics and Elections," *Comparative Connections* 3, no. 3 (October 2001), http://www.csis.org/pacfor.

18. Bruce Gilley and Maureen Pao, "Defenses Weaken," *Far Eastern Economic Review*, October 4, 2001, http://www.feer.com; Yu-Shan Wu, "Taiwan in 2000," *Asian Survey* 41, no. 1 (January–February 2001): 40–48.

19. David G. Brown, "Strains over Cross-Strait Relations," *Comparative Connections* 5, no. 4 (January 2004), http://www.csis.org/pacfor; T. J. Cheng, "China-Taiwan Economic Linkage," in *Dangerous Strait: The U.S.-Taiwan-China Crisis*, ed. Nancy Bernkopf Tucker (New York: Columbia University Press, 2005), 93–130.

20. Nancy Bernkopf Tucker, *Strait Talk: United States–Taiwan Relations and the Crisis with China* (Cambridge, MA: Harvard University Press, 2009); Philip Yang, "Cross-Strait Relations under the First Chen Administration," in Goldstein and Chang, *Presidential Politics in Taiwan*, 211–22.

21. Consultations with twenty U.S. officials with responsibility for assessing Taiwan–China relations and their implications for U.S. interests, October–November 2004; consultations and interviews with U.S. officials responsible for Taiwan affairs, Washington, DC, March–May 2005; interviews with Chinese officials and specialists in Vail, Colorado, (October 2003), Beijing and Shanghai (May–June 2004), and Washington, DC (August–November 2004); David G. Brown, "China-Taiwan Relations: Campaign Fallout," *Comparative Connections* 6, no. 4 (January 2005), http://www.csis.org/pacfor; Shi Yinhong, "Beijing's Lack of Sufficient Deterrence to Taiwan Leaves a Major Danger," *Ta Kung Pao* (Hong Kong), June 23, 2004.

22. Brown, "China-Taiwan Relations."

23. China's Anti-Secession Law of March 2005 was among the PRC pronouncements that displayed firmness against Taiwan's moves toward independence mixed with signs of flexibility on cross-strait issues. Notably, Chinese President Hu Jintao was said to have moved away from considering a timetable for Taiwan's reunification with China, which had been discussed during the leadership of Jiang Zemin (who left the last of his major leadership posts in 2004). Interviews with Chinese officials and specialists and U.S. government officials and specialists, Washington, DC, March–June 2005.

24. Thomas Christensen, "China," in *Strategic Asia 2001–2002*, ed. Richard Ellings and Aaron Friedberg (Seattle: National Bureau of Asian Research, 2001), 47–51; International Crisis Group, "Taiwan Strait I: What's Left of 'One China'?" *Asia Report* 53 (Brussels: International Crisis Group, June 6, 2003), 17–22; Alan Wachman, *Why Taiwan? Geostrategic Rationales for China's Territorial Integrity* (Stanford, CA: Stanford University Press, 2007).

25. Consultations with thirty Taiwanese government officials and specialists in Taiwan in May–June 2004, with twenty such officials and specialists visiting the United States in 2004–2005, and twenty such officials and specialists in Taipei in May–June 2005.

26. Brown, "China-Taiwan Relations"; interviews with Chinese government officials and specialists, Washington, DC, January–March 2004.

27. Interviews, Beijing and Shanghai, May 2004.

28. At that time, Taiwan media reported that George Bush had used an epithet to refer to Chen Shui-bian (Brown, "China-Taiwan Relations").

29. International Crisis Group, "China-Taiwan: Uneasy Détente," *Asia Briefing* 42 (Brussels: International Crisis Group, September 21, 2005).

30. Michael Swaine, "Managing Relations with the United States," in Goldstein and Chang, *Presidential Politics in Taiwan*, 197–98.

31. Steven Goldstein, "Postscript: Chen Shui-bian and the Political Transition in Taiwan," in Goldstein and Chang, *Presidential Politics in Taiwan*, 296–98.

32. Goldstein, "Postscript," 299–304.

33. David Brown, "Taiwan Voters Set a New Course," *Comparative Connections* 10, no. 1 (April 2008): 75.

34. For a comprehensive assessment of cross-strait relations under the Ma government, see Bush, *Unchartered Strait*; see also Dennis Hickey, "Beijing's Evolving Policy toward Taipei: Engagement or Entrapment," *Issues and Studies* 45, no. 1 (March 2009): 31–70; Alan Romberg, "Cross-Strait Relations: 'Ascend the Heights and Take a Long-Term Perspective,'" *China Leadership Monitor* 27 (Winter 2009), http://www.chinaleadershipmonitor.org; interviews and consultations with international affairs officials, including repeated meetings with senior officers up to minister level, Taipei (May, July, August, and December 2008; April 2009).

35. David Brown, "Economic Cooperation Framework Agreement Signed," *Comparative Connections* 12, no. 2 (July 2010): 77–79.

36. David Brown, "Looking Ahead to 2012," *Comparative Connections* 12, no. 4 (January 2011), http://www.csis.org/pacfor.

37. Donald Zagoria, *Trip to Seoul, Taipei, Beijing, Shanghai, and Tokyo—May 8–25, 2010* (New York: National Committee on American Foreign Policy, 2010), 2–6.

38. Interviews and consultations with international affairs officials, including repeated meetings with senior officers up to minister level, Taipei (May, July, August, and December 2008; April 2009).

39. Shirley Kan, *Taiwan: Major U.S. Arms Sales since 1990*, Congressional Research Service Report RL30957 (Washington, DC: Library of Congress, August 29, 2014); Kathrin Hille

and Demetri Sevastopulo, "U.S. and China Set to Resume Military Talks," *Financial Times*, June 21, 2009, http://www.ft.com.

40. Interviews and consultations, Taiwan, December 2008, April 2009; David Shear, "Cross-Strait Relations in a New Era of Negotiation," remarks at the Carnegie Endowment for International Peace, Washington, DC, July 7, 2010, http://www.state.gov.

41. Bonnie Glaser, "The Honeymoon Ends," *Comparative Connections* 12, no. 1 (April 2010): 23–27.

42. Kan, *Taiwan: Major U.S. Arms Sales*.

43. Shirley Kan and Wayne Morrison, *U.S.-Taiwan Relationship: Overview of Policy Issues*, Congressional Research Service Report R41952 (Washington, DC: Library of Congress, April 22, 2014), 26.

44. Jason Pan, "Reliance on China Makes Taiwan Vulnerable: Clinton," *Taipei Times*, June 25, 2014, 1.

45. Kan and Morrison, *U.S.-Taiwan Relationship*, 40–41.

46. Kan and Morrison, *U.S.-Taiwan Relationship*, 41–42.

47. Wei-chin Lee, *The Mutual Non-denial Principle, China's Interests, and Taiwan's Expansion of International Participation* (Baltimore, MD: University of Maryland Carey School of Law, 2014).

48. David Brunnstrom, "Taiwan Presidential Hopeful Seeks to Ease U.S. Concerns on China," *Reuters*, June 3, 2015, http://www.reuters.com/article/2015/06/03/us-taiwan-china-usa-idUSKBN0OJ30H20150603.

49. Taken from Sutter, "More American Attention to Taiwan."

50. Sutter, "More American Attention to Taiwan," 6.

51. Kan and Morrison, *U.S.-Taiwan Relationship*, 14.

52. "Upsetting China," *The Economist*, April 27, 2001, http://www.economist.com/node/594078.

53. William Lowther, "U.S. Senator Not Convinced on F-16 Bid," *Taipei Times*, September 23, 2010.

54. "Senator Questions Arms Sales to Taiwan," *Reuters*, June 16, 2010.

55. Kerry Dumbaugh, "Underlying Strains in Taiwan-U.S. Political Relations," Congressional Research Service Report RL33684 (Washington, DC: Library of Congress, April 20, 2007); Robert Sutter, "Taiwan's Future: Narrowing Straits," *NBR Analysis*, May 2001, 19–22.

56. "A Way Ahead with China: Steering the Right Course with the Middle Kingdom," recommendations from the Miller Center for Public Affairs Roundtable, Miller Center for Public Affairs, University of Virginia, March 2011; Charles Glaser, "Will China's Rise Lead to War?" *Foreign Affairs* 90, no. 2 (March–April 2011): 80–91; Michael Swaine, *America's Challenge* (Washington, DC: Carnegie Endowment for International Peace, 2011); Bill Owens, "America Must Start Treating China as a Friend," *Financial Times*, November 17, 2009, http://www.ft.com.

57. Daniel Russel, "Evaluating U.S. Policy on Taiwan on the 35th Anniversary of the Taiwan Relations Act," testimony before the Senate Committee on Foreign Affairs Subcommittee on East Asian and Pacific Affairs, April 3, 2014; Joseph Yeh, "Taiwan Lauded for Response to Beijing ADIZ Move: AIT," *China Post*, December 14, 2013, http://www.chinapost.com.tw.

58. Josh Hicks, "Obama Foreign Policy Sparks Bi-Partisan Criticism," *Washington Post*, August 31, 2014, http://www.washingtonpost.com; "Inviting an Asian Crimea," *Wall Street Journal*, April 6, 2014, http://www.wsj.com; William Lowther, "US Senator Rubio Seeks Answers on the 'Six Assurances,'" *Taipei Times*, April 5, 2014, 1; William Lowther, "US Academic Warns over Pace, Extent of Cross Strait Moves," *Taipei Times*, June 20, 2014, 3.

59. Dean Cheng, "Taiwan's Maritime Security," *Heritage Foundation Backgrounder*, March 19, 2014, http://www.heritage.org/research/reports/2014/03/taiwans-maritime-security-a-critical-american-interest.

60. William Lowther, "US Study Urges 'Offshore Control' Strategy for China," *Taipei Times*, January 12, 2014, 3.

61. Toshi Yishihara, *Going Anti-Access at Sea: How Japan Can Turn the Tables on China* (Washington, DC: Center for a New American Security, September 2014).

62. Wendell Minnick, "US Might Tap into Taiwan Early Warning Radar," *Defense News*, May 8, 2014.

63. Jeffrey Bader, "The U.S. and China's Nine-Dash Line," Brookings Institution, February 6, 2014, http://www.brookings.edu/research/opinions/2014/02/06-us-china-nine-dash-line-bader; Bonnie Glaser, "A Role for Taiwan in Promoting Peace in the South China Sea," *PacNet* 30, April 16, 2014.

64. The options noted below are discussed in Robert Sutter, "Dealing with America's China Problem in Asia—Target China's Vulnerabilities," *PacNet* 58, July 21, 2014.

65. The author thanks the Taiwan Economic and Cultural Representative Office (TECRO) in Washington, DC for their assistance in filling out the full scope of these interchanges.

66. Kan and Morrison, *U.S.-Taiwan Relationship*, 25.

67. Kan and Morrison, *U.S.-Taiwan Relationship*, 16; information provided by TECRO.

68. Kan and Morrison, *U.S.-Taiwan Relationship*, 15–16; 26–28.

69. William Lowther, "US Report Supports TPP Membership," *Taipei Times*, April 19, 2014, 1.

70. Author interviews, Washington, DC, August 22, August 28, September 5, 2014.

71. Jim Wolf, "Senior U.S. Senator Faults Taiwan over Arms 'Complacency,'" *Reuters*, February 11, 2013, http://www.reuters.com.

72. William Lowther, "Taiwan Slipping Off US Agenda: Panel," *Taipei Times*, April 13, 2013, 3.

73. Dan Blumenthal, "5 Faulty Assumptions about Taiwan," *Foreign Policy*, February 12, 2014.

74. John Mearscheimer, "Say Goodbye to Taiwan," *National Interest*, February 25, 2014.

75. Timothy Adamson, Michael Brown, and Robert Sutter, *Rebooting the U.S. Rebalance to Asia* (Washington, DC: George Washington University Elliott School of International Affairs, May 2014), 7.

76. James Lindsay, "The Shifting Pendulum of Power: Executive-Legislative Relations on American Foreign Policy," in *Domestic Sources of American Foreign Policy*, 6th ed., ed. James McCormick (Lanham, MD: Rowman & Littlefield, 2012), 235.

77. See a long list of sensible recommendations on what Taiwan could do to strengthen its position vis-à-vis an ever stronger and often intimidating China in Bush, *Unchartered Strait*, 159–98, and then compare the proposed options with actual behavior of Taiwan leaders. The conclusion points to an ever weaker Taiwan unwilling or unable to take the actions that would change circumstances that otherwise appear to point to closer dependency on and integration with China.

8. RELATIONS WITH JAPAN AND KOREA

1. See Zhao Shengnan, "Xi and Delegates Signal 'Thaw,'" *China Daily*, May 25, 2015, http://www.chinadaily.com.cn/china/2015-05/25/content_20805947.htm.

2. Andrew Scobell and Mark Cozad, "China's North Korea Policy: Rethink or Recharge," *Parameters* 44, no. 1 (Spring 2014): 51–63; Scott Snyder, *China's Rise and the Two Koreas: Politics, Economics, Security* (Boulder, CO: Rienner, 2009); Bonnie S. Glaser, "China's Policy in the Wake of the Second DPRK Nuclear Test," *China Security* 5, no. 2 (2009): 1–11; Yang Bojiang, "China and Its Northeast Asian Neighbors," *Xiandai guoji guanxi* (Beijing) 17 (January 2007): 56–63; Lian Degui, "Where Are Japan-U.S. Relations Heading?" *Foreign Affairs Journal* (Beijing) 95 (Spring 2010): 39–49; Wang Yusheng, "Some Thoughts on 'East Asia Community' and the Japanese and U.S. Factors," *Foreign Affairs Journal* (Beijing) 95 (Spring 2010): 31–38.

3. See, among others, Ming Wan, *Sino-Japanese Relations: Interaction, Logic, and Transformation* (Stanford, CA: Stanford University Press, 2006); Michael Yahuda, *Sino-Japanese Relations After the Cold War* (New York: Routledge, 2013); Greg Austin and Stuart Harris, *Japan and Greater China* (Honolulu: University of Hawaii Press, 2001); Christopher Howe, *China and Japan: History, Trends, Prospects* (New York: Oxford University Press, 1996).

4. Ma Licheng, "Duiri Guanxi Xinsiwei," *Zhanlue yu Guanli* (Beijing) 6 (2002); Shi Yin-hong, "Zhongri Jiejin yu 'Waijiao Geming,'" *Zhanlue yu Guanli* (Beijing) 2 (2003); Liu Tain-chun, *Riben Dui Hua Zhengce yu Zhongri Guanxi* (Beijing: Renmin Chubanshe, 2004).

5. Minxin Pei and Michael Swaine, *Simmering Fire in Asia: Averting Sino-Japanese Strategic Conflict*, Policy Brief 44 (Washington, DC: Carnegie Endowment for International Peace, December 1, 2005).

6. Mike Mochizuki, "Japan: Between Alliance and Autonomy," in *Strategic Asia 2004–2005*, ed. Ashley Tellis and Michael Wills (Seattle: National Bureau of Asian Research, 2004), 103–38; Ralph Cossa and Brad Glosserman, "U.S.-Japan Defense Cooperation: Has Japan Become the Great Britain of Asia?" *CSIS Issues and Insights* 5, no. 3 (2005), http://www.csis.org/pacfor.

7. T. J. Pempel, "Japan: Divided Government, Diminished Resources," in *Strategic Asia 2008–2009*, ed. Ashley Tellis, Mercy Kuo, and Andrew Marble (Seattle: National Bureau of Asian Research, 2008), 107–34.

8. Susan Shirk, *China: Fragile Superpower* (New York: Oxford University Press, 2007), 140–80; Mike Mochizuki, "Terms of Engagement: The U.S.-Japan Alliance and the Rise of China," in *The U.S.-Japan Relationship in the New Asia-Pacific*, ed. Ellis Krauss and T. J. Pempel (Stanford, CA: Stanford University Press, 2004), 87–115; "China and Japan: In the Pipeline," *The Economist*, April 29, 2004, accessed May 3, 2004, http://www.taiwansecurity.org.

9. Peter Ford, "Japan Abandons Bid to Make China a Key Pillar of Its Foreign Policy," *Christian Science Monitor*, November 17, 2010, http://www.csmonitor.com; James Przystup, "Japan-China Relations," *Comparative Connections* 12, no. 4 (January 2011), http://www.csis.org/pacfor.

10. Shirk, *China*; Robert Sutter, *China's Rise in Asia: Promises and Perils* (Lanham, MD: Rowman & Littlefield, 2005), 125–50.

11. Lian Degui, "Where Are Japan-U.S. Relations Heading?" *Foreign Affairs Journal* (Beijing) 95 (Spring 2010): 39–49; Wang Yusheng, "Some Thoughts on 'East Asia Community,'" 31–38.

12. Michael Green, "Managing Chinese Power: The View from Japan," in *Engaging China*, ed. Alastair Iain Johnston and Robert Ross (London: Routledge, 1999): 152–75; Benjamin Self, "China and Japan: A Façade of Friendship," *Washington Quarterly* 26, no. 1 (Winter 2002–2003): 77–88; Kent E. Calder, "China and Japan's Simmering Rivalry," *Foreign Affairs* 85, no. 2 (2006): 129–40; Richard Bush, *The Perils of Proximity: China-Japan Security Relations* (Washington, DC: Brookings Institution Press, 2010).

13. Pei and Swaine, *Simmering Fire in Asia*.

14. According to Japanese officials interviewed in Japan in May 2006, the Chinese international lobbying ranged widely and included governments in Africa and the Pacific Islands, among others (interviews, Japan, May 2006).

15. Dan Blumenthal, "The Revival of the U.S.-Japanese Alliance," American Enterprise Institute's *Asian Outlook* (February–March 2005).

16. S. Frederick Starr, "A Strong Japanese Initiative in Central Asia," *Central Asia–Caucasus Institute Analyst*, October 20, 2004; *U.S.–Japan–India Report* (Washington, DC: Center for Strategic and International Studies, August 16, 2007).

17. David Kang and Ji-Young Lee, "The New Cold War in Asia?" *Comparative Connections* 12, no. 4 (January 2011), http://www.csis.org/pacfor.

18. Yoshihisa Komori, "Rethinking Japan-China Relations: Beyond the History Issue," paper presented at scholarly conference at the Sigur Center for Asian Affairs, George Washington University, Washington, DC, December 5, 2001.

19. Wu Xinbo, "The End of the Silver Lining: A Chinese View of the U.S.-Japanese Alliance," *Washington Quarterly* 29, no. 1 (Winter 2005–2006): 119–30.

20. Green, "Managing Chinese Power"; Self, "China and Japan"; Shirk, *China*, 140–80; Denny Roy, *Stirring Samurai, Disapproving Dragon* (Honolulu: Asia Pacific Center for Security Studies, September 2003). See also "Noted Scholar Discusses 'New Thinking' in Sino-Japanese Relations," *Renmin Wang* (Beijing), January 1, 2004; Liu Xiaobiao, "Where Are Sino-Japanese Relations Heading?" *Renmin Wang* (Beijing), August 13, 2003; and Shi Yin-

hong, "On Crisis Formation, Control in Sino-Japanese Relations," *Wen Hui Po* (Hong Kong), June 1, 2005, cited in Sutter, *China's Rise in Asia*, 151.

21. Donald Klein, "Japan and Europe in Chinese Foreign Relations," in *China and the World*, ed. Samuel Kim (Boulder, CO: Westview Press, 1998), 137–46.

22. Robert Sutter, *Chinese Policy Priorities and Their Implications for the United States* (Lanham, MD: Rowman & Littlefield, 2000), 82.

23. *Japan-China Relations: Status, Outlook, and Implications for the United States*, Congressional Research Service Report 96-864F (Washington, DC: Library of Congress, October 30, 1996).

24. "The New Korea," *Asiaweek*, December 1, 1995, http://www.asia.com/asiaweek/95/1201/ed.html.

25. Sutter, *Chinese Policy Priorities and Their Implications for the United States*, 83.

26. Robert Sutter, *The United States and East Asia: Dynamics and Implications* (Lanham, MD: Rowman & Littlefield, 2003), 131–32.

27. Richard Samuels, *Securing Japan: Tokyo's Grand Strategy and the Future of East Asia* (Ithaca, NY: Cornell University Press, 2007).

28. Robert Sutter, "Japan-China: Trouble Ahead?" *Washington Quarterly* 25, no. 4 (Autumn 2002): 39.

29. Samuels, *Securing Japan*, 95.

30. Robert Marquand, "China Gains on Japan in Age-Old Rivalry for Asia Influence," *Christian Science Monitor*, October 29, 2003, 1; Pei and Swaine, *Simmering Fire in Asia*.

31. Chen Zhijiang, "Japan Accelerates Construction of Missile Defense System," *Guangming Ribao* (Beijing), June 24, 2003. See citation and discussion in Sutter, *China's Rise in Asia*, 152.

32. Marquand, "China Gains on Japan in Age-Old Rivalry for Asia Influence"; Pei and Swaine, *Simmering Fire in Asia*.

33. Chen Zhijiang, "Japan Accelerates Construction of Missile Defense System."

34. Wu Xinbo, "The End of the Silver Lining"; Ralph Cossa and Brad Glosserman, "More of the Same, Times Three," *Comparative Connections* 12, no. 4 (January 2011), http://www.csis.org/pacfor.

35. Shirk, *China*, 164–76.

36. Self, "China and Japan"; Sutter, "China-Japan."

37. *Senkaku (Diaoyu) Islands Dispute*, Congressional Research Service Report 96-798F (Washington, DC: Library of Congress, September 30, 1996).

38. James Przystup, "Japan-China Relations," *Comparative Connections* 12, no. 3 (October 2010), 105–8; Pei and Swaine, *Simmering Fire in Asia*.

39. Shirk, *China*, 160–61.

40. "China Cuts Rare Earth Export Quotas," *Los Angeles Times*, December 28, 2010, http://www.latimes.com.

41. "Japan-China Trade in 2010 Exceeds US$300 Billion to Set New Record," *JCN Newswire*, March 1, 2011, http://www.japancorp.net.

42. *"Asian Values" and Asian Assertiveness*, Congressional Research Service Report 96-610F (Washington, DC: Library of Congress, July 9, 1996).

43. Michael Yahuda, *The International Politics of the Asia-Pacific* (London: Routledge, 2011), 324–28; Yahuda, *Sino-Japanese Relations*.

44. James Przystup, "Abe Opens New Fronts," *Comparative Connections* 17, no. 1 (May 2015): 109.

45. Przystup, "Abe Opens New Doors," 108–9; "Japan-China Trade"; "Japanese Investment in China," *Konaxis*, accessed May 5, 2011, http://www.konaxis.com; Feng Zhaokui, "Japan's Role in China's Economic Reforms," *China Daily*, October 20, 2008.

46. Peter Ford, "For Study Abroad, More Japanese Prefer Chinese University to U.S. One," *Christian Science Monitor*, May 19, 2010, http://www.csmonitor.com; Zhao Xinying, "Tokyo Campus Aims to Lure Japanese," April 28, 2015, http://www.chinadaily.com.cn/china/2015-04/28/content_20559603.htm.

47. Marquand, "China Gains on Japan in Age-Old Rivalry for Asia Influence."

48. Lim Tai Wei, "Japan's Views of Ma Ying-jeou's Ascension to Power," *EAI Background Brief* 391, July 2, 2008, accessed May 5, 2011, http://www.eai.nus.edu.sg.

49. Kang and Lee, "The New Cold War in Asia?"

50. Jonathan Pollack, *No Exit: North Korea, Nuclear Weapons, and International Security* (London: Routledge, 2011).

51. Shirk, *China*, 166–74.

52. "Japan's PM Koizumi Continues High-Profile Diplomacy Challenged by China," Agence France-Presse, accessed May 9, 2005, May 8, 2005, http://www.taiwansecurity.org.

53. Thomas Christensen, "Have Old Problems Trumped New Thinking? China's Relations with Taiwan, Japan, and North Korea," *China Leadership Monitor* 14 (June 2005), http://www.chinaleadershipmonitor.org.

54. James Przystup, "Japan-China: Summer Calm," *Comparative Connections* 7, no. 3 (October 2005), http://www.csis.org/pacfor.

55. Shirk, *China*, 171–76.

56. "Hu's Points Show Way for Sino-Japan Ties," *China Daily*, June 21, 2005, accessed June 27, 2005, http://www.taiwansecurity.org.

57. Norimitsu Onishi, "Koizumi Provokes Anger around Asia," *New York Times*, October 17, 2005, accessed October 20, 2005, http://www.taiwansecurity.org.

58. Przystup, "Japan-China Relations" (October 2010).

59. Richard Armitage and Joseph Nye, *U.S.-Japan Alliance: Getting Asia Right through 2020* (Washington, DC: Center for Strategic and International Studies, 2007).

60. Robert Sutter, "The United States and Asia in 2006: Crisis Management, Holding Patterns, and Secondary Initiatives," *Asian Survey* 47, no. 1 (January–February 2007): 12.

61. Michael Green, "U.S.-Japanese Relations after Koizumi: Convergence or Cooling?" *Washington Quarterly* 29, no. 4 (Autumn 2006): 101–10.

62. Jeffrey Bader, *Obama and China's Rise* (Washington, DC: Brookings Institution, 2012), 42–43; David Allen, "Japan to Revisit Base Plan, SOFA," *Stars and Stripes*, September 11, 2009, http://www.stripes.com/news/japan-to-revisit-base-plan-sofa-1.94627.

63. John Hemmings, "Understanding Hatoyama's East Asia Community Idea," *East Asia Forum*, January 22, 2010, http://www.eastasiaforum.org/2010/01/22/understanding-hatoyamas-east-asian-community-idea.

64. James Przystup, "Japan-China Relations," *Comparative Connections* 14, no. 3 (January 2013): 109–11.

65. Kosuke Takahashi, "Shinzo Abe's Nationalist Strategy," *The Diplomat*, February 13, 2014, http://thediplomat.com/2014/02/shinzo-abes-nationalist-strategy.

66. Mark Valencia, "Asian Threats, Provocations Giving Rise to Wiffs of War," *Japan Times*, June 9, 2014, http://www.japantimes.co.jp/opinion/2014/06/09/commentary/world-commentary/asian-threats-provocations-giving-rise-whiffs-war/#.U6VP6JRdXxA.

67. White House Office of the Press Secretary, *Fact Sheet: U.S.-Japan Global and Regional Cooperation*, April 25, 2014; Matt Spetalnick and Nathan Layne, "Obama Accuses China of Flexing Muscles in Disputes with Neighbors," *Reuters*, April 28, 2015, http://www.reuters.com/article/2015/04/29/us-usa-japan-idUSKBN0NJ09520150429.

68. Andrew Davis, "Kennedy Urges Japan, South Korea to Resolve Diplomatic Row," *Bloomberg*, March 6, 2014, http://www.bloomberg.com/news/2014-03-06/kennedy-urges-japan-south-korea-to-resolve-diplomatic-tensions.html.

69. Shannon Tiezzi, "A China-Japan Breakthrough," *The Diplomat*, November 7, 2014, http://thediplomat.com/2014/11/a-china-japan-breakthrough-a-primer-on-their-4-point-consensus/; Michael Green, "Xi Meets Abe: Skillful Diplomacy But Tensions Remain," *CSIS Asia Maritime Transparency Initiative*, November 11, 2014, http://amti.csis.org/xi-meets-abe-skillful-diplomacy-but-tensions-remain.

70. Emma Chanlette-Avery, coord., *Japan-U.S. Relations*, Congressional Research Service Report RL33436 (Washington, DC: Library of Congress, April 23, 2015), 2.

71. Pei and Swaine, *Simmering Fire in Asia*; "China-Japan Dispute," *Wall Street Journal*, accessed June 22, 2014, http://stream.wsj.com/story/china-japan-dispute/SS-2-58300/SS-2-60993/?mod=wsj_streaming_china-japan-dispute.

72. Armitage and Nye, *U.S.-Japan Alliance*, 24; "Japan's Abe Turns to Southeast Asia to Counter China," *Reuters*, January 16, 2013,http://www.reuters.com/article/2013/01/16/us-japan-abe-asean-idUSBRE90F0LW20130116.

73. International Crisis Group, *North Korea's Nuclear Test: The Fallout*, Asia Briefing 56 (Brussels: International Crisis Group, November 13, 2006); Snyder, *China's Rise and the Two Koreas*; Samuel Kim, *The Two Koreas and the Great Powers* (New York: Cambridge University Press, 2006), 42–101; David Shambaugh, "China and the Korean Peninsula," *Washington Quarterly* 26, no. 2 (Spring 2003): 43–56; Denny Roy, "China and the Korean Peninsula: Beijing's Pyongyang Problem and Seoul Hope," *Asia-Pacific Security Studies* 3, no. 1 (January 2004); Jae Ho Chung, "From a Special Relationship to a Normal Partnership?" *Pacific Affairs* 76, no. 3 (Winter 2003–2004): 549–68; You Ji, "Understanding China's North Korea Policy," *Jamestown Foundation China Brief* (March 3, 2004); Ming Liu, "China and the North Korean Crisis," *Pacific Affairs* 76, no. 3 (Fall 2003): 347–73; Andrew Scobell, "China and North Korea," *Current History* 101, no. 656 (September 2002): 278–79; Fu Mengzi, "China and Peace Building on the Korean Peninsula," *Xiandai guoji guanxi* (Beijing) 17 (July 2007): 27–40.

74. Taeho Kim, "China's Evolving Bilateral Ties in Northeast Asia," in *Rising China*, ed. Jaushieh Joseph Wu (Taipei: Institute of International Relations, National Chengchi University, 2001), 205–6; Roy, "China and the Korean Peninsula"; Fei-Ling Wang, *Tacit Acceptance and Watchful Eyes: Beijing's Views about the U.S.-ROK Alliance* (Carlisle, PA: U.S. Army War College, 1997).

75. Samuel Kim, "The Changing Role of China on the Korean Peninsula," *International Journal of Korean Studies* 8, no. 1 (2004): 79–112.

76. Jason T. Shaplen and James Laney, "Washington's Eastern Sunset: The Decline of U.S. Power in Northeast Asia," *Foreign Affairs* 86, no. 6 (November–December 2007): 82–97; Evan Medeiros, *Pacific Currents: The Responses of U.S. Allies and Security Partners in East Asia to China's Rise* (Santa Monica, CA: RAND Corporation, 2008), 63–96.

77. Scott Snyder, "Post Olympic Hangover: New Backdrop for Relations," *Comparative Connections* 10, no. 3 (October 2008): 101–7; Scott Snyder, "DPRK Provocations Test China's Regional Role," *Comparative Connections* 12, no. 4 (January 2011), http://www.csis.org/pacfor; Scott Snyder, "South Korea's Diplomatic Triangle," *Comparative Connections* 17, no. 1 (January 2015): 94–95.

78. Scott Snyder, "Lee Myung-bak and the Future of Sino–South Korean Relations," *Jamestown Foundation China Brief* 8, no. 4 (February 14, 2008): 5–8; Megha Rajagopalan and Meeyoung Cho, "China, South Korea Sign 'Substantial Conclusion' of Free Trade Deal," *Reuters*, November 10, 2014, http://www.reuters.com/article/2014/11/10/us-southkorea-china-trade-idUSKCN0IU02Z20141110.

79. Snyder, "Lee Myung-bak and the Future of Sino–South Korean Relations"; Snyder, "DPRK Provocations Test China's Regional Role."

80. *South Korean Attitudes on China*, Asian Institute on Policy Studies, July 3, 2014, http://en.asaninst.org/contents/south-korean-attitudes-on-china.

81. Sutter, *Chinese Policy Priorities and Their Implications for the United States*, 101.

82. *Korea: Improved South Korean–Chinese Relations*, Congressional Research Service Report 97-681F (Washington, DC: Library of Congress, July 1997), 4.

83. Roy, "China and the Korean Peninsula."

84. Scott Snyder, "Sino-Korean Relations and the Future of the U.S.-ROK Alliance," *NBR Analysis* 14, no. 1 (June 2003): 55–59.

85. Consultations with fifteen South Korean officials and nongovernment China specialists, Seoul and Busan, South Korea, May–June 2004; consultations with fifteen South Korean officials and nongovernment specialists, Seoul and Taegu, May 2006.

86. Consultations with U.S. and South Korean officials, Seoul, May 31 and June 1, 2004; consultations with South Korean officials, Seoul and Busan, May–June 2004.

87. Scott Snyder, "Establishing a 'Strategic Cooperative Partnership,'" *Comparative Connections* 10, no. 2 (July 2008): 114.

88. The assessment of South Korean official views is based heavily on interviews and private consultations with South Korean officials and specialists between 1995 and 2005. The findings of those consultations are reviewed in Sutter, *China's Rise in Asia*, 155–76.

89. Robert Sutter, "China's 'Peaceful Rise': Implications for U.S. Interests in Korea," *International Journal of Korean Studies* 8, no. 1 (2004): 113–34.

90. Some of these steps were brought up by South Korean and U.S. officials during consultations with the author in Seoul, May 2006; *New Opportunities for U.S. Exporters Under the U.S.-Korea Trade Agreement*, Office of the U.S. Trade Representative, accessed June 16, 2015, https://ustr.gov/trade-agreements/free-trade-agreements/korus-fta.

91. Medeiros, *Pacific Currents*, xviii–xix.

92. Cossa and Glosserman, "More of the Same, Times Three."

93. Snyder, *China's Rise and the Two Koreas.*

94. Glaser, "China's Policy in the Wake of the Second DPRK Nuclear Test"; Michael Swaine, "China's North Korea Dilemma," *China Leadership Monitor* 30 (Fall 2009), http://www.hoover.org.

95. Christopher Twomey, "Chinese Foreign Policy toward North Korea," *Journal of Contemporary China* 17, no. 56 (August 2008): 422.

96. Kim, "China's Evolving Bilateral Ties in Northeast Asia"; Roy, "China and the Korean Peninsula"; Fei-Ling Wang, *Tacit Acceptance and Watchful Eyes.*

97. Jeremy Page, Jay Solomon, and Julian Barnes, "China Warns U.S. as Korea Tensions Rise," *Wall Street Journal*, November 26, 2010, http://www.wsj.com; Snyder, "South Korea's Diplomatic Triangle," 91–92.

98. This paragraph and the next two rely on Robert Sutter, *Chinese Foreign Relations: Power and Policy since the Cold War* (Lanham, MD: Rowman & Littlefield, 2010), 203–8.

99. Interviews with senior officials in charge of Chinese foreign relations, Beijing, May 30, 2006.

100. Wang Jisi, "China's Search for a Grand Strategy," *Foreign Affairs* 90, no. 2 (March–April 2011): 68–80.

101. This section is taken in part from Robert Sutter, "China and North Korea after the Cold War: Wariness, Caution, and Balance," *International Journal of Korean Studies* 14, no. 1 (Spring–Summer 2010): 19–34.

102. David Shambaugh, "Coping with a Conflicted China," *Washington Quarterly* 34, no. 1 (Winter 2011): 7–27.

103. Scott Snyder, "China-DPRK Relations: A Return to a Strategic Relationship?" January 22, 2010, accessed January 25, 2010, http://blogs.cfr.org/asia/2010/01/22/china-dprk-relations-a-return-to-a-strategic-relationship/.

104. Snyder, "DPRK Provocations Test China's Regional Role."

105. Snyder, "DPRK Provocations Test China's Regional Role"; Scott Snyder and See-won Byun, "Consolidating Ties with New DPRK Leadership," *Comparative Connections* 12, no. 3 (October 2010), http://www.csis.org/pacfor.

106. Snyder, "DPRK Provocations Test China's Regional Role," 91.

107. Snyder, "DPRK Provocations Test China's Regional Role," 94.

108. Snyder and Byun, "Consolidating Ties with New DPRK Leadership."

109. Ralph Cossa and Brad Glosserman, "U.S. Profile Rises, China's Image Falls, North Korea Changes," *Comparative Connections* 12, no. 3 (October 2010): 1–5; Snyder and Byun, "Consolidating Ties with New DPRK Leadership."

110. Mark Landler, "Obama Urges China to Check North Koreans," *New York Times*, December 6, 2010, http://www.nytimes.com.

111. Elisabeth Bumiller and David Sanger, "Gates Warns of North Korea Missile Threat to U.S.," *New York Times*, January 11, 2011, http://www.nytimes.com.

112. Cossa and Glosserman, "U.S. Profile Rises," 3–5.

113. Snyder, "South Korea's Diplomatic Triangle," 93–94; "The China-North Korea Relationship," *Council on Foreign Relations Backgrounder*, August 22, 2014, http://www.cfr.org/china/china-north-korea-relationship/p11097.

9. RELATIONS WITH SOUTHEAST ASIA, AUSTRALIA, NEW ZEALAND, AND THE PACIFIC ISLANDS

1. Harold Hinton, *Communist China in World Politics* (Boston: Houghton Mifflin, 1966), 394–441.

2. Donald Weatherbee, *International Relations of Southeast Asia* (Lanham, MD: Rowman & Littlefield, 2014); M. Taylor Fravel, "China's Strategy in the South China Sea," *Contemporary Southeast Asia* 33, no. 3 (2011): 292–319.

3. International Crisis Group, *Stirring Up the South China Sea I*, Asia Report 223 (Brussels: International Crisis Group, April 23, 2012).

4. Robert Sutter, *Foreign Relations of the PRC* (Lanham, MD: Rowman & Littlefield, 2013), 234–37.

5. Jay Taylor, *China and Southeast Asia*, 2nd ed. (New York: Praeger, 1976).

6. Nayan Chanda, *Brother Enemy* (New York: Harcourt, 1986).

7. Robert Ross, *Indochina Tangle* (New York: Columbia University Press, 1988).

8. Differing perspectives about the course and implications of China's rise in Southeast Asia and the role of the United States include Amitav Acharya, *The Making of Southeast Asia* (Ithaca, NY: Cornell University Press, 2013); Amitav Acharya, "Power Shift or Paradigm Shift? China's Rise and Asia's Emerging Security Order," *International Studies Quarterly* 58, no. 1 (March 2014): 158–73; Dennis Blair and John T. Hanley Jr., "From Wheels to Webs: Reconstructing Asia-Pacific Security Arrangements," *Washington Quarterly* 24, no. 1 (Winter 2001): 7–17; Rosemary Foot, "Chinese Strategies in a U.S.-Hegemonic Global Order: Accommodating and Hedging," *International Affairs* 82, no. 1 (2006): 77–94; Evelyn Goh, *The Struggle for Order: Hegemony, Hierarchy and Transition in Post–Cold War East Asia* (Oxford: Oxford University Press, 2013); Evelyn Goh, *Meeting the China Challenge: The United States in Southeast Asian Regional Security Strategies*, Policy Studies 21 (Washington, DC: East-West Center, 2006); Evelyn Goh, "The Modes of China's Influence: Cases from Southeast Asia," *Asian Survey* 54, no. 5 (2014): 825–48; Kishore Mahbubani, *The Great Convergence* (New York: Public Affairs, 2013); Evan Medeiros, "Strategic Hedging and the Future of Asia-Pacific Stability," *Washington Quarterly* 29, no. 1 (Winter 2005–2006): 145–67; Bronson Percival, *The Dragon Looks South: China and Southeast Asia in the New Century* (Westport, CT: Praeger Security International, 2007); Hugh White, *The China Choice* (Collingwood: Australia Black, 2012); Michael Yahuda, *The International Politics of the Asia-Pacific*, 3rd ed. (London: Routledge, 2011).

9. Chinese assessments on China-Southeast relations after the Cold War include Zhao Jinfu, "China, ASEAN Advance United," *Contemporary International Relations* (Beijing) 20, no. 5 (September–October 2010): 89–96; Zhang Yunling, "New Thinking Needed to Promote East Asian Cooperation," *Foreign Affairs Journal* (Beijing) 96 (September 2010): 17–23; Lu Fanghua, "An Analysis of U.S. Involvement in the South China Sea," *Contemporary International Relations* (Beijing) 20, no. 6 (November–December 2010): 132–41; Lu Jianren, "Evolution of Relations between China and ASEAN," in *Making New Partnership: A Rising China and Its Neighbors*, ed. Zhang Yunling (Beijing: Social Sciences Academic Press, 2008), 115–35; Tang Shiping and Zhang Yunling, "Zhongguo de Diqu Zhanlue," in *World Politics—Views from China* (Beijing: Xin Shijie Chubanshe, 2007), 119–31. On the past record of the People's Republic of China in Southeast Asia, see John Garver, *Foreign Relations of the People's Republic of China* (Englewood Cliffs, NJ: Prentice Hall, 1993).

10. Sophie Richardson, *China, Cambodia, and the Five Principles of Peaceful Coexistence* (New York: Columbia University Press, 2010); International Crisis Group, *China's Myanmar Strategy* Asia Briefing 112 (Brussels: International Crisis Group, September 21, 2010).

11. "China Reassures Neighbors, Deepens Engagement," *Comparative Connections* 13, no. 1 (May 2011), http://www.csis.org/pacfor; Brantly Womack, "China and Southeast Asia: Asymmetry, Leadership, and Normalcy," *Pacific Affairs* 76, no. 3 (Winter 2003–2004): 529–48; Alice Ba, *(Re)Negotiating East and Southeast Asia* (Stanford, CA: Stanford University Press, 2009); John Wong and Sarah Chan, "China-ASEAN Free Trade Agreement," *Asian*

Survey 43, no. 3 (May–June 2003): 507–26; Evelyn Goh and Sheldon Simon, eds., *China, the United States, and Southeast Asia* (London: Routledge, 2007); Stanley Foundation, *China and Southeast Asia*, Stanley Foundation Policy Bulletin (Muscatine, IA: Stanley Foundation, October 2003); Rosemary Foot, "China and the ASEAN Regional Forum," *Asian Survey* 38, no. 5 (May 1998): 425–40.

12. *China–Southeast Asia Relations: Trends, Issues, and Implications for the United States*, Congressional Research Service Report 97-553F (Washington, DC: Library of Congress, May 20, 1997): 3–6.

13. Wong and Chan, "China-ASEAN Free Trade Agreement," 514.

14. Robert Sutter, *Chinese Policy Priorities and Their Implications for the United States* (Lanham, MD: Rowman & Littlefield, 2000), 129; *China–Southeast Asia Relations*, 115; "Small Advances, Trouble with Vietnam," *Comparative Connections* 10, no. 3 (October 2008): 67.

15. Wong and Chan, "China-ASEAN Free Trade Agreement," 519; Sutter, *Chinese Policy Priorities and Their Implications for the United States*, 129; *China–Southeast Asia Relations*, 115; "Economic Concerns Begin to Hit Home," *Comparative Connections* 10, no. 4 (January 2009): 68.

16. Sutter, *Chinese Policy Priorities and Their Implications for the United States*, 129; *China–Southeast Asia Relations*, 116; "PRC Expands Cooperation with ASEAN," *Xinhua*, January 4, 1998, carried by FBIS, cited in Sutter, *Chinese Policy Priorities and Their Implications for the United States*, 129; *China–Southeast Asia Relations*, 129.

17. Robert Sutter, *China's Rise in Asia: Promises and Perils* (Lanham, MD: Rowman & Littlefield, 2005), 190.

18. Lyall Breckon, "China Caps a Year of Gains," *Comparative Connections* 4, no. 4 (January 2003), http://www.csis.org/pacfor; for background see Ian Storey, *Southeast Asia and the Rise of China* (New York: Routledge, 2013).

19. Bates Gill, *Rising Star: China's New Security Diplomacy* (Washington, DC: Brookings Institution, 2007).

20. Sutter, *Chinese Policy Priorities and Their Implications for the United States*, 129; *China–Southeast Asia Relations*, 116.

21. ASEAN, *Declaration on the Conduct of Parties in the South China Sea* (November 2002), accessed December 2002, http://www.aseansec.org/13163.htm; Breckon, "China Caps a Year of Gains."

22. Gill, *Rising Star*.

23. Bonnie Glaser and Evan Medeiros, "The Changing Ecology of Foreign Policy Making in China: The Ascension and Demise of the Theory of 'Peaceful Rise,'" *China Quarterly* 190 (June 2007): 291–310.

24. Robert Sutter, *The United States in Asia* (Lanham, MD: Rowman & Littlefield, 2009), 110–12; "U.S. Intervention Complicates China's Advances," *Comparative Connections* 12, no. 3 (October 2010): 65.

25. *Comparing Global Influence: China's and U.S. Diplomacy, Foreign Aid, Trade, and Investment in the Developing World*, Congressional Research Service Report RL34620 (Washington, DC: Library of Congress, August 15, 2008), 51, 53; "China Reassures Neighbors, Deepens Engagement"; Catherin Dalpino and Juo-yu Lin, "China and Southeast Asia," in *Brookings Northeast Asia Survey 2002–2003*, ed. Richard Bush and Catherin Dalpino (Washington, DC: Brookings Institution Press, 2003), 83.

26. "Trade Agreement Registers China's Prominence," *Comparative Connections* 12, no. 1 (April 2010): 58–59.

27. "China Reassures Neighbors, Deepens Engagement."

28. Elizabeth Economy, "Asia's Water Security Crisis: China, India, and the United States," in *Strategic Asia 2008–2009*, ed. Ashley Tellis, Mercy Kuo, and Andrew Marble (Seattle: National Bureau of Asian Research, 2008), 380–82; "China Reassures Neighbors, Deepens Engagement."

29. "Cyclone, Earthquake Put Spotlight on China," *Comparative Connections* 10, no. 2 (July 2008): 76–77; "From Bad to Worse," *Comparative Connections* 10, no. 4 (January 2009): 5–6.

30. The following 2012 events are explained in greater detail in "China Muscles Opponents on South China Sea," *Comparative Connections* 14, no. 2 (September 2012), http://www.csis.org/pacfor.

31. The 2014 events are explained in greater detail in "China Advances, More Opposition in South China Sea," *Comparative Connections* 16, no. 2 (September 2014), http://www.csis.org/pacfor.

32. "Top Ten ASEAN Trade Partner Countries/Regions, 2013," accessed June 19, 2015, http://www.asean.org/images/2015/January/external_trade_statistic/table20_asof04Dec14.pdf; "Top Ten Sources of Foreign Direct Investment Inflows in ASEAN," accessed June 19, 2015, http://www.asean.org/images/resources/Statistics/2014/ForeignDirectInvestment/Aug/Table%2027.pdf.

33. Robert Sutter, *The United States and Asia* (Lanham, MD: Rowman & Littlefield, 2015), 297–316.

34. Robert Sutter, *China's Rise and U.S. Influence in Asia: A Report from the Region*, Senior Fellows Program Issue Brief (Washington, DC: Atlantic Council of the United States, July 2006); *The Rise of China in the Pacific*, Policy Briefing Note 2 (Canberra: Australian National University, 2007); *China and Taiwan in the South Pacific: Diplomatic Chess versus Pacific Political Rugby* (Sydney: Lowy Institute, 2007); Tamara Shie, "Rising Chinese Influence in the South Pacific," *Asian Survey* 47, no. 2 (March–April 2007): 307–26; Linda Jakobson, "Australia-China Ties: In Search of Political Trust," *Policy Brief*, Lowy Institute, June 2012.

35. Interviews with twenty Australian officials, Canberra, June 2004; interviews with twenty-five Australian officials, Canberra, June 2006; interviews with twenty Australian officials, Canberra, August 2010.

36. "Senior Official Visits; South China Sea Tensions," *Comparative Connections* 12, no. 2 (July 2010): 70, 73; "Turning the Page on Sino-Australian Relations," *Jamestown Foundation China Brief* 8, no. 4 (February 14, 2008): 2; "Small Advances, Trouble with Vietnam," *Comparative Connections* 10, no. 3 (October 2008):68; "Australia-East Asia/US," *Comparative Connections* 16, no. 2 (September 2014), http://www.csis.org/pacfor.

37. Interviews with Australian officials cited in note 35; interviews with twenty New Zealand officials, Wellington, June 2006; interviews with fifteen New Zealand officials, Wellington, August 2010; "ASEAN and Asian Regional Diplomacy," *Comparative Connections* 11, no. 4 (January 2010): 69; Anne-Marie Brady, "New Zealand-China Relations," *New Zealand Journal of Asian Studies* 10, no. 2 (December 2008): 1–20.

38. Robert Sutter, *Historical Dictionary of Chinese Foreign Policy* (Lanham, MD: Scarecrow Press, 2011), 49; Jakobson, "Australia-China Ties."

39. This section is based on the interviews in Australia cited in note 35. I also conducted seminars in four Australian cities and had round-table discussions with Australian officials in separate weeklong visits in 2004, 2006, and 2010. See also the discussion of China–Australian relations in Australian Parliamentary Library Research Service, *Directions in China's Foreign Relations: Implications for East Asia and Australia*, Parliamentary Library Research Brief 9: 2005–2006 (Canberra: Australian Parliamentary Library Research Service, December 5, 2005), 51–66, and Thomas Lum and Bruce Vaughn, *The Southwest Pacific: U.S. Interests and China's Growing Influence*, Congressional Research Service Report RL34086 (Washington, DC: Library of Congress, July 6, 2007); *Turning the Page on Sino-Australian Relations*, 2; Zhai Kun, "China-Australia Ties Are of Strategic Importance," *China Daily*, September 4, 2008, 10; "ASEAN and Asian Regional Diplomacy," *Comparative Connections* 11, no. 4 (January 2010), http://www.csis.org/pacfor; "China Reassures Neighbors, Wary of U.S. Intentions," *Comparative Connections* 12, no. 4 (January 2011), http://www.csis.org/pacfor.

40. "China-Australia Free Trade Agreement Puts Local Jobs at Risk, Unions, Industry Groups Say," *ABC News*, June 17, 2015, http://www.abc.net.au/news/2015-06-17/free-trade-agreement-with-china-puts-local-jobs-at-risk-unions/6554460.

41. "Small Advances, Trouble with Vietnam," 68; "China Reassures Neighbors, Deepens Engagement."

42. *China: Fact Sheet* (Canberra: Australian Government Department of Foreign Affairs and Trade, 2008); *China: Fact Sheet* (Canberra: Australian Government Department of Foreign Affairs and Trade, 2014).

43. *China: Fact Sheet* (Canberra: Australian Government Department of Foreign Affairs and Trade, 2010); Zhong Nan, "China, Australia Sign Free Trade Agreement," *China Daily*, June 17, 2015, http://www.chinadaily.com.cn/bizchina/2015-06/17/content_21027815_2.htm; *China Country Brief* (Canberra: Australian Government Department of Foreign Affairs and Trade, 2014).

44. Interviews with Australian officials, 2006.

45. Interviews with Australian officials, 2010.

46. "ASEAN and Asian Regional Diplomacy"; "China Reassures Neighbors, Wary of U.S. Intentions."

47. "Beijing Sets Positive Agenda, Plays Down Disputes," *Comparative Connections* 16, no. 3 (January 2015), http://www.csis.org/pacfor.

48. Sutter, *Historical Dictionary of Chinese Foreign Policy*, 179–80.

49. Sutter, *Historical Dictionary of Chinese Foreign Policy*, 179–80; Mark Manyin, coord., *Pivot to the Pacific? The Obama Administration's "Rebalancing" Toward Asia*, Congressional Research Service Report R42448 (Washington, DC: Library of Congress, March 28, 2012), 2–6; Rebecca Howard, "China, New Zealand Trade Exceeds Hopes," *Wall Street Journal*, June 27, 2014, http://blogs.wsj.com/economics/2014/06/27/china-new-zealand-trade-exceeds-hopes/.

50. Manyin, *Pivot to the Pacific*; U.S. Embassy New Zealand, "Secretary of State Hillary Clinton in New Zealand," November 2010, http://newzealand.usembassy.gov/clinton_nz2010.html.

51. John Henderson and Benjamin Reilly, "Dragon in Paradise," *National Interest,* Summer 2003, 93–94; Australian Parliamentary Library Research Service, *Directions in China's Foreign Relations*, 51–54; *The Rise of China in the Pacific*; Shie, "Rising Chinese Influence in the South Pacific."

52. Sutter, *Historical Dictionary of Chinese Foreign Policy*, 193–94; ROC Foreign Ministry, accessed June 20, 2015, http://www.mofa.gov.tw/en/default.html.

53. "Military Diplomacy and China's 'Soft Power,'" *Comparative Connections* 8, no. 2 (July 2006), http://www.csis.org/pacfor.

54. Interview, Canberra, June 2006.

55. Henderson and Reilly, "Dragon in Paradise," 93–94; "China Has Become a 'Major Donor' in the Pacific Islands Region," [interview with Lowy Institute analyst Philippa Brant] *DW*, March 3, 2015, http://www.dw.de/china-has-become-a-major-donor-in-the-pacific-islands-region/a-18290737.

56. Australian Parliamentary Library Research Service, *Directions in China's Foreign Relations*, 51–54; "President Ma Praises ROC-Palau Ties," *Taiwan Today*, October 14, 2013, http://www.taiwantoday.tw/ct.asp?xItem=210435&CtNode=436.

57. Australian Parliamentary Library Research Service, *Directions in China's Foreign Relations*, 51–54.

58. "Beijing Shifts to the Positive, Plays Down Disputes."

59. Matthew Dornan, Denghua Zhang, and Philippa Brant, "More Chinese Loans to Pacific Islands But No Debt Forgiveness," *East Asia Forum*, November 20, 2013, http://www.eastasiaforum.org/2013/11/20/more-chinese-loans-to-pacific-islands-but-no-debt-forgiveness/.

60. "Beijing Shifts to the Positive, Plays Down Disputes"; "Ambitious Economic Initiatives Amid Boundary Disputes," *Comparative Connections* 17, no. 1 (May 2015),http://www.csis.org/pacfor.

61. Anne-Marie Brady, "China's Rise in Antarctica," *Asian Survey* 50, no. 4 (2010): 759–85; "Xi Jinping Visits Chinese and Australian Antarctic Scientific Researchers and Inspects Chinese Research Vessel 'Snow Dragon,'" Ministry of Foreign Affairs of People's Republic of China, November 18, 2014, http://www.fmprc.gov.cn/mfa_eng/topics_665678/xjpzxcxesgjtldrdjcfhdadlyxxlfjjxgsfwbttpyjjdgldrhw/t1212943.shtml.

10. RELATIONS WITH SOUTHERN ASIA AND CENTRAL ASIA

1. Chinese perspectives on these issues include "Initiative Offers Road Map for Peace, Prosperity," *China Daily*, March 30, 2015, http://europe.chinadaily.com.cn/china/2015-03/30/content_19950708.htm; Quang Xiaoyun, "China–Central Asia Natural Gas Pipeline and Multilateral Cooperation of the Shanghai Cooperation Organization," *Foreign Affairs Journal* (Beijing) 95 (Spring 2010): 50–58; Cheng Ruisheng, "China-India Diplomatic Relations: Six Decades' Experience and Inspiration," *Foreign Affairs Journal* (Beijing) 96 (Summer 2010): 59–70; Wang Shida, "The Way to a Secure and Stable Afghanistan," *Contemporary International Relations* (Beijing) 20, no. 6 (November–December 2010): 123–31; Feng Yujun, "Strategic Orientation and Prospects of the Shanghai Cooperation Organization," *Contemporary International Relations* (Beijing), special issue (September 2010): 121–28; Li Li, "India's Engagement with East Asia and the China Factor," *Contemporary International Relations* (Beijing) 20, no. 5 (September–October 2010): 97–109; Ye Hailin, "China and South Asian Relations in a New Perspective," in *Making New Partnership: A Rising China and Its Neighbors*, ed. Zhang Yunling (Beijing: Social Sciences Academic Press, 2008), 217–43; Ma Jiali, "Is Competitive Partnership between China and India Viable?" in Zhang Yunling, *Making New Partnership*, 177–89.

2. John Garver, *Protracted Contest: Sino-Indian Rivalry in the Twentieth Century* (Seattle: University of Washington Press, 2001); Francine Frankel and Harry Harding, eds., *The India-China Relationship: What the United States Needs to Know* (New York: Columbia University Press, 2004); Jing-dong Yuan, "The Dragon and the Elephant: Chinese-Indian Relations in the Twenty-first Century," *Washington Quarterly* 30, no. 3 (Summer 2007): 131–44; Jean-Francois Huchet, "Emergence of a Pragmatic India-China Relationship: Between Geostrategic Rivalry and Economic Competition," *China Perspectives* 3 (2008): 50–67; Jonathan Holslag, *China and India: Prospects for Peace* (New York: Columbia University Press, 2010); Shalendra Sharma, *China and India in the Age of Globalization* (New York: Cambridge University Press, 2009); Lawrence Saez and Crystal Chang, "China and South Asia: Strategic Implications and Economic Imperatives," in *China, the Developing World, and the New Global Dynamic*, ed. Lowell Dittmer and George T. Yu (Boulder, CO: Rienner, 2010): 83–108; John Garver and Fei-Ling Wang, "China's Anti-encirclement Struggle," *Asian Security* 6, no. 3 (2010): 238–63.

3. *South Asian Crisis: China's Assessments and Goals*, Congressional Research Service Memorandum (Washington, DC: Library of Congress, June 6, 1998).

4. Devin Hagerty, "China and Pakistan: Strains in the Relationship," *Current History* (September 2002): 289.

5. John Garver, "China's Influence in Central and South Asia: Is It Increasing?" in *Power Shift: China and Asia's New Dynamics*, ed. David Shambaugh (Berkeley: University of California Press, 2005), 213–18.

6. Wu Yixue, "U.S. Dreams of Asian NATO," *China Daily*, July 18, 2003, 4.

7. Abu Taher Salahuddin Ahmed, "India-China Relations in the 1990s," *Journal of Contemporary Asia* 26, no. 1 (1996): 100–115; Robert Sutter, *China's Rise in Asia: Promises and Perils* (Lanham, MD: Rowman & Littlefield, 2005), 231–48.

8. Gurpreet Khurana, "Securing the Maritime Silk Route: Is There a Sino-Indian Confluence?" *China and Eurasia Forum Quarterly* 4, no. 3 (August 2006): 89–103.

9. Denny Roy, *China's Foreign Relations* (Lanham, MD: Rowman & Littlefield, 1998), 170–74.

10. "Indian Prime Minister Ends China Visit," *China Daily*, January 15, 2008, 1; Fu Xiaoqiang, "Wen's Visit Benefits South Asia," *China Daily*, December 23, 2010, 8.

11. Robert Sutter, *Chinese Policy Priorities and Their Implications for the United States* (Lanham, MD: Rowman & Littlefield, 2000), 135.

12. Tarique Niazi, "Sino-Pakistani Relations Reach New Level after Zadari's Visit," *China Brief* 8, no. 24 (December 19, 2008): 7–9; Christopher Griffin, "Hu Loves Whom? China Juggles Its Priorities on the Subcontinent," *China Brief* 6, no. 25 (December 19, 2006): 1–3.

13. *Hong Kong AFP in English*, June 3, 1998, accessed June 4, 1998, http://www.afp.com, cited in Sutter, *Chinese Policy Priorities and Their Implications for the United States*, 135.

14. Stephanie Ho, "China to Sell Outdated Nuclear Reactors to Pakistan," VOANews.com, March 24, 2011, http://www.voanews.com; Li Xiaokun and Ai Yang, "Wen Delivers on Flood Aid as Visit to Pakistan Begins," *China Daily*, December 18–19, 2010, 1; L. C. Russell Hsiao, "China and Pakistan Enhance Strategic Partnership," *China Brief* 8, no. 19 (October 7, 2008).

15. J. Mohan Malik, "Chinese-Indian Relations in the Post-Soviet Era," *China Quarterly* 142 (June 1995): 317–55; Garver, *Protracted Contest*; Sutter, *China's Rise in Asia*, 233; Holslag, *China and India*; C. Raja Mohan, "Sino-Indian Relations: Growing Yet Fragile," *RSIS Commentaries* 174 (December 20, 2010); "India and China Eye Each Other Warily," IISS *Strategic Comments* 9, no. 27 (December 2010).

16. Robert Sutter, *The United States and East Asia: Dynamics and Implications* (Lanham, MD: Rowman & Littlefield, 2003), 116; Robert Sutter, *The United States and Asia* (Lanham, MD: Rowman & Littlefield, 2015), 233–68.

17. Yuan, "The Dragon and the Elephant"; Huchet, "Emergence of a Pragmatic India-China Relationship."

18. Sutter, *China's Rise in Asia*, 240; "India and China Eye Each Other Warily."

19. Sutter, *The United States and East Asia*, 117; Yuan, "The Dragon and the Elephant"; Huchet, "Emergence of a Pragmatic India-China Relationship"; Saez and Chang, "China and South Asia."

20. Preetam Sohani, "The New Superpower Coalition: Indian, Chinese, and Russian Foreign Ministers to Meet in Russia," *India Daily*, May 30, 2005, accessed February 10, 2009, http://www.indiadaily.com; "BRICS Group," *New York Times*, April 20, 2011, http://www.nytimes.com.

21. Huchet, "Emergence of a Pragmatic India-China Relationship," 66.

22. Sutter, *China's Rise in Asia*, 240–41; "Chinese President Makes Five-Point Proposal for Sino-Indian Economic Cooperation," *China Daily*, November 23, 2006, 1; Li Xiaokun and Li Xiang, "Trade Target Set at $100b," *China Daily*, December 17, 2010, 1; Han Hua, "China, India Vital to Asia's Growth Story," *China Daily*, May 15, 2015, http://www.chinadaily.com.cn/opinion/2015-05/15/content_20722050.htm.

23. Sutter, *China's Rise in Asia*, 239–46; "India and China Eye Each Other Warily."

24. Sutter, *The United States and East Asia*, 117.

25. Some of these interviews and consultations in Indian cities and Chinese cities on repeated occasions in recent years are reviewed in Sutter, *China's Rise in Asia*, xi, 239–48; Robert Sutter, *The United States in Asia* (Lanham, MD: Rowman & Littlefield, 2009), vii, 270–80; and Sutter *The United States and Asia*, 233–68.

26. Monika Chansoria, "The Changing Nature of Taiwan-India Ties," *Taiwan Today*, November 12, 2010, http://www.taiwantoday.tw.org.

27. Huchet, "Emergence of a Pragmatic India-China Relationship"; "India and China Eye Each Other Warily"; Satu Limaye, "Acting East under Prime Minister Modi?" *Comparative Connections* 16, no. 3 (January 2015): 141–60; Satu Limaye, "Back in the Same Orbit and Back on Earth," *Comparative Connections* 17, no. 1 (May 2015): 133–48.

28. Han, "China, India Vital to Asia's Growth Story."

29. Limaye, "Acting East under Prime Minister Modi?"

30. Marina Golovnina, "China Offers to Mediate in Stalled Afghan Taliban Peace Talks," *Reuters*, February 12, 2015, http://www.reuters.com/article/2015/02/12/us-pakistan-china-idUSKBN0LG1UP20150212; Sutter, *The United States and Asia*, 233–68.

31. Philippa Brant, "China Pledges $46 Billion for Pakistan, But Will Beijing Deliver?" Lowy Institute *Interpreter*, April 21, 2015, http://www.lowyinterpreter.org/post/2015/04/21/China-pledges-$46-billion-for-Pakistan-but-will-Beijing-deliver.aspx?COLLCC=866310007&.

32. Bates Gill and Matthew Oresman, *China's New Journey to the West* (Washington, DC: Center for Strategic and International Studies, August 2003); Garver, "China's Influence in Central and South Asia"; Kathleen Collins and William Wohlforth, "Defying 'Great Game' Expectation," in *Strategic Asia 2003–2004*, ed. Richard Ellings and Aaron Friedberg (Seattle: National Bureau of Asian Research, 2003), 291–320; Tang Shiping, "Economic Integration in Central Asia," *Asian Survey* 40, no. 2 (March–April 2000): 360–76; Philip Andrews-Speed and Sergei Vinogradov, "China's Involvement in Central Asian Petroleum," *Asian Survey* 40, no. 2

(March–April 2000): 377–97; Venera Galyamova, "Central Asian Countries and China: Managing the Transition," in Zhang Yunling, *Making New Partnership*, 282–323; Yitzhak Shichor, "China's Central Asian Strategy and the Xinjiang Connection," *China and Eurasia Forum Quarterly* 6, no. 2 (2008): 55–73; Chin-Hao Huang, "China and the Shanghai Cooperation Organization: Post-summit Analysis and Implications for the United States," *China and Eurasia Forum Quarterly* 4, no. 3 (August 2006): 15–21; Niklas Swanstrom, "China and Greater Central Asia: A New Great Game or Traditional Vassal?" *Journal of Contemporary China* 14, no. 45 (November 2005): 109–28; Jen-kun Fu, "Reassessing the 'New Great Game' between India and China in Central Asia," *China and Eurasia Forum Quarterly* 8, no. 1 (2010), http://www.chinaeurasia.com; Andrew Small, "China's Caution on Afghanistan-Pakistan," *Washington Quarterly* 33, no. 3 (July 2010): 81–97; Raffaello Pantucci, "China and Central Asia in 2013," *China Brief* 13, no. 2 (January 18, 2013), http://www.jamestown.org/programs/chinabrief/single/?tx_ttnews%5Btt_news%5D=40332&cHash=734a6e4544f563fb65d87ffdce73a63f#.VYgoI_lViko; Jean-Pierre Cabestan, "The Shanghai Cooperation Organization, Central Asia, and the Great Powers, an Introduction," *Asian Survey* 53, no. 3 (2013): 423–35; Marlene Laurelle and Sebastien Peyrouse, eds., *The Chinese Question in Central Asia: Domestic Order, Social Change, and the Chinese Factor* (New York: Columbia University Press, 2012); Wang Jisi, "'Marching Westwards': The Rebalancing of China's Geostrategy," *International and Strategic Studies Report* 73 (October 7, 2012); Zhao Huasheng, "China's View of and Expectations from the Shanghai Cooperation Organization," *Asian Survey* 53, no. 3 (2013): 436–60.

33. Gill and Oresman, *China's New Journey to the West*, viii–ix.

34. Zhou Yan, "A Lifeline from Central Asia," *China Daily*, February 17, 2011; Sebastien Peyrouse, "Sino-Kazakh Relations: A Nascent Strategic Partnership," *China Brief* 8, no. 21 (November 7, 2008): 11–15; C. Frederick Starr, "Central Asia: A Regional Approach to Afghanistan and Its Neighbors," in *Strategic Asia 2008–2009*, ed. Ashley Tellis, Mercy Kuo, and Andrew Marble (Seattle: National Bureau of Asian Research, 2008), 337–39.

35. Peyrouse, "Sino-Kazakh Relations," 12; Kevin Sheives, "China and Central Asia's New Energy Relationship: Keeping Things in Perspective," *China-Eurasia Forum Quarterly* (April 2005): 18; Stephen Blank, "The Strategic Implications of the Turkmenistan-China Pipeline Project," *China Brief* 10, no. 3 (February 4, 2010): 10–12.

36. "Year Ender on Peace in Afghanistan," *Xinhua*, December 8, 1997, carried by FBIS, cited in Sutter, *Chinese Policy Priorities and Their Implications for the United States*, 148.

37. "Chinese Foreign Ministry Delegation Arrives in Afghanistan," Kabul Radio, January 31, 1999, carried by FBIS, cited in Sutter, *Chinese Policy Priorities and Their Implications for the United States*, 148; Small, "China's Caution on Afghanistan-Pakistan"; "China Says Bin Laden's Death a Milestone for Anti-terrorism," *China Daily*, May 3, 2011, http://www.chinadaily.com.cn.

38. Guang Wan, "The U.S. New Central Asian Strategy," *Xiandai guoji guanxi* (Beijing) 11 (November 27, 1997): 13–16.

39. Sutter, *Chinese Policy Priorities and Their Implications for the United States*, 143.

40. Adapted from Gill and Oresman, *China's New Journey to the West*, viii–ix.

41. Garver, "China's Influence in Central and South Asia," 206–9; John Garver, "Development of China's Overland Transportation Links with Central, Southwest, and South Asia," *China Quarterly* 185 (March 2006): 1–22.

42. Wan Zhihong, "China Agrees on New Gas Line," *China Daily*, June 14, 2010, 6.

43. CIA *World Factbook*, accessed June 22, 2015, https://www.cia.gov/library/publications/the-world-factbook/fields/2061.html.

44. Justin Li, "Chinese Investment in Mongolia," *East Asia Forum*, February 2, 2011, http://www.eastasiaforum.org; "Mongolia: A Special Issue," *China Brief* 5, no. 10 (May 5, 2005): 1–12; "China, Mongolia Quietly Enhance Military Ties," *China Brief* 8, no. 17 (September 3, 2008): 2; "China, Mongolia Finalize 4,677-km Border," *China Daily*, December 1, 2005, accessed December 1, 2005, http://www.chinadaily.co.cn.

45. This discussion of Mongolia's economy is taken from *CIA World Factbook 2014*, "Mongolia Economy," https://www.cia.gov/library/publications/the-world-factbook/geos/mg.

html; see also Susan Lawrence, *Mongolia: Issues for Congress*, Congressional Research Service Report R41867 (Washington, DC: Library of Congress, June 14, 2011), 5–10.

46. Discussed in Lawrence, *Mongolia*, 10.

47. Yuriy Humber and Michael Kohn, "Few Roads Leading to China Tell Tale of Mongolian Fears," *Bloomberg*, July 4, 2013, http://www.bloomberg.com/news/articles/2013-07-04/few-roads-leading-to-china-tell-a-tale-of-mongolia-s-trad.

48. "China Vows to Deepen Friendship with Central Asian Countries," *Xinhuanet*, July 19, 2013, http://news.xinhuanet.com/english/china/2013-07/19/c_132556932.htm.

49. Yu Bin, "Russia's Pride and China's Power," *Comparative Connections* 16, no. 3 (January 2015): 124–25.

50. "China: Reproducing Silk Road Story," *China Daily*, June 5, 2001, accessed June 7, 2001, http://www.chinadaily.co.cn.

51. Gill and Oresman, *China's New Journey to the West*, 7.

52. Gill and Oresman, *China's New Journey to the West*, 6–10; Jianwei Wang, "China's Multilateral Diplomacy in the New Millennium," in *China Rising: Power and Motivation in Chinese Foreign Policy*, ed. Yong Deng and Fei-Ling Wang (Lanham, MD: Rowman & Littlefield, 2005), 177–87.

53. Qin Jize, "Wen: SCO Trade Is Set to Double," *China Daily*, September 16–17, 2006, 1.

54. *Chief Zhang Says SCO Will "Absolutely Never Become Euro-Asian Military Alliance,"* Report CPP20060116001017 (Washington, DC: FBIS, January 16, 2006).

55. Gill and Oresman, *China's New Journey to the West*, 10–12.

56. Yu Bin, "China-Russia Relations: A New World Order according to Moscow and Beijing," *Comparative Connections* 7, no. 3 (October 2005): 143–47.

57. "China: Reproducing the Silk Road Story."

58. "China: Reproducing the Silk Road Story."

59. Jyotsna Bashki, "Sino-Russian Strategic Partnership in Central Asia: Implications for India," *Strategic Analysis* 25, no. 2 (May 2001): 4.

60. "China: Reproducing the Silk Road Story."

61. "People's Daily Editorial Hails SCO Founding," *Xinhua*, June 15, 2001, accessed June 18, 2001, http://www.taiwansecurity.org.

62. "China: Regional Co-op Boosted," *China Daily*, June 15, 2001, accessed June 16, 2001, http://www.chinadaily.co.cn.

63. "People's Daily Editorial Hails SCO Founding."

64. "SCO Charter Adopted," *China Daily*, June 8, 2002, accessed June 9, 2002, http://www.chinadaily.co.cn.

65. Sergei Blagov, "Shanghai Cooperation Organization Prepares for New Role," *Eurasia Insight*, April 29, 2002, http://www.eurasianet.org/departments/insight/articles.

66. "SCO Opens Permanent Secretariat in Beijing," *Xinhua*, January 15, 2004, accessed January 18, 2004, http://www.taiwansecurity.org.

67. Yu Bin, "Party Time," *Comparative Connections* 5, no. 2 (July 2003), http://www.csis.org/pacfor.

68. Gill and Oresman, *China's New Journey to the West*, 7.

69. "'Shanghai Spirit'—New Banner of International Cooperation," *Xinhua*, June 15, 2001, accessed June 18, 2001, http://www.taiwansecurity.org.

70. Robert Sutter, "China's Recent Approach to Asia: Seeking Long-Term Gains," *NBR Analysis* 13, no. 1 (March 2002): 19.

71. Joseph Ferguson, "Disappointment in Dushanbe," *PacNet* 47 (September 9, 2008), accessed September 10, 2008, http://www.csis.org/pacfor; Zhu Feng, "Russia-Georgia Military Conflict: Testing China's Responsibility," *CSIS Freeman Report* (November 2008): 1–3.

72. Gill and Oresman, *China's New Journey to the West*, 17.

73. James Millward, *Eurasian Crossroads: A History of Xinjiang* (New York: Columbia University Press, 2007); Gill and Oresman, *China's New Journey to the West*, 18; Yu Bin, "Coping with the Post-Kosovo Fallout," *Comparative Connections* 1, no. 1 (July 1999), http://www.csis.org/pacfor.

74. Stephen Blank, "Central Asia's Strategic Revolution," *NBR Analysis* 14, no. 4 (November 2003): 51–77.

75. "SCO Officials Vow to Pursue Peace," *China Daily*, January 8, 2002, accessed January 9, 2002, http://www.chinadaily.co.cn.

76. "SCO Defense Ministers Sign Communiqué on Military Cooperation," *Xinhua*, May 15, 2002, accessed May 20, 2002, http://www.taiwansecurity.org.

77. "Shanghai Five Fight Terrorism," *China Daily*, August 12, 2003, accessed August 12, 2003, http://www.chinadaily.co.cn.

78. "Hijacked Airline Tests SCO's Anti-terror Skills," *Xinhua*, August 7, 2003, accessed August 8, 2003, http://www.xinhuanet.com/english; "China's Top Legislature Approves Treaty on SCO Joint Military Exercises," *Xinhua*, December 27, 2008, accessed January 2, 2009, http://www.chinaview.cn; Richard Weitz, "China's Growing Clout in the SCO," *China Brief* 10, no. 20 (October 8, 2010): 8–11.

79. Stephen Blank, "Recent Trends in Russo-Chinese Military Relations," *China Brief* 9, no. 2 (January 22, 2009): 6–8; Edward Wong, "China Quietly Extends Its Footprints into Central Asia," *New York Times,* January 2, 2011, http://www.nytimes.com.

80. Yu Bin, "Treaties Scrapped, Treaties Signed," *Comparative Connections* 3, no. 2 (July 2001), http://www.csis.org/pacfor.

81. "Roundup: Economic Cooperation to Add New Light to SCO," *Xinhua*, May 28, 2002, accessed May 29, 2002, http://www.xinhuanet.com/english.

82. Yu Bin, "The Russian-Chinese Oil Politik," *Comparative Connections* 5, no. 4 (October 2003), http://www.csis.org/pacfor.

83. Bernard D. Cole, *Oil for the Lamps of China: Beijing's 21st-Century Search for Energy* (Honolulu: University Press of the Pacific), viii, 70; Sheives, "China and Central Asia's New Energy Relationship," 18.

84. Yu Bin, "Russia's Pride and China's Power," 124–25.

85. Yu Bin, "Russia's Pride and China's Power," 124–25.

86. "SCO Charter Adopted."

87. Matthew Oresman, "The SCO: A New Hope or a Graveyard of Acronyms?" *PacNet* 21 (May 22, 2003), http://www.csis.org/pacfor.

88. Garver, "China's Influence in Central and South Asia," 213; European Commission, *Trade Issues: Central Asia*, accessed February 12, 2009, http://www.csis.org/media/csis/pubs/pac0819.pdf; CIA *World Factbook*, Export Partners, accessed June 23, 2015, https://www.cia.gov/library/publications/the-world-factbook/fields/2050.html.

89. Yu Bin, "China-Russia Relations."

90. Michael Mihalka, "Not Much of a Game: Security Dynamics in Central Asia," *China and Eurasia Quarterly* 5, no. 2 (2007): 21–39; Dan Burghart, "The New Nomads? The American Military Presence in Central Asia," *China and Eurasia Quarterly* 5, no. 2 (2007): 5–19; Sutter, *The United States and Asia*, 269–96.

91. Compare Susan Shirk, *China: Fragile Superpower* (New York: Oxford University Press, 2007), 140–254, with Matthew Oresman, "Repaving the Silk Road: China's Emergence in Central Asia," in *China and the Developing World: Beijing's Strategy for the Twenty-first Century*, ed. Joshua Eisenman, Eric Heginbotham, and Derek Mitchell (Armonk, NY: Sharpe, 2007), 60–83.

92. Kevin Sheives, "China Turns West: Beijing's Contemporary Strategy toward Central Asia," *Pacific Affairs* 79, no. 2 (Summer 2006): 205–24.

93. Swanstrom, "China and Central Asia," 569–84.

94. Celeste Wallander, "Russia: The Domestic Sources of a Less-Than-Grand Strategy," in *Strategic Asia 2007–2008*, ed. Ashley Tellis and Michael Wills (Seattle: National Bureau of Asian Research, 2007), 138–75.

11. RELATIONS WITH RUSSIA AND EUROPE

1. Chinese assessments and commentaries on these issues include Feng Yujin, "International Natural Gas Market and Prospects for Sino-Russian Cooperation," *Contemporary International Relations* (Beijing) 20, no. 6 (November–December 2010): 23–33; Chen Dongxiao,

"Opportunities and Challenges in China's Relations with Major Powers," *Foreign Affairs Journal* (Beijing) 97 (August 2010): 55–68; Ji Zhiye, "Strategic Prospects for Russia," *Contemporary International Relations* (Beijing) 20, no. 5 (September–October 2010): 1–16; Xing Guangcheng, "Work for Mutual Trust and Mutual Benefit in Deepening Sino-Russian Relations," *Foreign Affairs Journal* (Beijing) 80 (June 2006): 8–13; Li Shaoxian, "China-Russia Bond," *Xiandai guoji guanxi* (Beijing) 17 (January 2007): 5–21; Liu Mingli, "Reflection on EU-China Relations," *Contemporary International Relations* (Beijing) 20, no. 3 (May–June 2010): 115–22; Xia Liping, "Sino-EU Security Relations," *Contemporary International Relations* (Beijing) 20, no. 1 (January–February 2010): 102–8; Mei Zhaorong, "Sino-European Relations in Retrospect and Prospect," *Foreign Affairs Journal* (Beijing) 79 (March 2006): 17–27; Shen Qiang, "Properly Handle Problems Arising from Development of the Sino-EU Relations," *Foreign Affairs Journal* (Beijing) 90 (Winter 2008): 92–103; Feng Zhongping, "China-EU Relationship," *Xiandai guoji guanxi* (Beijing) 17 (January 2007): 47–55; Tang Xizhong et al., "Zhong E Guanxi," in *The Bilateral and Multilateral Relations between China and Her Neighbor Countries* (Beijing: Zhongguo Shehui Kexue Chubanshe, 2003), 186–99; and Zhou Hong, "Lun Zhong Ou Huoban Guanxi Zhong de Bu Dui Cheng Xing yu Dui Cheng Xing," in *World Politics—Views from China* (Beijing: Xin Shijie Chubanshe, 2007), 298–315.

2. Jeannne Wilson, *Strategic Partners: Russian-Chinese Relations in the Post-Soviet Era* (Armonk, NY: Sharpe, 2004); Yu Bin, "China and Russia: Normalizing Their Strategic Partnership," in *Power Shift: China and Asia's New Dynamics*, ed. David Shambaugh (Berkeley: University of California Press, 2005), 228–46; Robert Sutter, *China's Rise in Asia: Promises and Perils* (Lanham, MD: Rowman & Littlefield, 2005), 107–22; Peter Ferdinand, "Sunset, Sunrise: China and Russia Construct a New Relationship," *International Affairs* 83, no. 5 (2007): 841–67; Bobo Lo, *Axis of Convenience: Moscow, Beijing, and the New Geopolitics* (Washington, DC: Brookings Institution Press, 2008).

3. Lo, *Axis of Convenience*; Wilson, *Strategic Partners*; Yu Bin, "China-Russia: Embracing a Storm and Each Other?" *Comparative Connections* 10, no. 4 (January 2009): 131–40; Yu Bin, "Reset under Medvedev," *Comparative Connections* 12, no. 2 (July 2010): 135–45; Rajan Menon, "Sick Man of Asia," *National Interest*, Fall 2003, 93–105; Elizabeth Wishnick, "Russia and China: Brothers Again?" *Asian Survey* 41, no. 5 (September–October 2001): 797–821; Sherman Garnett, ed., *Rapprochement or Rivalry? Russia-China Relations in a Changing Asia* (Washington, DC: Carnegie Endowment for International Peace, 2000).

4. John Garver, *Foreign Relations of the People's Republic of China* (Englewood Cliffs, NJ: Prentice Hall, 1993), 31–39, 304–13; Lowell Dittmer, *Sino-Soviet Normalization and Its International Implications, 1945–1990* (Seattle: University of Washington Press, 1992).

5. Robert Ross, ed., *China, the United States, and the Soviet Union: Tripolarity and Policy Making in the Cold War* (Armonk, NY: Sharpe, 1993).

6. Rajan Menon, "The Strategic Convergence between Russia and China," *Survival* 39, no. 2 (Summer 1997): 101–25.

7. James Clay Moltz, "Regional Tension in the Russo-Chinese Rapprochement," *Asian Survey* 35, no. 6 (June 1995): 511–27.

8. Stephen Uhalley, "Sino-Soviet Relations: Continued Improvement amidst Tumultuous Change," *Journal of East Asian Affairs* 6, no. 1 (Winter–Spring 1992): 171–92.

9. Robert Sutter, *Chinese Policy Priorities and Their Implications for the United States* (Lanham, MD: Rowman & Littlefield, 2000), 65.

10. Menon, "The Strategic Convergence between Russia and China"; Stephen Blank, *Dynamics of Russian Weapons Sales to China* (Carlisle, PA: U.S. Army War College, Strategic Studies Institute, March 4, 1997).

11. Bates Gill and Matthew Oresman, *China's New Journey to the West* (Washington, DC: Center for Strategic and International Studies, August 2003), 5–6.

12. Moltz, "Regional Tension in the Russo-Chinese Rapprochement," 518.

13. Sutter, *Chinese Policy Priorities and Their Implications for the United States*, 66.

14. Blank, *Dynamics of Russian Weapons Sales to China*; *China's Rising Military Power*, Congressional Research Service Report 96-647F (Washington, DC: Library of Congress, July 31, 1998).

15. Sutter, *Chinese Policy Priorities and Their Implications for the United States*, 67.

16. Menon, "The Strategic Convergence between Russia and China."

17. Sutter, *Chinese Policy Priorities and Their Implications for the United States*, 67.

18. Sutter, *Chinese Policy Priorities and Their Implications for the United States*, 68.

19. Peter Rodman, "A New Russian-Chinese Alliance?" *Los Angeles Times*, March 25, 1996, accessed March 25, 1996, http://www.latimes.com; Alexander Nemets and Thomas Torda, *The Russian Chinese Alliance* (West Palm Beach, FL: Newsmax.com, 2002).

20. Peggy Falkenheim Meyer, "From Cold War to Cold Peace? U.S.-Russian Security Relations in the Far East," in *Russian Security Policy in the Asia-Pacific Region: Two Views*, ed. Stephen Blank (Carlisle, PA: U.S. Army War College, Strategic Studies Institute, May 1996).

21. Stuart Goldman, *Russian-Chinese Cooperation: Prospects and Implications*, Congressional Research Service Report 97-185F (Washington, DC: Library of Congress, January 27, 1997), 8–13.

22. Sutter, *Chinese Policy Priorities and Their Implications for the United States*, 68.

23. Gilbert Rozman, "Russian Foreign Policy in Northeast Asia," in *The International Relations of Northeast Asia*, ed. Samuel Kim (Lanham, MD: Rowman & Littlefield, 2004), 201–11.

24. Goldman, *Russian-Chinese Cooperation*, 13.

25. Rozman, "Russian Foreign Policy in Northeast Asia."

26. Rouben Azizian, "Russia's China Debate," in *Asia's China Debate* (Honolulu: Asia Pacific Center for Security Studies, December 2003), 6–7.

27. Sutter, *Chinese Policy Priorities and Their Implications for the United States*, 74–75.

28. William Wohlforth, "Russia," in *Strategic Asia 2002–2003*, ed. Richard Ellings and Aaron Friedberg (Seattle: National Bureau of Asian Research, 2002), 183–222.

29. Wohlforth, "Russia," 165–80; Joseph Ferguson, "Energizing the Relationship," *Comparative Connections* 5, no. 3 (October 2003), http://www.csis.org/pacfor.

30. Ching Cheong, "U.S.-Russia Summit Worries China," *Straits Times*, May 31, 2002, accessed June 5, 2002, http://www.taiwansecurity.org; Willy Wo-Lap Lam, "Moscow Tilts West, Beijing Worries," *China Brief* 12, no. 12 (June 6, 2002): 1–3; Yu Bin, "A 'Nice' Treaty in a Precarious World," *Comparative Connections* 3, no. 3 (October 2001), http://www.csis.org/pacfor.

31. Robert Sutter, *The United States and East Asia: Dynamics and Implications* (Lanham, MD: Rowman & Littlefield, 2003), 114.

32. Azizian, "Russia's China Debate"; Rozman, "Russian Foreign Policy in Northeast Asia"; Sutter, *China's Rise in Asia*, 121.

33. Yu Bin, "The New World Order according to Moscow and Beijing," *Comparative Connections* 7, no. 3 (October 2005), http://www.csis.org/pacfor.

34. Yu Bin, "Pragmatism Dominates Russia-China Relations," *PacNet* 11 (March 20, 2006), http://www.csis.org/pacfor.

35. The Putin visit received full coverage in *China Daily* and other official Chinese media on March 20, 21, and 22. Yu Bin, "China's Year of Russia and the Gathering Nuclear Storm," *Comparative Connections* 8, no. 1 (April 2006): 145–51.

36. Sutter, *The United States and East Asia*, 115; Azizian, "Russia's China Debate"; Yu Bin, "Reset under Medvedev"; Rozman, "Russian Foreign Policy in Northeast Asia."

37. Yu Bin, "Reset under Medvedev"; Yu Bin, "Guns and Games of August: Tales of Two Strategic Partners," *Comparative Connections* 10, no. 3 (October 2008): 131–38.

38. Yu Bin, "Putin Invited Xi; Overture to 2012," *Comparative Connections* 12, no. 1 (April 2010): 119; "China-Russia Economic, Trade Co-op New Starts: Minister," *China Daily*, November 25, 2010, http://www.chinadaily.com.

39. "China, Russia Sign $25-Billion Loan-for-Oil Deal," *Financial Times*, February 18, 2009, accessed February 19, 2009, http://www.ft.com.

40. Michael Richardson, "China and Russia Spread Their Influence over Central Asia," *Canberra Times*, August 2, 2007, accessed February 16, 2009, http://www.canberratimes.com.au.

41. Yu Bin, "China-Russia: Embracing a Storm and Each Other?" 135; Stephen Blank, "Recent Trends in Russo-Chinese Military Relations," *China Brief* 9, no. 2 (January 22, 2009): 6–8.

42. Jeremy Page, "China Clones, Sells Russian Fighter Jets," *Wall Street Journal*, December 6, 2010, http://www.wsj.com; Minnie Chan, "Russia Will Sell Beijing Hi-Tech Jets," December 2, 2010, *South China Morning Post*, http://www.scmp.com.

43. "The Crisis in Ukraine Is Drawing Russia Closer to China, But the Relationship Is Far from Equal," *The Economist*, May 9, 2015, http://www.economist.com/news/china/21650566-crisis-ukraine-drawing-russia-closer-china-relationship-far-equal; "49 Deals Cement Partnership," *China Daily*, May 21, 2014, 1; June Teufel Dreyer, "China and Russia: A Limited Partnership," Foreign Policy Research Institute *E-Notes*, February 2015.

44. Zachary Keck, "Putin Approves Sale of S-400 to China," *The Diplomat*, April 11, 2014, http://thediplomat.com/2014/04/putin-approves-sale-of-s-400-to-china/; "The Crisis in Ukraine Is Drawing Russia closer to China."

45. "Chinese Warships to Join Russian Navy in Black Sea, Mediterranean for Historic Drill," *RT*, May 7, 2015, http://rt.com/news/256573-russia-china-novorossiysk-ships.

46. Gilbert Rozman, "Asia for Asians: Why Chinese-Russian Friendship is Here to Stay," *Foreign Affairs*, October 28, 2014, https://www.foreignaffairs.com/articles/east-asia/2014-10-29/asia-asians.

47. "China Opposes Alliance with Any Other," *China Daily*, May 11, 2015, http://www.chinadaily.com.cn/opinion/2015-05/11/content_20677200.htm.

48. David Shambaugh, "China and Europe: The Emerging Axis," *Current History* 103, no. 674 (September 2004): 243–48.

49. Jean-Pierre Cabestan, "European Union–China Relations and the United States," paper prepared for the fifty-eighth annual meeting of the Association for Asian Studies, April 6–9, 2006, San Francisco; Jean-Pierre Cabestan, "European Union–China Relations and the United States," *Asian Perspective* 30, no. 4 (Winter 2006): 11–38.

50. David Shambaugh, "China-Europe Relations Get Complicated," *Brookings Institution Northeast Asia Commentary*, May 2007, accessed May 17, 2007, http://www.brookings.edu; David Shambaugh, "The 'China Honeymoon' Is Over," *International Herald Tribune*, November 26, 2007, accessed November 26, 2007, http://www.iht.com.

51. Pu Chendong, "European Trip Yields Ripe Fruit," *China Daily*, April 3, 2014, http://www.chinadaily.com.cn/world/2014xivisiteu/2014-04/03/content_17402630.htm; European Commission, "Joint Statement: Deepening the EU-China Comprehensive Strategic Partnership for Mutual Benefit," press release, March 31, 2014; Wu Jiao, "France Welcomes China with Massive Deals," *China Daily*, November 11, 2010, http://www.chinadaily.com; Philippa Runner, "EU-China Relations Continue to Fray," *EU Observer*, December 1, 2008, accessed December 1, 2008, http://www.euobserver.com; "Wen Ends EU Tour with Optimism," *China Daily*, February 3, 2009, 1; Edward Wong, "Nobel Prize Is Seen as Rebuke to China," *New York Times*, October 8, 2010, http://www.nytimes.com; Xu Xianping, "Li's Visit Pushes China-EU Ties toward New Stage," *China Daily*, January 6, 2011, 8; "China's Attitude on Libya: Give Peace a Chance," *People's Daily Online*, March 31, 2011, http://www.peoplesdailyonline.com.

52. Michael Yahuda, "China and Europe: The Significance of a Secondary Relationship," in *Chinese Foreign Policy: Theory and Practice*, ed. Thomas W. Robinson and David Shambaugh (New York: Oxford University Press, 1994), 266–82; David Shambaugh, "The New Strategic Triangle: U.S. and European Reactions to China's Rise," *Washington Quarterly* 29, no. 3 (Summer 2005): 7–25; Lanxin Xiang, "China's Eurasian Experiment," *Survival* 46, no. 2 (Summer 2004): 109–22; Hou Yousheng, "Oumeny yu Meiguo dai Hua zhanlue bijiao," *Xiandai guoji guanxi* (Beijing) 8 (August 2006): 1–6; Hou Zhengdo, "Guanyu Zhong Ou zhanlue guanxi jige xiangfa," *Guoji Wenti Yanjiu* (Beijing) 2 (April 2005): 22–25. Recent publications resulting from dialogues among European, Chinese, and other specialists examining the status and outlook of China–Europe relations include Bates Gill and Melissa Murphy, *China-Europe Relations: Implications and Policy Responses for the United States* (Washington, DC: Center for Strategic and International Studies, May 2008); David Shambaugh and Gudrun Wacker, eds., *American and European Relations with China* (Berlin: Stiftung Wissenschaft und Politik, 2008); David Shambaugh, Eberhard Sandschneider, and Zhou Hong, eds., *China-Europe Relations: Perceptions, Policies, and Prospects* (London: Routledge, 2007); and Jing Men and Guiseppe Balducci, eds., *Prospects and Challenges for EU-China Relations in the Twenty-first*

Century (Brussels: PIE–Peter Lang, 2010); European Commission, "Joint Statement: Deepening the EU-China Comprehensive Strategic Partnership for Mutual Benefit," press release, March 31, 2014; "Full Text of China's Policy Paper on the EU," *Xinhuanet*, April 2, 2014; Theresa Fallon, "China's Pivot to Europe," *America Foreign Policy Interests* 36 (2014): 175–82.

53. "Ambassador: China-Portugal Strategic Partnership Will Be More Fruitful," *Xinhua*, February 7, 2009, accessed February 20, 2009, http://www.xinhuanet.com/english.

54. Jean-Pierre Cabestan, "A European Role in Cross-Strait Relations?" paper presented for the Fifth Northeast Asian Forum titled "The Taiwan Strait and Northeast Asian Security," Stiftung Wissenschaft und Politik, Berlin, December 15–17, 2005, 2.

55. Cabestan, "European Union–China Relations and the United States"; Francois Godement, *A Global China Policy* (Paris: European Council on Foreign Relations Policy Brief, 2010).

56. Sutter, *Chinese Policy Priorities and Their Implications for the United States*, 150.

57. "Text of China-EU Summit Statement," *Xinhua*, April 2, 1998, carried by Foreign Broadcast Information Service, cited in Sutter, *Chinese Policy Priorities and Their Implications for the United States*, 173.

58. "China Posts First EU Trade Surplus in Five Years," *Reuters*, February 4, 1998 (Internet version); "PRC-EU Trade Growth in 1999," *Xinhua*, January 22, 1999. Both sources are cited in Sutter, *Chinese Policy Priorities and Their Implications for the United States*, 172.

59. Lanxin Xiang, "China's Eurasian Experiment."

60. Sutter, *Chinese Policy Priorities and Their Implications for the United States*, 151, 172.

61. *"Towards a New Asia Strategy"* (Brussels: Commission of the European Communities, July 13, 1994); *"A Long-Term Policy for China-Europe Relations"* (Brussels: Commission of the European Communities, July 5, 1995); *"Regarding the Asia-Europe Meeting (ASEM) to Be Held in Bangkok on 1–2 March 1996"* (Brussels: Commission of the European Communities, Communication of the Commission to the Council and Parliament, 1996); *"Building Comprehensive Partnership with China"* (Brussels: Commission of the European Communities, June 29, 1998); "Text of China-EU Summit Statement."

62. Feng Zhongping, "EU's China Policy Analyzed," *Contemporary International Relations* (Beijing) 8, no. 4 (April 1998): 1–6; Yahuda, "China and Europe"; Michael Yahuda, *Europe and America in Asia: Same Bed, Different Dreams,* Sigur Policy Paper 18 (Washington, DC: George Washington University, Sigur Center for Asian Studies, 2004); Sutter, *Chinese Policy Priorities and Their Implications for the United States*, 151–53.

63. Shambaugh, "China and Europe," 243.

64. Hou Na, "Fifth China-EU Strategic Dialogue Calls for Closer Ties," *CCTV*, May 6, 2015, accessed June 24, 2015, http://english.cntv.cn/2015/05/06/VIDE1430891651506439.shtml.

65. "EU Becomes China's Largest Trade Partner," *Xinhua*, January 10, 2005, accessed January 19, 2005, http://www.taiwansecurity.org.

66. Stanley Crossick, Fraser Cameron, and Alex Berkofy, *EU-China Relations: Toward a Strategic Partnership*, Working Paper (Brussels: European Policy Centre, July 2005), 26; "Senior Chinese Official Calls for Enhanced Trade, Economic Cooperation with EU," *Xinhua*, December 29, 2010, http://www.xinhua.com; "Full Text of China's Policy Paper on the EU"; "Fifth China-EU Strategic Dialogue Calls for Closer Ties."

67. "Senior Chinese Official Calls for Enhanced Trade, Economic Cooperation with EU"; Crossick et al., *EU-China Relations*, 26–27; Xu, "Li's Visit Pushes China-EU Ties toward New Stage"; European Union, "EU_China Trade (11/03/2015)," http://eeas.europa.eu/delegations/china/press_corner/all_news/news/2015/20150311_en.htm.

68. Cabestan, "European Union–China Relations and the United States," 18–19; Crossick et al., *EU-China Relations*, 26–27; "Senior Chinese Official Calls for Enhanced Trade, Economic Cooperation with EU"; European Commission, *Trade—China* accessed June 24, 2015, http://ec.europa.eu/trade/policy/countries-and-regions/countries/china/.

69. "EU Policy Paper Stresses Closer China Relations," *China Daily*, October 25, 2006, 1; Jonathan Stearns, "Three China Solar Panel Firms Lose EU Tariff Exemptions," *Bloomberg*,

June 15, 2015, http://www.bloomberg.com/news/articles/2015-06-05/three-china-solar-panel-groups-lose-eu-tariff-exemptions.

70. Cabestan, "European Union–China Relations and the United States," 19–20.

71. *EU-China Trade in Facts and Figures*, EUROPA MEMO/09/40, January 30, 2009, accessed February 16, 2009, http://europa.eu.

72. Sun Shangwu, "Asia, Europe Eye Bigger Global Role," *China Daily*, September 11, 2006, 1; Qin Jize, "Sino-EU Talks Set to Take Relationship to 'New High,'" *China Daily*, September 2–3, 2006, 2; *Seventh Asia-Europe Meeting*, accessed February 20, 2009, http://www.asem7.cn; "Premier Li Keqiang visits Europe October 9–18, 2014," *Beijing Review*, October 25, 2014, http://www.bjreview.com.cn/Cover_Stories_Series_2014/premier_li_keqiang_visits_europe.html.

73. "Full Text of Joint Statement Issued at 8th China-EU Summit," *Xinhua*, September 5, 2005, accessed September 9, 2005, http://www.xinhuanet.com/english; Huang Shuo, "New Year, Old EU Woes for China," *China Daily*, January 7, 2011, http://www.chinadaily.com.cn; "Premier Li Keqiang"; Pu, "European Trip Yields Ripe Fruit."

74. Yahuda, *Europe and America in Asia*, 5.

75. People's Republic of China Ministry of Foreign Affairs, *China's EU Policy Paper* (Beijing: Ministry of Foreign Affairs, October 13, 2003), http://www.fmprc.gov.cn/eng/zxxx/t27708.htm.

76. Cabestan, "European Union–China Relations and the United States," 6–8.

77. Neil King and Marc Champion, "EU, U.S. Policy on China Converges on Key Issues: Trade, Defense Spats Foster Alignment, Worrying Beijing," *Wall Street Journal*, May 4, 2006, accessed May 4, 2006, http://www.wsj.com; Cabestan, "European Union–China Relations and the United States," 7.

78. Shambaugh, "China and Europe," 243–44.

79. *China Outbound Tourism 2014*, accessed June 24, 2015, http://www.travelchinaguide.com/tourism/2014statistics/outbound.htm.

80. Riazat Butt, "A Class Act—UK Universities Attract More Chinese Students," *China Daily*, April 13, 2015, http://europe.chinadaily.com.cn/business/2015-04/13/content_20419388.htm.

81. Francois Godement, "China's Apparent Cost-Free Slight to Europe," *PacNet* 65 (December 9, 2008), http://www.csis.org/pacfor; "Wen Ends EU Tour with Optimism," *China Daily*, February 2, 2009, 1.

82. Tania Branihan and Jonathan Watts, "Chinese PM Rebuts Criticism over Copenhagen Role," *The Guardian*, March 14, 2010, http://www.guardian.uk.com; Goeff Dyer and Andrew Ward, "Europe Defies China's Nobel Threat," *Financial Times*, November 5, 2010, http://www.tf.com.

83. "China's Attitude on Libya: Give Peace a Chance."

84. Robert Sutter, *Historical Dictionary of Chinese Foreign Policy* (Lanham, MD: Scarecrow Press, 2011), 60.

85. Francois Perreault, "Can China Become a Major Arctic Player?" *RSIS Commentaries* 073/2012, April 24, 2012, accessed July 8, 2012, http://www.rsis.edu.sg/publications/Perspective/RSIS0732012.pdf.

12. RELATIONS WITH THE MIDDLE EAST, AFRICA, AND LATIN AMERICA

1. A Chinese government specialist wrote in an editorial in 2010 that China "consumed 0.82 ton of standard oil for every $1,000 increase in GDP value" while "in the U.S. and Japan, the figure was 0.20 ton and 0.10 ton respectively." Feng Zhaokui, "China Still a Developing Nation," *China Daily*, May 6, 2010, 12. Chinese perspectives on relations with the Middle East, Africa, and Latin America include the following: Li Shaoxian and Wei Liang, "New Complexities in the Middle East since 9.11," *Contemporary International Relations* (Beijing) 20, special

issue (September 2010): 22–32; Li Shaoxian and Tang Zhichao, "China and the Middle East," *Xiandai guoji guanxi* (Beijing) 17 (January 2007): 22–31; Tang Jizan, "The Middle East Situation Is Full of Variables," *Foreign Affairs Journal* (Beijing) 79 (March 2006): 63–72; "White Paper on China-Africa Economic Cooperation and Trade Cooperation," *China Daily*, December 24, 2010, 9; Zeng Qiang, "FOCAC: A Powerful Engine for the Continued Development of Friendship between China and Africa," *Contemporary International Relations* (Beijing) 20, no. 6 (November–December 2010): 45–59; Xu Weizhong, "Beijing Summit Promotes Sino-African Relations," *Xiandai guoji guanxi* (Beijing) 17 (January 2007): 72–79; "Full Text of China's Africa Policy," *People's Daily*, January 12, 2006, accessed January 12, 2006, http://www.peoplesdaily.com.cn; He Wenping, "The Balancing Act of China's Africa Policy," *China Security* 3, no. 3 (Summer 2007): 23–41; Wu Hongying, "Latin America: Key Trends and Challenges," *Contemporary International Relations* (Beijing) 20, special issue (September 2010): 33–42; and Wu Hongying, "A New Era of Sino-Latin American Relations," *Xiandai guoji guanxi* (Beijing) 17 (January 2007): 64–71.

2. Phillip C. Saunders, *China's Global Activism: Strategy, Drivers, and Tools*, Occasional Paper 4 (Washington, DC: National Defense University, Institute for National Strategic Studies, June 2006), 2; Thomas Lum, coord., *Comparing Global Influence: China's and U.S. Diplomacy, Foreign Aid, Trade, and Investment in the Developing World*, Congressional Research Service Report RL34620 (Washington, DC: Library of Congress, August 15, 2008); Lowell Dittmer and George T. Yu, eds., *China, the Developing World, and the New Global Dynamic* (Boulder, CO: Rienner, 2010); "China in Africa: One Among Many," *The Economist*, January 17, 2015, http://www.economist.com/news/middle-east-and-africa/21639554-china-has-become-big-africa-now-backlash-one-among-many; *2013 China-Latin America Bulletin*, accessed June 5, 2015, http://www.bu.edu/pardee/files/2014/01/Economic-Bulletin-2013.pdf.

3. John Garver, *China and Iran: Ancient Partners in a Post-imperial World* (Seattle: University of Washington Press, 2006).

4. Jon B. Alterman and John Garver, *The Vital Triangle: China, the United States, and the Middle East* (Washington, DC: Center for Strategic and International Studies, 2008); John Garver, "Is China Playing a Dual Game in Iran?" *Washington Quarterly* 34, no. 1 (Winter 2011): 75–88.

5. Wenran Jiang, "China's Growing Energy Relations with the Middle East," *China Brief* 7, no. 14 (July 11, 2007): 12–15.

6. Lillian Harris, *China Considers the Middle East* (London: Tauris, 1993); Guang Pan, "China's Success in the Middle East," *Middle East Quarterly* (December 1997): 35–40; Lillian Harris, "Myth and Reality in China's Relations with the Middle East," in *Chinese Foreign Policy: Theory and Practice*, ed. Thomas W. Robinson and David Shambaugh (New York: Oxford University Press, 1994), 322–47; Alexander Lennon, "Trading Guns, Not Butter," *China Business Review* (March–April 1994): 47–49.

7. Robert Sutter, *Chinese Policy Priorities and Their Implications for the United States* (Lanham, MD: Rowman & Littlefield, 2000), 156.

8. Han Xiaoxing, "China–Middle East Links," *China Business Review* (March–April 1994): 44–46.

9. Lennon, "Trading Guns, Not Butter"; Guang Pan, "China's Success in the Middle East."

10. Guang Pan, "China's Success in the Middle East"; Harris, *China Considers the Middle East*; Wenran Jiang, "China's Growing Energy Relations with the Middle East"; Xia Liping, "Sino-Israeli Contacts as Seen from Declassified Foreign Ministry Files," *Dangdai Zhongguoshi yenjiu* [Contemporary China History Studies] 12, no. 3 (May 2005): 76–82; Sutter, *Chinese Policy Priorities and Their Implications for the United States*, 157.

11. Huai Chengbo, "Why Do Arab Nations Widen the Gap with the United States?" *Liaowang* 11 (March 16, 1998): 42; Yitzhak Shichor, "China and the Role of the United Nations in the Middle East: Revised Policy," *Asian Survey* 31, no. 3 (March 1991): 255–69.

12. Evan Medeiros, *Reluctant Restraint: The Evolution of China's Nonproliferation Policies and Practices, 1980–2004* (Stanford, CA: Stanford University Press, 2007), 58–65, 81–82; "U.S. Lists Accords with China at Summit," *Reuters*, June 27, 1998, http://www.reuters.com; "Qian Qichen Speaks to Chinese Reporters, Concludes Trip," *Xinhua*, December 26, 1997, carried by Foreign Broadcast Information Service (Internet version).

13. Sutter, *Chinese Policy Priorities and Their Implications for the United States*, 158.

14. Sutter, *Chinese Policy Priorities and Their Implications for the United States*, 158.

15. Fu Quangheng, "Use of Force Has Little Support," *Xinhua*, February 4, 1998, http://www.xinhuanet.com/english; "Russia-China Reject Use of Force against Iraq," *Reuters*, February 17, 1998, http://www.reuters.com; Rong Song, "Iran's New Gulf Diplomatic Offensive," *Xinhua*, November 7, 1997, http://www.xinhuanet.com/english; "Tomur Dawamat, Tang Jiaxuan Meet Libyan Deputy Minister," *Xinhua*, May 12, 1998, http://www.xinhuanet.com/english.

16. "Russia-China Reject Use of Force against Iraq."

17. Tang Jian, Wang Yadong, and Hou Jia, "Qian Qichen's Tour of the Middle East Is a Complete Success," *Xinhua*, December 26, 1997, http://www.xinhuanet.com/english.

18. Sutter, *Chinese Policy Priorities and Their Implications for the United States*, 160.

19. Tang et al., "Qian Qichen's Tour of the Middle East Is a Complete Success."

20. B. Rena Miller, "Israeli Source on Netanyahu Meetings," Agence France-Presse, May 26, 1998, http://www.afp.com.

21. Chas W. Freeman Jr., "The Middle East and China," remarks to a Conference of the U.S Institute of Peace and Georgetown University, February 17, 2015; Alterman and Garver, *The Vital Triangle*; Garver, "Is China Playing a Dual Game in Iran?"; Mao Yufeng, "China's Interests and Strategy in the Middle East," in *China and the Developing World: Beijing's Strategy for the Twenty-first Century*, ed. Joshua Eisenman, Eric Heginbotham, and Derek Mitchell (Armonk, NY: Sharpe, 2007), 113–32; Yitzhak Shichor, "China's Middle East Strategy," in *China and the Developing World*, ed. Lowell Dittmer and George Yu (Boulder, CO: Rienner, 2010), 157–76; Daniel Blumenthal, "Providing Arms," *Middle East Quarterly* (Spring 2005): 11–19; Jing-dong Yuan, "China and the Iranian Nuclear Crisis," *China Brief* 6, no. 3 (February 1, 2006): 6–8; Yitzhak Shichor, "China's Kurdish Policy," *China Brief* 6, no. 1 (January 3, 2006): 3–6.

22. SUSRIS interview with Jon Alterman, October 13, 2008, accessed October 14, 2008, http://www.saudi-us-relations.org/articles/2008/interviews/081013-alterman-interview.html.

23. Flynt Leverett and Jeffrey Bader, "Managing China–U.S. Energy Competition in the Middle East," *Washington Quarterly* 29, no. 1 (Winter 2005–2006): 187–201.

24. John Calabrese, "Saudi Arabia and China Extend Ties beyond Oil," *China Brief* 5, no. 12 (May 24, 2005): 1–4.

25. "The Great Well of China," *The Economist* June 20, 2015 http://www.economist.com/news/middle-east-and-africa/21654655-oil-bringing-china-and-arab-world-closer-economically-politics-will; Fatah Al-Rahman Youssef, "Saudi Arabia, China Sign Nuclear and Renewable Energy Agreement," *Asuarq Al-Awsat*, August 11, 2014, http://www.aawsat.net/2014/08/article55335276/saudi-arabia-china-sign-nuclear-and-renewable-energy-agreement; "Saudi Arabia Ties Get a Boost," *China Daily*, February 12, 2009, 1; Calabrese, "Saudi Arabia and China Extend Ties beyond Oil"; Australian Parliamentary Library Research Service, *Directions in China's Foreign Relations: Implications for East Asia and Australia*, Parliamentary Library Research Brief 9:2005–2006 (Canberra: Australian Parliamentary Library Research Service, December 5, 2005), 16–20.

26. "China-Saudi Trade Reached Record High in 2010," Chinese Embassy in Saudi Arabia, February 9, 2011, http://sa2.mofcom.gov.cn/article/chinanews/201102/20110207391731.shtml; "The Great Well of China."

27. Borzou Daragahi, "Iran Signs $3.2 Billion Natural Gas Deal with China," *Los Angeles Times*, March 14, 2009, accessed March 18, 2009, http://www.latimes.com; Garver, "Is China Playing a Dual Game in Iran?"

28. "Iran-China Trade Volume Reaches $38 Billion," Press TV, February 13, 2011, accessed May 18, 2011, http://www.presstv.ir/detail/165011.html.

29. Michael Richardson, "Middle East Balancing Act Is Becoming Harder for China," *International Herald Tribune*, July 28, 2008, accessed August 3, 2008, http://www.IHT.com; "The Great Well of China."

30. Interview with Chinese Ambassador Hua Liming, cited in Shuang Wen, "From Brothers to Partners: The Evolution of China's Foreign Policy to the Middle East," master's thesis, American University of Cairo, 2008, 75; Yufeng Mao, "Beijing's Two-Pronged Iraq Policy," *China Brief* 5, no. 12 (May 24, 2005).

31. Bonnie Glaser, "Pomp, Blunders, and Substance: Hu's Visit to the U.S.," *Comparative Connections* 8, no. 2 (July 2006): 35–36, 40; and Bonnie Glaser, "Cooperation Faces Challenges," *Comparative Connections* 12, no. 2 (July 2010): 38–39.

32. Blumenthal, "Providing Arms," 6.

33. Chris Zambelis, "China's Palestine Policy," *China Brief* 9, no. 5 (March 4, 2009): 9–12; "China Welcomes Hamas-Fatah Unity Deal," *China Daily*, April 29, 2011, http://www.chinadaily.com.cn.

34. Yitzhak Shichor, "Silent Partner: China and the Lebanon Crisis," *China Brief* 6, no. 17 (August 16, 2006): 2–4.

35. Consultations with Chinese diplomats, Washington, DC, December 18, 2006.

36. Yu Bin, "SCO Five Years On: Progress and Growing Pains," *Comparative Connections* 8, no. 2 (July 2006): 140. "Hu Slams Use of Force, Seeks Libyan Ceasefire," *China Daily*, March 31, 2011, http://www.chinadaily.com.cn.

37. "Smooth Evacuation," *People's Daily Online*, March 6, 2011, http://www.peoplesdaily.com.cn; Yun Sun, "China's Acquiescence on UNSCR 1973: No Big Deal," *PacNet* 20 (March 31, 2011), http://www.csis.org/pacfor.

38. Mu Chunshan, "Revealed: How the Yemen Crisis Wrecked Xi Jinping's Middle East Travel Plans," *The Diplomat*, April 22, 2015, http://thediplomat.com/2015/04/revealed-how-the-yemen-crisis-wrecked-xi-jinpings-middle-east-travel-plans.

39. Gerald Segal, "China and Africa," *Annals of the American Academy of Political and Social Science* 519 (January 1992): 115–26; Philip Snow, "China and Africa: Consensus and Camouflage," in Robinson and Shambaugh, *Chinese Foreign Policy*, 283–321; Deborah Brautigam, *Chinese Aid and African Development* (New York: St. Martin's, 1998).

40. Philip Snow, *The Star Raft: China's Encounter with Africa* (Ithaca, NY: Cornell University Press, 1988); Alaba Ogunsanwo, *China's Policy in Africa, 1958–1971* (New York: Cambridge University Press, 1979); Christopher Alden, Daniel Large, and Ricardo de Oliveria, *China Returns to Africa: A Superpower and a Continent Embrace* (New York: Columbia University Press, 2008); Ian Taylor, *China's New Role in Africa* (Boulder, CO: Rienner, 2008).

41. Sutter, *Chinese Policy Priorities and Their Implications for the United States*, 163–64.

42. Sutter, *Chinese Policy Priorities and Their Implications for the United States*, 164.

43. Snow, "China and Africa," 318–21.

44. For daily coverage of Qian's visit, see *China Daily*, http://www.chinadaily.com.cn; Sutter, *Chinese Policy Priorities and Their Implications for the United States*, 164.

45. These visits were covered extensively in *China Daily* and other official Chinese media.

46. Xiong Guangkai, "China's Defense Policy and Sino-African Relations—Speech at Zimbabwean Defense Staff College on June 2, 1997," *International Strategic Studies* (Beijing) 3 (July 1997): 1–5.

47. "Sudanese Minister on Growing Trends with China," *Xinhua*, February 24, 1998, http://www.xinhuanet.com/english; "Jiang Zemin–Democratic Congo President Hold Talks," *Xinhua*, December 18, 1997, http://www.xinhuanet.com/english; "Official Comments on Sino-African Trade Cooperation," *Xinhua*, January 14, 1998, http://www.xinhuanet.com/english; "China to Set Up Investment Promotion Center in Zambia," *Xinhua*, April 3, 1998, http://www.xinhuanet.com/english; *Conventional Arms Transfers to Developing Countries, 1990–1997*, Congressional Research Service Report 98-647 (Washington, DC: Library of Congress, July 31, 1998).

48. "Official Comments on Sino-African Trade Cooperation"; "News Analysis on Sino-African Ties," *Xinhua*, January 23, 1999, http://www.xinhuanet.com/English.

49. Liu Yegang, "'Roundup' on Criticism of New U.S. Africa Policy," *Xinhua*, March 30, 1998, http://www.xinhuanet.com/english; Yang Rusheng, "Analysis of 'New Partnership,'" *People's Daily*, December 23, 1997, 6.

50. Sutter, *Chinese Policy Priorities and Their Implications for the United States*, 167–68.

51. Deborah Brautigam, *The Dragon's Gift: The Real Story of China in Africa* (New York: Oxford University Press, 2009); George Yu, "China's Africa Policy," in *China, the Developing World, and the New Global Dynamic*, ed. Lowell Dittmer and George Yu (Boulder, CO: Rienner, 2010), 129–56; Alden et al., *China Returns to Africa*; Taylor, *China's New Role in Africa*; Robert I. Rotberg, ed., *China into Africa: Trade, Aid, and Influence* (Washington, DC:

Brookings Institution Press, 2008); David Shinn and Joshua Eisenman, *Responding to China in Africa* (Washington, DC: American Foreign Policy Council, July 2008); Council on Foreign Relations, *More Than Humanitarianism: A Strategic U.S. Approach toward Africa*, Independent Task Force Report 56 (New York: Council on Foreign Relations, January 2006); "Full Text of China's Africa Policy"; *China and Sub-Saharan Africa*, Congressional Research Service Report RL33055 (Washington, DC: Library of Congress, August 29, 2005).

52. Brautigam, *Dragon's Gift*; David Shinn and Joshua Eisenman, *China and Africa* (Philadelphia: University of Pennsylvania Press, 2012); Howard French, *China's Second Continent* (New York: Random House, 2014).

53. "China in Africa: One Among Many."

54. *Africa and China: Issues and Insights—Conference Report* (Washington, DC: Georgetown University, School of Foreign Service, Asian Studies Department, November 7, 2008); Shinn and Eisenman, *China and Africa*; "China in Africa: One Among Many."

55. Chin-Hao Huang, *China's Rising Stakes in Africa*, Asian Studies Research Paper (Washington, DC: Georgetown University, April 2006), 7.

56. *China's African Policy* (Beijing: State Council Information Office, January 2006), http://english.people.com.cn/200601/12/print20060112_234894.html; Yan Yang, "China-Africa Trade Prospects Look Promising: President Hu Jintao Promotes Nation on Tour of the Continent," *China Daily*, April 26, 2006, 9; "Support for Africa 'Not a Temporary Measure,'" *China Daily*, July 3, 2006, 3; Wenran Jiang, "China's Booming Energy Relations with Africa," *China Brief* 6, no. 13 (June 21, 2006): 3–5.

57. Sun Shangwu, "Bright, Prosperous Relations," *China Daily*, November 6, 2006, 1.

58. Yan Yang, "China-Africa Trade Prospects Look Promising."

59. Le Tian, "UN Official Praises Nation's Role in African Development," *China Daily*, August 16, 2006, 2.

60. Xing Zhigang, "Leaders Call for Closer Cooperation," *China Daily*, November 3, 2006, 2.

61. Council on Foreign Relations, *More Than Humanitarianism*, 43.

62. See the discussion of this problem in Saunders, *China's Global Activism*, 13–14.

63. Ding Qingfen, "Countries 'Seek More Investment for Development,'" *China Daily*, April 27, 2011, 1.

64. Saunders, *China's Global Activism*, 2; Lum, *Comparing Global Influence*, 62, 65.

65. Lum, *Comparing Global Influence*, 33; Claire Provost, "China Publishes First Report on Foreign Aid Policy," *The Guardian*, April 28, 2011, http://www.guardian.co.uk; Council on Foreign Relations, *More Than Humanitarianism*, 42.

66. "Appendix: Selected PRC Interactions with Countries in Sub-Saharan Africa, 2003–July 2005," in *China and Sub-Saharan Africa*, 13–18.

67. Council on Foreign Relations, *More Than Humanitarianism*, 42.

68. For discussion of the previously noted investment and foreign assistance questions related to Chinese involvement in Africa, see Jian-Ye Wang, *What Drives China's Growing Role in Africa?* Working Paper WP/07/211 (Washington, DC: International Monetary Fund, August 2007); Vivien Foster, William Butterfield, Chuan Chen, and Nataliya Pushak, *Building Bridges: China's Growing Role as Infrastructure Financier for Sub-Saharan Africa* (Washington, DC: World Bank, 2008); and Brautigam, *Dragon's Gift*.

69. Ding, "Countries 'Seek More Investment for Development'"; Zeng Qiang, "FOCAC"; "White Paper on China-Africa Economic Cooperation and Trade Cooperation," *China Daily*, December 23, 2010, http://www.chinadaily.com.cn; David Smith, "China Poised to Pour $10bn into Zimbabwe's Ailing Economy," *The Guardian*, February 1, 2011, http://www.guardian.co.uk; He Wenping, "Equal Platform, Mutual Benefit," *China Daily*, July 17, 2010, 5; "China-Africa Trade Hits Record High," *China Daily*, December 24, 2010, 3.

70. Elleka Watts, "As Xi Jinping Visits Africa, What Are China's Intentions?" *The Diplomat*, March 25, 2013, http://thediplomat.com/2013/03/as-xi-jinping-visits-africa-what-are-chinas-intentions/1/; "Li Pledges Larger Credit Line, High-Speed Rail Technology to Africa," *South China Morning Post*, May 7, 2014, http://www.scmp.com/news/china/article/1506229/li-pledges-larger-credit-line-high-speed-rail-technology-africa; Zhong Nan and Yan Yiqi, "Africans' Fatter Wallets Shift Focus of Bilateral Trade," *China Daily*, February 2, 2015, http://

/english.gov.cn/news/international_exchanges/2015/02/02/content_281475049021958.htm; Lauren Johnston, "China's Road to Growth in Africa, *East Asia Forum*, February 7, 2015, http://www.eastasiaforum.org/2015/02/07/chinas-road-to-growth-in-africa.

71. Yun Sun, *Xi Jinping's Africa Policy: The First Year* (Washington DC: Brookings Institution, April 14, 2014), http://www.brookings.edu/blogs/africa-in-focus/posts/2014/04/10-jinping-africa-policy-sun; Kevin Wang, "Yemen Evacuation a Strategic Step Forward for China," *The Diplomat*, April 10, 2015, http://thediplomat.com/2015/04/yemen-evacuation-a-strategic-step-forward-for-china/; Nicholas Bariyo, "China Deploys Troop in South Sudan to Defend Oil Field Workers," *Wall Street Journal*, September 9, 2014, http://www.wsj.com/articles/china-deploys-troops-in-south-sudan-to-defend-oil-fields-workers-1410275041; "China 'Negotiates Military Base' in Djibouti," *Aljazeera*, May 9, 2015, http://www.aljazeera.com/news/africa/2015/05/150509084913175.html.

72. Robert Rotberg, "China's $1 trillion for Africa," *China-U.S. Focus*, November 26, 2013, http://www.chinausfocus.com/finance-economy/chinas-1-trillion-for-africa.

73. "Li Pledges Larger Credit Line"; Johnston, "China's Road to Growth."

74. Johnston, "China's Road to Growth."

75. "Nigerian Railway Project: Derailed Too Many Times," *Notes by Nigeria Civil Rights Movement*, June 19, 2011, https://www.facebook.com/notes/nigerian-civil-right-movement/nigerias-railway-project-derailed-too-many-times-any-possible-logg-out-from-the-/1368583 96392560.

76. Lillian Wong, "The Impact of Asian National Oil Companies in Nigeria," *Nigerian Muse*, January 4, 2009, accessed April 9, 2009, http://www.nigerianmuse.com; Wang Ying, "CNOOC Buys Share in Nigerian Oil Mining License," *China Daily*, April 21, 2006, 9; Kate Linebaugh, "CNOOC Is Buying a 45% Stake in Nigerian Oil Field," *Wall Street Journal Online*, January 7, 2006, accessed January 9, 2006, http://www.wsj.com; Adam Wolfe, "The Increasing Importance of African Oil," *Power and Interest News Report*, March 2005, accessed April 2, 2006, http://www.pinr.com; "Nigeria Bilateral Trade with China: Increased by 76.3 Percent," *Vanguard*, June 23, 2010, accessed July 14, 2010, http://allafrica.com.

77. Johnston, "China's Road to Growth"; "China in Africa: One Among Many."

78. "Angola Asks China for Two-Year Freeze on Debt Repayments," *Reuters*, June 11, 2015, http://www.reuters.com/article/2015/06/11/ozatp-uk-angola-china-idAFKBN0OR13W20150611.

79. "China in Africa: One Among Many"; Johnston, "China's Road to Growth."

80. Cecil Johnson, *Communist China and Latin America* (New York: Columbia University Press, 1970); Samuel Kim, *The Third World in Chinese World Policy* (Princeton, NJ: Princeton University Press, 1989); Frank O. Mora, "Sino–Latin American Relations: Sources and Consequences," *Journal of Interamerican Studies and World Affairs* 41, no. 2 (Summer 1999): 91–116; Chein-hsun Wang, "Peking's Latin American Policy in the 1980s," *Issues and Studies* 27, no. 5 (May 1991): 103–18.

81. Jorge Dominguez, *China's Relations with Latin America: Shared Gains, Asymmetrical Hopes*, Working Paper (Washington, DC: Inter-American Dialogue, June 2006); R. Evan Ellis, *U.S. National Security Implications of Chinese Involvement in Latin America* (Carlisle, PA: U.S. Army War College Strategic Studies Institute, June 2005); R. Evan Ellis, *China in Latin America* (Boulder, CO: Rienner, 2009); Kerry Dumbaugh and Mark Sullivan, *China's Growing Interest in Latin America*, Congressional Research Service Report RS22119 (Washington, DC: Library of Congress, April 20, 2005); Riordan Roett and Guadalupe Paz, eds., *China's Expansion into the Western Hemisphere* (Washington, DC: Brookings Institution Press, 2007); Robert Delvin et al., *The Emergence of China: Challenges and Opportunities for Latin America and the Caribbean* (Cambridge, MA: Harvard University Press, 2006); David Shambaugh, "China's New Foray into Latin America," *YaleGlobal Online*, November 17, 2008, accessed November 18, 2008, http://www.yaleglobal.com; Cynthia Watson, "Adios Taipei, Hola Beijing: Taiwan's Relations with Latin America," *China Brief* 4, no. 11 (May 27, 2004): 8–10, and "A Warming Friendship," *China Brief* 4, no. 12 (June 10, 2004): 2–3.

82. As discussed below, China used its veto power to pressure both Guatemala and Haiti to alter their pro-Taiwan policies.

83. Peter Van Ness, *Revolution and Chinese Foreign Policy* (Berkeley: University of California Press, 1971).

84. Chein-hsun Wang, "Peking's Latin American Policy in the 1980s."

85. Mora, "Sino–Latin American Relations."

86. "China to Boost Trade with Latin America," *Xinhua*, January 10, 1999, http://www.xinhuanet.com/english.

87. "Officials Sign Agreements Worth over $19 Million," *Prensa Latina* (Havana), March 27, 1998, cited in Sutter, *Chinese Policy Priorities and Their Implications for the United States*, 175.

88. "NPC's Tian Visits Brazil," *Xinhua*, May 8, 1998, http://www.xinhuanet.com/english; "CPC Senior Official Meets Guatemalan Party Leader," *Xinhua*, February 27, 1998, http://www.xinhuanet.com/english.

89. "NPC Delegation to Visit Latin America," *Xinhua*, April 30, 1998, http://www.xinhuanet.com/english.

90. "Chi Haotian Leaves Beijing," *Xinhua*, February 19, 1999, http://www.xinhuanet.com/english.

91. "Chinese Defense Minister Meets Venezuelan Visitor," *Xinhua*, March 25, 1998, http://www.xinhuanet.com/english; "Chinese Air Force Commander Visits Brazil," *Xinhua*, March 11, 1998, http://www.xinhuanet.com/english; "PLA Commander Leaves Beijing for Cuba, Mexico," *Xinhua*, April 28, 1998, http://www.xinhuanet.com/english.

92. Robert Sutter, *Historical Dictionary of Chinese Foreign Policy* (Lanham, MD: Scarecrow Press, 2011), citations for "Guatemala" and "Haiti."

93. Li Zhiming, "Dialogue and Not Confrontation," *People's Daily*, April 30, 1998, 6; Yuan Bingzhong, "Why Did the U.S. Ease Sanctions on Cuba?" *Xinhua*, March 21, 1998, http://www.xinhuanet.com/english.

94. Yuan Bingzhong, "Albright's Caribbean Trip," *Xinhua*, April 8, 1998, http://www.xinhuanet.com/english.

95. Dominguez, *China's Relations with Latin America*; Ellis, *U.S. National Security Implications of Chinese Involvement in Latin America*; Dumbaugh and Sullivan, *China's Growing Interest in Latin America*; Shambaugh, "China's New Foray into Latin America."

96. *Asia and Latin America and the Caribbean: Economic Links, Cooperation, and Development Strategies*, discussion paper for annual meeting of governors (Washington, DC: Inter-American Development Bank, March 21, 2005).

97. *Asia and Latin America and the Caribbean*; John Paul Rathbone, "China Is Now Region's Biggest Partner," *Financial Times*, April 26, 2011, http://www.ft.com.

98. "Strengthening of Peru-China Trade Relations," U.S. Department of State Cable 5816 from U.S. Embassy, Lima, December 16, 2004.

99. *Asia and Latin America and the Caribbean.*

100. Ruth Morris, "China: Latin America Trade Jumps," *Latin Business Chronicle*, May 9, 2011, http://www.latinbusinesschronicle.com; "China Vows New Brazil Trade Ties," *China Daily*, April 13, 2011, 1.

101. Dumbaugh and Sullivan, *China's Growing Interest in Latin America.*

102. Andres Oppenheimer, "China Seeks Materials, Political Allies," *Miami Herald*, September 25, 2005, accessed September 26, 2005, http://www.miami.com.

103. Dumbaugh and Sullivan, *China's Growing Interest in Latin America.*

104. Wang Xiaotian and Chen Ma, "RMB Fund Planned to Aid Latin America," *China Daily*, April 29, 2011, 13; Brian Winter and Brian Ellsworth, "Brazil and China: A Young Marriage on the Rocks," *Reuters*, February 3, 2011, http://www.reuters.com; "Brazil Leads Surge in LatAm Foreign Investment," *UV10*, May 18, 2011, accessed May 18, 2011, http://www.uv10.com/brazil-leads-surge-in-latam-foreign-investment_800548463/.

105. *China's Growing Interest in Latin America.*

106. Shambaugh, "China's New Foray into Latin America."

107. Thomas Lum, *China's Foreign Aid Activities in Africa, Latin America, and Southeast Asia*, Congressional Research Service Report R40361 (Washington, DC: Library of Congress, February 25, 2009), 15; Erica Downs, *Inside China, Inc: China Development Bank's Cross-*

Border Energy Deals, John Thornton China Center Monograph Series 3 (Washington, DC: Brookings Institution Press, March 2011), 1.

108. "Magic or Realism: China and Latin America," *The Economist*, December 29, 2004, accessed January 10, 2005, http://www.economist.com; Stuart Grudgings, "Analysis: Surge in Chinese Investment Reshapes Brazil Ties," *Reuters*, August 10, 2010, http://www.reuters.com.

109. Inter-American Development Bank in Delvin et al., *The Emergence of China*, 85, 111; and Sutter, *Historical Dictionary of Chinese Foreign Policy* (for Mexico).

110. Larry Rohter, "China Widens Economic Role in Latin America," *New York Times*, November 20, 2004, accessed November 20, 2004, http://www.nytimes.com; Winter and Ellsworth, "Brazil and China."

111. "Chile and China Sign Trade Deal," *BBC News*, August 22, 2006, http://www.bbc.com.uk; "China Inks FTA with Costa Rica," *China Daily*, April 9–11, 2010, 5; "Imports Set to Soar on China-Peru FTA," *China Daily*, March 2, 2010, 10; Shambaugh, "China's New Foray into Latin America."

112. Sun Hongbo, "Tapping the Potential," *China Daily*, April 16, 2010, 9.

113. "Taiwan Is Largest Aid Donor in Many Caribbean Nations," *Caribbean News*, December 9, 2003, accessed December 10, 2003, http://www.caribbeannews.com.

114. "Any Port in a Storm," *The Economist*, December 29, 2004, accessed January 5, 2005, http://www.economist.com.

115. "Ma Reaffirms 'Modus Vivendi' Diplomatic Approach," *China Post*, March 15, 2011, http://www.chinapost.com.tw.

116. Carey, "Sino–Latin American Relations and Implications for the United States."

117. Sutter, *Historical Dictionary of Chinese Foreign Policy*, citations for "BRIC" and "BASIC."

118. William Ratliff, "Pragmatism over Ideology: China's Relations with Venezuela," *China Brief* 6, no. 6 (March 15, 2006): 3–5; "Venezuela's Crude Oil Exports to U.S. Average 1 Million BPD," *El Universal*, April 4, 2011, accessed May 18, 2011, http://eluniversal.com.

119. Guillermo R. Delamer et al., "Chinese Interest in Latin America," in *Latin American Security Challenges: A Collaborative Inquiry from North and South*, ed. Paul D. Taylor, Newport Paper 21 (Newport, RI: Naval War College, 2004), 94; Shambaugh, "China's New Foray into Latin America."

120. Stephen Johnson, *Balancing China's Growing Influence in Latin America*, Heritage Foundation Backgrounder 1888 (Washington, DC: Heritage Foundation, October 24, 2005), 4.

121. "Testimony of Rogelio Pardo-Maurer, Assistant Secretary of Defense for Latin America, before the House Committee on International Affairs, Subcommittee on Western Hemisphere Affairs," April 6, 2005, accessed May 7, 2005, http://www.house.gov.

122. Johnson, *Balancing China's Growing Influence in Latin America*, 5.

123. "Backgrounder: China's Cooperation with Latin America," *Xinhua*, July 17, 2014, http://news.xinhuanet.com/english/china/2014-07/17/c_133491300.htm; "Recent High-Level Visits Showcase Strengthening Ties with Latin America," *China Daily*, May 27, 2015, http://wo.chinadaily.com.cn/view.php?mid=138660&cid=80&isid=1887; "China's Financial Diplomacy: Rich but Rash," *The Economist*, January 31, 2015, http://www.economist.com/news/finance-and-economics/21641259-challenge-world-bank-and-imf-china-will-have-imitate-them-rich.

124. Evan Ellis, "The China-CELAC Summit," *The Manzella Report*, January 13, 2015, http://www.manzellareport.com/index.php/world/945-the-china-celac-summit-opening-a-new-phase-in-chi.

125. "Recent High-Level Visits Showcase Strengthening Ties with Latin America."

126. "Backgrounder: China's Cooperation with Latin America."

127. "The Dragon and the Gringo: Latin America's Shifting Geopolitics," *The Economist*, January 17, 2015, http://www.economist.com/news/americas/21639549-latin-americas-shifting-geopolitics-dragon-and-gringo.

128. "Exports and Imports for Latin America and the Caribbean," *World Integrated Trade Solution*, accessed June 28, 2015, http://wits.worldbank.org/CountryProfile/Country/LCN/Year/2013/Summarytext.

129. Rebecca Ray and Kevin Gallagher, *2013 China-Latin America Economic Bulletin*, accessed June 28, 2015, https://ase.tufts.edu/gdae/Pubs/rp/wg/WG_ChinaLA_Bulletin_2013.pdf.

13. PROSPECTS

1. Aaron L. Friedberg, *Contest for Supremacy: China, America and the Struggle for Mastery in Asia* (New York: Norton, 2011); Andrew Nathan, review of *The China Choice*, by Hugh White, *Foreign Affairs*, January–February 2013, http://www.foreignaffairs.com/articles/138661/hugh-white/the-china-choice-why-america-should-share-power.

2. *The Economist*, "China in Africa: One Among Many," January 17, 2015, http://www.economist.com/news/middle-east-and-africa/21639554-china-has-become-big-africa-now-backlash-one-among-many.

3. Some specialists are more moderate; see Lyle Goldstein, *Meeting China Halfway* (Washington, DC: Georgetown University Press, 2015).

4. Robert Sutter, *The United States and Asia* (Lanham, MD: Rowman & Littlefield, 2015), 297–316.

5. Robert Sutter, *China's Rise in Asia* (Lanham, MD: Rowman & Littlefield, 2005), 266–67.

6. For a recent discussion by a prominent American China specialist on how the United States could go about shaping China's rise, see Thomas Christensen, *The China Challenge: Shaping the Choices of a Rising Power* (New York: Norton, 2015).

Selected Bibliography

Acharya, Amitav. "Power Shift or Paradigm Shift? China's Rise and Asia's Emerging Security Order." *International Studies Quarterly* 58, no. 1 (March 2014): 158–73.

Alden, Christopher, Daniel Large, and Ricardo de Oliveria. *China Returns to Africa: A Superpower and a Continent Embrace.* New York: Columbia University Press, 2008.

Alterman, Jon, and John Garver. *The Vital Triangle: China, the United States, and the Middle East.* Washington, DC: Center for Strategic and International Studies, 2008.

Austin, Greg, and Stuart Harris. *Japan and Greater China.* Honolulu: University of Hawaii Press, 2001.

Ba Zhongtan et al. *Zhongguo Guojia Anquan Zhanlue Wenti Yanjiu.* Beijing: Zhongguo Junshi Kexue Chubanshe, 2003.

Bader, Jeffrey. *Obama and China's Rise.* Washington, DC: Brookings Institution, 2012.

Beckley, Michael. "China's Century? Why America's Edge Will Endure." *International Security* 36, no. 3 (Winter 2011–12): 41–78.

Bergsten, C. Fred, et al. *China's Rise: Challenges and Opportunities.* Washington, DC: Peterson Institute for International Economics and Center for Strategic and International Studies, 2008.

Bhattasali, Deepak, Shantong Li, and Will Martin. *China and the WTO.* Washington, DC: World Bank, 2004.

Blasko, Dennis. *The Chinese Army Today.* London: Routledge, 2012.

Brautigam, Deborah. *The Dragon's Gift.* New York: Oxford University Press, 2009.

Brown, Kerry. *China and the EU in Context.* London: Palgrave Macmillan, 2014.

Bush, Richard. *The Perils of Proximity: China-Japan Security Relations.* Washington, DC: Brookings Institution, 2010.

———. *Unchartered Strait: The Future of China-Taiwan Relations.* Washington, DC: Brookings Institution, 2012.

———. *Untying the Knot: Making Peace in the Taiwan Strait.* Washington, DC: Brookings Institution, 2005.

Bush, Richard, and Michael O'Hanlon. *A War Like No Other: The Truth about China's Challenge to America.* Hoboken, NJ: Wiley, 2007.

Cabestan, Jean-Pierre. "European Union-China Relations and the United States." *Asian Perspective* 30, no. 4 (Winter 2006): 11–38.

———. "The Shanghai Cooperation Organization, Central Asia, and the Great Powers, an Introduction," *Asian Survey* 53, no. 3 (2013): 423–35.

Carlson, Allen. "More Than Just Saying No: China's Evolving Approach to Sovereignty and Intervention." In *New Directions in the Study of China's Foreign Policy*, edited by Alastair Iain Johnston and Robert S. Ross, 217–41. Stanford, CA: Stanford University Press, 2006.

Center for a New American Security. *More Willing and Able: Charting China's International Security Activism*. Washington, DC: Center for a New American Security, 2015.

Cha, Victor. *The Impossible State: North Korea Past and Future*. New York: HarperCollins, 2012.

Chanda, Nayan. "China and Cambodia." *Asia-Pacific Review* 9, no. 2 (2002): 1–11.

Cheng Ruisheng, "China-India Diplomatic Relations: Six Decades' Experience and Inspiration," *Foreign Affairs Journal* (Beijing) 96 (Summer 2010): 59–70.

Cheung, Joseph Y. S. "Sino-ASEAN Relations in the Early 21st Century." *Contemporary Southeast Asia* 23, no. 3 (December 2001): 420–52.

Chi, Su. *Taiwan's Relations with Mainland China: A Tail Wagging Two Dogs*. New York: Routledge, 2008.

Christensen, Thomas. *The China Challenge: Shaping the Choices of a Rising Power*. New York: Norton, 2015.

———. "Fostering Stability or Creating a Monster? The Rise of China and US Policy toward East Asia." *International Security* 31, no. 1 (Summer 2006): 81–126.

———. "Windows and War: Trends Analysis and Beijing's Use of Force." In *New Directions in the Study of China's Foreign Policy*, edited by Alastair Iain Johnston and Robert S. Ross, 50–85. Stanford, CA: Stanford University Press, 2006.

Chu Shulong. "Quanmian jianshe xiaokang shehui shiqi de zhongguo waijiao zhan-lue." *Shijie Jingji yu Zhengzhi* 8 (August 2003).

Chung, Jae Ho. *Between Ally and Partner*. New York: Columbia University Press, 2007.

———. "From a Special Relationship to a Normal Partnership?" *Pacific Affairs* 76, no. 3 (2003): 549–68.

Clough, Ralph. *Cooperation or Conflict in the Taiwan Strait?* Lanham, MD: Rowman & Littlefield, 1999.

Cohen, Warren I. *America's Response to China: A History of Sino-American Relations*. New York: Columbia University Press, 2010.

———. "China's Rise in Historical Perspective." *Journal of Strategic Studies* 30, nos. 4–5 (August–October 2007): 683–704.

Cole, Bernard. *Great Wall at Sea*. Annapolis, MD: Naval Institute, 2010.

Council on Foreign Relations. *U.S.-China Relations: An Affirmative Agenda, a Responsible Course*. New York: Council on Foreign Relations, 2007.

Cui Liru. "A Multipolar World in the Globalization Era." *Contemporary International Relations* (Beijing) 20, Special Issue (September 2010): 1–11.

Dai Bingguo. "Stick to the Path of Peaceful Development." *Beijing Review* 51 (December 23, 2010). http://www.Beijingreview.com.cn.

Dahlman, Carl. *The World under Pressure: How China and India Are Influencing the Global Economy and Environment*. Stanford, CA: Stanford University Press, 2011.

Deng Hao. "China's Relations with Central Asian Countries: Retrospect and Prospect." *Guoji Wenti Yanjiu* (Beijing), May 13, 2002, 8–12.

Deng, Yong. *China's Struggle for Status: The Realignment of International Relations*. New York: Cambridge University Press, 2008.

———. "The Chinese Conception of National Interests in International Relations." *China Quarterly* 154 (June 1998): 308–29.

———. "Hegemon on the Offensive: Chinese Perspectives on U.S. Global Strategy." *Political Science Quarterly* 116, no. 3 (Fall 2001): 343–65.

Deng, Yong, and Thomas Moore. "China Views Globalization: Toward a New Great-Power Politics." *Washington Quarterly* 27, no. 3 (Summer 2004): 117–36.

Deng, Yong, and Fei-Ling Wang, eds. *China Rising: Power and Motivation in Chinese Foreign Policy*. Lanham, MD: Rowman & Littlefield, 2005.

Dittmer, Lowell. *Sino-Soviet Normalization and Its International Implications, 1945–1990*. Seattle: University of Washington Press, 1992.

Dittmer, Lowell, and George T. Yu, eds. *China, the Developing World and the New Global Dynamic*. Boulder CO: Rienner, 2010.

Downs, Erica. *Brookings Foreign Policy Studies Energy Security Series: China*. Washington, DC: Brookings Institution, 2006.

————. *Inside China, Inc: China Development Bank's Cross-Border Energy Deals*. John Thornton China Center Monograph Series 3. Washington, DC: Brookings Institution, March 2011.

Dumbaugh, Kerry. *China-U.S. Relations: Current Issues and Implications for U.S. Policy*. Report RL32804. Washington, DC: Library of Congress, Congressional Research Service, June 8, 2006.

————. *Taiwan-US Relations: Recent Developments and Their Policy Implications*. Report RL34683. Washington, DC: Library of Congress, Congressional Research Service, October 27, 2008.

Economy, Elizabeth. "China's Environmental Challenge." *Current History* 105, no. 692 (September 2005): 278–79.

Eisenman, Joshua, Eric Heginbotham, and Derek Mitchell, eds. *China and the Developing World*. Armonk NY: Sharpe, 2007.

Ellis, R. Evan. *China in Latin America*. Boulder, CO: Rienner, 2009.

Fang Ning, Wang Xiaodong, and Qiao Liang. *Quanqihua Yinying xia de Zhongguo Zhilu*. Beijing: Chinese Academy of Social Sciences, 1999.

Feng Zhongping. "China-EU Relationship." *Xiandai guoji guanxi* (Beijing) 17 (January 2007): 47–55.

————. "EU's China Policy Analyzed." *Contemporary International Relations* (Beijing) 8, no. 4 (April 1998): 1–6.

Fewsmith, Joseph. *China since Tiananmen*. New York: Cambridge University Press, 2008.

Fewsmith, Joseph, and Stanley Rosen. "The Domestic Context of Chinese Foreign Policy: Does 'Public Opinion' Matter?" In *The Making of Chinese Foreign and Security Policy in the Era of Reform*, edited by David Michael Lampton, 179–86. Stanford, CA: Stanford University Press, 2001.

Finkelstein, David. *China Reconsiders Its National Security: The Great Peace and Development Debate of 1999*. Alexandria, VA: CNA, December 2000.

Foot, Rosemary. "China and the ASEAN Regional Forum." *Asian Survey* 38, no. 5 (1998): 425–40.

————. "Chinese Strategies in a U.S.-Hegemonic Global Order: Accommodating and Hedging." *International Affairs* 82, no. 1 (2006): 77–94.

————. *The Practice of Power: U.S. Relations with China since 1949*. New York: Oxford University Press, 1997.

Foot, Rosemary, and Andrew Walter. *China, the United States and the Global Order*. New York: Cambridge University Press, 2011.

Fravel, M. Taylor. "China's Search for Military Power." *Washington Quarterly* 33, no. 3 (Summer 2008): 125–41.

————. "China's Strategy in the South China Sea." *Contemporary Southeast Asia* 33, no. 3 (2011): 292–319.

————. *Strong Borders, Secure Nation: Cooperation and Conflict in China's Territorial Disputes*. Princeton, NJ: Princeton University Press, 2008.

Fravel, M. Taylor, and Evan Medeiros. "China's Search for Assured Retaliation." *International Security* 35, no. 2 (Fall 2010): 48–87.

French, Howard. *China's Second Continent*. New York: Vintage, 2014.

Friedberg, Aaron. *A Contest for Supremacy: China, America, and the Struggle for Mastery in Asia*. New York: Norton, 2011.

————. *Beyond Air-Sea Battle: The Debate over US Military Strategy in Asia*. Adelphi Paper 444. London: International Institute for Strategic Studies, 2014.

————. "The Future of U.S.-China Relations: Is Conflict Inevitable?" *International Security* 30, no. 2 (2005): 7–45.

————. "'Going Out': China's Pursuit of Natural Resources and Implications for the PRC's Grand Strategy." *NBR Analysis* 17, no. 3 (September 2006): 1–40.

Fu Mengzi. "China and Peace Building on the Korean Peninsula." *Xiandai guoji guanxi* (Beijing) 17 (July 2007): 27–40.

————. "Sino-US Relations." *Xiandai guoji guanxi* (Beijing) 17 (January 2007): 32–46.

Gao Lianfu. "East Asia Regional Cooperation Entered the Stage of Institutionalization." *Taipingyang Xuebao* 2 (2001).

Gao Zugui. "An Analysis of Sino-U.S. Strategic Relations on the 'Western Front.'" *Xiandai guoji guanxi* (Beijing) 12 (December 20, 2004).

Garnett, Sherman, ed. *Rapprochement or Rivalry? Russia-China Relations in a Changing Asia.* Washington, DC: Carnegie Endowment for International Peace, 2000.

Garver, John. *China and Iran: Ancient Partners in a Post-Imperial World.* Seattle: University of Washington Press, 2006.

———. "Development of China's Overland Transportation Links with Central, Southwest, and South Asia." *China Quarterly* 185 (March 2006): 1–22.

———. *Face-Off.* Seattle: University of Washington Press, 1997.

———. *Foreign Relations of the People's Republic of China.* Englewood Cliffs, NJ: Prentice Hall, 1993.

———. "Is China Playing a Dual Game in Iran?" *Washington Quarterly* 34, no. 1 (Winter 2011): 75–88.

———. *Protracted Contest: Sino-Indian Rivalry in the 20th Century.* Seattle: University of Washington Press, 2001.

Gill, Bates. "China's Evolving Regional Security Strategy." In *Power Shift: China and Asia's New Dynamics*, edited by David Shambaugh, 247–65. Berkeley: University of California Press, 2005.

———. *Rising Star: China's New Security Diplomacy.* Washington, DC: Brookings Institution, 2007.

———. "Two Steps Forward, One Step Back: The Dynamics of Chinese Nonproliferation and Arms Control Policy-Making in an Era of Reform." In *The Making of Chinese Foreign and Security Policy in the Era of Reform*, edited by David Michael Lampton, 257–88. Stanford, CA: Stanford University Press, 2001.

Gill, Bates, and Melissa Murphy. "China's Evolving Approach to Counterterrorism." *Harvard Asia Quarterly* (Winter–Spring 2005): 21–32.

Gill, Bates, and Matthew Oresman. *China's New Journey to the West.* Washington, DC: Center for Strategic and International Studies, August 2003.

Glaser, Bonnie, and Evan Medeiros. "The Changing Ecology of Foreign Policy Making in China: The Ascension and Demise of the Theory of 'Peaceful Rise.'" *China Quarterly* 190 (2007): 291–310.

Glaser, Charles. "Will China's Rise Lead to War?" *Foreign Affairs* 90, no. 2 (March–April 2011): 80–91.

Glosny, Michael. "Heading toward a Win-Win Future? Recent Developments in China's Policy toward Southeast Asia." *Asian Security* 2, no. 1 (2006): 24–57.

Godwin, Paul. "China as a Major Asian Power: The Implications of Its Military Modernization (a View from the United States)." In *China, the United States, and Southeast Asia: Contending Perspectives on Politics, Security, and Economics*, edited by Evelyn Goh and Sheldon Simon, 145–66. New York: Routledge, 2008.

Goh, Evelyn. *Meeting the China Challenge: The United States in Southeast Asian Regional Security Strategies.* Policy Studies 21. Washington, DC: East-West Center, 2006.

———. "The Modes of China's Influence: Cases from Southeast Asia." *Asian Survey* 54, no. 5 (2014): 825–48.

———. "Southeast Asia: Strategic Diversification in the 'Asian Century.'" In *Strategic Asia 2008–2009*, edited by Ashley Tellis, Mercy Kuo, and Andrew Marble, 261–96. Seattle: National Bureau of Asian Research, 2008.

———. *The Struggle for Order: Hegemony, Hierarchy and Transition in Post–Cold War East Asia.* Oxford: Oxford University Press, 2013.

Goldstein, Avery. *Rising to the Challenge: China's Grand Strategy and International Security.* Stanford, CA: Stanford University Press, 2005.

Goldstein, Lyle. *Meeting China Halfway.* Washington, DC: Georgetown University Press, 2015

Goldstein, Lyle, and Vitaly Kozyrev. "China, Japan, and the Scramble for Siberia." *Survival* 48, no. 1 (Spring 2006): 163–78.

Goldstein, Steven. *Taiwan Faces the Twenty-First Century*. New York: Foreign Policy Association, 1997.

Goldstein, Steven, and Julian Chang, eds. *Presidential Politics in Taiwan: The Administration of Chen Shui-bian*. Norwalk, CT: Eastbridge, 2008.

Gong Li. "Deng Xiaoping Dui Mei Zhengce Sixing yu Zhong-Mei Guanxi." *Guoji Wenti Yanjiu* 6 (2004): 13–17.

———. *Kuayue: 1969–1979 nian Zhong Mei guanxi de yanbian* [Across the Chasm: The Evolution of China-US Relations, 1969–1979]. Henan: Henan People's Press, 1992.

———. "The Official Perspective: What Chinese Government Officials Think of America." In *Chinese Images of the United States*, edited by Carola McGiffert, 25–32. Washington, DC: CSIS, 2006.

Green, Michael. *Japan's Reluctant Realism*. New York: Palgrave, 2003.

Green, Michael, and Benjamin Self. "Japan's Changing China Policy: From Commercial Liberalism to Reluctant Realism." *Survival* 38, no. 2 (Summer 1996): 34–58.

Gries, Peter. *China's New Nationalism*. Berkeley: University of California Press, 2004.

Guoji Zhanlue yu Anquan Xingshi Pinggu 2001–2002. Beijing: Shishi Chubanshe, 2002.

Guoji Zhanlue yu Anquan Xingshi Pinggu 2003–2004. Beijing: Shishi Chubanshe, 2004.

Guoji Zhanlue yu Anquan Xingshi Pinggu 2004–2005. Beijing: Shishi Chubanshe, 2005.

Hachigian, Nina. *Debating China*. New York: Oxford University Press, 2014.

Hagerty, Devin. "China and Pakistan: Strains in the Relationship." *Current History* (September 2002): 284–89.

Halper, Stefan. *The Beijing Consensus*. New York: Basic, 2010.

Harding, Harry. *China's Foreign Relations in the 1980s*. New Haven, CT: Yale University Press, 1984.

———. *China's Second Revolution*. Washington, DC: Brookings Institution, 1987.

———. *A Fragile Relationship: The U.S. and China Since 1972*. Washington, DC: Brookings Institution, 1992.

Harris, Lillian Craig, and Robert Worden, eds. *China and the Third World*. Dover, MA: Auburn House, 1986.

Heginbotham, Eric, and George Gilboy. *Chinese and Indian Strategic Behavior: Growing Power and Alarm*. New York: Cambridge University Press, 2012.

Henderson, John, and Benjamin Reilly. "Dragon in Paradise." *National Interest*, Summer 2003, 93–102.

Herberg, Mikkal, and Kenneth Lieberthal. "China's Search for Energy Security: Implications for U.S. Policy." *NBR Analysis* 17, no. 1 (April 2006): 1–54.

Holslag, Jonathan. *China and India: Prospects for Peace*. New York: Columbia University Press, 2010.

Hou Yousheng. "Oumeny yu Meiguo dai Hua zhanlue bijiao." *Xiandai guoji guanxi* (Beijing) 8 (August 2006): 1–6.

Hou Zhengdo. "Guanyu Zhong Ou zhanlue guanxi jige xiangfa." *Guoji Wenti Yanjiu* (Beijing) 2 (April 2005).

Hu Angang. *Daguo Zhanlue Liyi yu Shiming*. Liaoning: Liaoning Renmin Chubanshe, 2000.

Hu Angang and Meng Honghua. "Zhongmeiriieying youxing zhanlue ziyuan bijiao." *Zhanlue yu Guanli* 2 (2002): 26–41.

———, eds. *Jiedu Meiguo Dazhanlue*. Hangzhou: Zhejiang Renmin Chubanshe, 2003.

Hu Guocheng. "Chinese Images of the United States: A Historical Review." In *Chinese Images of the United States*, edited by Carola McGiffert, 3–8. Washington, DC: CSIS, 2006.

Huang Renwei. *Zhongguo Jueji de Shijian he Kongjian*. Shanghai: Shanghai Academy of Social Sciences, 2002.

Huchet, Jean-Francois. "Emergence of a Pragmatic India-China Relationship: Between Geostrategic Rivalry and Economic Competition." *China Perspectives* 3 (2008): 50–67.

Hunt, Michael H. *The Genesis of Chinese Communist Foreign Policy*. New York: Columbia University Press, 1996.

Institute for International and Strategic Studies. *China's Grand Strategy: A Kinder, Gentler Turn*. London: Institute for International and Strategic Studies, November 2004.

Institute of Strategic Studies, CCP Central Party School. *Zhongguo Heping Jueji Xindaolu.* Beijing: Zhonggong Zhongyang Dangxiao Chubanshe, 2004.

International Crisis Group. *China and North Korea: Comrades Forever?* Asia Report 112. Brussels: International Crisis Group, February 1, 2006.

———. *China's Growing Role in UN Peacekeeping.* Asia Report 166. Brussels: International Crisis Group, April 17, 2009.

———. *China's Myanmar Strategy.* Asia Briefing 112. Brussels: International Crisis Group, September 21, 2010.

———. *China's Thirst for Oil.* Asia Report 153–59. Brussels: International Crisis Group, June 2008.

———. *China-Taiwan: Uneasy Détente.* Asia Briefing 42. Brussels: International Crisis Group, September 21, 2005.

———. *North Korea's Nuclear Test: The Fallout.* Asia Briefing 56. Brussels: International Crisis Group, November 13, 2006.

Jakobson, Linda, and Dean Knox. "New Foreign Policy Actors in China." SIPRI Policy Paper 26. Stockholm: Stockholm International Peace Research Institute, September 2010.

Ji Zhiye. "Strategic Prospects for Russia." *Contemporary International Relations* (Beijing) 20, no. 5 (September–October 2010): 1–16.

Jia Qingguo. "Peaceful Development: China's Policy of Reassurance." *Australian Journal of International Affairs* 59, no. 4 (December 2005): 493–507.

Johnson, Christopher. *Decoding China's Emerging "Great Power" Strategy in Asia.* Washington, DC: Center for Strategic and International Studies, June 2014.

Johnston, Alastair Iain. "How New and Assertive Is China's New Assertiveness?" *International Security* 37, no. 4 (Spring 2013): 7–48.

———. "Is China a Status Quo Power?" *International Security* 27, no. 4 (Spring 2003): 5–56.

———. *Social States: China in International Institutions, 1980–2000.* Princeton, NJ: Princeton University Press, 2008.

Johnston, Alastair Iain, and Paul Evans. "China's Engagement." In *Engaging China: The Management of an Emerging Power,* edited by Alastair Iain Johnston and Robert Ross, 235–72. New York: Routledge, 1999.

Johnston, Alastair Iain, and Robert S. Ross, eds. *New Directions in the Study of China's Foreign Policy.* Stanford, CA: Stanford University Press, 2006.

Kan, Shirley. *China and Proliferation of Weapons of Mass Destruction and Missiles: Policy Issues.* Report RL31555. Washington, DC: Library of Congress, Congressional Research Service, January 3, 2014.

Kan, Shirley, Christopher Bolkcom, and Ronald O'Rourke. *China's Foreign Conventional Arms Acquisitions.* Report RL30700. Washington, DC: Library of Congress, Congressional Research Service, November 6, 2001.

Kang, David. *China Rising: Peace, Power, and Order in East Asia.* New York: Columbia University Press, 2007.

———. "Getting Asia Wrong: The Need for New Analytical Frameworks." *International Security* 27, no. 4 (2003): 57–85.

Keefe, John. *Anatomy of the EP-3 Incident.* Alexandria, VA: Center for Naval Analysis, January 2002.

Keller, William, and Thomas Rawski, eds. *China's Rise and the Balance of Influence in Asia.* Pittsburgh, PA: University of Pittsburgh Press, 2007.

Kim, Samuel. *China, the United Nations and World Order.* Princeton, NJ: Princeton University Press. 1979.

———, ed. *China and the World: New Directions in Chinese Foreign Relations.* Boulder, CO: Westview, 1989.

———. "Chinese Foreign Policy Faces Globalization Challenges." In *New Directions in the Study of China's Foreign Policy,* edited by Alastair Iain Johnston and Robert S. Ross, 276–308. Stanford, CA: Stanford University Press, 2006.

———. *The Third World in Chinese World Policy.* Princeton, NJ: Center of International Studies, Woodrow Wilson School of Public and International Affairs, Princeton University, 1989.

———. *The Two Koreas and the Great Powers*. New York: Cambridge University Press, 2006.

Kim, Taeho. "Sino-ROK Relations at a Crossroads: Looming Tensions amid Growing Interdependence." *Korean Journal of Defense Analysis* 17, no. 1 (2005): 129–49.

Kissinger, Henry. *On China*. New York: Penguin, 2011.

Kitano, Naohiro, and Yukinori Harada. *Estimating China's Foreign Aid 2001–2013*. Tokyo: JICA Research Institute, June 2014.

Kleine-Ahlbrandt, Stephanie, and Andrew Small. "China's New Dictatorship Diplomacy." *Foreign Affairs* 87, no. 1 (January–February 2008): 38–56.

Kurlantzick, Joshua. *Charm Offensive: How China's Soft Power Is Transforming the World*. New Haven, CT: Yale University Press, 2007.

Lampton, David Michael. *Following the Leader: Ruling China from Deng Xiaoping to Xi Jinping*. Berkeley: University of California Press, 2014.

———, ed. *The Making of Chinese Foreign and Security Policy in the Era of Reform, 1978–2000*. Stanford, CA: Stanford University Press, 2001.

———. *Power Constrained: Sources of Mutual Strategic Suspicion in US-China Relations*. NBR Analysis (June 2010): 5–25.

———. *Same Bed, Different Dreams*. Berkeley: University of California Press, 2001.

———. *The Three Faces of Chinese Power: Might, Money, and Minds*. Berkeley: University of California Press, 2008.

Lancaster, Carol. *The Chinese Aid System*. Washington, DC: Center for Global Development, June 2007.

Lardy, Nicholas. *Integrating China in the Global Economy*. Washington, DC: Brookings Institution, 2002.

Laurelle, Marlene, and Sebastien Peyrouse, eds. *The Chinese Question in Central Asia: Domestic Order, Social Change, and the Chinese Factor*. New York: Columbia University Press, 2012.

Lawrence, Susan. *U.S.-China Relations: An Overview of Policy Issues*. Report R41108. Washington, DC: Library of Congress, Congressional Research Service, August 1, 2013.

Lee, David Tawei. *The Making of the Taiwan Relations Act*. New York: Oxford University Press, 2000.

Lee Teng-hui. *Creating the Future: Towards a New Era for the Chinese People* (a compilation of speeches and remarks by President Lee Teng-hui). Taipei: Government Information Office, 1992.

Leverett, Flynt, and Jeffrey Bader. "Managing China-U.S. Energy Competition in the Middle East." *Washington Quarterly* 29, no. 1 (Winter 2005–2006): 187–201.

Lewis, Joanna. "China's Strategic Priorities in International Climate Change Negotiations." *Washington Quarterly* 31, no. 1 (Winter 2007–2008): 155–74.

———. "The State of U.S.-China Relations on Climate Change." *China Environmental Series* 11 (2010–2011): 7–39.

Li, Cheng, ed. *China's Changing Political Landscape: Prospects for Democracy*. Washington, DC: Brookings Institution, 2008.

———. *China's Leaders: The New Generation*. Lanham, MD: Rowman & Littlefield, 2001.

Li Li. "India's Engagement with East Asia and the China Factor." *Contemporary International Relations* (Beijing) 20, no. 5 (September–October 2010): 97–109.

Li Shaoxian. "China-Russia Bond." *Xiandai guoji guanxi* (Beijing) 17 (January 2007): 5–21.

Li Shaoxian and Tang Zhichao. "China and the Middle East." *Xiandai guoji guanxi* (Beijing) 17 (January 2007): 22–31.

Li Shaoxian and Wei Liang, "New Complexities in the Middle East since 9.11," *Contemporary International Relations* (Beijing) 20, Special Issue (September 2010): 22–32.

Li Shengming and Wang Yizhou, eds. *Nian quanqiu Zhengzhi yu Anquan Baogao*. Beijing: Shehui Kexue Wenxian, 2003.

Lieberthal, Kenneth. "Preventing a War over Taiwan." *Foreign Affairs* 84, no. 2 (March–April 2005): 53–63.

Lieberthal, Kenneth, and Mikkal Herberg. "China's Search for Energy Security: Implications for U.S. Policy." *NBR Analysis* 17, no. 1 (April 2006): 1–54.

Lieberthal, Kenneth, and David Sandalow. *Overcoming Obstacles to US-China Cooperation on Climate Change*. John L. Thornton China Center Monograph Series, no. 1. Washington, DC: Brookings Institution, January 2009.

Lieberthal, Kenneth, and Wang Jisi. *Addressing U.S.-China Strategic Distrust*. Washington, DC: Brookings Institution, March 2012.

Liu Baolai. "Broad Prospects for China-Arab Relations." *Foreign Affairs Journal* (Beijing) 79 (March 2006): 38–44.

Liu Jianfei. *Meiguo yu Fangong Zhuyi: Lun Meiguo Dui Shehui Zhuyi Guojia de Yishixingtai Wijiao*. Beijing: Chinese Social Science Press, 2001.

Liu Ming. "China and the North Korean Crisis." *Pacific Affairs* 76, no. 3 (Fall 2003): 347–73.

Liu Tainchun. *Riben Dui Hua Zhengce yu Zhongri Guanxi*. Beijing: Renmin Chubanshe, 2004.

Lo, Bobo. *Axis of Convenience: Moscow, Beijing, and the New Geopolitics*. Washington, DC: Brookings Institution, 2008.

Lou Yaoliang. *Diyuan Zhengzhi yu Zhongguo Guofang Zhanlue*. Tianjin: Tianjin Press, 2002.

Lu Fanghua, "An Analysis of U.S. Involvement in the South China Sea." *Contemporary International Relations* (Beijing) 20, no. 6 (November/December 2010): 132–41.

Lu Gang and Guo Xuetang. *Zhongguo Weixie Shui: Jiedu "Zhong Weixie Lun."* Shanghai: Xueling Chubanshe, 2004.

Lu Ning. *The Dynamics of Foreign Policy Decision Making in China*. Boulder, CO: Westview, 1997.

Lum, Thomas, coord. *Comparing Global Influence: China's and U.S. Diplomacy, Foreign Aid, Trade, and Investment in the Developing World*. Report RL34620. Washington, DC: Library of Congress, Congressional Research Service, August 15, 2008.

Luthi, Lorenz M. *The Sino-Soviet Spilt: Cold War in the Communist World*. Princeton, NJ: Princeton University Press, 2008.

Ma Jiali. "Emerging Sino-Indian Relations." *Xiandai guoji guanxi* (Beijing) 17 (May 2007): 71–80.

Ma Licheng. "Duiri Guanxi Xinsiwei." *Zhanlue yu Guanli* 6 (2002): 41–47.

MacFarquhar, Roderick, and John K. Fairbank, eds. *The Cambridge History of China*, vol. 15: *The People's Republic, Part 2: Revolutions within the Chinese Revolution, 1966–1982*. Cambridge: Cambridge University Press, 1991.

MacFarquhar, Roderick, and Michael Schoenhals. *Mao's Last Revolution*. Cambridge, MA: Harvard University Press, 2006.

Malik, J. Mohan. "The China Factor in the India-Pakistan Conflict." *Parameters* (Spring 2003): 35–50.

———. "Chinese-Indian Relations in the Post-Soviet Era." *China Quarterly* 142 (June 1995): 317–55.

Mann, Jim. *About Face: A History of America's Curious Relationship with China, from Nixon to Clinton*. New York: Knopf, 1999.

McGiffert, Carola, ed. *Chinese Images of the United States*. Washington, DC: CSIS, 2006.

Medeiros, Evan. "Is Beijing Ready for Global Leadership?" *Current History* 108, no. 719 (September 2009): 250–56.

———, ed. *Pacific Currents: The Responses of U.S. Allies and Security Partners in East Asia to China's Rise*. Santa Monica, CA: RAND Corporation, 2008.

———. *Reluctant Restraint: The Evolution of China's Nonproliferation Policies and Practices, 1980–2004*. Stanford, CA: Stanford University Press, 2007.

———. "Strategic Hedging and the Future of Asia-Pacific Stability." *Washington Quarterly* 29, no. 1 (2005–2006): 145–67.

Medeiros, Evan, and M. Taylor Fravel. "China's New Diplomacy." *Foreign Affairs* 82, no. 6 (November–December 2003): 22–35.

Mei Zhaorong. "Sino-European Relations in Retrospect and Prospect." *Foreign Affairs Journal* (Beijing) 79 (March 2006): 17–27.

Men Honghua. *China's Grand Strategy: A Framework Analysis*. Beijing: Beijing Daxue Chubanshe, 2005.

Menon, Rajan. "The Strategic Convergence between Russia and China." *Survival* 39, no. 2 (Summer 1997): 101–25.

Miller, Alice Lyman, and Richard Wich. *Becoming Asia*. Stanford, CA: Stanford University Press, 2011.

Miller, H. Lyman, and Liu Xiaohong. "The Foreign Policy Outlook of China's 'Third Generation' Elite." In *The Making of Chinese Foreign and Security Policy in the Era of Reform*, edited by David Michael Lampton, 123–50. Stanford, CA: Stanford University Press, 2001.

Mitter, Rana. *A Bitter Revolution: China's Struggle with the Modern World*. New York: Oxford University Press, 2004.

Mochizuki, Mike. "Terms of Engagement: The U.S.-Japan Alliance and the Rise of China." In *The U.S.-Japan Relationship in the New Asia-Pacific*, edited by Ellis Krauss and T. J. Pempel, 87–115. Stanford, CA: Stanford University Press, 2004.

Moltz, James Clay. "Regional Tension in the Russo-Chinese Rapprochement." *Asian Survey* 35, no. 6 (June 1995): 511–27.

Moore, Thomas. "Chinese Foreign Policy in an Age of Globalization." In *China Rising: Power and Motivation in Chinese Foreign Policy*, edited by Yong Deng and Fei-Ling Wang, 121–58. Lanham, MD: Rowman & Littlefield, 2005.

Morck, Randall, Bernard Yeung, and Minyuan Zhao. *Perspectives on China's Outward Foreign Direct Investment*. Working Paper. Washington, DC: International Monetary Fund, August 2007.

Morrison, Wayne. *China's Economic Conditions*. Report RL33534. Washington, DC: Library of Congress, Congressional Research Service, June 26, 2012.

———. *China's Economic Rise*. Report RL33534. Washington, DC: Library of Congress, Congressional Research Service, October 9, 2014.

———. *China-U.S. Trade Issues*. Report 33536. Washington, DC: Library of Congress, Congressional Research Service, May 21, 2012.

Murray, William S. "Revisiting Taiwan's Defense Strategy." *Naval War College Review*, Summer 2008, 13–38.

Nathan, Andrew, and Robert Ross. *The Great Wall and Empty Fortress*. New York: Norton, 1997.

Nathan, Andrew, and Andrew Scobell. *China's Search for Security*. New York: Columbia University Press, 2012.

Naughton, Barry. *The Chinese Economy*. Cambridge, MA: MIT Press, 2007.

Niu Haibin. "China's International Responsibility Examined." *Xiandai guoji guanxi* (Beijing) 17 (July 2007): 81–93.

Niu Jun. *From Yan'an to the World: The Origin and Development of Chinese Communist Foreign Policy*. Edited and translated by Steven I. Levine. Norwalk, CT: Eastbridge, 2005.

O'Rourke, Ronald. *China's Naval Modernization*. Report RL33153. Washington, DC: Library of Congress, Congressional Research Service, June 15, 2015.

Pang Guang. "An Analysis of the Prospects of 'Shanghai Five.'" In *Thinking of the New Century*, edited by Ling Rong. Beijing: Central Party School Press, 2002.

———. "China's Asian Strategy: Flexible Multilateralism." *World Economy and Politics* (Beijing) 10 (2001).

———, ed. *Quanqiuhua, Fanquangiuhua yu Zhongguo: Lijie Quanqiuhua de Fuzhanxin yu Duoyangxin*. Shanghai: Renmin, 2002.

———. "SCO under New Circumstances: Challenge, Opportunity and Prospect for Development." *Journal of International Studies* (Beijing) 5 (2002): 40–52.

Paulson, Henry. "The Right Way to Engage China: Strengthening U.S.-Chinese Ties." *Foreign Affairs*, September–October 2008. http://www.foreignaffairs.org.

Pearson, Margaret. "China in Geneva: Lessons from China's Early Years in the World Trade Organization." In *New Directions in the Study of China's Foreign Policy*, edited by Alastair Iain Johnston and Robert S. Ross, 242–75. Stanford, CA: Stanford University Press, 2006.

Pei, Minxin. *China's Trapped Transition: The Limits of Development Autocracy*. Cambridge, MA: Harvard University Press, 2006.

Pei, Minxin, and Michael Swaine. *Simmering Fire in Asia: Averting Sino-Japanese Strategic Conflict*. Policy Brief 44. Washington, DC: Carnegie Endowment for International Peace, December 1, 2005.

People's Republic of China Ministry of Foreign Affairs. "China's Africa Policy." *People's Daily*. http://www.peoplesdaily.com.cn, January 12, 2006.

———. *China's EU Policy Paper*. Beijing: Ministry of Foreign Affairs, October 13, 2003.

People's Republic of China Ministry of Foreign Affairs, Department of Policy Planning. *China's Foreign Relations 2010*. Beijing: World Affairs Press, 2010.

People's Republic of China State Council Information Office. *China's Foreign Aid*. Beijing: People's Republic of China State Council Information Office, April 21, 2011.

———. *China's National Defense in 2002*. Beijing: People's Republic of China State Council Information Office, December 9, 2002.

———. *China's National Defense in 2004*. Beijing: People's Republic of China State Council Information Office, December 27, 2004.

———. *China's National Defense in 2006*. Beijing: People's Republic of China State Council Information Office, December 29, 2006.

———. *China's National Defense in 2008*. Beijing: People's Republic of China State Council Information Office, January 2009.

———. *China's National Defense in 2010*. Beijing: People's Republic of China State Council Information Office, March 2011.

———. *China's Peaceful Development Road*. http://www.peoplesdaily.com.cn, December 22, 2005.

People's Republic of China State Council Taiwan Affairs Office and Information Office. *The One-China Principle and the Taiwan Issue*. http://www.gwytb.gov.cn, February 21, 2000.

———. *The Taiwan Question and the Reunification of China*. http://www.gwytb.gov.cn, September 1, 1993.

Percival, Bronson. *The Dragon Looks South: China and Southeast Asia in the New Century*. Westport, CT: Praeger, 2007.

Pillsbury, Michael. *The Hundred Year Marathon*. New York: Holt, 2015.

Plesner, Jonas Parello, and Mathieu Duchatel. *China's Strong Arm: Protecting Citizens and Assets Abroad*. London: International Institute for Strategic Studies, 2015.

Pollack, Jonathan. *No Exit: North Korea, Nuclear Weapons, and International Security*. New York: Routledge, 2011.

———. "The Transformation of the Asian Security Order: Assessing China's Impact." In *Power Shift: China and Asia's New Dynamics*, edited by David Shambaugh, 329–46. Berkeley: University of California Press, 2005.

Qian Qichen. "Adjustment of the United States National Security Strategy and International Relations in the Early New Century." *Foreign Affairs Journal* (Beijing) 71 (March 2004): 1–7.

———. "Xinshiji de Guoji Guanxi." *Xuexi Shibao*, October 18, 2004.

Ranganathan, C. V. "India and China: 'Learning to Learn.'" In *Prime Minister Vajpayee's China Visit June 2003*. Occasional Studies 1, 45–54. New Delhi: Institute of Chinese Studies, October 2003.

Reilly, James. *China's Economic Statecraft: Turning Wealth into Power*. Sydney: Lowy Institute, November 2012.

Richardson, Sophie. *China, Cambodia, and the Five Principles of Peaceful Coexistence*. New York: Columbia University Press, 2010.

Rigger, Shelley. *Taiwan's Rising Rationalism: Generations, Politics, and "Taiwanese Nationalism."* Washington, DC: East-West Center, 2006.

Robinson, Thomas W., and David Shambaugh, eds. *Chinese Foreign Policy: Theory and Practice*. New York: Clarendon, 1997.

Rose, Caroline. *Sino-Japanese Relations: Facing the Past, Looking to the Future*. New York: RoutledgeCurzon, 2005.

Rosen, Daniel, and Thilo Hanemann. *An American Open Door: Maximizing the Benefits of Chinese Foreign Direct Investment*. New York: The Asia Society, 2011.

Ross, Robert S., ed. *After the Cold War*. Armonk, NY: Sharpe, 1998.

———. *The Indochina Tangle*. New York: Columbia University Press, 1988.

———. *Negotiating Cooperation: The United States and China, 1969–1989*. Stanford, CA: Stanford University Press, 1995.

———. "Taiwan's Fading Independence Movement." *Foreign Affairs* 85, no. 2 (March–April 2006): 141–48.

Ross, Robert, and Zhu Feng, eds. *China's Ascent: Power, Security and the Implications for International Politics*. Ithaca, NY: Cornell University Press, 2009.

Roy, Denny. *China's Foreign Relations*. Lanham, MD: Rowman & Littlefield, 1998.

———. *Return of the Dragon: Rising China and Regional Security*. New York: Columbia University Press, 2013.

———. "Rising China and U.S. Interests: Inevitable vs. Contingent Hazards." *Orbis* 47, no. 1 (2003): 125–37.

———. *Taiwan: A Political History*. Ithaca, NY: Cornell University Press, 2003.

Rozman, Gilbert. *Chinese Strategic Thought toward Asia*. New York: Palgrave Macmillan, 2010.

Sa Benwang. "Some Observations on Building a Harmonious World." *Foreign Affairs Journal* (Beijing) 80 (June 2006): 37–42.

Saich, Tony. *Governance and Politics of China*. New York: Palgrave, 2010.

Samuels, Richard. *Securing Japan: Tokyo's Grand Strategy and the Future of East Asia*. Ithaca, NY: Cornell University Press, 2007.

Saunders, Phillip. "China's America Watchers: Changing Attitudes toward the United States." *China Quarterly* (March 2000): 41–65.

———. *China's Global Activism: Strategy, Drivers, and Tools*. Occasional Paper 4. Washington, DC: National Defense University Institute for National Strategic Studies, June 2006.

Scobell, Andrew. "Terrorism and Chinese Foreign Policy." In *China Rising: Power and Motivation in Chinese Foreign Policy*, edited by Yong Deng and Fei-Ling Wang, 305–24. Lanham, MD: Rowman & Littlefield, 2005.

Self, Benjamin. "China and Japan: A Façade of Friendship." *Washington Quarterly* 26, no. 1 (Winter 2002–2003): 77–88.

Shambaugh, David. *Beautiful Imperialist*. Princeton, NJ: Princeton University Press, 1991.

———. "China and Europe: The Emerging Axis." *Current History* 103, no. 674 (September 2004): 243–48.

———. *China Goes Global: Partial Power*. New York: Oxford University Press, 2013.

———. *China's Communist Party: Atrophy and Adaptation*. Washington, DC: Woodrow Wilson Center, 2008.

———. "Coping with a Conflicted China." *Washington Quarterly* 34, no. 1 (Winter 2011): 7–27.

———. *Modernizing China's Military*. Berkeley: University of California Press, 2002.

———, ed. *Power Shift: China and Asia's New Dynamics*. Berkeley: University of California Press, 2005.

———, ed. *Tangled Titans*. Lanham, MD: Rowman & Littlefield, 2012.

Sheives, Kevin. "China Turns West: Beijing's Contemporary Strategy toward Central Asia." *Pacific Affairs* 79, no. 2 (Summer 2006): 205–24.

Sheng Lijun. *China's Influence in Southeast Asia*. Trends in Southeast Asia Series 4. Singapore: Institute of Southeast Asian Studies, 2006.

Shi Yinhong. "Zhongri Jiejin yu 'Waijiao Geming.'" *Zhanlue yu Guanli* (Beijing) 2 (2003): 71–75.

Shie, Tamara. "Rising Chinese Influence in the South Pacific." *Asian Survey* 47, no. 2 (March–April 2007): 307–26.

Shinn, David, and Joshua Eisenman. *China and Africa*. Philadelphia: University of Pennsylvania Press, 2012.

Shirk, Susan. *China: Fragile Superpower*. New York: Oxford University Press, 2007.

Snyder, Scott. *China's Rise and the Two Koreas: Politics, Economics, Security*. Boulder, CO: Rienner, 2009.

Stahle, Stefan. "China's Shifting Attitude towards United Nations Peacekeeping Operations." *China Quarterly* 195 (September 2008): 631–55.

Storey, Ian James. "Living with the Colossus: How Southeast Asian Countries Cope with China." *Parameters* (Winter 1999–2000), 111–25.

———. *Southeast Asia and the Rise of China*. London: Routledge, 2011.

————. *The United States and ASEAN-China Relations: All Quiet on the Southeastern Asian Front*. Carlisle, PA: Strategic Studies Institute, U.S. Army War College, 2007.

Su Ge. *Meiguo: Dui hua Zhengce yu Taiwan wenti* [America: China policy and the Taiwan issue]. Beijing: Shijie Zhishi Chubanshe, 1998.

Suettinger, Robert. *Beyond Tiananmen*. Washington, DC: Brookings Institution, 2003.

Sun, Yun. *Chinese National Security Decision-making: Process and Challenges*. Washington, DC: Brookings Institution, May 2013.

Sutter, Robert. "Assessing China's Rise and U.S. Leadership in Asia—Growing Maturity and Balance." *Journal of Contemporary China* 19, no. 65 (June 2010): 591–604.

————. *China's Rise: Implications for U.S. Leadership in Asia*. Washington, DC: East-West Center, 2006.

————. *China's Rise in Asia: Promises and Perils*. Lanham, MD: Rowman & Littlefield, 2005.

————. *Chinese Foreign Relations: Power and Policy Since the Cold War*. Lanham, MD: Rowman & Littlefield, 2012.

————. *Foreign Relations of the PRC*. Lanham, MD: Rowman & Littlefield, 2013.

————. *U.S.-Chinese Relations: Perilous Past, Pragmatic Present*. Lanham, MD: Rowman & Littlefield, 2013.

Swaine, Michael. *America's Challenge: Engaging a Rising China in the Twenty-First Century*. Washington, DC: Carnegie Endowment for International Peace, 2011.

————. "China's Regional Military Posture." In *Power Shift: China and Asia's New Dynamics*, edited by David Shambaugh, 266–88. Berkeley: University of California Press, 2005.

Swaine, Michael, and Ashley Tellis. *Interpreting China's Grand Strategy, Past, Present and Future*. Santa Monica, CA: RAND Corporation, September 2001.

Swaine, Michael, Tousheng Zhang, and Danielle F. S. Cohen. *Managing Sino-American Crises: Case Studies and Analysis*. Washington, DC: Carnegie Endowment, 2006.

Swanstrom, Niklas. "China and Central Asia: A New Great Game or Traditional Vassal." *Journal of Contemporary China* 14, no. 45 (November 2005): 569–84.

Tang Shiping and Zhang Yunling. "Zhongguo de Diqu Zhanlue." *Shijie Jingli Yu Zhengzhi* 6 (2004): 8–13.

Taylor, Ian. *China's New Role in Africa*. Boulder, CO: Rienner, 2008.

Taylor, Jay. *The Generalissimo*. Cambridge, MA: Harvard University Press, 2009.

————. *The Generalissimo's Son: Chiang Ching-kuo and the Revolutions in China and Taiwan*. Cambridge, MA: Harvard University Press, 2000.

Tellis, Ashley. *Balancing without Containment*. Washington, DC: Carnegie Endowment for International Peace Report, January 22, 2014.

Tian Peiliang. "China and Africa in New Period." *Foreign Affairs Journal* (Beijing) 70 (December 2003): 36–42.

————. "Nationalism: China and Japan." *Foreign Affairs Journal* (Beijing) 63 (March 2002): 63–83.

Tain Zengpei, ed. *Gaige kaifang yilai de Zhongguo waijiao* [Chinese diplomacy since reform and opening]. Beijing: Shijie Zhishi Chubanshe, 1993.

Tiang Zhongqing. *East Asia Cooperation and China's Strategic Interest. Dangdai Yatai* (Beijing) 5 (2003).

Tucker, Nancy Bernkopf. "China-Taiwan: U.S. Debates and Policy Choices." *Survival* 40, no. 4 (Winter 1998–1999): 150–67.

————, ed. *Dangerous Strait: The U.S.-Taiwan-China Crisis*. New York: Columbia University Press, 2005.

————. *Strait Talk: United States-Taiwan Relations and the Crisis with China*. Cambridge, MA: Harvard University Press, 2009.

————. *Taiwan, Hong Kong, and the United States, 1945–1992: Uncertain Friendships*. New York: Twayne, 1994.

United States–China Economic and Security Review Commission. *Report to Congress 2014*. http://www.uscc.gov.

U.S. Department of Defense. *Military and Security Developments Involving the People's Republic of China, 2012*. http://www.defense.gov/pubs/pdfs/2012_CMPR_Final.pdf.

U.S. National Intelligence Council. *China and Weapons of Mass Destruction: Implications for the United States*. Conference Report. Washington, DC: U.S. National Intelligence Council, November 5, 1999.

———. *China's Future: Implications for U.S. Interests*. Conference Report CR99-02. Washington, DC: U.S. National Intelligence Council, September 1999.

U.S. Senate, Committee on Foreign Relations. *China's Foreign Policy and "Soft Power" in South America, Asia, and Africa*. Washington, DC: U.S. Government Printing Office, 2008.

Wachman, Alan. *Why Taiwan: Geostrategic Rationales for China's Territorial Integrity*. Stanford, CA: Stanford University Press, 2007.

Wan, Ming. *Sino-Japanese Relations: Interaction, Logic, and Transformation*. Stanford, CA: Stanford University Press, 2006.

Wang, Fei-Ling. "Beijing's Incentive Structure: The Pursuit of Preservation, Prosperity, and Power." In *China Rising: Power and Motivation in Chinese Foreign Policy*, edited by Yong Deng and Fei-Ling Wang, 19–50. Lanham, MD: Rowman & Littlefield, 2005.

Wang Gungwu. *China and Southeast Asia: Myths, Threat, and Culture*. EAI Occasional Paper 13. Singapore: National University of Singapore, 1999.

———. "The Fourth Rise of China: Cultural Implications." *China: An International Journal* 2, no. 2 (September 2004): 311–22.

Wang Jianwei. "China's Multilateral Diplomacy in the New Millennium." In *China Rising: Power and Motivation in Chinese Foreign Policy*, edited by Yong Deng and Fei-Ling Wang, 177–87. Lanham, MD: Rowman & Littlefield, 2005.

Wang Jisi. "China's Search for a Grand Strategy." *Foreign Affairs* 90, no. 2 (March/April 2011): 68–79.

———. "China's Search for Stability with America." *Foreign Affairs* 84, no. 5 (September–October 2005): 39–48.

———. "'Marching Westwards': The Rebalancing of China's Geostrategy." International and Strategic Studies Report 73 (Beijing: Peking University), October 7, 2012.

———. "Xinxingshi de Zhuyao Tedian he Zhongguo Waijiao." *Xiabdai Guoji Guanxi* (Beijing) 4 (April 2003): 1–3.

Wang Shida, "The Way to a Secure and Stable Afghanistan," *Contemporary International Relations* (Beijing) 20, no. 6 (November–December 2010): 123–31.

Wang Shuzhong, ed. *Mei-Su zhengba zhanlue wenti* [The question of contention for hegemony between the United States and the Soviet Union]. Beijing: Guofang daxue chubanshe, 1988.

Wang, T. Y. "Taiwan's Foreign Relations under Lee Teng-hui's Rule, 1988–2000." In *Sayonara to the Lee Teng-Hui Era*, edited by Wei-chin Lee and T. Y. Wang, 250–60. Lanham, MD: University Press of America, 2003.

Wang Xiaolong. "The Asia-Pacific Economic Cooperation and the Regional Political and Security Issues." *Dangdai Yatai* (Beijing) 4 (2003).

Wang Yizhou. *Quanqiu zhengzhi he zhongguo waijiao*. Beijing: Shijie Zhishi Chubanshe, 2004.

Weatherbee, Donald. *International Relations in Southeast Asia: The Struggle for Autonomy*. 3rd ed. Lanham, MD: Rowman & Littlefield, 2014.

———. "Strategic Dimensions of Economic Interdependence in Southeast Asia." In *Strategic Asia 2006–2007*, edited by Ashley Tellis and Michael Wills, 271–302. Seattle: National Bureau of Asian Research, 2006.

Weiss, Jessica. *Nationalist Protests in China's Foreign Relations*. New York: Oxford University Press, 2014.

White, Hugh. *The China Choice*. Collingwood: Australia Black, 2012.

Whiting, Allen S. *China Crosses the Yalu*. New York: Macmillan, 1960.

———. *The Chinese Calculus of Deterrence: India and Indochina*. Ann Arbor: University of Michigan Press, 1975.

Wilson, Jeanne. *Strategic Partners: Russian-Chinese Relations in the Post-Soviet Era*. Armonk, NY: Sharpe, 2004.

Wishnick, Elizabeth. "Russia and China: Brothers Again?" *Asian Survey* 41, no. 5 (September–October 2001): 797–821.

Womack, Brantly. *China and Vietnam: The Politics of Asymmetry.* New York: Cambridge University Press, 2006.

———."China and Southeast Asia: Asymmetry, Leadership and Normalcy." *Pacific Affairs* 76, no. 3 (Winter 2003–2004): 529–48.

Wong, John, and Sarah Chan. "China-ASEAN Free Trade Agreement." *Asian Survey* 43, no. 3 (May–June 2003): 507–26.

Wu Hongying. "A New Era of Sino-Latin American Relations." *Xiandai guoji guanxi* (Beijing) 17 (January 2007): 64–71.

———. "Latin America: Key Trends and Challenges." *Contemporary International Relations* (Beijing) 20, Special Issue (September 2010): 33–42.

Wu Xinbo. "Chinese Perspectives on Building an East Asian Community in the Twenty-First Century." In *Asia's New Multilateralism*, edited by Michael Green and Bates Gill, 55–77. New York: Columbia University Press, 2009.

———. "The End of the Silver Lining: A Chinese View of the U.S.-Japanese Alliance." *Washington Quarterly* 29, no. 1 (2005): 119–30.

———. "Four Contradictions Constraining China's Foreign Policy Behavior." *Journal of Contemporary China* 10, no. 27 (May 2001): 293–302.

Xing Guangcheng. "Work for Mutual Trust and Mutual Benefit in Deepening Sino-Russian Relations." *Foreign Affairs Journal* (Beijing) 80 (June 2006): 8–13.

Xiong Guangkai. "Dongqian Quanqiu Fankongxing shi Jiqi Qiying Zhanwang." *Guoji Zhanlue Yanjiu* (Beijing) 2 (2003).

———. "A Review of International Strategic Situation and Its Prospects." *Guoji Zhanlüe Yanjiu* [*International Strategic Studies*, English version] 71, no. 1 (January 2004): 3.

Xu Weizhong. "Beijing Summit Promotes Sino-African Relations." *Xiandai guoji guanxi* (Beijing) 17 (January 2007): 72–79.

Yahuda, Michael. *The International Politics of the Asia-Pacific.* 3rd ed. London: Routledge, 2011.

———. "The Limits of Economic Interdependence: Sino-Japanese Relations." In *New Directions in the Study of China's Foreign Policy*, edited by Alastair Iain Johnston and Robert S. Ross, 162–85. Stanford, CA: Stanford University Press, 2006.

———. *Sino-Japanese Relations after the Cold War.* London: Routledge, 2013.

Yan Xuetong. "The Instability of *China-US* Relations." *Chinese Journal of International Politics* 3, no. 3 (2010): 1–30.

———."The Rise of China and Its Power Status." *Chinese Journal of International Politics* 1 (2006): 5–33.

Yan Xuetong et al. *Zhongguo Jueji—Guoji Huanjin Pinggu.* Tianjin: People's Press, 1998.

Yang Jianmian. *Da Mo He.* Tianjin: Renmin Chubanshe, 2007.

Yang Wenchang. "Sino-U.S. Relations in Retrospect and Prospect." *Foreign Affairs Journal* (Beijing) 80 (June 2006): 1–7.

Ye Zicheng. *Xin Zhongguo Waijiao Sixiang: Cong Maozedong dao Dengxiaoping.* Beijing: Beijing Daxue Chubanshe, 2001.

———. "Zhongguo Shixing Daguo Waijiaozhanlue Shizai Bixing." *Shijie Jingli yu Zhengzhi* 1 (2000): 5–10.

Yee, Herbert, and Ian Storey. *The China Threat: Perceptions, Myths, and Reality.* London: Routledge, 2002.

Yu Bin. "China and Russia: Normalizing Their Strategic Partnership." In *Power Shift: China and Asia's New Dynamics*, edited by David Shambaugh, 228–46. Berkeley: University of California Press, 2005.

Yuan, Jing-dong. "China's Role in Establishing and Building the Shanghai Cooperation Organization (SCO)." *Journal of Contemporary China* 19, no. 67 (November 2010): 855—70.

———. "The Dragon and the Elephant: Chinese-Indian Relations in the 21st Century." *Washington Quarterly* 30, no. 3 (Summer 2007): 131–44.

Yuan Peng. "9.11 Shijian yu Zhongmei Guanxi." *Xiandai guoji guanxi* (Beijing) (November 11, 2001): 19–23, 63.

———. "A Harmonious World and China's New Diplomacy." *Xiandai guoji guanxi* (Beijing) 17 (May 2007): 1–26.

Zeng Qiang. "FOCAC: A Powerful Engine for the Continued Development of Friendship between China and Africa," *Contemporary International Relations* (Beijing) 20, no. 6 (November–December 2010): 45–59.

Zhang Biwu. "Chinese Perceptions of American Power, 1991–2004." *Asian Survey* 45, no. 5 (September–October 2005): 667–86.

Zhang Wenmu. "Quanqiuhua Jincheng Zhong de Zhongguo Guojia Liye." *Zhanlue yu Guanli* 1 (2002): 52–64.

Zhang Yunling. "East Asian Cooperation and the Construction of China-ASEAN Free Trade Area." *Dangdai Yatai* (Beijing) 1 (2002): 20–32.

———, ed. *Huoban Haishi Duishou: Tiao Zheng Zhong de Mei Ri E Guanxi.* Beijing: Social Science Departments Press, 2000.

———, ed. *Making New Partnership: A Rising China and Its Neighbors.* Beijing: Social Sciences Academic Press, 2008.

———. "New Thinking Needed to Promote East Asian Cooperation." *Foreign Affairs Journal* (Beijing) 96 (September 2010), 17–23.

———, ed. *Weilai 10-15 Nian Zhongguo Zai Yatai Diqu Mianlin de Guoji Huanjing.* Beijing: Zhongguo Shehui Kexue Chubanshe, 2003.

Zhang Yunling and Tang Shiping. "China's Regional Strategy." In *Power Shift: China and Asia's New Dynamics*, edited by David Shambaugh, 48–70 Berkeley: University of California Press, 2005.

Zhao, Huasheng, "China's View of and Expectations from the Shanghai Cooperation Organization," *Asian Survey* 53, no. 3 (2013): 436–60.

Zhao, Suisheng. "Chinese Nationalism and Its International Orientations." *Political Science Quarterly* 115, no. 1 (Spring 2000): 1–33.

———. *A Nation-State by Construction: Dynamics of Modern Chinese Nationalism.* Stanford, CA: Stanford University Press, 2004.

———, ed. *China in Africa.* New York: Routledge, 2015.

Zheng Bijian. "China's 'Peaceful Rise' to Great-Power Status." *Foreign Affairs* 84, no. 5 (2005): 18–24.

Zheng Ruixiang. "New Development of Relations between China and South Asian Countries." *Foreign Affairs Journal* (Beijing) 76 (June 2005): 40–46.

Zhou Gang. "Status Quo and Prospects of China-ASEAN Relations." *Foreign Affairs Journal* (Beijing) 80 (June 2006): 14–21.

Zhou Yuhao. *Liyi Youguan.* Beijing: Zhongguo Chuanmei Daxue Chubanshe, 2007.

Zhu Feng. "Zai Lishi Gui yi Zhong Bawo Zhong Mei Guanxi." *Huanqiu Shibao Guoji Luntan*, February 28, 2002.

Zhu Tingchang et al., eds. *Zhongguo Zhoubian Anquan Huanjin yu Anquan Zhanlue.* Beijing: Shishi Chubanshe, 2002.

Zou Jingwen. *Li Denghui Zhizheng Gaobai Shilu.* Taipei: INK, 2001.

Index

About the Author

Robert G. Sutter has been professor of practice in international affairs at the Elliott School of International Affairs (ESIA) at George Washington University since 2011. He also directs the ESIA program of Bachelor of Arts in International Affairs, involving over 1,000 students.

A PhD graduate in History and East Asian Languages from Harvard University, Sutter taught full-time at Georgetown University (2001–2011) and part-time during the previous thirty years at Georgetown, George Washington, Johns Hopkins Universities, or the University of Virginia. He has published twenty-one books, more than 200 articles, and several hundred government reports dealing with the United States, China, and contemporary Asian and Pacific affairs. His most recent book is *The United States and Asia: Regional Dynamics and Twenty-First-Century Relations* (Rowman & Littlefield, 2015).

Sutter's government career (1968–2001) involved work on Asian and Pacific affairs and U.S. foreign policy. He was for many years the senior specialist and director of the Foreign Affairs and National Defense Division of the Congressional Research Service. He also was the national intelligence officer for East Asia and the Pacific at the U.S. government's National Intelligence Council, the China Division director at the Department of State's Bureau of Intelligence and Research, and a professional staff member of the Senate Foreign Relations Committee.